Effective Teaching in Secondary Schools

Rinehart Books in Secondary Education

WILLIAM M. ALEXANDER AND PAUL M. HALVERSON
Effective Teaching in Secondary Schools

WILLIAM M. ALEXANDER AND J. GALEN SAYLOR
Secondary Education: Basic Principles and Practices

R. WILL BURNETT
Teaching Science in the Secondary Schools

WILL FRENCH, J. DAN HULL, AND B. L. DODDS
American High School Administration: Policy and Practice

LUCIEN B. KINNEY AND C. RICHARD PURDY
Teaching Mathematics in the Secondary School

J. PAUL LEONARD
Developing the Secondary School Curriculum, Revised

J. GALEN SAYLOR AND WILLIAM M. ALEXANDER
Curriculum Planning: For Better Teaching and Learning

ROBERT S. GILCHRIST, WILBUR H. DUTTON, AND WILLIAM L. WRINKLE
Secondary Education for American Democracy, Revised

Effective Teaching

in Secondary Schools

WILLIAM M. ALEXANDER

Professor of Education and Coordinator of In-Service Education
University of Miami

PAUL M. HALVERSON

Professor of Education, Syracuse University

Rinehart & Company, Inc., New York

Preface

*E*ffective Teaching in Secondary Schools is intended to be used as a textbook in courses in methods of secondary school teaching and as a reference for all teachers in junior and senior high schools who are interested in study and improvement of their work. We hope that it will be found useful in understanding both the theory and the practice of modern teaching. We have stated principles and illustrated them by examples, presented our point of view and expressed it in terms of classroom operation, and in general tried to describe a sound, workable philosophy and practice of teaching adapted to the schools of democratic America.

The authors do not advocate any narrow "method" in the sense that the term has frequently been used to identify a particular pattern of teacher activities. Rather, we see method in the context of an interaction process of pupils and teacher. In this process, appropriate teacher actions make a significant difference in the learning experiences of boys and girls. These actions have to do with understanding boys and girls and helping them to carry on problem-solving activities. Effective teaching results, we believe, in learning experiences which change the behavior of learners. Such teaching is grounded in democratic philosophy and scientific method, and we have drawn principles from these fields to explain how teachers can guide the problem-solving processes of adolescents.

Part I is devoted to explaining the nature of effective teaching and the critical factors involved. This part provides the theoretical bases of the teaching actions described in subsequent parts. Part II deals with the organization of the classroom environment and analyzes the dynamics at work in the classroom group. Part III describes the techniques effective teachers use in working with groups of learners, both the total class group and small groups within the class, in the classroom situation and elsewhere. Part IV is concerned especially with the guidance role of teachers as they work with individual learners. Part V presents the specific jobs of teachers in planning instruction and in working for improvement. This organization of the book is designed to help readers appreciate the interrelatedness of different phases of dynamic teaching as well as develop increased understanding of the specifics of each phase.

The ideas and suggestions contained in *Effective Teaching in Secondary Schools* are based on our experiences as teachers in junior and senior high schools, as supervisors and administrators of programs of secondary education, as supervisors of student and beginning teachers, and as teachers of teachers. We gratefully acknowledge the help given us by our colleagues and students in clarifying our ideas and strengthening our insights about the nature of teaching method. We are specially grateful to the following educators, who reviewed the preliminary outline of this book: Professor Walter A. Anderson, Chairman of the Department of Administration and Supervision, School of Education, New York University; Dean Stephen M. Corey of Teachers College, Columbia University; Professor Earl M. Ramer, Head of the Department of Curriculum and Instruction, The University of Tennessee; and Professor William Van Til, Chairman of the Division of Curriculum and Teaching, George Peabody College for Teachers; and to Professor J. Donald Neill of Rutgers University, who reviewed the entire manuscript at a late stage in its development. We also wish to express appreciation to the various publishers who have given permission to quote from certain copyrighted publications, and to the individuals, school systems, and organizations which have made available some of the photographs and other illustrative materials used in our book.

W. M. A.
P. M. H.

Coral Gables, Florida
Syracuse, New York
January, 1956

Table of Contents

List of Figures

List of Tables

Part I The Teaching-Learning Process

What makes the difference between good and poor teaching? Between effective and ineffective learning? How does one teach pupils so that they will really behave differently? What is the relation between teaching and learning? What is the right method of teaching? These are the questions to which Part I of this book is devoted as an introduction to the specific activities of teachers described in the other parts.

The authors hope that Part I will help the reader understand the nature of modern teaching method and its critical elements. Since we regard the relation of teacher and pupils as central in the teaching-learning process, the two chapters in Part I give major attention to this relation. Teaching method in secondary schools, as we see it, is the process of guiding the problem-solving activities of adolescents. The nature of this process, the role of the teacher therein, and the factors which make a difference in teaching are described. Chapter 1 defines teaching method and the teacher's job, and Chapter 2 deals with three critical factors in the teaching-learning process: the teacher's personality, the nature of effective learning, and the characteristics of adolescence. A summary section in Chapter 2 states the authors' conclusions as to the significant characteristics of good teaching in secondary schools.

1. The Nature of Teaching Method

WHAT DO YOU THINK about teaching method? Is it just a necessary evil, or an unnecessary evil, or is it perchance the basis of our teaching profession? Is method a means of teaching, or is it teaching itself? What is the relation of method and content? Is there more than one teaching method? Perhaps your point of view may be found in one of those expressed in the following dialogue of some teachers-to-be.

WHAT ABOUT METHODS?

THE TIME: About 3:30 of a May afternoon

THE PLACE: "The Grotto"—a student hangout on the campus of Dearborn University

THE PRINCIPALS: Marj Smith, a history major; Jim Drake, a science major; and Lucile Johnson, an English major—all senior students in the College of Education. They are entering the hangout after the final meeting of their seminar on Problems of Secondary Education.

. . . . .

JIM: Boy, will a coke taste good after a session like that one! Let's sit over here in the corner where we can talk awhile. I've got some things I need to get off my chest.

LUCILE: What's bothering you, Jim? I noticed you seemed more restless than usual today—which is saying a lot.

MARJ: I thought you were going to explode when Doc Archer said that the teacher's primary job is to help kids solve their problems.

JIM: What a bunch of tripe that is. Here I am, a major in physical sciences after four years of training in my field, and it looks like my knowledge is only incidental to what the kids think they need or want. I don't get it!

MARJ: I get rather worried, too. I just love my world history, particularly the Renaissance period; but the way Prof Archer talks, there isn't any guarantee my kids at Wellsville will like it. Maybe that's why his

3

discussion and description of student committee work fascinated me. I think I'll start using that idea right away next fall.

JIM: Doc Walsh in chemistry was right. He warned me there wouldn't be much content in my education courses. Thank goodness, I know my subject. These theory and methods courses don't add up for me. I want to teach physics and chemistry.

LUCILE: You know, it's funny—during the last year I've realized how some of these education courses begin to fit together. I can't agree with you. I'm beginning to see the relation of ed psych courses, philosophy of education, mental hygiene, and others to how and what I'm going to teach in English.

JIM: Aha—another progressive has been spawned. Let's start with the kids where they are. To heck with subject matter.

MARJ: Relax, Jim. Lou, I'm not sure I see how these theories apply, but I certainly need all the techniques for teaching I can lay my hands on. I get scared to death when I think of my kids not liking history. I've got to fill my bag of tricks to interest them. I think history is awfully important, but anything I can pick up right now to interest them is very welcome.

JIM: I say that physics and chemistry are important. I know my subject, I put it out for them to learn; they can take it or leave it. None of this sugar-coating for me.

LUCILE: Jim, I bet you will find them both taking it and leaving it. But you are not practicing the things you say you believe about the importance of science in the modern world if you just leave it to the students to take it or leave it. Or do you think science is important for just a select few who are interested?

JIM: No, but I want to produce more than dabblers in science. I think kids ought to be subjected to a systematic, logical presentation of scientific facts and ideas, and I think I'm the guy who can do it.

LUCILE: Speaking of science—or more especially, the scientific method—do you as a scientist suggest that we keep on doing the same things in teaching even though the evidence is that we aren't achieving what we hope for? Can't we experiment with various methods to see which ones are more effective, and with which children?

MARJ: I think you're right, Lou. I'm willing to try anything.

LUCILE: But you're going to try to get some evidence, aren't you, on the effectiveness of these methods?

MARJ: I suppose so, if I have time. But my main concern is to keep kids interested and working.

JIM: Time—there's the rub. If I have so much physics to teach in a year, I've got to cover it. So many of these things we've talked about in Doc Archer's seminar take longer, and there's no guarantee kids will learn anyway.

LUCILE: But you just said that kids will take or leave your science, that is, learn it or not learn it. So you have no guarantee there either.

JIM: Which reminds me of one sure thing—I've got an exam tomorrow in organic—so I've got to run. Excuse me, gals—see you in Utopia where all kids are ready and anxious to learn and where we can really teach them what they ought to know. Bye now.

Conversations such as the above have taken place countless times among pre-service students of education. Their counterparts among in-service educators are legion. We might observe, however, that Lucile is found less frequently in both the pre-service and in-service ranks. Suppose we analyze further these three people to determine whom and what they represent. Maybe we can find clues in their backgrounds which may account for the attitudes they expressed toward teaching, students, and themselves. Maybe you can find some similarities in your beliefs and your background to those of Jim, Marj, or Lucile.

WHERE DO THESE ATTITUDES COME FROM?

Jim. Jim is an engaging, forthright young man with very positive ideas about the contribution which he and his subject field can make to the education of adolescents. In high school he was the salutatorian of his class, and received one of the highest grades ever recorded on the college board examination in science. He was active in science clubs, had his own "ham" radio station, and worked in a laboratory as a chemist's helper during the summer months.

It is rather interesting to speculate on why Jim chose the teaching of science as his lifework rather than research, engineering, or some allied activity. One should know that Jim has a highly altruistic side to his nature which forces him to espouse causes and ideals somewhat in advance of their time. The "atomic age" began when Jim was in high school, and Hiroshima left an indelible mark on his consciousness. Two years of military experience further convinced him of the need for a more common understanding of modern, technological society, both in war and peace. He saw in teaching an opportunity to make a contribution to such understanding.

Such drives in Jim have made his college work, particularly after his military service, a very challenging experience. He has been on the dean's list from the outset, and has served as a paid assistant for two years to the chairman of the Department of Physical Sciences. In such a setting he has had a chance to learn of differences in philosophy existing among the various departments and colleges on a university campus.

Marj. Marj is an attractive, poised young woman who has spent much of her time in college with social affairs and student service organizations. Her father is a history professor in a small private college, and her mother also attended college. During Marj's high school days, her father took his family with him for a year of study and travel in Europe. At that time Marj developed an interest in the history and culture of other nations and times which carried over into her college study. For several years she was undecided about her career, but finally chose teaching because it seemed to represent to her an opportunity for using her cultural interests and background. She is engaged to a premed student who still has five years of study before him. Following their marriage on graduation day, Marj plans to teach until her husband can set up his practice.

Marj is surprised and disillusioned by the failure of her younger brothers and sisters to share her enthusiasm for history and by the antagonism she encountered on the part of students while practice teaching. She is anxious to succeed, both because of her feeling about the importance of history, and because of her need to support her husband while he is preparing for medical practice.

Lucile. Lucile is a vivacious, friendly person with many interests— sports, reading, and volunteer community service organizations. She is the daughter of a carpenter-contractor who attended a trade school and a mother who did not finish high school. While in high school, Lucile was active in journalism, music, and sports, and finished in the upper third of her class in scholarship. Early in high school, she planned on taking secretarial training, but in her junior year the promise of an aunt to assist her financially and the moral support of her parents caused her to plan for a college training. Early in her college career, she chose teaching as a profession, partly because of the influence of one of her high school teachers, and also because she saw in it an outlet for her interest in literature, speaking, and writing.

During the summer months she has served as counselor at a girls' camp in Maine, and has tutored high school students in English. One of her great disappointments was the dropping out of her younger brother from high school. During her practice teaching experience, she interviewed sixty-five juniors and seniors on their future plans and how they saw the study of English contributing to those plans. She also experimented with several classes in English, using one to try out student correction of themes; with the other class, she was entirely responsible for correction of the themes.

TO THE READER

What is your idea now about methods? Is it like that of Jim or Marj or Lucile, or is it still different? And why is it what it is? What in your background of experience has made you arrive at a point of view on what teachers should do? Is one's experience an adequate basis for one's attitude toward teaching? Is it true that "teachers are what they have experienced"?

All students, including those planning to be teachers, are influenced greatly by their purposes and these in turn by their past experiences. Although we hope the experience of reading this book may change some attitudes, we must and do recognize that teachers, both present and prospective, differ in their points of view. We believe a first step in studying teaching method is to identify your ideas and attitudes about method. This is why we have begun this chapter and book as we have.

Whatever your point of view, the authors hope you approach this book with a real desire to teach and to teach well. If in addition to this desire you can look at the facts and principles of methodology with an open, inquiring mind, you are certain to profit from study of our material. Good luck!

A DEFINITION OF TEACHING METHOD

The reader may be surprised at our approach thus far with its emphasis on personalities—the backgrounds, interests, and purposes of prospective teachers. We believe that this approach is an appropriate keynote to a book on teaching method, for method is a highly personalized process involving people—teachers and pupils. From what we know about school situations, it seems that teachers and pupils are the most important elements in education. All other elements—supplies, subject matter, buildings, administrators, supervisors, parents, and so forth—important as they are, are subsidiary to the fundamental human relationships which exist between teacher and learners in an educative situation.

Teaching method, as we see it, embodies the teacher's efforts in the teacher-pupil relations to bring about individual and group problem-solving activities. These teacher efforts are almost inextricably related to pupils' activities. In the very best teaching-learning relation, teacher and pupils alike are searching for tenable solutions of mutually recognized problems—searching through individual reflection and group sharing. But we must seek a definition of teaching method which makes clear and specific the teacher's role. Accordingly, in this section we explore several theories of method to arrive at a working definition.

We often hear definitions such as

1. Subject matter is *what* we teach, method is *how* we teach.

2. The *ends* are learning, the *means* the way we achieve such learning.

3. The *product* is the outcome of a learning experience, the *process* is how we provide for the experience to take place.

Such definitions account for the pitfalls into which many teachers fall as they think about educational methods. Jim, confident of the efficacy of his subject matter, found it difficult to see and appreciate the need for consideration of appropriate settings for learning to take place. Marj, less confident of her subject matter, sought teaching panaceas in techniques and gadgets of method. Have you had teachers like these?

For purposes of their discussion, this separation of means and ends, of process and product, might have assisted Jim and Marj in coming to grips with specific value judgments of the *what* and *how* of teaching. But when entangled with their own backgrounds of experiences and their resulting biases and prejudices, Jim and Marj lost their objectivity. They became inconsistent and muddled, and eventually resorted to what seemed to be the safest position to take—an absolute.

JIM: Thank goodness, I know my subject.
MARJ: I've got to fill my bag of tricks to interest them.

Similarly, many teachers retreat from inconsistencies in their points of view to dogmatic reliance on authority or techniques. Only Lucile was beginning to see the relation of method to outcomes, of process to product, of means to ends.

LUCILE: I'm beginning to see the relation of ed psych courses, philosophy of education, mental hygiene, and others to *how* and *what* I'm going to teach in English.

Unlike Jim, who rejected the problem of the *how* in favor of the *what*, or Marj, who hoped to get security in the *how*, perhaps at the expense of the *what*, Lucile was beginning to see the essential unity of means and ends, of teaching and learning. One sees why Jim and Marj, with their concepts of the role of the teacher and teaching, could not understand Doc Archer's statement, "The teacher's primary job is to assist pupils in solving problems." Can you understand it?

THE ROLE OF METHOD IN FUNCTIONAL LEARNING

The central emphasis of newer pedagogical method is that "true" learning is always purposeful. Without purpose, a learner retains mere facts for only a short time, and obviously never incorporates in his behavior real understanding based on such facts. For learning to be efficient in respect to time and energy, and permanent to the point where it is useful, the purposes of the learner must be involved in the learning situation. The method of teaching then becomes at best the teacher's effective ways of helping learners employ some material or experience for some end or purpose. Unless that material or experience is seen by the learner as important for his purposes, learning will be inefficient in respect to time and energy, and short-lived.

This fact is hard for Jim to assimilate, because *his* purposes make science so important that he fails to recognize the need for looking at content in relation to other people's purposes. And the baffling dilemma is that the more he learns because of *his* purposes, the more he is convinced that his pupils should learn what he has learned. This is a frustrating desire, because pupils will never be so obliging! Until Jim can be convinced that pupils learn in terms of solving problems important to them, his role will be that of telling them what they ought to learn. Teaching method is bound up with people and their purposes, and the fact that the *what* and *how* of teaching are inseparable appears to be Jim's greatest ignorance.

Marj likewise views method as extraneous to content. While concerned over the lack of interest of students in her subject, she is willing for various reasons to settle for methods which will "interest" them. Her assumption is that students will expend time and energy and will learn because of the method employed. Many teachers have overworked tricks and techniques in just this belief. Marj places, as does Jim, the *what* of learning apart from the *how*. Even though personally convinced of the value of her subject, she fears that history will not sell itself on its own merits. Her anxiety prompts her to look toward techniques and devices as means to the interests of learners. She is sure that pupils will see values and purposes for them in the Renaissance if only she can interest them. Whereas Jim believes that learners should have purposes related to science and therefore that methods are unimportant, Marj is not sure that students see their purposes relating to her subject. She views methods therefore as very important in creating purposes, or "interests," as she terms them.

Both Jim and Marj are troubled by the same fallacy that prevails among large numbers of teachers—the view that subject matter in a ready-made systematized framework can be imposed upon learners. Jim has faith that his expertness in the subject, plus the inevitable presence of problems which science can solve, will result in learning— ergo, his impatience with methods of teaching. Marj, less sure of herself and the learners' purposes, sees methods as tricks of the trade which will sell her subject. To Jim, only subject matter is necessary;

to Marj, subject matter needs "sugar-coating." Many teachers of Jim's beliefs simply assign and lecture, while those like Marj persuade, coerce, and "motivate."

In contrast, Lucile for a variety of reasons sees the *what* and *how* of teaching as closely bound together. Certain experiences, both in her professional courses and her everyday life, have given her some ideas on the content of her English teaching. At the same time, her experience also tempers her enthusiasm for the ends she has in mind to the point where she mentions the *how* of her teaching in the same breath. Just as she sees the unitary relation of educational psychology and philosophy of education, so she sees content and method as mutually supportive to her role as a teacher. She refuses to place her confidence in either subject matter or methodology per se, but sees them as interacting elements in a good learning situation. She will not determine content first and let method develop as it will, as Jim proposes. Nor will she prescribe methods unrelated to subject matter, as Marj is tempted to do. The Luciles in teaching try to help learners find content which relates to their recognized needs.

Lucile hopes to remain sufficiently flexible in her own thinking and in her relation to learners to make content and method the joint concerns of teacher and pupil. This demands of Lucile a measure of security which is found infrequently in teachers. She must understand and accept herself, must really know and accept the learners for what they are. In such a climate, content and method are more likely to develop harmoniously, although, to be sure, less logically than in Jim's classroom and perhaps with less teacher direction than in Marj's room. The *how* of learning will develop automatically as Lucile studies content, as she plans with pupils in the light of problems which suggest the purposes for learning.

But the fundamental difference between the approach of Lucile and that of her two friends will be her experimental attitude to teaching. With her there will be no adamant attitude toward methods as sugar-coating, nor will there be a frantic adoption of any idea or innovation that comes along. At all times Lucile will get evidence on the relative success of the methods which she and the pupils employ, always in relation to their purposes. Thus the method itself, the way of solving problems reflectively, becomes content for teacher and learner alike to the point where eventually many pupils will learn how best to solve their own problems. This *scientific method* is really the only way of learning and must be the basis of teaching method.

The problem-solving approach to teaching is highly desirable for adolescent learners who are preparing for the time when they must

increasingly solve their own problems with less and less adult direction or guidance. And therein, we believe, resides the strongest argument for the unity of means and ends, of content and method. The
argument is soundly conceived from a pragmatic standpoint, both for
efficiency of learning at the moment and for future utility of adults
who must be better equipped to solve problems in terms of facts and
skills.

CONTRASTING THEORIES OF THE TEACHING-LEARNING PROCESS

Although we believe that our point of view regarding the unity of
content and method is well supported by the research and theory concerning learning and teaching,[1] it must be noted that the actual practice of teaching in the classrooms of American secondary schools does
not universally reflect this point of view. Observation of prevailing
teaching methods indicates at least three different interpretations of
the teaching-learning process. Brief review of these may help the
teacher clarify his understanding of the nature of teaching method.

Pupils Absorb What Teachers Tell. The predominant method of
teaching in higher education is the lecture. Unfortunately, the same
procedure is used in one form or another by many high school teachers.
The familiar definition of a lecture as the process whereby the teacher's
notes are transferred from his notebook to those of his students without passing through the minds of either may be more fact than fiction.
Critical analysis of the lecture method reveals the following assumptions, each of which may be questioned:

1. The teacher's role is to *tell* pupils what they need to know.
2. The pupil learns by listening to the teller, reviewing notes taken
on the lecture, perhaps thinking, but usually memorizing what is told,
and thereby *absorbing* what he needs to know.

The fallacy of this point of view lies in the phrase "what he needs to
know." Learning takes place only when the individual learner consciously seeks to satisfy a need that he believes is important to him. It is
highly unlikely that any lecture can be so presented that all hearers will
actively seek to understand all the material as satisfying their needs.
A good lecturer does attempt to establish reasons why what he has to
tell is important. If these reasons are accepted, if the telling is done in
such a manner that there is a clear relation between what is told and
why it is important, then learners may follow the telling through
thinking processes. If the telling is based on learners' questions, if

[1] See Walter S. Monroe, *Teaching-Learning Theory and Teacher Education,
1890 to 1950* (Urbana: University of Illinois Press, 1952), Part I, for a review
of the major theories of the learning-teaching process held during recent
educational history.

there is frequent opportunity for further questions, the learners' purposeful activity can be utilized.

However, even under best conditions, telling is a highly limited teaching method. Since learners listen in terms of their individual interests and in the light of their individual experiences, what is heard is not identical with each learner. Except for his questions, the individual learner has no opportunity to direct his listening activities to his own problems. Since listening is only one of many learning activities, overuse of the telling method neglects the possibilities of learning through varied activities. Since the idea of learning by absorption is wholly inconsistent with the facts of learning, it is understandable that most of what pupils hear through lectures is not long remembered, perhaps not longer than the final examination!

The telling method is used in ways other than the traditional lecture. Question periods in which the teacher is always relied upon for the correct answer is essentially a telling procedure, although use of pupil questions may make for more active learning processes than absorption. The use of committee and individual reports is a telling method for those merely listening, and the evident boredom observed on the part of many listeners is indication enough of the inadequate involvement of the latter in purposeful activity. The recitation procedure so commonly employed in high school is considered below as a separate method, but it does have some of the telling approach because the teacher is usually telling by approval or disapproval what is correct.

Pupils Learn by Memorizing and Reciting What Teachers Assign. Despite the many professional criticisms directed against it in this century, the question-answer recitation is probably still used more extensively than any other procedure in high school classrooms. The procedure is usually like this:

1. Pupils are given an assignment of materials to read, terms to learn, questions to answer, exercises to work out, and so forth, either out of class or during supervised study periods.

2. When the class convenes, the teacher hears pupils recite on their assignment—that is, questions are asked by the teacher and answered by the pupils, or the exercises or definitions or questions are gone over one by one.

Underlying this procedure is generally the assumption that pupils will learn by memorizing the answers and definitions. There is the further idea that the recitation helps fix these "learnings" in pupils' minds. The fallacy of the procedure lies in the fact of forgetting, for there is very little permanent retention of material so memorized. Also to be noted is the fact that the assign-memorize-recite procedure, like the lecture, ignores basic processes of learning. An assignment to learn given all members of the class in no way assures that each will accept as his goal the acquisition of the facts or concepts to be learned, nor does it take into account the varying experiences which individual pupils can apply to the assignment. The reciting of answers to teachers' questions is not an activity of sufficient interest to learners in general to make reasonable any assumption that each will be following actively the recitation and engaging in considering, applying, and testing the material recited. More likely, even attentive learners are more occupied with learning how to anticipate and answer the questions so as to make an acceptable impression.

The authors do not mean to suggest the complete elimination of memorizing and reciting activities. Once learners wish to acquire skills of working in mathematics, science, or languages, for example, and after understanding how to use these skills, practice periods may be highly desirable. Such practice or memorization may be occasionally aided by a type of oral drill like the recitation. However, individual memorizing and group drill on skills in handling scientific equipment, the use of which is understood and practiced, is quite a different matter from memorizing fixed answers to questions, neither questions nor answers being understood, in the civics textbook. Mathematical operations may be used sufficiently frequently by the learner to become a part of his behavior pattern, but such memorized matter as "the functions of the legislative branch" is likely to be a combination of words that once repeated a few times becomes a set phrase without particular meaning, to be forgotten as soon as the necessity for repetition in class disappears.

Pupils Learn from Experiences Guided by Teachers. Although listening, if this is the meaning we attach to absorption, and memorizing are learning experiences too, they have significance only as they are a part of a problem-solving process important to the learner. Learning is significant, we believe, only if it affects the individual's behavior. In fact, it follows from the concept of learning in terms of problem solving that learning is a change in behavior, that is, a modified or new behavior which solves the individual's problem. Every experience has some effect, however slight or negative, on the individual, but as teachers we are interested in learners having significant and positive effects from their learning experiences. Therefore our concern is properly with the learner's purposeful experiences which can be guided to result in desirable changes in behavior. Our job as teachers is to help learners formulate problems and carry on problem-solving activities that will result in better behavior than we would expect to come from boys' and girls' unguided experiences. Our guidance or help is "teaching."

The fact is clear that boys and girls learn with or without teachers. They learn from experience, and experience is continuous with life. But experiences are appropriate and inappropriate, desirable and undesirable, effective and ineffective, in changing people's behavior

PLATE 1. DISCUSSION AND PLANNING RATHER THAN RECITATION ARE CHARACTERISTIC OF EFFECTIVE LEARNING SITUATIONS. Teachers can guide more purposeful experiences in these situations. (Courtesy of the Oak Ridge, Tennessee, Public Schools)

for the better. Schools exist to affect the quality of learners' experiences—to provide appropriate, desirable, and effective experiences. Likewise, teachers are employed to guide these experiences. The challenge of teaching is to guide boys and girls to have the most appropriate, desirable, and effective learning experiences possible— that is, to solve their most important problems by the best activities possible. It may be important to point out here that problem solving at its best is an act of reflective thinking. The individual does not just happen on to a solution; he tries out, reflectively, various possible solutions until he arrives at the solution which he has no reason, from past experience or present tryout, to reject. The critical intellectual activity we call reflection is most likely to occur in a problem situation, and is man's most effective method of problem solving. From such reflections, learners secure insights that guide their actions in future, similar problem situations. Hence our most effective teaching actions are those which stimulate and give direction to pupils' reflective processes.

METHOD OR METHODS?

It is to be emphasized that teaching method is inclusive. It may on occasion involve lectures and hearing of recitations. Good teachers follow no one narrow set of techniques, but instead use whatever means seem best to help learners become increasingly effective persons. Thus the teacher's choice is not what method is best, but what techniques will work best for the particular combination of individuals and situations. Some learners may need a great deal of direct help. Some problems may be of such common concern that brief, interesting lectures (explanations) may be economical. Many problems may be best attacked through work by small groups. Drill in needed skills, once their use is understood, may be helped through occasional recitationlike procedures. Pupils' previous experiences must be known so that changes can be made in techniques in the light of pupils' readiness for different ones. Always the *method* of teaching is the process of guiding learners' problem-solving activities, but the techniques of effective guidance of these activities vary greatly.

Thus there is the broad, inclusive concept of "teaching method" which we have presented and there are also the specific "methods" teachers use in their total job of guiding learning. It may be helpful, at least semantically, to keep in mind a distinction between *technique* and *method*. The former we may consider as a specific way of doing a particular task in the methodology of education—for example, the technique of organizing a committee of learners, of recording a summary on the blackboard, or of conducting a discussion. The latter we have already defined as the process of teacher guidance of pupils' problem-solving activities.

We should note here that there have been many patterns of techniques to which particular names have been given in educational methodology: the Morrisonian plan, the Dalton plan, the socialized recitation, the laboratory method, the demonstration method, the project method, the recitation, and many others. In recent years, however, the practice of naming particular patterns of techniques seems to have declined. According to Monroe's review of teaching-learning theory, "there appears to be a tendency to think of a 'method of teaching' in terms of an ordered enumeration of the teacher's instructional responsibilities rather than of 'methods of teaching,' each defined in terms of an organization of teaching 'devices.' "[2] This tendency does not justify the adoption of a particular set of minute steps that must be taken in like fashion in every situation, for situations and human interactions in these situations differ. We can and do distinguish, however, certain general responsibilities which are described in a subsequent section and illustrated in Table 1 (see pages 20–21)

THE METHOD OF DEMOCRATIC EDUCATION

Before concluding this introductory discussion of the meaning of method, it seems wise to relate it to American public schools and their role in our democracy. There are persons who would insist that educational methods should rise or fall on their demonstrated efficiency alone. That is, a method is considered good only if it produces learning of predetermined material.

Under this philosophy, many sincere teachers, desirous of achievement for learners and imbued with almost fanatical zeal for what they deem to be the contribution of their subjects, could justify unwholesome means to reach desirable ends. Our Jim and Marj might become such teachers. The entire range of extrinsic motivation—praise and blame, reward and punishment, promises and threats—may well drive learners to achieve, for the moment at least. Aside from the matter of the permanence of such learning, there is the fundamental question: Does one demonstrate democratic faith in the integrity and potentialities of human beings by resorting to such methods? That is, can we teach people democratic values through undemocratic procedures? Can we teach values at all unless learners have or accept the need for values?

Again we bring up the cogency of *purposeful* learning and the support it lends to fundamental learning, as well as to democratic beliefs concerning the dignity and worth of the individual. American education cannot afford to by-pass the question of democratic method any more than it can neglect the testing of the efficiency of teaching methods. It is hoped that we can demonstrate in this book that democratic teaching methods are pragmatic; that is, they are most efficient, both from the standpoint of pupil learning in school situations and, more important, in subsequent changed behavior as adults when confronted with problems pressing for solution.

[2] Monroe, *op. cit.*, p. 177.

A SUMMARY OF WHAT TEACHING METHOD IS

We hope that the foregoing statements have clarified our position regarding the essential unity of means and ends in education. What is learned and how it is learned are not discrete phases of education, for

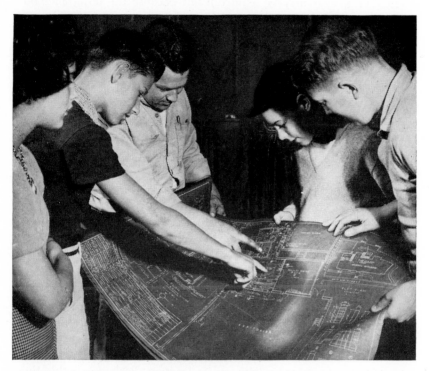

PLATE 2. EFFECTIVE TEACHING IS SPARKED BY THE INTERESTS AND PROBLEMS OF PUPILS. The teacher and pupils work together in a good learning situation. (Courtesy of the Portland, Oregon, Public Schools)

the *how* of learning is also an end result or a *what* of learning. The authors regard teaching method as all the techniques teachers use to guide pupils in achieving their learning purposes, in solving their problems. The scientific method of thinking is the method of learning. Its counterpart, from the teacher's standpoint, is the problem-solving approach to teaching. The ultimate goal of teaching method is the better use of the scientific method of problem solving, that is, orderly reflection, by pupils. Thus ways of working on problems, as well as verbal concepts and discrete skills, are the learnings of the teaching-learning process.

We have emphasized the teaching-learning process as one of interaction between learners and teachers, which is sparked by the learners' purposes rather than by the teacher's bag of tricks. This concept of the interaction process may be a bit difficult because the term "method" to most teachers means what they do rather than what *teachers and pupils do together.* This is why we just defined method as the composite of techniques that the teacher uses in guiding the learning process. The important point is to recognize that teaching method which works involves what learners do as well as what teachers do.

WHAT DOES THE TEACHER DO?

Although method involves the activities of both learners and their teacher, there are definite responsibilities and jobs for the teacher. These tasks in teaching method constitute the major subject matter of this book and we now turn to their classification.

THE TEACHER'S RESPONSIBILITIES

The responsibilities of secondary school teachers from the time standpoint as revealed by a 1950 survey conducted by the National Education Association are shown in Figure 1. This figure shows that on the average in 1950, 25 per cent of the teacher's time was spent in miscellaneous duties not necessarily related to classroom instruction. It is with the remaining 75 per cent of his time that we are primarily concerned in this book, although we should note that some of the non-instructional time, such as that for club sponsorship and report cards, may have an important relation to instruction. Perhaps all this time should be related to maintaining good planning and working conditions for learning in the school as a whole.

Many studies have been made of the detailed activities teachers carry on. As an extreme example, the comprehensive *Commonwealth Teacher-Training Study* used a check list of teachers' activities that included 1,010 items.[3] Although teachers may find interesting and useful the reports of such studies for comparison with or in anticipation of their own duties, we believe that a more significant need is that of understanding the various phases of guiding pupil learning. It is important, we believe, for the teacher to be able to fit activities into their proper place in relation to the basic job of helping boys and girls

[3] W. W. Charters and Douglas Waples, *The Commonwealth Teacher-Training Study* (Chicago: University of Chicago Press, 1929), pp. 254–303.

achieve learning purposes. The major phases of this job are briefly described in the following paragraphs, and reference is made to the later sections of this book dealing with each phase and the many subordinate activities included.

HOW THE SECONDARY-SCHOOL TEACHER DIVIDES THE WEEK

(Average work-week of 47 hours, 58 minutes)

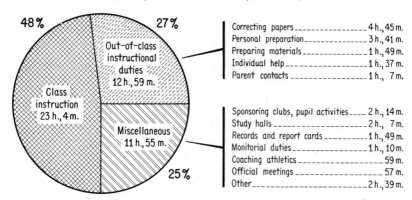

Correcting papers	4 h., 45 m.
Personal preparation	3 h., 41 m.
Preparing materials	1 h., 49 m.
Individual help	1 h., 37 m.
Parent contacts	1 h., 7 m.

Sponsoring clubs, pupil activities	2 h., 14 m.
Study halls	2 h., 7 m.
Records and report cards	1 h., 49 m.
Monitorial duties	1 h., 10 m.
Coaching athletics	59 m.
Official meetings	57 m.
Other	2 h., 39 m.

Fig. 1. The Teacher's Week. (Courtesy of Research Division, National Education Association, *Research Bulletin*, 20:19, February, 1951)

THE PHASES OF TEACHING METHOD

In considering these major aspects of teaching method, readers may find helpful the brief enumeration of items under "What Does the Good Teacher Do?" contained in the check list in Table 1. This check list, prepared by a group of teachers and supervisors doing graduate work in the field of secondary school supervision at the University of Miami, indicates six phases of the teacher's job. As the authors see it, there are four discrete aspects of teaching method, and we now describe each of these briefly in relation to corresponding divisions of our book.

Organizing the Learning Situation. Both the novice and the experienced teacher sometimes operate under the assumption that once there is a class roll and a textbook and a seat for everybody the learning situation is organized. We believe that the physical characteristics and arrangement of the classroom, with which we deal in Chapter 3, are much more complex and highly important factors in learning. For effective group relationships, there must be study of the interpersonal relationships and other factors involved in the dynamics of the learn-

Table 1

What Does the Good Teacher Do?

Directions: Check your performance on each item according to
how you rate yourself in comparison with the performance of
the poorest (1) and best (5) teachers you have known.

	(Poorest)				(Best)
	1	2	3	4	5

I. PREPARING FOR THE TEACHING SITUATION

    A. Maintains records of appropriate teaching resources

    B. Participates in faculty planning for the total school program

    C. Makes adequate, sound, and flexible plans for each learning situation

    D. Coordinates his plan of work with that of teachers of same or related fields

    E. Studies the backgrounds of pupils

II. ORGANIZING THE LEARNING SITUATION

    A. Organizes classroom procedure early

    B. Arranges for distribution of routine classroom responsibilities

    C. Adapts physical facilities to group needs

    D. Organizes such small groups as needed

    E. Identifies and uses wisely pupil leaders

    F. Guides cooperative planning of standards of behavior

III. GUIDING THE LEARNING ACTIVITIES OF THE WHOLE CLASS

    A. Establishes worth-while goals and means through pupil-teacher planning

    B. Provides for total class participation

    C. Helps pupils to develop effective communication skills

    D. Suggests materials and resources to pupils to be used in problem solving

    E. Plans culminating activities which evaluate and summarize each unit of work

    F. Provides adequate opportunity for socializing experiences

IV. GUIDING THE LEARNING ACTIVITIES OF SMALL GROUPS

    A. Attempts to understand each group's purpose

    B. Helps the pupils become well acquainted with each other

(*Poorest*) (*Best*)
1   2   3   4   5

C. Promotes pupil participation in various types of group activities . . . .

D. Makes effective use of individual abilities in the small group . . . .

E. Helps group members to clarify their problems . . . .

F. Encourages creative ideas in group activities . . . . . .

G. Serves as consultant or resource person for the group . . . .

H. Develops skills more effectively through use of small groups . . . .

V. GUIDING THE LEARNING ACTIVITIES OF INDIVIDUALS

A. Stresses individual recognition and participation in class situations . . . .

B. Shows sympathetic understanding of needs and problems of the individual . . . .

C. Helps pupils develop new interests . . . .

D. Aids pupils in formulating and developing desirable sets of values . . . .

E. Makes available time for pupils to pursue their own individual interests . . . .

F. Provides time for individual help in learning problems . . . .

G. Guides pupils in understanding their needs and progress . . . .

VI. GUIDING EVALUATIVE ACTIVITIES

A. Provides opportunity for frequent and critical self-evaluation . . . .

B. Provides for pupil-teacher evaluation of the learning situation . . . .

C. Uses a variety of means to evaluate pupil progress . . . .

D. Encourages improvement through use of evaluative techniques . . . .

ing group (Chapter 4). In the light of this study the group must be organized for effective work (Chapter 5), and agreements and plans must be made for how the group and its members work together, that is, for discipline (Chapter 6).

Guiding Group Learning Experiences. In common practice most high school classes are taught on the basis of the group's working as a whole. For effective work by groups of the size usually found in high school classes, there must be a considerable degree of skill in group work on the part of the members. The teacher's responsibility for de-

veloping these skills and for leading groups in cooperative planning
for their learning experiences is developed in Chapters 7 and 8. In
better practice there is also extensive use made of small groups or
committees within the total class. Chapter 9 deals with the guidance

PLATE 3. EFFECTIVE TEACHING INCLUDES WORK WITH SMALL GROUPS.
Extensive use is made of such small groups for more effective
teacher-pupil relationships. (Courtesy of the Phoenix, Arizona,
Union High School)

of these subgroups. Effective learning also involves extensive use of
learning experiences outside the classroom, and the teacher's job in
this connection is explained in Chapter 10.

Helping Individual Learners. Although individuals do learn effectively, in some respects more effectively, in group situations, they
require the teacher's direct help in many instances. In order to give
individuals help, indeed to teach effectively, teachers must study the
needs of their individual pupils (Chapter 11). The whole problem of
providing for the great range of individual differences in any class-

room group is a challenging one with which we deal in Chapter 12. The teacher's function in evaluating pupil progress (Chapter 13) is also a matter of studying and helping individual learners.

Planning and Improving Instruction. The preplanning of instructional units is a rather specialized job of cooperative curriculum planning of teachers as distinct from the pupil-teacher planning dealt with in Part III. This preplanning process is described in Chapter 14, and Chapter 15 is devoted to the teacher's day-by-day tasks of planning and preparation. The final chapter (16) of this book presents our ideas and suggestions on ways and means of continuing improvement of the teacher's work.

HOW DO TEACHERS LEARN ABOUT TEACHING METHOD?

The teacher in training or in service must realize that his learning how to teach is acquired through the same teaching-learning process as that with which we deal in this book. There must be first of all a real desire on the part of the prospective teacher to learn how to do a good job or on the part of the teacher in service to do a better job. Once there is a purpose on the part of the teacher-learner, the know-how can be acquired. There is needed only a process of experiencing or learning wisely guided by your college teacher and/or school supervisor to solve your problems in teaching and thereby achieve your purposes in this learning process. Some of the usual better experiences through which teaching method is learned are summarized in subsequent sections. The authors hope that each reader-teacher may have a maximum of effective experiences of these types.

COURSES IN TEACHING METHODS

Probably many of the readers of this book will be taking courses in methods of teaching in high school, or in general methods, or in student teaching or internship, or courses of related title. Such courses are universally offered in teacher-education institutions and may contribute a great deal to the learning of teachers. They frequently include such experiences as study of a textbook like this one, readings about the theory and practice of teaching in supplementary sources like those listed at the end of our chapters, observation of teaching practices, viewing of films and other visual aids showing teaching practice, participation in sociodrama dealing with methods of teaching, and, during student teaching, actual teaching. All these experiences can help the teacher answer his questions about the elements of method.

OBSERVATION OF TEACHING PRACTICE

There is no adequate substitute for firsthand experience in seeing teaching-learning processes at work. For the prospective teacher, this may mean a definite program of observation of various high school classes as a part of the study of teaching. If definite provision is not made by the college for observation in secondary school classrooms, the teacher in training will find it highly profitable to arrange, perhaps through his college instructor or perhaps through some principal or teacher he knows, for some observation. If the observation is to be worth while, there should be some definite plan that includes specifics to be looked for and a chance to discuss what was observed with the teacher and/or another observer. Many written guides for observation are used in teacher-education classes. The check list in Table 1 may be used for this purpose, but better as a guide in discussion of what was observed.

For teachers in service, observation is usually easily arranged with other teachers either by the teacher directly or through a principal or supervisor. Many schools encourage intervisitation of teachers to promote the exchange of ideas and experiences. Again there is needed a purpose for observation and an opportunity to discuss what is observed.

Although college classes (and high school classes also) may not demonstrate well the teaching method described in this book, teachers in training should realize that every class of which they are members is an opportunity to observe the teacher-learning process in action. Systematic evaluations of the classes in which they are enrolled may sharpen their understandings of teaching method as well as improve the teaching and learning involved and are frequently encouraged in teacher-education classes. Similarly, retrospection about classes in high school which prospective teachers once attended may be helpful.

USE OF DESCRIPTIONS OF TEACHING PRACTICE

A variety of published, filmed, and recorded descriptions of classroom practices may be effectively used by teachers to get help in their acquisition of know-how in teaching. Many of the books cited at the end of this and other chapters include descriptions of actual practice, and we are including in this book as many descriptions as our space permits. Such a casebook of practices as *Toward Better Teaching* (1949 Yearbook of the Association for Supervision and Curriculum Development, National Education Association) is especially helpful. A very fruitful source of others' experiences is periodical literature.

Such professional journals as *NEA Journal, Educational Leadership, School Review,* and *Clearing House* carry many articles of general interest dealing with descriptions of classroom practice. Each of the major subject areas is represented nationally by an organization which publishes a journal including articles describing practices in the area concerned. Information about these organizations and their publications is included in Appendix II. In addition, the journals of the state educational organizations include many descriptive materials.

A number of significant audiovisual aids for teacher education are now available. A selected list of those dealing with teaching method is also included in Appendix I of this book. Use of these materials in teacher-education classes or in-service study groups, faculty meetings, or workshops may be an effective means for teachers to learn about the practices of others.

LEARNING HOW TO TEACH BY TEACHING

The theory of "learning by doing" is as applicable to teaching method as it is to any other field of learning. However, it is not to be loosely interpreted in teaching method any more than elsewhere. One learns effectively by doing only as one has valid purposes and necessary background information, and then consciously evaluating one's learning and seeking for ever more satisfying learning. The teacher who teaches the same way day in and day out is not learning how to teach better any more than the pupil who makes the same errors in his written work repeatedly is learning to write better. Evaluation and experimentation must be continuous parts of the process of learning how to teach.

The beginning teacher, including the student teacher or intern, can learn a great deal about how to teach from his own experience. In fact, there is no better source of know-how, *provided* the beginner goes at his job with an inquiring mind and a disposition to find fault with his own work and make corrections therein. Hence the authors suggest very frequent use of some evaluation guide. The critic teacher, supervisor, or other person can help, but the most effective evaluation will be that which the teacher makes of his own work. For this purpose, some written guide can be most helpful. So can careful reflection on the question, "How am I doing?" provided again there is an attitude of inquiry which seeks to get evidence about how one is doing. This evidence may come from learners, from persons in supervisory capacities, and from the teacher's own sincere application of such criteria as pupil interest and effort in the classroom situation.

Whatever method the teacher uses to evaluate his own work, the essential step in improvement is that of continuous seeking of better ways when it is evident that existing ways are inadequate. The zeal to try something better, the will to modify what one does for something that may be better even if more difficult, the energy to search for new practices and answers to questions—these are the *sine qua non* of the good teacher. Teaching as one knows best, getting evidence regarding how the process is working, and experimenting with promising, different ways—this is the essence of the teacher's own learning process and of the approach to methodology which this book makes. In Chapter 2 we turn to more systematic examination of the critical factors in teaching method from the standpoint of teachers and learners in secondary schools, and in the remainder of the book to the specifics of the teacher's job in guiding learning.

FOR FURTHER STUDY

Alexander, William M., and Samuel Ersoff, "Schools for Adolescents: Instructional Procedures," *Review of Educational Research*, 24:54–65 (February), 1954.
　Review of significant research studies pertaining to teaching method in secondary schools. Bibliography includes eighty-one items.

Bode, Boyd H., *How We Learn*. Boston: D. C. Heath & Company, 1940.
　See Chapters 10, 13, and 15 for Bode's analysis of problem-solving processes.

Brownell, William A., "Learning Theory and Educational Practice," *Journal of Educational Research*, 41:481–497 (March), 1948.
　Points out the gap between learning theory and teaching practice.

Burton, William H., *The Guidance of Learning Activities*. 2nd ed.; New York: Appleton-Century-Crofts, Inc., 1952.
　See Part I for Burton's analysis of learning as an introduction to methodology.

Cantor, Nathaniel, *The Teaching-Learning Process*. New York: The Dryden Press, Inc., 1953.
　Based on discussions of the author and groups of teachers, this book describes the teaching-learning process from the point of view of the teacher.

"Creative Teaching," *Educational Leadership*, 10:138–200 (December), 1952.
　This issue contains several significant articles on methodology.

Dewey, John, *How We Think*. Boston: D. C. Heath & Company, 1933.
　Dewey's conception of thought processes is basic in the theory of learning as problem solving.

Doll, Ronald C., "High-School Pupils' Attitudes toward Teaching Procedures," *School Review*, 55:222–227 (April), 1947.

Study of pupils' attitudes toward low-level and high-level democratic, laissez-faire, and autocratic procedures of teachers.

Kelley, Earl C., and Marie I. Rasey, *Education and the Nature of Man.* New York: Harper & Brothers, 1952.
Treats methodology critically in the light of modern knowledge about the nature of man.

Marshall, Max S., *Two Sides to a Teacher's Desk.* New York: The Macmillan Company, 1951.
See for a well-written, somewhat challenging philosophy of methodology, relevant to higher education.

Melvin, A. G., *General Methods of Teaching.* New York: McGraw-Hill Book Co., Inc., 1952.
Presents a modern philosophy of teaching method.

Monroe, Walter S., *Teaching-Learning Theory and Teacher Education, 1890–1950.* Urbana: University of Illinois Press, 1952.
Part 1 is an excellent source on the historical development of the modern theory of teaching and learning.

Passow, A. Harry, and Gordon N. Mackenzie, "Research in Group Behavior Shows Need for New Teaching Skills," *Nation's Schools,* 49:71–73 (April), 1952.
Indicates types of teaching skills necessary in organizing for effective group work.

Rasey, Marie I., *This Is Teaching.* New York: Harper & Brothers, 1950.
Written as a record of a college seminar conducted on a cooperative-planning basis, and centered around students' problems, this book both illustrates problem-solving processes and presents a basic philosophy of methodology.

Simpson, Ray H., *Improving Teaching-Learning Processes.* New York: Longmans, Green & Co., Inc., 1953.
Deals with the problem-solving nature of learning and the teacher's role in aiding learners' problem-solving processes.

Spears, Harold, *Principles of Teaching.* New York: Prentice-Hall, Inc., 1951.
Treats teaching from the position of the schools (Part I), the pupil (Part II), and the teacher (Part III).

Stiles, Lindley J., "Methods of Teaching," in Walter S. Monroe, ed., *Encyclopedia of Educational Research.* Rev. ed.; New York: The Macmillan Company, 1950, pp. 745–753.
Stiles' review of the research is presented in terms of three general categories of teaching method: teacher-centric, pupil-centric, and cooperative-group method.

————, and Mattie F. Dorsey, *Democratic Teaching in Secondary Schools.* Chicago: J. B. Lippincott Company, 1950.
Part I, especially its Chapters 4 and 5, presents an excellent analysis of methodology.

Thelen, Herbert A., and Ralph W. Tyler, "Implications for Improving Instruction in the High School," in *Learning and Instruction.* Forty-ninth

Yearbook of the National Society for the Study of Education; Chicago: University of Chicago Press, 1950, Part I, Chap. 12.
   Defines methodology as a set of procedures for dealing with problem-solving processes and describes phases of this methodology.

Wiles, Kimball, *Teaching for Better Schools*. New York: Prentice-Hall, Inc., 1952.
   See Chapters 1 and 2 for Wiles's inviting interpretation of methodology.

2. Critical Factors in
Teaching Method

Ɪɴ Cʜᴀᴘᴛᴇʀ 1 we dealt with the nature of teaching method, and described its major phases: organizing the learning situation, guiding group-learning experiences, helping individual learners, and planning and improving instruction. In all four phases, that is, in method as a whole, there are certain basic factors which make a significant difference in teaching success even among teachers who try to follow the same general procedures. In this chapter we shall describe these critical factors. First, we need to see what they are, what it is that makes for successful method.

WHAT MAKES FOR SUCCESSFUL TEACHING?

Many research studies have shown rather clearly several factors which make for success in teaching. One effective way to study the problem is to determine the difficulties of teachers or the causes of their failure. For example, one such study collected statements of 2,537 difficulties from eighty-five beginning teachers and their principals. A tabulation of these difficulties showed the following items as being reported more than one hundred times each:

Handling problems of pupil control and discipline, reported 270 times
Adjusting to deficiencies in school equipment, physical conditions, and materials, reported 234 times
Difficulties related to the teaching assignment, reported 179 times
Adapting to the needs, interests, and abilities of pupils, reported 127 times
Motivating pupil interest and response, reported 116 times[1]

[1] Herbert W. Wey, "Why Do Beginning Teachers Fail?" *Bulletin,* No. 180, National Association of Secondary-School Principals, 35:56 (October), 1951. Italics ours.

Although the second and third items involve factors partially beyond the teacher's control, certainly the italicized items and to some extent the former are inextricably involved in the relations of teachers and learners in the teaching-learning process.

Similarly, other research studies reveal that the item of greatest importance in teaching success is that of the nature of the pupil-teacher relation. These studies, as well as the authors' experience in teaching, supervising, and training teachers, show at least three critical factors in these relations which secondary school teachers should recognize. The first of these is the teacher's own personality, and we do believe that a degree of personality change can be effected. A second important factor is the teacher's understanding of the general nature of effective learning in relation to teaching method. A third factor closely identified with the other two is that of the teacher's insight into the characteristics and problems of adolescent learners. Although extended treatment of these factors is beyond the scope of this book, we have selected some especially pertinent and important data regarding each to present in subsequent sections of this chapter.

TEACHING METHOD AND THE TEACHER'S PERSONALITY

Who was the best teacher you had in high school? Why was he or she best? If the reader answers these questions like the large majority of prospective teachers from whom we have received actual answers, you will say you liked Miss or Mrs. or Mr. X because she or he was "friendly," or "considerate," or "fair," or "interesting," or "human." That is, the odds are that you will indicate a personality trait of the teacher as your most important criterion of judgment. This fact is supported by various studies as to the differences between teachers considered "best" and "poorest." Hence, it seems appropriate to identify the teacher traits which are most significant in effective teacher-pupil relations.

WHAT PERSONALITY TRAITS ARE MOST IMPORTANT?

In view of the relation of teaching success and the quality of pupil-teacher interaction, pupils are the logical persons to tell us what personal qualifications they find most important in teachers. For who can know better than learners themselves what attracts them most to teachers? In general, it seems a fair assumption that teachers whom learners like best are those who have the best interaction with pupils and therefore the potentiality for greatest success in teaching method.

The foregoing assumption is supported by Hart's pioneer study, published in 1934, of high school seniors' evaluation of teachers. Among other interesting data, he found that 80 per cent of these pupils said that the teacher they liked best was also their best teacher (defined as "the one who taught you most effectively").[2] The characteristics of "the best teacher" (called "Teacher H" in this study), according to the 20 per cent, were the same as those for the "teacher liked best" ("Teacher A"), with the significant difference in Hart's summary that the former had "most of those generally attractive, likable human qualities of friendliness, good cheer, companionship, and understanding *left out*."[3] In view of the preponderance of evidence indicating that these "human qualities" count most of all, we are inclined to believe that the 20 per cent were influenced by the once popular belief that good teachers must be feared and disliked.

The more significant data of Hart's study are shown in Tables 2 and 3, which respectively report his summary of the responses of 3,725 high school seniors to the following directions:

(1) Consider all of the teachers you have had in high school, and think of the one *you have liked best*. Without mentioning the teacher's name, write down in the space below as accurately as you can your *reasons for liking this teacher best*. Call this teacher "Teacher A." Note: this is to be the teacher you *liked best,* not necessarily the *best teacher*.

(2) Now think of the one *you have liked least of all,* and write down as accurately as you can your reasons for *not liking* this teacher. Call this teacher "Teacher Z."

The overwhelming preponderance of various personality traits of teachers, or at least of the pupils' interpretation of these traits, as controlling factors in pupil evaluation of teachers, is obvious from these data. Even the most frequently mentioned reason for liking Teacher A —"is helpful with schoolwork, explains lessons and assignments clearly and thoroughly, and uses examples in teaching"—indicates "helpfulness" as a definitely liked characteristic in pupil-teacher relations.

The findings of Hart's study have been in general confirmed by various other studies of pupil evaluations of teachers. One somewhat similar, more recent study may be noted. Witty's analysis of 33,000 letters, submitted by high school pupils in the Quiz Kids annual radio program contests to award scholarships to the teachers most convincingly described as "The Teacher Who Has Helped Me Most," revealed the following traits: (1) cooperative, democratic attitude; (2) kindli-

[2] Frank W. Hart, *Teachers and Teaching* (New York: The Macmillan Company, 1934), p. 256.
[3] *Ibid.,* p. 279. Italics ours.

TABLE 2

WHAT TEACHER CHARACTERISTICS DO PUPILS LIKE?

(Reasons for Liking "Teacher A" Best, Arranged in Order of Frequency of Mention, as Reported by 3,725 High School Seniors)

Reasons for Liking "Teacher A" Best	Frequency of Mention	Rank
Is helpful with school work, explains lessons and assignments clearly and thoroughly, and uses examples in teaching	1950	1
Cheerful, happy, good-natured, jolly, has a sense of humor, and can take a joke	1429	2
Human, friendly, companionable, "one of us"	1024	3
Interested in and understands pupils	937	4
Makes work interesting, creates a desire to work, makes class work a pleasure	805	5
Strict, has control of the class, commands respect	753	6
Impartial, shows no favoritism, has no "pets"	695	7
Not cross, crabby, grouchy, nagging, or sarcastic	613	8
"We learned the subject"	538	9
A pleasing personality	504	10
Patient, kindly, sympathetic	485	11
Fair in marking and grading, fair in giving examinations and tests	475	12
Fair and square in dealing with pupils, has good discipline	366	13
Requires that work be done properly and promptly, makes you work	364	14
Considerate of pupils' feelings in the presence of the class, courteous, makes you feel at ease	362	15
Knows the subject and knows how to put it over	357	16
Respects pupils' opinions, invites discussion in class	267	17
Not superior, aloof, "high hat," does not pretend to know everything	216	18
Assignments reasonable	199	19
Is reasonable, not too strict or "hard boiled"	191	20.5
Helpful with students' personal problems, including matters outside of class work	191	20.5
Dresses attractively, appropriately, neatly, and in good taste	146	22
Young	121	23
Work well planned, knows what class is to do	110	24
Enthusiastically interested in teaching	108	25
Gives students a fair chance to make up work	97	26
Home-work assignments reasonable	96	27

Reasons for Liking "Teacher A" Best	Frequency of Mention	Rank
Recognizes individual differences in ability	86	28
Frank, "straight from the shoulder," a straight shooter	78	29.5
Personally attractive, good-looking	78	29.5
Teaches more than the subject	74	31
Interested in school activities	68	32
Sticks to the subject	53	33
Modern	52	34
Sweet and gentle	50	35.5
Pleasing voice	50	35.5
Intelligent	42	37
Prompt and businesslike	41	38
Sincere	36	39
Knows more than the subject	32	40
Has pep	31	41
Uses good judgment	22	42
Cultured and refined	20	43

Source: Frank W. Hart, *Teachers and Teaching* (New York: The Macmillan Company, 1934), pp. 131–132. Reprinted by permission.

ness and consideration for the individual; (3) patience; (4) unusual proficiency in teaching a particular subject; (5) wide interests; (6) interest in pupils' problems; (7) fairness and impartiality; (8) sense of humor; (9) good disposition and consistent behavior; (10) use of recognition and praise; (11) flexibility; (12) pleasing personal appearance and manner.[4] By another analysis of the statements in regard to "I like ——— because she does *not*," the negative traits were determined as follows: (1) bad-tempered and intolerant; (2) unfair and inclined to have favorites; (3) disinclined to show interest in the pupil and to take time to help him; (4) unreasonable in demands; (5) tendency to be gloomy and unfriendly; (6) sarcastic, and inclined to use ridicule; (7) unattractive appearance; (8) impatient and inflexible; (9) tendency to talk excessively; (10) inclined to talk down to pupils; (11) overbearing and conceited; (12) lacking in a sense of humor.[5] Witty concluded that "the teacher most admired is usually a well-adjusted individual who is genuinely responsive in human relations."[6]

From such studies as these and in the light of our own experiences, the authors conclude that the teacher's personality traits which really make a difference in pupil-teacher relations are these:

[4] Paul Witty, "Some Characteristics of the Effective Teacher," *Educational Administration and Supervision*, 36:199 (April), 1950.
[5] *Ibid.*, p. 200.
[6] *Ibid.*, p. 203.

Alertness	Patience
Cooperativeness	Personal appearance
Emotional stability	Respect for personality of others
Fairness and impartiality	Self-confidence
Friendliness	Sense of humor

These traits are too closely related for any rank to be given them, and we have therefore listed them alphabetically.

DEVELOPING AN EFFECTIVE TEACHING PERSONALITY

Although innate characteristics are important and difficult to modify, teachers in secondary schools are especially fortunate in having the continuous contact with learners which permits them to project their attempts at modification on the critical but easily read screen of adolescent reactions. It is not difficult to find out what boys and girls think of teachers, and, *if teachers really think it matters,* to work for desirable improvements in adolescent reactions.

TABLE 3

WHAT TEACHER CHARACTERISTICS DO PUPILS DISLIKE?

(Reasons for Liking "Teacher Z" Least, Arranged in Order of Frequency of Mention, as Reported by 3,725 High School Seniors)

Reasons for Liking "Teacher Z" Least	Frequency of Mention	Rank
Too cross, crabby, grouch, never smiles, nagging, sarcastic, loses temper, "flies off the handle"	1708	1
Not helpful with school work, does not explain lessons and assignments, not clear, work not planned	1025	2
Partial, has "pets" or favored students, and "picks on certain pupils"	859	3
Superior, aloof, haughty, "snooty," overbearing, does not know you out of class	775	4
Mean, unreasonable, "hard boiled," intolerant, ill mannered, too strict, makes life miserable	652	5
Unfair in marking and grading, unfair in tests and examinations	614	6
Inconsiderate of pupils' feelings, bawls out pupils in the presence of classmates, pupils are afraid and ill at ease and dread class	551	7
Not interested in pupils and does not understand them	442	8
Unreasonable assignments and home work	350	9
Too loose in discipline, no control of class, does not command respect	313	10

Reasons for Liking "Teacher Z" Least	Frequency of Mention	Rank
Does not stick to the subject, brings in too many irrelevant personal matters, talks too much	301	11
"We did not learn what we were supposed to"	275	12
Dull, stupid, and uninteresting	275	13
Too old-fashioned, too old to be teaching	224	14
Not "fair and square" in dealing with pupils	203	15
Knows the subject but "can't put it over"	193	16
Does not hold to standards, is careless and slipshod in her work	190	17
Too exacting, too hard, gives no chance to make up work	183	18
Does not know the subject	170	19
Does not respect pupils' judgments or opinions	133	20
Too changeable, inconsistent, unreliable	122	21
Lazy, not interested in teaching	115	22
Not friendly, not companionable	98	23
Shows boy or girl favoritism	95	24
Dresses unattractively or in bad taste	92	25
Weak personality	85	26
Insincere	75	27
Personally unattractive	65	28
Does not recognize individual differences in pupils	64	29
Voice not pleasant	63	30

Source: Hart, *Teachers and Teaching*, pp. 250–251. Reprinted by permission.

Frequently, teachers in service and even those just beginning in the profession are so thoroughly oriented to the concept of teaching method as dosage of subject matter, perhaps with appropriate sugar-coating and punishment measures, that a completely new orientation is necessary before they accept the importance of interpersonal relations and teaching personality. That is, these teachers, not sensing the importance of interpersonal relations in teaching, *do not really think personality matters.* Thus a first step in personality change for many teachers is the understanding of the teaching-learning process we are dealing with in this book. The critical factors of teacher personality, the nature of learning, and the characteristics of adolescence are somewhat inseparable lines of study for the secondary school teacher who seeks improvement. In his penetrating study of teacher growth, Sharp describes the process of change as re-education and emphasizes the role of a person such as a curriculum coordinator to help teachers in the process:

The reorientation of the traditional teacher can come about only through a slow process of re-education in which the teacher is helped by someone else to achieve new insights into children and their needs and to discover new ways of teaching that will relate the classwork to those needs. In this way, the teacher may, after a period of time, come to accept fully the modern conception of the curriculum and *change his teaching behavior in accordance with that conception.*[7]

Whether for the many teachers who do not need the re-education Sharp describes, the teachers just beginning and anxious to adapt themselves to their work, or the teachers, experienced and inexperienced, who must first see the need for more effective pupil-teacher relations, there are several specific steps that may develop personality traits conducive to effective pupil-teacher relations. Some of these steps are described in the following paragraphs.

Analyzing One's Own Personality Traits. An important step in personality improvement, as in behavioral change of any type, is the identification of behavior which needs change. Although no mere check list of personality traits can resolve the complex problems involved, some teachers may find it a helpful beginning to appraise their personalities through use of published personality inventories.[8] It may be fruitful also for teachers to do some self-analysis by reference to the studies by Hart and Witty described earlier in this chapter.

Such self-checks may be particularly helpful to the prospective teacher in locating areas of possible difficulty in his chosen profession. One of us has worked with some prospective teachers who prepared as a class project their own check lists of desirable personal characteristics. They found this a helpful experience, and we hope some of our readers will have similar opportunities. The process in these classes included class agreement on major characteristics, listing of questions under each characteristic, and class discussion and revision of the lists, with each individual being given a copy of the final check list for any use desired. A sample check list prepared by members of a class in secondary education is shown in Table 4. We believe that such a process involves considerable thinking about personality traits and may provoke desirable self-analysis. It is hoped that readers may find the list and especially the process whereby it was prepared useful in studying their own fitness for teaching.

Perhaps a more significant type of self-analysis may come through

---

[7] George Sharp, *Curriculum Development as Re-education of the Teacher* (New York: Bureau of Publications, Teachers College, Columbia University, 1951), p. 4. Italics ours.

[8] See the current *Mental Measurements Yearbook* (Oscar Krisen Buros, ed.; Highland Park, N.J.: The Gryphon Press) and current publications on personality analysis and evaluation for lists of available inventories.

what Sharp classifies as "opportunities for fresh perceptions of the teaching role." The opportunities he describes are

Opportunities for informal discussion (of teaching problems).

Receiving visitors (who ask questions about the teacher's work).

Observation of classroom teaching (which illustrates effective pupil-teacher relations).

Film showings (of modern teaching).

Role-playing (of teaching situations).

Reading books about teachers.

Reading descriptions of modern teaching.[9]

Such means of seeing, reading, and talking about good pupil-teacher relations may help many teachers to see themselves more clearly and critically. If help is received, however, teachers who participate must approach these opportunities with the purpose of identifying better ways of working and not merely of finding fault either with themselves or others.

Getting Learners' Reactions. As stated earlier, it is both important and possible for teachers to know what personality factors interfere with their effectiveness in interpersonal relations and therefore in teaching method. Even though adolescent boys and girls may not generally volunteer their criticisms of teachers' personal traits, they do reveal their feelings in many overt ways such as their enthusiasm, friendliness, exchange of confidences, or lack thereof. If it is difficult to explain the presence or absence of such overt signs of pupil-teacher relations, there are more direct ways of getting reactions such as

1. Use of personality inventories checked anonymously by pupils.
2. Role-playing skits in which pupils impersonate the teacher.
3. Interviews with individual pupils to find out their suggestions on how the teacher and pupils can get along together better.
4. Pupils' written responses to such questions as "What I Like Most" and "What I Like Least" (about the teacher concerned).
5. Use of group evaluations of questions about how the teacher helped or could have helped more.
6. Asking other teachers or the principal to observe pupils' reactions so as to help identify problems of pupil-teacher relations.

Working on Specific, Obvious Problems. For those who have no real emotional disturbances and personality disorders, it is possible to suffer undue difficulty and loss of time by endless pondering over fancied or actual personality difficulties. For those who do have such disturbances

[9] Sharp, *op. cit.*, pp. 115–120.

Table 4

PERSONAL CHARACTERISTICS OF EFFECTIVE TEACHERS

(A Sample Check List Prepared by a Class of Prospective Teachers)

I. HEALTH. Do I have
    1. good general health?
    2. good hearing?
    3. good eyesight?
    4. freedom from health handicaps or habits which would limit my effectiveness?

II. GROOMING AND APPEARANCE. Do I keep
    1. clothing well pressed, clean, and properly fitted?
    2. adequate changes of clothing?
    3. within conventional modes of dress?
    4. my posture good?
    5. hair trim and neat?
    6. fingernails clean?
    7. shoes clean and in good repair?
    8. teeth clean and in good repair?

III. VOICE AND SPEECH. Do I have
    1. good enunciation?
    2. a resonant voice?
    3. variable pitch?
    4. good command of the English language?
    5. a well-modulated voice?
    6. a knowledge of correct pronunciation of words?
    7. poise in speaking before a group?

IV. MANNERS. Do I know and practice such basic rules of etiquette as
    1. saying "Please" when I ask someone to do something for me?
    2. holding my remarks until the person speaking has finished?
    3. saying "Thank you" when a favor is done for me?
    4. rising to greet persons entering a room?
    5. practicing good table manners?

V. SINCERITY. Am I
    1. sincerely interested in the welfare of others?
    2. a sincere listener to the problems of another person?
    3. always sincere when I give advice to those who seek it?
    4. really a sincere person, even in my thoughts?

VI. EMOTIONAL STABILITY. Do I
    1. remain even-tempered under adverse conditions?
    2. have ideals that are high and within reason?
    3. take "constructive criticism" kindly?

    4. keep my criticisms objective?

    5. admit it when I don't know the answer?

    6. admit it, when I am wrong?

    7. keep free from excessive egotism?

    8. strive to correct my shortcomings?

    9. adjust to necessary supervision and routine easily?

   10. willingly accept responsibility?

   11. accept sympathetically human failings?

   12. avoid excessive and extreme moods?

VII. GETTING ALONG WITH OTHERS. Am I

    1. able to make my own decisions?

    2. self-confident?

    3. attracted in a positive way to most personalities?

    4. able to recognize individual rights of others?

    5. congenial with members of my own groups?

    6. careful to discharge my responsibilities to others?

VIII. SENSE OF HUMOR. Am I able to

    1. take a joke that is directed to me personally?

    2. laugh with others instead of at them?

    3. sense when and when not to introduce humor?

    4. fit my humor to the occasion?

IX. DEMOCRATICNESS. Am I

    1. always fair?

    2. able to recognize the needs of both the majority and the minority?

    3. unprejudiced?

    4. respectful of others as individuals?

    5. tolerant of the opinions of others?

    6. free from being dictatorial?

    7. a good participant in committees and other groups?

    8. able to cooperate with others?

and disorders, professional help is needed. But for the general run of teachers, we believe the essential steps in improvement of pupil-teacher relations are (1) identify any one specific, obvious problem that is a chief source of difficulty; (2) work out the best program of remediation possible; and (3) follow the program. To illustrate these steps of learning in this connection, note the case of Miss Smith.

Miss Smith was doing very well as a beginning teacher except that she noticed several of her pupils became less and less friendly as the year wore on. Other pupils, she felt, were increasingly appreciative and intimate. This cleavage bothered her and she asked her principal, Mr. Jones, who had shown great interest and had been helpful with her work, what the trouble might be. He offered to observe her classes a few days and then afterward in their discussion led her to see that some pupils felt she played favorites. Looking backward, she realized that she had increasingly leaned on some of the more responsive learners in her classes. To remedy the situation, she and Mr. Jones set up a program whereby leadership and recognition would be more generally distributed in her classes. After a period of experimentation with this approach, Miss Smith found not only that some of the unfriendly pupils had become friendly but that the general interest and energy of the classes had substantially increased.

In this instance, Miss Smith and Mr. Jones spent very little time trying to decide whether it was her nature to be unfair or intolerant in her human relationships. Once the reaction of pupils was accepted as a barrier in effective teaching method, steps were taken to remove the barrier. This is the method of problem solving which must be relied upon in seeking to improve teacher-pupil relations and all other phases of methodology.

Securing Wise Counsel. Miss Smith's experience illustrates another important way of seeking personality improvement. She went to Mr. Jones for help, and this very way of seeking help is frequently a long step toward the solution of one's problem. Some personality difficulties, such as those of personal appearance, health, and speech, may be greatly helped by use of technical advice. Clinical assistance may be necessary with some problems. But wise counsel on many personality difficulties may be available from a fellow-teacher, principal, or supervisor. Prospective teachers frequently get real help from their college instructor or counselor or their directing teacher (in student teaching). Like Miss Smith, one frequently needs only to recognize that there is a problem and then seek experienced help in its diagnosis and solution.

Following Sound Methodology. Teachers who really practice scientific method will eventually solve their problems of personal relations with boys and girls. This method applied to the teaching-learning process places paramount importance on the role of the learner, with the teacher serving as a guide and helper. As teachers try to serve in this capacity, they have to seek ways of involving learners in planning, of giving due regard to each learner, of attracting learners' interests. Hence sound methodology both emphasizes and makes possible a type of pupil-teacher interaction in which the teacher finds pupil reactions warmly responsive to his leadership. The teacher therefore needs to have faith in this method, use it devotedly, and follow through on the avenues of evaluation and experimentation it opens. This methodology itself is the fundamental approach to good teacher-pupil relations and effective teaching.

TEACHING METHOD AND THE NATURE OF EFFECTIVE LEARNING

As pointed out in Chapter 1, teaching method is not a series of discrete steps in teaching which the teacher takes to achieve some goal or goals determined at another prior step. Rather, method is the sum total of the teacher's work with learners to determine the latter's goals, to plan and carry on their goal-seeking activities, and to evaluate their goal accomplishments. Hence method should be considered in relation to the learning process it seeks to help. This relation is described in this section.

Learning is generally considered to be a change in behavior. That is, a thing is not "learned" until the learner behaves differently. He behaves differently, we know, because of experience, or interaction with his environment. For experience to make a difference in how a person behaves, he must become consciously involved; in other words, the experience must be purposeful. A learner does not become a better person by being told how to be good unless he wishes to be told, that is, unless he wishes to be better. He has to want to change, and then try to find out how. Only then does the experience of being told become purposeful and meaningful; in fact, only then does it become an experience if we define experience as interaction.

From the standpoint of teaching, we conceive of learning as a process of deliberate problem-solving activity—the problem as the motive for learning, the solution as the learning product or the change in behavior or the "learning." The learner is the problem-solver, and the teacher is his helper at any and all of the various steps in the process.

Problem solving occurs in any phase of the curriculum as well as in any life activity in general. Wherever choices must be made—and we Americans have great freedom of choice and therefore need great ability in choice making—the scientific method of weighing alternative courses of action may be followed.

Problem solving as critical thinking is frequently considered as a particular type of learning, but our reference is to learning in general, for we are assuming as a problem any desire, difficulty, interest, or need that motivates the process of learning. Critical reflection is simply problem solving at its best. Thus learning a football play, a musical score, or a dance step is a problem-solving process, just as is thinking through the reasons for selecting a particular high school course. The various elements of the process of solving problems, as just defined, are analyzed in the following paragraphs.

Boys and girls in high school are experiencing problems at every hand. These problems arise in varying forms: longings, immediate difficulties, disturbances, wishes, pressing needs, physical discomforts, emotional stresses, lack of know-how, and so forth. Sometimes the problem seems so remote or so impossible of solution that it is simply pushed aside. Sometimes it cannot be pushed aside and something has to happen. What happens is the effort we think of as problem-solving activity. The first step in this activity is a clarification and identification of the problem.

For example, Mary Smith longs for recognition from other students in her classes. She is very successful in her schoolwork, but her classmates usually pay little attention to her because, Mary suspects, of her plain face and good marks. Mary is not quite sure whether her problem is to make herself more attractive physically, like Susan Eager, or to make the others recognize her academic abilities or to do both. But she gives a good deal of thought to this problem, and the teacher notices Mary's evident preoccupation during the English class. Mary is working hard in sizing up her problem and in jumping from one possible idea to another about how to work it out.

On a more academic level, Johnny Jones is encountering some problems of adjustment in this new class. In his previous English class, his teacher had read literary pieces to the students most of the time and Johnny had given very little thought to the kind of questions and suggestions the new teacher kept making about writing and speaking. He was especially worried about the time when he would have to stand before the class and give a report on the book he had selected to read. Johnny felt perplexed by many problems, and was having a hard time deciding whether to concentrate on reading the book, listening to and observing other students make their reports, preparing his own report, or doing all these things. But as he worries along about these matters, he decides the real problem is to learn how to make an acceptable report.

Susan Eager has a problem, too. All the boys seem to be interested in her and she is proud of this, but her family is in financial difficulty and she wants to go to work as soon as she can complete the commercial course and find a secretarial job. Right now she is having a miserable time in shorthand and she doubts whether she will ever be able to take dictation. "Why should I be trying to read these old English books," she wonders, "when I need to spend all my time on shorthand?" And she tries while returning the boys' smiles to plan ways and means of doing better in shorthand—when to drill, how to drill and also read the books, and especially, how to buy the new clothes and things she needs.

The problems of boys and girls in high school may be quite different from those which the teachers want them to solve. In fact, one of the high school pupil's greatest problems is how to do things he wants to do and also those the teachers want him to do! But even in the midst of the conflicts and varying longings, interests, and difficulties, there are forces which cause boys and girls to identify problems to be solved, problems which have worth-while and important places in the learning situations of the classroom. Thus Mary Smith may identify her problem as one of making herself more attractive, and with this problem her homemaking teacher or perhaps her counselor can give help in problem solving. Johnny's problem of making an acceptable report is just the place for his English teacher to start work with him. And Susan may need some help from the shorthand teacher and perhaps some consultation with the counselor. But in each case and in all the other infinite number of problem-solving activities going on in schools with and without teachers' help, there must first be a thinking-through, an identification of the problem to attack *now* out of all the varying and conflicting forces which affect boys and girls. Other problems can be cast aside or mentally noted for consideration some other time, but conscious learning must be concerned with solving *a* problem at *a* particular time. The process is halted frequently for work on another problem, and sometimes it is halted because the learner loses interest or feels unsuccessful. Whatever happens, however, there is first the problem identification and then the choice of goals and plans of action.

IDENTIFYING GOALS AND PLANS OF ACTION

Many factors may enter into the choices Johnny, Mary, and Susan make as they ponder their difficulties—previous experience, opportunities at school and elsewhere, relations with teacher and other learners, and the like. If Mary has been influenced greatly by certain movies and books she has read, she may decide to attract recognition through playing a sophisticated role beyond her years. If she has seen friendliness operate at school, she may decide to ask Johnny Jones, the new classmate, if she can help him get acquainted with procedures in the room. If she knows that her homemaking teacher will help with problems of personal appearance, she may venture to ask for suggestions on how she can make a better appearance. Thus these and all the other alternative goals she might choose in the new situation or problem are based largely on her previous experiences and relationships.

Similarly, Johnny may choose to ask some other boy or girl, or perhaps his parents, to help him with his report, or maybe he has learned that he had best work out things for himself. And Susan may decide to spend a little more time drilling on her shorthand at home, if home conditions permit; or she may ask the English teacher if she can work on shorthand instead of English if she thinks this request would be considered; or she may decide to forget about shorthand and concentrate on getting married.

Fortunately, not all learning problems are as involved as these, and not all learners have to work things out with as little help from teachers and counselors as these situations indicated. Each of these three learners might have been spared some concern by earlier intervention of teachers, but when to intervene in suggesting courses of action and in helping identify problems is a problem of considerable moment for a teacher. The teacher's problem is greatly aggravated by his usual lack of knowledge of the many factors which have made Mary, Johnny, and Susan what they are, and these are the factors which have most to do with learners' choices of goals. Previous learning, relations with others, family backgrounds, general personality structure—these are the important items with which teachers must deal as they help learners identify goals and select means of attainment.

CARRYING ON GOAL-SEEKING ACTIVITY

Once learners have at least a partial understanding or recognition of their problems or motives and have identified goals which seem to be toward solution of their problems, goal-seeking activities may proceed. For example, if Mary settles on the goal of helping the new classmate, she may stop Johnny at the first opportunity to ask if she can explain anything about the procedures in English class. If Johnny says "Yes," she tells him about the teacher, the assignments, types of reports, and methods of preparation. Johnny's grateful "Thank you" is her reward and her first goal satisfaction in this learning process.

Johnny has engaged in goal-seeking activity, too. He had set as his goal to learn how to make a book report, and listening attentively to Mary is a learning activity for him. His next step is to ask Mary whether she would help him actually prepare a report. Their work together on an outline, his practicing of the report by presenting it to Mary, his changes at her suggestions, are all activities whereby Johnny gains self-assurance and a degree of satisfaction in attaining his goal.

Susan decides to concentrate on memorizing the shorthand symbols and keeps drilling herself in the study hall period. But in the short-hand class she does no better, for her goal-seeking activity is neither well motivated nor properly carried on. At the end of the period she asks her teacher about her problem, and the teacher arranges a special help session for Susan. Susan is pleased at this consideration and profits greatly from the session. Now she believes she knows how to learn shorthand—and she will not have to give up her job hopes after all.

Goal-seeking activities do get tied up in these emotional and con-flicting tensions. Rarely are we able to set up clear-cut goals and march undistractedly toward their solution. Some goals present fewer com-plications than others, and some persons have greater powers of con-centration (undistracted goal seeking) than others. But learners in general have difficulty in clarifying the real problem or motive, in identifying a goal which will be in the direction of solving the prob-lem, and in following courses of action related to the goal. The less the difficulty, the more direct the learning. Thus the necessity of hitting the baseball (an immediate goal) in order to make the team (the prob-lem or motive) may bring about successive batting-practice sessions (goal-seeking activity) which are carefully and successfully followed to satisfy the learner's motive. But Mary's problem of attracting others cannot be solved by such obvious and direct activities, and may involve many inconsistent trial-and-error activities over several years before she is able to attain reasonable security in the problem. In all these activities reflective thinking is essential, and the higher its quality the less wasted motion.

THE SOLUTION OR LEARNING PRODUCT

The examples we have used have indicated the learning products. Thus Mary learned that helping Johnny brought his favor; Johnny that listening to Mary helped in preparing his reports; Susan that sharing her problem with the teacher got results; the baseball player that practice caused improvement. Each series of goal-seeking activi-ties brings results, not always so positive. Thus Susan also learned that self-drill in the study hall did not help. Mary may find that Johnny's attention veers after his book report is given and that she must look for new ways to attract people. And Johnny may find that his notes and practice of his report make it boresome and stilted for the class. And with these perceptions, each learner will need to formulate new goals and activities to solve his or her problem.

We teachers need to see learning as a circuitous route rather than a straight line. The solution of the problem may be thought of as the destination, the intermediate goals as landmarks of the route, and goal-seeking activities as steps along the route. A more difficult concept to understand is that the entire route may be somewhat different for each learner because of differences in experience which create for each his own goals and ways of proceeding. The ultimate destinations differ less. That is, we may expect all youth to have some problems in common, such as achieving status in their groups, having satisfactory relations with the opposite sex, acquiring a means of livelihood, and so forth. From day to day each learner is setting out toward such destinations and selecting his own landmarks as assurance that he is on the right route. Landmarks may be mischosen or not reached, and this makes for circuitous routes and retracing of steps. Learners may also make such poor choices of landmarks as to get completely lost and never reach their destinations. But in all their experiences of goal selecting and seeking, they are achieving learning products: satisfactions and dissatisfactions, understandings and confusions, skills both good and poor. As their satisfactions overcome the dissatisfactions, their understandings the confusions, and their skills the lack of skills, their problems are being solved and they can reach generalizations. Thus, when Johnny has learned to read a book and prepare a report which is approved by his fellows, he can tell others how to solve this problem. That is, he can "generalize" on how to make a good book report. If his procedures have become a part of his working pattern so that he outlines and talks with very little error, we say this learning has been "efficient." If he has succeeded in learning to read, even to make a report, with enjoyment, to do his own work, to give and take in the discussion of his report, we can also say that his learning is properly organized in relation to other values and therefore is "integrated."

THE ELEMENTS OF EFFECTIVE LEARNING

At this point it is appropriate to define rather specifically certain concepts—the elements of learning—which we have been using and shall continue to use in our treatment of the teaching-learning process. These concepts are briefly stated in the following paragraphs.

Learning Situation. The learning situation is the environment in which learning experience occurs. From the standpoint of learning in school, it is the classroom, library, playground, auditorium, gymnasium, or other school facility in which the learner is located. The situation includes the learner and other people as well as physical objects, and it also includes the intangible drives within the learner and in his relations with others which stimulate learning. Of greatest importance in this situation are the group influences on the individual.

Motives. All individuals have several basic drives, wants, needs, and interests which constitute motives. Certain primary needs which individuals have in common, such as hunger, are modified by experience and social acceptance. Many secondary or acquired motives arise from an individual's experience. Whatever their origin, these motives are those drives which cause a particular individual to engage in goal-seeking activities.

Goals. Within the learning situation, there are incentives to seek goals related to the learner's basic motives or problems. For example, the typical high school youth wants to have status in his group. The approval of his peers is a goal of an individual boy or girl, and their smiles or lack thereof thus become an incentive to action. Identification of the goal is the problem clarification step.

Goal-Seeking Activity. When the learner becomes aware of an incentive toward a goal he finds desirable, he may be considered to be stimulated to goal-seeking activity. That is, his awareness of the desirability of approval from others means that he has not as yet secured a satisfactory degree of approval. Hence he engages in various trial efforts to secure approval. At first his behavior may be irrelevant, confused, inefficient. Successive efforts to secure approval through loud talk, winks, courtesies may result in success. Smiles and words of approval from others satisfy the original motive, and learning has occurred.

Mental Processes. Experience which changes behavior, that is, results in learning, is characterized by certain mental processes we may further identify as *differentiation, efficiency, integration,* and *generalization.* Behavior becomes differentiated when the learner is able to distinguish between the success of different activities in goal attainment: when the boy realizes that courtesies bring smiles and loud talk does not, he has attained a degree of differentiation. When he practices various courtesies until they become more typical of his behavior than discourtesies, he has acquired some efficiency in this particular learning. When he is able to attach particular relations between the responses of individuals to specific courtesies, he is developing some integration of the whole idea. His conclusions regarding what courtesies to use when and with whom represent his generalization of the learning. These mental processes represent ultimate goals of effective learning, and are important considerations in teaching method. They would not necessarily occur in teaching aiming at absorption or memorizing, for they follow active problem-solving efforts of the learner.

The foregoing discussion of effective learning suggests the teacher's role as that of helping the problem-solving process we call learning. Since learning is an individual's own pattern of activity in relation to his own problems or motives, no one other than the learner can com-

PLATE 4. TEACHERS CAN HELP PUPILS CLARIFY THEIR OWN PROBLEMS. Choice of careers and courses is important to adolescents. (Courtesy of the Board of Education, City of New York)

pletely control his learning. However, there are very important ways of helping learners in their problem-solving processes. Obviously, this fact is the justification of the teaching profession and of teaching method. Illustrations of the help teachers can give follow in connection with each of the major steps of learning or problem solving.

In Clarifying Problems. A major fallacy in much teaching is the notion that problems once "assigned" become learners' problems. It is true that boys and girls may accept assigned problems as their own, more likely that they will go through the motions of solving assigned but unaccepted problems, and most probable that assigned problems are simply hurdles boys and girls jump in the process of solving their own problems. For example, many high school pupils are assigned topics for term papers or other written work. Even though the topics may be stated in "how" or "why" terms, whether the students become personally involved in seeking out the "how" or "why" of the problem is questionable. More likely the learner is basically concerned with how to write a term paper which will assure his status in the class. If this is the basic problem, he may find copying another's paper a short cut to the solution.

A different approach in the English class is to survey the kinds of jobs students hope to undertake after high school, to review with the group the types of written reports if any that may be customary in each kind of job, and then to give directions for preparing such reports. For those pupils who expect to continue their formal education in college, experience in writing term papers may be desirable, and for them the problem of preparation for college may be sufficiently real to make such writing a desirable problem-solving process. For others, writing committee reports, sets of minutes, letters of application, newspaper articles, or letters to the editor may be goals with more apparent relationship to recognized motives.

The teacher's role in learners' problem clarification has three major aspects. First of all, the teacher needs to know as much as possible about the problems that really drive his pupils into learning activities. Although he can anticipate many common problems of adolescents, such as those defined later in this chapter, there is need to check this list against the real problems of every learning group. Additional problems, clusters of interest, and other such information can be secured through careful observation and interviews of individual pupils, published lists and inventories of pupils' problems, the teacher's own check lists, and oral and written problem censuses taken on a free response basis, such as, "What are your most important problems?" No one basis for identifying problems is wholly adequate; the most skillful teachers use a combination of procedures to make as certain as possible that their pupils' real problems are identified and that these problems are understood by both teacher and pupil.

Another aspect of problem clarification is the relating of pupils' problems to educational purposes. We should note here that most curriculum areas or subjects truly abound in problems of potential concern to youth. Teachers have only to bridge the gap between pupils' present and future concerns and the guides to action available in such areas as science, social studies, homemaking, language arts, and others. Returning to the cases of Mary, Susan, and Johnny, there might be a question in the minds of many teachers as to whether Mary's problem had much to do with school. The authors feel that personal relations is a problem area of great importance to high school youth, that better learning in school in regard to many other learning problems, as well as ultimately better 'relationships outside school, may result from successful attention to it, and that good teaching must and does tie many specific learning activities to this drawing card. Thus a good teacher would probably encourage Mary's help to Johnny in preparing his book report. Perhaps he would also use Mary as a tutor for other pupils who are new or having difficulty. The idea here is not to sugar-coat book reports, but rather to provide substantial and satisfactory bases for pupils' relations with each other. The whole matter of which problems of learners are suitable for consideration in school is an issue of considerable interest in educational philosophy and in actual curriculum planning. Briefly, we see three possible positions teachers may take on the issue. One very common one, which we find untenable in the light of learning theory, is the idea that the only problems that can be considered are those presented in the adopted textbook or other official curriculum guide. Another equally untenable position, we feel, is the uncommon practice of discussing in the classroom any problems boys and girls propose without respect to curriculum limitations. We ourselves believe that the problems dealt with should represent the best possible selection based on pupils' interests, the basic curriculum goals and framework, and the availability of resources, including the teachers' own competence, to help in solving the problems considered in making the selection. Reaching these judgments is the important task of curriculum planning at all levels, and is dealt with in more detail in Chapter 14.

In problem clarification, the teacher also helps learners translate their basic drives into appropriate goals. He must be constantly helping learners decide whether the next steps they wish to take on the learning route are possible and worth while. Thus Susan might learn how to type well enough to get a typist's job even without knowing shorthand. This learning activity might be psychologically appropriate—that is, Susan might learn to type rapidly—but be inappropriate philosophically because she would be placing unnecessary limitations on her employment possibilities. Similarly, any problem of a pupil must be identified with some immediate goal that seems attainable and profitable. Susan's problem can be approached through her immediate goal, a method of studying shorthand that she can use with much more effectiveness than her former methods.

In Selecting Goals and Courses of Action. Traditional concepts of teaching give little consideration to goal selection by learners, since they involve passive learning in which the learner's goal is to acquire the information given or assigned by the teacher. Teachers know how unrealistic this assumption is, for learners do not passively accept or learn assignments. Under great compulsion most or all may, but the real learning going on in many cases is concerned with how to evade punishment or failure rather than with how to acquire any desired knowledge. In more permissive learning situations, learners are encouraged to formulate goals and courses of learning activity in relation to goals.

For example, we can imagine that the English class of which Mary, Susan, and Johnny were members began its year's work by some cooperative stating and clarifying of problems these girls and boys felt important. One problem might have been how to speak effectively to a group of people. Once such a general problem is identified and understood by the pupils, the teacher properly directs attention to ways and means of working it out. For example, such specific goals as these might have been mentioned by members of the class: how to present an interesting book report; how to make a report without notes; how to read a set of minutes aloud; how to make a report for a committee; how to secure audience interest in a speech; how to address a group as large as the student body; how to be a good chairman. After all these goals are identified, the teacher may then direct discussion to the question of whether these competencies would help with the general problem of speaking effectively before a group. Perhaps it is decided that the competency of speaking before a group as large as the student body is needed by few people and those who wish it can get help. This comment might lead to some differentiation between goals all people should seek and those in which only some are interested. Perhaps all feel that they need to learn how to make an interesting book report, so plans are made as to the nature, preparation, and presentation of book reports—which brings us to Johnny's arrival!

Thus the teacher's role is that of helping learners identify goals of personal importance as landmarks in solving the major problem. The foregoing illustration possibly oversimplifies the process, as group agreement cannot always be reached so easily on basic problems or on goals related to these problems. Many basic drives of learners are highly personal and individual, and teachers can merely attempt to know these and help individual learners plan learning routes toward their destinations. Some pupils may learn at such an advanced or retarded rate that it is virtually impossible for them to participate effectively in many group activities. Recognizing all these factors, the skillful teacher wherever possible helps learners set up common goals, which also permit sufficient flexibility in courses of action to allow learners to travel at their own speed and not necessarily toward the same goal. Most of all, this teacher is trying to help *each* boy and girl find a way of working effectively toward a goal that is important to him or her and is possible and worth while.

In Goal-Seeking Activity. Even though all learners identify as a goal related to the effective speaking problem that of making interesting oral reports, individual learners vary greatly in the past experiences and the abilities they bring to this goal. Some have already learned how to identify important themes, ideas, and issues in the books they read, and others have not. Some have well-modulated voices, and others have real speech difficulties. Some rely on notes, and others do not know how to prepare and use notes. The teacher will have to help each individual identify the types of activity which will best develop his ability in preparing an interesting book report. Actually, the individual learners will be identifying somewhat different goals: some to read with better understanding, some to overcome speech difficulties, some to speak with more poise.

Some of these goals are conducive to group activity, others to individual practice, and some to both. Thus the teacher may work with a reading group to guide their identification of important points and with another to show how to prepare good outlines. Teams such as that of Mary and Johnny, described earlier, may be organized for drill on preparing and using notes and practicing oral reports. Some individual learners may be given help in learning correct pronunciation, silent reading, and use of reference materials on authors and their works. The entire class may be helped in developing good listening habits by the teacher's guidance, and at the same time notes taken by the teacher on each individual report may be a help to the individual learner in identifying further goals and courses of action. Thus teaching must include work with the entire class, small groups, and individuals.

In Evaluating Learning Products. Comments by teacher and classmates on the individual's book report may help him evaluate his own learning. The skillful teacher can use class discussion of a report both to help the reporter identify his strengths and weaknesses in writing and to help the other learners compare their own development with whatever standards are stated or implied in the discussion.

Evaluation is a constant aspect of our personal experience. We are continually sizing up our satisfactions and dissatisfactions and reaching judgments as to how well we are doing. Usually this is just a mental process and we have no help from another person. Sometimes, however, a friend's question as to how we like this or that or how we feel about something we have tried stimulates our evaluative thinking. The friend's role in our personal experiences approximates that of the teacher in the classroom. The Marys, Susans, and Johnnys can and do

PLATE 5. PUPILS NEED HELP IN SECURING INFORMATION FROM VARIED SOURCES. The effective teacher works with groups like this as well as with the total class and individual members. (Courtesy of the National Education Association)

decide for themselves whether they are succeeding in reaching their goals and solving their problems, but teachers can help greatly by raising thought-provoking questions, supplying critical comments, and using various evaluative devices to give Mary, Susan, and Johnny information about their progress.

Teachers can be particularly helpful in the evaluative process by guiding groups and individuals in the establishment of criteria for judging accomplishment. Group goals are in themselves criteria but it may be further desirable to establish standards whereby individual learners can decide for themselves how well goals have been achieved. Thus a set of standards for appraising book reports might well have been developed by the class we have been describing. These standards might be applied by the person to his own report, by other pupils, or by the teacher, or by all. For evaluation to be an effective drive to establishment of learning goals and courses of action, however, the individual must ultimately do his own evaluation. However much he may be influenced by the teacher's and others' judgments, only his own decision that he needs further study will make that study a profitable goal-seeking action.

GROUP INFLUENCES ON LEARNING

Throughout this discussion of learning we have been dealing with learning as an individual matter. But teachers talk of teaching classes, and indeed the basis of instructional organization in American high schools is the class of some thirty or so individual learners. The real dilemma of teaching is this matter of individual learning versus group organization for instruction. The easy thing for teachers to do is to teach the class as a whole—easy, that is, if teachers ignore the basic facts of learning and assume that individuals have the same interests and work at the same rate toward the same goals. The obvious fact that they do not learn in these ways explains the frustrations teachers experience when learners are disinterested and unsuccessful in achieving the goals that teachers expect to be reached uniformly.

The easiest way to teach might be the tutorial method, except for one very important factor in learning, that of group influence on the individual. Although a teacher could work very effectively with one learner, the latter would miss all the stimulation and help that comes from learning as a member of a group. Economy is an obvious explanation for the group organization of schools, but there is a very real argument for group organization as an aid to efficient learning and teaching. Individuals can learn better in groups provided the group is so organized and the teacher's guidance so used that each individual is helped to more effective learning than he could acquire on his own. Teachers need to understand how to apply principles of learning in group organization and instruction so as to make for effective learning by individuals.

The role of the problem or motive in learning is all important. Teachers' conceptions of how to build on learners' motives and how to shape these motives into ever better ones constitute their philosophy of teaching. Under earlier theories of learning, such motives as rewards and punishment were given high place, but more recent research has discounted all types of artificial motivational devices and placed greatest emphasis on the personal-social needs of learners.[10] We pointed out by illustrations earlier in this chapter how learners' relations with each other affected their problem-solving activities, and may summarize here certain major influences:

1. Individual learners are motivated to a considerable extent by the desire to be accepted and recognized by their associates, and to this end will adopt as problems of their own those which have group sanction.

2. The desire to be accepted and recognized is itself a problem of major concern and constitutes a drive to learning those types of behavior which seem to secure acceptance and recognition within the group.

3. Learners' likes and dislikes for each other may strongly affect the choice of problems and activities in learning; that is, a learner may select a problem or activity because it is selected by a friend or reject one because it is selected by a person he dislikes.

4. Group listing of possible goals helps individual learners identify goals which would not have occurred to them individually. Similarly, group discussion of possible goal-seeking activities helps individuals select activities.

5. When individuals feel a part of, and a responsibility for, group enterprises, their activities are motivated to an extent by these feelings and become better organized and controlled than if the students felt responsibility to the teacher alone.

6. Group situations produce the opportunity for leadership and provide motivation for individuals to seek leadership roles.

7. Group planning situations make it possible for individuals to make choices, and the act of making a choice itself motivates problem-solving thinking.

None of the foregoing motivating influences can be present in the tutorial situation, except as the teacher-pupil relation creates motives for the pupil. But in the group situation there are exerted not only the motivating influences of the teacher but the more compelling influences of the total group. Particularly with adolescents, who dearly crave recognition and approval of their age-mates, this influence is of the utmost importance in the selection and pursuit of learning goals.

[10] According to Hilgard and Russell's analysis of motivation in school learning, "All learning is energized and directed by the social-personal relations of the school." See Ernest R. Hilgard and David H. Russell, "Motivation in School Learning," in *Learning and Instruction* (Forty-ninth Yearbook of the National Society for the Study of Education; Chicago: University of Chicago Press, 1950), Chap. 2, p. 65.

Hence the individual may learn better in the group situation than as an isolate.

Group organization also greatly extends the variety of learning experiences which individuals may engage in as they seek to solve problems in which they are interested. The individual learner is limited to his own reading, observation, and reflection, but as a group member he has the advantage of sharing the reading, observation, and reflection of others. Furthermore, many desirable learning experiences are more feasible for groups than individuals: excursions, dramatization, discussion, debate; production of newspapers, exhibits, collections; service and work projects. Although the learning in these group experiences varies with each individual, it is the group situation which makes possible whatever learning accrues. Certain particular principles of learning best served in group situations may also be noted.

Problem-Solving Skills. The skills involved in problem-solving activities are acquired in part through participation with others in such activities. That is, the individual learner sharpens his own ability to define his problems and related goals by seeing how other learners do this, and especially through being one of a group of learners planning together (Chapter 8). In the group situation each learner may find his own reasoning challenged and thereby may come to clearer thinking about his problem definitions. Faulty logic in assigning causes and reasons, in relating goals to problems, and in planning activities to achieve specific goals is revealed through the process of group discussion. Evaluative procedures may be more adequately planned by several learners trying out their ideas and their conclusions on each other than by one learner who evaluates without any test of his conclusions. The ability to generalize, a higher learning product, is stimulated by the reactions of others to the individual's trial generalizations.

Practice. Although drill or practice is traditionally an individual matter, modern teaching provides many opportunities for learners to help each other in drill situations. Once the reason for learning a particular skill is understood by a group of learners, and once each understands how to perform the skill, learners may help each other. Thus pairs of learners may help in drill on vocabulary, mathematical operations, use of study aids, paraphrasing, and similar skills in which one may check the other. Groups of learners may help individuals practice skills of speaking, group leadership, or physical performance by providing the practice situation. Frequent use of such practice situations helps learners acquire a degree of efficiency in their learning that might not occur under conditions of self-drill alone.

Meaningful Learning. Individual learners can memorize material without actually understanding it, either because they do not want to understand or because they have no help in reaching understanding. When the emphasis is placed instead on understanding, and learners help each other through discussion and explanation, the number to whom the material has meaning is much greater than would be true under assign-memorize-recite learning and teaching procedures. In a sense, a true recitation procedure is a matter of tutorial teaching taking place in a group situation; that is, there is no group discussion, sharing, or challenging. But in group situations where questions and comments are encouraged, learners have the opportunity to ask about what they do not understand, to get others' ideas, to attach meaning to what might otherwise be meaningless. Forgetting comes because the learner fails to understand a term or idea in relation to other terms and ideas. Hence, as learners challenge each other to understand these relations, forgetting is minimized and integration of learning is secured.

These statements of the advantages of group situations for learning in no way imply that individuals learn simply because they are group members. Even under best practices of group organization, learning is uneven for each individual. The argument is simply that learners in general are more likely to carry on effective learning processes in group situations than in isolation. Alone or in a group, the learner does not learn unless he consciously goes through the steps of problem solving. And in these steps he needs periods of work by himself as well as with others, the extent of such need being another factor unique to each individual's own learning equipment.

GROUP ORGANIZATION AND DEMOCRACY

Although sound psychological principles strongly support the practice of teaching pupils in groups, the principles of American democracy demand that our citizens be proficient group members. Americans must make many choices and take many actions in groups controlled by the respective members. Our public schools are truly laboratories for training children and youth in the give-and-take, the principle of majority rule, the choice of leaders and representatives, the development and use of group regulations, and all the other procedures characteristic of democratic organization. It is a "must" for the fullest adherence to democratic principles that teachers use to maximum advantage the cooperative procedures which are possible in every teaching-learning situation.

TEACHING METHOD AND THE
CHARACTERISTICS OF ADOLESCENTS

The authors recognize that the process of learning is the same at one age as another and accordingly that the nature of teaching method as guidance of problem solving is the same at every level. However, as we have already emphasized, the nature of the individual has a great deal to do with his problem-solving activities. Although adolescents vary greatly in their unique characteristics, certain characteristics which are typical of adolescents in general do have rather definite effects on the problem-solving activities of individuals at this age. These characteristics have been carefully studied in a considerable number of research studies. Here we shall briefly summarize the more significant characteristics of adolescents with particular attention to their implications for adolescents' learning processes

PHYSICAL CHARACTERISTICS

The most striking characteristics of adolescence relate to the physiological change occurring in this period. The advent of puberty occurs for girls at the average age of about thirteen, although the range is from about ten to sixteen. Boys usually attain puberty from one and one-half to two years later than girls. The growth spurt starts with girls at about nine or ten years of age and on the average slows down about two or three years later; with boys, the growth spurt occurs about two years later. All the associated physical changes have great significance for learning.

One of the great concerns of the adolescent is whether or not he is developing normally. Too early or too late pubescence, too great or too little body changes, too much or too little total growth, as compared with average or with what seem typical patterns of the adolescents each student knows, are problems which create intense interest in understanding of self, sexual development and relationships, and proper care of the changing body. Teachers can build upon these questions in developing problem-solving activities that have personal interest to adolescents.

Related to sexual maturity is the aroused interest in boy-girl relations. The new interest in the opposite sex is another driving force which for many adolescents dominates almost every social situation as well as his reflections when alone. Here again is a powerful motive upon which skillful teachers build goal-seeking activities of a wholesome nature.

But sexual maturity and related boy-girl interests come at different times, and the difference in growth between the sexes is also a challenging problem to teachers of adolescents. Teachers are familiar with the usual situation of having young women in junior high school classes learning side by side with little boys. From even the fifth through the ninth or tenth grade there are rather obvious differences in the physical maturity of girls and boys, and instruction in these grades cannot assume equal and uniform interest in the problems just mentioned. Not only is there the rather typical difference between girls and boys, but there is the considerable range of differences within each sex. These factors emphasize again the necessity of understanding each individual and the forces which drive his activities.

The physical development of adolescents also has other significant aspects for teachers' recognition. The rapid growth during this period makes attention to diet, exercise, and rest very important, and teachers need to give due consideration to these physiological needs in developing daily programs for youth. Personal appearance, neatness, and clothing become important considerations that provide opportunities for teachers to give individual help and recognition which cement teacher-pupil relations. The typical restlessness of the adolescent demands that classroom arrangements and procedure provide plenty of opportunities for normal movement.

PERSONAL-SOCIAL CHARACTERISTICS

Perhaps the dominant personal-social characteristic of an adolescent is the desire for recognition from his peers. More than almost anything else, adolescents want to be accepted within their group, and to win acceptance they conform by and large to whatever standards of behavior and to whatever agreements are reached for learning experiences. This desire for group sanction and approval is a powerful instrument for teachers to use in guiding groups to choices which are consistent with educational purposes. Effective group organization and teaching fully utilizes group planning procedures to capitalize upon this drive of youth to conform, and provides wholesome goals for cooperative seeking rather than almost forcing youth to join together to overcome unacceptably restrictive school policies.

Their concern for recognition from their peers is associated with a decline in adolescents' dependence on parental and other approval. The adolescent is achieving maturity and seeking independence. Unlike the child he was in elementary school, he no longer eagerly seeks goals which his parents and other adults urge; in fact, he may actively and aggressively initiate contrary behavior. The teacher of adolescents appeals to their own needs and judgments rather than just to their knowledge of parental and social expectations. Adolescents are rightly encouraged to assert their personal ideas, and wise teachers help find common ground for these with social ideals and expectations rather than emphasizing conflicts and inconsistencies.

Their interest in each other and their feelings about achieving independence produce the strong tendency for adolescents to band together in cliques, gangs, clubs, and so forth. Rather than forcing these associations underground, effective teaching capitalizes on gregarious interests by capable organization and guidance of small groups in the classroom, extra-mural clubs and leisure-time organizations, and in desirable community projects and programs.

Along with the self-assertive tendencies there is also a quest for security and affection. Though adolescents look toward home for this, they also look toward each other and the teacher. Warm personal relations between teachers and adolescents provide a source to which the learner can go with his personal problems, and also make it possible for teachers to advise parents on how to help their adolescent children achieve independence and at the same time have security in family relations.

Although their emotions are being influenced by all the other changes of adolescence, emotional disturbance is not characteristic of adolescence. Its indication is a factor to be investigated by teachers and to be used as a basis for work with individual learners. Emotional disturbance frequently occurs in those adolescents whose physical development deviates sharply from the group average, and teachers need to find special compensations for those learners who are denied the feeling of normality and the consequent sense of well-being.

Adolescents have very real problems in achieving moral and ethical standards. The handling of sexual drives is itself a problem that must be recognized in organizing school activities and programs so as to provide adolescents proper heterosexual relations. Conflicts with parents and adults may create powerful drives to aggressive action that eventually appear as delinquent behavior. The drive to conformity creates financial problems for adolescents whose family incomes are inadequate to make possible the clothes, spending money, and advantages of other class members. Rejection by the group may stimulate unwholesome assertive behavior that is marked as delinquency. Restrictions on normal social activities superimposed by overzealous parents and teachers create rebellious behavior which we recognize too late as immorality. Unsupervised clubs, cliques, and gangs may pattern their behavior upon what appears so attractive in movies and books, and crime eventuates. All of these possibilities merely underline the need for teachers to understand adolescents, to know them individually, and to plan and conduct their classes with full recognition of the factors which constitute the learners' basic motives. In teaching in this way, teachers will be helping adolescents establish and maintain acceptable moral and ethical standards, and will be meeting and dealing forthrightly with the influences which encourage immoral and unethical behavior.

To summarize, adolescence is a period of adjustment, and good teaching method seeks to utilize and build upon the problems of personal-social adjustment. Effective teachers are concerned with ways and means of helping adolescents arrive at educationally desirable solutions of these and related problems which may be defined in learning situations.

INTELLECTUAL CHARACTERISTICS

Intellectual development in the sense of "ability to learn" continues, although unevenly, through adolescence. The peak of an individual's intellectual development, that is, his power to learn, is usually reached at from eighteen to twenty years of age, although there may be a slight increase thereafter. Hence continuing challenge in the form of increasingly complex understandings and skills is desirable. Because of the great variations in individual intellectual ability (as much as eight years in mental age within the same chronological age group), and also because of the widening range of learnings being acquired at a particular stage of development, it is impossible to anticipate uniform accomplishment in verbalistic and reasoning processes. That is, adolescents vary intellectually and physically, and good teaching simply recognizes the variations and also the increasing capacity of all learners. It follows that individual learners will not be able to engage equally well in the same problem-solving activities but also that each may improve in his problem-solving processes.

Perhaps these facts of intellectual development more than any other have been neglected in teaching method. Physical development is easily enough observed. Personal-social drives to action are somewhat common in nature and may be generalized upon in planning learning experiences. But learners have differences of mental ability which are not so readily observed and which are peculiarly difficult to serve. We believe that this fact can be met best through reliance on problem-solving processes in learning and teaching. The cooperative determination of learning problems and goals gives each adolescent an opportunity to set up goals which have meaning to him, and his own selection of problem-solving activities is more likely to result in work at his level than his forced conformance to some uniform assignment. Close observation and assistance from his teacher, supported by adequate guidance and testing services, should help in detecting profitable and unprofitable activities and in the choice of activities of increased difficulty as his intellectual powers grow.

THE PROBLEMS OF ADOLESCENTS

For effective teaching, it is essential that we have some basis for anticipating the major problems of those we teach. That is, we need to anticipate problems or areas in which we may expect youth to have interests, or teaching is perforce on an unplanned basis or unrelated to the natures of those we teach. Two courses seem desirable therefore: (1) to have a general understanding of the characteristics of adolescents as just presented; and (2) to pinpoint these characteristics into a tentative list of major problems with reference to which planning can take place. In connection with this pinpointing process, study of the literature concerning adolescence and secondary education is very helpful. Two sources are especially noted here for the teacher's consideration.

Studies of human development carried forward by Havighurst and others at the University of Chicago have presented the concept of the developmental tasks which individuals must master to be successful human beings. These tasks, which necessarily change as the individual ages and meets new demands, may arise "from physical maturation, from the pressure of cultural processes upon the individual, from the desires, aspirations and values of the emerging personality, and they arise in most cases from combinations of these factors acting together."[11] In *Human Development and Education,* the developmental tasks of adolescence are described as follows:

1. Achieving new and more mature relations with age-mates of both sexes
2. Accepting a masculine or feminine social role
3. Accepting one's physique and using the body effectively
4. Achieving emotional independence of parents and other adults
5. Achieving assurance of economic independence
6. Selecting and preparing for an occupation
7. Preparing for marriage and family life
8. Developing intellectual skills and concepts necessary for civic competence

[11] Robert J. Havighurst, *Human Development and Education* (New York: Longmans, Green & Co., Inc. 1953), p. 5.

9. Desiring and achieving socially responsible behavior
10. Acquiring a set of values and an ethical system as a guide to behavior[12]

Closely paralleling the developmental tasks is a list of "imperative educational needs of youth" first published by the Educational Policies Commission in 1944[13] and subsequently widely used in educational planning in the United States. These needs are listed and illustrated in the accompanying figure. The authors believe that full understanding of these developmental tasks and educational needs and frequent reference to them is essential in instructional planning which gives due attention to the problems of adolescent learners.

THE CHARACTERISTICS OF GOOD TEACHING

Somewhat in summary of the theory of methodology we have presented, the authors suggest the following as characteristics of good teaching:

1. The maintenance of an atmosphere, social and physical, in the classroom which stimulates and encourages problem-solving activity
2. The functioning of the teacher as a guide and helper rather than as a taskmaster and dictator
3. The encouragement of friendly and efficient sharing and cooperation in all phases of classroom activity
4. The use, so far as feasible, of pupils' own motives as guides in the selection of learning goals and experiences
5. Careful understanding of and attention to the needs of individual learners
6. Patterns of group organization which utilize fully group influences on learning
7. The use of evaluative processes and devices to help learners make optimum progress
8. Emphasis on and respect for accomplishment in the acquisition of understandings and skills needed by learners in solving problems attacked in learning situations

[12] *Ibid.*, Chaps. 9, 10, and 11.
[13] See Educational Policies Commission, *Education for All American Youth* (Washington, D.C.: National Education Association, 1944), pp. 225–226, for the Commission's listing of these needs. Also see the revised edition, *Education for All American Youth—A Further Look*, 1952, pp. 215–216. These two volumes are basic sources for secondary school teachers.

All youth need to develop saleable skills and those understandings and attitudes that make the worker an intelligent and productive participant in economic life. To this end, most youth need supervised work experience as well as education in the skills and knowledge of their occupations.

All youth need to develop and maintain good health and physical fitness.

All youth need to understand the rights and duties of the citizen of a democratic society, and to be diligent and competent in the performance of their obligations as members of the community and citizens of the state and nation.

All youth need to understand the significance of the family for the individual and society and the conditions conducive to successful family life.

All youth need to know how to purchase and use goods and services intelligently, understanding both the values received by the consumer and the economic consequences of their acts.

FIG. 2. THE IMPERATIVE NEEDS OF YOUTH. (Courtesy of *Planning for Ameri-*

All youth need to understand the methods of science, the influence of science on human life, and the main scientific facts concerning the nature of the world and of man.

All youth need opportunities to develop their capacities to appreciate beauty in literature, art, music, and nature.

All youth need to be able to use their leisure time well and to budget it wisely, balancing activities that yield satisfactions to the individual with those that are socially useful.

All youth need to develop respect for other persons, to grow in their insight into ethical values and principles, and to be able to live and work co-operatively with others.

All youth need to grow in their ability to think rationally, to express their thoughts clearly, and to read and listen with understanding.

can *Youth,* rev. ed., National Association of Secondary Principals, 1951, p. 9)

9. Adequate and definite plans and resources for instruction which insure desirable learning experiences and permit flexibility in the classroom development of plans

10. Use of an experimental approach that continually seeks better procedures and also evidence regarding the effectiveness of procedures tried

THE CHALLENGE OF TEACHING METHOD

The conclusion we hope teachers will reach from study of this chapter is that they must be learners themselves to do an effective job of teaching adolescents. When learning and teaching are considered to be the dynamic processes we have described, it follows that a teacher cannot use fixed, unchanging procedures. There is the challenge to find ever better ways of guiding learning as well as that of meeting the unpredictable aspects of every learning situation. These challenges add up to the necessity for successful teachers to face each situation as a problem which requires goal-seeking activity or learning on their own part. We may now summarize some of these factors which challenge teachers to carry on learning activities of their own.

Although there are the typical characteristics of adolescents which we presented, it does not follow that every adolescent exhibits these characteristics in the same pattern or at the same time as others. Quite to the contrary, each individual has a distinct personality which he expects to be recognized and dealt with as such.

Since each class is composed of different individuals, each has its unique pattern of interpersonal relationships. As we have pointed out, the teacher's own personality is of great importance in establishing the quality of these relations. Establishing favorable reactions to his own personality is an exacting but most rewarding task for the teacher. There is also the necessity to discover and influence the pattern of social relations among boys and girls.

Although the basic process of learning remains constant, its content varies greatly with each group, individual, and year. Even if the teacher taught the same group of individuals for several consecutive years, there would be differences in the problems of these students which determine their goals, activities, and products in learning. Furthermore, the types of learning experiences possible vary from time to time as new resources and opportunities become available. Add to this the great turnover in individuals whom the teacher actually teaches from period to period and year to year, and the potential variations in the content of teaching method adapted to a problem-solving learning process become almost infinite.

All these facts add up to making teaching method an exciting venture in guiding adolescents into being informed, successful American citizens. We hope our readers take to their further study a bit of the spirit of adventure, inquiry, and enthusiasm which makes successful teaching a significant service to humanity.

FOR FURTHER STUDY

Ausubel, David P., *Theory and Problems of Adolescent Development.* New York: Grune & Stratton, Inc., 1954.
This comprehensive treatment of adolescent development analyzes the psychological and psychosocial problems of adolescents.

Cantor, Nathaniel, *Learning through Discussion.* Buffalo: Human Relations for Industry, 1951.
Analysis of the psychological implications of group discussion.

Cole, Luella, *Psychology of Adolescence.* 4th ed.; New York: Rinehart & Company, Inc., 1954.
Treats all phases of adolescent growth, with considerable attention to recent studies in personality and sociometry.

Hart, Frank W., *Teachers and Teaching.* New York: The Macmillan Company, 1934.
Reports 3,725 high school pupils' reasons for liking and disliking teachers.

Havighurst, Robert J., *Human Development and Education.* New York: Longmans, Green & Co., Inc., 1953.
Part III, Chapters 9–15, deals with the developmental tasks of adolescence and includes three case studies (Chapters 13, 14, and 15) to show the role of the school in adolescents' development.

Hilgard, Ernest R., *Theories of Learning.* New York: Appleton-Century-Crofts, Inc., 1948.
Detailed analysis of ten different systems of learning theory.

Kinney, Lucien B., *Measure of a Good Teacher.* San Francisco: California Teachers Association, September, 1952.
As a result of a five-year study by the California Council on Teacher Education, this monograph presents a check list of "Factors in Teaching Competence."

Landis, Paul H., *Adolescence and Youth.* 2nd ed.; New York: McGraw-Hill Book Co., Inc., 1952.
Treats the problems of adolescents and youth from a sociological point of view.

Malm, Marguerite, and Olis G. Jamison, *Adolescence.* New York: McGraw-Hill Book Co., Inc., 1952.

Deals with the adolescent and his world, his adjustment, and the major influences on him.

Mursell, James L., *Developmental Teaching*. New York: McGraw-Hill Book Co., 1949.
See Chapters 1–4 for Mursell's interpretation of learning theory and its implications for teaching method.

National Society for the Study of Education, *Learning and Instruction*. Forty-ninth Yearbook of the Society; Chicago: The University of Chicago Press, 1950, Part I.
Comprehensive review and interpretation of theory and research on learning problems and their implications for instruction.

Sharp, George, *Curriculum Development as Re-education of the Teacher*. New York: Bureau of Publications, Teachers College, Columbia University, 1951.
Indicates directions and processes needed in the re-education of teachers for curriculum change.

Sugarman, Myrtle F., ed., *Effective Learning for Use in Junior High Schools*. Denver, Colo.: The Public Schools, 1949.
Problems of learning as analyzed in a hypothetical discussion reported as held by a group of teachers in a workshop.

Trow, William Clark, *The Learning Process*. "What Research Says to the Teacher Series," No. 6 of the Department of Classroom Teachers and the American Educational Research Association, National Education Association; Washington, D.C.: The Association, 1954.
A brief synthesis of research findings on the learning process.

Wey, Herbert, "Why Do Beginning Teachers Fail?" *Bulletin*, No. 180, National Association of Secondary School Principals, 35:55–62 (October), 1951.
Report of a follow-up study of eighty-five first-year teachers.

Witty, Paul, "Some Characteristics of the Effective Teacher," *Educational Administration and Supervision*, 36:193–208 (April), 1950.
Report of an analysis of papers submitted in the Quiz Kids annual radio program contests to award scholarships to teachers most convincingly described as "The Teacher Who Has Helped Me Most."

———, "The Mental Health of the Teacher," in *Mental Health in Modern Education*. Fifty-fourth Yearbook of the National Society for the Study of Education; Chicago: The University of Chicago Press, 1955, Part II, Chap. 13.
See for a review of studies of the characteristics of good teachers and also for Witty's suggestions regarding the improvement of teacher personality.

Part II Organizing the Classroom for Learning

Part I has given the reader our point of view on what we believe is a sound teaching method. The difference between a method *and* techniques *of a method was established. Part II focuses on certain organizational techniques in the teaching-learning situation which are consistent with our definition of method—the process of interaction between teacher and pupils through which they are guided in achieving their teaching and learning purposes.*

In Chapter 3 attention is paid to the provision of a physical setting and a psychological climate which characterize "a laboratory for learning."

Chapter 4 examines the dynamics of classroom groups and discusses their implications for teaching and learning.

Chapter 5 gives suggestions for organizing the classroom group for more effective use of resources for learning, and defines the issues, problems, and possible solutions in group planning and action for learning.

Chapter 6 concentrates on problems of adolescent behavior in teaching-learning situations, with control of behavior in the light of learners' purposes being offered as the basic principle of discipline.

The reader should not believe that organizing a classroom for our ideal teaching-learning situation is something which is done at the beginning and thereafter is no longer a problem. Reorganization of the learning environment and experience is implied in the method of learning we espouse. This is only consistent with the over-all premise of learning through problem solving, and the least of the problems is not the setting for learning.

3. *The Classroom as a*
Learning Laboratory

INTRODUCTION

IN PART I the method of problem solving has been described as central to good teaching and learning processes, and we have discussed the roles and relations of teachers and learners in problem solving. Our emphasis thus far has been on the interpretation of theory and research which underlie and support a general method of education and the procedures of scientific thought and activity.

The appeal of the scientific method as a guide to good teaching and learning processes may be recognized, but the difficulties in using it are apparent when we think about typical school situations. There are many forces which militate against a conscious and consistent use of problem-solving procedures in our schools. The traditional role of the teacher as an authority, the expectations of parents and pupils, the nature of many of our instructional materials, and the environment of the typical classroom, to mention a few—all make the use of problem solving as the basic educational method a difficult task to accomplish.

Method has focused on the procedure of the teacher. While activities for students have been sensed as being important, the teacher "ran the show," so to speak. . . . Instruction is defined today as the process of guiding and directing experiences of children to the end that they learn. . . . Schools should be learning laboratories. . . . Classrooms, which have been the chief centers of instruction, should cease to be lesson-hearing rooms. Rather, they should be centers where children engage in the activities that will lead to the learning which is socially desirable.[1]

[1] G. Lester Anderson, Gertrude Whipple, and Robert Gilchrist, "The School as a Learning Laboratory," in *Learning and Instruction* (Forty-ninth Yearbook of the National Society for the Study of Education; Chicago: University of Chicago Press, 1950), Part I, Chap. XIII, p. 337.

One common complaint of teachers is, "I'd like to try some of these approaches, but our classrooms just aren't set up in our schools to do the job." To be sure, few schools have the optimum physical setting for the kind of teaching and learning activities we have been describing. But most schools could do more with their present facilities if the classroom were seen as a laboratory for learning. This chapter suggests things teachers might do with present facilities, or the kinds of physical facilities they might request. Attention will also be paid to certain nonphysical concomitants of the "classroom laboratory."

WHAT IS A LABORATORY?

Certainly the term "laboratory" has greater meaning in a school where the scientific method is basic to teaching and learning. When we think of a laboratory, a room comes to mind where experiments are conducted, where hypotheses are tested, and where answers to problems are sought. Such activity is more likely to take place in a certain kind of room, with special types of equipment, and with expert assistance. Facilities and their uses differ from those found in lecture-recitation rooms because of the differences in kinds of activities appropriate for each. Several examples may clarify possible relations between facilities and the nature of learning experiences.

In one classroom where there are movable seats and work tables, and varied resources for learning are readily available in storage cabinets, the class may engage in a variety of activities simultaneously —small group discussions, construction projects, drill groups, and the like. Yet in such a setting we have also seen a very rigid lecture or recitation process of teaching and learning. Likewise, in unattractive, inflexible physical settings we have seen dynamic teachers provide a variety of learning experiences, even though under the most adverse conditions.

In other words, flexible and attractive classroom appointments are important but not sufficient. The use made of the classroom environment presents a wide range of imaginative and creative possibilities for students and teachers.

Some of the differences in appearance and use between typical laboratory-type rooms and lecture-recitation rooms are described as follows in Table 5.

TABLE 5

CHARACTERISTICS OF LECTURE-RECITATION AND
LABORATORY-TYPE CLASSROOMS

Lecture-Recitation	*Laboratory-Type*
1. Uniformity in size and shape	1. Diversity in size and shape depending on nature of instruction
2. Rigidity in seating arrangement	2. Flexibility in arrangement of pupil stations and their use, depending on needs and activities of learners
3. Lack of opportunity for movement around room by pupils	3. Considerable movement and activity, less sitting
4. Paucity of materials and equipment, mostly uniform for each pupil	4. Varied materials and equipment, depending on need and activity of individual pupils
5. Adaptable primarily to listening, reciting, and uniform activities for total group	5. Geared to "doing things," and to various kinds of activities by individual pupils and small groups
6. Forces teacher into "telling" or "listening" role	6. Allows teacher to "do things" together with pupils, to act as assistant, as expert, or as co-learner
7. Emphasis on acquisition of facts and skills as ends in themselves	7. Primary emphasis on facts and skills as they relate to solution of problems
8. Use of blackboard for drill on facts and skills	8. Use of blackboard for making a record of problems, purposes, plans for action, or summaries of decisions and responsibilities
9. Class time assigned arbitrarily by teacher for recitation and study	9. Class time used flexibly, depending on group and individual needs and activities

A TRADITIONAL CLASSROOM

Because of its characteristics listed above, one would find in the typical lecture-recitation room a teacher standing or sitting in the front of the room. He faces a group of from thirty to forty pupils seated in five or six straight rows of seven or eight stationary desks each. Typically, he is lecturing or asking questions based on reading which all pupils have done (he hopes) from a common textbook. Pupils listen, recite when called on, or occasionally volunteer a question or answer. Study time in the classroom is marked by quiet,

PLATE 6. A TRADITIONAL SECONDARY CLASSROOM IS UNINVITING. Such an environment inhibits creativity and restricts activity. (Courtesy of the Kenton, Kentucky, County Schools)

lack of movement, and highly individualistic effort, mostly of a reading or writing nature. Other equipment consists of blackboards on two or three sides of the room and a combination bookcase and cupboard which houses a few reference books, boxes of chalk, several reams of paper, and several "projects" done by students two years ago for "extra credit." Hardly a setting for creative thinking, experimentation with things or ideas, and activity geared to the solution of problems!

A FUNCTIONAL SETTING FOR LEARNING

In contrast, the laboratory-type classroom would infrequently find the teacher in front of the room because the focus would not be on him and what he is saying. Rather, attention would be focused on what students are saying and doing, individually or in smaller groups. The teacher's role is that of consultant, adviser, assistant, and coordinator to the varied activities going on in the room. Movable seats allow for teams, committees, and subgroups to form in various parts

PLATE 7. A MODERN CLASSROOM ALCOVE ENCOURAGES COMMITTEE
WORK. Semiprivacy allows pupils to pursue special interests in
small groups. (Courtesy of the Birmingham, Michigan, Public
Schools)

of the room, and also permit the arrangement of the entire group in
a circle, oval, or rectangle when the time has come for sharing individual or subgroup activities and learnings.

One is impressed with the physical activity and hum of voices
present in the room. Even more interesting is the variety of activity.
One boy is writing a news story describing what has happened in
class the past two weeks; three students are preparing a model on
a small table in one corner; three others are preparing a chart for
presenting an idea to the total group; one group of six is not in the
room because it is readying itself for a debate by reading in the
school library; another girl is painting an impression of the story
read to the class the day before by a student who had written it;
the rest of the class is reading books from the classroom library at
the rear of the room. For this unit of work the library numbers over
150 volumes, selected cooperatively by teachers and students from
the school and public libraries.

In a storage cabinet there are a record player and a tape recorder which have been borrowed for several days from the central store-room of the school. The cabinet also houses ten or twelve individual and committee projects for this unit of study. The bulletin boards are full to overflowing with articles and pictures from current maga-zines, and reports and bits of writing from class members. The rolling book cart contains the three basic textbooks of the class in numbers sufficient for one-third to one-half of the class.

A person might suggest a bias on our part because of the greater space devoted to a description of the laboratory-type classroom. We can only reply, "What else can be said about the lecture-recitation room? The possibilities are limited in such a setting, whereas the description we have given of the laboratory-type classroom only begins to suggest the infinite potentialities of that type of facility."

EFFECTS OF TRADITIONAL
CLASSROOM ARRANGEMENTS

The above comparisons between lecture-recitation rooms and laboratory-type rooms may explain the fact that traditional teaching methods are inconsistent with problem-solving procedures. Most class-rooms discourage movement, activity, or "doing" on the part of learners by the nature of the size, shape, and seating arrangements of the rooms. Such classrooms encourage "teaching as telling," and the proof of learning becomes reciting, writing, and the passing of pencil-and-paper tests. This does not mean that such teaching and learning activities have no place in the classroom, but it does suggest that in the typical classroom they play a part out of proportion to what we know about the nature of learning as described in Chapter 2.

Such inflexible classrooms make the use of varied teaching and learning materials very difficult. They argue for uniformity of class-room activity and experience, based on a single textbook and on verbal facility alone. In such rooms there are few opportunities for more active types of behavior which are concomitants and products of learning activity geared to the solution of problems.

Perhaps most serious are the implications of the typical lecture-recitation room for the roles of teacher and learner. In such a setting the learner is cast as a "know-nothing," and the teacher as a "know-everything." This may seem to be an overstatement, but observa-tions of many classrooms and the behavior of teachers and pupils support this idea. Such a climate for learning frequently develops authoritarian attitudes in teachers and habits of overdependence in learners, neither of which is conducive to the problem-solving approach to learning.

It is hoped that the foregoing analysis of a typical lecture-recitation classroom, contrasted with the classroom as a laboratory for learning, may help the reader account in part for the infrequent use of problem solving in classrooms, and may serve as a basis for understanding the significance of the recommendations which follow.

THE CLASSROOM—SIZE, SHAPE, AND FUNCTION

In its broadest definition, curriculum would include the methods of facilitating the learning process as well as the necessary and desirable learning experiences to be provided by the school. The curriculum finds its physical expression in the construction and organization of the school plant. Following this line of reasoning it becomes apparent that the school plant can be defined as the space interpretation of the curriculum.[2]

In most cases, teachers have little to say about the over-all size and shape of their classrooms. They inherit classrooms which are standard in size. Fifteen to twenty square feet of space per pupil have until recently been considered ample, with a resulting rectangular or square room of 22 by 30 or 25 by 25 deemed more than ample for a class size of thirty. Such a room also allows the crowding in of five or ten more pupils by placing seats closer together. We are referring here to general classrooms rather than to rooms for special subjects and activities like shop, music, and home economics.

It is not surprising under such circumstances that many classrooms have become unbearable from the standpoint of health and safety, and have fostered conditions where classroom control has become difficult except by very authoritarian measures. Obviously, there is little chance for pupils to do much more than hear lectures or read, write, and recite under these conditions. Rooms of this type are the product of teachers, the public, architects, superintendents, and boards of education whose concept of the learning process demands uniformity and limiting of activity. They are traditional classrooms and as such seem to have an aura of respectability which makes their perpetuation desirable, regardless of changes in educational aims and methods.

However, as we have pointed out previously, creative teachers can vitalize the most austere and rigid classroom environment. Problem-solving activity can go on in such a setting under great difficulty.

[2] Stephen J. Knezevich, "Curriculum and the School Plant," *Educational Leadership*, 10:496 (May), 1947.

But teachers above all others should demonstrate and argue for the need of larger and more flexible classrooms.

Some teachers have the good fortune to be in school systems where alterations or new units are planned. They can exercise leadership by assisting building planners in determining appropriate classroom sizes and shapes which will provide for more flexibility in teaching and learning procedures. Many school systems are now involving classroom teachers on building committees, and the results are encouraging for teachers and pupils alike. Newer general classrooms are allowing for 25 to 35 square feet per pupil, resulting in greater variety of activities and in potentialities of adapting the classroom to various functions within the basic shape of the room.[3] More will be said of these possibilities in the section immediately following.

WHY LARGER CLASSROOMS?

It seems safe to generalize that most classrooms are too small for the kind of teaching and learning experiences we envision, at least for groups of the usual size of thirty or more. If the size of classroom is only a matter of "containing" a number of pupils, then the size can be the conventional 22 by 30 or smaller. If the classroom is thought of as a place to release teachers and learners in a creative problem-solving experience, then most classrooms need to be larger.

Teachers and pupils can use more classroom space in many creative ways.

1. Work areas are needed with tables, chairs, and display spaces for individuals or small groups, where materials can be spread out during the process of development or where exhibits, projects, and the like can be displayed for periods of time. Many teachers suggest that their classrooms are lacking in pupil activity because they lack the space required for developing such a learning situation. Spacious facilities encourage individualization of instruction, adaptation to small groups, and provision of socializing experiences which are at a premium in a crowded, traditional classroom.

2. Storage cabinets, drawers, and files are helpful for student work in the form of charts, mock-ups, drawings, models, maps, posters, and other pupil productions. Most teachers and pupils are discouraged from this kind of creative work by the fact that the work lies around in places where it may be damaged or lost, or requires carrying to hall

[3] Ernest Hayes, "A Study of the Problems of Space Allocation in New High School Buildings to Meet the Needs of the Various Departments," *College of Education Record,* University of Washington, 21:10–12 (November), 1954.

PLATE 8. DISPLAY AREAS FACILITATE LEARNING. Exhibits stimulate activity and provide wholesome recognition for achievement. (Courtesy of the Board of Education, City of New York)

lockers or to their homes. Adequate storage space takes care of these problems and in addition allows a resource file of student work to be built over the years which can be invaluable for indicating student growth.

3. Alcoves or conference rooms should be provided for individual or group meetings with teacher, consultants, parents, and others, where quiet or privacy can be assured. Increasingly as teachers see themselves as an integral part of the guidance program of the school, space must be provided where they can visit informally with pupils and parents.

4. Classroom libraries are part of the modern classroom. These demand shelving or cabinet space and a "browsing" area. Problem-solving activity, as well as greater individualization of instruction, demand varied materials close at hand in order to be functional in this kind of learning laboratory.

5. Movable desks and tables are important, but sufficient space

must be available after rearrangement of furniture to provide for considerable freedom of movement and a variety of total group experiences.

6. Filing-cabinet space is a prerequisite for cumulative records of pupils, samples of individual work, and the like, as they become part of a continuous, cooperative evaluation procedure by pupils and teachers. There are few who would argue against the importance of better guidance for evaluation of pupil growth and achievement. This better guidance requires space for orderly storage and maintenance of records and other evidence, readily available for use by all concerned with the progress of the learner.

7. Informal group discussions become very important, either as a total group or in subgroups. These are facilitated by moving furniture about to achieve desired groupings. The problem-solving, laboratory approach to learning requires much more group activity at all stages of the process—problem identification, planning, implementation, and evaluation. The opportunity and desirability of being able to group pupils effectively for these kinds of discussions require flexible furniture and adequate space.

All of the above advantages for a creative, problem-solving classroom atmosphere cannot be provided adequately in the average size classroom. Provisions like those listed above make possible more varied group and individual activities by which teachers and learners work together on the solution of problems. It is interesting to note that trends in building construction at the elementary school level where the self-contained classroom is recognized as desirable embody many of the above features. Secondary school building planners would do well to move in these directions by making rooms more self-sufficient, at the same time striving for more class "living room" and a maximum class size of thirty.

As mentioned before, most teachers find that the size and shape of the classroom are factors in instructional conditions beyond their control. However, even in smaller classrooms creative teachers can make adaptations to their limiting surroundings. Perhaps their most obvious concern should be with classroom arrangement, equipment, and the materials of instruction.

CLASSROOM EQUIPMENT AND ITS USES

The type and use of permanent equipment is often an index of the degree of problem-solving activity employed in a classroom. In most classrooms the basic equipment has been pupils' desks and seats, teacher's desk and chair, and the blackboard. Many classrooms today have gone beyond this minimum, but as far as learning *activity* is concerned, they still remain the focal points in the teaching-learning process.

It would seem that equipment for a modern classroom would include the following as a minimum:

1. Movable seat-desks or tables and chairs which can be shifted into various patterns of seating arrangements for the total group or subgroups, depending on the needs and purposes involved in the learning situation.

2. Several work tables around which individuals or subgroups can engage in projects or discussions, apart from the rest of the class.

3. Bulletin boards, blackboards, and/or display cases for use by students and teacher to display learning materials or products of individual and group activity.

4. Storage cabinets, drawers, or cupboards where pupils' projects can be kept—a natural outgrowth of creative, problem-solving teaching and learning.

5. Audiovisual equipment, including radio, television, record player, recording machine, films, projector, screen, dark shades, maps, globes, pictures, and charts. Ideally, these would be available for each room, but realistic planning by a building staff will make their shared use possible, on a total building, department, building wing, or floor basis.

6. Filing cabinets for pupils' and teacher's use. New methods of teaching and learning demand new methods of evaluation. Other kinds of records of pupil activity and progress must be kept. Cumulative records, samples of pupils' work, contributions to resource files (clippings, pictures, and so forth)—all demand a place to be kept. In such a setting the teacher's class record book is less important, and a file of records showing pupil progress, activity, and achievement become a necessary part of the permanent equipment.

SUGGESTIONS FOR IMPROVING THE PHYSICAL ENVIRONMENT

It is important to consider the plight of the teacher whose classroom falls far short of these recommendations, and who finds that no funds can or will be spent for improvement of the environment for learning. The blocks facing the teacher in such a situation are often so frustrating that no attempts are made to improvise. We feel, however, that the best hope for eventually getting the kind of physical setting he needs lies in demonstrating his own resourcefulness in creating a better environment and in proving the value of better facilities.

In respect to the seating arrangements, one should investigate whether present stationary seating can be detached from the floor to provide greater flexibility. Caution is necessary here because some types of seats are not safe unless bolted down; others are too heavy to be moved around easily. However, frequently seats may be unscrewed from the floor to allow shifting as the need arises, or they may be regrouped in other patterns than rows if they must be fastened to the floor. Such changes require only effort and initiative on the part of a teacher to determine the possibilities and to secure permission and aid for the shifts.

Additional seating may be secured by rounding up little-used tables and chairs in the building for use at the back and front of the room. If such are not available, pupils and parents may assist in locating little-used chairs and tables in their homes, churches, or other places in the community. Such activity on the part of teachers, pupils, and parents will focus attention on the need for facilities and may result in increased demand and support for better classroom equipment.

Other kinds of equipment, such as bulletin boards, display cases, cupboards, and cabinets, can well become the concern of pupils, particularly boys. If the need is apparent, they will contribute their time and effort in shop classes or in the classroom by building these pieces of equipment. Materials used may be discarded orange crates, packing boxes, and scrap lumber, decorated by a little bright paint or stain and varnish. Rougher and less permanent perhaps, these additions to the classroom will still be functional not only in their use but in signifying the contribution and worth of certain individuals in the group.

Given the above equipment to a greater or lesser degree, pupils and teachers would be in a better position to approach learning on a problem-solving basis than in a room where the activity is limited by stationary seats, the teacher's rostrum, and the blackboard space. All of the above recommendations are geared to available room space and class size as suggested previously. Proper use of these facilities does not follow automatically, but is the product of in-service education programs which explore the potentials of such equipment for problem-solving teaching and learning.

In addition to a more creative use of existing classroom space and facilities, many teachers have found that areas outside the classroom can be employed to give some flexibility to classroom activities.

The descriptions of the following two schools and what pupils, parents, and teachers did about them may encourage teachers who find themselves in classrooms which are not conducive to learning:

The Pepperdine School in Springfield, Missouri, was built in the days when schools were constructed with a huge rotunda in the center. There is much extra space in halls leading out from the center foyer, on the wide stair landings, and in corners which could become dark and dismal. By making use of this space, this school has made its architecture an educational asset. Painted and cushioned benches have been placed on the landings, and the extra hall space is used for hobby or reading corners. These nooks make good work places for small committees, or serve as places of retreat for individuals who want to read alone when others are doing group work in the classroom. One corner is furnished with an old round dining table, cut down and painted white. Plants abound, but they are not huge ferns and unchanging foliage plants alone; they are flowering plants, cared for by the children, and interesting because they grow rapidly and change their appearance. In the spring and fall, this school has a house cleaning day. Children come in jeans and old clothes and go over the entire school to get it ready for the school year in September, and in the spring clean it again before the vacation. The teachers and parents see this as an opportunity to teach care of property and to give the children a chance to make the school into the kind of place in which they feel at home. Parents and children have worked together to build the benches, paint the bookcases and do the other work necessary for making this school such a pleasant place in which to live and learn.

A rural school in Bucks County, Pennsylvania, has a similar atmosphere. It is a one-room school with old-fashioned desks fastened to the floor; but there are curtains at the windows and a cut-down table with a rocking chair and a small rug at the back of the room. Children paint the windows at various seasons of the year. A plank bookcase runs the full length of the room, and a show table borders the other side of the room under the window. A flower box has been made from the top of an old mechanical phonograph. The room looks homelike as one enters, even before the children arrive.[4]

THE MATERIALS OF INSTRUCTION

Given a classroom of functional size, shape, and equipment to carry on a modern program of teaching and learning, the teacher is still faced with the problem of choice and use of instructional materials. (See Chapter 15 for a more detailed discussion of the problem of choosing materials.) It is at this point where American education

[4] Association for Supervision and Curriculum Development, National Education Association, *Creating a Good Environment for Learning* (Washington, D.C.: The Association, 1954), pp. 202–204. Reprinted by permission.

has standardized the learning process to a uniformity which goes even beyond the concept of the classroom as a lecture and recitation hall. We refer to the use of the textbook.

THE TEXTBOOK

The typical secondary academic classroom uses a single textbook as the basic material of instruction, supplemented by teacher lectures, pupil recitations, some class discussion, and occasional use of reference materials. Out of this context has come the "assign-recite-test" method of teaching, with emphasis on a body of subject matter to be covered, but generally not placed in the framework of problem solution. The basic assumption underlying this procedure is that the content or subject matter will be learned for its own sake, or retained for possible future use in solving problems *if* and *when* they arise. Subject matter as such becomes an end in itself, and not instrumental to the solution of immediate problems faced by the learner.

Sharp divisions of opinion have arisen, both within the profession of education and outside, as to the place of subject matter. To many teachers and most lay people, education has come to mean the mastery of subject matter or skills found within the confines of textbooks. And yet most critics of education worry about the behavior of learners, that is, what people *do* as a reflection of what they have learned.

Advocates of learning as problem solving assert that learners who are assisted in scientific methods of solving problems learn not only subject matter but also appropriate behavior when faced with a similar or new problem in the future. And they support with evidence the contention that the subject matter is learned more economically from the standpoint of time and with greater possibilities of retention to the degree that the problems are lifelike and of importance to the learner.

It is at this point that the subject matter of textbooks bears examination. No one will deny that textbooks contain much important subject matter which can assist in the solution of problems. We quarrel with the organization and use of textbooks which are prescribed as a teaching-learning process and not oriented to the solution of the problems of learners. The result is that the use of a basic textbook makes the content of that book synonymous with what needs to be learned in a given area of educational experience. The most scholarly and zealous of textbook writers would say that theirs is not a completely definitive statement of what is known about the area under consideration, that many other sources need to be consulted and various kinds of activities need to be engaged in other than reading for one to become proficient in the area.

We propose the use of the textbook as a capstone to an educational experience, involving the prior use of many resources and materials. Typically, the textbook is used as an introduction to a unit of work. Most textbooks are compact treatments of a body of subject matter, tightly packed with generalizations and highly selected content. As such, it is hardly appropriate to use a textbook as a student's first exposure to a unit of work.

We suggest that pupils do better to have first an organized sequence of varied readings, discussions, and other kinds of activities built around the central problem or theme. The reading of the textbook then becomes a culminating experience in which the important ideas, facts, and generalizations are distilled for the learner. With the previous background of classroom experiences leading up to the reading of the text, a learner has a better chance of understanding and using these contributions made by a textbook.

All this seems to us to argue for a policy on use of instructional materials that allows and urges the utilization of varied materials *and* activities, geared to the solution of practical problems. Even the use of several textbooks does not do justice to the wealth of human knowledge at our disposal, nor does it provide for the solution of problems as a focus for learning activity. It also by-passes the question of individual differences in learners—their interests, needs, and abilities.

Again, as in the case of classroom equipment and physical surroundings, the presence of a "lush environment" with respect to instructional materials does not guarantee good teaching and learning. Creative supervision and in-service education programs will do much to exploit the possibilities of varied materials of instruction in problem-centered teaching.

OTHER MATERIALS

The reader at this point will again wish to refer to Chapter 15, which deals more completely with planning the materials of instruction. The introduction of multiple textbooks and varied materials into the learning experience obviously provides a wider base for data gathering on problems and introduces the element of evidence weighing to the learner. Almost any problem-oriented learning experience, if it utilizes varied materials—magazines, newspapers, standard reference sources, pamphlets, films, human resources (parents, community members, expert consultants)—will provide a wider understanding of the problem and alternative solutions than if a single textbook is used. But tradition, vested interests, and lack of professional knowledge and know-how continues to strait-jacket learning experiences in the classroom within the confines of the single textbook. The danger also exists that learners may gain a point of view and emphasis which is narrow or biased, hardly a desirable outcome for either a traditional classroom or a problem-centered learning situation.

The advantages of using varied materials in the classroom can be seen in the following discussion of classroom resources:

Providing a variety of instructional materials makes possible a variety of learning experiences. We do not all learn through the same approaches or at the same rate. Reading, discussing, writing, observing, using films or slides, illustrating, listening, constructing, painting, drawing, experimenting, manipulating, practicing are avenues of learning used in all curricular areas at all levels. . . .

Many audio-visual aids should be used in every classroom program. It may be necessary to use another place in the building for the showing of films, slides, and filmstrips, but such a schedule can be set up. Flat pictures, charts, models, and graphs are particularly helpful in developing concepts. A word about charts, prepared either by teachers or students. They can be used for a variety of purposes: To set up standards of performance for work; record group experiences; set up guides for day-by-day activities; show progress in a given field; show operational processes, such as grading of lumber, finishing methods, preparing soil for planting; give directions or summaries; present data in sequence as a time line; or show organization or structure of a subject. Charts can organize material for a class, as well as carry individuals along with the class. . . .

In more recent years, transcriptions and recordings of all types are used to enhance learning in many fields, not just in music. The tape recorder is coming into common use for recording discussions that can be played back for evaluation; preserving important happenings, as a choral reading or rhythm band to be shared later with others; helping children improve their speech or reading by listening to themselves or a group. Earphones attached to the tape recorder can play back an individual student's reading so he may listen and correct his own problems without embarrassment.

We should mention felt boards, stereographs, opaque projectors, tachistoscopes, radio, and our newest vehicle, television. These media cannot carry the burden of instruction in themselves, but they can be real aids to instruction.[5]

THE CLASSROOM LIBRARY

Many teachers admit the soundness of the arguments advanced for a great variety of learning materials, but raise budgetary limitations as an excuse for staying with the single textbook. This may be a realistic excuse, but we suggest that the decentralization of school libraries

[5] Robert S. Gilchrist and Dorothy M. Swatszel, "The Room That Helps Good Teaching," *Educational Trend*, November, 1954, p. 2. Reprinted by permission from *The Educational Trend,* an Arthur C. Croft publication.

into mobile classroom libraries could do much to provide varied instructional materials. The concept of the school library as a repository of books for safekeeping and the librarian as "the keeper of the books" is becoming outmoded. The library is becoming a special service of the school and the librarian an instructional services person whose

PLATE 9. LEARNERS NEED CLASSROOM LIBRARIES. Research activity and browsing are both encouraged by readily accessible books. (Courtesy of the Denver, Colorado, Public Schools)

responsibility it is to get books, pamphlets, and other materials into the mainstream of the instructional program in great variety of content and difficulty, geared to the problems under consideration in the classroom.

A classroom library might include textbooks at various reading levels, reference books on special topics and interests, and related fiction and nonfiction, pamphlets, clippings, pictures, maps, and charts. Such facilities do not preclude the use of the central library for research purposes, but experience has shown greater use of varied materials when they are readily available in the classroom under the supervision of the teacher.

The following description suggests a setting for a classroom library other than just a collection of books to be placed on a shelf:

A planned reading center invites students to use many types of books. Two or three books can be fastened open to alluring pictures, placed on a book rack with snap clothespins with an invitation, "Have you seen this?". Book jackets can be placed on a bulletin board above the bookshelves with such catchy questions as "Who is Little Britches?" or "Have you met the Americans who fought *against* the Revolution?". A card file near the reference material giving exact information and page numbers indicating where to find discussions of specific subjects can lead a less able student to find material. A wide range of reading material—books, magazines, pamphlets, and newspapers—should be provided. Students need to be encouraged to read both sides of a problem as a basis for critical thinking.[6]

In such a setting, teachers, pupils, and librarians may cooperate in the establishment of materials, facilities, and procedures for the use of varied resources in all classrooms. If such planning is done, the day of "outside reading" and "book reports" is past, and more reading will be geared to real interests and needs developed and pursued in the classroom for the solution of problems. Such a policy concerning classroom libraries again calls for in-service education and for the provision of space, shelving, and records of circulation.

Fundamental to the successful organization of classroom libraries is a good rapport between teachers and the librarian. The teacher must be able to propose a pattern of requests for books and for their circulation which librarians will see as a systematic attempt by teachers and pupils to use books wisely and economically. The librarian must have as much confidence in the motivations of teachers and pupils toward books as he has desire to develop broad reading habits among pupils. This applies to both public and school librarians.

Cooperative planning among teachers, pupils, and the librarian ought to result in policies something like the following:

1. Classroom libraries may contain two kinds of books—those related to a specific unit of work in progress, and those which are intended for free, recreational reading. Probably these two kinds of collections should be separated.

2. Requests from a classroom for a library collection should be given to the librarian several days before it will be needed. This will avoid unnecessary rush and delays.

3. Certain agreements should be made regarding each collection of books sent to a classroom. These include the length of time they will be needed and the part pupils may play in administering the collection.

[6] *Ibid.,* p. 2.

4. In connection with the latter, planning of teachers and pupils should result in shared responsibilities for keeping the collection in order, for checking books in and out, and for repair of any books which may be damaged. Committees for this kind of responsibility have been found very helpful.

5. Opportunities should be afforded for teachers and pupils to recommend purchases by the librarian of new materials for classroom libraries.

6. Although some loss and damage may be expected and justified in any kind of library service, classroom libraries may invite more of this sort of thing than usual. Agreements should be developed explicitly on the nature of teacher and pupil responsibility. In addition, a class group does well to consider ways of replacing lost books or repairing damaged materials.

7. In general, classroom libraries may have the same problem as central libraries in accelerating the circulation of books. Realistic agreement should be reached on time limits for individuals to use a book.

8. Finally, the development, free procurement, or even purchase of additional materials for classroom libraries should be encouraged in classroom groups. This results in greater involvement and interest in finding resources for learning, a basic attitude in learning which we frequently fail to develop in learners.

Teachers who have sensed the possibilities inherent in classroom libraries are enthusiastic about the contribution they make to the learning situation, particularly in three respects: (1) the ready availability of materials for research by students under the supervision of the teacher, (2) the increase in quantity and quality of "free reading" by students, (3) the development of pupil responsibility for the discovery, use, and evaluation of classroom materials which seldom characterizes the learner in the typical schoolroom.

NONPHYSICAL FACTORS IN THE ENVIRONMENT

Having developed at some length the importance of the physical factors in the classroom setting, we turn now to the psychological elements of the teaching-learning situation which are basic to the problem-solving method.

Important as are pleasant, flexible surroundings and a wealth of instructional materials, even more conducive to learning is the general psychological atmosphere which pervades the relations of teachers and pupils. The climate of a problem-oriented classroom situation is characterized by certain attitudes, habits, and behaviors which are both the motivation of a group of learners and a teacher working together cooperatively and, at the same time, the products of the situation.

We believe that the chief psychological concomitants of the problem-solving method of teaching are as follows:

1. The utilization of the spirit of inquiry in both teachers and learners which charges them with energy to pose problems, to develop hunches on how to solve the problems, to test these hunches in reality or vicariously through the experience of others, to evaluate the experience, and to generalize to the point where learning takes place

2. The attachment of value and respect to the individual—his problems, his fears, his hopes and aspirations—to the point where the fundamental worth and integrity of the individual learner prescribes the *what* and *how* of learning, rather than prescribed content and teaching methods circumscribing the learner and his educational experience

These attitudes, habits, and behaviors are so much a part of the problem-solving approach to learning that they seldom are found in classrooms where the scientific method is not employed as the basis for teaching methodology. It is true that in some classrooms they may exist through a combination of fortuitous circumstances such as the personality of the teacher and the experiential backgrounds of the pupils. But then they are present, not because of the methods of teaching and learning, but in spite of them. As such, they cannot be planned for or taught systematically, but develop haphazardly. Yet even in these cases, they at times provide a spark for teachers and pupils which lights up otherwise drab and enervating classroom routines.

If these are factors important enough to make the difference between a humdrum, routine "lesson" and a stimulating, creative educational experience, what are the specific things that must be given attention if these desirable outcomes are to be achieved?

THE SPIRIT OF INQUIRY

We believe that one of the sharpest indictments that can be made of most education is related to the increasing absence of inquisitiveness on the part of boys and girls as they go through the schools. The young preschool child burns with curiosity, reflected in his questions of *what, how,* and *why.* In the early years of elementary education much use is made of these questions as they relate to himself, his family, and his more immediate environment. But as he climbs the educational ladder, these questions tend to become fewer as teachers define the problems, ask the questions, and spoon-feed the answers. By the time pupils reach the secondary school and the age of adolescence, their questions persist outside the school, but find little response within the school. Consider the dilemma of the adolescent as his teachers and parents say on the one hand, "Why don't you grow up?" This, in reality, means, "Why don't you become more mature in sensing and solving your problems?" On the other hand, they often say, "You aren't old enough," when he raises his problems and asks for help in their solution. The latter response of adults really means, "You aren't mature enough to know what the problems are or how to solve them. We know your problems and how to solve them."

Small wonder that the adolescent becomes confused as to his role, both in school and in the larger society. The problems he faces in school become, for a large part, his problems as a pupil, not as a human being. He learns to accept the problems posed for him, the methods of solving the problems, and the answers which ready-made solutions give him.

As a result, adolescents in our secondary schools display little curiosity about the subject matter of their lessons but exhibit the appropriate behavior of docility as they listen, read, and reproduce what is determined by others to be the content of an educational experience. If they become hostile or rebel against the adult-determined curriculum, they are the "problem children" of our schools. We suggest, rather, that they are children with problems other than those posed by the school. The developmental tasks of youth which were suggested in Chapter 2 are set aside as inappropriate, and in their place curriculum content develops which for many students is only remotely related to their problems, present or future. In order to accomplish the "learning" of this content, we are forced to introduce materials and methods which must seem unrealistic to the learner. For example, listen to a seventh-grader as he soliloquizes about his school experience:

. . . I don't know why the teachers don't like me. They never have very much. Seems like they don't think you know anything unless you can name the book it comes out of. I've got a lot of books in my own room at home —books like POPULAR SCIENCE, MECHANICAL ENCYCLOPEDIA, and the Sears' and Ward's catalogues, but I don't very often just sit down and read them through like they make us do in school. I use my books when I want to find something out, like whenever Mom buys anything secondhand I look it up in Sears' or Ward's first and tell her if she's getting stung or not. I can use the index in a hurry to find the things I want.

In school, though, we've got to learn whatever is in the book and I just can't memorize the stuff. Last year I stayed after school every night for two weeks trying to learn the names of the Presidents. Of course I knew some of them like Washington and Jefferson and Lincoln, but there must have been thirty altogether and I never did get them straight.

I'm not too sorry though because the kids who learned the Presidents had to turn right around and learn all the Vice Presidents. I am taking the seventh grade over but our teacher this year isn't so interested in the names of the Presidents. She has us trying to learn the names of all the great American inventors. . . .[7]

Serious as is the failure of our schools to meet the real needs of learners, we believe that equally important is the tremendous waste of energy which results when this natural curiosity is not exploited. It is here that the school's greatest contribution lies—namely, in helping learners to define more clearly the nature of their problems, and to provide materials and environment for a systematic attack on these problems. Skills of thinking and action can be introduced so that the trial-and-error method of coping with problems is replaced by a systematic approach to learning, which, in the final analysis, is one of the products of problem solving. Therein lies the hope of more functional education for youth, both in terms of meeting their needs and in giving them methods of facing up to problems, present and future, with the expectation of more economical and safe learning from experience.

Teachers frequently are distressed by the thought of giving free rein to learners' questions, problems, and desires to "find out." Such student involvement may do violence to the scope and sequence of a teacher's plan or of a course of study. For example, presidential elections do not, unfortunately, fall at the time when classes are studying matters related to nominating conventions, campaigns, the electoral college, and the like. Interest and a spirit of inquiry during such an event may run high among students, but many teachers refuse to capitalize on them, saying, "That comes later."

Other teachers, deciding to utilize student interest and concern about a current problem, introduce "respectable" material to students who are asking for experiences of a more contemporary and meaningful nature. Witness the "bootlegging" of *Silas Marner* as "a novel portraying the problems of the Industrial Revolution"! Small wonder that

[7] Stephen M. Corey, "Poor Scholar's Soliloquy," *Childhood Education*, 20:219–220 (January), 1944. Reprinted by permission.

the spirit of inquiry and the desire to solve problems is lost for many pupils.

The teacher who realizes the importance for real learning of the desires of students to "find out," or to solve problems important to them, will accept at the outset the problems *as students see them.* He will respect their hypotheses on how to solve the problems and the materials and activities they propose. From that point, the teacher is in a better position to introduce other materials and activities and to raise levels of insight and aspiration—in short, to guide learning.

In summary, we believe that only through capitalizing on the curiosity of learners about themselves and their world, and by assisting them in developing rational approaches to the solution of their problems, will education become exciting and functional for boys and girls. An excellent example of teachers' and pupils' capitalizing on their curiosity about themselves and their environment can be seen in the following description:

Monday, September 8, the first day of school, was one of routine organization. In one seventh-grade core class there were forty children, while in the other there were thirty-nine. In size, each core classroom was nineteen feet wide and twenty-eight feet long. In each were forty movable desks, book shelves, blackboards and a small bulletin board. Obviously, the physical conditions in these rooms were hardly of the best for carrying on a core program.

Next day, the pupils discussed some of the problems which were facing them as seventh graders entering junior high school. Their basic problem, they decided, was that they had to learn to live in a different school setting from the one to which they had been accustomed. As far as the teachers were concerned, it seemed necessary to choose a learning unit in which pupils would get to know each other better, in which they would learn to understand better their new school and its program, and in which they would have ample opportunity to practice good citizenship and develop language arts skills.

The teacher asked the pupils to tell some of the things they liked about their new school. They named a variety of things, one of which was the appearance of the school and its grounds. Through discussion, the class brought out facts relating to the school's age and history. Most of these items were recalled from stories told by their parents and from older brothers and sisters. Some children said that they had studied about their community while attending the elementary school. They were anxious to contribute any information they could for the benefit of some of the new children who were attending school in this community for the first time.

As an outgrowth of the discussion concerning the beauty of the front campus, some of the children remarked that they had noticed several unattractive bare spots. The teacher then suggested that during their leisure at lunch time and after school they might survey the campus to see what improvements might be made.

Recognizing the importance of fundamental skills in a core program, the teacher next asked the pupils to write two paragraphs: the first, to describe the specific poor conditions they had discovered; the second, to explain what should be done to correct these conditions. Some children who rode buses thought that they might not have time to survey the campus and asked whether they could use a home situation on the same basis. It was agreed that they might do so.

The following morning, class members shared their findings. Some pupils proposed unique solutions to cope with situations they had found; some frankly said they did not know what should be done; and some children presented solutions thought by the class to be promising. Then the children began to realize that the approach to the problem should be made carefully and scientifically. Some felt that the science teacher would surely have some helpful material. Recognizing that pupil learning has more continuity when teachers plan together, the science teacher agreed to plan his science unit to correlate with the core unit.[8]

We suggest the following questions which a teacher may use to determine whether or not he is capitalizing on pupil interests and curiosity:

1. Do I recognize and accept the urgency of learners' *immediate problems, interests,* and *questions* by providing the opportunity to explore, seek answers, and test their ideas in active, lifelike situations?

2. Do I give learners the opportunity to remember and reconstruct their past experience and that of others in the light of present problems, interests, and needs?

3. Do I assist learners to broaden their horizons of interests by looking to the future in terms of what they see their present problems and interests to be?

4. Do I assist learners to see shortages in their experience, information, and skills and provide for their improvement in these areas, as far as possible in relation to their perceptions of need for these facts, experiences, or skills to solve their problems?

5. Do I recognize that I cannot function as an expert in all areas, admit at times that I do not know the answer, and suggest that we need the assistance of other people? Do I provide that assistance?

6. Do I give ample opportunity for learners to share their interests, problems, and needs and to profit from the many experiences which

---

[8] Association for Supervision and Curriculum Development, National Education Association, *op. cit.,* pp. 89–92. Reprinted by permission.

individuals or groups have in attempting to solve their problems and pursue their interests?

If all teachers did this consistently, we contend that classroom experiences would be more vital and that the classroom would approach the setting of a laboratory for cooperative problem solving.

THE IMPORTANCE OF THE INDIVIDUAL

By the very nature of the American ideal of free public education for all youth, we find that group teaching and learning are central to our system of instruction. We plan, organize, and administer our schools in terms of groups of children. The tutorial system is impossible in mass education. Even if it were possible, we are more enthusiastic about the values of social instruction in groups and argue that group experiences in education are important in preparation for life. Our culture is group-minded, and the best education is in terms of group living in our schools.

The fact remains, however, that learning is a highly personal matter, both in content and method. Experiential background, abilities, interests, and aptitudes combine to make an educational experience meaningful or insignificant for a learner. With mass education as now conceived have come group procedures, materials, standards, and measurements which do not take into account sufficiently the individual differences of pupils. Teachers and learners alike are conscious of this situation, and teachers in particular are constantly harassed by the problem of providing for individual differences. Typically, the search for answers to the problem has been made in the field of special methods and materials, rather than in looking at the nature of the learning experience and what is appropriate for learning. We do not mean to imply that special methods and materials are not helpful in instruction. Rather, we suggest that more basic is a consideration of general methods and particularly the problem-solving approach to learning.

We have suggested previously that the spirit of inquiry is a natural phenomenon of a human being and that schools can do much to exploit the curiosity of learners as they struggle to cope with their problems. We also believe that such an emphasis in teaching-learning situations will lead to greater concern with individual perceptions of need, and more respect for pupils' problems as they see them. This, to us, is a fundamental precept in democratic education—the respectability of the individual and his problems as he sees them.

Much of education fails to take into account the individual's unique problems, or at best, places a value judgment on them as being real or respectable. From many state departments of education, from pressure groups, from local administrators and supervisors, and from parents and teachers comes a flood of prescriptions for the education of youth—all of them suggesting a magic elixir which can be swallowed by all pupils, transforming them into better citizens, better wage earners, better family members, and better individuals. It is as though a group of specialists in pharmacopoeia had concocted a new wonder drug which purports to cure the ills of all people at any time in any place. This would hardly be accepted as possible, much less scientific.

The authors argue that the scientific approach to problem solving supplies the context for learning which places a premium on the individual and his problems as he sees them; on the teacher as an expert who can assist him in clarifying the problems and providing him with ways and means for solving them; and on cooperative assessment of the outcomes of attempts to solve the problems. We hope the analogy is not lost between this kind of teaching and learning and the new approaches to clinical therapy in which the client-centered approach is central. To be sure, the clinical approach of the psychologist has fewer limitations than those imposed upon teaching methods; but education as therapy is one concept of the school's function which cannot be overlooked.

The typical classroom experience in the past has been conceived primarily in terms of criteria extraneous to the individual learner— what society says or does, or perhaps more accurately, what the teacher or course of study says about society. We are not suggesting that education has no social function. We do insist that the greatest hope for integrating individuals with society lies in starting with the individual and *his* perceptions, rather than rejecting them as immature, unreal, or unworthy. Only when they are accepted *as a starting point* can there be hope for relating the individual to a larger society and his role in it.

The skillful teacher accepts the spontaneous question, remark, or action of the learner as a clue to an interest, need, or problem, not as a spurious phenomenon of immaturity. For such a teacher, the challenge is clearer to guide the learner to more mature, realistic, and socially acceptable behavior, based on growth and expansion from the point at which he found the learner.

The great need of American classroom is an atmosphere where pupils are liked and accepted for themselves as they are, together with their weaknesses and strengths, problems and potentialities. In such a background the stage is set for teachers and learners to work together on the solution of problems, with learning the end product more surely than in classrooms where tailor-made problems and pre-fabricated solutions are the stock in trade of teachers.

Such a classroom is well illustrated in the following description:

In a particular twelfth-grade social-studies class, the educational objectives of the course are: (a) To develop understanding of the problems involved in the operation of a democratic government and the methods by which these problems are being attacked at the local, state, and national levels. (b) To develop an attachment for the general principles of the democratic system with its emphasis on the worth of the individual responsibility for fellowmen, freedom, and equality. (c) To develop skill in critical thinking about civic problems.

One of the major units is entitled, "How May We Crystallize Public Opinion into Law in a Representative Democracy?" The teacher in introducing this unit, showed a cartoon from a current magazine which illustrated some fantastic laws still on the statute books. The discussion began with the question, "Why should such silly laws be enacted?" The discussion brought out a number of hypotheses regarding the school-achievement problem, and it also indicated several group-process problems. Several members of the group did not express themselves in the discussion. Certain members of the group were using the discussion for the expression of aggression toward other members of the group. The control of aggressive behavior was not yet established in the group. These problems the teacher noted because there would likely be need to deal with them at a conscious level later on.

During the preliminary discussion, two questions emerged which continued to involve a large majority of the group. They were: "Do we have silly laws in force here in our community?" and "How do laws get on the books and get off the books?" As it became clear to the teacher that these questions were challenging to the group, the additional question was raised: "How can we find out whether we have silly laws in force and how laws get on and off the books?" This question turned attention of the group to problems of process: What could be done? Who could do it? How could the various tasks be carried out? The motivation of the class was high and could be maintained by continuing analysis and interpretation.

In particular, the teacher had the insight to suspect that some of the discussion about silly laws and ways of changing them actually might be reflecting a variety of feelings in the class about some of the classroom and school regulations. He felt that the civics discussion was, in effect, not only a discussion of civics but a cloak under which was occurring a circuitous, semiconscious probing of the teacher's attitudes toward rules. The question of the right of designated authorities to pass laws seemed particularly intriguing to several of the students, and they returned again and again to different ways of raising this question.

The teacher decided to explore the situation further, on the grounds that civics-learning would be interfered with if the major preoccupation during civics discussion was the relationship between teacher and class. He, therefore, found occasion to point out rather casually that even teachers regulate some matters by rules and that it is not always easy to know if the rules are fair or if they are really needed. He was able to make this comment in a nondefiant, calm, objective manner that did not make the class feel that he was merely fishing for reassurances. A couple of students responded to the statement by attacking directly the rules governing homework assignments; but the lack of support from the class as a whole discouraged this sort of open attack. The class as a whole seemed unwilling to consider specific teacher rules—at least, not in the presence of the teacher—and, instead, they discussed how they might help the teacher set up fair rules. This led to the setting up of an advisory board and to the definition of its function as a steering committee for planning homework assignments with the teacher.

This board functioned rather formally for about a month. Its members, of course, had contacts with the other students outside of class, and they did a good deal of interpreting to the others of what sort of person the teacher was and how sincerely he was concerned with having a pleasant working relationship in the class. By the end of the second month, the board had almost ceased functioning. It was seldom called on by either teacher or class. This produced guilt feelings in the teacher and some anxiety in the class until someone pointed out that, for the last couple of weeks, the class had been arriving at its homework assignments by open discussion during the class period rather than by considering the committee's suggestions at the end of the class hour. The effort to deal with the feeling of resentment by the class against arbitrary teacher rulings had, in this case, led not only to a solution of the group-process problem, but along with it, to the release of considerably more energy for attacking the school-achievement problem, as shown by the change in the method of arriving at homework assignments.

Under the freer climate resulting from the students' recognition of the teacher's objectivity, flexibility, and nondefensiveness, there developed not only a heartening acceptance of the teacher as a friendly and fair-minded person but also much greater involvement in the schoolwork as significant in itself. The method of getting assignments through class agreement during discussion seemed satisfactory for a couple of months, and then it began to run into snags. It seemed harder and harder to find agreement. It was only after several days of tension at assignment times that the teacher made the interpretation that the trouble was no longer that people didn't want to work but that different individuals were motivated to work on different aspects of the problem. Acceptance of this interpretation led eventually to the formation of subcommittees on such occasions, and they operated in this manner from time to time from then on, being reconstituted on each occasion when differentiation of work seemed desirable either as a way of covering more material or as a way of adjusting the content of the individual student's needs.

These changes came about because the teacher was sensitive to the class feeling and because he felt it was important to take feeling into account (i.e., to accept the students as people).[9]

We suggest the following as questions a teacher might ask to determine the importance attached to the individual and his ideas in the learning situation:

1. Are individual differences in learners respected and used as starting points for progressive learning toward individual and group goals?

2. Are these goals based on varying abilities, interests, and needs of individuals rather than entirely on what is commonly accepted as appropriate for a grade level?

3. Do I use varied materials and activities as a result of accepting 1 and 2?

4. Is the atmosphere of the classroom free from tension and fear, not least because of my attitudes and behavior?

5. Do I seek for and gain evidence that pupils feel important and respected?

6. Do pupils have a part in determining what is happening in the learning experiences by participating actively rather than listening passively, and by becoming increasingly self-directive?

By capitalizing on learners' inquiring attitudes rather than submerging them and by accepting the worth of individual ideas, we submit that the classroom teacher creates the psychological climate of a laboratory consistent with the method of teaching and learning we have expounded. This climate, coupled with a physical environment conducive to problem solving, will result in the most efficient and permanent learnings.

SUMMARY

In this chapter we have attempted to look at the classroom as a laboratory for learning in which the principles of the scientific method of problem solving, discussed in Chapter 2, guide teachers and learners. The classroom setting and its physical arrangements were described, with suggestions for exploiting certain characteristics of a good learning environment.

[9] Herbert A. Thelen and Ralph W. Tyler, "Implications for Improving Instruction in the High School," in *Learning and Instruction* (Forty-ninth Yearbook of the National Society for the Study of Education; Chicago: University of Chicago Press, 1950), Part I, Chap. 12, pp. 314–316. Reprinted by permission.

Attention was then paid to certain psychological conditions which should pervade a problem-centered classroom—the spirit of inquiry and respect for the uniqueness of individual problems and needs. Chapters 4, 5, and 6 will develop more in detail the specifics which teachers and learners may employ in organizing a classroom for learning experiences.

FOR FURTHER STUDY

American Association of School Administrators, *American School Buildings.* Twenty-seventh yearbook; Washington, D.C.: National Education Association, 1949.

The first seven chapters relate school personnel and educational program to the development of an appropriate school plant for modern America.

Combs, Jane, Michael Graycar, and Irene Priddle, "The School with Built-in Ideas," *National Education Association Journal,* 44:73–75 (February), 1955.

An interesting story of how a school staff planned together for a new building, and what kinds of decisions they had to make, based on curriculum and teaching practices to which they subscribed.

Engelhardt, N. L., Jr., "Laboratories for Learning," *School Executive,* 74:63–66 (November), 1954.

A persuasive argument for high school classrooms which can accommodate many activities, provide varied research materials, and include display space for completed work. Illustrated with four helpful drawings, suggesting how classrooms can be arranged if such facilities are available.

Fawley, Paul C., and Roald F. Campbell, "Classroom Environment Has Measurable Effect upon the Learning Situation," *Nation's Schools,* 49:76–78 (May), 1952.

Reports interesting results of an evaluation of classroom environment in a school system, and furnishes the scale which was used. Focuses on both the social and physical environment.

Hamon, Ray L., John H. Herrick, and William G. Eckles, "Planning the Secondary School Plant," *Bulletin,* National Association of Secondary School Principals (Proceedings of the thirty-second annual convention), 32:202–227 (March), 1948.

Practical suggestions offered on what constitutes school-building essentials for a functional program of education, including attention to activity program, methods of teaching, and type of daily schedule.

Miller, Ward I., "Requirements of the Modern Secondary School," in *American School and University,* 1948–1949. New York: American School Publishing Corporation, 1948, pp. 77–85.

A stimulating proposal for a new kind of instructional facility, based on new instructional theories and techniques which are derived from new needs of secondary school youth.

Moore, Harold E., "The Modern Secondary School Building," in *American School and University,* 1948–1949. New York: American School Publishing Corporation, 1948, pp. 70–76.

After a review of emerging trends in the population and needs of secondary school youth, the author presents what he believes are the implications for the building of secondary schools. Flexibility is the keynote in planning for modern classrooms and other school facilities.

National Society for the Study of Education, *Learning and Instruction.* Forty-ninth Yearbook; Chicago: University of Chicago Press, 1950, Part I.

An outstanding collection of articles on teaching-learning theories and practices by leading educators.

Neutra, Richard J., "A Theory of School Design," *American School Board Journal,* 130:58–59, 114 (January), 1955.

A challenging proposal to make the school a more indigenous part of the context in which it is found. This is a striking statement by an architect of his beliefs, which he maintains have significance for teaching and learning.

Nulton, Lucy, "A Classroom for Living," *Educational Leadership,* 11:291–295 (February), 1954.

Analyzes a classroom, typical of too many schools, and suggests how and why the room should be improved to provide a better learning environment.

Perkins, Lawrence B., and Walter D. Cocking, *Schools.* New York: Reinhold Publishing Corporation, 1949.

An exciting and profusely illustrated book on new functions and designs in modern educational buildings, together with some attention to classroom equipment (Chapter 9).

Vincent, William S., "Tomorrow's School Building," *School Executive,* 67:25–27 (November), 1947.

The author lists and develops twelve principles of planning school buildings, most of which are appropriate for consideration of classroom teachers as they assist in helping to plan buildings or attempt to make full use of existing facilities.

Whitehead, Willis A., and W. R. Flesher, "Designing Secondary School Classrooms for General Use," *School Executive,* 66:57–60 (November), 1946.

The authors look ahead fifty years and predict certain outcomes in classroom design which seem to be indicated by present trends, for example, emphasis on "life experience" as an approach to learning, the extension of laboratory method to all areas of instruction, and more widespread use of school facilities by adult groups.

4. Studying the Dynamics
of the Classroom Group

A CONSTANT SOURCE of surprise and concern for teachers is the variations existing among classroom groups. These differences appear in any given school year and also between groups in different years. Teachers remark, "How I wish my problem class during period III were like my period IV class! I just can't get those youngsters to work together."

"I know what you mean. Last year I had a couple of groups like that. This year I'm happy about all of my classes."

One might suppose that adolescents would be enough alike in their characteristics to make their groups fairly homogeneous. A mistaken assumption is that if a teacher and a class engage in a problem-solving approach to learning, difficulties related to classroom management, discipline, and morale will be eliminated. We have suggested that the employment of the scientific method in teaching and learning will create a better over-all situation for instruction. However, this method causes many kinds of individual and group dynamics to come into play which in more traditional classrooms are inhibited, disregarded, or regarded as minor in importance.

We suggest that all adolescents must come to grips at some time with certain developmental tasks, such as adjusting to their body changes, to the opposite sex, to their growing independence, to their more mature roles as potential wage earners, and to conflicting value patterns. These supply a common frame of reference for secondary school youth, but do not account for more subtle differences in personal and interpersonal affairs, which are difficult to detect even though they play a large part in the way a classroom group functions.

102

The aim of this chapter is to define some of these dynamics which operate in classrooms and to suggest how they may be detected and studied.

THE LIMITATIONS AND POTENTIALITIES OF GROUP TEACHING AND LEARNING

As mentioned before, American education today has primarily a group orientation, even as does our total culture. We live and move in groups, both in and out of school. This is not to say, however, that we understand the dynamics which may operate in group situations, or that we operate intelligently in groups. We express our doubts and frustrations or our faith and satisfactions in group life in terms of what we consider to be its limitations and potentialities.

LIMITATIONS

Most of us have had at times as a result of group experiences in education such reactions as "I can't. . . . I'm not interested. . . . I don't see the reason for this. . . . I resist what we are doing."

Such reactions are symptomatic of differences which exist among people when confronted by group situations. Whether these differences are real or not, objective assessments of the people and situations are beside the point. These reactions represent people's perceptions, and operate to their advantage or disadvantage as surely as the objective facts.

Such differences between objective reality and individual perceptions are often lost in group situations to the point where a person is out of touch with the situation. In classrooms the result is poor learning, frustration, retardation, and eventual failure. The attention to individuals which seems to be needed as an antidote for such differences is difficult to achieve in a classroom group of thirty or more people, and as such remains one of the teaching dilemmas of modern education.

Closely allied to the problem of individual differences in ability, aptitude, interest, needs, and purposes of pupils is the possibility in group situations of failure to recognize explicitly individual expressions of effort and achievement. In classroom groups where the opportunity is present to operate in terms of group goals, standards, projects, and activities, the individual's unique capabilities and limitations may not be recognized or may be lost in the larger complex of group operation. There are many who believe that lack of opportunity for the individual to express himself in his own unique fashion and to gain recognition for his personal contributions results in lack of motivation and a mediocre achievement level. The latter may be an overstatement of what really takes place, but we know enough about human behavior to be sure that all of us need recognition for our own efforts. It seems that group living must always provide opportunity for meeting this need. If it does not do this consistently, the advantages of group endeavor may not outweigh those of highly individual effort and achievement.

Also akin to the matter of the individual and his role in the group is the possibility of individuals developing overdependence on the group. Although most of our waking hours are spent in group situations involving group deliberations and action, a considerable part of our time involves highly personal, private thoughts and behavior. If group education develops in individuals a lack of initiative, fear of making decisions, and blind obeisance to majority rule, then a stern criticism can be made of this emphasis in education. Such developments might occur if a balance between group and individual thinking and action is not maintained.

An outgrowth of this last questionable phenomenon of group life is the fear of being different or unique. Mob psychology and mob rule are to be decried, less perhaps in the realm of minor judgments such as appropriate dress and speech, but more certainly in areas of values involving morals and citizenship. The peer acceptance concept of adolescents is a powerful drive which cannot be dismissed as unimportant; but group living within and without the classroom can provide a setting which accentuates this drive out of proportion to other values for youth.

Briefly, then, the limitations of group life in the classroom and the pitfalls which may arise stem from the potential conflicts which may develop between the group as an entity and the individual member of the group.

These dangers may be summarized as follows:

1. Failure to recognize and provide for individual differences among learners
2. Failure to give recognition to individual effort and achievement
3. Development of overdependence of individuals on the group
4. Lack of courage and responsibility for one's own ideas and values

The thoughtful teacher should recognize these potential problems, be alert for their appearance, and be willing to attack them with the help of the group as threats, first to the individual, and eventually to the success of the group as a whole.

POTENTIALITIES

Those who argue for the group emphasis in education point out that such teaching and learning capitalize on a fundamental need of people—the sense of belonging. They suggest that this drive is as powerful as the need for individual recognition—in fact, that unless recognition takes place in a setting where a person feels that he belongs and is liked, recognition for individual achievement is a hollow satisfaction. Small wonder then that gifted pupils frequently place their peers' acceptance of them as people above adults' recognition of their achievement. We believe that classroom groups provide a setting for adolescents to learn how to evaluate individual success and achievement against a backdrop of cooperative activity in which each person is accepted for his own unique abilities and problems. Here the individual can maintain a feeling of integrity and worth, can feel that he belongs to the group, and yet not excel to the point where he demands recognition based on a preordained standard.

We have said before that our lives are spent for the most part in groups of varying sizes. Yet our behavior frequently suggests that we have not learned how to act intelligently or gracefully in groups. How does one learn group skills? We believe that classroom groups offer the best opportunity for learning the skills of cooperative planning and action. Traditional classrooms have been preparing youth for a highly competitive, individualistic society which is rapidly disappearing because of new survival needs. Modern education must assume the responsibility for preparing pupils to live cooperatively, now in the classroom, and later in society as wage earners, family members, and citizens. No other institution is able to offer this education to all the children of all the people. This seems to be the greatest potential contribution of group living in the classroom.

Inevitably, in a setting where great emphasis is placed on group planning and action and where opportunity is given for a maximum of interaction among learners, a natural concomitant is the recognition and acceptance of differences among people. Thrown into such a situation where success or failure depends on one's ability to get along, not alone with the teacher but with each other, pupils respond by testing and practicing skills of human relationships. In both traditional and experimental classrooms, there exist potentialities for competition and cooperation, for aggression and withdrawal, for faith and fear, and for likes and dislikes of people. Only in classrooms where cooperation and group problem solving are the accepted procedures do these dynamics become explicit and are they tested under varying situations with learnings the result.

Finally, we suggest that modern classrooms are incorporating some learnings which have always existed in schools in extracurricular activities. These learnings can also take place in the classroom. We refer to the group unity and feeling engendered by cooperative planning and action. Athletic teams, school publications, clubs, and other forms of extracurricular participation have furnished for many pupils the spark of enthusiasm for school which classrooms lacked. In many instances this spirit and feeling for the group working on projects or objectives of common concern and interest have been transplanted into the classroom from the extracurricular program. Involving learners in setting the goals and objectives of a class and in developing the procedures and activities for achieving their purposes have become the basic element in the teaching-learning situation. Out of this have come team play, high morale, motivation, and standards far beyond the expectations of teachers accustomed to other ways of teaching.

The potentialities of group work in the classroom can be summarized as follows:

1. Contributions of the group to the individual's need for a sense of belonging
2. Development of cooperative skills in planning and action
3. Opportunities for practice in good human relationships
4. Development of unity among learners around common ideals and goals

By way of summary, it can be said that classroom groups have limitations and pitfalls, particularly as they relate to the individual as a unique personality. But skillfully handled by teacher and group, the potentialities of cooperative classroom group work far outweigh the limitations. They can result in successful and happy experiences in group life, a prerequisite for learning in formal education and for a mature and satisfying life in adulthood.

DYNAMICS AT WORK IN CLASSROOM GROUPS

There are many ways to define and categorize the factors present in classroom groups which may retard or accelerate learning. For our purpose in assisting teachers to detect, study, and provide for these dynamics, we suggest the following factors: differences, both innate and acquired, which exist among individuals in respect to their mental, physical, social, and emotional capacities; varieties of interpersonal relations between individuals and subgroups which may be likened to chemical valences; and the presence or absence of positive and negative forces which activate behavior—drives and motivations, fears and frustrations. Our purpose in the rest of this chapter is to describe and define these dynamics, suggest ways for teachers and learners to become aware of these forces, and point out their implications for improving the learning environment.

INDIVIDUAL DIFFERENCES

Intellectual. Teachers are dealing with a commonly recognized, but less frequently accepted, phenomenon of groups when they study individual differences of pupils in mental ability. That is, in our present context of values in education, all teachers are conscious of differences in the intellectual equipment of pupils, but by the nature of their concepts of the curriculum and of learning they find it difficult really to accept the less intellectually able student. The standardization of curriculum, teaching methods, and evaluation techniques gives the advantage to the intellectually capable pupils, and penalizes the learners with less verbal facility.

These differences in intellectual capacity are also fully recognized by pupils. There are some teachers who are fearful that unless high intellectual standards are maintained with resulting failures by many learners, false notions of success and ability are engendered. We submit that presently constituted classrooms provide ample opportunity for less able pupils to sense their deficiencies and to experience failures. Life outside the school also furnishes pupils with evidence on their differences.

It is not alone the sensing of differences which provides a potential threat-to learners, important as that is for adolescents who want to be "like each other," not "different." It is, rather, the preoccupation of the classroom with intellectual pursuits and the attachment of primary value to them that frustrate the less endowed student. This, added to the accent on intellectual achievement and an evaluation of it, creates real barriers among "slow," "average," and "gifted" students to the point where cooperative approaches to learning become difficult.

We do not mean to suggest that intellectual activity is unimportant, or that we do not need it in our schools or adult society. We plead, rather, for a curriculum and a teaching method which gives opportunity for all levels of intellect to work together on common problems, each making its best unique contribution to their solution. The alternative is a stratification of classroom groups, with a range of reactions by students from self-deprecation to snobbery.

Some educators, baffled by the problem of individual differences and fearful of the development of such attitudes, suggest homogeneous grouping as the answer. This mechanical approach to the problem evades the larger issue, "How can a society, within or without the school, recognize and accept the challenge of differences among people?" We believe that this can be accomplished not by segregation, but by facing up to these differences as part of the basic problem of learning to live together.

In respect to differences in mental ability, we suggest that their existence is real and significant for teaching and learning. However, provision for them is best begun not by disregarding or by accentuating them. Rather, they become part of any problem which a classroom group attempts to solve, and should receive attention by teachers and learners alike. Only then individual differences become respectable, with the possibility of being a positive dynamic for better learning which culminates in behavior and attitude change.

Physical-emotional. The age of adolescence is marked by significant physical growth and certain accompanying emotional developments. The acquiring of secondary sex characteristics and the questions which may stem from these body changes create certain dynamics in adolescent groups which are more pronounced and yet more subtle than for most other age levels.

These problems are known as "developmental tasks"—coming to terms with one's own body, and assuming a new relation with the opposite sex. As is true with all other aspects of human growth, these changes do not come at the same time for all people. The variations present in the psychobiological development of any classroom group of fourteen-year-olds, for example, are tremendous. They can account for as many varieties of interest, effort, and achievement as do the differences in intellectual abilities.

The problem once again is not to disregard or overemphasize these adolescent growth factors in the teaching-learning situation. By using observation, interviews, questionnaires, and check lists, the problems of adolescents and their intensity can be assayed. A teacher who knows these for his class in more than general terms is in a good position to develop a more helpful program of learning, and is in a better position to explain and provide for this factor in his group.

Economic-social. Also more subtle than problems arising from differences in mental ability are those related to varying socioeconomic backgrounds of pupils. It should be expected that democratic schools for all the children of all the people include boys and girls from all walks of life. As such, they reflect American society, including the tensions which exist between the "haves" and "have-nots," between those from the "wrong side of the tracks" and those from the "country club set."

Here in America we are blessed with less class consciousness than anywhere in the world. Our high standard of living, our relative social mobility, and most of our institutions have over the years tended to minimize the effects of definite social classes. And yet recent studies in educational sociology have demonstrated that these differences in socioeconomic class do affect the mores of school life, instructional programs, and the very composition of the secondary school population.[1] As teachers, we are blind if we fail to recognize differences in economic and social levels which are seen and felt in our classrooms.

Again, as in the case of differences in mental ability, these dynamic factors in the classroom climate are not dangerous unless they are disregarded or are accentuated by school traditions and practices. If the curriculum or teaching methods assume a common background of experience, based on middle-class standards or higher, then these differences in socioeconomic class may present a real problem as many students will resist or reject the experiences and values which the school offers. Much of the curriculum content, as well as our teaching and evaluation procedures, are based on situations and values which are new or opposed to many learners' previous experience. Perhaps the most challenging investigation in this area has been done by Havighurst and his associates on the nature of items in intelligence tests. He has found that many intelligence tests penalize students from lower socioeconomic groups because the test items demand certain experiences and value patterns which these pupils do not have.[2]

Almost as serious as the failure to take into account these socioeconomic differences in our curriculum and our teaching method are the instances in many schools when attention is drawn to these differences or where they are exploited. Many phases of our school life are still not free of cost, both within and without the classroom.

The Illinois Secondary School Study has revealed some startling figures on what it costs pupils to engage in school life. These "hidden

[1] The reader is urged to become acquainted with one or more of the following: Robert J. Havighurst, Martin B. Loeb, and William L. Warner, *Who Shall Be Educated?* (New York: Harper & Brothers, 1944); A. B. Hollingshead, *Elmtown's Youth: The Impact of Social Classes on Adolescents* (New York: John Wiley & Sons, Inc., 1949); Celia B. Stendler, *Children of Brasstown: Their Awareness of Social Class* (Urbana, Illinois: University of Illinois Press, 1949); William L. Warner, Paul S. Lunt, and others, *Yankee City Series* (4 vols.; New Haven, Connecticut: Yale University Press, 1941–1947).

[2] Kenneth Eells, Allison Davis, Robert Havighurst, and others, *Intelligence and Cultural Differences* (Chicago: University of Chicago Press, 1951), pp. 16–21.

costs" are for materials, equipment, activities, yearbooks, and the like. The alarming fact, of course, is that 72 per cent of all pupils in this study who dropped out of high school came from low-income groups.[3] This suggests a possible cause-effect relation between cost of attending high school and dropout. We are not arguing the pros and cons of completely free public education, but suggest that when these factors exist they tend to create feelings within individuals and to differentiate between "active" and "nonparticipating" pupils on the basis of ability to pay.

One of the most contradictory social phenomena in American public secondary schools is the presence of sororities and fraternities. It seems hard to justify such organizations in democratic schools. Their secrets, their membership qualifications, and their political machinations in school life are undemocratic and have caused untold difficulty and problems in maintaining good school morale. They are a dramatic evidence of cleavages which exist between individuals and groups in school life, and are symptomatic of social and economic differences in the school and the larger society.

As mentioned before, these differences among pupils on a social and economic basis are subtle and therefore more difficult to treat. The first step certainly is recognition by teachers and administrators of these forces. It seems that an indirect approach to the problem through democratizing the total life of the school is next. But we believe that even more important is the day-to-day life in the classroom where no problems of any individual are too insignificant for consideration and where every individual's efforts and contributions are respected. Such a climate is inherent in the problem-solving approach to learning.

Religious and Moral. Finally, the differences existing among pupils in a classroom may be seen in respect to their religious and moral values. Public schools, enrolling all the children of all the people, find their pupils with widely differing religious backgrounds and personal-social codes of ethics. Historically, the public school of America has always been troubled by the problem of what its role is and can be in the teaching of moral and spiritual values.

It is difficult to determine the effect of religious and moral differences on the efforts of democratic schools to unify our society. Some, but not all, of our democratic values have their counterparts in religious codes, and American public schools cannot disregard religion as a vital factor in our lives. At the same time they must guard against sectarian teaching.

[3] Harold Hand, "Do School Costs Drive Out the Youth of the Poor?" *Progressive Education*, 28:89–92 (October), 1950.

Regardless of how well a school handles its curriculum and teaching problem with respect to moral and spiritual values, the fact remains that these differences exist among pupils and can be one of the dynamics which operate to inhibit or facilitate classroom learning. Most teachers have at some time or other experienced unfortunate situations arising in the classroom because of dislikes, tensions, and bitterness stemming from pupils' differences in religious and moral values. Unfortunately, in such situations teachers often have not faced up to the problems of differences. By not recognizing them and not making these differences understandable, pupils have developed narrow and ignorant perceptions of each others' values. Out of such a setting come misunderstanding, intolerance, and eventually strife.

The presence of religious and moral differences in a classroom group can provide a great opportunity for study and interpretation of differences in a sympathetic manner. Such study cannot and should not erase the differences, but should create understanding of the reasons for differences and more acceptance of them. This is a difficult thing to do and requires creativity on the part of the teacher in the use of materials and human resources.

But perhaps even more important than a formal approach to this problem are the everyday attitudes of the members of the classroom group toward each other. In this respect the teacher sets the example of understanding acceptance of differences rather than distrust, fear, or dislike of them.

INTERPERSONAL RELATIONS

Out of such a constellation of individual differences in any classroom—physical, intellectual, economic, social, emotional, and moral—are bound to arise many likes and dislikes, acceptances and rejections among the members of the group. These factors in classroom life may result in "stars" and "isolates" among pupils.

They may be seen in a pupil who leads in all activities because he is seen by his class members as endowed with attributes fitting him for leadership in all situations. The truth of the matter may be that he is not "the best" in all the desirable characteristics, but his excellence in some transfers to other attributes and situations.

As a result, the athlete endowed with only average academic and social intelligence is elected to the presidency of his class. Another pupil who may excel in certain manual or artistic skills may be overlooked in the preparation of stage sets for the class play because he is much slower in history and English. Another youth, competent in intellectual and social skills, may be turned down for a leadership role in student government because "he doesn't travel with the right set."

Such occurrences take place in the schools of our country, stemming from personal likes and dislikes among pupils. They, in turn, arise from the differences among pupils which have been delineated earlier in this chapter. The problem for the teacher and the class group is to prevent these likes and dislikes from creating a school atmosphere which is not conducive to good teaching and learning or to the fullest utilization of human resources available.

Many of these personal and social relations develop in situations outside the school. For that reason, some teachers feel it is hopeless to combat these factors in the school. We submit, however, that unless some of these personal-social relations are bettered in the classroom, there is little chance for real learning, either on a factual level or in respect to attitudes, appreciations, and understandings.

Again, as in other problems of classroom management, we suggest that this becomes a problem for study by the group and teacher. These are factors to be considered in the problem-solving approach to learning. How do we assess the human resources in our group? What are the relations which exist among group members, and what provision should be made for more interaction among members and for the sharing of leadership as learning situations change and vary in the classroom?

All of these factors are the raw materials out of which better conditions must arise, conducive to learning in group situations. Without them, teachers and learners will constantly be faced by situations which defeat cooperation, group morale, and a healthy environment for learning. These are not matters which are easy to cope with, and attention to them requires time. In the long run, we believe that time spent in consideration of such matters results in better learning, both of the usual content and, more important, of attitudes and understandings which are required if democratic ideals are to prevail in practice as well as in theory.

DRIVES AND MOTIVATIONS

Up to this point we have considered dynamics of the classroom group which are either obvious or can be detected by teachers and learners if some attention is given to them. Most subtle, however, are those dynamics of a personal, private nature which pervade every individual personality in varying degrees of intensity. Their manifestations in behavior are often misleading and prompt teachers to treat symptoms rather than causes of behavior. In discussing these matters, we shall attempt to look at several fundamental drives of the individual, their often misleading behavior manifestations, and finally their implications for classroom groups.

In the social context of the classroom, the potentialities of competition and cooperation are always present and need constant consideration by teachers and learners. At first thought, the reader may question the consideration of these factors as personal motivations or drives. Often they are thought of as external factors introduced by our culture and supplying extrinsic motivation. For many teachers, they become "tricks of the trade" to give meaning to activities which otherwise might have less appeal to learners.

We should like to consider competition and cooperation as basic drives of human personality which exist side by side in an individual, and may cause conflict unless recognized for what they are and how they may be employed to give energy and meaning to human activity. As such, we do not accept either factor as good or bad in itself, but ascribe value in terms of situations which render them appropriate for use as dynamics in group behavior.

Competition. How shall competition be used? No one can deny that competition, if between individuals or groups which are evenly matched, can supply interest and energy for a learning situation. However, for unmatched groups or individuals, competition supplies a setting for disappointment, chagrin, and self-abnegation for some; for others it provides an exhilaration and sense of achievement and pride, all out of proportion to the situational factors. As a result, unfortunate attitudes develop, both for "winners" and "losers." It becomes increasingly difficult for the loser to win, and for the winner to lose. Talk of "good sportsmanship" or "you can't always win" may salve feelings but does not repair loss of self-esteem or an unrealistic attachment of importance to the event.

Several suggestions can be given. First, teachers can see to it that individuals perform at a suitable ability level, and *with*, not *against*, others of similar capacities, so that achievement is geared to potentialities, not impossibilities. Then achievement and recognition are more assured, which in turn may supply impetus for greater effort toward higher levels of achievement.

Second, pupils can be helped to recognize and accept their limitations and assets, and to gear them to reasonable expectations. As such, they compete against themselves as well as with others of like abilities. The feeling of adequacy resulting from achievement of reasonable goals is basic to raising levels of aspiration to the point of capacity.

Third, competition between comparable groups, as well as between comparable individuals or against oneself, gives a feeling of security and worth to learners. That is, even though one group "wins," the support which one receives from his group, even in a "losing cause," bolsters self-esteem and allows the group to continue as a force for further effort and achievement.

It is true that in our society a premium has been placed on competition which has resulted in progress and achievement; often, however, such advances have been at the expense of individuals and not always for the greatest good of the greatest number. Increasingly in our culture, because of our greater interdependence on one another, competition has seemed less appropriate, at least between widely differing groups in capacities, endowments, and interests. Competition remains as a possible motivation and drive for self-improvement, but increasingly it is seen in the larger setting of common social needs which affect everyone in our interdependent world. Teachers have not always seen this trend toward cooperation, and have clung to older patterns of competition between individuals. "Everyone for himself, and may the best man win" may have been more appropriate in earlier days of selective secondary schools; but in these days of "education for all American youth" our practices in competition must be geared to new social needs and realities.

Cooperation. "Working together" is another basic motivational factor which can be employed, particularly with adolescents who prize the group, its values, and its recognition. The desire of youth "to belong," to identify with group goals and activities is recognized. Perhaps it provides youth with a transition from the dependence of childhood to the independence and responsibility of the adult. We submit that the classroom can utilize this desire more than has been the case in the past.

The whole process of problem identification, hypothesizing, testing, and generalizing lends itself to cooperative group situations. To be sure, the individual does well to approach individual learning situations in this fashion. But a class which is thought of as a group, not as a collection of individuals, gives the opportunity to supply a more thoughtful, systematic approach to group activity which is sorely needed in our culture. Given such experience in the classroom, adolescents are satisfying a basic need of that age level—group activity—and at the same time are learning much-needed skills for adult life. The findings of many studies on job failure in adult life testify to the fact that the greatest barrier to occupational success and satisfaction is not the lack of individual, technical skills but the inability of people to get along with one another. Classrooms which do not supply opportunities for youth to plan, act, and evaluate together are not only failing to capitalize on an adolescent need but are neglecting the preparation of pupils for an important phase of adult activity.

It should be pointed out, however, that pupils in school and adults in later life cannot always be involved in group deliberation and action. There is a danger when an individual becomes so group-identified that he cannot think or act alone. This overdependence on the group may well destroy initiative and self-reliance so that he is not even willing to compete against himself—"to do his best." He may choose to lose himself in the anonymity of the group, and coast on the efforts and recognition of others.

Such events need not develop if competition and cooperation are seen in their supplementary relations and functions. The skillful teacher and the maturing pupil can forestall such outcomes if they too are a part of the conscious consideration of a group.

Challenge and Threat. Closely associated with concepts of competition and cooperation in educational practice are the perceptions of youth about themselves and their environment. Competition may be associated with threat—of failure, of punishment and lowering of self-esteem—or it may be seen as a challenge to success, to rewards, and to justifiable pride. Whether or not a person sees an experience as a threat or challenge is largely a function of his past experience. It follows then that for students to grow in their capacity to face new situations, they need to be bolstered by many successful experiences. We can learn from our mistakes, but if we have nothing but mistakes and failures we eventually are immobilized for further learning by the weight of past failures.

As such, our previous comments about competition and cooperation are related to how we see ourselves in new situations. To the degree that we have competed against uneven odds, have experienced repeated failure, and have accumulated feelings of unworthiness and inability, to that degree we are threatened by the present and future.

To the extent that we have competed against ourselves and our capabilities, or have been bolstered and supported by cooperative undertakings, to that extent the present and future appear as a challenge, not a threat. Such an attitude toward the present and future and what it holds for the individual in the way of learning experiences requires self-understanding on the part of teachers and learners, and appreciation of others' perceptions. These insights come only through deliberate attention to these matters on the part of understanding teachers, counselors, and parents.

Having acquired these understandings, pupils, parents, and teachers are in a better position to look at educational experiences in the school more realistically. Expectations, levels of aspiration, and evaluations will be more appropriately conceived, and the total environment for learning will be enhanced because these dynamics are understood and taken into account.

Aspirations. Finally, we should consider the end product of competition or cooperation, of threat or challenge, as it affects the hopes and aspirations of the individual. Most teachers are quick to sense in students varying levels of aspirations for themselves, both for the present and future. Many teachers despair of youths who aspire to heights beyond them, or of pupils who are content to settle for achievement and goals below their capabilities. We are assuming that teachers are not willing to make these judgments without adequate information about the intellectual, social, economic, emotional, and physical factors applying to a pupil. Yet even with a great deal of information such as the above, we find pupils with unrealistic aspirations and goals, bolstered by parents' attitudes toward the school and life.

These, too, may be related to competition and cooperation, to threat and challenge. A parent concerned about his child's achievement compared with that of the neighbor's child, or disappointed that his child does not demonstrate the academic ability he himself displayed, appeals to the competitive side of his child, or motivates by threat or punishment or promise of reward. The pupil comes to school convinced that he *can* if he *will*, regardless of his level of abilities; or he may know himself better than his parent and yet feels he *must* achieve above his level. These are dynamics of classroom groups which often are not known by teachers or are applauded as praiseworthy.

By the same token, there may be pupils who, lacking home motivation or an understanding and appreciation of their own abilities, are not working up to their capacity. Competition or threat in such cases is generally inappropriate because the pupil's value system may be different from the teacher's. If other interests and values are supplied more closely allied to his own, and if his normal adolescent desires for group approval and activity are met, the chances for raising his level of aspiration are greater.

In the case of both the "underaspiring" and "overaspiring" pupil, competition and threat are generally inadequate for fundamental changes in attitude and behavior. Challenge and cooperation give greater promise of developing better understanding of potentialities or limitations, with better learning the result as evidenced by changed behavior.

The last statement brings us to certain overt aspects of classroom behavior which are readily recognizable as dynamics affecting the learning situation. The withdrawing, shy, reticent personality as well as the aggressive and boisterous individual are well-known extremes in pupil behavior. Study of these types reveal, however, that both can be related to competition, threat, and subsequent unrealistic levels of aspiration. A withdrawing pupil can react in such a fashion because of his fear of failure in competition. He may escape into silence when threatened, or he may be so frustrated in his drive for achievement above his ability level that he becomes introvertive. Another youth may become aggressive or even openly hostile, and may attempt to cover up his insecurity by boisterous, antisocial behavior.

Either kind of behavior presents a dilemma to teachers and groups on how to analyze it and, more important, what to do about it. Unfortunately, teachers and groups often double their measures in the direction of competition and threat by using even more rigid standards, double-barreled threats, and exhortations.

The alternative of supplying more opportunities for cooperation, challenging of interests, and better understanding of assets and limitations might well be tried. This new set of dynamics for individuals and groups has often made a great difference in the morale of a classroom group, and has resulted in greater achievement.

Summary. Up to this point, we have attempted to define and explain the importance of a number of factors in classroom groups which supply the dynamic energy for group activity, either in a positive or negative direction for learning. It should be apparent to the reader that for a teacher to be aware of these factors in a particular class and to be able to assess the valence of them in various group situations requires skills and techniques. The next portion of this chapter proposes to describe various ways of discovering the dynamics which operate in groups.

DISCOVERY OF DYNAMICS AT WORK IN CLASSROOM GROUPS

Although we have suggested that pupils as well as teachers should be aware of the dynamics which operate in them as individuals and are manifest in group situations, the teacher remains the central figure in the discovery of these factors. The teacher's level of maturity, his access to measures and records of pupil growth and behavior, and his concern for the total development of the learner should make the study of individuals and groups one of his chief responsibilities.

However, a teacher's age may serve to make him insensitive to adolescent needs and problems. Lack of interest in measures and records of pupil development, or unawareness of their existence, may also characterize a teacher, as may intense preoccupation with teaching of subject matter to the exclusion of concern with all aspects of the learner's existence.

The Dynamics	Methods of Discovery
1. Intellectual Differences	1. Intelligence tests, achievement records (teachers' marks), standardized achievement tests, teacher-made tests, case conferences and studies
2. Physical-Emotional Differences	2. Health record, anecdotal records, case studies and conferences, projective techniques, personality inventories, observation, attendance records, parent conferences
3. Economic-Social Factors	3. Records of extracurricular participation, data on family background, sociometry, observation
4. Religious-Moral Differences	4. Data on family background, observation, projective techniques, interviews, parent conferences
5. Interpersonal Relationships	5. Sociometry, observation, extracurricular participation, problem check-lists, projective techniques
6. Drives and Motivations	6. Interest finders, autobiographies, attitude inventories, check lists, interviews, parent conferences

Fig. 3.   Classroom Dynamics and Methods for Their Discovery

We believe, however, that modern teachers are increasingly aware of the importance of knowing pupils better, both as individuals and in group situations. Frequently, however, teachers are baffled by the problem of getting information which will provide them with insights about the dynamics which operate in individual and group behavior. How may teachers come to know more about the pupils they have in their classes? A great deal of attention is paid in Chapter 11 to the study of the individual learner. Our purpose here is only to relate methods of individual study and knowledge resulting from that study to the contributions of group life in the classroom. Figure 3 lists some of these more important dynamics in the classroom and relates them to methods for their discovery.

CUMULATIVE RECORDS

Most schools accumulate in folders assorted bits of information about a student over the years of his schooling. Intelligence data, achievement test scores, attendance records, and scholastic marks are the most commonly available information about pupils. In recent years many schools have gone beyond these matters to investigate the health, home and family background, vocational and avocational interests, friendships, personality factors, extracurricular participation, work experience, and other facets of pupils' make-up and experience. Anecdotal descriptions by teachers are also included in such collections of information.

Certainly these kinds of information combine to give teachers insights into pupils' backgrounds which are helpful in accounting for their behavior and in planning appropriate group experiences. For example, a teacher planning for group activity early in the school year may find cumulative records helpful in identifying group leaders, in locating special competencies in the class, and in safeguarding the feelings of class members who might be baffled by too sudden an introduction to the responsibilities of group planning and action. Placement of pupils in subgroups or the establishment of seating arrangements may well be affected by the teacher's knowledge of friendships, economic differences, personality factors, and individual interests as revealed by cumulative records.

CASE STUDIES AND CASE CONFERENCES

Of comparatively recent development in educational circles are the case study and case conference. In the case study one or two teachers, or the principal or counselor, may volunteer to assemble all available information about an individual pupil from cumulative records and other sources such as parents, social agencies, and the like. The following case study report is an example of material which in part may be helpful to a teacher in making judgments and adjustments in a pupil's group relations. The potentially significant material is *italicized*. How might the *italicized* material be particularly significant to group experiences in the classroom?

CASE STUDY REPORT—*John Doe*

Recently, John Doe has been referred to me by several teachers because they have been disturbed by John's *lack of achievement in classwork* and

PLATE 10. TEACHERS CONDUCT A CASE CONFERENCE DURING PRE-SCHOOL WORKSHOP. Cooperative consideration by teachers of students' problems develops new insights. (Courtesy of the Oak Ridge, Tennessee, Public Schools)

his *generally listless attitude.* We are asking all of John's teachers to observe him in their classes and around the building for the next week, reporting to me any observations or information which may be helpful as background for this period of observation. The following data may be helpful:

Name—John Doe   *I.Q. 117* (Otis) (7th grade)
Age—14–9   *110* (Kuhlman-Anderson) (9th grade)
Height—5′ 8″   Kuder Preference Record
Weight—107   *Mechanical—1st*
                                             Aesthetic—2nd
                                             Social Service—lowest

Physical Defects. Extreme astigmatism, corrected by glasses. Underweight, subject to headaches frequently. Absent 24 days this year.

School Record. Generally mediocre to poor, failed grade 8 the year before last. Takes part in no extracurricular activities.

Interests. Likes to tinker with motors, bicycles, scooters, etc. *Likes hunting and fishing.* Has paper route.

Family. Father separated from mother three years ago. John lives with mother, a younger sister, and an older brother. Mother works at laundry, older brother quit school last year and works in local garage as mechanic helper. Younger sister in junior high school. Live in rented flat on Second Street.

School Behavior. Says he hates school except for shop and art. Generally causes no discipline problems for teachers. Just sits or sleeps and does little or no work. Accused by another student last year of stealing from gym locker, but investigation proved him innocent.

PLATE 11. CASE CONFERENCE IN A TEACHERS' LOUNGE. The informality of the teachers' lounge during free periods can be used to good advantage. (Courtesy of the North Phoenix, Arizona, High School)

This information may be duplicated, and copies given to teachers who have the pupil. Sometimes no follow-up is suggested, and the results are varied in the use made of the case study. In the case of the teacher interested in the possible dynamics at work in his classroom, he would see the *italicized* material as significant in planning John's roles in the total group and in subgroups. He knows, for example, that John is above average in intelligence, has strong mechanical interests and abilities, and likes outdoor sports. These are facts which make John a potential resource to the group and a person who no doubt can find classmates with common interests.

In addition, John's achievement record suggests a complete resistance to both the content and method of his previous learning experience. Certainly a teacher in John's case could do no worse than to try some innovations in classroom organization and to give him more recognition for his interests and capacities. Much might be gained and nothing lost in giving John a greater role in determining cooperatively the *what* and *how* of his learning experiences. Other data in this report have additional implications for John's group life in the classroom.

Generally, a case conference is a more fruitful approach to the study of a pupil. A typical group for such a study might consist of the principal, counselor, nurse, and the teachers who have the pupil in their classes. The advantage of the case conference is that it provides for a more extensive exploration of the problems of a pupil through the sharing of experiences with the pupil in a variety of situations. At the same time, information of the case study type may be brought to bear upon the discussion. Most significant in the case conference is the opportunity for sharing opinions and for consensus on constructive measures to help the pupil with the problems which prompted calling the case conference. Note the additional information which is gained from the conference and the implications drawn for John's individual and group adjustment.

Case Conference Record—*John Doe*

Present. English teacher, science teacher, shop teacher, counselor, nurse, principal

Conference Information and Opinions. Nurse volunteered that a recent dental inspection revealed John had several badly infected teeth which would be taken care of at once at the clinic.

English teacher said John had failed to turn in a book report due this week and had failed his written test on *Julius Caesar*.

Counselor reported that John had come to him, asking for help in getting an after-school job. Said he needed money for buying a new motor for his scooter. Rejected idea of cutting lawns, said he wanted work which would allow him to be around cars, a gas station job if possible. Was told he could get working papers for such a job.

Principal said he had noticed John loafing in lavatories and around locker areas during classes several times during the past week.

General agreement was had that something different must be attempted for and with John; that certain health and family problems contributed to John's attitudes but basically that the school's job was to capitalize on his interests and abilities.

The shop teacher said that some of the motors in the electric shop needed cleaning and reconditioning. Would it be possible to hire John for after-school work on these motors?

The science teacher said he had not been aware of John's interest and ability in mechanical things, and said he could use John as a "consultant" to explain the workings of a single-cycle gasoline engine in class demonstrations. Someone suggested that he might be interested in reading biographies of Ford, Edison, or Steinmetz as more closely related to his reading interests. The science teacher said he could ask John to give a talk on hunting and fishing before the Hobby Club next week.

Conference Agreements. The teachers involved agreed to try the things suggested, and to report any changes in attitude and behavior which might be forthcoming. They also agreed to meet in two weeks to compare notes.

(Time of conference—35 minutes)

Equipped with new insights about the pupil and possible approaches to be used with him, the teacher in such a case as this is in a better position to give him help in his individual and group adjustment. We do not imply that such study and procedure are a magic wand which will produce wonders overnight. We do suggest that teachers involved in such activity are in a better position to approach John and eventually to create more receptive attitudes toward teaching and learning.

AUTOBIOGRAPHIES, UNFINISHED STORIES, REACTIONS TO PICTURES

Another cluster of information-gathering devices is found in what are known as projective techniques. Many of these procedures require training in their use and interpretation beyond the preparation of most teachers. However, the autobiography, the pupils' reactions to pictures, and unfinished stories can be employed intelligently by teachers if used with reservations or combined with other information.

Autobiographies are frequently used as exercises in composition. Their greater value would seem to be in giving background information about a pupil, and in raising questions for the teacher as to why some experiences and ideas are emphasized by the pupil and others are avoided or glossed over. Consider the implications of the following, taken from the closing lines of an autobiography of a ninth-grader: "As I look back over the early years of my life and look ahead to the future, I have only two wishes. One is that I may never see my father again; the other is that I may spend my life in the service of the church."

Such a statement may be more dramatic than most found in autobiographies of adolescents, but it serves to illustrate the kinds of insights a teacher may gain about the conflicts and attitudes of pupils which more often than not affect their individual and group behavior. Caution must be exercised to avoid too hasty conclusions about such evidence and to prevent ill-conceived dabbling in therapy for students who may have serious behavior disorders. Consultant help must be used if available, or referrals be made to a person competent to handle seriously maladjusted people. Such cautions do not mean, however, that the intelligent teacher cannot profit from pondering how autobiographical comments such as the above might account for the writer's withdrawal from group activity, for his cynical attitude toward classmates and general antisocial spirit in the classroom. They may also make the need for group experience and approval all the more important for this pupil.

Another simple device is the unfinished story. The teacher reads or puts on the blackboard a brief description of a situation and persons involved in an experience which pupils would regard as lifelike (family life, boy-girl relation, choice of values, school situation or relation). The "story" is built up to the point where a decision, choice, action, or judgment is about to take place. The pupils are asked to complete the "story" in any way they choose. Study of these completions by the teacher may indicate pupils' projection of belief, attitudes, and values which are at stake in the situation described. Here again caution must be exercised in interpretation, and must be checked with other evidence. But this device has provided many teachers with clues on attitudes and behavior of pupils which could not be gained by direct methods. Given these clues, a teacher must look for opportunities to meet needs which have been uncovered and to provide experiences which seem appropriate for the group in the light of evidence gleaned from their reactions.

Another variation is the reaction to pictures. A picture of a person, perhaps most often an adolescent, with some recognizable setting as background (family, school, church, and so forth) and with an emotional reaction or feeling of some kind on the person's face, is placed before the group. The pupils are then asked to write a paragraph on questions such as, "How does he feel? What is he thinking? Why does he react this way? What took place just before this picture was made?"

To the degree that the picture represents an experience which a pupil has had, or thinks he has had, to that extent he may project his own feelings, attitudes, and understandings into the responses he makes to the questions. Again, as in the case of the other techniques, care must be taken to avoid overinterpretation of responses and consideration of the responses in isolation from other data on the pupil. But here also an intelligent teacher can see opportunities for meeting individual needs through group situations in the classroom.

INTEREST-FINDERS AND CHECK LISTS

More direct approaches to getting information about pupils may be used. Increasingly we find teachers who are concerned with gearing instruction and classroom activity to pupil interests and problems. A teacher may devise his own interest-finder or use an instrument which is produced commercially. In any case, this approach can attempt to get at, among other things, both general (outdoor activity versus reading) and specific (baseball versus hiking) interests; those related to the class (history, for example, stories of heroes, descriptions of customs and traditions, various legal methods of punishment); and vocational interests.

Teachers vary greatly in their ability and willingness to adapt their instruction to these interests. We suggest, however, that even though no direct provision is made for these interests, a teacher's awareness of the pupils' interests will make him more sensitive to pupils' reactions, and occasionally he may even be reminded of a pupil interest which can be exploited and developed through the subject matter of the course.

Problem check lists can be teacher-devised or they can be purchased. The focus of the problem check list is on students' perceptions of what they consider their problems to be—physical, mental, social, emotional, family, community, moral and religious, vocational, avocational, and so forth. Such lists again are used in various ways. Some teachers are content to teach their subject, but highlight and enlarge areas of instruction which they believe can contribute to the solution of indicated problems. Others more daring make these problems the organizing centers for the subject matter of the course, with some subject matter omitted, or treated less intensively, as less germane to the problems.

Here, as in the case of interest-finders, the use of such approaches depends in large part on a teacher's philosophy of education and his knowledge and commitment to the findings of research in the psychology of learning. A major contribution has been made, we believe, if teachers arrive only at a better understanding of students' interests and problems as a backdrop against which teaching and learning take place in small and large groups. Obviously, if these problems and interests are respected, the opportunities for total class or subgroup activity become apparent.

SOCIOGRAMS

Although our attention has been focused on techniques of understanding individual pupils, we feel that they contribute much to understanding behavior of groups. Recently much attention has been directed to the study of group structures, group forces, and their relation to individual dynamics. Much of the research in this area is still not definitive, particularly as it applies to classroom groups. However, the sociogram is a technique for studying relations among individuals in groups which gives great promise for better understanding of group behavior.

The sociogram is a technique whereby a teacher gets information from pupils on their attitudes toward and understandings of other

	Jim	Brad	Rose	Alex	John	Janet	Louise	Ruth	Steve	Alice	Anne	Tom	Jean	Stuart	Philip	Sidney	Karen	Helen	Bob	Roberta	Sarah
Jim		3							2			1									
Brad			1												2					3	
Rose					1	2							3								
Alex	1		2										3								
John			1								2		3								
Janet							1	2			3										
Louise								1			2	3									
Ruth							1						2					3			
Steve			1	2																3	
Alice			1								2	3									
Anne							1						2					3			
Tom			1								2			3							
Jean							1				2							3			
Stuart				1							2		3								
Philip			1	2															3		
Sidney	1																2	3			
Karen								2		1	3										
Helen														1	2						3
Bob		1		3	2																
Roberta					3						2		1								
Sarah					1						3		2								

FIG. 4. A SUMMARY SHEET OF SOCIOMETRIC SCORES

pupils. From this information, he can plot a diagram of relations which exist among pupils. Such a diagram reveals degrees of acceptance and rejection of individual pupils by their classmates, and establishes some as "stars," others as "isolates." These peer judgments may help a teacher understand the tensions which exist in the classroom and the failure of a group to work together. Briefly, the procedure for constructing a sociogram is as follows:

1. It is important that this technique is introduced in a normal situation. A common situation is one in which there is a need for

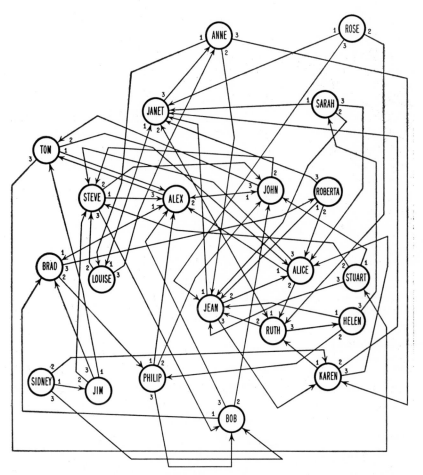

Fig. 5. A Sample Sociogram Based on Scores Found in Figure 4

committees, either for class responsibilities or for an outside function such as a picnic, party, etc. The teacher asks each member of the class to put his own name on a sheet of paper, and then list in order of preference the names of three persons with whom he would like to work on a committee. The teacher should point out the value of getting pupils on committees who can work together. These papers are collected and set aside to pursue discussion of the project at hand.

2. The data are later tabulated by the teacher on the form shown in Figure 4. A complete tabulation will reveal the number of times each pupil was chosen, and how many times he was a first, second, or third choice.

3. As the tabulation proceeds many questions will occur to the teacher. How many reciprocated choices are there? Who and what proportion are "stars"? Who and what proportion are "isolates"? Do choices cross sex lines, and are such choices reciprocated? These and many other questions in the process of tabulation might be noted for more careful analysis.

4. A sociogram may then be constructed from the tabulation form. An illustration of a sociogram is found in Figure 5. The pictorial representation of pupil choices may then be studied for implications of these choices, not only for the formation of committees and leadership designation but also for wider implications for classroom behavior and management such as seating arrangements, causes of discipline problems, and aggression or withdrawal on the part of students. A host of other questions may be raised about the evidence on socioeconomic factors in choices, extent of participation in class activities, and the like.

The bibliography at the end of the chapter supplies the reader with a number of references for further study. It is hoped that by our introduction of the reader to some of these techniques, we have suggested the need for further study and more experimentation with these devices, and the possibilities in them for developing a better understanding of individual and group behavior.

PARENTS AND OTHER AGENCIES

At several earlier points in this chapter we thought of suggesting the importance of involving parents and other people interested in pupils and the study of their problems. However, our focus was on what the teacher and other school personnel can do. It remains to be said that the school cannot and should not attempt to do this kind of study alone. And yet there are obstacles to parent or agency involvement, such as the time factor, the resistance of adolescents to parent participation, the traditional remoteness of the high school from the families and agencies of the community, and not least, the unfortunate attitudes which frequently prevail among teachers, parents, and social agencies.

Somehow these must be broken down, and the best way we know is to start this involvement on a small scale, but with a plan for expan-

PLATE 12. INFORMAL SOCIAL SITUATIONS PROVIDE TEACHERS WITH OBSERVATIONS. In such settings, teachers can often see pupils in a different light from that of the classroom. (Courtesy of the Milwaukee, Wisconsin, Public Schools)

sion through parent-teacher conferences, parent-teacher association activities, case conferences involving parents and social workers, and finally an "open-door policy" for parents and others to collaborate with teachers, principal, and counselors on the solution of *their* children's problems.

In addition, many schools have found that conferences of parents around common problems such as discipline, homework, teen-age dating, and the like have provided much help and understanding to parents and teachers alike. Out of such conferences may come sound insights into adolescent behavior which can provide better guidance by parents and teachers in individual and group situations. This is no small task, and requires some fundamental shifts in community-school traditions, policies, and procedures. Without it, the process of studying pupil problems in learning and adjustment will be, at best, fragmentary and frustrating to all concerned.

Good teachers have always employed other techniques for getting to know and understand pupils, such as observation, extracurricular participation, studying the research on adolescent development, and the like. The procedures and techniques we have suggested go beyond what most teachers are doing. As such, they are a challenge to pre-service students of education as well as to experienced teachers. Whether they become the professional equipment of most teachers and how soon the development takes place will be determined by two factors: (1) the degree to which teachers see and understand the full implications of the dynamics of individual and group behavior for good teaching and learning situations; and (2) the time which is made available for teachers to carry on the kinds of activities leading to better pupil adjustment and subsequent improved learning.

IMPLICATIONS FOR CLASSROOM METHOD

At this point, we hope that the reader is more conscious of the nature of some of the dynamics operative in a classroom situation, and is acquainted with a few of the techniques for discovery and study of these dynamics. Chapter 5 will devote attention to problems of organizing a classroom group for effective learning, based in part on our discussion of group and individual factors present.

Before we conclude this discussion, however, an attempt should be made to relate the dynamics of a classroom group to our central proposal for teaching method—the problem-solving approach to learning. Once again the stepwise procedure for this method might be reviewed:

1. Problem identification—getting out the problems, clarification of problems, establishing priorities, selecting the problem
2. Exploration of the problem for further clarification and understanding
3. Establishing some hypotheses or "hunches" on how the problem might be solved
4. Testing the hypotheses through activity and direct or vicarious experience
5. Generalizing from the experience, direct or vicarious, and making judgments on the need for further study

Committed to such a setting for teaching and learning, teachers and pupils are of necessity prompted to get facts. This problem-solving process is based on the importance of getting and interpreting facts. Our difficulty frequently lies in what we consider to be appropriate or respectable facts to be taught or learned. Too frequently we limit ourselves to facts which are extraneous to ourselves, our own situations, and our own behavior. We tend, in our search for objective facts, to disregard the facts close at hand or within ourselves which may be as significant for teaching and learning as those which we originally set out to learn. The extraneous facts may seem to be more clear and therefore simpler to describe, learn, and use. The other factors within the group or individuals are more subtle, more difficult to assess and make ready for learning or understanding, and most difficult to use in changing behavior.

Nevertheless, the latter are inescapable facts which must be tapped for a completely significant learning situation, that is, one which results in insight, understanding, and changed behavior. Our hope is that in this chapter we may have created a greater awareness of the dynamics of classroom groups, and that we may have persuaded the reader of the importance of knowing the many facts about a classroom group. We have tried to give some techniques for discovering and interpreting these facts. Finally, we have made some suggestions how teachers and learners may better incorporate these facts into their learning situations. Much of what has been developed in this chapter contributes to Chapters 11 and 12 in Part IV and to the following chapters in Part II. How do a teacher and his group organize a classroom for teaching and learning? How do they develop a code of procedures and policies for the group which serves to control the behavior of individuals and the group in such a way as to insure greatest productivity in learning?

FOR FURTHER STUDY

Caswell, H. L., ed., *The American High School.* New York: Harper & Brothers, 1946, Chap. 5.
This chapter furnishes a very readable account and some apt illustrations of the developmental tasks of youth.

Cummings, Howard H., ed., *Improving Human Relations.* Bulletin 25, National Council for the Social Studies, 1949.
Analyzes intercultural and intergroup pressures which exist in our society, and proposes methods for reducing tension and developing understandings in school situations.

Cunningham, Ruth, and Associates, *Understanding Group Behavior of Boys and Girls.* New York: Bureau of Publications, Teachers College, Columbia University, 1951.
A "must" for people interested in studying the dynamics of school groups; filled with excellent illustrative material from real classrooms and written in nontechnical language.

Hopkins, Carl L., and W. I. Stevenson, "What Are the Most Effective Methods for Dealing with Fraternities and Sororities?" *Bulletin,* No. 202, National Association of Secondary School Principals, 38:218–221 (April), 1954.
A concise statement of the claims made for and against secret societies

in the high schools, followed by various approaches to their control and elimination.

Horace Mann–Lincoln Institute of School Experimentation, *How to Construct a Sociogram.* New York: Bureau of Publications, Teachers College, Columbia University, 1947.

A simple step-by-step description of how teachers may use sociograms to plot the interrelationships in classes for studying the dynamics present in the classroom.

Kuhlen, Raymond G., *The Psychology of Adolescent Development.* New York: Harper & Brothers, 1952.

An excellent summary of theories and research on the nature of adolescent characteristics and their development.

Jersild, Arthur T., *In Search of Self.* New York: Bureau of Publications, Teachers College, Columbia University, 1952.

A challenging proposal that good teachers must aid pupils in discovering, understanding and accepting themselves; without such discovery, the author believes learning can only be sporadic and ineffective.

Lindgren, Henry Clay, *Mental Health in Education.* New York: Henry Holt & Co., 1954, Chap. 9.

A discussion of factors, such as anxiety, cohesiveness, morale, and emotional climate, operating in classroom groups, and the effect they may have on learning.

Lloyd-Jones, Esther, and Margaret R. Smith, eds., *Student Personnel Work as Deeper Teaching.* New York: Harper & Brothers, 1954, Chap. 6.

An excellent chapter for introducing teachers to the use of certain techniques for gaining better understanding of students, both by the teacher and by the students themselves.

Northway, Mary L., *A Primer of Sociometry.* Toronto: Toronto Press, 1952.

Introduces students to basic principles and practices of sociometry for use in classroom groups and elsewhere.

Reid, Chandos, "The Classroom Teacher and Adolescent Adjustment," *Teachers College Record,* 52:500–511 (May), 1951.

Describes the use of unfinished stories as a technique for teachers to assess individual and group dynamics which may operate in the classroom.

Thelen, Herbert A., *The Dynamics of Groups at Work.* Chicago: The University of Chicago Press, 1954, Chap. 2.

Argues that the education of children comes about best through development of activities which meet their needs; states their needs and the kinds of group interaction which can fulfill them.

Wiles, Kimball, *Teaching for Better Schools.* New York: Prentice-Hall, Inc., 1952, Chaps. 3 and 4.

These chapters furnish provocative material on the questions: "What quality of human relations do we seek, and how can we improve human relations in the classroom?"

5. *Organizing the Classroom Group for Effective Learning*

INTRODUCTION

ONE COMMON COMPLAINT heard among undergraduate students of professional education is that they do not feel secure about their responsibilities on the first day and during the first weeks and months of working with classes. They ask, "How do we organize our groups? What about seating the pupils? How do we break the ice and get acquainted? How about keeping attendance records? How are committees selected? How are leaders chosen?" These and a host of other questions are uppermost in the minds of many beginning teachers.

To instructors in education departments and to experienced teachers in the field, these questions may not seem as significant as other larger issues of curriculum and teaching method. Yet they represent to the neophyte a source of real concern. This chapter attempts to give certain general principles and illustrative practices which may be of assistance to persons who are troubled by problems of classroom organization.

At the outset, the reader must understand that local policies and practices vary widely in respect to these minutiae of classroom organization. It is for this reason perhaps that many instructors in education classes hesitate to spend too much time on specific procedures and techniques, and prefer to examine the principles underlying classroom management. It is our purpose to alternate between principles and practices in such a way as to suggest guides for appropriate action, but not to argue for one pattern of organization.

THE GENERAL SETTING

The nature of his concern over problems of classroom organization will be determined by the teacher's attitudes toward the teaching-learning process. In earlier days, the teacher generally was more positive about *what* was to be taught and learned and *how* it was to be taught and learned. Classroom procedures and organization followed naturally from this concept of education, and tended to be rigid and authoritarian for the most part. More recently, as democratic problem solving has become a basic method for consideration by teachers, old patterns of classroom management have not seemed as appropriate. The beginning teacher today, perhaps affected by his own experience as a pupil with more permissive relations in the classroom and by his introduction to the problem-solving method of teaching and learning, is puzzled by what all this means for his behavior and the behavior of his pupils, particularly with respect to organizing the group for learning.

This, we suggest, is as it should be. That is, as a teacher approaches the teaching-learning situation with an experimental point of view, it is reasonable to expect some changes in classroom procedures. At least, it seems consistent that as new goals are envisioned for democratic classrooms, some new relations and organizational features are indicated. But these new facets of classroom management are hardly reducible to formulas which have universal application. They must be tried on the basis of the needs and abilities of individual teachers and groups. They become the patterns for a group and teacher if they work—that is, if they produce effective learning in a democratic problem-solving setting.

This experimental approach to teaching and learning procedures can be dignified by the term "action research." Experimentation engaged in by persons interested in improving their own procedures is "research in action." More attention will be paid to this important concept in Chapter 16. For the present, we suggest only that all teachers, new and experienced, should approach all matters of classroom practices with an experimental attitude, searching for evidence on the basis of which they continue or discard what they have been doing.

THE FIRST DAY

The old adage, "First impressions are the most lasting," applies to the first day of a class, the first attitudes of a group of students toward a teacher, and vice versa. A teacher may think, "Shall I let them know from the outset that I am boss in this room? Or shall I be more relaxed and friendly to test the possibilities of our relations? Shall we get right down to work on history so that they know I mean business? Or shall we proceed at a more leisurely pace to get acquainted with each other, our resources, our interests, the possibilities of this class, and so forth?"

It is true that in some schools an edict from the administrator may make it necessary to get formal study and work under way during the very first hour. But in most situations teachers are given great freedom in the first few days. The decision then rests with the teacher.

We propose that in line with the democratic problem-solving approach to learning, great importance should be attached to getting acquainted, to an orientation period or periods. This approach to teaching and learning demands a relaxed, friendly atmosphere in which everyone is worthy of being heard and where individual needs, interests, and abilities are assessed as a diagnostic measure. How much time can be used for this purpose will depend on the teacher's attitude toward its importance, the pupils' readiness for this kind of activity, and the skill with which the orientation is planned. We suggest a minimum of two or three days, but as much as several weeks can be used profitably.

ADMINISTRATIVE ACTIVITIES FOR THE FIRST DAY

There are always some administrative matters to be taken care of at the outset of the first class meeting. Roll call should be taken if a prepared class list has been furnished to the teacher. If such a list is not available, students may sign up on a sheet which is circulated through the class while other matters are taken care of. In any case, a teacher should have some kind of record of the first day's attendance so that early in the first week some study can be made of his pupils' personnel records. This is a responsibility teachers should not postpone.

Most schools will have a number of routine announcements which may be made during the first class period. Certain fees may be collected, and books may be distributed if they are furnished by the school. It is impossible to indicate the wide range of administrative duties which may fall to the teacher during the first few days of school. Their extent will depend on the traditions of the local school in part and on the amount of planning administrators have done to relieve teachers of this kind of activity. It is likely that most teachers can expect considerable activity and interruption of this kind for the first several weeks. Beginning teachers, in particular, do well to keep check lists of these kinds of responsibilities as often they may cause considerable embarrassment if they are not discharged.

Most of the above first-day activities and additional responsibilities later in the year apply to strictly departmentalized high schools. That is, many of these responsibilities would fall upon the teacher in the first period class, for example, school announcements, collections for drives such as Red Cross and March of Dimes, school banking, and the like. Other matters such as attendance check and book fees may apply to all teachers throughout the day.

If these administrative functions annoy teachers, certain arrangements can be made. Some schools have homeroom periods early in the day in which many of these details can be taken care of. Other schools schedule pupils in blocks of twenty-five to thirty-five for part or all of the day. This arrangement facilitates the discharge of many of these duties at one time for a group of pupils. Provisions such as these require considerable administrator-staff planning. In any case, many kinds of duties when assumed by the teacher alone are irksome and take much of his time which could be employed to better advantage. We suggest that there are some learning potentialities in many of the activities which we have been discussing. If they are incorporated into the classroom planning and are seen by the pupils as part of their problem of living and learning together, individuals and committees can be given direct experiences in certain language and number skills and in assuming responsibility; at the same time the teacher's burden is lightened. More will be said of these developments later in this chapter.

It should be possible during the first full-length class period to devote a portion of the time to a start toward getting acquainted. The teacher might remember at the outset that he too has an obligation in that respect. Pupils like to know about their teachers as people, and here is a good opportunity for a teacher to tell of his background— family, experiences, interests, and the whole range of attributes which make him a human being. The teacher's introduction may serve to break the ice and suggest a pattern for the class members.

The class members' participation in this activity is crucial. Some will enter in wholeheartedly; others will lack confidence or understanding of what is taking place. For the less verbal members, a brief outline as follows, or any number of variations of it, may be of assistance if placed on the blackboard:

1. Name
2. Number of brothers and sisters (other family information perhaps)
3. Recent travel or other interesting experience
4. What I like best about school
5. What I like least about school
6. Hobbies and interests
7. Vocational interests and plans

The above outline is only suggestive. The teacher must be careful in setting up such a device to guard against asking for information which might be seen by students as damaging to prestige or reputation—for example, location of home, occupation of parents, etc. These are important facts, but they might better be determined from personnel records.

Another variation of this procedure is to ask sets of two students to interview each other, take notes on the interviews, and then introduce each other to the class. This may help some shy students who find it difficult to talk about themselves, and may develop some socialization at the very outset of the class activity.

Many other devices can be used to get acquainted—the writing and reading of autobiographical sketches, sharing of student scrapbooks, talks on hobbies, preparation of personal data sheets for the teacher, and the like. Most of the latter extend over a period of time, and for the first day or two of a class self-introductions or interviews followed by introductions seem to be the most usable devices.

The teacher must be alert during all of these activities for clues to varying needs, interests, and abilities of students. These become the basis for teacher understanding and for provision for individual differences. The teacher may wish to take notes and record observations during these early days of the class to be placed in individual folders of the pupils. Personal data sheets for each pupil have been found to be helpful to the teacher during these first few days of school.

However, the chief contribution of this "getting-acquainted activity" is to provide a setting for learning in which individuals are honored for their uniqueness, where similarities are recognized, and where a feeling exists that a group is forming which is going to live and work together for a year around organized learning experiences. We submit that if such insights develop through this direct approach to self and group orientation, a class is off to a good start, particularly if subsequent activity is in the framework of democratic problem solving.

THE FIRST WEEK AND MONTH

We caution that the development of these basic attitudes toward individuals and the group is not a matter of a day, a week, or a month of attention. This must be worked out continuously, but the first few days are crucial in providing the relations and organization for such attitudes to develop.

ATTENDANCE ACCOUNTING

Early in the life of any class must come some decisions on routine management. For example, regular attendance and punctuality are important matters, both from the standpoint of achievement and of attitudes. The development of responsibility for promptness and regularity in attendance is something to be cherished for all adolescents. The question arises whether this is achieved best by involvement of pupils directly in the process of checking attendance and tardiness, or by having the teacher serve as the person responsible for this phase of classroom management. There are things to be said on both sides.

Rotation of responsibility for checking attendance and tardiness can be set up by the teacher and class. Certainly this kind of shared responsibility should not be undertaken without some thoughtful discussion of the merits of regular and prompt attendance, of the importance of accuracy in reporting absence and tardiness, and of the value of relieving the teacher of this purely administrative routine. Whether or not the responsibility for this task develops must be checked by the teacher, and in some cases may involve more effort to begin with than if he took the roll himself. Then a judgment must be made on whether the time involved is justified in terms of the learnings, or whether the pupils have demonstrated by a growth in responsibility a readiness for this kind of activity.

SEATING ARRANGEMENTS

Closely related to the attendance problem is the matter of the seating arrangement for pupils. Assigned seating, perhaps by alphabetical order, may facilitate attendance checking. Whether an assigned seating arrangement is always the most appropriate in terms of learning activities is another matter. Some insist that the flexibility gained by not assigning seats can be gained by regrouping after attendance has been taken or when the need arises. Others say that permanent seating arrangements tend to crystallize patterns of interaction among and between students and teacher.

Surely in a problem-solving approach to learning more activity and flexibility of pupils and their relations are necessary. Here again, though, experimentation is needed by teachers to determine what administrative arrangements in seating pupils are most productive. Perhaps a middle ground between permanent and arbitrarily assigned seats and no seating pattern whatsoever is wise. This might take the form of changing seating arrangements periodically on the basis of pupil choice, learning activities in progress, or sociometric data (Chapter 4) at the disposal of the teacher.

In any event, seating arrangements can be used experimentally and always should be open to change occasioned by the demands or the best interests of the group in terms of learning. If the classroom has movable seats, much can be done to vary seating arrangements. Besides the formal, traditional seating arrangement in rows facing the teacher, the group may wish to experiment with a large circle, several concentric semicircles, hollow squares and rectangles, and subgroups within these larger patterns. There is something to be said for changing the seating for the sake of variety alone. However, the chief justification should be in terms of adapting the seating facilities and the arrangement of class members to the various kinds of learning activities.

ESTABLISHING GROUND RULES FOR THE CLASS

Early in the life of any class, a teacher may anticipate questions from students on procedural matters related to individual and group requirements, discipline, use of classroom materials, and other related problems. A teacher may choose to state what he expects to follow as rules on these matters, or he may decide that the setting up of some kind of code is a valuable learning experience. Some classes develop a set of bylaws or a constitution as the basis for classroom activity.

If this kind of activity is seen as potentially a good learning experience, time must be devoted to it. Some class time seems justified, with perhaps out-of-class activity indicated for a committee which in turn might propose to the entire group a set of bylaws for consideration. The degree to which this activity is formalized will vary according to the maturity level of the pupils, the degree of importance attached to it in comparison with other activities, and the pupils' previous experience with this kind of learning situation. In any case, it seems wise rather early in the school year for a classroom group to give some attention to the limits within which it must operate. The degree of involvement in this process and subsequent understanding and commitment to the class's decisions may well determine the morale of the group for the rest of the year.

We believe that this attempt to establish rules for a class must be approached cautiously if cooperation is solicited from pupils. If the teacher sees his role as that of setting arbitrary standards, then perhaps the sooner this is done, the better. If he chooses to involve pupils in establishing class policies and procedures at the outset of the class, only a short time can be devoted to it. This is because pupils and teachers do not know each other well enough to arrive at conclusions to govern themselves. These develop as purposes and goals are set, arising from common problems defined by teacher and learners.

The minimum set of ground rules to govern the class in the interim before it is acquainted and learning purposes are clearly set might cover the following:

I. Attendance and tardiness
   A. Make-up of work missed when absent
   B. Penalties for tardiness
II. Materials needed and furnished by pupil
   A. Kind of writing material and equipment preferred
   B. Other material and equipment needed (books, rulers, and so forth)
III. Use of materials and equipment furnished by school
   A. Standards and penalties
   B. Regulations governing sharing of reference books, other materials and equipment
   C. Care of desks, tables, and so forth
   D. Use of bulletin board
IV. Classroom conduct
   A. Moving around classroom
   B. Speaking to other students with and without permission
   C. Recitation or discussion manners

The above list does not offer specific recommendations of what the rules should be, and covers only four aspects of classroom life which can be sources of disagreement and tension. As said before, arbitrary rules from the teacher or commonly agreed-upon regulations in these areas may help a class get started. But eventually, a more thorough look at these ground rules becomes necessary, particularly in a problem-solving classroom.

The reader will notice that the suggested areas above are either ambiguous or negative in their implications for behavior. Also it should be realized that most of them may be related to all-school policies. As such, any set of ground rules like the above must be only a stopgap measure, to be revised as the classroom group becomes more unified in purposes and goals. These in turn will indicate the need and extent of rules to govern behavior. More of this point of view is expressed in Chapter 6.

CLASS OFFICERS AND ELECTIONS

A class constitution suggests, among other things, the assignment of certain duties and privileges to the people involved. The bylaws can establish policies and practices about which decisions need to be made frequently in the life of a group. Some attention might also be given to more or less permanent organizational features of the class.

For example, some classes have found that periodic election of three of four officers for the class will provide pupil personnel to take care of certain duties that many teachers frequently assume. A president and vice-president may serve as chairmen for general class sessions involving announcements and routine class matters, or they may act in the teacher's place if he is out of the room. The secretary and/or treasurer can function as record-keeper both of class deliberations and of accounts related to fees, special activities, and the like. On paper, such officers may seem to have minor functions. Most teachers who have committed themselves to democratic procedures in the classroom have found such student leaders to be of great help to them. In addition, the rotation of such leadership periodically can provide opportunities for many students to learn responsibility by practicing it.

Although many teachers say that class officers and organizations for every period in the day are helpful, their most common use is found in schools where homerooms are provided. Such a group as a homeroom develops a unity and a need for an organization and for student officers more rapidly than many classroom groups devoted to a study of a subject field. Pupil activity, responsibility, organization, and leadership are seen as more meaningful in many homerooms. The various projects, interest discussions, and socializing functions of the homeroom encourage teachers and pupils to organize efforts and to choose and develop leadership. Greater freedom exists in their operations because of the absence of need for "ground to be covered" in a subject. We believe homerooms can be the best training ground for leaders in the entire school.

However, in connection with both class constitutions and officers, it can be said that one must guard against the machinery getting in the way of the program of the class. No one can deny that students can learn much of democratic process from opportunities to practice it in the way we have described. If learning how to work together democratically is one of secondary education's goals, then such activity seems promising and justified. At the same time, overorganization and overdependence on codes of behavior and structures of personnel may well inhibit a group from a more natural, creative atmosphere for group activity. Teachers and students alike must constantly evaluate the advantages and limitations of structuring a class as highly as we have suggested it.

CLASS COMMITTEES

Perhaps more closely allied with group activity and class goals is the question of committee organization. As a group develops its purposes and acts to achieve them, it soon recognizes that all members cannot do all things at all times. Delegation of responsibility is indicated for individuals and subgroups.

Although class committees generally should arise out of need which is indicated in a specific learning activity, there are some general committees which might be elected or appointed early in the year at the suggestion of the teacher. Figure 6, which follows, illustrates the nature and relations of these committees.

The Steering Committee. This group might act in an advisory capacity to the teacher. Called into session at the request of either the teacher or a committee member, it serves as a small discussion group in which the teacher may learn of the general morale of the class and of problems of which he may not be aware. He may see the committee as a sounding board for testing his own ideas. Students can regard the group as an opportunity to know the teacher and his ideas better, to channel to the teacher ideas about the class activity, to voice opinions more freely than in the total group, and to represent the ideas of their classmates.

This kind of advisory group is increasingly used in civic affairs, religious activities, business and industrial relations, and even in family situations. We suggest that adolescents can gain much for both present and future by being involved in such a relation. And for the teacher it can be a real boon by providing closer liaison with students and their ideas, besides giving testimony to the fact that he is sincere about the idea of democratic involvement.

Materials Committee. In any classroom committed to democratic problem solving, the procurement and utilization of materials is a pressing concern for the teacher. The single textbook with a few standard references will hardly suffice for an involved, eager group

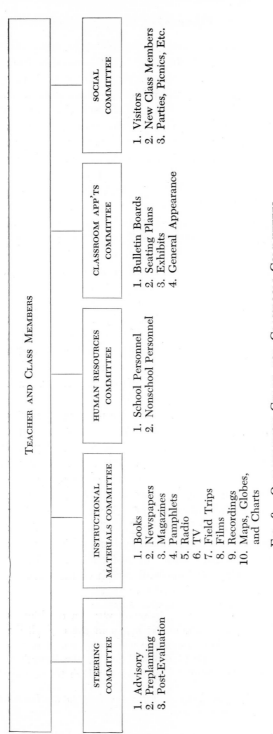

Fig. 6. Organization Chart for Classroom Committees

143

of adolescents who want to "know." Although early in the year pupils may not be so impressed with the need for such a committee, it will not be long before the need arises and is seen. The election or appointment of such a group, either permanently or as varying kinds of material needs develop, is suggested as a "must." Under considerable supervision of the teacher at the outset, members of this committee can be instructed to employ the standard library research devices for locating pertinent material. But even more helpful is their constant surveillance of current, timely materials and events which can be brought in for class consideration—books, newspapers, magazines, pamphlets, radio and TV programs, lectures, forums, and the like.

It should be made clear that the function of such a committee is not "to do the work"; that is, do the research, read the magazines, listen to the radio programs, and the like. The committee is only a watchdog for materials and experiences which can be reported to the class for possible use. The expansion of the classroom library becomes the chief tangible outcome. The enrichment of the total group is the net product of its endeavors. Without such a constantly functioning group, the problem-solving approach to learning may become sterile for lack of facts, information, ideas, and understandings which grow out of varied experiences. As more and more pupils become members of this committee, they are constantly alerted to varied sources of material for study and thought.

Human Resources Committee. One of the most encouraging recent developments in curriculum and teaching methods has been the increased use of human resources in the classroom. Many schools are attempting to systematize these resources into a file whereby teachers and pupils can readily locate people in their community who can be brought into the classroom as experts or specialists on some topic.

Interesting examples of this kind of systematic planning can be found in the brochure, *Fifty Teachers to a Classroom.*[1] Accounts are given of a number of New York school systems which have exploited human resources in the community to assist teachers. For example, the following paragraph is a thumbnail sketch of the development of Manhasset's resource file:

The procedure in Manhasset was, in many ways, a combination of the Great Neck and Essex Falls methods. It began in the over-all Curriculum Committee of the schools. This committee was composed of representatives from the elementary schools and high school and an equal number of interested people from the community. A card upon which to record pertinent

[1] Metropolitan School Study Council, *Fifty Teachers to a Classroom* (New York: The Macmillan Company, 1953).

information in concise form was first devised. The next step was to get together a master list of the names of people who had special interests, experiences, or hobbies and who could talk effectively to children. To get this information, teachers suggested names of parents who had already visited classrooms or parents whose work or hobbies were of such a nature that they would be of interest to children. The lay members of the committee were also asked to suggest "leads." Since it was considered of prime importance that each individual on the master list be approached personally, this work was divided among the members of the committee, with the laymen undertaking the greater share. The questions of an individual's willingness to serve, the particular aspect of his subject that he would like to discuss, the age level to which he would prefer to speak, were decided through this personal contact. It was carefully explained to all contributors that they would be called upon only when the need arose. The committee realized that valuable people might escape its notice but was constantly watchful for new leads to useful talent. When the classification was complete, the file was put in charge of a standing committee of the Curriculum Committee which was responsible for keeping it active and up-to-date. A copy of the resource file is housed in the library of each school.[2]

Figure 7 is a sample of the kind of resource file card which may be used.

We suggest that this kind of activity by teachers and supervisors might well be engaged in by pupils. The establishment of a human resources committee of pupils for each classroom would open up a whole range of people with varying specialties and competencies. Besides the values derived from such resources in the classroom, one can add the feeling of importance and contribution which pupils and lay people alike feel as they have a part in developing the instructional program.

Classroom Appointments Committee. In Chapter 3 we spoke at length about the importance of the classroom environment. Pupils can have a large part in developing classroom conditions conducive to learning. Infrequently do we find teachers encouraging students along these lines, except by general exhortations to the total group.

A committee elected by the class or appointed by the teacher early in the year might begin by making a survey of the classroom's appointments, with suggestions for improvement. Some recommendations would be to the custodial or maintenance staff, others to the teacher, and others to themselves as pupils.

Teachers who have experimented with such committees have found that their contributions have been as follows:

1. Pressure brought to bear upon administration, board members,

[2] *Ibid.*, pp. 15–16. Reprinted by permission of The Macmillan Company.

(Front)

Area of Interest	WEST LINCOLN	Card Prepared by
Grade Level	PUBLIC SCHOOLS	Date

NAME OF RESOURCE—

ADDRESS—

TELEPHONE NO.—

SPECIFIC INTEREST,
   COMPETENCE, OR
   EXPERIENCE—

ADDITIONAL INFORMATION
   (Equipment, transportation
   needed, etc.)

(Back)

EVALUATION OF RESOURCE PERSON (CHECK ONE)

1. DATE_____

2. EXCELLENT_____ GOOD_____ FAIR_____ POOR_____

3. SUGGESTIONS FOR IMPROVEMENT OR COMMENTS

4. NAME OF EVALUATOR_____

1. DATE_____

2. EXCELLENT_____ GOOD_____ FAIR_____ POOR_____

3. SUGGESTIONS FOR IMPROVEMENT OR COMMENTS:

4. NAME OF EVALUATOR_____

FIG. 7. HUMAN RESOURCES FILE CARD

and parents for the improvement of classroom equipment, size, general appearance, lighting, ventilation, and the like

2. The improvement of pupil attitudes toward room housekeeeping and increased respect for school property
3. The initiative taken by some classes to improve conditions themselves by painting, dusting, making cabinets, making or buying drapes for windows, and the like

PLATE 13. RESPONSIBILITY FOR BULLETIN BOARDS MAY BE DELEGATED. Teachers generally find their bulletin boards to be of greater variety and creativity when this is done. (Courtesy of the Oak Ridge, Tennessee, Public Schools)

Social Committee. We suggest that as a classroom group works cooperatively on the solution of problems of mutual concern, there develops both the need for closer socializing influences and the opportunity to capitalize on friendships which develop in the process of group work. As a result, a social committee seems a feasible recommendation.

Many school social functions range from the one extreme of very large, costly, elaborate, and time-consuming parties to small, poorly planned, and poorly executed affairs. In either case the net results are not wholesome, primarily in terms of pupil attitudes which develop.

We would like to see more continuous, planned socialization of smaller, natural groups in the school. The social committees of classes might well serve to bring about such events.

Classroom parties, picnics, and excursions of many kinds can furnish friendly ties among students and between students and teacher which stand in good stead when relations become strained in the regular routine of the school day. Many teachers testify that they learn more of real importance about their pupils at such social affairs than they can in the more formal setting of the school. Given such advantages, a social committee for a classroom seems a good investment of time and effort.

As in the case of class elections, the use of a social committee may well be most applicable to homeroom groups or to classes which are scheduled as a block throughout the day. In these kinds of groups, the degree of acquaintance and unity developed may motivate socializing activities such as parties and picnics more than in the typical classroom. A social committee, however, can assume responsibilities of various kinds, such as welcoming and orienting new pupils, greeting visitors to the classroom and making them comfortable, remembering class members who are ill or bereaved, and acting as a liaison between the class and the parent-teacher organization when the need arises.

OTHER KINDS OF COMMITTEES

The kinds of committees we have suggested up to this point are only suggestive of possibilities for involvement of pupils and for organizing the classroom group as a functioning unit. Many other types can be added, both permanent and *ad hoc;* however, we suggest that the five we have recommended are crucial to the success of a democratic, problem-solving approach to learning.

In addition, teachers and pupils will find need and opportunity to use other committees as specific learning experiences are planned and carried out. For example, pupil subgroups for bulletin boards, field trips, and evaluation procedures may grow out of certain kinds of learning activities. These need to be provided consistently as an integral part of the learning experience rather than as a concern during the first few days or weeks of a class. More will be said of this kind of committee in Chapter 9.

SOME ISSUES IN CLASSROOM ORGANIZATION

Lest the reader feel that we have oversimplified the processes and patterns of classroom organization, we discuss at this point some of the

PLATE 14. STUDENT CHAIRMAN AND SECRETARY ARE A LEADERSHIP
TEAM FOR CLASS DISCUSSION. Note the intense concentration on real
problems. (Courtesy of the North Phoenix, Arizona, High School)

issues and problems involved in this facet of classroom management.
We believe that our opinions and recommendations should be only
suggestive to the reader, and that they need verification by individual teachers and classes as they proceed to set up their own room
organizations.

1. *Who Shall Select Committee Members, and Who Shall Make
Policy and Procedural Decisions?* In general, we believe that pupils
themselves should increasingly elect the membership of their subgroups. It may be that early in the year when students are not well
acquainted the teacher may wish to appoint members or ask for volunteers. But as the group plans and works together during the year,
student election of committees and student decisions on classroom
policies and procedures are surely desirable. This belief is in line with
our contention that classrooms committed to democratic problem solving should provide actual experiences in cooperative planning, decision
making, and action.

2. *How Shall Teachers and Students Engage in Cooperative Activity
on Classroom Organizational Matters?* Two cautions are necessary.
First, without some guidance adolescents may make thoughtless selections and immature decisions. Teachers can assist pupils in developing
understanding of effective cooperative methods by two means. One is

by helping pupils arrive at criteria for selection of their peers or for making decisions. This process of involvement carries with it great responsibility, and adolescents need help in developing attitudes and habits which will enable them to assume responsibility thoughtfully.

For example, the following describes how criteria might be developed by a group of ninth-grade students to assist them in the selection of a unit of work to be studied:

CHAIRMAN: Yesterday we decided that we were ready to pick out the topic we want to work on for the next few weeks. We agreed that we would each make a list of the topics we were most interested in at home last night. What should we do now?

JANE: I think we should put them all on the board and then vote for the ones we want most.

DON: I think a committee should take everyone's list and put them all together first.

ELSIE: That would take too long. Why don't we divide into groups of seven or eight and each group can put the lists of its members together?

BILL: That will take too long, too.

TEACHER: Do you want to put every topic that is suggested on the list?

BILL: Sure, why not?

MARY: I think every one should be on.

CHAIRMAN: I showed my list to Doug and he thought a couple of mine shouldn't be on the list and I thought a couple of his shouldn't. I'll bet we have trouble that way.

DOUGLAS: I've been thinking. Is there any way we could decide ahead of time whether a topic should go on the list? Some of mine are sort of silly, I guess.

CHAIRMAN: Has anybody any suggestions?

Silence. No suggestions.

CHAIRMAN: Miss ———, what do you think?

TEACHER: Well, when people want to judge whether a thing is to be used or not, they decide on ways to measure its usefulness. We say that they decide on criteria for judging it. Maybe we could go at this by asking ourselves this question: "How can we tell whether or not a topic is a good topic to work on?" What would you say to this question?

JACK: I think a topic is good if knowing about it is going to tell me things that are useful to me. That's most important, I think.

CHAIRMAN: Helen, will you put these on the board? Then we can all see them.

JOY: I think it's just as important to learn about some things that are going to be useful to us later on in our lives too.

CHAIRMAN: Are there any others to be added? Margaret?

MARGARET: A topic should be interesting, too, if you are going to work on it for a long time.

STANLEY: I want to learn about things that are happening in the world today. Maybe that's what Jack meant when he said it should tell us things that are useful. But that might be something like learning how to make a soapbox racer if you wanted to enter the Derby. But I want to be able to understand a lot of other things that are happening too.

CHAIRMAN: Maybe we had better make Jack's point and yours separate even if they sound a lot alike. But I don't know how to say it.

JOY: Could Stanley's point be said this way: "Helps us to understand the world around us"?

STANLEY: That's it.

SUSAN: We had better be pretty sure we can find enough material on the topic we choose, too.

MARY: That's right. If we don't, we'll have trouble.

CHAIRMAN: Any others?

Silence

TEACHER: How about choosing a topic that you haven't studied before? Would it be a good idea to add that?

HUGH: I think that should go on the list. If it doesn't, we might choose something like Transportation and we studied that for a long time last year.

SUSAN: I don't think it should go on the list because we might study a different problem about transportation and then we would be learning something new.

HUGH: That's different. If we haven't studied that problem and we want to, it's O.K. because then we aren't studying the same thing over at all.

CHAIRMAN: Any other points? If not, will you read the list of points for us, Helen?

HELEN: Criteria for Choosing a Topic
1. Knowledge of the topic should be useful to us now.
2. Knowledge of the topic should be useful to us later in our lives.
3. A topic should be interesting.
4. Knowledge of the topic should help us to understand the world around us.
5. We should be able to find enough material on the topic.
6. It should be a subject we haven't studied before.

CHAIRMAN: Now that we have that done, we still have to decide how to select our topic to work on. But I guess that will have to wait till tomorrow.[3]

A teacher's responsibility is to assist pupils in making wiser judgments, based on some criteria which they have developed and understand. This skill, of course, goes beyond the mere organizational

[3] Roland C. Faunce and Nelson L. Bossing, *Developing the Core Curriculum* (New York: Prentice-Hall, Inc., 1951), pp. 113–115. Reprinted by permission of Prentice-Hall, Inc., and Dr. Rosalind Zapf, with whom most of the material originated.

features of the classroom and is a crucial and integral aspect of all democratic problem solving. We must teach it directly rather than hoping it will eventuate or will be seen by students as they go about their affairs in the classroom.

In the case of elections, certain criteria as follows might be developed to assist in selecting committee members:

1. Has this person displayed interest or ability along the lines needed for effective membership on this committee?

2. Does he have too many other interests and responsibilities so that he cannot give the time required?

3. Has he had an opportunity to work on other committees? Do we wish to spread participation more?

4. Are there other facts of interpersonal relations or committee composition which would make his election a good or poor choice?

Pupils can be assisted in developing and utilizing such criteria. Of course, their ability to develop such skills is a function of maturity, previous experience, and practice. A start must be made sometime if we hope to develop pupils who think in an orderly fashion about their democratic responsibilities.

Other assistance which the teacher can provide is in terms of evaluating procedures and policies effected by students. Pupils in adolescence need help in assessing the outcomes of their deliberation and action. This, too, is an integral part of democratic problem solving and cannot be overstressed. Too often teachers and classes enthusiastically embark on cooperative ventures without thoughtful consideration of alternative courses of action and criteria for decision making in respect to the alternatives. Infrequently do we find that classes are given the opportunity to evaluate their planning, decisions, and actions.

This, to be sure, is an indictment which can be made of adult behavior. If we are anxious to prepare adolescents for more intelligent problem solving as adults, we must be willing to give time and effort to the practice of evaluation procedures. This is particularly true of cooperative ways of working about which we know comparatively little. Through evaluation of democratic action we might learn a great deal more.

Early in the life of a classroom group, the teacher should give leadership to pupils in thinking about the organizational features of the class along the lines we have been proposing but with many variations in terms of specific classes and situations. However, it is most important at the planning stage that all concerned understand that all proposals for policies and procedures of classroom organization are tentative, subject to review, and finally open to revision if the evidence indicates the need of change.

3. *How Shall Teachers and Pupils Evaluate Classroom Organizational Policies and Procedures?* We submit that evaluation should go on continuously during the life of a committee or during the period a policy or decision is being implemented. But there comes a time when direct attention needs to be focused on the question, "How are we doing?" Then, by total class discussion or by subgroup consideration which then is pooled for the entire class, attention can be paid to the successes and failures of the venture. This should involve both self-evaluation and group evaluation. The degree to which peer evaluation is possible will be a function of the general climate of the group.

At times a written evaluation, perhaps with a five-point scale, is desirable. Here, for the record but anonymously, pupils register their opinions on a scale on some decision, policy, or action. In addition, they can elaborate on their reasons for the rating, in respect to both good and bad points. This kind of activity dramatizes evaluation, and the findings when collected and reported may serve as a good springboard for an evaluation discussion. For an example of the form which can be developed for this purpose, see Figure 8 in Chapter 7.

4. *What Is the Relation of These Kinds of Classroom Organizational Features to the Ability Levels of the Class?* This question brings up the old issue of heterogeneous vs. homogeneous grouping of classes. At the outset, we should point out that on the basis of research, our own experience, and democratic philosophy, we subscribe to the concept of heterogeneous grouping of pupils in classes. We need not rehearse the arguments pro and con on grouping by various kinds of criteria—age, sex, intellectual ability, social development, and the like. We only say that for certain kinds of choices and purposes which are related to special education (college preparatory, trade training, development of proficiency in certain aptitudes and interests), grouping by these criteria may have some values. But for general education in our society we need and want a cross section of all students' needs, interests, abilities, and understandings.

Furthermore, the problem-solving approach to learning suggests that we need all kinds of interests, competencies, and motivations, just as our larger society demands them in order to function. The fundamental methodological issue is *where* and *how* do we group pupils—or how do we organize the classroom group for various kinds of learning experiences?

When the curriculum and teaching methods of a school are crystallized and placed in a nonexperimental approach to learning, it is possible that we might group pupils by any number of different criteria. When the school is committed to a democratic, problem-solving approach to learning, classroom groups cannot be neatly set up by any one criterion or any combination of criteria. This does not say, however, that differences dissolve among pupils. It only suggests that the place for grouping to be effected is in the classroom and not on the principal's schedule board or at a meeting of the board of education or faculty. We suggest that grouping must and will take place if a cooperative, experimental approach to teaching and learning develops in the classroom. The grouping, however, will be effected and understood by those in the best position to see the need and purpose of the grouping—the teachers and pupils.

At this point, we are not suggesting that this "natural grouping" will take place automatically. It will receive tremendous impetus from the pupils themselves, based on their own self-understanding, peer choices, and felt needs and interests. But it will need guidance from the more mature teacher who will help the "under-achiever" and "over-achiever" to find their proper niches, who will enable students to avoid cliques, and who will minimize domination by an individual or a subgroup.

All of this demands a teacher who is sensitive to pupils' behavior, aware of pupil-personnel information which is available, and has at his fingertips varied materials and methods of instruction. This important concept is related to the authors' argument that homogeneous grouping of class sections is not necessary to achieve an optimum setting for learning.

5. *Can We Justify Time for Meetings of Committees and Other Organizational Features?* This issue involves a number of value judgments. If a teacher sees as his primary function the imparting of a set body of subject matter, largely from a textbook, he may well question the enthusiasm we have for involving students and using time in organizing the classroom group for effective learning. In fact, such a teacher will not need much organizational skill as the kinds of learning experiences he promotes lack variety and pose no great problems in organizing the classroom, except for having at pupils' disposal the textbooks and the seats in which to sit.

On the other hand, a teacher committed to problem solving must face some realistic questions on the amount of time he and his class can use on organization and procedural matters. Again, it is the old process-product issue we heard Jim, Marj, and Lucile discuss in Chapter 1. There are realistic limits to the amount of time which can be spent on planning processes, but we contend that most teachers could devote more time with pupils than at present on cooperative organization of the classrooms and learning experiences. We believe that in the long run time will be saved because of better motivation of learners in such a setting.

For example, in the use of classroom committees decisions must be made on their meeting time. Certainly it must be stated that a portion of the class period, or sometimes an entire period, should be devoted to committee work. If this does not take place, unwholesome attitudes of pupils will develop toward committees; for example, they will think of some committees as activities less important than others or as making unreasonable demands on their out-of-school time. Yet it should be assumed that if the problem-solving setting is present, learners will be motivated more strongly to pursue, both in and out of school time, the activities leading to problem solution. It seems fair to suppose, too, that committee work outside the classroom is legitimate "homework"—or must homework be study at home?

All of the above concepts suggest to us that a balance can be maintained between committee work in and outside the classroom, but with more time devoted to it in the classroom than at present. This will also allow the teacher to function in the appropriate roles developed in Chapter 9. If all small group work takes place outside the classroom, adequate consultation will not be given to learners, or an unfair demand on the teacher's time will result. Of course, in the case of committees meeting outside the class period, some chance should be given to pupils for working independently of the teacher.

CONCLUSION

We have attempted in this chapter to direct our attention to matters of classroom organization for learning. Throughout we have advanced suggestions based on the assumption that the method of learning toward which organizational features were directed was that of cooperative problem solving. By way of summary and conclusion, it can be said again that a teacher's views on classroom organization and management will be a reflection of his understanding and beliefs about the nature and purposes of learning.

If a teacher believes that the purpose of teaching and learning is to amass facts, and that the best method for achieving this purpose is by absorption of facts through lecture, memorization, and recitation, then the appropriate classroom organization and management is a simple, rigid authoritarian setup. If, on the other hand, a teacher believes that the chief goal of education is to develop competent thinkers, equipped with the skills and knowledges necessary for the solution of present and future problems in our society, then a more flexible and cooperative organization and relation within a classroom is necessary. The teacher is in a key position to decide what procedures and practices are to govern the operation of the group, and the values he holds will affect his decisions. We come back again to broad principles which govern action rather than specific patterns which grow out of one set of values or another.

We hope that this chapter has caused the reader to consider methods of classroom organization and management as only means to ends which must be clearly in mind. The alternatives we have proposed as methods or techniques must always be chosen with the educational goals determining the selection in mind.

FOR FURTHER STUDY

Bartels, M. H., and O. E. Peterson, "Student Participation in Classroom Management," *American School Board Journal*, 125:23–24 (July), 1952.
　　Furnishes principles underlying participation and gives examples of how these principles may be applied to organizing and managing the classroom.
Faunce, Roland C., and Nelson L. Bossing, *Developing the Core Curriculum*. New York: Prentice-Hall, Inc., 1951.
　　An excellent volume for teachers interested in both the philosophy and techniques of teaching through problem solving.
Gordon, I. J., "Class as a Group: The Teacher as Leader; Some Comments and Questions," *Education Administration and Supervision*, 27:108–118 (February), 1951.
　　Raises some pertinent questions about the expectations of pupils in regard to their own roles and the role of the teacher.
Grambs, Jean D., "Group Techniques in High School Classes," *California Journal of Secondary Education*, 26:277–282 (May), 1951.
　　Considers the use of "long-run" group techniques for purposes such as continuing class projects, standing committees, skill development, and the like.
————, "Using Group Work in High School Classes," *California Journal of Secondary Education*, 26:232–238 (April), 1951.
　　Analyzes the use of "short-run" group techniques for such purposes as discussion of controversial topics, group reading of material, group evaluation, participation in course planning, and the like.
————, and William J. Iverson, *Modern Methods in Secondary Education*. New York: The Dryden Press, Inc., 1952, Chap. 10.

Contains helpful suggestions on organizing the facilities, materials, and time available in the classroom for their most efficient use.

Helseth, I. O., "Off to a Good Start," *National Education Association Journal*, 37:342–343 (September), 1948.

Stresses the importance of a teacher's preplanning the organization and administration of the first days of school.

Keliher, Alice V., "Mental Hygiene in the Day's Work: A Day in the Life of a Teacher," *Mental Hygiene*, 34:455–464 (July), 1950.

Lists and discusses the many demands made on teachers which may bear little relation to teaching, but which must be met efficiently if teachers are to be happy and well adjusted in the classroom situation.

Kettelkamp, Gilbert C., *Teaching Adolescents*. Boston: D. C. Heath & Company, 1954, Chap. 5.

An excellent treatment of the importance of planning carefully for classroom routines and for the best use of the classroom environment.

Kinnick, B. J., "Groping My Way through Group Methods," *Clearing House*, 26:95–97 (October), 1951.

A word of caution to teachers that group planning and organization for learning in the classroom are no magic formula for success, and that variety through individual and group approaches is desirable.

Klausmeier, Herbert J., *Principles and Practices of Secondary School Teaching*. New York: Harper & Brothers, 1953, Chap. 7.

A general treatment of organizing and initiating classroom activities, part of which is devoted to the use of student committees.

Rivlin, Harry N., *Teaching Adolescents in Secondary Schools*. New York: Appleton-Century-Crofts, Inc., 1948, Chap. 11.

Describes organizational and clerical routines of the typical classroom and offers suggestions for the teacher's part in attending to these details.

Webber, Frank D., and Byron H. Atkinson, "Dynamic Classroom Control," *California Journal of Secondary Education*, 24:350–352 (October), 1949.

Urges careful establishment of classroom routines and limits as basic to good learning situations; cooperation between teacher and pupils in such planning is held to be of the greatest importance.

Wiles, Kimball, *Teaching for Better Schools*. New York: Prentice-Hall, Inc., 1952, Chap. 6.

A wide range of suggestions is offered on how a teacher can work with a class so that it becomes a group, including the development of responsibility for planning and executing group decisions.

6. Classroom Discipline for Adolescents in a Democracy

INTRODUCTION

A CHAPTER on pupil discipline is a difficult one to place in a sequence which develops general methods for teaching in the secondary schools. In fact, some would argue that separating discipline as a topic for treatment from the framework of the psychology of human development as developed in Chapter 2 is a poor procedure. Others would say that good or bad discipline is a matter of classroom organization and management and should be treated in that context. Still others would point out that the control of pupil behavior is an integral part of individual and group participation in the problem-solving approach to learning and should be discussed at many points where appropriate.

We believe that all of these contentions have merit, and we attempt to point out implications for student control at a number of other places in this book. However, the importance of this topic, both from a theoretical and a practical standpoint, justifies in our minds a direct attack on the problem of discipline at this point.

In this chapter we hope to analyze some of the faulty thinking which pervades adolescent-adult relations in and out of school and substitute what we consider to be appropriate theories of classroom control. These theories will be advanced in the light of what we know about human behavior and learning, and what we believe is consistent with democratic tradition. Attention will also be given to causes and treatment of common pupil behavior problems in the classroom.

158

WHAT IS DISCIPLINE?

The behavior of children and youth has always been a source of worry to their elders. From classical literature of Greece and Rome through the writings of contemporary authors, one can find the fretful indictments of youth for their wayward manners and activities and the critical catalogues of examples and causes of delinquency. There are some who would take refuge in the fact that, like the poor, delinquents we always have with us. Others take a dim view of youth, and say that they are getting worse, not better. Many, perhaps most, resort to wishful thinking and crossed fingers for the future of our youth.

In such a setting, it is not surprising that today also we hear much about adolescent behavior problems in the home, school, and community. Scapegoats are sought, and education comes in for its share of criticism. We believe the school must take its share of the responsibility, but not for the reason many advance. We do not blame the schools for a lack of discipline, but for the wrong kind of student control in a day when fundamental human relationships are being subjected to new problems, tensions, and dilemmas. In a few cases, parents and educators have misinterpreted certain new theories of discipline as meaning no discipline. Many teachers are judged to be competent or incompetent on the basis of their classroom discipline, with teacher and critics holding two or more different concepts of discipline. For these reasons we believe an intensive consideration of discipline in the schools is justified.

As a starting point, we believe that the best definition is as follows: *Discipline is the control of their behavior on the part of individuals or groups in order to attain their goals and purposes.* The emphasis is on discipline from *within* the individual or group rather than from without, and focuses on *their* purposes and goals. So we are agreed that discipline means control, restraint, or even inhibition. The difference between this concept and others commonly held lies in the amount of importance and degree of value attached to the source of control and purposes of it.

CHARACTERISTICS OF GOOD DISCIPLINE

Let us consider two people: A who is to be disciplined, B who is to do the disciplining. Traditional concepts of discipline suggest that control be imposed upon A by B, and should be related to the purposes of B or to the purposes which B wants A to have.

A modern concept of discipline does not suggest that such a

disciplinary relation has no value or should never exist. It does argue that the extent to which A controls his behavior in terms of purposes which he understands and values, to that degree a better disciplinary relation exists between A and B.

What then is the relation of A and B in the latter case? Ideally, B is a person who assists A to consider alternative purposes and alternative behavior to achieve those purposes. The choice of purposes and behavior, to be sure, involves value judgments by A which may be in conflict with those of B. The showdown comes when B either allows or forbids A to choose goals and appropriate behavior. Discipline moves toward self-control when A becomes more and more skillful in weighing alternatives and consequences, resulting in choices by him which are both socially and personally acceptable. It moves toward authoritarianism on the part of B, and dependence on B by A, as B makes the decisions on purposes and behavior and controls A in their light.

At this point the reader may have concluded that we have not considered the possibly greater maturity, wisdom, and foresight of B. Obviously, there are differences among people in ability to weigh alternatives, make decisions, and act. These differences are a function of intelligence, maturity, and emotional balance. But we must come back to the definition of discipline—control of behavior—which brings us to the second big idea in our philosophy of discipline.

"Discipline," from the standpoint of word derivation, is closely allied to "teaching" and "learning." It is also related by usage to the word "punishment," but the basic stem meaning is "learning." Now we come to a consideration once again of how people learn. It is true that earlier concepts argued that learning was associated with pain, difficulty, defeat, and chastisement. Much of our current research in learning disproves the "failure and frustration" concept of learning and substitutes a "success and enjoyment" theory of learning.

The basis for this latter theory is that all human behavior is goal-oriented; in other words, that as human beings move in their environment they test behavior in relation to satisfying needs, wants, and wishes out of which stem their goals. As they move toward achieving their purposes, their behavior becomes adjusted until they change it sufficiently to achieve fully their goals. *At this point they have learned.* Repeated research shows that speed, permanence, and quality of learning are related to the learner's ability to differentiate purposes in terms of needs, desires, wants, etc.

What we have been leading toward should be apparent now. If discipline is control or change of behavior, which we have shown is also learning, then we ask ourselves the same questions about discipline that we do about learning. What are the conditions conducive to discipline? How do we know when discipline has been effected? Just as in the case of learning, these answers are complex. We propose at this point to discuss them at some length.

DISCIPLINE MUST HAVE CLEARLY DEFINED PURPOSES

Control or change of behavior is best effected when reasons are seen for such control or change. This is a fundamental law of learning and discipline. Reasons for changing or controlling one's behavior are best understood and accepted when they relate to the fulfillment of purposes or goals of the persons involved in the change or control of their behavior.

We can agree on the meaning of these words, but may fail to see what they denote for classroom learning situations. Much of classroom behavior should be directed toward specific learning outcomes. The desirability of the behavior will be judged in terms of whether it assists in achieving the goals of the specific learning experiences. Conflict arises among students and between students and teachers when goals are not similar, commonly accepted, or even perceived. Because of differences in goals and purposes, differences in behavior may be expected.

All this may lead to the question—so what? So—the alternatives are (1) to demand common acceptance of goals and appropriate behaviors; (2) to attempt a reconciliation of differences in goals to the point where the group is ready to move ahead together; (3) to accept differing goals and differing behavior as permissible and desirable.

In the case of the first alternative, it can be said that this procedure works—on the surface. That is, out of desperation over how to use the other two approaches, a teacher may insist on certain purposes and appropriate behavior and may achieve a measure of surface control. This kind of control we often need, both in schools and in our larger society, for the benefit of all concerned. We should not be deluded, however, that we have achieved discipline in the best sense, or that learning has taken place. Removal of the external controls of teacher, school and group, and the individual may well revert to behavior which is in line with his purposes. What then can be done about the other alternatives?

In the case of the second possibility, we suggest that too often teachers and parents do not have the patience or take the time to attempt a reconciliation of differences in purposes. Discussion, explanation, and trying out behavior can go far to help all understand the

differences in values which account for differences in goals. Such
sharing, in the home or in the classroom, may often lead to a change
of purposes, or at least a more wholesome attitude toward differences
and a willingness to act in terms of other kinds of goals, tentatively

PLATE 15. A FRIENDLY ATMOSPHERE MAY EXIST IN DISCIPLINARY
SITUATIONS. In fact, without this acceptance of pupils, if not of their
behavior, good discipline cannot be developed. (Courtesy of the
Baton Rouge, Louisiana, Public Schools and of the National
Education Association)

accepted. But this takes time and patience from parents and teachers.
Furthermore, it asks them to abrogate their traditional role, "I know
best for you—therefore you *must* do as I say." Many parents and
teachers find it difficult to give up this role and what it does for their
ego needs.

The third alternative is even more difficult. This demands, in the
first place, a willingness to accept goals and values of people which
may be opposed to our own. It asks that individuals and their ideas
be respected for their own sakes, even though we "know" that they
are wrong. And it requires a willingness and helpfulness on our part
to assist the person in the achievement of goals which we consider less
respectable than ours. This is almost a superhuman demand to be
placed on oneself in terms of skills and attitudes. But it is the earmark

of a great teacher, and prepares the learner to consider the teacher's goals after he has found his own to be impossible of achievement or less satisfying than he imagined they would be.

To many readers, what we have been saying may appear to be too idealistic. To be sure, it is an ideal we have presented in respect to teacher, pupil, and situation. There are many things which militate against teachers believing and acting in these ways with children and youth. But we submit that the best hope for creating good learning situations out of which come changes in behavior, or control of it, lies in recognizing and exploiting the concept of goal-oriented learning and discipline.

DISCIPLINE MUST BE FLEXIBLE IN APPROACH AND OUTCOMES

This statement may sound like heresy to some, as it suggests possibilities of unfairness toward pupils and vacillation in policies. For many teachers and parents, the qualities of mercy, judgment, and tolerance are less desirable than uniformity, justice, and legalism.

Incorporating the question of appropriate behavior into a learning situation will of necessity mean flexibility by reason of the differences in learners. In no other place than the school is such a premium placed on uniformity and conformity in behavior. Elsewhere recognition is given to varying purposes of individuals and groups, and unless they run counter seriously to the rights of others, behavior manifestations are allowed great variations. We believe such a viewpoint might find a more prominent place in teaching, learning, and discipline.

Consideration of differences in goals and thoughtful analysis and planning of the behavior required of learners should lead to variations in behavior patterns and controls. Too often the matter of behavior is considered as something outside the learning situation. As a result, absolutes and rigidity develop in the minds of teachers and learners, regardless of the situation at hand. Such unexamined and habitual behavior control does not develop self-discipline, and will almost always result in inappropriate behavior when external pressures are absent.

The problem of this viewpoint lies, of course, in whether the individual and his unique behavior infringe upon other individuals or the group. It is the old question of the individual versus the group.

One can well imagine or remember instances when a learning situation might eventuate in discipline for an individual, but might retard or disrupt the processes of the group. By the same token, attention to the "common denominator" needs of the group may often develop group morale and behavior but slight an individual or two in the group. An excellent example of the need for variations in diagnosis and treatment of behavior problems may be seen in the following cases:

Example 1A: Johnny is just at the stage of his development in which a lot of clowning is frequently used by children in order to gain group prestige. There is nothing really wrong with this. In fact, knowing Johnny, we are glad this happened "at last." However, it is also usually unavoidable that children overdo this ambition of group effect at times and become so intense in their wish for applause that they really disturb every serious teaching situation in class.

In this case it is not sufficient to know that Johnny's behavior is all right, normal, and understandable, even desirable from the angle of his own development. The teacher is still confronted with the job of limiting it, or else her whole teaching situation goes to pot.

Example 1B: The teacher notices that Mary is sitting back, obviously daydreaming. After awhile she finds that the child is seriously disturbed about some family situation or whatnot. However, Mary's behavior is restricted to her fantasy life. She does not act in any way which would disturb the group or the teacher on the job. Her behavior remains, from a group angle, innocuous, though it is alarming as far as her own case history goes.

In that case there is no *disciplinary* need for the teacher to interfere, but Mary's behavior is still an important educational challenge, for she needs help.[1]

As Sheviakov and Redl point out,[2] the teacher's problem is how to help these individuals with the least disturbance to the group, and at the same time not to lose Johnny and Mary in an attempt to influence the behavior of the group. The teacher finds that Johnny's case is more group-relevant than Mary's. He also should recognize that the discipline techniques for handling attention-getters and daydreamers must be different. Therefore, choices must be made for treatment of these cases which, if beneficial to the group, must be harmless to Johnny and Mary. At the same time, measures taken to assist these two youngsters must not be harmful in their effect on the total group. Much of this dilemma of choice can be handled by anticipating situations and appropriate disciplinary measures.

For example, in the case of Johnny, his dismissal from the room or the use of sarcasm will probably not solve his basic problem. In fact, it may accentuate it, for he has achieved his goal of getting attention and finds the behavior appropriate for his goal. One technique which

[1] George V. Sheviakov and Fritz Redl, *Discipline for Today's Children and Youth* (Washington, D.C.: Association for Supervision and Curriculum Development, National Education Association, 1944), p. 24. Reprinted by permission.

[2] *Ibid.*, pp. 24–25.

has worked in cases of this type has been the cooperation of Johnny's classmates in helping him understand the limits to which he can go. Peer disapproval may mean much more to him than the sarcasm of the teacher or the threat of having to leave the room.

In the case of Mary, who is really a much more serious problem even though she does not disturb the class, other measures are needed. Obviously, the use of her peer group as in Johnny's case might cause her to withdraw even more from the group. The teacher probably will begin by not calling attention to her daydreaming in the class, but ask for special assistance in the form of personnel records, home visitation, or expert psychological consultation.

These two cases illustrate the need for skill and creativity in diagnosis and treatment. Certainly the teacher who uses the word "discipline" loosely would make some hasty judgments about the behavior of these youngsters, and resort to prescribed forms of punishment for "disturbing the class" in the case of Johnny and for "not paying attention" in Mary's instance. Instead, a skillful, sensitive teacher would recognize that these cases demand complex decisions for which patient, thought-requiring procedures are needed. No rule-of-thumb or legalistic approach will suffice. Out of such insights might come wide varieties of treatments and outcomes.

DISCIPLINE MUST BE INCREASINGLY SELF-IMPOSED

As in the case of learning, so in discipline the individual should increasingly assume responsibility for himself, his decisions, and his actions. This is the essence of self-discipline, of self-control. This is in opposition to older concepts of discipline which result in ever increasing provisions for control in the form of laws, personnel for enforcement, and punishments.

Most people would say that the prevalence of externally imposed controls over adults is the product of the greater complexity of adult society or of the eternal struggle between right and wrong. We are not suggesting that problems of the modern day do not pose new and more difficult problems for adults and children alike. But new problems demand new procedures and solutions. We have not learned how to adapt our individual and social control systems to modern day demands.

Nor do we argue that there is no value conflict in our society—a struggle between "good" and "evil." The moral content of education must be examined and inspected for its contribution to modern discipline problems.

But we do insist that centuries of authoritarian control of children, youth, and adults have not supplied us with evidence that this kind of discipline produces constantly developing, self-reliant people who can be responsible for their own actions in the best interests of all. We suggest that homes and schools need increasingly to test ways of exerting their influence so that learners have an opportunity to develop and practice self-discipline.

This opportunity for practice must be provided by skillful teachers, committed to classrooms where all learners have a recognized stake in the goals, activities, and outcomes of the learning situations. Self-discipline will never result in schools where youngsters react, "School's okay, I guess. The teacher tells us exactly what we are to do, how we are to do it, when we are to do it, with whom we are to do it—and then if anything goes wrong, we just blame the teacher."

This increasing propensity for self-discipline is surely a function of maturity as well as of practice. Any parent and teacher knows the differences in ability of the six-year-old and the twelve-year-old to direct his own activity and behavior. The fact is, though, that at any age level there are certain kinds of responsibilities which are appropriate and can be developed. They are developed best in terms of the learner seeing the need and purposes of such responsibilities, not simply being told, "You must do this, because I say so."

And so a parent or a teacher is torn between conflicting facts and desires. He wants the child to "grow up," to be self-disciplined; at the same time he is fearful that the learner will make mistakes in practice. Faced with such a dilemma, we only say that in no better place can a child or youth learn the lessons of "mistakes" than in the home or school. Here "the chips are not down," so to speak; here he can practice, and profit by assistance from adults when he makes mistakes.

Instead, we prepare youth for life, either by creating an educational vacuum where there is no opportunity for planning, deciding, and acting, or by setting up a rigid pattern of behavior in which they have little participation, assuming that by some magic at high school graduation, or at age eighteen or twenty-one, they will become self-disciplined, adult citizens. Small wonder we have more laws, more enforcement personnel, and more problems of human relationships for the governing of adults.

Ultimately, the question becomes "Discipline for what?" We suggest that as good teaching eventually makes the learner capable of teaching himself, so the best discipline eventually should result in people responsible for their own control. Without such an outcome resulting from efforts of parents, teachers, and all others placed in positions of leadership with children and youth, we will be fighting a losing battle against the problems of individual and group relations which are constantly becoming more complex.

We hope that this discussion of various concepts of discipline, and of what some theories of the development of sound discipline mean to us, will furnish the reader with a setting for a consideration of some common school discipline problems—their causes and treatment.

SCHOOL DISCIPLINE PROBLEMS— CAUSES AND TREATMENT

We come now to a consideration of various kinds of specific behavior problems. Even as we have varying opinions about the nature and purpose of discipline, so we find many conflicting ideas about what constitutes a problem in pupil behavior. Many studies have been made of the attitudes of teachers and principals toward various kinds of aberrant behavior.

ATTITUDES TOWARD SCHOOL DISCIPLINE PROBLEMS

A number of years ago both Wickman[3] and Garinger[4] reported that even though principals and teachers were asked to judge the seriousness of various kinds of behavior problems for the future adjustment of pupils, their responses indicated that teacher and school routine were of primary concern. That is, discipline problems which seemed to be offenses against the established order—stealing, truancy, impertinence, cheating, obscenity—were considered much more serious than lying about other pupils, inattention, giggling, carelessness in work, and the like. These researchers concluded that for that time (1925–1935) at least, teachers and principals thought more seriously of their own welfare and the established routines of the school than of the pupils' problems which indicated lack of personal adjustment which might lead to disabling habits and attitudes.

We have some reason to believe that modern teachers and administrators increasingly are seeing behavior deviations as symptoms of poor pupil adjustment which need diagnosis for determining the cause, rather than punishment to secure docility, obedience, and conformity. These changed attitudes of many educators are the result of the research and writing in human development and mental hygiene.

[3] E. K. Wickman, *Children's Behavior and Teachers' Attitudes* (New York: Commonwealth Fund, 1928), pp. 117–130.

[4] Elmer Henry Garinger, *The Administration of Discipline in the High School* (New York: Bureau of Publicatons, Teachers College, Columbia University, 1936), pp. 81–83.

Encouraging as this more humane and intelligent approach to discipline may be, the problems still remain; and for classroom teachers, particularly beginners, discipline continues to be an important aspect of their success or failure.

We submit that the best hope for the solution of most of these problems lies in the improvement of the teaching-learning situation. At the same time, we recognize that many problems of student control stem from causes outside the classroom or even the school. In any case, a teacher must be willing to attempt a diagnosis of behavior symptoms in a search for causes of the problem.

Since this is a book on classroom method, our major emphasis is on analyzing possible causes of misbehavior which relate to the learning situation. However, some attention must be given to causes which lie outside the classroom and school.

EXTRA-SCHOOL PROBLEMS

Our purpose here is not to catalogue all possible kinds of adolescent misbehavior which can be attributed to nonschool factors. This is a temptation into which educators frequently fall. "Oh, it's not the child's fault—or the school's. What can you expect—coming from a home and community setting like that?"

It is true that home, neighborhood, and total community factors affect behavior at school. But the multiplicity of factors and behavior manifestations make a discussion of them impossible and perhaps not too valuable, as most teachers become aware of them only by firsthand investigation of the community, by sharing of information, and by becoming better acquainted with pupils. We have mentioned case conferences and case studies elsewhere in this book as excellent ways to keep abreast of this kind of information.

CONFLICTS BETWEEN ADOLESCENTS AND SOCIETY

More significant, we believe, is the role of any adolescent in our society at the moment. We place the teen-ager with his fundamental, developmental needs in the context of contemporary America, and we find many possible reasons for his behavior.

Consider the following:

1. The adolescent must understand and accept his changing body and its functions. And yet we have not in our society come to a point either in home, church, or school where the adolescent is consistently given the help he needs to make a graceful adjustment in becoming an adult physically. The range of practice in this respect is still largely from strict taboos to "programs" of sex education.

2. The adolescent must develop gracefully new heterosexual interests and attitudes, culminating during late adolescence or early adulthood in courtship, marriage, and family life. This, by and large, is considered by home, church, and school as subject matter which is not quite respectable—or something which "comes naturally," or as

PLATE 16. STUDENTS' ASKING FOR ASSISTANCE REFLECTS A GOOD CLIMATE FOR DISCIPLINE. Most pupils desire help in decision making, and wish to know what limits exist. (Courtesy of the Oak Ridge, Tennessee, Public Schools)

by-products of other kinds of teaching and learning. Add to that the fact that our culture for social and economic reasons prolongs adolescence in respect to marriage, to making a livelihood, and to becoming independent long after the teen-ager is ready for such adult activity.

3. In speaking of independence, we refer to both psychological and

economic ability to "go it alone." The adolescent himself vacillates between the feeling of need for support from parents and other adults and his aggressive desire to assert himself and break away from childhood restraints. Add to that the mixed feelings and actions of parents and other adults toward adolescents, and it is not difficult to understand the confusion in the minds of teen-agers. It also accounts for their desire to test limits of their freedom and to experiment with their behavior. Here again, the guidance which adults give youth is "catch-as-catch-can" at best. This applies both to vocational and personal-social guidance. Schools have advanced greatly in the past few years in this respect, but greater cooperation among all institutions and agencies interested in youth is needed.

4. Finally, consider the alternatives facing youth today as they strive to build a code of values and beliefs. Confronted with conflicts in basic values and with contradictions between the preachments and practices of adults, it is not suprising that many adolescents become cynical about morality, accepted behavior, and the institutions which are unable to cope with modern problems of human relationships.

Let us hasten to add that these basic needs of adolescents are not new phenomena. But placed in the complex of modern life where alternatives are so numerous, the choices are more difficult. As a result, behavior manifestations vary more widely than in the past. This fact gives meaning to the statement, "We don't have more problem youths than before; we do have youths with more problems."

A commonly used and seemingly trite statement we hear is, "Behavior is caused." If the causes of adolescent behavior are found in large part in teen-agers' attempts to satisfy these basic needs, then it seems fair to suggest that nonacceptable behavior according to society's standards is caused by failure to accomplish these developmental tasks. It follows then that home, school, church, and all agencies interested in youth might well begin to face up to the "youth problem" by direct attention to these basic developmental needs. For the school this becomes a school-home relations problem, a curriculum problem, a guidance problem, and an in-service education problem for teachers.

Many individual schools, some school systems, and even some states have faced up to this problem of closer integration of all agencies interested in youth. It is certain that the school alone can never solve the problem of juvenile delinquency, or for that matter, routine problems of misbehavior in school without cooperation from all concerned. But basic to all groups' understanding of the problem is a recognition and acceptance of the nature of adolescent needs.

CLASSROOM PROBLEMS IN DISCIPLINE

All of the problems arising from failure to meet his developmental needs come to school with the adolescent. The disquieting attitudes about his physical development, his feelings of unrequited love toward his girl friend, his desire to quit school so that he can earn money for his own car, his mother's disappointment because he stays out late—all of these he brings to school with him. They are with him in algebra, in English, in study hall, at all times when he is sufficiently quiet to contemplate. The frustration he experiences when other demands are placed on his thinking may result in withdrawal or aggression.

We do not mean to imply that all teen-agers have such traumatic experiences in going through adolescence. In fact, it is likely that for most youth these developmental needs occasion only vague uneasiness which does not of itself erupt into serious behavior manifestations. But for purposes of creating problems when subjected to restrictions of authority in home, school, and community, these nebulous misgivings about self, other people, and life in general are very important. They account for sudden outbursts of anger, unpredictable fits of moodiness, and various kinds of unsocial or antisocial behavior at the strangest times, at least to adults. They do not approach delinquency, but are troublesome for all adults who contact youth with established purposes and programs.

It is in this regard that the classroom teacher becomes a focal person in the experience of the adolescent. The teacher symbolizes authority and requires respect. In addition, our culture promises that from education will come the realization of economic and social prestige. On the one hand, the teen-ager has the need for meeting these developmental tasks, and on the other he sees the school as the avenue toward the satisfaction of his needs, the social and economic ones being those of which he is most conscious.

The stage seems set, therefore, for a happy experience of teacher and learner working together. What happens? Typically, the adolescent is confronted with a series of requirements in terms of learning methods and content which seem completely divorced from his immediate and not so distant needs and plans. For a while, he may be respectful, hoping that this class and teacher are going to be different. In most cases, he is disappointed and lapses into docile boredom or open hostility, or he may exhibit surface interest and enthusiasm because this pays off in rewards and recognition, even though unrelated to what he considers important.

This may seem to be a harsh indictment of secondary schools and teachers. We are testing this concept of the behavior reactions of adolescents in school because we believe that while the secondary school cannot be blamed alone for aberrant adolescent behavior, it helps to aggravate the problems in many ways. We are suggesting that the curriculum and teaching methods of secondary schools contribute to the manifestation of problems in adolescents which are present in them when they come to school. These we have discussed earlier in this chapter. Now we propose to look at the classroom and teaching methods for sources and aggravation of discipline problems.

POSSIBLE CAUSES FOR CLASSROOM DISCIPLINE PROBLEMS

Sheviakov and Redl suggest some areas of classroom life which can create problems in discipline among pupils and between pupils and teacher. The following seem particularly suggestive to us of methodological weaknesses:

Subject matter much too easy. Too much of the work ability of the students remains unchallenged and has to search for other outlets.

Subject matter much too difficult. The emotion of frustration accompanies great stretches of the work. Research has proved beyond doubt that exposure to the frustration of not being able to do things well will produce tremendous aggression or restlessness in *normal* children. The result will be unavoidable diversions, taking pokes at each other, dropping and throwing things, irritability, and I-don't-care attitudes, which lower behavioral inhibitions all over the place.

Language of teachers too remote from the child's developmental level, or from the native tongue ordinarily used on his social plane. If that is the case, the child feels out of place, not really wanted, or even looked down upon, and begins to show signs of social-outcast reactions and protest.

Load of assignments too heavy, in which case the school hour is loaded with the emotional strain of guilt feelings, criticisms, and a general impression of not being up to what is expected, or an attempt is made to catch up on lost play time by having a good time during class.

Load of assignments too light. Then the feeling of progress in learning is lacking, which again reflects itself in a growing unwillingness to do any work for that subject because the time spent on it does not seem profitable in the end.

Assignments badly planned, poorly explained, unfairly judged—with the result that typical "resentment behavior" pops out in little irritations all over the place.

Type of work or way of presentation too advanced—not clicking with the developmental needs of the children. For instance, lectures on nature in general are given at an age where a strong curiosity about animals' bodies could easily be utilized for motivation.

Type of work and presentation too infantile, compared to development level on which children happen to move emotionally. For instance, talks about sex and the flowers are too childlike, when youngsters are full of pride about their newly acquired pre-adolescent daring in sex exploration on a very different level, indeed.

Activities too much on a merely verbal level, leaving the normal motoric needs of growing children unchallenged for long stretches of time. Thus, we frequently find restlessness, noise, shuffling of feet, falling of chairs, and pushing each other where too much discussion or lecturing substitutes for real participation and manipulative activities.

Work badly scheduled as to sequences of different types, or ill-placed in terms of exhaustion and fatigue. For instance, the English poetry class is at the end of a long day after a baseball game, at which moment it seems to be especially hard to excite manipulation-greedy sixth-graders about Shelley or Keats.[5]

These characteristics of "work process," as Sheviakov and Redl express it, or of teaching-learning method as we have described it, are recognizable by teachers and learners alike. In a classroom we often hear things which are clues to mistakes in teaching and learning methods. The following are typical behavioral examples of weaknesses in teaching and learning methods:

TEACHER: I am simply disgusted with this class today. No concentration, poor work habits. John, what's the trouble with you?

JOHN: I'm through with your assignment on the Boer War.

TEACHER: Well, you might look it over to be sure it is complete. Jane, why aren't you working?

JANE: I don't understand the assignment on the reading. I've gone over it three times and it doesn't make sense to me.

TEACHER: James, you haven't been working.

JAMES: I can understand what I read, but what's the good of it? I'd rather study the problem they're having now in South Africa.

ALEX: I'm just tired—can't concentrate on this reading. Why couldn't we have a movie on this? Is there one?

Here we have all the telltale reactions of a group of students to a learning experience arbitrarily decided upon, planned, implemented, and no doubt, evaluated at its conclusion. This is not to say that no learning will take place. There will be some learning of facts, no doubt; but, in addition, for some there will be developed and learned a distaste for history, for reading, for the teacher, and perhaps for the school in general. And through it all will run for the teacher and the class a series of disciplinary crises or the terrible boredom of conformity.

[5] Sheviakov and Redl, *op. cit.,* pp. 45–46. Reprinted by permission.

What is the alternative? We suggest, as previously, that in the light of viewing discipline and learning as synonymous, we must alter the teaching-learning situation to improve the class morale and its behavior. In contrast to the previous class, consider this sequence of discussion in a classroom subgroup under the leadership of a student:

EDITH: Is everyone who is supposed to be in our group here now?

JACK: Tom was going to be in our group, but he decided that he would rather work on the problem of how to prevent juvenile delinquency.

DON: Well, then I guess we're all here. How about having Bill act as chairman of the group?

STANLEY: I second that. How about the rest of you? In favor? (All heads nod except Bill's. He shakes his violently, but agrees to take the job. He appoints Shirley to act as secretary for the group.)

BILL: Well, let's see. We chose the problem of finding out what the causes of juvenile delinquency are. How should we go about it?

MARGARET: Miss ——— said the other day that there are those steps to guide us in solving a problem and that we should try to follow them.

BILL: That's right, but I can't remember them. Anybody write them down?

EDITH: I did. Here they are. (1) What do we already know about the problem? (2) What do we think the answer is? (3) How can we get reliable data? (4) What facts have we found? (5) What conclusions can we draw from these facts?

DON: We can't do all that in one day, that's sure.

BILL: No, but we can get started at any rate. The first one is, What do we already know about the problem? I don't know very much except things I've heard. How about you, Jack?

JACK: My dad says it's because kids have too much money, but I heard a friend of his say it was because they didn't have enough.

DON: I read an article that said it was all the parents' fault.

SHIRLEY: My mother thinks it's because boys and girls don't go to Sunday school and church as much as they used to.

(Margaret and Edith are talking together in an undertone and obviously not about the problem.)

BILL: Come on, Margaret. We'll never get this done if you don't pitch in and help. We've got to stick together. Stanley, you haven't said anything yet. What have you heard about this?

STANLEY: I heard a fellow on the radio blame it on poor homes. He said home environment. I think he meant homes where kids aren't happy and things go all wrong.

EDITH: That makes sense. I read some place that it was the school's fault when kids went wrong. But I think it's more likely to be the way Stanley said, because you can take a lot outside if just your folks stick by you and things go all right there.

BILL: That sounds as if you were working on our second question, What do you think is the answer to the problem? Does anyone have any more on the first one before we go on to the second?

(Several voices—Let's go on.)

BILL: O.K. Edith and Stanley think the cause of juvenile delinquency is unhappy homes. What about the rest of you?

MARGARET: I agree with that, but it isn't always true. Sometimes there is some other reason.

DON: I read that when kids didn't have enough chance at decent recreation they often got into trouble and I think that's true too.

JACK: I think those two are the main reasons—being unhappy at home and not having a chance for decent fun outside.

SHIRLEY: Should I write those two down as the things our group believes are the biggest causes of juvenile delinquency?

BILL: How about it? Should Shirley record those or are there others as big as those?

DON: I think that's good.

(Others show agreement.)

BILL: The third step then is to plan how to get information about this. It's the end of the period, though, so we'll have to get together first thing tomorrow and make our plans.[6]

IMPROVING CLASSROOM DISCIPLINE

The differences represented between the first and second classroom lie in the role of the teacher, the involvement of the pupils, and the active character of the learning process. In the former instance, the teacher dominated rather than guided, the learners were obviously lacking in interest rather than being drawn together toward a common goal, and the learning process was largely verbalization through reading rather than through varied activities and experiences in the solution of a problem. The chief difference in appearance would be the presence of cooperative and overtly active behavior in the latter case and competitive, hostile, and covert behavior in the former.

What we are saying is that the solution of many classroom discipline problems lies in the reorganization of classroom experiences and teaching methods. We suggest that the problem-solving approach to learning is the basic method of teaching conducive to high learner morale and disciplined behavior related to his individual purposes and those of the group. The method of cooperative problem solving leads to control of behavior in the light of behavers' purposes, is flexible in

[6] Roland C. Faunce and Nelson L. Bossing, *Developing the Core Curriculum* (New York: Prentice-Hall, Inc., 1951), pp. 116–118. Reprinted by permission of Prentice-Hall, Inc., and Dr. Rosalind Zapf, with whom most of the material originated.

content and method of learning and therefore in appropriate behavior, and finally, results in tangible learning outcomes through the solutions of problems—the change in behavior during and after the learning experience because that experience has purpose and meaning to the learners.

All of these facets of learning method are also characteristic of our definition and description of democratic discipline. Therefore we submit that the greatest hope for the ultimate improvement of individual and group morale and behavior lies in the classroom where teachers and learners work together cooperatively on the solutions of problems of mutual concern to them. It is true that guidance services of school, home, church, and other agencies are necessary and important. But the schoolteacher is fundamental to the improvement of the behavior of children and youth. He may at times be able only to stem the tide of forces inimical to the best development of his pupils; at other times he will be a positive force in the reconstruction of personalities and characters.

However, we again say that the greatest promise for his achievement lies in making discipline an integral part of teaching and learning through problem solving, not by divorcing it from the ongoing activities of the classroom or from the classroom entirely.

THE TEACHER'S PERSONALITY AND DISCIPLINE

We have discussed as basic causes of discipline problems in classrooms (1) the conflicts between the strivings of adolescents to meet their developmental needs and our cultural patterns which retard or deny the satisfaction of those needs and (2) the teaching-learning content and method of many classrooms which is authoritarian, rigid, and lacking in meaning to numerous teen-agers. In the case of the former, it was suggested that the teacher alone cannot solve the behavior problems which stem from these adolescent developmental needs, but must work with all concerned, in and out of school, to provide the necessary understanding, guidance, and adjustment for the pupils. In the case of the second, the teacher is in a key position to alter teaching and learning processes so that behavioral problems do not arise from these factors.

Finally, there is one other factor over which the teacher has control. We refer to his own personality and behavior. All the discipline techniques in the world will not assist a teacher who lacks certain traits of personality and character. Disciplinary gadgets and tricks are interesting, can be helpful at times, but are not the answer to control problems. Teachers in training and in service need constantly to study the situational and pupil factors in classrooms which give rise to control problems, but constantly they must look within themselves for possible improvements they might make in their own behavior.

High on the list of desirable traits we place a sense of humor which allows a teacher to see events in their proper perspective. Closely allied with this quality is the ability to act naturally in human relationships. That is, lack of affectation or mannerisms in speech, appearance, and other clearly discerned aspects of behavior will prevent a teacher from creating a false dignity, a fatal characteristic for critical teen-agers. Self-control is a requirement in any classroom, preventing punitive outbursts in the form of sarcasm, corporal punishment, or precipitous discipline decisions. Finally, a teacher who analyzes and understands himself and his reactions is in a better position to work with youth than one who constantly looks outside himself for causes.

The combination of the above personality traits, knowledge of the developmental needs of adolescents, skill in assisting teen-agers toward solving their developmental problems, and finally a commitment in the classroom to democratic procedures in the solution of meaningful problems will put a teacher well on the way toward intelligent and humane discipline of pupils.

SOME DISCIPLINE CASES TO PONDER

We believe that to this point we have given the basic understandings and principles which should underlie the development of discipline in democratic schools. Adolescent behavior has many causes, some of which are outside the control of the school. Increasingly the school is cooperating with other agencies and institutions to effect the best possible solutions of problems in aberrant adolescent behavior. And yet teachers may expect control problems in the classroom to continue, either because all causes outside the classroom are not known and treated or because the intraclass situation is not conducive, and perhaps never can be, to perfect behavior as seen by the teacher.

What we are saying is that teachers must expect in the daily routine of living and working with 150 or more teen-agers a day to face some problems in student control. Some of these represent serious social and personal dislocations and need referral to competent specialists within or without the school. More of these instances represent chance combination of factors which produce irritating but not serious problems, requiring patience and a sense of humor on the part of the teacher for their adjustment. And finally, there are problems created by teachers and the learning situation by lack of motivation, failure to provide for individual differences, and other aspects of an inadequate teaching and learning situation.

The following brief descriptions of discipline problems come from students preparing to be teachers. They are recollections of classroom experiences which they had while in high school, and can serve as the basis for discussion in education classes along the following lines:

1. What are the significant personal characteristics, group phenomena, and behavior symptoms present in this situation which need to be recognized and understood by the teacher?

2. What are possible *causes* of the behavior?

3. Analyze and criticize the teacher's behavior in this situation.

4. How serious is this situation for individual pupils, for the teacher, for the total learning situation?

5. What other information might be needed in this case?

6. In the light of the above, what improvements would you recommend in teacher behavior, classroom arrangements, learning situations, or other factors which you believe have a relation to the incident described?

We suggest that these cases may be used for class discussion in general methods courses or for consideration by individual student teachers and small groups of teachers in service who are concerned with problems of control. Practice on these cases should lead to the use of these questions in their own cases of classroom control.

Richard:

Roosevelt High School had been in session for less than a week when our homeroom teacher announced at the beginning of our homeroom period that she had received word from the principal's office that a new boy was starting school and had been assigned to our room. Just as she finished her sentence, the door opened and we all turned in unison toward the back to witness the new arrival. He was an extremely tall boy for his age, who evidently was passing through the awkward stage. Our teacher, Miss Larkin, smiled at him and said graciously, "You must be Richard Jones; we've all been looking forward to meeting you."

Perhaps a less self-conscious boy or girl would have been sufficiently in control of the situation to respond in an acceptable manner, but not so with Richard. He mumbled something under his breath and began to move toward the front of the room. He never quite made it, as he tripped over the outstretched leg of one of the other students and fell flat on his face with his long, clumsy legs sprawled out in a ridiculous manner. One of the boys began to guffaw. The other boys followed him. Many of the girls began to titter and giggle until our teacher silenced the class room with a loud shout. Richard pulled himself off the floor with as much dignity as he could muster, which was not much, and red-faced walked to the front of the room where his seat was assigned.

Now, to start the reader off with the use of these cases, we suggest a few leads for the six questions above:

1. Richard's awkwardness, his mumbling speech, the group laughter, the teacher's shouting.

2. Richard's stage of adolescent development, the group psychology of adolescents, the teacher's anger, pity, or embarrassment.

3. Shocked by the group's raucous (by her standards) reception of Richard and torn between anger at the class, pity for Richard, and her embarrassment, she shouts down the class to order.

4. Not a serious discipline situation. Some possible serious implications for Richard as a new student and an awkward adolescent, but the teacher's action did not help Richard's problem.

5. This class needs to consider, if it has not done so before, the responsibility it has to help new members feel at home. A person or a committee to take care of visitors or new members might make entrances of this kind less embarrassing for all.

6. For suggestions of improvement, the student teacher reporting this situation said,

Miss Larkin said or did nothing to relieve the air of tension which prevailed. I believe that she failed to fulfill her obligation to Richard as his teacher, in this moment. Her loud shout which silenced us made us feel that we had all been extremely cruel to him, which was probably the case; but she should have realized that our guilty recognition of this fact would give birth to considerable resentment toward him on the part of the class. This was the time for understanding and a sense of humor on her part to come into play, but it did not. She might have said, "Well, Richard, that was quite an entrance," with a smile directed toward him. This might have provoked a laugh from the class that told him we were laughing with him and not at him. And then, "I'll bet that added height is quite an advantage on a basketball court." We wouldn't have felt so guilty and Richard would have been made to feel as though he was one of us.

John:

In his first year of junior high school, John's history teacher was a pretty, soft-voiced, friendly young woman. John, newly arrived in the community, soon was drawn to her. Only an average student, he began to work very hard on his history and even did extra, outside projects. In this he was only moderately successful, but the added pressure seemed to make him tense and strained. He also dressed up for school, slicked down his hair, and washed his hands and face more than was customary among boys of his age. He behaved himself in class until he came to be considered a "goody-goody" by his classmates.

The teacher, seeing this, scrupulously divided her attention equally among all her pupils. Whereupon John began to try other more obvious and less desirable methods of attracting attention. He spoke loudly and "showed off" in the classroom so that the teacher found it necessary to reprimand him. He became the class wit, raising his hand to answer questions and making accompanying noises, even when he had no idea of the answer; and when the other children teased him about his different behavior, he beat them up.

The more he misbehaved, the more unpopular he became with his teacher and classmates. The more his attempts to gain attention failed, the worse his behavior became until he had a problem of adjustment with his peer group as well as a frustrating experience with his teacher. His school work and his social development suffered, and he became the scapegoat of his class and a general troublemaker.

Ken:

Mrs. Jones, a social studies teacher in Wilson High School, felt she had to direct her subject matter to a fifth or sixth grade level because of many average and slow learners in her classes. Students in her class had to raise their hands for permission to leave the room. Her tests for some of us students were snaps! A test, too easy to challenge even the average student, was given on a Friday afternoon. Two boys who were both on the honor roll finished long before the period was over. In their boredom they started talking and laughing.

Mrs. Jones, becoming very angry, reprimanded them quite severely, and in a nervous manner accused them of cheating on her exam. Ken, one of the students, became angry at the accusation of dishonesty and talked back to his instructor, saying, "I'm sorry, Mrs. Jones, but you see I learned my nursery rhymes last week, and so I don't have to cheat on your test." The class, hearing the argument between Ken and Mrs. Jones, started talking to one another and laughing. They were soon making comments to the point where the instructor had a difficult discipline problem on her hands. Ken received an "F" on the test and had to stay after school for a week.

Bobby:

When the family moved to the suburbs, Bobby entered the seventh grade at a new school. On the first day of school the pupils were asked to stand and recite to the class their names, addresses, and hobbies. Bobby rose in turn and started to speak in his high, rather affected voice. The first few sentences were met with snickers and giggles from the class and when he said that his main interests were voice and the drama, peals of laughter resounded.

The teacher immediately quieted the class and asked that the new pupil be seated without disturbing the class. Bobby sat with eyes lowered and cringed at every escaping giggle of his classmates.

After several occurrences of the same type, and overhearing some of the students imitating his voice and manner, he refrained from reciting in class and from making conversation with classmates. Although he seemed to know the proper answers to questions, he responded with a low-voiced "I don't know" or a shrug of the shoulders. The teacher called on him less frequently, preferring to ignore the boy rather than disrupt the class by having to quiet the other pupils. He became more and more secluded within himself, and then began to skip school, taking walks in the parks.

For each of these cases above, the same procedure of using the six suggested questions should reveal differences in teacher, pupils, and situations; therefore, the fallacy of absolute standards, definite "foolproof" techniques, and hard and fast rules and penalties becomes apparent. What is needed by teacher and pupils is a sensitivity to situational factors, personal needs, and the best interests of the group as a whole.

Perhaps a final note on which to end a discussion of discipline might be the question and suggested answers of Sheviakov and Redl: "What do you want to be anyway, an educator, or an angel with the flaming sword? It is upon your answer to this question that your decisions about discipline techniques will finally depend. For it requires one type of person to be the proud avenger of infantile wrongs and sins against defined rules and regulations, and another to be the guide of human beings through the turmoil of growth. You have to make up your mind."[7]

FOR FURTHER STUDY

American Council on Education, *Helping Teachers Understand Children.* Washington, D.C.: The Council, 1945.
An outstanding resource for case studies of behavior problems, theories of adjustment, methods for study of individuals and groups, and techniques in helping pupils adjust to school life.
Association for Supervision and Curriculum Development, National Education Association, *Fostering Mental Health in Our Schools.* 1950 Yearbook; Washington, D.C.: The Association, 1950.
One of the classics in the interpretation of the behavior of children and youth, and its meaning for teaching and learning.
Baruch, Dorothy, *New Ways in Discipline.* New York: Whittlesey House, 1949.
Argues for better self-understanding of adults about their own motivation and feelings as they go about the task of disciplining children.

[7] Sheviakov and Redl, *op. cit.*, p. 64.

Bond, J. R., "Analysis of Observed Traits of Teachers Who Were Rated Superior in School Discipline," *Journal of Educational Research,* 45:507–516 (March), 1952.

Serves as an interesting point of departure for a discussion of teacher characteristics which may be related to good classroom control.

Butterworth, Ivan, "Discipline," *Bulletin,* No. 205, National Association of Secondary School Principals, 38:70–76 (November), 1954.

Contains an excellent check list for teachers on factors which encourage and inhibit good teacher-pupil relations.

Christophe, LeRoy M., "The Principal's Responsibilities for Developing and Maintaining Discipline in the High School," *Bulletin,* No. 192, National Association of Secondary School Principals, 37:37–44 (February), 1953.

A proposal for a positive approach to school discipline, with emphasis on cooperation between teachers and administrators in evolving principles, practices, and activities that promote high student morale.

Driscoll, Gertrude, *How to Study the Behavior of Children.* New York: Bureau of Publications, Teachers College, Columbia University, 1941.

Although techniques and examples cited are most often in terms of preadolescents, many approaches and methods are equally suggestive for high school teachers. A practical, "down-to-earth" book.

Good, W. R., "Discipline in Relation to Creative Teaching," *Educational Leadership,* 10:173–175 (December), 1952.

Argues that good discipline is an integral part of good teaching, not something apart from the teaching-learning situation.

Hymes, James L., Jr., *Behavior and Misbehavior—A Teacher's Guide to Action.* New York: Prentice-Hall, Inc., 1955.

Suggests possible diagnostic approaches for teachers to various kinds of classroom discipline problems, and discusses potentialities and limitations of remedial measures. Throughout, the ingredients of good teaching are related to discipline problems.

Langdon, Grace, and Irving W. Stout, *The Discipline of Well-adjusted Children.* New York: John Day Co., Inc., 1952, Chap. 4.

Analyzes the responses of 414 parents of well-adjusted children about what they did in bringing up their children. Chapter 4 deals directly with preteacher-pupil-parent relations in school discipline.

National Association of Secondary School Principals, National School Public Relations Association, National Congress of Parents and Teachers, *It's High Time.* Washington, D.C.: National Education Association, 1955.

Although intended to be a handbook for parents of adolescents, this forty-page pamphlet should be of value to high school teachers in understanding what makes teen-agers "tick," and how parents and teachers can help adolescents grow up more gracefully.

Ojemann, Ralph H., *Personality Adjustment of Individual Children.* Washington, D.C.: Department of Classroom Teachers and American Educational Research Association, National Education Association, 1954.

An effort to report to classroom teachers the most important suggestions from research bearing on the personality adjustment of individual childen, with practical implications for classroom teaching.

Sheviakov, George V., and Fritz Redl, *Discipline for Today's Children and Youth.* Washington, D.C.: Association for Supervision and Curriculum Development, National Education Association, 1944.
One of the most provocative treatises available on theories and practices of behavior control.

Yeager, William A., *Administration and the Pupil.* New York: Harper & Brothers, 1949, Chap. 16.
Discusses the role of administrators and administrative practices in helping to determine the most wholesome environment for learning behavior.

Zachry, Caroline B., *Emotion and Conduct in Adolescence.* New York: Appleton-Century-Crofts, Inc., 1940.
A standard work on adolescent feelings and behavior which illuminates the teacher's understanding of the kind of boys and girls with whom he is working.

Part **III** Guiding Group
Learning Experiences

The American public school system is committed to accepting all the children of all the people and to providing the best possible education in the light of their needs. This is more than a lofty ideal, as any teacher can testify. It has hard, practical meaning for the curriculum, and raises real problems in teaching and learning method. Chief among these is the question of the most effective means of employing groups in the learning situation.

Part III of this book attempts to assist the teacher in developing concepts and practices of group work which may serve as guides to group learning experiences.

Chapter 7 names and illustrates the skills which are central to effective group work in the classroom. Some attention is also paid to how a teacher and a class may learn these skills as part of the problem-solving approach to learning.

Chapter 8 focuses on the importance of the planning phase of co-operative learning, and suggests both general principles and specific practices for classroom use.

Chapter 9 introduces and develops the important contribution which small groups within the total class can make to effective learning. Illustrations are given of varied uses of small groups in a number of subject areas.

Chapter 10 closes our consideration of group learning experiences as we analyze and illustrate the potentialities for learning when a class moves out of its own room into the larger school and community.

7. Developing Skills of Group
Work in the Classroom

INTRODUCTION

As MENTIONED PREVIOUSLY, we live in a group culture. Public education has been forced increasingly to use group methods of instruction. We live and learn in groups, but frequently we must admit that our group experiences are ineffective and frustrating. Such events are written off largely as inevitable, the product of too large or too small groups, of inadequate group leadership, of poor environment for group work, or of a host of other reasons. Seldom do we find group leadership or membership taking a long look at its own ways of working, with a view toward improving its methods of operation.

We believe that if group life in the classroom plays an important role in education, it merits systematic study and evaluation. What better setting for such a study could exist than in a classroom where the problem-solving method is used? Teachers and students, motivated by a curiosity about people, things, and circumstances, and working on individual and group problems which furnish goals and purposes controlling individual and group behavior, should also consider the means by which they hope to attain their purposes. And this is no small task!

In our concern for the end product of a learning experience, we infrequently evaluate it in terms of how well the group planned and organized its procedures. If we do show concern about these matters, it frequently comes too late to do anything constructive about them. A class and a teacher engaged in the problem-solving approach to learning will take into account *at the outset* of a learning experience their "ways of working." Decisions will be made on the appropriateness of various individual and group efforts, but always related to

187

the purposes in mind. Such planning will avoid indiscriminate use of techniques such as panels, discussion groups, debates, and the like. Techniques will not become ends in themselves but will be related to goals. Evaluation of the total experience at the end will be more significant because all concerned will be in a better position to answer, "How could we have approached this problem better? How better could we have organized our group for learning?"

Only in the scientific approach to teaching and learning does this concern for group process become an integral part of the learning experience. It does not become the end in itself, but assumes its rightful place in planning, organizing, and implementing a cooperatively designed classroom lesson, unit of work, or year's program.

It seems to us that until teachers do recognize the importance of the group skills required for planning and executing classroom activities, the old mistakes will continue to be made because insufficient attention will be paid to these matters. In the problem-solving method they fit naturally into the scheme of things when questions about methods of attaining goals are raised following the cooperative defining of problems by teachers and pupils. The purpose of this chapter is to propose and describe certain skills involved in cooperative group work and to suggest ways in which teachers and learners can make these skills part of the outcomes of educational experiences in the classroom.

ADOLESCENTS' INTEREST IN GROUP SKILLS

Teachers who are interested in helping boys and girls develop cooperative ways of working in the classroom will be pleasantly surprised by their enthusiastic response and interest, particularly if the group skills are always related to the achieving of purposes which learners themselves have set. The following needs and drives contribute to this interest in becoming more proficient in group situations:

1. Teen-agers like to express themselves, and generally in no uncertain terms. Their feelings and ideas often lie very close to the surface, but their expression of them is often faltering and frustrating. Opportunities to express themselves in situations where they know their opinions are accepted can be a factor in helping them mature, particularly if they see their ideas related to a group problem or interest.

2. Adolescents are very conscious of their own peer group and its judgments, and are eager to secure its recognition and approval. Often boys and girls clamor for recognition by attention-getting behavior

PLATE 17. COOPERATIVE SKILLS ARE NEEDED IN PROBLEM SOLVING.
Even in modern laboratories, the team approach is used. (Courtesy
of the Long Beach, California, Public Schools)

unrelated to the group's purposes. They need help in knowing how to
gain the respect of their peers in a fashion which is constructive for
the best interests of the group.

3. Teen-agers need to have an opportunity to test their ideas. Adults
frequently despair of adolescents' erratic thinking and their garbled
expression of ideas. The need is obvious, but often we do not give
boys and girls the chance to clarify and organize their thinking. Good
group discussion and activity assist learners in doing this.

4. Adolescents test the limits of their independence of adults. They
typically resent adult domination and yet need support from their
peers. The group setting of the classroom can provide boys and girls
with not only a feeling of growing independence but also the need for
putting this new responsibility to constructive purposes.

We suggest to the reader that he check his own classroom experience as a learner against these four needs. Usually the lecture method

or the assign-recite-test procedure characterized classroom practice. We submit that these teaching-learning approaches do not give adolescents the opportunity to satisfy the above needs. In fact, more often than not, learners in traditional classrooms are thwarted in respect to these drives.

LEADER-MEMBER ROLES IN GROUP WORK

We hope that our introductory remarks in this chapter have created a readiness in the reader for a consideration of certain concepts of group work in the classroom which at first reading may seem rather theoretical. It is true that some of the ideas presented are drawn from a new area of the social sciences—group dynamics. This recent development is so new that its theories and practices are still in a formative stage. The interesting fact is that many of these theories and proposed procedures seem obvious, and are things which many teachers have done for a long time without dignifying them with new terminology such as we use. As a result, we hope that the reader will not be distracted from our central purpose of providing a systematic treatment of the need for and the means of direct attention to skill development in classroom group work.

At the outset it should be said that we do not argue for sharp distinctions between leader and group-member roles and responsibilities. Throughout this book our theme is cooperative problem solving as a basic method of teaching and learning. Therefore we do not assign to certain kinds of people attitudes and behavior which are those of leaders only, nor do we ascribe certain skills and understandings alone to other kinds of persons known as followers or members.

Our concept of leadership is based less on personality traits, general intelligence, and other inherited characteristics, and more on situational factors which demand varied kinds of skills, attitudes, habits, understandings, and appreciations seldom found in one individual. That is, leadership is a function earned by a person from a group which sees this person as possessing the kinds of skills, facts, attitudes, and understandings necessary to assist the group in achieving its purpose at the time. This concept argues against a generalized kind of leadership for all times, places, and circumstances. It suggests the sharing of leadership depending on the situation which a group faces.

This is in contrast to many classrooms where the rigidity of the curriculum and classroom procedures allows only certain kinds of people to emerge as leaders, capable of teaching in rather narrow areas of learning activity. The resulting dichotomy between leaders

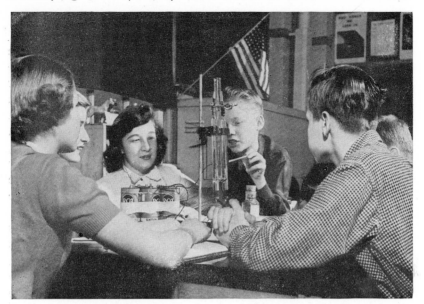

PLATE 18. PUPILS CAN SERVE AS TEACHER'S ASSISTANTS. Mass education demands the use of emerging classroom leaders. (Courtesy of the Board of Education, City of New York)

and followers is a natural product of classroom teaching and learning methods which are inflexible by nature of their not being cooperative or problem-centered.

This does not mean that factors of intelligence and personality do not play a part in either assigned or emerging leadership. Rather, situational leadership gives greater recognition and acceptance to individual differences, and is more appropriate to the flexibility which is both a prerequisite and an outgrowth of cooperative problem solving. Therefore as we discuss leader-member roles we intend the hyphenation to suggest skills, understanding, facts, and attitudes which all group members should develop to the level of their ability. These leadership attributes will then be available as leadership passes around the group, depending on the nature of the problem and the kinds of special competencies evidenced by the leader of the moment. The resulting level of leadership potential in the group will be higher as a result; and in the process of utilizing more people, more leadership will be developed—something which is constantly being urged as a purpose of education.

What then are some of the crucial skills which pupils should develop as effective class leader-members?

THE LEADER GIVES FACTS AND OPINIONS

Any member of a classroom group should at times be in a position to give facts or opinions pertinent to the solution of a problem. The fact-giver may draw upon generalizations from his own experience, or he may furnish findings which he has at his disposal from study in preparation for the solution of the problem. In either case he is a leader because, by our definition, he assists the group in the solution of a problem. Pupils should be encouraged to share facts and opinions, not in the spirit of competition for recognition or of proving that they have studied their lesson. These latter elements may creep into the classroom climate, but are not consistent with the spirit of cooperative problem solving.

Pupils should be able to differentiate between facts and opinions and be urged to label their contributions as one or the other. This process will lead to greater importance attached by pupils to sources of facts and to the nature of and reason for opinions. Certainly no greater outcome could be cherished for learners than the ability to sift and evaluate facts and opinions, not for the skill as an end in itself but as a means to better solutions of problems.

THE LEADER AS A SEEKER OF FACTS AND OPINIONS

Closely related to the giving of facts and opinions is the inclination and skill in asking for facts and opinions. Class members who learn to ask questions, either of fact or opinion, are assuming a leadership role because they are pushing for necessary data to assist in the solution of a problem. Here desire for recognition is less a prompting motivation for seeking information than in the case of giving facts or opinions. Too often pupils are reticent in asking questions because they are fearful of the reactions of teachers or classmates to what they feel might be interpreted as ignorance, lack of intelligence, or failure to have studied the lesson.

The general classroom climate has much to do with the degree of freedom pupils feel in seeking information or opinions. In a classroom geared to the solution of problems, the spirit of inquiry is viewed by teachers and pupils as a real asset and contribution to the class.

The following example of a class discussion may serve to give the reader the significance of the leadership role in giving and seeking of facts and opinions:

TEACHER: I believe Louise is chairman of our discussion today on the problem, "How may we secure better health for our citizens?" Will you take over, Louise?

LOUISE: Yesterday we decided that our interest today would be the discussion of present facilities and conditions for promoting better health in our country. Am I right?

JOHN: Yes, but I have a note here that we also decided to compare various parts of the country and to compare the United States with other countries.

LOUISE: I believe that's right. Does the rest of the class agree that we have this topic for today? (Pause) O.K. I see heads nodding, so let's go.

BILL: After school yesterday I was getting a cold shot at my doctor's office, so I asked him what he thought was the best way of promoting health. He said we ought to have a law requiring everyone to have a medical examination every six months. I think he was kidding about the law, but. . .

ANDY: Sure, a doctor would say that. Think of the business he would get.

BILL: I think he would lose business. The early diagnosis of health problems might prevent operations, sickness. . . .

MARY: Anyway, how could we get enough doctors to do this when now we have to wait weeks for appointments?

BILL: Oh, you can always get a doctor if you are sick enough.

MARY: But that's not what we were talking about.

LOUISE: It seems that we are talking about a lot of things. Let's get back to Bill's first idea—more frequent health examinations. Is that the answer?

JOE: There are many people who can't afford examinations periodically and treatment which they may need. I think they could if somehow they could be insured for health needs, including examinations.

SUE: Why not take out of every person's wages a certain amount, just like withholding tax. Then the government could furnish these health services to everybody.

LOUISE: Are you suggesting compulsory insurance or what's the name—socialized medicine?

SUE: England has that system and it works very well.

BILL: Where did you find that out?

SUE: My aunt in England wrote us saying that she had just had an operation which cost her practically nothing.

JOE: I saw a TV show on that kind of stuff—and boy, did it take apart the idea! They said the service was poor, you had to go to the doctor the government assigned. . . .

ANDY: Probably just propaganda to scare us away from that kind of doctors and government control.

BILL: Is there any place we can get facts on both sides of this question?

ANNE: My uncle is an officer in the County Medical Society. Maybe he would talk to us.

SUE: I don't know of anybody except my aunt in England who could tell us—but maybe we can find some books or magazines in the library.

LOUISE: Before we go on to other possibilities of improving health, can we have some volunteers to check on getting some facts, either from people or books?

This hypothetical example of what might transpire in a classroom where fact finding and opinion seeking are important illustrates the shared leadership roles we have discussed. We also should note that the giving of facts and opinions led to examination of sources and the need for more facts, under the insistent leadership not only of Louise but other members of the group as this leadership role was assumed by other members of the class. We suggest that for such leadership to develop and be exhibited by learners, certain kinds of direct attention must be paid to the process involved in such discussion. After other roles have been described and illustrated, we shall have more to say about how a teacher and class may develop an awareness of and skill in these roles.

THE LEADER CLARIFIES AND SUMMARIZES DISCUSSION

This role, too, is one which should not be assumed by one person. All members have the right and some skill to rephrase what others have said, either by way of summary to help the group see where it is going or for purposes of making more clear certain ideas for themselves and others. This is a skill which good leaders and participants in group discussion frequently employ. Almost without fail, certain members or the entire group take on new interest and enthusiasm for the proceedings, either because some accomplishment is noted or because some things make more sense.

Caution must be exercised that this role is not played too often. That is, the person who summarizes may be detrimental if he does it too often and impedes the flow of talk. A person may clarify the obvious or rephrase an idea in a condescending way. These roles call for sensitivity to timing and to the needs of himself and others.

The following example may be helpful:

TEACHER: And now let's go on to a discussion of the next experiment on oxygen.

BOB: Before we do, I want to be sure that I understand the last problem. I think we said that covering a burning person with a blanket was better than trying to beat the flames out. And the reason was that fire cannot burn without oxygen. When we beat the flames, we really stir up the oxygen supply, but in a blanket the fire loses its source of oxygen. Am I right?

TEACHER: Very good. Are there any other questions?

JILL: I still don't see why the glowing ember bursts into flame when dropped into the flask of oxygen.

JOE: May I explain? It simply lies in an ember state because the burning has reduced the wood to a point where flames cannot be seen. But when plunged into pure oxygen it momentarily burns brightly, almost explodes.

Here is a discussion which may be symptomatic of previous inadequate summary and clarification by both teacher and class. The teacher is ready to go on, but the request for summary by Bob and for clarification by Jill suggests that the teacher's move to the next problem is premature. The class members show some skill in seeking summaries or clarifications.

This kind of situation is often more serious in cases where pupils are acting as discussion leaders. Frequently, they are not as sensitive to the need for summary and clarification as more experienced teachers. This, too, is a role which needs identification for students and practice by them. As in the case of other roles, more attention will be given later to how this is done.

THE LEADER TENDS TO HUMAN RELATIONSHIPS

No classroom is without tensions and conflicts within its ranks at times. Feelings may flare, and cooperative activity is threatened. A leadership role which is sorely needed in schools, and in society generally, is the attending to interpersonal conflicts, tensions, and rivalries. We are not arguing against sincere, intellectually honest, and courageous differences of opinion. But adolescents are often tempted to feel, rather than think, their decisions and actions. This is not to be frowned on entirely, as feelings can be respectable facts too. But when a cooperative problem-solving venture is threatened for its existence by the presence of tension and conflict, all members must rally for the best interests of achieving a common goal.

Humor, summarization, restatement, and attempted reconciliation of opposing positions can be tried by leader-members interested in preserving the group. Consider the following example:

JOE: I don't care what you say. You're prejudiced and stubborn, and won't look at the facts.
SUE: Facts! Do you call facts the things you have been citing?
JOE: Well, why don't you come back with better facts if you know the answers? You can't, that's why.
SUE: If you gave me a chance to talk without interrupting . . .
CHAIRMAN: Speaking of interrupting, this last discussion reminds me that girls are always supposed to have the last word. Well, Sue has had it— at least for today. So why don't we stop for a minute and review what we have been arguing about? First, I think Joe's point is that . . .

Thus, a chairman might stop the rising tension, for a moment at least, by injecting a little humor and calling for a summary. The latter might give the two contestants a chance to cool off and listen to how other class members heard their arguments. Perhaps the basic disagreement would remain, but a setting would be introduced where a more dispassionate look at facts and opinions might be gained.

Frequently, when such development of tension and animosity occurs, the teacher sees it as an occasion for her action alone. More often than not, the leadership of the contestants' peers in restoring a better climate for work is more effective than remonstrances or discipline by the teacher. Such a process requires an awareness of what is happening and what to do about it on the part of all concerned. More will be said later of techniques for developing this awareness and for skills in good human relationships.

The leader-member roles discussed thus far are of the type which individuals play in cooperative group work. Others are mentioned and developed by researchers in group dynamics.[1] For our purposes, the ones we have discussed are most crucial, at least for pupils who are just beginning to pay attention to skills of group work.

NONCONSTRUCTIVE LEADER-MEMBER ROLES

The more obvious manifestations of poor group climate and skills can be seen in certain roles which impede the progress of a group toward the solution of problems. Some direct attention to these destructive roles may prove beneficial to a group. This requires tact and humor, however, lest such preoccupation with antisocial behavior appears as threat and nonacceptance to those who may be assuming these roles. Briefly, several of these roles have been described as follows:

1. The playboy—the pupil who sees himself as the wit of the group, and by "wisecracks" disturbs the group to the point of distraction
2. The blocker—the person who is "agin everything," be it the purposes, activities, or outcomes of the learning experiences
3. The hair-splitter—the argumentative type who is unwilling to settle for anything but complete consensus on everything involved in class endeavors[2]

Again, as in the case of certain constructive roles, the use of humor by the teacher and of group pressure by his peers will do much to assist the destructive group member. We suggest that any group interested in studying its own work processes does well to begin with the earlier positive and constructive roles, and wait for analysis of the latter destructive roles until they appear.

[1] Kenneth D. Benne and Paul Sheats, "Functional Roles of Group Members," *Journal of Social Issues*, 4:42–45 (Spring), 1948.
[2] *Ibid.*, pp. 45–46.

GROUP-BUILDING SKILLS

Up to this point our emphasis has been on the roles and responsibilities which individual pupils assume. That is, these are the parts which learners play as individuals to help or hinder the group in its progress toward goals. There is also a cluster of roles contributing to group success which cannot be played individually but require collaboration if the group is to be able to think and act together. They may be called group-building and maintenance roles. In these cases, too, leadership must be spread for the full effectiveness of the group to develop. That is, in the case of the following skills, the effectiveness of the group will depend on the degree to which all members of the group are conscious of these skills and are responsible for seeing that they are exploited to the fullest.

PROBLEM DEFINITION

Certainly in a classroom group committed to the problem-solving approach to learning, the skill in clearly defining the problem to be solved is a crucial one. Many times a group will define a problem or a set of problems in such global terms that it is not manageable. For example, it is doubtful that a unit of work called "Political, Social and Economic Problems of Modern American Democracy" lends itself to manageable proportions for a group of adolescents. They need help in seeing that the time factor, the complexity of the problems, and the lack of definition about what is involved for the solution of any or all of these problems will lead to confusion on how to begin and how to plan.

Such a statement might serve as an overarching theme for a year or a semester of work in social studies. But at this point decisions must be made on how to limit and define these problems so that one or several constitute a starting point. For example, a more appropriate problem might be, "What are current trends in respect to concentration of authority and responsibility at local, state, and national levels of government, and what can be done to keep our government closer to the grass roots?"

Such a problem in turn needs further definition in connection with specific governmental activities such as education, law enforcement, social security, regulation of business and industry, and the like. If such an approach to learning is made, one can readily see that the subject matter necessarily will include the history of trends in respect to these facets of government from colonial days to the present. But it is geared to a current problem of concern to Americans, and can be recognized as such by learners much more readily than can subject matter taught in chronological sequence. However, all the value of this approach is lost if the skill of problem definition is not present to make the problems meaningful and manageable for the group.

CONSIDERATION OF ALTERNATIVES

This is a group skill which frequently is not developed. Too often because of teacher domination or lack of understanding by the pupils of their role in planning the learning experience, quick choices are made of procedures, activities, materials, and the like which do not tap all the resources available. The skill of a group in considering alternatives is related to the step of hypothesis formulation in the problem-solving approach to learning. That is, what a teacher and class are really doing as they consider alternatives is the posing of hypotheses about how they can solve the problem—by reading, by interviews, by discussion, by field trips, by a movie, etc.

It is important that the class and the teacher recognize the importance of delaying the decision on whether alternatives are to be chosen, or whether all may be used. This is difficult under the pressure of time and the desire to "get going." However, in the long run, the use of time for getting out all alternatives and in careful selection pays dividends subsequently in providing for individual differences and in gaining the most creative thinking of the group.

ORDERING OF SEQUENCE OF ACTIVITIES

Following a consideration and selection of alternatives, there is created a need for careful recognition of an orderly procession of events. In more traditional teaching and learning, this is a matter of teacher concern only, resulting in assignments of both long-range and daily type. In a cooperative group approach to the solution of problems, it is crucial that all class members participate in structuring the sequence of pupil activities, individual and group.

This involvement makes clear the reason for work to be done *in relation to the advantage of the class.* Flexibility in assignments, deadlines, and methods of reporting individual and group progress seems to be indicated. The premium in the decision making on sequence and timing of learning activities should be placed on pupil needs and differences, rather than on arbitrary and convenient arrangements by the teacher. This is only reasonable if we are consistent at this step with the problem-solving approach to learning, and are truly desirous of making this method of teaching really operate at optimum efficiency.

SECURING WIDESPREAD PARTICIPATION

Another skill is that of securing widespread participation in discussion. In traditional classrooms, the teacher "calls on" pupils and secures varying degrees of participation. In a problem-centered group as hitherto described, we submit that widespread participation is more likely to occur by reason of the involvement of all in the planning. And yet there are dynamics which militate against full participation. The shy pupil and the domineering talker are two types who reduce spread of participation. Sensitive use of participation charts may bring this problem to the attention of the class. More will be said of this technique when we discuss methods of developing group skills.

The importance of widespread participation relates to the attachment of worthiness to everyone's contribution, the need of pooled thinking from everyone, and the "feeling of belonging" which accompanies participation. This does not insure quality of participation, which is a matter of individual differences and of other skills of cooperative thinking and action.

We simply are suggesting that good group members are conscious of the spread of participation and induce widespread participation by encouragement of classmates through seeking facts and opinions, by giving approval or at least recognition to their contributions, and by rationing their own talk at times.

GAINING CONSENSUS

Still another skill, and a very difficult one, is that of gaining consensus. The problem-solving approach to learning inevitably leads to the need for corporate decision making. The obvious pattern of action is voting. Naturally there follow majority and minority opinions which create possible cleavages in class attitudes and action. One can always point out the possibility of a "loyal opposition" and of the need for "being good sports." Adolescents can learn these attitudes, both for the present and future. However, one must raise the question whether this is a good setting for learning.

We suggest that a group must mature in its ability to reconcile differences in values, opinions, judgments, and decisions. This is a time-consuming process but should be a recognized need for good class morale. That is, group members on seeing division of opinion should delay voting by asking for more facts, by trying to persuade each other, or by attempting compromise. Out of such activity, mature groups arrive at the point where more general agreement is reached.

This requires overt behavior on the part of class members in registering opinions. Head nodding or shaking, facial expressions, and general appearance often are more significant in appraising real group opinion than a vote. Sensitivity to these cues and willingness to give them when requested are skills in group work which tend to bind members together more and more as they live and work together. Most of us have had experiences in some groups when constant voting was not necessary because we knew each other well enough and were free enough to register feelings to obviate the need for a formal vote.

However, it is seldom that a group achieves full consensus. As a group matures in its deliberations, it will achieve greater consensus and more quickly than it did when first convened. But in all cases, provisions must be made for reconsideration of issues if minorities desire it or if subsequent experience proves the need for it.

CERTAIN GROUP ATTITUDES

Accompanying these discussion skills are several attitudes basic to the effective functioning of a group. Two of them may be considered together—*the willingness to volunteer* and *the assumption of responsibility for interim activity*.

The former is a product of a general feeling on the part of group members that they have a stake in the problems and processes of the group. Too often in classes, volunteering is practically nonexistent, either because of the lack of interest and concern in the class activity or because such volunteering may be interpreted as "apple polishing." This applies to volunteering both for participation in the current discussion or activity or for responsibilities in the future. In either case, the lack of such a spirit in a class is symptomatic of certain problems in class attitudes and morale which suggest the need for a different approach to learning.

The assumption of responsibility for interim activity is even more a test of class morale. To the despair of teachers, pupils report a wide variety of reasons for failure to "do the work." We submit that most of the excuses are subterfuges for lack of interest, failure to understand the meaning and sequence of learning activities, and a general feeling of unrelatedness between pupils' goals and the activities of the class.

In a well-conceived and implemented problem approach to learning, learners see need, reason, and meaning for "assignments"; but even more, willingness to volunteer for and carry through activities outside the classroom is likely to develop.

A final attitude which is basic to good group work is an *appreciation of freedom* and the responsibilities it entails. Many readers will say that the kinds of group activity and skills we have been describing place a tremendous amount of freedom at the disposal of learners. We agree, but add that freedom is learned. Unless pupils are given opportunities to experience freedom of choice and action in ever increasing

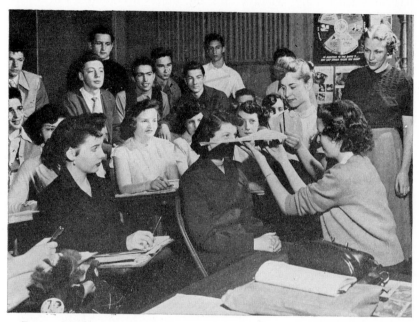

PLATE 19. PARTICIPATION IN GROUP DEMONSTRATIONS MAKES LEARN-ING MORE MEANINGFUL. No problem here of concentration or behavior control! (Courtesy of the Board of Education, City of New York)

amounts, we doubt that adolescents can cope with the still greater freedom that adult life entails.

So we suggest that a recognition of what freedom means for the individual and what limits and responsibilities are attendant upon freedom is basic to good group work. We begin as teachers by granting freedom and making the grant explicit, together with what it involves in responsibility to individuals and the group. This is only a beginning, however, as eventually the adolescent must learn how to take freedom without specific grant or supervision. This is the mark of maturity, both for individuals and groups. But the crucial point is that constant recognition and evaluation must be given to the factor of freedom in the classroom procedures and environment lest learners begin to take it for granted. This progressive achieving of freedom has as its ultimate goal the self-discipline which we prize so highly.

GENERALIZING AND EVALUATING

In any cooperative problem-solving approach to learning, all that has preceded is only "window dressing" unless it culminates in learning. That is, in the scientific method the point at which generalizations are made from reading, research, field trips, interviews, tests, and other forms of learning activity becomes the stage at which we learn. This is a personal, private outcome for the individual which cannot be completely measured, no matter how extensive the battery of tests. But we often fail to use an important device of group generalization, that is, pooling the individual reactions to an educational experience, both for comparison purposes and for supplementing the learnings of each other. The method is group discussion, but the nature of the discussion calls for special skills in weighing sources and kinds of data, in judging conflicting data, and most important, in asking and answering questions such as, "What does all this mean? for me? for others? for all of us? for my family? for my future? for the state, nation, world? What can I or we do about it?"

This is the pay-off—the development of meanings, the implications for behavior. It is the most sophisticated skill for individuals and groups to develop, and requires patience and practice from teachers and learners alike. Without the development of this skill, however, and explicit outcomes emanating from the skill of generalizing, all that precedes this step is meaningless as far as real learning is concerned. It may serve to keep pupils busy and even interested up to a point. But learning does not follow unless this kind of generalization and application takes place as a culmination. In other words, the problem which motivates all the activity really is not solved.

Any teacher and group falls short of the potentialities of cooperative group work if they do not incorporate in their planning some provision for discussion of the generalizations from a learning experience. It is true that tests, written work, reports, and other forms of evaluation give clues to teachers and learners on the nature and extent of learning. But these contrived measures of learning at best are status indicators of the moment and are less suggestive of permanent gains in facts, attitudes, and behavior. We need a direct attack through discussion of the *meanings* of the educative experience to reinforce them. If some outcomes cherished by the teacher do not become apparent in such discussion, it signifies that they were not meaningful to the learners. This suggests that the nature of the experience was inappropriate or that the outcomes were too elementary or advanced to be grasped as significant by the learners. In either case the teacher can learn much to assist him in subsequent guidance of the group.

Consider the following discussion of a class in ninth-grade social studies which has just completed an exploratory unit on vocations.

TEACHER: Before we turn our attention to our next unit of work, let's consider for a little while what we have learned during the past four weeks. You remember that the problems we suggested for study were (1) What are the kinds of opportunities in the world of work? (2) What are requirements for success in various fields? (3) How does one go about choosing a vocation?

BOB: We sure covered a lot of different vocations—but I don't think I'll remember much about them except for forestry, photography, and aviation.

TEACHER: But you think you know more about those?

BOB: Sure, and a lot about whether I have the requirements for a job in those vocations.

PAT: Why do we have to study a minimum of six different vocations, and listen to reports on a lot of others? I'd rather spend more time on one or two by myself or with kids interested in the same things.

TEACHER: That's a good question, Pat. Who else thinks the same way?

SALLY: I don't. When we began our study, I hadn't given much thought to anything but modeling. By listening to other reports, I think I see other opportunities as good or better. . . .

JOAN: That's the trouble, I'm more confused now than when we started.

TEACHER: I wouldn't worry too much, Joan. We don't want you to choose your vocation on the basis of this study. We hope you will be thinking more and in a better fashion about your vocational future as a result of our study.

JIM: I liked our tests which we took on interests and abilities. It helped me see that I need to have a lot more than an interest in a vocation.

ALEX: One fact I won't forget for a long time is that employers fire many more people for not getting along with their fellow-workers than for lack of skill or ability.

JOHN: How about the importance of attitudes like honesty?

BOB: Of course. Everybody knows that, but honesty here means things like a full day's job for a day's pay. I never thought of it that way before.

Here is reflected a wide variety of learnings, many of which could hardly be measured by objective tests. Even if they were measurable, it is unreasonable to expect uniformity in learning or expression of what was learned. Such a discussion allows for reinforcement of learnings already present, some initial learning by sharing in the experience of others, and finally a feeling of group achievement as individual learnings are pooled and compared.

Note, too, that in this discussion the products of the learning experiences were not divorced from the process. Pat was critical of a certain procedure and called for an evaluation of it. As pointed out previously, this kind of evaluation is more likely to take place when pupils and teachers have cooperatively planned goals and procedures. Ultimately, as a problem-solving group becomes more sophisticated, it will pay as much attention to the evaluation of learning procedures as to outcomes. Therein lies the best hope for progressive, intelligent improvement of learning processes, and thereby of learning outcomes.

HOW MAY GROUP SKILLS BE DEVELOPED?

Up to this point we have defined and illustrated certain skills of cooperative group work which seem basic to the efficiency of a problem-solving class. Many teachers can see the efficacy of such abilities and fervently desire to incorporate them into their classrooms. However, they are doubtful about methods of initiating such activity and of sustaining effort along these lines. Attention will now be given to some suggestions for moving in the direction of these kinds of skills and attitudes.

BREAKING THE ICE

Depending upon the teacher's knowledge and experience in group procedures and the previous experience of the class about which he may know, it may be wise to begin in a small way to plan cooperatively and to focus attention on group skills. Too abrupt a shift from the experience of other classes may prove to be disconcerting to teachers and pupils alike. However, we believe that an early start in the life of a class is necessary before old patterns of authoritarian, individualistic, and competitive activities become established.

Most teachers begin a school year by talking about the total year's work in terms of goals, subject matter, materials, evaluation, standards, and the like. Seldom, however, is there any attention paid to ways of working. Teachers and pupils easily fall into an expected pattern of assign-recite-test. Although most teachers cannot suddenly change to the extent of involving pupils in setting goals based on their individual or common interests, we believe a small start can be made in asking for their assistance on how to study a topic, how to collect information, how to report, and such procedural matters. This, too, may be surprising or even disconcerting to pupils, and the teacher must be able to convince the class of his sincerity. He can point out that he believes pupils have good ideas, that he welcomes variety too, and that there are many ways of learning.

It may be worth while to demonstrate a variety of activities on a narrow segment of a learning experience, for example, how does our society recognize and provide for old age? Individuals and/or groups may be assigned to get information on this topic through a variety of media—books, movies, and interviews of aged people or welfare officials.

Sharing the learnings from these varied experiences may create acceptance both of the teacher's sincerity and of the efficacy of various methods. It may well be that at this point the teacher and class can see no opportunity for cooperative planning other than procedures to achieve preordained objectives. Nevertheless, the ice has been broken and as this climate is fostered subsequent expansion of cooperation is possible.

Thus, we suggest that the most realistic approach to the initiation of cooperative group work is on a small scale, devoted to a consideration of ways of arriving at the facts, skills, attitudes, and understandings necessary to achieve goals set by someone other than the learners themselves.

DEVELOPMENT OF LEADER-MEMBER ROLES

One dilemma facing the teacher relates to the introduction of individual roles in group work. We began by suggesting that a focus on a task of the group—the establishment of learning activities and procedures—might be the least difficult way of initiating group deliberation. Although this step is not in proper sequence for the cooperative problem-solving approach to learning, it is probably easiest from the standpoint of teacher and pupil security. A next step might be to move in the direction of establishing group goals by the group itself. This is a big step, however, and may run completely counter to pupil expectations, community traditions, or legal curriculum provisions. Furthermore, any attempt at cooperative planning, even at the less difficult level of procedure planning, soon makes the group recognize certain individual deficiencies in group skills. Therefore we suggest a logical next step may be some attention to leader-member roles.

It is likely that most groups in their initial attempt at group planning will experience some frustration. More often than not, competition and antagonisms may develop, or withdrawal and apathy may be present. Continuous group evaluation of these early attempts at group planning will make explicit individual behavior which inhibits the group.

Fact and Opinion Roles. At this point the teacher can characterize certain roles which we have described earlier in this chapter. The tags of *fact-giver, fact-seeker, opinion-giver,* and *opinion-seeker* can be suggested with appropriate behavior in each case and their contributions to group work. Simple illustrations of verbal behavior can be put on the board as follows:

FACT-GIVER. There are several books in the library on this topic.

FACT-SEEKER. What do we have to furnish the class by tomorrow?

OPINION-GIVER. I think books are better sources of information than interviews.

OPINION-SEEKER. Do you think we should try to get Dr. Johnson to speak to the class?

Although these four roles may appear to be rather stilted in this form of presentation, they can serve to clarify four kinds of verbal behavior which contribute to group thinking and action. However, these roles can be vitalized by the use of role playing before the total group.

This device calls for a deliberate "acting out" of these roles to make more apparent how they operate to move a group ahead. In any class there will be some members who are more verbal than others, more able and willing to subject themselves to this kind of practice before a group, and therefore more suitable persons to be selected or to volunteer for role playing. Two alternative suggestions may be made by the teacher. One is to act out impromptu a group discussion on some simple problem such as, "How shall we divide responsibility for our report tomorrow?" Or it may be wise for the first time to ask a group to rehearse such a scene before presenting it the next day.

In either case, we can expect varying degrees of skill to be exhibited in these roles. The important thing to remember is that "the play is *not* the thing." By that we mean that too much attention should not be focused on the length or the quality of the role playing. The learning comes from the analysis through discussion after the role playing has taken place for perhaps two or three minutes. Questions should be raised such as, "How typical was this scene of the problems we faced when we tried to plan? What examples of specific roles can you point out? What ones seem overplayed? underplayed? How might this situation have been improved?"

Such objective questioning by teacher and class of the role-players and of each other can do much to make these roles more tangible and meaningful for the group. The teacher has a special responsibility as a more mature person to point out the strengths and limitations of role

PLATE 20. ROLE PLAYING MAY MAKE JOB INTERVIEWS EASIER. Here the interviewee can make mistakes and learn from them without unhappy consequences. (Courtesy of the Board of Education, City of New York)

playing. In such circumstances, role playing may be used to provide a common, visible experience for all to evaluate, and by eventually involving more and more pupils in it, to give practice in situations where "the chips are not down." That is, in these situations pupils are not really solving problems but are practicing roles which are seen as contributory to good group work.

Other Constructive Roles. We have thus far spoken only of the roles pertaining to facts and opinions. Caution must be given against introducing too many roles at one time. At the same time, the teacher must be alert to opportunities for introducing other roles, such as clarifier, summarizer, and tender to human relationships.

As cooperative group work continues with frequent evaluation of it, certain other problems will be reflected in such statements as, "We weren't talking about the same things. I couldn't get his idea. We spent too much time saying the same things over and over. We disagreed, got mad, and settled nothing."

At points such as these, the alert teacher will conceptualize the

roles for the group, give examples, and better yet, suggest role playing
of situations in which these problems arise. These are more sophisticated roles and may require the teacher's participation in order to carry
them off. It is gratifying to see the nods of approval from students as
a teacher demonstrates an awareness of these problems and some skill
in meeting them.

Many teachers may resist the foregoing suggestions as representing
too much expenditure of time and effort, and as perhaps being too
artificial. We submit that if a teacher devotes as much time to the
development of group skills as he might otherwise in the attempt to
secure cooperation and skill in recitation and other formal classroom
procedures, significant gains will be made. Consider how much time
many teachers and classes use in listening to more formal oral presentations. In addition, teachers expend considerable time in arriving at
evaluations and keeping records of recitations.

The important element, however, is to give "reality practice." Talk
about, but no practice in, the skills of group work will be no more
beneficial than the exhortation "Think" unrelated to the "How" and
the "About what?"

We believe that the role playing of concrete action situations involving cooperative procedures will go far toward developing an awareness of these group skills for pupils. Good judgment must be exercised
in respect to its introduction and the frequency of its use. Without this
kind of practice, group skills are likely to remain as nebulous as any
of the personal-social skills about which we talk much but do little.

Destructive Roles. Mention was made earlier in this chapter of
certain destructive roles which group members may assume. The
"blocker," the "playboy," and the "hairsplitter" are types of group
members who evidence symptoms of poor social adjustment. As such,
they must be viewed in a light other than simply impediments to group
progress. Extreme care must be taken in analyzing such behavior so
that direct attention does not isolate these members from the group.
Personal conferences with these people can be of some assistance;
however, group pressure at appropriate times can be helpful. For
example, early identification of such anti-group behavior through description or role playing may put such types in proper perspective,
particularly if they are seen as group problems and not just as a
source of teacher concern. Some teachers have found that cartoons on
bulletin boards which depict destructive group roles may call attention to such behavior more effectively than attempting to handle it
when it arises. However, like many of the decisions required for the
timing and nature of skill development, this attention to nonconstruc-

tive roles requires sensitivity and guidance on the part of the teacher. He must more frequently than not emphasize the positive aspects of group work. The resulting productivity and feeling of achievement is probably the best antidote for anti-group behavior.

THE DEVELOPMENT OF GROUP-BUILDING SKILLS AND ATTITUDES

Our focus again returns to the skills which group members need for effective participation in group problem solving. The development of individual roles discussed thus far are valuable for group membership, whether the group is problem-oriented or not. That is, such skills are appropriate for participation in informal conversational groups, in groups organized for exploration and sharing of ideas, and in groups highly structured in purpose and procedure by someone other than the group itself.

But even more crucial to the classroom situation are those skills which build and maintain a group which has as its chief excuse for being the solution of common problems. The distinction between individual and group roles may be slight, but certainly in the case of the development of the following skills it is of prime importance that they be seen primarily in the context of group problem solving.

Therefore we suggest that in developing the following skills, pupils see their relations to the scientific method.

Problem Definition. Previously we suggested that perhaps the easiest way to begin a development program in group skills was to gain the assistance of pupils in determining activities and procedures for learning. This is generally seen as less of a departure from traditional classroom procedure than the suggestion of participation in problem identification and the establishment of goals.

However, the teacher who is committed to cooperative group problem solving must ultimately ask, "How may pupils learn the skills of problem identification and goal setting?" It is at this point where direct attention to the scientific method is appropriate. To some teachers, this may appear to be too abstract and difficult for the comprehension of adolescents. We believe that they will be pleasantly surprised by the persuasiveness for pupils of the problem approach to learning.

The first step in this method is a process of identifying and clarifying questions which pupils frequently raise but for which they seldom receive answers: "Why do we study this? What's the purpose of this unit? Why can't we spend more time on this instead of that?"

The problem-identification phase needs only to be tried to be appreciated for its efficacy in supplying interest, motivation, and effort. Whether the problems are circumscribed by subject matter limits or are unlimited in nature and scope, the appeal is there for pupils. They see a chance for learning that which is meaningful to their concerns, interests, and values. Even when areas of concern are prescribed, they recognize greater freedom and opportunity than is typically allowed in the classroom.

This does not mean, however, that they possess the skills required for intelligent problem census and selection. We refer later to the assistance pupils can be given in setting of criteria for selection of a problem (Chapter 8). However, prior to the utilization of such criteria for selection, there needs to be a climate of self-acceptance and acceptance of others. The problem census which teachers may suggest can result in only the "respectable" problems being named, those which pupils think a teacher would like.

Rejection by a teacher of pupils' interests and problems accounts for the difficulty many pupils have in believing the sincerity of teachers who ask for cooperation in problem identification. Such ingrained doubts may be minimized by utilizing anonymous check lists of possible topics within a prescribed area, or by asking students to list the problems in which they are interested if less subject-matter structure is possible. Another variation is to give small groups of five or six an opportunity to list together problems of interest to them. These can then be pooled to form a class census.

In any case, when problems of a restricted or an unlimited nature have been identified, the selection process becomes crucial. Through application of criteria for selection which have been developed by the class, some priority and sequence can be given to the problems for a week, a month, a term, or even a year. At this point, students can be helped to recognize that a list of problems for study need not be final. Subsequent study and discussion may suggest a revision of the sequence of problems, or even the introduction of new ones.

This skill, like any of the individual or group roles, is not learned at once. Only by practice and evaluation of the process will greater skill develop, coupled with a growing recognition of the fact that this teacher means what he says and accepts pupils' interests and problems as important.

Establishing Hypotheses. Of course, this term is probably not used with pupils in describing the next step of problem solving. Actually, the teacher and class turn to a consideration of alternatives in respect to possible solutions of the problems. For example, in connection with the problem, "How can we cope with the threat of world communism?" several alternatives may be suggested. The possibilities of all-out war, of collective security through a world organization, of raising the world standard of living, of peaceful coexistence—all may appear as separate hypotheses or in combination. The role of the teacher in suggestion and rephrasing of alternatives is important at this point for systematic progression to the next consideration of alternatives.

Before engaging in cooperative planning of learning activities related to the various hypotheses, a word should be said about the nature of hypotheses. In some areas, the alternatives may be more action-oriented; that is, pupils may do something very specific or concrete in the way of formal behavior, as in the case of language experiences, science experiments, health habits, and the like. In other cases, the alternatives may be tested through vicarious experience or in hypothetical situations. In the case of the problem of communism, pupils are not in a position to test alternatives directly or immediately. These variations in the nature of hypotheses do not detract from the importance of setting one's thinking and ordering of experiences in the problem-solving sequence.

Testing Hypotheses. Having proceeded from cooperative problem identification to a consideration of alternative solutions, the next step is the consideration of alternatives in nature and sequence of activities which test the hypotheses. At this point, the alternatives in hypotheses suggest alternatives in learning activities necessary to the solution of the problem. Whether these be direct personal actions taken by pupils to test the hypotheses, or indirect vicarious experiences through reading, films, interviews, discussions, reports, and the like, the important thing is to keep the activities in constant relation to the problems to be solved. This requires recurring attention to the statement of the problem and the related hypotheses. Frequent evaluation sessions of the total group will bring these first two elements of the scientific method into focus with what individuals and groups in the class are doing.

To some teachers this may appear to be a rather artificial, rigid format for structuring learning experiences. Actually, there is greater freedom in this process than in situations where teachers choose the problem, the hypotheses, and the procedures and activities. The only formalizing of the process is necessary when pupils seem to be out of focus with the problem or hypotheses or learning activities. They need to know where they are in the process and how well they are proceeding. In every other way, greater flexibility is provided for individuals and groups, and individual differences can be accounted for.

Developing Concomitant Skills and Attitudes. The problem-solving skills which we have just been discussing must be fortified by certain other individual and group skills. Some of these have already been described and suggestions given for their development under the heading of leader-member roles. In addition, there are the skills and attitudes represented by widespread participation, volunteering for individual and group activity, "keeping on the beam," assuming responsibility for interim activity, and gaining consensus.

WIDESPREAD PARTICIPATION

Widespread participation is in part a product of the degree of involvement of group members and skills in leader-member roles. But also important is the responsibility all members assume for spreading participation.

Direct attention to this phenomenon of group discussion can be systematized. The teacher or a pupil observer should occasionally keep a record of the frequency and length of contributions to class discussion. This may then be reported to the group in gross percentage terms. Whether names of pupils should be used in discussion of these participation analyses is questionable. The chief purpose of this kind of periodic record keeping is to focus attention on the degree to which overparticipation and underparticipation exist and possible reasons for the situation. We do not argue for equal participation on the part of all concerned. But in a cooperative group discussion, we submit that greater spread of participation than can usually be found in classrooms is desirable. Having become aware of the problem of participation, improvement can be sought through self-stimulation, through encouragement of silent members by more vocal individuals in the groups, or by a reconsideration of the group problem and goals.

VOLUNTEERING

Volunteering is a characteristic of an involved, enthusiastic member of a group. It is more an attitude than a skill and can be considered directly at some point of the activity phase of problem solving. The alternative is a directive or an assignment from the teacher or group. Although the act of volunteering is largely a reflection of attitude toward the total classroom situation—teacher, fellow-pupils, problems, activities, and so forth—much can be achieved by raising the desirability of volunteering in cooperative group work. If volunteering for responsibility is not seen as a natural outgrowth of personal involvement in the learning experience, questions may well be raised by the teacher or group as to the shortcomings which probably exist in the earlier phases of problem identification, hypothesizing, and ordering of activities. Such questions may at times be answered only by backtracking to the point where involvement on the part of nonvolunteers was lost.

Of course, there are some pupils who may be labeled as timid, lazy, or too busy with other things. These may be valid descriptions of some pupils on their first experience with cooperative problem solving. But we believe that if the earlier phases of the process are successfully concluded, volunteering follows as a basic attitude because the experience has real meaning and value to the individual to the point where he can and will contribute his efforts.

ASSUMING INTERIM RESPONSIBILITY

The assumption of responsibility is closely allied to volunteering. This too is more an attitude than a skill. Often a person in the flush of enthusiasm for a class project or desirous of group or teacher approbation may volunteer for a responsibility to be discharged a day or a week hence. This involves a carry-over of the volunteering attitude into the future. Circumstances or his enthusiasm may change. Even though the person finds it difficult, a good group worker feels his responsibility and carries through to completion what is expected of him. If he does not, circumstances must be considered. If waning enthusiasm and interest are the cause of his lack of responsibility, once again an examination of the problem, hypotheses, and procedures is in order.

In both the case of volunteering and of assumption of responsibility, teachers may feel that these behaviors are more inherent factors in pupils than in the nature of the learning experience. We believe that these two characteristics of individuals, if present to a large degree, are indices of group maturity and of the degree of success with which the problem-solving method is being used. For a group to mature in this respect, it is not unreasonable for it to devote time occasionally to a consideration of these attitudes and their importance to group success.

"KEEPING ON THE BEAM"

The expression "keeping on the beam" is a good term to use with adolescents in discussing the importance of orderly, progressive discussion of a topic. They recognize it as a term applied to an aircraft as it is guided toward a destination by a pilot. Most pupils will also recognize the problems created in a classroom discussion by failure of participants to relate their contributions to the topic at hand.

The role playing of such a development in a class may provide an insightful if humorous experience. Such a "drama" might take this form to begin with:

TEACHER: Our topic for today is the mayor-council form of government compared with the city-manager or commission form of local government. Tom?

TOM: Did you know that Mayor Jones appointed his own sister-in-law as clerk of court? I heard my Dad say that if such things took place, what chance . . .

TEACHER: I wonder if we might organize our discussion around three or four points; for example, what are the strong points of the mayor-council system?

JOE: This system around here sure hasn't worked—I remember a couple of years ago Miss Smith, our civics teacher, said that mayor-council plans in large cities were . . .

TEACHER: Can't we follow my suggestion that we begin by discussing strengths of this system?

SUE: Well, one good point is that it allows frequent elections when people can continue in office or disapprove the present mayor. I heard that in some cities where they have managers, it takes practically a revolution to get a change in leadership. In the mayor-council plan when elections are held frequently and each party has a candidate . . .

TEACHER: Well, it's easy to see that we aren't getting any place in this discussion. Everyone seems intent on pursuing some ideas that he has regardless of . . .

One can see what is happening here. The exasperated teacher is at a loss, and yet the class members seem interested and motivated. What can be done about such situations?

In the first place, it is clear that no pattern of discussion has been determined, either by the class or teacher. At the signal from the teacher, the discussion began, or rather talk began. The subsequent confusion in thinking suggests the need for some outline of the nature and sequence of discussion. Someone needed to get the attention of the class focused on what was happening, and what needed to be done in order to channel the enthusiasm of the class along more productive lines. Even the teacher's plea for beginning on the strengths of the mayor-council plan was not sufficient, because the class could not see the over-all pattern of the discussion.

This suggests that a class leader should prepare participants in the discussion by offering a structure for their remarks. Some may object that this approach limits participants. It does not limit discussion if provision is given later for digressions to take place after the orderly sequence of talk has resulted in a problem being solved or next steps being projected. The task of the group is important and should not be lost sight of in rambling forays down perhaps interesting but unproductive paths.

In addition to careful planning of discussion and the guiding of it according to an agreed-upon pattern, the teacher or a student as a group observer can comment upon the quality of group discussion from time to time. Such an observer, intent on such matters as spread of participation, evidence of group feelings, and "keeping on the beam," can interrupt occasionally to point out things which are happening, not observed by the group in their concentration on the subject under discussion.

A word of caution might be added here. Occasionally, departures from a logical, orderly discussion may open up a new avenue of interest and activity which needs exploring. When this happens, the teacher and class should knowingly explore the new area for its possibilities. But attention should be called to this tangent from the topic, and agreement should be had on the desirability of pursuing it. Such development of tangents in the discussion may indicate a poor problem identification or clarification, and adds further to our contention that cooperative planning should be flexible in the plan which eventuates; without flexibility, we may encounter resistance such as in the above discussion, partly because there was no shared plan for discussion, and also because the teacher rejected the contributions made as not germane to *her* idea of what the discussion should be.

GAINING CONSENSUS

Finally, any group needs to develop *skill in achieving consensus.* We already have discussed the consensus gained by voting and the consensus which does not depend on voting for its recognition. The more mature group needs to vote less, as it has other cues for determining extent of agreement. In either case of voting or of gaining consensus by other cues, the timing is important. Many groups almost disintegrate waiting for a decision to be made. Leadership residing either in the official-status person, such as chairman, or in any member of the group needs to be sensitive to the time at which consensus should be requested. Certain clues can be helpful and should be recognized by all the class members:

1. Obvious restlessness occasioned by the fact that there is no call for consensus, even though everyone sees that the group is ready to act
2. Obvious boredom, lack of attention, and side attractions which arise because the discussion has passed the stage at which a decision could be made

3. Repetition of ideas which means that all that needs saying has been said, but some feel uneasy about lack of action to the point of repeating what they or others have said

When such group phenomena appear, it becomes the responsibility of any group member to call for some evidence of the extent of agreement or for a decision on a course of action. If this is not forthcoming, a group loses its effectiveness in solving problems. Only by analysis of such group dilemmas can there be created a consciousness of their seriousness. Again, as in the case of the development of other skills, role playing, observation of the group's processes by one designated to perform such duties, or total class discussion of the particular group skill in question—all may assist in the improvement of the group's skills along these lines.

Generalization and Evaluation. The final step in the scientific approach to problems is the appraisal of the learning experience, both in terms of product and process. The product of the experiences, which are set up as hypotheses for the solution of problems, becomes what is learned. This is a conscious, deliberate step if it is to be meaningful for future events. That is, all of us generalize more or less from all our experience. The unique function of schools is to make that generalization process more explicit, both in terms of product and process.

For example, a child can and does learn much of simple computation skill by himself without a teacher. But the amount, speed, and quality of learning can be improved considerably by the teacher's assistance in making explicit what and how he has learned. Unfortunately, many teachers are content to settle for a minimum of facts and skills as products of learning experiences. A little more effort by teacher and learners at the conclusion of a problem-solving experience would pay dividends in added facts, attitudes, skills, habits, understandings, and appreciations.

The key to such enrichment of the learner lies in shared evaluation and generalization, a natural outgrowth of the cooperative approach to problem solving. Such evaluative and generalizing activity should be continuous through an experience, but should be a culminating activity also to bring together in a more complete fashion the learnings of a group.

The need for sharing evaluative judgments and for accepting as individual or group values the learnings which are made explicit can be seen from the remark of the youngster who said, "After four weeks of work the only thing we have learned is how to work together better as a group."

The second-rate value which this youth attached to that kind of learning reminds us of how various people perceive differently the same experience. It suggests that broadening and strengthening of values can be achieved by jointly evaluating a group's experience in the classroom. For some, certain facts and skills will be paramount; for others, attitudes and appreciation will seem more valuable. Until teachers give the opportunity for something more than an individual test of an objective type, pupils can hardly supply the kind of evidence on the quality of a learning experience, helpful to the teacher in planning future experiences with learners, and helpful to pupils in seeing the whole range of educational outcomes which could exist for them.

The following description of a science teacher's efforts to involve his class in generalizing and evaluating activities should give the reader a clearer conception of the importance of this phase of the problem-solving method:

Mr. Allen was able to discover much about the attitudes of his students toward learning by asking them to evaluate carefully an experience they had just undergone. After he had experimented with pupil-teacher planning and small-group work in one unit in science, he asked the group certain questions.

I asked them how they liked this group method, what they liked or did not like about it, and would they like to continue it in the next unit. Their opinions on the method were all very favorable. There was not one who did not wish to continue with it in the next unit.

The reasons for liking the group method ran like this:

"We are more interested when we select our topics."

"It gives us responsibility."

"We can study more things than are in the book."

"I like to work with my friends."

"We can talk things over better in a small group and understand them better."

"Some of my group helped me get things which I couldn't get myself."

After work was in progress on the second unit, in which small-group attack was encouraged, Mr. Allen asked the students for another evaluation.

I was not satisfied that the groups were doing as good a job as in the previous unit. The unit is much more complex and difficult. I decided to see how the students felt about it, so I asked how many thought the work not as good as last time. Almost half the class thought it better! About a fourth thought it not as good and the rest were undecided. Those who thought it not as good said that they couldn't get enough reference material which they could understand or that the topics which they had chosen were too hard to understand. The ones who said it was better than last time said that they found the work more interesting and that there were better experiments to do. I guess the background has a lot to do with the amount of interest and understanding. I suggested that those who were not satisfied with their topics get together and decide on new ones. This seemed to be satisfactory, and they went to work on the idea at once.

By asking a loaded question, "How many think the work not as good as last time?" instead of asking a neutral question like "How do you compare our two units?" the teacher ran the risk of influencing the replies. Fortunately, the students were able to think for themselves.

Mr. Allen also secured evidence from the National Council on Education Cooperative Science Test given at the end of the term, which enabled him to write:

These were the results of the test:

> 2 were in the 100th percentile
> 4 were in the 95–99th percentile
> 8 were in the 85–94th percentile
> 6 were in the 75–84th percentile
> 2 were in the 50–74th percentile
> 2 were in the 40–49th percentile

This indicates to me that these pupils did as well under the group process as they probably would have done under the more formal type, and, in addition, they gained much more in real personal and social growth and had a lot of fun doing it, teacher included.[3]

Mr. Allen demonstrates an interest in both the factual learnings of his class in general science and the other outcomes such as social development, greater interest, and enjoyment of the unit of work.

End-of-Meeting Evaluations. We should like to suggest here the importance of frequent, possibly daily, evaluations as a means whereby the teacher can sense the interest and achievement of the group. Of the various devices, possibly two seem to have special merit for this purpose.

First, the group summary may be extended to include such questions as "How did we do today? What did you like most (least) about this meeting? What can we do to have a better meeting tomorrow?" That is, a rapid discussion by the group of individual reactions to the meeting may readily identify satisfactions and dissatisfactions. The group summary is itself a type of evaluation in that group agreements and accomplishments are identified, but more direct statements of how members like and dislike the meeting are needed to insure interest.

Second, to save the time a discussion takes and also to elicit the

---

[3] Alice Miel and Associates, *Cooperative Procedures in Learning* (New York: Bureau of Publications, Teachers College, Columbia University, 1954), pp. 469–471. Reprinted by permission.

more critical statements some learners will not make to the group, some type of end-of-meeting evaluation form may be helpful. These should be so developed and used that as accurate reactions as possible are secured, that a minimum of time is needed for their completion by pupils and tabulation by the teacher or a committee, and that they are clearly understood. We have found a simple form like that shown in the accompanying figure to be useful. A supply of these can be mimeo-

---

POST-MEETING EVALUATION

‾‾‾‾‾‾‾‾‾‾
Date

Please leave your name off this evaluation unless there is some very good reason for the evaluation committee knowing who you are. Check your feeling about the meeting today and add any comments you care to make, explaining why you feel the way you do about the meeting. Use the reverse side of the sheet if you need more room.

I. Our meeting today was:

_____ Excellent

_____ Good

_____ So-So

_____ Rather Poor

_____ Terrible

II. Explain why you feel the way you do.

III. Any suggestions for improvement?

FIG. 8. SAMPLE OF A FORM FOR POST-MEETING EVALUATION

graphed on half-sheets and made available for the teacher's use whenever he wishes to check pupils' reactions to particular meetings. See Figure 8 for the example.

Some teachers are skeptical about the usefulness of pupil reactions, whether secured in group discussion or on anonymous forms. Many adolescents have never been consulted about their reactions to their classes, and it is to be expected that some of them will give exaggerated, ridiculous, or inaccurate reactions. Many of them also will have become so accustomed to the pressure of grades as the measure of their own success that they may react in ways calculated to bring the teacher's approval. Nevertheless, our experience indicates that once adolescents are convinced of the teacher's sincerity and of the importance he attaches to their reactions, they will generally supply honest, thoughtful expressions. Teachers who seek pupils' reactions will have to meet these problems of their lack of previous experience in evaluation and of the influence of the marking system. Careful explanation of the purposes of the reaction forms or evaluation discussions, plus specific demonstration by the teacher of the use to which reactions are put, will solve these problems in time. Learners will then become more conscious and active participants in the planning and evaluation processes.

The test for all of our proposals for cooperative group work in problem solving is the extent to which they contribute to better learning of facts, attitudes, skills, habits, appreciations, and understandings. Much research needs to be done on basic learning problems and outcomes involving various group skills and techniques. But each teacher who employs group work to any degree will be motivated to check up both on the product and the process of such learning procedures.

The usual sought-for products of learning such as facts and skills must certainly measure up as well in this method of learning as in any other. If they do not, further refinement and practice of group skills are indicated. But in addition, the evaluation of other outcomes in attitudes, habits, understandings, and appreciations must be included in evaluation.

The following check list may be suggestive of outcomes which any teacher should include in a total evaluation:

1. Was the level of complexity of the problems such that students might be expected to handle them? Were the questions so open and undefined that students never knew where to start or were they so specific that they could usually be answered by a single word or a very brief reply?
2. Who did the talking—the teacher, a few students, or most of the students? Did the group as a whole participate in the discussion?
3. Did the discussion move forward? Was there some progress from one idea to another?
4. What was the role of the teacher—to raise problems, limit irrelevant material, keep the group from straying away from the main problem of the discussion, or keep individuals from dominating the group?
5. What was the role of the students—active participants in an exchange of views or mere spectators?
6. How were students' answers treated—judged as correct or incorrect, accepted without comment, or used as a basis for further development of the topic?
7. To what extent did the discussion center on the main topic or problem?

Did it frequently stray into irrelevant areas, and how much effort and authority were necessary to secure a return to the central issue?

8. What encouragement did the teacher give the students? Were they encouraged to express their views even though contrary to those of the teacher or other students? Did the teacher help create a friendly and receptive atmosphere in which everyone felt a desire to participate and in which no one was made to feel insecure or inferior?

9. How enthusiastically did students participate in the discussion?

10. Did students exhibit adequate preparation for the discussion? Were advance assignments in terms of the different students' abilities and interests?[4]

By using such criteria, we believe any teacher can more skillfully evaluate group learning procedures and can move ahead toward greater competence on his part and by learners in developing the skills of working together on the solution of learning problems.

FOR FURTHER STUDY

Benne, Kenneth, and Bozidar Muntyan, *Human Relations in Curriculum Change*. New York: The Dryden Press, Inc., 1952, Part III.
An excellent resource for teachers interested in helping groups improve their operation; deals with diagnosis of group difficulties, training methods for group procedures, the use of group observers, and the process of self-evaluation.

Elliot, Lawrence, "Unsettled Issues in the High School," *Educational Leadership*, 8:340–344 (March), 1951.
Proposes that problem solving will inevitably raise controversial issues, and that teachers and pupils need security in their right and ability to handle these issues in the classroom.

Grambs, Jean D., and William J. Iverson, *Modern Methods in Secondary Education*. New York: The Dryden Press, Inc., 1952, Chaps. 7 and 8.
Two helpful chapters on specific techniques for the use and improvement of group discussion, recorders and observers, sociodrama, group evaluation, and the like.

Hanson, John W., "A High School Experiment," *Educational Leadership*, 6:220–227 (January), 1949.
A description of a social studies class which tackled a big problem and successfully solved it; attention is also given to the processes of the group in its classroom activity.

Kight, Stanford S., and John M. Mickelson, "Problem vs. Subject," *Clearing House*, 24:3–7 (September), 1949.

[4] Russell Shull, *Techniques of Discussion with Teen-Agers* (Chicago: National Forum, Inc., 1951), p. 29. This check list is reprinted by special permission of the Junior Town Meeting League, 356 Washington Street, Middletown, Conn., from their booklet, *Learning through Group Discussion*, pp. 26–27, in which it was originally published.

Reports the relative effects on learning of problem-centered and subject-centered units of instruction, involving twenty-four teachers and 1,415 pupils.

Klausmeier, Herbert J., *Principles and Practices of Secondary School Teaching.* New York: Harper & Brothers, 1953, Chap. 9.

Discusses the need for integration of individual and group activities, with many suggestions for specific skills and situations needed for the development of good learning situations.

Miel, Alice, and Associates, *Cooperative Procedures in Learning.* New York: Bureau of Publications, Teachers College, Columbia University, 1954.

One of the best books on cooperative group work in the classroom, much of it in the words of teachers who describe their experiences.

Mowrer, O. Hobart, "Learning Theory," *Review of Educational Research,* 22:478–481 (December), 1952.

Summarizes theory and research on learning as problem solving; of value to those sufficiently interested to consult original researches, briefly reported.

Reid, Chandos, "Instructional Materials and Problem-centered Teaching," *Teachers College Record,* 52:24–33 (October), 1950.

Delineates the relation of appropriate learning materials to problem solving, and gives criteria for selection and use of such materials.

Sobel, Morton J., "Sociodramas: An Aid in Classroom Discipline," *Clearing House,* 26:235–238 (December), 1951.

An interesting account of how one teacher made visible and solved through role playing the problems which a group had in maintaining a good climate for learning.

———, "Sociodrama in the Classroom," *Social Education,* 16:166–168 (April), 1952.

Suggests sociodrama or role playing as helpful in developing communication skills, in fact finding, in problem solving, and in developing intergroup understanding; basic steps in its use are listed.

Thorndike, Robert L., "How Children Learn the Principles and Techniques of Problem-Solving," *Forty-ninth Yearbook of the National Society for the Study of Education,* 1950, Part I, pp. 192–216.

An excellent treatise on the development of problem-solving skills in the classroom.

Umstattd, J. G., *Secondary School Teaching.* 3rd ed.; New York: Ginn & Co., 1953, Chap. 5.

This chapter presents an interesting analysis of various facets of adolescent personality and their implications for classroom activities.

Wiles, Kimball, *Teaching for Better Schools.* New York: Prentice-Hall, Inc., 1952, Chap. 5.

Speaks in general terms of how teachers and pupils may use group work in promoting learning experiences.

8. Cooperative Planning of
Learning Experiences

INTRODUCTION

THE PURPOSE of this chapter is to assist the reader in considering the pains and pleasures of teacher and pupils as they plan together for problem-solving experiences in the classroom. Through the use of anecdotes and illustrations we hope to point up the advantages and pitfalls of this kind of activity, and also to give insight and understanding to those who are not quite sure of "how it works." Finally, we hope that out of this chapter will emerge a recognition for the reader that such an approach to teaching and learning requires some daring, a great deal of faith in people, and most of all, some skill in securing evidence on which to evaluate progress through such a method.

MEETING THE NEED FOR PLANNING AND ORGANIZATION

DOES PROBLEM SOLVING DEMAND MORE TIME?

The great degree of involvement of pupils is the distinguishing feature in cooperative problem solving, in contrast with the teaching methods employed in many classrooms where chiefly the teacher is deeply concerned with setting the stage for learning. In the latter case, the teacher decides the *what* and the *how* of the learning experience based on local and/or state requirements, his own experience and training, the materials at hand, or combinations of these factors.

But cooperative problem solving is not an all-or-none process. We

223

submit that few teachers, if any, approach the point where pupils are continuously involved in all the phases of initiating, planning, implementing, and evaluating a learning experience. Pressures, insecurities, uncertainty in values, lack of skills—all combine from time to time to prevent a teacher from being completely consistent at all the steps of problem-centered teaching. Likewise, there are few teachers who never engage pupils in planning and carrying through at least some aspects of a learning experience, or who never see the advantages of greater involvement of learners in identifying and working on their problems and interests.

Most of us teachers find ourselves at various points along a continuum at various times. The questions we should ask are perhaps: "Are we moving in one direction or the other as a general trend in our teaching? Do we recognize contradictions and inconsistencies, and can we account for their presence?"

Another question which can be raised is the amount of planning necessary. There are many who would say that cooperative problem solving by teacher and pupils is marked by little or no planning, a fact which argues against it as a basic teaching method. "Laissez faire" and aimlessness characterize it, they say. We suggest that *more* planning is necessary in the cooperative problem-solving approach. If such a viewpoint is held to be false, it would seem that there exist misunderstandings of scientific method, or that only lip service is being given to it as a way of teaching.

Consider the differences in degree and spread of planning apparent in the two following approaches:

Teacher A, anticipating a period of time to be spent on the period of Reconstruction (1865–1890) in American history, uses his state course of study and his local guides and materials for the ingredients of his plan for two weeks of work. Opinions may differ on what length of time he would need to lay out his purposes, activities, materials, and evaluation procedures. It would seem safe to say that a conscientious teacher, particularly after some experience, would be able to do this over-all job in two to five hours at the most.

Teacher B, in a setting which also requires the teaching of this period of American history, attempts to involve his class in some planning for this unit of work. Even assuming that the group has had previous experience in cooperative planning, we would predict that a minimum of two class periods might be necessary for problem definition, discussion of goals which might be reached, and agreement on possible activities and materials needed to achieve the goals. We would also guess that student participation might broaden the problem defined by Teacher A, "How did our country achieve the unity and phenomenal growth which characterized the United States after the Civil War? What kinds of problems did it face, and how were they handled?" to "How do our present problems correspond to or differ from those faced by the United States in 1865 and 1920, following the Civil War and World War I?" The greater scope and significance of the second problem would demand much more time in planning for Teacher B and for his class, both at the outset of the unit and subsequently. It is impossible to predict what amount of time would be necessary for all the planning by teacher and pupils in the latter case, but it is certain that Teacher B and his group would be forced to plan and organize better the work contemplated than would Teacher A.

These examples are by no means intended to give a picture of all the issues and problems faced by these two teachers at different places on a continuum of teacher-pupil planning. But they represent the dilemma faced by teachers who take the time to think, "Shall I involve pupils more consistently in the planning of this educational experience through getting their assistance in the problem approach to learning? How do I get this involvement? Do I have the time to use on this approach?" We also believe they support our contention that more careful planning by teachers and pupils is needed when problem solving becomes the basic educational method.

CAN WE USE PLANNING TIME BETTER?

Even though we see the need for more planning in the problem-solving method on the part of everyone concerned, all would agree that there are practical limitations to the amount of time which can be used for this purpose. Too long periods of planning by teacher and group before actual study and activity begin will be frustrating to everyone. The initial "preplanning" phase of a class embarking on a problem solution should be limited by a consideration of questions such as "What do we know now about the problem? What more do we need to know? What shall we do first? Who shall do what?" Out of such consideration may come both long-range and short-term goals.

For example, a science class interested in the problem of community health and its improvement might well settle for such long-range problems and interests as

1. The health status of our own community
2. The factors in our community which contribute to poor health
3. Present attempts in our community to improve health through governmental controls, social agencies, and the like

4. What other communities are doing about health improvement
5. Health conditions in our own school

This kind of problem identification comes rather easily and should not be too time-consuming. Teachers and classes often falter at the next step which relates to short-term or "enabling" goals—those which allow learners to move toward their long-range purposes. Rather than "overplanning" the total learning situation at this point, we suggest that the group turn to the question of getting the facts, skills, and understandings by exploration in books, through interviews and trips, by using consultants in the classroom from the community—in other words, get started on the solution of the problems. This does not mean that the teacher and class will be finished with planning at this point. Rather, it suggests that probably several additional periods will be necessary later on to evaluate progress and to replan.

The latter suggests caution that the classical five steps of problem solving—(1) problem identification, (2) problem exploration and definition, (3) hypothesizing, (4) action, and (5) generalizing—should not be regarded as a hard-and-fast sequence. That is, a class may early in its planning talk about the last step—"How do we evaluate? What may we expect to learn? How can we determine what we have learned?" Certainly, a scientific approach to a problem suggests frequent evaluation and possible replanning. We say this lest the reader imply that the problem-solving approach is a cut-and-dried method. If this approach becomes stereotyped, it can be as inflexible and deadly as any teaching and learning method.

Another factor to consider in planning and organizing a class for effective learning is the possibility for division of labor, especially in the initial phases. This is different from most learning situations where a premium is placed on uniformity of activity among students. By recognizing at this point differences in interest and ability, better provision can be made for division of responsibility in getting started on the solution of the problem. That is, every person does not have to read the same book or do the same thing; by pooling the contributions of individuals and subgroups on varied approaches to the goals, time can be saved. Provisions must be made, of course, for sharing and communicating the findings of individuals and subgroups, so that eventually there are some common facts, skills, insights, understandings, and appreciations developed. More will be said on this matter in Chapters 9 and 10, which deal with guiding the total learning experience through the problem-solving approach. At the moment, our emphasis is on the planning and organizing phase of the experience.

PLATE 21. TOTAL CLASS PLANNING OF FUTURE UNITS OF WORK. In such activity are found the real problems of adolescents on which they wish to work. (Courtesy of the Board of Education, City of New York)

Another factor related to the planning and organization of a group for a learning experience is the differences in quality and quantity of effort among learners and the varieties in kinds of activity. The cooperative planning of a learning situation would make these differences apparent to some pupils. For others, this fact would have to be made explicit and provision made for it. That is, learners should soon come to recognize that although their interests and abilities make them more receptive to certain responsibilities than others, the fact is that learning involves change and improvement in all aspects of one's behavior. A learner should not be content always to contribute in the same fashion to the group solution of a problem. At this point, guidance by the teacher and group is important so that rotation of duties and responsibilities is an accepted pattern of procedure. More will also be said of this facet of group planning in Chapters 9 and 10.

One final word needs to be said about the initial planning and organization phases. In any working group involving thirty or more individuals, there is always the danger of failure on the part of individuals to see growth, achievement, or productivity. In traditional classrooms, the prevailing assign-recite-test pattern of procedure gives the teacher and learner evidence of a kind that something is being achieved, or that nothing is being learned. Since the problem-solving situation presents a fundamentally different approach to learning, other kinds of evidence are needed as pencil and paper evaluations are not as appropriate or possible.

This fact argues all the more for careful initial planning, so that learners recognize long-range and short-term goals and that provisions are made for making progress in the learning process visible and acceptable. Without such provisions, the classic remark of a learner who was frustrated by the problem-solving approach is understandable: "After two weeks, the only things we have learned is how to plan together, where to get the information we need, and how to assemble the reports of our committees for class presentation."

In this case, it would appear that the differences between long-range and short-term goals were not apparent to this pupil, and that perhaps too long a time had transpired without a "stocktaking" by the class. This recognition of progress toward goals is fundamental to the morale of the group, besides being an integral part of scientific method. It may well be the chief responsibility of the teacher to provide awareness of progress for the learners.

WHAT IS THE TEACHER'S ROLE IN PLANNING?

Although more detailed suggestions will be given in Part V on the role of the teacher, it seems wise at this point to consider this question in relation to the job of planning with the classroom group for learning. This question always excites discussion among teachers. Do you remember Jim in Chapter 1? He, like many others, interprets the problem-solving approach to mean a lesser role for the teacher. Such is not the case. In fact, we believe the role of the teacher in the problem-solving approach requires more creativity and makes more of a difference for learning than in more traditional methods.

Consider first the maturity of a teacher. It is hoped that the teaching profession attracts people with good emotional stability, broad interests, and an awareness of present and future needs of learners. As such, the teacher is in a position of great responsibility toward less mature pupils. The difficulty arises in the interpretation of his role in assisting learners to broaden their horizons, in recognizing their needs, and in providing a setting which motivates the pupils without threat. The "telling role" is an easy one for a teacher to assume, particularly in a situation where problem solving is not the basic method and where the "ground-to-be-covered" concept of teaching and learning is followed.

In contrast, a teacher who works with a group on the solution of problems senses early the need for a new role. We suggest three components—the teacher as a resource person, as a guide, and as an authority.

A Resource Person. The concept of the teacher as a resource person is fundamental. It recognizes him as a person with certain facts, skills, insights, and understandings not shared with the pupils, at least in the same degree. That is, in any group of thirty pupils there may be learners who possess certain facts, skills, insights, and understandings not held by the teacher. And yet, by reason of his greater experience, training, and maturity, the sum total of the teacher's attributes is greater than those of any individual learner and possibly than those of the entire class.

The artistry of the teacher in a problem-solving approach to learning lies in his ability to function as a resource person when the class lacks certain skills, facts, insights, and understandings, and at the same time to use class members as resource persons when they have the required attributes for a specific situation. All teachers function in this manner to some degree, but many teachers find it difficult to view themselves in this role consistently. They may not be able to do this by reason of their preconception of the importance of *their* contribution, their feeling that it is more economical of time for them to "tell" pupils, or because their personality demands a more dominant role in the situation. Whatever the reason, many teachers find it difficult to assume the role of resource person and consultant.

A Guide. Closely related to this role of resource person is that of guidance. This, too, is viewed by many teachers as inappropriate. Perhaps an understanding of the word "guidance" is necessary. We suggest that guidance implies assistance in making choices and decisions. If teachers believe that pupils either should not or cannot make choices and decisions in their learning experiences, much of the problem-solving approach to learning is vitiated.

A belief on the part of the teacher that choice and decision are fundamental to learning requires opportunity for learners to make choices and decisions. This, too, is hard for teachers to translate into classroom procedure. It is difficult because "they may make mistakes," or "I know better." Here some value judgments must be made by a mature teacher: "Can more be learned by testing pupils' choices and decisions, even though mistakes are made? Do I really 'know better'—for this group, for this situation?"

Speaking realistically, such judgment must always be qualified by concern for the group's best interests in terms of its safety, development of good habits of thinking and action, and the feelings of the learners about the teacher's role. Most pupils need the security of adult direction, at least at points. Here the creativity of the teacher is taxed to the limit. He must assay the possibility of "letting learners carry the ball"—and perhaps fumbling or feeling inadequate—versus creating a situation where he as teacher can guide the planning and direction of individual and group problem solving without dominating their purposes and activities. The line between the two is narrow, and perhaps the alternatives are not so clear. We believe that constant attention must be given by the teacher to his role in this regard if problem solving is to result in increased responsibility being assumed by learners as they mature.

An Authority. There is another supporting role which a teacher must assume from time to time in the teaching-learning process; that of being an authority. This prerogative is appropriate again because of the greater maturity of the teacher. In many classes when increasing involvement is allowed in the setting of purposes, conflict arises out of disagreement within the group or between the group and the teacher over appropriate goals and activities.

A teacher may feel that ample opportunity for exploration and decision has been given but no thoughtful consensus has been reached. Unity of purpose and action are lacking, and there seems to be little chance for the resolution of differences. Class morale and discipline may be suffering. At that point the teacher's responsibility is to provide a setting where pupils look directly at the course of events and are forced to reconcile differences in purposes, plans, and activities. The teacher may have to exert a more direct influence than guidance, bordering perhaps on what may seem to be authoritarianism.

It is at this point that we may have a symptom of poor previous planning. It may mean that a realistic appraisal of the practical limits of the situation has not taken place. Learners must always take into account the limits within which they can operate. These may include school policies, the time factor, available materials, and a host of other exigencies.

There are such limits within our larger society, and learners do well to recognize and operate within those which the school society sets. In fact, we believe that any problem-solving approach which does not take into account these restraints is unrealistic, and is damaging to the basic method and, more important, to learners themselves.

For that reason, we believe that there are situations and circumstances when the teacher can and must be arbitrary in the best interests of the individual and the group. However, placing this concept in the setting where the teacher is also a resource person and a guide will tend to reduce the prominence of this role. We believe this because of our faith in the ability of learners to grow in the skills of rational thinking necessary for problem solution. One outgrowth of these skills will be a recognition of the existence and importance of certain external authorities which may affect the purposing, planning, and activity of individuals and groups. This, we submit, is a more wholesome view than blind obedience and unquestioned acceptance of authority.

In summary, we suggest that the role of the teacher in the problem-solving approach to learning is a more significant one than the traditional part he plays in the assign-recite-test method of teaching. It calls for more creativity, more sensitivity, and most important, more good judgment in maintaining a realistic balance among the functions of resource person, guide, and authority.

WHAT IS THE LEARNER'S ROLE?

The burden which is placed on the teacher by the foregoing discussion of his role in the problem-solving approach to learning may seem to be a heavy one. We feel, however, that eventually this kind of responsibility will be lightened as individual learners assume new roles appropriate for this kind of educational experience. However, the initial contact of the learner with this basic method of teaching and learning may be frustrating for both him and the teacher. Again, therefore, the teacher is responsible for developing certain understandings and competencies required of the learner. But with this development will come greater responsibility and self-discipline on the part of the learner, leading to a more wholesome and happy situation for everyone concerned.

What are the roles of the individual learner in respect to this kind of teaching and learning? How may they be developed for the individual by the teacher and the group? We deal here with many subtleties of individual differences in ability, expectations, and concepts of self. We need to know much more about these matters, and at best our suggestions can only be pondered, refined, tested, and revised.

The Learner Is a Source of Problems and Purposes. At the outset the scientific method as applied to the solution of problems is offered as a basic method of learning. This proposal has its basis in logic, but even more so, it is founded on certain psychological bases. The chief one is that all learning is gained from the organism striving to reach goals. Between the organism and the goal are certain barriers which must be overcome. As the individual strives to attain his goals, he must surmount these barriers.

Rational thinking and the application of a systematic approach to these barriers offers the greatest promise of the individual's activity being something more than hit and miss or trial and error. To be sure, the individual learns by a haphazard approach to these barriers or problems, but he does it with less economy of time, less safety, and with more frustration unless he happens to make a lucky guess as to the solution of the problem.

One can agree with all of the above analysis of the learning process, and yet not see its most significant relation to the learner. We refer to the fact that the activity of the organism must be in terms of its purposes, so that it will be of the highest order. By high-order activity, we refer to intensity and consistency of effort. This brings us to the problem of the relation of learners' activity in the classroom to the purposes of the activity.

The above condensed analysis of the learning process has been developed more thoroughly in Chapter 2. We hope that it points up the importance of the learner seeing the learning activity of the classroom related to his purposes and goals. One of the arts of teaching is that of capitalizing on the felt and expressed goals of learners, and of making explicit and meaningful those goals which he may not feel or express as important. We propose to start with the former—capitalizing on the expressed needs, wants, desires, interests, goals, purposes—all of which may be lumped together as the motivating forces for activity. We could go to great lengths with what all this means for the problem of individual needs versus societal needs. Instead, we propose to cut through to the fundamental questions: How do we involve learners in naming their problems related to the seeking of certain goals? What is the role of the learner in this process?

Fundamental to this role is the feeling of worth attached to the goals of the learner and the problems he faces in achieving them. This calls for acceptance both on his part and by the teacher. To the degree that the general climate of the classroom is conducive to free expression of problems and purposes, the role of learner becomes central in problem solution. Often teachers, by the narrowness of *their* prescribed goals and their failure to accept and take into account the learner's problems and goals, discourage this expression.

We know of no other way to change this uncongenial climate than to begin the search for and the acceptance of learners' problems and purposes. It may be wise to begin on a limited basis—that is, by involving them in cooperative planning for a limited area of study and for a short period of time. Plunging a group into such an experience without background for it may prove to be traumatic. But if over a limited period a teacher may demonstrate his sincerity and skill in drawing out pupil concerns and goals through discussion and in using them for planning an educational experience, the first step has been taken.

Teachers may also use other sources for clues to class and individual interests and concerns. Interest check lists, problem inventories, interviews, and the other devices discussed in Chapters 4 and 11 as means of understanding pupils—all can contribute to the role of the learner as sources of problems and purposes for educational planning. We believe, however, that in the long run the direct approach through class discussion is most conducive to generating confidence in the teacher and in the learner.

Gradually the role of the learner will become more central in the problem approach. To be sure, there will be variations in ability, interest, security, and achievement, but this applies also to teaching methods which do not capitalize on the learner's problems. Patience, sincerity, and awareness of progress will combine to make teacher and learners a team in building educational experiences through the problem-solving approach.

The Learner Develops Individual Responsibility. Assuming that the teacher and the class members have arrived at a set of goals and purposes for a learning experience, we find that they are in a position to develop activities for their achievement. This, too, is a cooperative process involving the give-and-take of teacher and learners on the appropriateness of such activities, both individual and group. It is at this point that many alternatives are necessary to provide for individual differences in ability, interests, and aptitudes. Teachers frequently can accept the idea that learners have a contribution to make in respect to the establishment of goals. They find it difficult, however, to accept the necessity of involvement on the part of learners in defining the methods by which goals are to be reached. We believe that the perception of learners on the appropriateness of means as well as ends is fundamental to good learning. To be sure, the teacher has a role because of his greater maturity in guiding the thinking of pupils in respect to means. But unless the learners see and accept the means as appropriate to the solution of their problems there will be a decline in interest, effort, and activity on their part.

The latter development is often a source of disillusionment to teachers. That is, a real effort may have been made to involve learners in the naming of problems and the setting of goals for learning experiences. The teacher becomes frustrated when pupils do not follow through on assignments which he makes. The clue to this situation lies in the fact that the teacher typically makes the assignment without regard for the learners' perceptions of its appropriateness. It may be seen by them as too difficult, too long, unrelated to their goals, or in some cases, so easy as to be lacking in challenge. All of these reactions are symptoms of the individual differences in learners and cannot be eliminated without greater involvement on their part in the planning of activities.

Teachers define the failure of pupils to "do assignments" as their lack of responsibility. It can be described as such, but merely describing it does not alter the situation. The crucial question is how to develop responsibility in learners so that they follow through on activities which lead to learning. *To the degree that learners are involved in the planning and evaluation of their activities, they will assume responsibility for their own activities.*

The attitude of many youngsters in our schools is their feeling that they have no real stake in the educational program. It is not surprising that out of such an attitude rises lack of responsibility, negativism toward school, and ultimately a stereotyped, uniform kind of achievement. In such a setting, extrinsic motivations become necessary and important. Competition among learners and highly individualistic efforts are at a premium.

Discipline problems are more likely to follow in such a situation. The learner sees himself as moving toward goals which may seem to be important to him, but they involve activities for him which place greatest importance on pleasing the teacher and doing better than the next person. Such an environment for learning produces tension, and tension in turn breeds relations within a group leading to control problems.

In contrast, a learning experience based upon the goals and purposes of teachers and learners arrived at cooperatively and achieved through agreed-upon activities develops self-respect in the learner and motivates him to do his best for himself and the group. Out of such experiences come high quality learning, both in respect to the purposes and goals set by teachers and pupils, and many concomitant learnings, not the least of which is growth in self-direction and responsibility for one's own actions.

The Individual Has a Group Role. Up to this point in our discussion of the individual, we have stressed the importance of providing appropriate goals and learning activities for him as an individual. This emphasis is sound, because it is he who learns. That is, the group cannot learn for him, and yet it is important to relate the individual and the group in such a way that there is constant interaction between them in a two-way process. The group has contributions to make to the individual, but likewise the individual has many things he can do for the group.

Many classrooms tend to isolate individuals from other individuals in such a way that whatever learning takes place depends primarily upon individual effort. However, it would seem that our objective is learning—using all situations, kinds of experiences, and resources for that purpose.

Individual research and study have a role to play in learning, both within schools and in our larger society. But an analysis of how people learn in out-of-school situations reveals a great majority of learning situations as cooperative undertakings. Competition among the group members is unimportant and greatest stress is placed upon achievement in a corporate sense. This does not mean that the corporate achievement is something other than the sum total of individual achievements. However, it does suggest a different setting for the learning experiences of individuals.

In classrooms increased attention should be given to what individual learning can mean to others in the class group. That is, an individual is not to learn for himself alone, but in order that he may share his learning with others. This applies both to what he has learned before the particular experience in the classroom and what he gains as a result of the particular classroom experience. Many teachers have experienced the improvement in class morale and subsequent learning because a group of pupils has seen itself in the light of commonly held goals. The real upsurge has come, however, when the group has realized the many potentials within the group and that these potentials can be coordinated for the best interest of the group. Learning in such a situation becomes exciting, not only because pupils are taking from others things which they have not known before, but also because they are putting back into the reservoir of potential learnings for the group some of their own individual strengths and competencies.

As has been suggested previously, the elementary school provides many of these kinds of opportunities for learning. It is when we come to the secondary school that we find more rigidity and uniformity in classroom experiences, primarily because learning has come to be thought of in individual terms only. That fact, plus the domination by the teacher at all stages of the learning experience, tend to make secondary classrooms something less than desirable in terms of the individual's expression of purposes and goals, his responsibility for self-direction, and his coordination of effort with other members of the classroom group.

COOPERATIVE PLANNING IN ACTION

At several points, we have suggested that good rapport is a prerequisite before cooperative planning is undertaken. Therefore we assume in the following examples and analyses that the teacher has provided an orientation period for his classes during which time the pupils have learned to know him and each other a little better. We take for granted that the teacher has studied whatever pupil personnel information is available about the students in his classes. Several kinds of general measures of intelligence, achievement level, personality, and interest may have been used to give the teacher more insight into the nature of the pupils with whom he is working. The school environment, too, in and out of the classroom, has been studied for its potentialities for learning, and perhaps certain plans are already under way to improve the physical setting.

We are suggesting that the setting for cooperative problem solving must be warm, friendly, and comfortable for teacher and learners alike. Whether cooperative problem solving is the basic method of teaching and learning or not, the above attributes are desirable. For democratic classrooms devoted to problem solving, they are fundamental.

Having reviewed the prerequisites for problem solving which were developed earlier in this book, we move to a stepwise consideration of the method. However, again we say that these steps are not always taken in sequence by a group of learners, particularly in their early experiences with the method. But for our purposes of analysis and illustration, the following sequence is used.

COOPERATIVE PROBLEM IDENTIFICATION

This first step will vary greatly in the form it takes, depending on the degree of freedom teachers and pupils have. That is, if a prescribed course of study is demanded, either of local or state origin, of necessity the problems are fairly well established and circumscribe the scope of the learning experiences. It is not our purpose here to inveigh

PLATE 22. PLANNING FOR THE STUDY OF IMMEDIATE INTERESTS. High morale and genuine interest follow when purpose and need are seen clearly. (Courtesy of the San Francisco, California, Unified School District)

against domination of the classroom by outside authorities, be it real or imagined by teachers. We do argue that even in such a setting much cooperative planning may be done through a problem approach. That is, even within the limits set by subject fields or courses of study, that which has been mandated for learning can be put in a problem setting. For example, after a period of orientation as suggested earlier, the teacher might point out:

"As we approach our study of English this year, we have a course of study which the State Department of Education asks that we follow. However, it leaves us much freedom in respect to how long we should spend on various topics, what specific books we should use, and so forth. I have put on the front board the major topics which the state wishes us to cover and suggest that we divide into five or six groups for about a half-hour to discuss what particular interests you might have under each topic, what you think we might do as individuals and as a class to study these topics, and what books or other materials you already know about or have read. After about thirty minutes in groups, let's come back together to share our ideas. I will go around the groups to see if I can be of any help. Why don't we divide into groups by rows, and will the first person in each row be responsible for reporting back to us at the end of thirty minutes? O.K.—let's go into our groups."

Such an approach, while limited by ideas of what state or local authorities believe appropriate for content, still attempts to develop a feeling among the students that they have a stake in the decisions to be made about activities, materials, human resources, time to be spent, sequence of units, and so forth. What will eventuate from such activity may be seen from the following outline of a junior high school class's deliberations, which developed cooperatively the approaches to be used in a required unit on transportation:

I. Arriving at the topic to be studied by:
   A. Asking children which of the remaining areas of man's life they wished to explore next
   B. Agreeing on transportation
II. Discussing possible angles of approach and means of securing information
III. Deciding to search for "ads" in magazines; locating addresses in phone directories, visiting all possible travel information bureaus, checking files in classroom and library, in order to obtain information
IV. Writing letters requesting information and materials
V. Setting up reasons for studying transportation, such as:
   A. Gaining an understanding of the development of transportation through the ages
   B. Learning the influence of natural resources, geographical barriers upon land and water development
   C. Appreciating the work done by pioneers in transportational development
   D. Realizing the value or the influence of railroads upon the development of our early history
   E. Noting the use of the simple tools as means of aiding in transportation in earlier times
   F. Following the progress made in transportation by men and machines to note the effect of the Machine Age on transportation
   G. Learning different countries and making studies and comparisons of their modes of life, climate, weather, and effects on their transportation
   H. Discussing reasons for progressive and retarded methods of transportation
   I. Gaining an over-all picture of the importance of all means of

transportation in order to develop a better understanding of nations and our shrinking world

VI. Deciding upon the procedure (how to study it) by:
  A. Hearing many children submit ideas
  B. Listing five that seemed most reasonable
  C. Voting on one idea (Majority voted to take an imaginary trip)
VII. Preplanning for the imaginary trip by:
  A. Seeing the need
  B. Deciding how long I can stay
  C. Planning the destination
  D. Seeing all possibilities of travel
  E. Examining the possibilities for:
    1. Time; cost; clothing
    2. Pleasure to be derived; weather
  F. Deciding how to go
  G. Mapping out full plan of trip
    1. Getting tickets, making reservations, passports, visas
    2. Getting checkups, tests, health certificates
    3. Buying appropriate clothing
VIII. The trip
  A. Keeping daily accounts
  B. Writing letters home, to friends
  C. Sending cablegrams, telegrams
  D. Collecting for hobbies
  E. Observing scenery, people, customs, climate, methods of transportation, industries, products, elevation, rainfall, and population[1]

This report shows the limitations of the choices which the pupils made; however, they planned the means of studying the topic and decided how to share their individual and group efforts. Although there is no evidence of an evaluation of the worth of their work, this account illustrates the opportunities available for cooperative pupil involvement even when the choices are limited. In a sense, the real problem of this group was, "How can we study transportation (which we must) in a way which will be most interesting and valuable to us?"

A science teacher tells of having a little more freedom in his hygiene classes which allowed him and the class to set up the topics under the general heading of personal and community health. He writes,

When I meet with my hygiene classes each year, the beginning weeks are used to plan the year's study under the title of "Health Problems of Society." I try to guide them in their planning, but also try not to dominate. At the end of two weeks this year we had included the following

[1] Alice Miel and Associates, *Cooperative Procedures in Learning* (New York: Bureau of Publications, Teachers College, Columbia University, 1952), pp. 84–85. Reprinted by permission.

topics: juvenile delinquency, poverty, crime, venereal disease, sex education, etiquette, and vocational information. I think that the above demonstrates that a class, with guidance, will want to talk about topics which are important to society. In many instances they will probably make a wiser selection than many adults.[2]

In this instance, the teacher was able to operate with the pupils on much more of a problem-solving level. The problem in part was to remain within a subject-matter field, but the problems inherent in that field were not delimited to the point where pupil choices were forced. They were able to come closer, as a result, to the developmental problems of adolescents which we have discussed earlier.

Most teachers in training and in the field will probably react to the above examples in one of two ways: "My courses of study are more detailed and do not leave me as much latitude as found in the above examples," or "What is so different about these procedures from what most teachers do?"

In response to the first reaction, it must be said that many teachers still are bound by detailed syllabi which are highly prescriptive. For them the degree of freedom and the opportunity for cooperative planning will be small. But such courses of study are decreasing in number, and more freedom and initiative are given to teachers and pupils if they will seize them. This greater freedom is a natural outgrowth of better teacher preparation and of a recognition of research in the psychology of learning.

We also have found that many teachers *think* they are bound by prescriptions of content and method. The facts often are that syllabi are suggestive rather than prescriptive. They are intended as minimum programs; the enriched programs which can be built upon state or local courses of study by greater use of teacher-pupil planning are typically encouraged by curriculum authorities. But many teachers find greater ease and security by offering a syllabus as an excuse for not teaching creatively.

To the second reaction, there is the rejoinder that in most secondary classrooms the process is taken for granted—that process being primarily the reading of a textbook, the recitation from it, and the testing based upon it. In contrast, the foregoing examples stress a cooperative attack on the question, "How best can we approach the study of what has been prescribed for us? Let's cooperate on some purposes for our being together in this class and the ways we may achieve those purposes—but all within the framework of the subject field and, more or less, the course of study."

[2] *Ibid.*, p. 92. Reprinted by permission.

This, we suggest, is a fundamental difference. Perhaps it can be seen only by direct observation of such a class, or better, by one's testing out this approach for himself. Certainly the differences are more apparent when we consider how a class identifies its problem for cooperative attack in a setting which is not limited by subject fields or courses of study. The following report of opinion and experience comes from a group of teachers engaged in an experimental general education course for sophomores called Basic Living:

. . . The central importance of problem-solving and group work was recognized early by the Basic Living teachers and is reflected in the aims and purposes stated earlier. It was also recognized early that the building of problem-centered groups would require changes in the ways of working in the classroom and new roles for the teachers and students. . . .

The term "problem-centered group activities" is one of convenience and is used to designate an educational process by which teachers and students work cooperatively to solve problems related to the experience, interests, and concerns of young people. Although the Basic Living work is at present limited largely to the more personal problems of students, there is no theoretical or methodological reason why the same process could not be employed in any situation where problems of interest and concern to youth exist. We have in mind, for example, community problems such as health, housing, juvenile delinquency, and recreation.

The problems of young people have their source in situations where individual and group adaptive behaviors are inadequate. For example, patterns of behavior learned in the elementary school with respect to the peer group and to teachers are more than likely to prove inadequate in the junior and senior high school where multi-group membership is encountered and several teachers are met daily. Problem-solving may be seen as a process of reconstructing individual or group behavior, reconstructing the situation, or more likely both. This point of view in general defines the position of the Basic Living teachers with respect to problem-solving. . . .

The importance of the problem approach in Basic Living work may be realized by comparison with another methodology. At one time the Basic Living teachers thought that the problems of young people could be discovered through empirical studies and other means, and that when these problems were listed and categorized, appropriate content materials and experiences could be organized and structured in terms of content fields. For example, it was known that many young people have health problems of considerable concern to them. The health content and health materials which it was thought would serve best to meet these problems would be presented to the group in an organized, systematic manner and the teacher would in most cases organize these materials in the form of a unit of instruction on health. Known problems of young people concerning their own bodies would be similarly treated by way of a unit on the function and structure of the human body. Actual experience with this type of prestructured approach convinced the Basic Living teachers of its ineffectiveness in helping young people to deal more adequately with their personal-social problems.

The problem-centered group approach is in a sense the reverse of the above procedure. Two variations have been considered and used by the Basic Living teachers. One variation is to determine, as well as possible beforehand, just what the characteristic problems of young people in the sophomore group are likely to be. These problems are then structured in terms of problem areas and presented to the student group for consideration. Each problem area is discussed and analyzed by the teacher and the group, and plans are laid for dealing with specific problems within the area which seems most significant to the young people at the time.

The procedure in the second variation involves a somewhat more "open-end" approach. Knowledge concerning the most likely problems of the sophomore student is acquired as in the first case. But instead of structuring the problem areas beforehand, this is done with the group as it explores and identifies problems of concern to the group members. It can be seen that the second variation may offer more flexibility in the group work. It has been the experience of the Basic Living teachers that the second variation requires more time and is perhaps less efficient in the light of the total situation. Both variations are currently in use, but it is likely that a modification of the first variation will be developed in the near future as the more common approach.[3]

Out of the first variation, that of structuring the problem areas according to adolescent interests and needs, came the following topics: orientation, human growth and development, boy-girl relations, intergroup relations, family relations. Out of the second variation came a wide range of problem areas such as manners, speech, and dress; universal military training; juvenile delinquency; use of alcohol, tobacco, and narcotics; use of leisure time; movies and radio in our culture; propaganda analysis; communism and democracy; and mental hygiene.[4]

PROBLEM CLARIFICATION AND GOAL SETTING

One of the chief difficulties for both an adult and an adolescent is that of clarifying and delineating a problem to the point where it is manageable, where something can be done about it. Most of us in thinking about our human endeavors, in and out of the classroom, can readily set down problems if we take time to think about them. They range all the way from global-size dilemmas to petty worries.

[3] "The Problem-Centered Group and the Personal-Social Problems of Young People," *Teachers College Record*, 51:438–440 (April), 1950. Reprinted by permission of the Bureau of Publications, Teachers College, Columbia University.
[4] *Ibid.*, pp. 440–441.

The first important step is to make some decisions about the size and appropriateness of the problem. Is it too big so that we cannot attack it within our limitations? Is it so small that given a little concentration we can dispose of it in a short time? Is this problem of real concern to us now and probably in the future? These are the kinds of questions which beg for criteria to aid in decision making. As we said earlier, creating awareness of the need for developing these criteria is one contribution which mature teachers can bring to the thinking of less mature learners. Many criteria will come from pupils, but the teacher has an obligation to point out for consideration criteria which grow out of his greater experience and knowledge. The following criteria developed by a group of ninth-graders bear testimony to the fact that even this age level is capable of doing some constructive thinking about choice and clarification of problems:

1. Knowledge of the topic should be useful to us now.
2. Knowledge of the topic should be useful to us later in our lives.
3. A topic should be interesting.
4. Knowledge of the topic should help us to understand the world around us.
5. We should be able to find enough material on the topic.
6. It should be a subject we haven't studied before.[5]

Equally important at this stage of the problem approach is the need for establishing some common and individual purposes for the solution of the problem. That is, the chief purpose is to solve a problem, but instrumental to this end are many skills, attitudes, habits, and understandings which are enabling purposes. Direct attention must be given to these goals if they are to be meaningful.

For example, one teacher attacked the problem of making explicit the individual goals of her pupils in the following manner:

At the end of a period of personal exploration and of inventories and tests, I collected each pupil's material in a folder and made arrangements to have a conference with him. Since daily schedules had shown that the majority of the class had no out-of-school free time, conferences had to be held during regular class time. While a student-teacher librarian conducted free-reading periods in the library, I called individuals from the larger group and talked with them in the classroom.

During the conference time, I went over the material in the individual's folder—omitting his intelligence tests—and discussed with him: early anecdotal records I had made concerning him; interests indicated thru personality inventories; test scores in reading, mechanics and effectiveness

[5] Roland C. Faunce and Nelson L. Bossing, *Developing the Core Curriculum* (New York: Prentice-Hall, Inc., 1951), p. 115.

of expression; study-habit inventories; daily schedules, which indicated the time the individual had for studying.

At the end of the conference period, I asked each individual to answer this question in writing: "If I could use my English class for working on those things that are most important to me, what would be my goals?"

The goals that individuals wrote in answer to my questions were simply expressed. These excerpts are taken from their writing:

"Learn to explain myself better in talking."

"Learn to be responsible about things."

"Be successful in my future vocation and get the necessary equipment for starting my career."

"Improve my personality."

"Be a faster reader."

"Have more friends; meet people more easily and learn to get along with them."

"Be a good conversationalist."

"Know more about what is going on in the world."[6]

These goals, as stated by pupils, are simple and recognizable. They might have been kept in the mind of the teacher or made explicit in writing or lecture. Rather, this teacher called forth from the student these goals, stated in their terms. As such, they were more meaningful and more readily capable of being reduced to behavioral terms. The means and ends relation of specific learning goals to the solution of problems can be seen in this context. Students are less likely to be doubtful about the values involved in certain activities when they see their relation to the solution of a meaningful problem. These goals and their attainment also provide some intermediate steps for evaluation along the way to the final objective—the solving of a problem.

Without such cooperative planning of personal and group goals and their relation to the attainment of a problem solution, we doubt that teachers and pupils can employ this method of teaching and learning. Either the teacher will prescribe the goals and gain only partial acceptance of them, or the pupils will hold only their own so that cooperative activity will be in name only. Cooperative goal setting is a necessary part of problem definition and refinement which must take place both before and during the activity phase.

PLANNING AND DEVELOPING THE LEARNING EXPERIENCES

After a teacher and a class have cooperatively identified a problem area, have delimited and refined the problem to be studied, and have

---

[6] Association for Supervision and Curriculum Development, National Education Association, *Toward Better Teaching* (Washington, D.C.: The Association, 1949), pp. 55–56. Reprinted by permission.

PLATE 23. A CLASS CONSIDERS PROPOSALS FOR NEXT STEPS IN A UNIT OF WORK. Identification of problems is not enough; methods of attack must be planned. (Courtesy of the Oak Ridge, Tennessee, Public Schools)

established their learning goals and purposes, they are ready to turn to the joint planning of experiences which will promote learning related to the solution of the problem. It is at this point where many teachers leave the problem approach to learning.

Many see the values inherent in the process of democratic planning as it applies to the naming and clarifying of problems, and even to the setting of educational goals. But they find it hard to believe that pupils can or should be engaged in the planning of what they should do or of how they should learn. This, they believe, is the job of the professional teacher.

We would certainly agree that a teacher should be well prepared with many alternatives of methods, materials, human resources, and pupil activities. Unfortunately, the average teacher knows a great deal more than she uses; that is, instead of serving as a consultant to a group on alternative ways of working on the problem, most teachers select for the group *one* way and impress it upon the class. A few may attempt differentiated assignments, but it is a one-way process—from teacher to pupils.

In contrast, pupils can be used to assist in the planning of individual and group activities. The following is an example of a high school class facing up to the planning of learning activities:

MARTHA: Why not let the class work together on the goals everybody has mentioned? Then divide the class up according to goals a few have set. Then let certain ones work on goals they alone have set.

TEACHER: What would be the advantages of the plan, Martha? It would be easier for everybody to work together on the same goals.

MARTHA: Well, if we did that, we would waste each other's time. Some would be working on things they already know.

RUTH: I don't think the plan would work. Everybody will get all mixed up.

ROY: It will work if we plan careful enough.

TEACHER: How would we plan it, Roy, so that we won't get "all mixed up," as Ruth said?

ROY: Well, we could have one day in the week when everybody will be working on goals in speaking—since that was a goal everybody had.

MIRIAM: We could organize like a club and have a chairman and let everybody talk—say, on books or movies or radio programs.

MARTHA: That will give us a chance to improve in listening, too.

ROY: Then on some days we could divide into small groups and work at different tables. We could have one or two days a week for people to work on separate goals.

TEACHER: I believe the plan may work. But does anyone else have a better plan? (silence). . . . Then suppose we begin with the plan Martha has suggested, and Roy and Miriam have supported. If we find that it isn't working, we can try another way. Does everyone understand the plan? (It is summarized.)

The details for a whole-group, small-group, and individual work were planned by a committee appointed by the class to work with the teacher. A week's schedule was suggested and submitted to the class for approval. The schedule included two days a week for the class to work as a whole on common goals (one of these two days the class would meet as a club); one day a week for free-reading; one day for small groups to work on special goals; one day for individuals to pursue particular aims. If an individual did not have an aim common to a small group, it was suggested that he might work on particular aims two days a week.

In order that the whole group, small groups, and individuals might have clearer directions in their work, the students made detailed plans in writing for every separate study. Each plan included: What I (or we) expect to gain from my (or our) study; how I (or we) plan to go about gaining my (or our) purposes; ways I (or we) will use to measure my (or our) progress toward my (or our) goals. In the beginning, slow learners needed much help in making their plans, but as they had further experience in planning, they grew in ability to plan more carefully.[7]

[7] *Ibid.*, pp. 61–62. Reprinted by permission.

Another example can be seen in the varied learning activities developed by teachers and pupils for the study of their home state:

The bulk of the work was "group projects." It was interesting as well as stimulating to watch the way groups were organized. One boy said he'd like to make a chart for future use in the classroom to show how Connecticut laws are made. He asked for co-workers who had the same interest. He found none in his class but he did in another. I met with the groups to help them evaluate their progress. Since these projects were not due until March, there was ample time for reading, research investigations, interviews, and visits to factories, museums, and other places.

The student's plans varied; they demonstrated initiative, ingenuity, and willingness to cooperate. Here are a few of the Connecticut "creations":

_____Three-dimensional scale-map showing state parks, state forests, state forest-fire look-out stations and main waterways, with a folder giving all explanations in detail. (Three boys and a girl.)

_____Scrapbook, maps, and drawings showing the development of transportation in Connecticut. (Two boys.)

_____Education in the state, including colleges and universities. (Two boys.)

_____A chart and map on industry in Connecticut. (A popular choice; five groups selected industry.)

_____"Connecticut, the Beautiful," a booklet containing photographs of beautiful and interesting spots, accompanied by descriptions.

_____Pencil drawing of lakes and mountains.

_____Diagrams showing the super-highways.

_____Scrapbook on agriculture in Connecticut, with a composition on "The Important Part the Farmer Plays in Connecticut Life."

_____Survey of Connecticut State Institutions.

_____Charts showing the types of city government in Connecticut and how they function.

_____Two "Waterbury Industrial" groups had a great field for their work. They traced the growth and development of the principal industries of our Brass City. One group contacted executives of the various factories for information. They had interviews and visits in one factory from the "rolling mills to the finishing rooms." Another group collected manufactured articles as far back as they could get them. What they couldn't obtain, they reproduced.[8]

These instances of cooperative development of learning experiences, following the naming and clarification of a class problem and the setting of individual and group goals, illustrate the potentialities inherent in a group of adolescents for planning both the process and product of education. These are in startling contrast to the teacher and classroom where assignments in a textbook and recitation upon them are the

[8] *Ibid.*, pp. 69–70. Reprinted by permission.

typical teaching-learning procedure, and where kinds of learning experiences as mentioned in the examples are usually for "extra credit."

One final point needs to be said in connection with this phase of problem solving. The point at which activities are planned by a group in a classroom corresponds to the hypothesizing step in scientific method. After a problem area has been indicated and a problem has been defined and clarified, the researcher may say, "If we do this, we predict that . . . ." The test follows—that is, what is hypothesized is carried into action to find out if the test supports or denies the hypothesis.

Or a group may say, in effect, "If we have these facts, we may be able to arrive at a solution."

Another kind of hypothesis is offered other than testing of action. This type suggests a vicarious experience through somebody else's action which resulted in facts or data.

However, in either case, the cogency of cooperative planning of the learning experience or activities lies in the relation of the three elements below:

1. *Our* problem
2. *Our* hunch or hypothesis to be tested
3. *Our* own experience yielding *our* data or *our* facts needed to understand or solve *our* problem

These relations are substantiated empirically in the research on motivation and in the experience of countless teachers who have dared to have faith in adolescents enough to allow them some freedom in the planning of their educational experiences.

As we have said before, there is danger that these steps in problem solving may become as rigid and inhibiting as any approach. There will be many times for many teachers that this orderly procedure resulting in the solution of problems will not be possible. For example, pupils may be encouraged to begin at the step of generalizing, or they may begin spontaneously at that point. This is a common characteristic of all ages—to generalize without having established clearly for themselves the nature of the problem, the facts which are available, or how those facts came into being. The absence of these steps in our thinking does not discourage us from making sweeping generalizations as though we had arrived at them in a very orderly fashion.

For example, when discussing current events a class in social studies may lead into a unit of work suggested by such a series of ideas as follows:

TEACHER: The railroad strike which we have been discussing is caused by the struggle between the owners and the workers. How many would agree or disagree?

BOB: I don't agree. I think this strike is an example of a small group of labor leaders raising a fuss with management. Most of those guys haven't done a decent day's work in years. They are racketeers who don't represent the workers' best interests.

JOHN: Where do you get that stuff? Labor unions have improved working men's wages and working conditions.

BOB: No, they haven't. Management has done that.

JOHN: But only under pressure of labor union leaders.

JEAN: That's right. My dad says that we didn't have any labor troubles until Roosevelt and the New Deal came in. He supported labor unions in return for their vote.

JOHN: Oh, we had strikes and labor unrest long before 1930. This kind of thing goes way back in history, I think.

BILL: Anyway, the laborer had more coming to him in better wages, working conditions, health insurance, and paid vacations. Why should management get so much of the profit? Why, I read in my dad's labor paper that——

BOB: That's the trouble. Lots of people don't read fair write-ups on labor problems.

LARRY: I'm not sure what is fair or what isn't. Why can't we have a debate on this topic?

TEACHER: I've been interested in seeing and hearing your reactions to this important problem. Many of you hold opposite views, and most of you seem quite sure of your opinions. Perhaps we need more facts. How can we get them?

BOB: I'd like to hear a representative of management—say a personnel director from downtown—talk about labor-management relations, unions, and so forth.

JOHN: Why not get a labor union leader in too?

JEAN: Let's get some of their publications—and some regular union members too—not just the leaders.

LARRY: I'd like to visit a union meeting. Do you suppose we could?

TEACHER: Our period is about over. Suppose we discuss this again tomorrow. We have some work left to do on our conservation unit. Why don't we think about this labor-management idea as a possible topic for a new unit? Let's discuss for a few minutes tomorrow how we might go about such a study. Let's see then how many would be interested in pursuing this topic further.

Here is a group which plunges into a problem analysis at the generalization stage. Sweeping statements are made, influenced no doubt by family attitudes, reading, current events, and the like. The interest is here, but the teacher's guidance is necessary to bring them to the point of recognizing differences in facts and opinions, the need for more facts, and a clarification of what the problem really is. This is moving the group to an orderly problem-solving approach even though the spark of enthusiasm which kindled the interest about the problem came from the generalizations bandied about, some without basis in fact.

A teacher may find that classes often evince interest and plunge into a problem approach at other points than naming and clarifying the problem. It is then that the skillful teacher puts the class interest and motivation in the setting of orderly problem solving, much as this teacher did, in as graceful and natural a manner as possible.

THE STEPS REMAINING

We hope that by now the problem identification, problem clarification, and hypothesizing phases of cooperative problem solving are better understood by the reader. The next step, of course, is to engage in the action proposed up to this point, collecting all the data available to bring to bear on the hypothesis.

In traditional classrooms, the teacher selects and assigns activities which he hopes will promote the kinds of learning he thinks will contribute to the solution of the problems he has posed for the class. These activities tend to be limited to verbal, individualistic behavior which can be evaluated more easily than cooperative, nonverbal behavior. Effort by learners is expended largely in the classroom under close supervision of the teacher.

In contrast, the teacher who experiments with the cooperative problem-solving method will in the first place have allowed pupils to name problems and to clarify them. Provision will also have been made for pupils to engage in offering alternative ways of approaching and solving the problems. Under the guidance of the teacher, some decisions will have been made on the appropriateness of the alternative proposals for action.

Even after possible elimination of some of the hypotheses for action, there remain several ways of working toward the solution of the problem. Some activities may be individual efforts, some will be small group endeavors, and others will be total class ventures. Some will be reading; others will involve construction, creative writing, and various kinds of research such as interviewing and experimentation. These are only a few samples of varied activities which will develop when learners are allowed to participate in their planning.

Putting these diverse activities into motion requires cooperation, self-discipline, and responsibility from the pupils. The activities by their nature must frequently move out of the classroom, and give greater freedom and responsibility to learners. Within all learners must run the spirit of inquiry, prompted by a desire to solve their problems. The data rendered by such a spirit and through such varied activities will necessitate much sharing, coordination, evaluation of activities, and the findings which result from these endeavors. These kinds of activities make cooperation so crucial to the success of the entire problem-solving approach that the next two chapters are devoted to their successful development.

Finally, there remain the collecting of all data for generalizations and the assessment of learning. In traditional classrooms the nature and setting of the teacher-dominated learning situation can result only in a narrow range of learning and measurement of outcomes by pencil and paper tests. Reports to parents and records of achievement will also be formal and lacking in communication value.

In contrast, the teacher who engages with his class in a cooperative problem-solving approach to learning will find older methods of evaluation and reporting of educational outcomes inadequate. A whole new range of learning is opened up in this method of teaching, and new evaluation devices must be developed. Cooperation must be exercised at this phase of the method also.

The result is teacher-pupil evaluation, peer evaluation, self-evaluation, and parent-teacher-pupil evaluation, in addition to the usual measurements of educational outcomes. A premium is placed on behavior and attitude changes which means that observation and records of behavior and inventories of attitudes become central to the evaluation. Much remains to be done in this area of development and use of a broader kind of evaluation. This is so vital to the understanding and use of problem solving as a teaching method that Chapter 13 is devoted exclusively to it.

CONCLUSION

In this chapter we have defined the initiating and planning phases of the problem-solving approach to learning. Certain issues have been delineated in its use, and dangers and pitfalls have been described with measures suggested for their avoidance. The fundamental roles of teacher and learner have been described. Finally, a number of examples were given of teachers and pupils initiating and planning their approach to the solution of problems.

With this setting established, we move on in Chapter 9 to a consideration of the use of small groups in implementing the planning of learners and to other uses of small groups in the classroom. It is in this phase of problem solving that many teachers feel the greatest need of help, because most classrooms at the secondary level have usually seen the total class functioning in concert. Much experimentation needs to be done in the high school to realize the contribution of small group work.

FOR FURTHER STUDY

Alberty, Harold, *Reorganizing the High School Curriculum*. New York: The Macmillan Company, 1953.
    Part III offers suggestions on the role of the teacher in cooperative planning.
Association for Supervision and Curriculum Development, National Education Association, *Creating a Good Environment for Learning*. 1954 Yearbook; Washington, D.C.: The Association, 1954, Chaps. 4, 5, 6.
    These chapters furnish vivid accounts of cooperative planning of certain educational experiences in a suburban junior high school and in a large city senior high school.
——, *Toward Better Teaching*. 1949 Yearbook; Washington, D.C.: The Association, 1949.
    Chapters 2, 3, 4, and 5 emphasize the importance of classroom atmosphere and the use of the problem-solving technique.
Collier, Calhoun C., "We Believe in Teacher-Pupil Planning," *National Education Association Journal*, 43:315 (May), 1954.
    A brief discussion of cooperative classroom planning by a teacher who has been successful in its use.
Department of Supervision and Curriculum Development, National Education Association, *Group Planning in Education*. 1945 Yearbook; Washington, D.C.: The Association, 1945.
    Chapter 2 is a discussion of some misunderstandings of cooperative planning. Chapter 19 describes the principles of cooperative group work. Other chapters provide concrete illustrations of successful teacher-pupil planning.
Faunce, Roland C., and Nelson L. Bossing, *Developing the Core Curriculum*. New York: Prentice-Hall, Inc., 1951.
    Perhaps the most comprehensive treatment available of theory and practice in cooperative problem solving in education.
Giles, Harry H., *Teacher-Pupil Planning*. New York: Harper & Brothers, 1941.
    Includes statements from schools where teacher-pupil planning has been used successfully. Offers specific suggestions to teachers to use in planning work with pupils.
Horace Mann-Lincoln Institute of School Experimentation, "Cooperative

Research and Curriculum Improvement," *Teachers College Record,* 51:407–474 (April), 1950.

The story of the early development of a problem-centered, cooperatively planned sophomore orientation course.

Leonard, J. Paul, *Developing the Secondary School Curriculum.* New York: Rinehart & Company, Inc., 1953, Chap. 4.

A thorough analysis of the "core idea" in curriculum development and teaching method, with emphasis on teacher-pupil planning.

Miel, Alice, ed., *Cooperative Planning.* New York: Teachers College, Columbia University, 1953.

A complete reference on teacher-pupil planning.

Noar, Gertrude, *Freedom to Live and Learn.* Philadelphia: Franklin Publishing & Supply Co., Inc., 1948.

A good discussion of pupil-teacher planning techniques.

————, *The Junior High School—Today and Tomorrow.* New York: Prentice-Hall, Inc., 1953.

Chapter 4 discusses some applications of the nature of the learning process. Chapter 7 describes the teacher's role of leadership in the classroom. Chapter 12 answers practical questions about the problem-solving technique.

Rasey, Marie I., *This Is Teaching.* New York: Harper & Brothers, 1950.

The description of a college seminar taught on a cooperative-planning basis with an emphasis on student problems; has some carry-over value to secondary school teaching.

Saylor, J. Galen, and William M. Alexander, *Curriculum Planning.* New York: Rinehart & Company, Inc., 1954.

Chapter 13 includes a description of criteria for effective pupil-teacher planning.

Spears, Harold, *The Teacher and Curriculum Planning.* New York: Prentice-Hall, Inc., 1951.

An emphasis on the teacher's role in curriculum planning.

Wiles, Kimball, *Teaching for Better Schools.* New York: Prentice-Hall, Inc., 1952, Chap. 8.

A very persuasive and readable argument for the social and psychological basis of group planning in the classroom.

9. *Working with Small Groups*
in the Classroom

INTRODUCTION

BY NOW, the reader must realize the importance we attach
to group skills and to their development for effective teaching and
learning. Our basis for this belief is derived first from the practical
demands of the public schools which are engaged in mass education
and therefore of necessity must use group methods rather than tutorial. Secondly, we believe that education in a democracy has a responsibility for the development of skills in cooperative problem solving,
because in such a context we live as individuals and make our contribution to society.

At the secondary level of education, classroom group work has
largely been construed as the activity of the total class in discussions
and projects. As a result, secondary teachers have been more interested in group methods appropriate for twenty-five to fifty pupils
planning and acting in concert. Although these skills and abilities are
important, the secondary school teacher is losing great opportunities
for vitalizing learning experiences if he does not break down the total
class into small groups for various purposes. In this chapter we will
explore the uses of small groups in the secondary school classroom.

ADMINISTRATIVE COMMITTEES

In Chapter 5 we have already commented upon the contributions
which various pupil committees can make to the over-all planning of
learning experiences. The steering, materials, human resources, classroom appointments, and social committees are all good examples of

254

small classroom groups which have special responsibilities for planning and administering larger phases of the classroom operation. By rotating membership on these committees, many pupils can have the valuable experience of participation. However, these are generally thought of as policy-making groups which will need to have special groups designated from time to time to carry out decisions and plans.

Figure 9 illustrates the kinds of administrative committees a teacher and a classroom group might well consider, together with their functions.

These small administrative groups represent the need for certain jobs to be done systematically in the interests of all. This division of labor is not only efficient but also teaches responsibility for a job well done if properly supervised by the teacher and made responsive to peer pressures. Many elementary school teachers spend much time organizing and supervising small groups for discharging certain routine responsibilities. Committees taking care of plants, keeping the sink clean, cleaning blackboards, arranging movable chairs, meeting visitors, and the like may seem to secondary school teachers less important than certain more academic responsibilities and activities.

Even in secondary school classrooms these things need attention by someone. More often than not they are handled by the teacher or custodian. We suggest that the appearance of many secondary school classrooms belie the idea that pupils have developed any responsibility for the attractiveness of their school environment. In schools whose teachers and custodians assume major responsibility, they fight a continuing battle against pupil irresponsibility which might well be improved through classroom committees.

We may say that we wish to develop responsibility in adolescents, but we might also examine whether we exploit all the opportunities for teaching this important facet of living. Six or seven years of this kind of direct experience in the elementary school are not enough. As pupils enter the secondary school, exhortations for responsible behavior will not replace adequately the opportunity for direct experience in behaving responsibly. We believe the pressure of adolescents' peer groups will make these committees function more effectively than at an earlier age. The decision needs to be made by the teacher that spending some time on organizing and supervising such committees is sound education.

It may well be that many of the administrative duties of classroom committees which we have discussed need to have a greater air of sophistication and maturity than their elementary school counterparts. We recall, for example, one school where homeroom committees

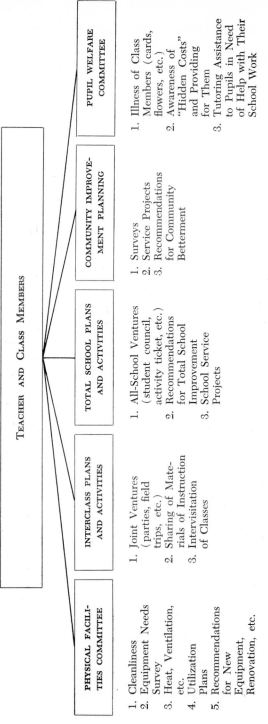

TEACHER AND CLASS MEMBERS

PHYSICAL FACILI- TIES COMMITTEE

1. Cleanliness
2. Equipment Needs Survey
3. Heat, Ventilation, etc.
4. Utilization Plans
5. Recommendations for New Equipment, Renovation, etc.

INTERCLASS PLANS AND ACTIVITIES

1. Joint Ventures (parties, field trips, etc.)
2. Sharing of Mate- rials of Instruction
3. Intervisitation of Classes

TOTAL SCHOOL PLANS AND ACTIVITIES

1. All-School Ventures (student council, activity ticket, etc.)
2. Recommendations for Total School Improvement
3. School Service Projects

COMMUNITY IMPROVE- MENT PLANNING

1. Surveys
2. Service Projects
3. Recommendations for Community Betterment

PUPIL WELFARE COMMITTEE

1. Illness of Class Members (cards, flowers, etc.)
2. Awareness of "Hidden Costs" and Providing for Them
3. Tutoring Assistance to Pupils in Need of Help with Their School Work

FIG. 9. A CHART OF SMALL ADMINISTRATIVE COMMITTEES FOR CLASSROOMS

assisted in the selection of new furniture and in choosing the color schemes for painting of classrooms. In another school, committees representing classrooms made studies of heating, ventilation, and lighting needs and offered recommendations for consideration by the board of education.

Regardless of the level of maturity of the pupils, the same fundamental needs and purposes are involved. Boys and girls need to learn responsibility. They learn by practice, by assuming responsibility, not by being told that they should be responsible. Likewise, they need the feeling of worthiness which comes through worth-while, satisfying group participation, not by being told that they are wanted for their contributions which they have not been able to demonstrate.

These are the questions which teachers need to ask when pondering the organization of small classroom groups for administering duties:

1. What are the routine jobs in the classroom which can be done by pupils?

2. Are these jobs seen by pupils as important to the efficient functioning of the classroom and how can such an attitude be developed?

3. Can we set up a schedule of rotation of committee responsibilities so that jobs do not become repetitive and therefore lacking after a time in learning potential?

4. Do I feel that in addition to getting certain jobs done, there are in small group work the values of developing responsibility and creating a feeling of worthy participation?

5. Do I feel these values to be of sufficient importance to give class time and time of my own to organizing and supervising such committee activity?

To the extent that a teacher's answers to these questions are in the affirmative, he will provide for continuous small group involvement in these routine, quasi-administrative phases of classroom life. Perhaps more important, however, is the training such activity provides for engaging in small group activities more directly related to the specific learning outcomes of a particular class. These uses of small groups will be developed subsequently.

SMALL GROUPS FOR SKILL DEVELOPMENT

Historically, the use of small groups for practice in skill development stems from the elementary school, particularly in the teaching of reading. In this kind of situation, a class is divided into three or four groups, based on their stage of development in reading skills. Varied materials are provided suitable to varying levels of ability. The teacher divides his time among the groups, listening to the reading and doing whatever teaching is necessary. While the teacher is with one group, the other groups may be practicing their reading or engaging in some other kind of learning activity.

The point to be made here is that small groups allow for meeting differences in ability, not by completely individualizing instruction, but by grouping pupils according to their level of development into three or four subgroups. This has become a fairly common elementary school practice, particularly in reading and arithmetic.

This practice is in sharp contrast to older elementary schools where all pupils tried to read the same book at the same time and in the same place. It is in even sharper contrast to most secondary schools today where we see total classes using the same textbooks, following the same assignments, and reciting or discussing the assignment as though everyone were at the same stage of skill development, be it in English, social studies, science, or mathematics.

It can be said that many of the special subjects in the secondary school have adopted small groups in classroom activities, differentiated by a number of criteria such as ability, interest, aptitude, and the like. We refer to art, music, industrial arts, physical education, home economics, and other "nonacademic" areas where creative teachers often use small groups in the classroom rather than having everyone do the same thing at the same time in the same way.

Why does not more of this grouping take place in the secondary school? In part, it is a matter of training. Many elementary teachers seem more cognizant of the nature and extent of individual differences and have been given experiences in providing for these differences in their student teaching. Armed with this knowledge and experience, they are more ready to accept varying levels of development and not to assume a sixth-grade or fourth-grade or second-grade ability or achievement level for all their pupils.

One must also remember that the teaching of certain basic skills is seen as central to the elementary school job alone. "Readin', writin', and 'rithmetic" are assumed to have been taught by the first six grades. This leaves subject matter or content to be the chief concern of the secondary teacher; if the skills for gaining subject matter cannot be guaranteed for all pupils by grades 7 or 9, one can understand the alarm of the secondary teacher and his inability or reluctance to provide for differences.

Finally, it should be said that secondary school materials have tended to be more rigid in content and form than elementary materials. That is, it is more difficult at the secondary level to find materials varying in both concept level and reading difficulty. The high school teacher therefore tends to use *a* basic text, and hopes for the best by going more slowly with some or by not requiring the same standards of everyone.

We submit that skill development is a province of the secondary school as well as of the elementary school. It ought always to have been so; but now with increased holding power of the secondary school, it is imperative that secondary school teachers work at all levels of skill development and in all subjects to raise proficiency in the basic skills to the capacity of individual learners.

Again, because of the nature of public education, this development will have to be done for the most part in small groups, even in schools where so-called "homogeneous grouping" is practiced to form class sections. The job of the secondary school teacher, in-service and pre-service, is to learn as much as possible from elementary school teachers about techniques of forming small groups within the classroom and of using these groups for skill development. Visitation of elementary school classrooms where small groups are used, conferring with elementary school teachers, and constant administrative provision for elementary and secondary teachers to meet jointly around common areas of interest will do much to help secondary school teachers. But even more important is the willingness of the secondary teacher to experiment with small groups.

A SOCIAL STUDIES CLASS DEVELOPS A NEW SKILL

We suggest a look at the experience of Mr. Grant, a social studies teacher of the ninth grade. As a teacher of community civics, he desires for his classes an increased awareness of their own city and its historical background. Someone suggests that a good way to get this kind of history is to talk to some "old-timers." As a result, an assignment is made for everyone to interview at least three "old people" by the following day, and to bring reports to class.

The next day Mr. Grant is disappointed by the number of students who have not done their assignment, by the lack of significant information brought in by those who have conducted interviews, and by the general letdown in enthusiasm from the day before. The student who proposed the interviews suggests that the trouble probably lies in the fact that this is the first time they have ever been asked to interview someone.

In quick succession come several suggestions why the interview idea did not work. Mr. Grant sees this as a chance to get real involvement in the development of interview skills. It is clear that skill in interviewing is a general need in this class. In another class some pupils might be very skillful, and would need no assistance in developing an ability to interview; others could be grouped on the basis of the kinds of problems they expressed in talking about their interview experiences or about reasons for not interviewing anyone.

But in this class Mr. Grant suggests that they spend ten minutes in groups organized at random, listing all the problems which might be encountered in conducting an interview.

A summary after ten minutes turns up the following:

1. How old are "old people"? Forty years, fifty, sixty, seventy, or older?

2. What do we want to find out? How far back?

3. Some of us are bashful about talking to older people we don't know very well.

4. After one or two questions I don't know what to say or ask.

5. Are we to have a written or oral report?

It is apparent that the group needs to have some practice and training in interviews. For the rest of the period groups divide up, again on a random basis, to discuss possible questions which might be asked in an interview and to arrange them in a logical order. The assignment for the following day is to be ready to discuss the other questions which had been raised.

The next class period is spent as follows:

1. Deciding on general age classifications to be interviewed
2. Listing in order questions which might be asked, suggested by the facts the class wants to find out
3. Agreeing that probably a written summary of the interview is desirable and also usable as an outline for an oral report
4. Practicing interviews in small random groups for fifteen or twenty minutes
5. Deciding that students not interested in interviewing or not having people to interview might seek out the information by other means—reading, using the library, visiting the local museum, and so forth

The following day small groups again meet to hear reports from interviewers. These are summarized and shared with the total class. Opportunity for reporting is also given to pupils who had chosen other means of gaining information. The high level of class morale, the quality of the facts and information, and the general satisfaction with the interview process gives Mr. Grant a good opportunity to point out the importance of learning the *how* as well as trying to get at the *what*.

This is what one high school teacher might do, confronted with the problem of skill development. It requires of him a sensitivity to the reasons for the initial failure at interviewing, a willingness to spend some time and effort on something which perhaps did not originally appear in his plans, and a recognition of the fact that he cannot by himself develop these skills for individual pupils. The use of small groups lends itself to his problem, and the subsequent decisions, learnings, and improved outcomes bear testimony to the efficacy of the small group approach.

The above example was given purposely because it represents a somewhat more complex kind of problem in the use of small groups, and therefore may be more typical of their use in the secondary schools for skill development. At a less complex level of skill development, similar groups might be used to provide drill in spelling, vocabulary, pronunciation, recall of facts, and other skills which need practice.

AN ENGLISH CLASS DEVELOPS SPELLING ABILITY

For example, in most secondary schools English teachers find a wide range of spelling ability. Frequently, attempts to improve in spelling are concentrated on the poorest spellers, or a total class approach is used with all pupils studying and being tested on the same word lists. In the former case, the attention focused on the poorest spellers results in the average or good spellers being neglected in their development of spelling skill. In the latter case, all levels of spelling proficiency are reduced to a common denominator with a waste of time and effort in skill improvement for everyone concerned.

In this setting a teacher might well employ small groups for drill on spelling at several levels of proficiency. Some diagnosis is necessary to answer the questions of how to group learners for drill and what spelling words are to be studied in the small groups. This diagnosis can be made by the use of standardized tests and the analysis of errors in teacher-made quizzes or in other written work by pupils. This kind of study should reveal quickly the need for three or four groupings.

One or more groups, composed of learners with persistent spelling disabilities, may be put to work on spelling lists below their grade level. The need for this would be apparent from standardized test results, quizzes, and other written work. These pupils need a great deal of help from the teacher in understanding the nature of their spelling problem and in developing certain basic phonetic skills. That is, putting these poor spellers in a group will not assist them unless they are given assistance in overcoming their faulty habits, inadequate understanding of spelling skills, and inappropriate attitudes toward spelling. If changes are made along these lines prior to or as concomitants of drill, there will be greater chance for improvement.

The other groups are better able to take care of themselves. These average and good spellers stand up rather well on standardized tests, but their written work reveals carelessness in writing habits or lack of continuous development in spelling new and more difficult words. Analysis of other written work by teachers and themselves, the furnishing of new word lists to master which are taken from all their subject fields, and setting up competition and word games will serve these average and good spellers better than subjecting them to study grade-level lists or to drill with poorer spellers.

What we are saying here is not that drill is to be avoided but that it should be used in appropriate groupings where pupils see meaning and relation between their lacks or skills and the learning activity in which they are engaging.

Obviously, the same basic requirement for effective drill applies here as in the case of individuals or large groups: *practice must be preceded by an understanding for the learner of the principles involved in what he is learning by drill.*

In summary, it can be said of the use of small groups in the development of skills:

1. That secondary teachers must assume responsibility for the teaching of skills—both skills which have already been presented and those which are new to the pupils.

2. That one way to lighten the load of this responsibility, and at the same time provide for differences in stages of skill development, is to use subgroups.

3. That small groups may be set up on the basis of differences in skill development if these are clearly known by the teacher. At other times, random groups may serve the purpose if there are no sharp differences in achievement or if a new skill is being introduced.

4. That a teacher must learn how best to share his time with groups, according to the needs of the groups and his responsibility for general supervision of this process.

5. That this process depends for its effectiveness upon pupils' increasingly directing their own learning after they understand the principles involved in what they are practicing. This also means that pupils' helping each other is to be encouraged as desirable and worthy.

6. That the use of small groups is only one way of providing for skill development, and by reason of its not having been used generally in

PLATE 24. IDEAS COME FAST IN SMALL GROUP WORK. Small committees develop participation at the idea level. (Courtesy of the Board
of Education, City of New York)

the secondary school, it is in need of careful experimentation and
evaluation.

EXPLORING INTERESTS AND
SHARING INFORMATION

One of the greatest concerns teachers have as they consider teacher-
pupil planning of learning experiences is the multiplicity of interests
represented in any class. Some teachers, of course, do not respect
learners' interests, at least to the point of making them motivational
factors for learning. Others see the power of interest in focusing and
directing learning experiences, but are unable to capitalize on interests
because of their number and variety. Still other teachers regard learning as something outside the question of interests, and relegate them
to extra-credit work or even to the extracurriculum.

Increasingly, however, teachers are recognizing that interests of
learners can be related to significant learning experiences, that interests can be classified so that small groups of learners can exploit them,

and that these small groups in their cooperative activity can supply vitality and a unification of the total class around the very interests which the teacher may have originally considered too diverse for organization. This means that the teacher as a more mature person has a very important role to play in assisting pupils in identifying interests, in relating them, and in applying criteria for selection of interests to be pursued.

At this point, we should relate interests to the problem-solving approach to learning. In fact, we believe that problem identification in the scientific method more often than not is synonymous with interest identification. For example, a junior high school student may have asked himself, "How far away are the stars? Why do some twinkle, others not? Do stars rotate like the earth? Where do stars fall?"

We might ask whether these questions represent to this eighth-grader a number of problems for which he would like answers or whether they are only casual, transitory interests. These questions have occurred to most people at one time or other. That is, these questions have a general, but not a consuming kind of interest. However, a sizable number of youngsters at this age, in response to the stimulation of a general science teacher, will make these interests so central for a period of time that they become real problems for study. For a very few, this interest will become so important that a vocational drive toward astronomy and related fields may develop.

Such an analysis of interests and their relation to learning as problem solving may only complicate the problem of interest identification and exploration for teachers. We suggest, however, that the above example of the junior high school student illustrates that expressed interests generally are not spurious or feigned; but they cannot always be taken as compelling enough to build upon for educative experiences. This only suggests that freedom to choose under the guidance of the more mature teacher may well be the principle to employ for selection of interests and problems for study.

The degree of freedom granted learners in self-selection of interests and problems for study will vary greatly, depending on the freedom the teacher enjoys curriculumwise, the expectation of pupils and parents, and his own feeling of security in dealing with learning situations in this fashion. In any case, the use of small groups suggests itself early in any consideration of pupil interests, as once again we must remind the reader that in public schools complete individualization of instruction and learning is neither possible nor wise.

As a result of this rationale for the use of small groups, we submit several examples of teachers and pupils engaging in interest groups.

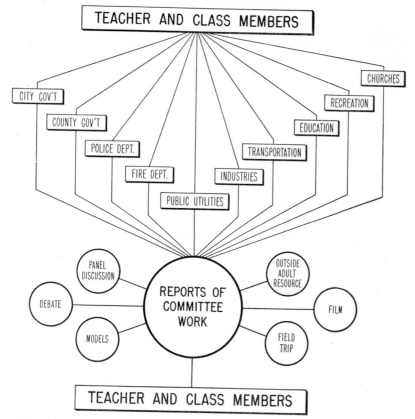

Fig. 10. A Social Studies Class Uses Small Groups for Community Study

A simple use of subgroups can be seen in a seventh-grade social studies class engaging in a unit entitled "Our Community" (Fig. 10). Early in the development of this unit, class discussion reveals the following interest areas:

city government
county government
police department
fire department
public utilities

industries
transportation
educational system
recreation
churches

Rather than having all pupils study all areas, opportunity is given for each pupil to choose his special interest. The resulting groups form the center for study and activity in this unit, although other kinds of experiences are provided too. Central to this whole procedure is the reporting phase of the unit in which each group presents its findings through models, panel discussions, a debate, consultant visits from the community, and the like. Thus the interest groups do not have the narrowing effect which many teachers fear, and at the same time the special interests of pupils are pursued far beyond what they can do if all topics are required of everyone.

At the senior high school level, the following account is revealing, both of the techniques employed for small groups, and of some of the feelings of the teacher involved:

Today I decided to take the plunge. I told the students that in our next unit, light, they were going to be able to select any topic or problem and work on it as they wished. Since many of the problems which they would select would be related, I suggested that they might like to work in groups so that they could help each other in preparing and presenting their topics. They seemed quite anxious to do this.

In order to stimulate their thinking and to open up the subject, I asked them to describe their experiences with light. Almost everyone volunteered some experiences. Questions were brought up but not answered by me. I suggested they note them down and save them. Each experience seemed to stimulate others and soon we were ready to list all the problems which were welling up.

A volunteer was selected to write on the board all the problems which the group thought might be of interest and on which they would like to work. Since I thought their knowledge of the scope of light would be somewhat limited, I suggested that they skim through the unit in their texts as the next assignment and that the next day we would add any new questions or problems which had been stimulated by the description in the text.

When we had finished our listing, there were thirty-six entries. Since the group was not advanced enough to recognize relationships, I said I would classify the problems and topics in related groupings and around these we would form our work-study groups. I then listed the main headings and the subtopics in related groups. Each student wrote on a piece of paper the main heading and the particular topic of his choice. These were then sorted and the groups were formed. We were now ready to start work.[1]

Both of these illustrations will be seen as having settings in which the over-all structure of the curriculum has been determined by the teacher or by some authority outside the learners themselves. This is typical of most secondary school curricula. And yet one is impressed

[1] Alice Miel and Associates, *Cooperative Procedures in Learning* (New York: Bureau of Publications, Teachers College, Columbia University, 1952), p. 380. Reprinted by permission.

by these teachers' willingness and ability to capitalize on individual and small group interests within the required framework to the point where great respect was given to interests and problems *as learners saw them.*

These, then, are the contributions of breaking down large classes into smaller groups according to interests. It allows, first of all, for more widespread participation in whatever activity is selected; secondly, it makes respectable and capitalizes on differing interests of learners; and third, it gives learners experiences in cooperative approaches to learning through problem solving rather than by highly individualistic, competitive methods.

USE OF SMALL GROUPS IN VARIOUS SUBJECT AREAS

Although the above basic principles of small group work apply to all subject areas, our examples to illustrate the use of classroom subgroups have not touched all fields. The following are illustrations from areas other than those already covered and may serve to reinforce the concepts of small group work which we have developed to this point.

AN EIGHTH-GRADE HOME ECONOMICS CLASS

The twenty-two girls in my class meet only two hours each week and the lapse of time between class periods makes it very difficult to keep interest and continuity constant. Earlier in the year the girls had planned their large topics to be covered during the year. Now the question was: what was the best procedure for accomplishing the work they had planned?

Since I had joined the group in cooperative planning, I told the girls about that procedure. They were interested and wished to try it. They chose a recorder, and began discussing and attacking the problem before them. They listed several areas that would be included in grooming and personality.

When these were listed, each girl chose her field of study. Thus groups were formed on an interest basis. Each group obtained as much source material as possible. Reading and discussion followed. Later activity groups were formed. Some made scrapbooks on personality and good grooming. Others prepared effective bulletin board displays. Showcases in the halls were used. Girls shampooed one another's hair and tried different hair styles. Reports on personality were given and demonstrations of posture were carried on. Personality tests were run by the students. They also wrote a skit, "The Sad Sacks."

In order to keep up interest and provide a sense of continuity and progress each recorder was asked to give a weekly report of her group in rather detailed form. At the end of the fourth week, the class evaluated

their work and procedure. They realized they had made many errors. They
listed suggestions for better procedures for their next unit. However, they
decided that this cooperative method was really the best way to work.
They had fun in sharing interests, materials, and ideas.[2]

A JUNIOR HIGH SCHOOL ENGLISH CLASS

The opening discussion grew out of the display of Book Week posters
and book jackets which greeted the pupils on coming to class. What kinds
of books do different people think make reading fun? Which books represented in the book jackets had they enjoyed? Soon a list of many kinds
of books was drawn up, and the boys and girls divided themselves into
groups according to their choice of topic—adventure and mystery, sport
stories, science fiction, teen-age-girl books, hobbies, and the like.

Next, pupils discussed how to find the books they wanted in the library
catalogue and on the shelves, in useful reading lists such as *Leisure Reading*
and *Books For You* by the National Council of Teachers of English,
Gateways to Readable Books by Ruth Strang and others, *Books for Reluctant
Readers* by Anita E. Dunn, Mabel Jackman, and members of the staff of the
Albany State Teachers College in New York, and similar lists loaned to
them by the librarian. After several class periods in the library with the
help of both teacher and librarian, each pupil prepared a list of books on
his topic and began reading the ones in which he was most interested.

During this time each of them developed a notebook in which he wrote
evaluations of the books he read and the criteria on which he would judge
them. He pasted in it clippings from newspapers and magazines in his home
library about books and authors and forthcoming Book Week events.

In the beginning some reading was done in class and some at home.
When each person had read one book, the pupils met together in groups
to decide how they could best share their reading with others. Some
retold humorous, thrilling, or unusual incidents; others discussed standards
for judging their books; some dramatized stories; others put on a panel or
a radio program. The group studying books that have been made into
motion pictures arranged to have sections of the film, *Two Years before the
Mast,* shown at the school.

Most of these reports were on individual books or authors. Eventually,
each group was to present to the class a brief program representing the
area of reading on which it was working—the best to be woven into a
Book Week Assembly for the entire school. Each group also was to file
in the school library a composite list of the best books in its field for use
in other classes. Each was to prepare a poster and one exhibit case of books
for the hall during Book Week. . . .

The sports fans presented their report in three sections: (1) why junior
high school pupils should be interested in sports stories such as Howard M.
Brier's *Phantom Backfield,* Philip Harkins's *Southpaw from San Francisco,*

[2] *Ibid.,* p. 272. Reprinted by permission.

Jackson V. Scholz's *Gridiron Challenge*, Caary P. Jackson's *Shorty Makes First Team*, and John Tunis's *The Kid from Tompkinsville* or *All-American;* (2) how to tell a good sport story from a poor one (in this pupils were helped by Miss Scury's article in the *Horn Book* for October, 1952); and (3) what sports heroes one can become acquainted with through biography. They introduced these men to the class and let them tell their own stories: Babe Ruth, Lou Gehrig, and Joe Louis.

Next, the group on science fiction broadcast from space—from Mars, from the moon, or from some other planets—telling of their experiences in getting there. Franklyn M. Branley's *Lodestar, Rocket Ship to Mars*, Robert A. Heinlein's *Farmer in the Sky*, Leslie Greener's *Moon Ahead*, and similar titles proved useful. At the end, they presented their reading list to the class with some ideas for their evaluation from August Derleth's article in *The English Journal* for January, 1952, which the teacher helped a superior reader among the boys to summarize.

Books about teen-age girls were popular with a group of girls who presented a program on "Find Yourself in Books." Among the most liked were Betty Cavanna's *A Girl Can Dream*, Adele L. DeLeeuw's *With a High Heart*, Mary Medearis's *Big Doc's Girl*, and Mary S. Stolz's *Organdy Cupcakes*. The talks were grouped around such teen-age problems as deciding what one wants to be, getting along with the family, and dating.

Another group introduced books that have been made into motion pictures—among them, *Alice in Wonderland, Tom Sawyer, The Yearling, Two Years Before the Mast*, and *Lassie Come Home*. They tried to decide why these particular books had been filmed, what kinds of people would like them, what happens to a story when it is filmed, and why. Finally, they discussed what a book has to offer that a moving picture has not and what a motion picture has that a book cannot furnish. The aim was to recognize the values of each.

Historical fiction, biography, sea stories, adventure, and mystery were also presented. Finally, groups concerned with nonfiction, chiefly mechanics and hobbies, gave their reports.[3]

A HIGH SCHOOL SHOP CLASS

In classrooms where there is much group business to transact, teachers and pupils have to learn short cuts to planning that still maintain the interest and concern of the entire group.

One such short cut is for the group to plan a way of rotating jobs. When this happens the major time investment is given to making the initial plan. An example is a scheme used in a high school shop for cleanup at the end of each class period. The plan, worked out by teacher and boys together, is reported by a high school counselor.

[3] The Commission on the English Curriculum of the National Council of Teachers of English, *Language Arts for Today's Children* (New York: Appleton-Century-Crofts, Inc., 1954), pp. 307–308, 310–311. Reprinted by permission.

"A list of the jobs to be done is printed on a sheet and each boy rotates in the different jobs. One boy acts as superintendent each week and checks the sheet when each job has been done satisfactorily."

That the teacher rarely had to intervene is undoubtedly a result of the fact that a cooperative decision had been made.[4]

A MATHEMATICS CLASS

I decided that since regular classroom procedure had failed, I would try cooperative planning with them.

We discussed as a class the topics to be covered in mathematics for the year. One of the students listed the topics on the board and the individual members decided what they were interested in studying. The topics were: (1) budgets and family spending, (2) buying and selling, (3) money and banking, (4) geometric figures, (5) measuring time, (6) figuring the cost of things we want to make (boats, wagons, etc.).

We discussed working in groups and settled on a common organization. Each group elected a chairman and recorder. Each group met and made plans for carrying out their work. Reports were made to the class by the recorder of each group about once a week. All students were very interested and the plans as outlined by each group were well thought out.[5]

A PHYSICAL EDUCATION CLASS

The breakdown of physical education classes into smaller subgroups is rather commonplace for teachers who desire to vary activities, to teach skills, and to provide for services to students. A class of thirty-five pupils in physical education, for example, could be grouped in this fashion:

Group I	10 boys using mat for tumbling
Group II	5 boys using the horse
Group III	5 boys using parallel bars
Group IV	5 boys using trampoline
Group V	5 boys taking hearing tests
Group VI	5 boys taking eye tests

By rotation of the groups during the class period, it would be possible for a boy to engage in three or possibly four of the above activities. The teacher, having designated for each group student-leaders who demonstrate competence and responsibility, is free to move from group to group for over-all supervision and inspection.

This kind of planning for utilization of small groups is feasible for many kinds of activity in physical education. It tends to destroy the

[4] Miel, *op. cit.*, p. 32. Reprinted by permission.
[5] *Ibid.*, p. 270. Reprinted by permission.

stereotype of gym classes in which large groups of students are inactive by reason of lack of interest, or because of waiting for their turn at an activity in which the whole group is participating.

The above examples of small group work, drawn from a number of subject areas, are intended to illustrate the varied uses to which sub-groups can be put. These could be multiplied manifold, but more illustrations would serve only to illustrate further the basic principles which have been elaborated thus far. All teachers should constantly check their planning by asking these questions:

1. Is our classroom organized into functional groups which discharge routine responsibilities for the good of all?

2. Have we developed all the potentialities in this unit of work for small groups to function in skill development through practice and drill?

3. Are we exploiting the varied interests, aptitudes, and needs of the learners by providing opportunity in subgroups for their expression and development?

4. In all of our classroom activity, are we seeing the possibilities in small groups for reducing boredom, providing variety, gaining wider participation, and developing spontaneity and responsibility?

The authors hope that up to this point they have provided the reader with a theoretical basis for small group work in the classroom and with enough examples to prove that it can be practical. What remains for teacher and students to initiate small groups and to safeguard their continued and efficient use?

GETTING STARTED IN THE USE OF SMALL GROUPS

The first attempt on the part of a teacher and a class to use small groups is frequently a difficult hurdle. Many teachers confess that they do not feel competent to organize and supervise a classroom on a small group basis. To such people, we can only say that early efforts should be on a small scale.

For example, it may become apparent during some general class activity that a small minority seems disinterested, or perhaps strongly interested in a related problem or topic which the entire class will not pursue. This gives the opportunity for the teacher to suggest the formation of a small group to pursue a common interest. Such a development leaves the classroom with two groups—the main body of the class and a small interest group. As an initial attempt, this kind of simple class-room arrangement may pose fewer problems in supervision for the

PLATE 25. SMALL BUZZ GROUPS PROVIDE GREATER OPPORTUNITY FOR PARTICIPATION. In large classes, frequent use of small groups is necessary to maintain pupil involvement. (Courtesy of the Phoenix, Arizona, Union High School)

teacher, and fewer for the pupils in terms of acceptance of the idea of grouping.

This brings us to an important consideration. Any deviation from normal classroom routine is a source of surprise and some concern to teacher and pupil alike. We are creatures of habit, and we have habitually seen classrooms as places where either total groups operated together on a single activity or where individuals engaged in highly personal and often competitive efforts. The presence of small groups is a departure, and as such may seem strange. Unfamiliarity may beget uneasiness which is not conducive to good learning.

The teacher can do much to alleviate this uneasiness and lack of readiness on the part of pupils. Perhaps the most important thing is to conceal as far as possible any doubts he has about small group organization. A teacher's insecurity transfers easily to students in any area where he feels less competent. We are not suggesting here that a teacher at all times should pose as authority or expert. But he may lack complete confidence without begetting doubt or indecision in the learners. Perhaps the difference can be illustrated.

TEACHER I. Today we are going to try to use small groups for discussion which you can elect to join on the basis of your particular interest in our general topic—weather. I haven't seen this kind of thing work very well, and if we fail, we can always go back to studying the text together. All those interested in studying various kinds of storms meet me in this corner, all who want to study weather forecasting over here. . . .

TEACHER II. Our topic for the next two or three days is weather. Yesterday in our short discussion of it, we saw that we have many different interests in weather. Some are interested in kinds of storms, others in forecasting, and there were several other interests mentioned. Since yesterday I thought about the possibility of allowing each of you to select among a half-dozen topics. We could organize a group to study each topic. I haven't done this in any of my classes before, but I am sure we can work out some ideas and plan for this kind of activity, don't you? Let's spend a little time talking about what we need to do. . . .

Note the negative, apprehensive attitude of Teacher I in contrast to the positive, confident spirit of Teacher II. Many teachers convey to the class the feelings of Teacher I without meaning to develop in the group these feelings. One also gets the impression from Teacher II that in the lead-up discussion the day before, more attention had been given to the various interests of the group in the broad topic; that is, there had been some analysis of the existing differences in interests, backgrounds, and possibly skills. This analysis and acceptance of differences makes the idea of grouping seem more reasonable, in fact, even desirable.

We do not wish to belabor unduly the importance of pupil readiness, but we feel very strongly the importance of creating pupil acceptance of an innovation in classroom organization and procedure. Without this willingness and understanding, pupils do not give small groups a chance to succeed. Teachers therefore should attempt the following:

1. Create an awareness and acceptance of the necessity for grouping because of differences in interests, needs, and abilities.

2. Adopt a positive, constructive attitude toward the potentialities of small groups.

3. Give ample opportunity for clarification of small group purpose, procedures, and the like by the pupils, lest they plunge into such activity in a confused state of mind.

Early in the experience of a class with the use of small groups, evaluation should be made of the activity. That is, this small group process becomes part of the total learning experience, and before a group goes too far it should become cognizant of successes and failures. The cumulative effect of evaluation, reconsideration of purposes and procedures, and some redirection if deemed necessary is to build on strengths and gradually to eliminate weaknesses in small group procedures. More attention is paid to evaluation of small group work later in this chapter. At this point, we only urge evaluation of the process soon after initiation. We caution against the expectation of or the desire for uniformity in the experiences of small groups. Rather, we ask for careful consideration of pupil opinions and attitudes about their group experiences as a basis for future growth and improvement.

One final suggestion remains for getting off to a good start with small groups. Understanding and acceptance of this kind of classroom procedure by pupils can quickly be negated by negative attitudes toward it by other teachers, parents, the principal, and "outsiders." This suggests that attempts be made by pupils and teacher alike to interpret, if asked, what they are doing in the way of group work. A good use of time would be to discuss with a class the kinds of questions which might be asked by others who have not been concerned with the planning of the group, and how best these questions might be answered. This is no program of indoctrination or the development of a cult. Rather, it should be seen as the sincere effort of a class and a teacher to interpret what lies back of some experimental activities in teaching and learning. Such preparation will never completely satisfy the questions of people who do not understand what is being attempted. It can result in suspended judgment until the time when more evidence is available on which to judge the efficacy of small group procedures.

MAINTAINING SMALL GROUPS

Assuming that a classroom group has initiated subgroup activity, there remain many problems for pupils and the teacher in maintaining the morale and productivity of small groups. Many teachers are tempted into thinking that once groups are formed and jobs assigned, these groups will run by themselves. On the contrary, the initiation phase may come rather easily because of the novelty. To maintain consistently a feeling of satisfaction with the process and to be able to point to tangible evidence of group productivity is another matter.

The teacher's role in supervision of small group work is crucial. After committees or subgroups in a classroom are under way, the teacher serves in the following ways:

1. The *stimulator* role is one marked by the raising of issues, questions, and alternatives by the teacher. As he moves among the groups, listening to their deliberations and plans, the teacher has a responsibility to function as a more mature person. At times he may

urge or demand a certain procedure, decision, or action in the best interests of the group. At that point he is reverting to the more traditional role of a teacher. In small group work, however, he must as far as possible serve only to raise the issues, questions, and alternatives, leaving their disposition to the group.

2. The *expert* role is an authoritative position which the teacher inherits and must fill to satisfy the expectations of most pupils. However, the nature of the expertness must be considered. Certainly as a teacher, he possesses certain facts and skills which he ought to furnish the group on some occasions. We refer here particularly to skills which most often can be taught and demonstrated in a more economical fashion by the teacher. Factual information at his disposal must be considered more carefully. The teacher's resorting to "telling" is probably no more effective in small groups than in a lecture to the total class. Therefore, the teacher's suggestions and help to a group on how to secure information and facts is the more desirable alternative.

3. The *resource* role is closely related to the expert role; in fact, it may be the same if used in connection with content or subject matter. We here are referring to the teacher more as an expert in process. That is, increasingly students in small groups, if given freedom to select the *what* of their experience, ask questions which relate to the *how*, the *where*, and the *when* of the problem or interest under study. The teacher in this connection also can go too far in supplying what the students themselves should discover. These process problems, however, are matters on which most students need help, because they involve skills which too often have not been developed or used in more typical large group or individualistic procedures. They relate to sources, research skills, and cooperatively arrived-at commitments on responsibility, deadlines, sharing, and the like. The teacher can be a source of real help to most small groups in this area, particularly in the early stages of the life of a group.

4. The *conscience* role is one which most teachers find is absolutely necessary at the outset of the use of small groups. Pupils embarking in this kind of classroom organization can early develop poor habits in respect to responsibility for work, punctuality, concentration, cooperation, and the like—the very attitudes and habits at which the setting up of small groups was aimed. The anonymity of the group, the less close supervision, and some confusion and doubt about the whole process may tempt some pupils to evade responsibility, disturb group discussion, or develop a general apathy toward the group. Close and frequent contact by the teacher with all groups provides opportunity to observe these developments, to call attention to them, and to raise

with the group the question of how to cope with these problems of pupil attitudes. At times the teacher will be forced to take disciplinary action himself. The experience of most teachers is that if a group has been organized around a problem or interest which is truly significant to them, these disciplinary actions by the teacher become less frequent. The group develops its own conscience which operates through peer pressure to help the deviate from the group's objective see his place in the picture.

5. The *coordinator* role is one which only the teacher can play because of his greater maturity and because he alone is acquainted with the activities of all groups. This is an extremely important responsibility, because it governs the sharing of subgroup's activities, learnings, and other outcomes. That is, a class which operates on a small group basis must provide for sharing experiences, lest learnings be narrow and total group unity be lost. Small group operation is only one method of organizing learning experiences. Individual and total group experiences will always be necessary to supplement small group work. The timing, purpose, and nature of individual and large group work must constantly be in the mind of the teacher as the over-all coordinator of the class.

These roles and responsibilities of the teacher seem to us to be the most crucial in small group work. Through the activities suggested by these roles, a teacher relates himself constantly to the subgroups and makes his greatest contribution to this kind of classroom procedure.

THE CULMINATION OF SMALL GROUP WORK

In the process of initiating and maintaining small groups in problem-solving activity, attention necessarily will be given to matters of concluding activity in data gathering and to the generalizing phase of the experience. This includes the question, "What have we learned?"

In individual and large group learning experiences, the requirements of sharing what one has learned are less complex and perhaps for that reason not as attractive to learners. In the individual learning experience, a written or oral report is the most common device. In the case of total classroom group experience, questions and answers and class discussion are the more typical practices.

In the case of the individual, his attempt to share may be dull, either because his problem or interest is so specialized as to be lacking in general interest, or because the sharing devices of an individual are more limited in appeal and variety. In the case of a total group's

PLATE 26. A SMALL WORK GROUP REPORTS TO THE CLASS BY TRAN-
SCRIPTION. Variety must be planned in the reports or pupils will
leave an experience with inadequately shared learnings. (Courtesy
of the Oak Ridge, Tennessee, Public Schools)

sharing a learning experience, the assumption that there is any
problem or interest which appeals to all needs to be examined. It is
unlikely therefore that the culminating experience will be interesting.

In contrast, assuming that small groups have been initiated and
maintained along the lines which we have described, we submit that
the reporting and sharing phase of small group work will be exciting
and will serve to unify the group after some time spent apart on
discrete problems and interests. The culmination phase of small group
work in reporting and sharing experiences becomes crucial for both
broadening of learnings and for total group unity and morale.

Creative teachers and pupils, motivated by the impact of small group
study and experiences, have reflected very effectively in the reporting
and sharing phase the varied learnings which they have gained. The
task is one of communication. Small group experiences as described
result in new kinds of experiences, and it is appropriate and necessary
that new kinds of communication be used to report and share them.
Direct oral or written reports can serve to convey learnings, but more
effective are the following:

1. Plays, skits, and other forms of dramatization
2. Slides, pictures, and movies
3. Maps, charts, and models
4. Simulated radio broadcasts and television shows
5. Tape recordings
6. Newspapers and other forms of creative writing
7. Debates
8. Panels and round-table discussions
9. Murals, drawings, and other forms of pictorial art

Other methods of reporting and sharing could be added. However, all others would only add to the contention that much creativity can and must be exercised at this stage of cooperative group work. Without it, a sag in interest and achievement develops among groups. With such creative efforts, high interest is maintained throughout the life of the small group and better communication established between it and the rest of the class.

EVALUATING SMALL GROUP EXPERIENCES

Many readers by now may be saying, "This sounds good. I think I would like to try small groups. But—do they really produce learnings?" This is a fair question. In addressing ourselves to the question, we must insist that thinking through the process of evaluation of small group work demands that the reader keep in mind the procedures we have recommended and a teacher with the skills, motivations, and ideals we have described. Otherwise, the contentions made for small group work in terms of evaluation procedures and outcomes are not valid. That is, we say that given teachers and methods as described, small groups will work well, and evaluation will disclose learnings equal to or surpassing those resulting from other classroom methods.

We do not supply the evidence for the above contentions at this point. Studies of modern methods of education, including cooperative group work, as listed in the bibliography at the end of this chapter, should suffice. We are concerned with suggesting to the reader what evaluation in this kind of classroom procedure looks like.

THE CONTINUOUS EVALUATION

Earlier in this chapter we suggested that evaluation must be continuous, beginning immediately after the initiation of small group work. A verbatim evaluation discussion of a small group of students and comments by their teacher are suggestive in this connection:

"Seldom have I seen youngsters get more done," thought Miss White as she watched a small group clean up at the end of the hour. Bob, Jane, Mary, Paul, and Ronald, who was chairman, had their papers picked up, their books put away and still had some time left. Instead of drifting away, the group collected again.

PAUL: The teacher said we'll have another work period tomorrow—at least the class steering committee approved one. Do you think we'll be ready to plan our final report then?

JANE: Mary and I would.

BOB: Paul and I need more time. We ought to go to the library tomorrow.

RONALD: Well, I guess we won't be ready. Anyway, I could use some more time myself.

PAUL: I think we wasted some time today that Bob and I could have used to work in the library. We just didn't get started because we didn't seem to know what we were doing.

There was a pause, and finally—

RONALD: We didn't have a plan so it took too long to set up an agenda.

PAUL: Yeah. And if Jane and Mary could use tomorrow to plan our—to make tentative plans for our final report, based on what we accomplished so far, we'd get started better next time.

MARY: I'd be willing if you'd really let us present it to start the meeting.

Jane agreed. Several heads nodded in agreement.

"Good evaluation," thought Miss White, "and done without the teacher's help. Their training has brought them to the point where they know how to criticize themselves. Let's see what they've learned.

(1) To measure their progress in terms of standards.
(2) To plan better as the result of self-criticism.
(Criticism and planning were practically merged.)
(3) To analyze the job to be done in terms of time limits."[6]

This kind of thoughtful self-evaluation reflects some growth and maturity in this kind of small group procedure. It takes place early in all groups in some form or other. It may be only in the form of such statements as "Wow, was that a terrible meeting!" "Boy, we really cooked with gas today!" "What's wrong with you people? We aren't getting anywhere!"

The need is for periodic, planned evaluations with an attempt to get some kind of consensus on how the group is doing and why, and what this means for the future. In this connection the teacher may have to lead in suggesting a systematizing of continuous evaluation efforts.

[6] Ned A. Flanders, *Teaching with Groups* (Minneapolis: Burgess Publishing Company, 1954), pp. 31–32. Reprinted by permission.

THE TERMINAL EVALUATION

Evaluation which comes at the end of an educative experience can be of two types. The first is more objective measurement and tends to emphasize specific learnings in terms of skills and facts. The second is more subjective and deals with attitudes, insights, understandings, and appreciations.

We think that neither type of terminal evaluation should be slighted. Most emphasis is given at present in typical evaluation procedures to measurements of facts and skills. If the procedures and attitudes prevail which we have described, and if skills and facts are part of the explicit objectives of the group, a teacher may expect to find similar or better achievement in mastery of skills and facts when compared with more formal, total class provisions for teaching and learning.

Much evidence, gathered from testimony of teachers who have tried experimental methods such as small group procedures, and from more formal research studies, indicates that pupil achievement in skills and information is not lowered, *providing sound principles of teaching and learning are incorporated into the experimental techniques.* We submit that small group procedures as we have outlined them are based on sound principles which stem from research in learning and human development.

In addition, however, there are many "intangibles" of which we have urged consideration that are included in the objectives of small group teaching and learning. Responsibility, cooperation, initiative, objectivity, social and personal adjustment are important concomitant learnings. How do you evaluate for these things? In Table 6 an evaluation instrument for these "intangibles" is found that may be helpful for use both during small group experiences and at their conclusion.

TABLE 6

How Did Our Meeting Go?

Did members work well so that no one had to carry		
more than his share of work?	Yes_____	No_____

How many worked? All_____Most_____Half_____
Few_____

| Did you work to your own satisfaction? | Yes_____ | No_____ |

Source: Dade County Schools, *Tentative Guide for Basic Education in Dade County Junior High Schools* (Bulletin No. 10; Miami: The Schools, 1952), p. 29. Reprinted by permission.

Did we know what we were going to do when we started?	Yes_____	No_____
Did you get said what you wanted to say?	Yes_____	No_____
Did you catch yourself talking more than you intended to talk?	Yes_____	No_____
Did you feel that the good points you made were fully considered?	Yes_____	No_____
Did you succeed in helping other pupils?	Yes_____	No_____
Did you succeed in helping everyone move forward?	Yes_____	No_____
Do you feel that you had to carry more than your share of work in the meeting?	Yes_____	No_____
Do you feel that you did as good a job as you usually do?	Yes_____	No_____
Did the chairman do a good job?	Yes_____	No_____
Did the group give him help in deciding the order of business?	Yes_____	No_____
Did the group help in summarizing the work?	Yes_____	No_____
Do you think we did in this meeting what we started out to do?	Yes_____	No_____
What does this group need to watch for next time as far as habits of work are concerned? Comment on back of page if you will.		

Again, if small group procedures are employed skillfully, utilization of data-gathering instruments such as this will hearten teachers, both in respect to the testimony of learners and in providing leads for improving teaching and learning methods.

SO—WHY NOT TRY SMALL GROUPS?

By way of conclusion, we hope that our discussion of small group methods has created sufficient interest in the concepts to stimulate experimentation with them by the reader. We use the word "experimentation" advisedly, because there is still much to learn about this kind of teaching and learning.

However, we know enough by now to encourage even beginning teachers to try small group procedures in a limited way. As these attempts are carried through carefully and thoughtfully, with a sense of professional responsibility, we are confident that success will beget more experimentation and success. Out of such activity will arise a more comprehensive and definitive rationale for the use of group procedures in the classroom. This is the challenge and the opportunity for professional teachers.

FOR FURTHER STUDY

Association for Supervision and Curriculum Development, National Education Association, *Toward Better Teaching*. 1949 Yearbook; Washington, D.C.: The Association, 1949.
Chapters 3 and 4 include discussions of group work in the classroom.

Benne, Kenneth D., "More Learning Takes Place," *National Education Association Journal*, 43:205–208 (April), 1954.
An analysis of the various roles in the classroom group.

Betzner, Jean *et al.*, "Meeting the Needs of the Whole Child through Group Participation," *Teachers College Record*, 50:295–302 (February), 1949.
Includes discussion on how the teacher can work effectively with small groups in the classroom.

Bradford, Leland P., and Gordon L. Lippitt, "The Individual Counts," *National Education Association Journal*, 43:485–487 (November), 1954.
A discussion of nine principles to show some of the ways in which the emphasis and concern of the social sciences with the study of group relations have at their core the importance of the individual.

Department of Supervision and Curriculum Development, National Education Association, *Group Planning in Education*. 1945 Yearbook: Washington, D.C.: The Association, 1945.
Includes illustrations of group activity in the secondary school.

Flanders, Ned A., *Teaching with Groups*. Minneapolis: Burgess Publishing Company, 1954.
An excellent handbook of techniques of small group work for teachers and pupils.

Heisler, Walter, Marion Smedling, and Clyde M. Campbell, "Group Dynamics: A Junior High Class Experiments," *Clearing House*, 24:151–154 (November), 1949.
The report of an experiment conducted in a junior high school. The experiment was undertaken to determine whether group processes could be taught effectively to seventh-grade pupils.

Kaminsky, Albert, "Committee Activities in Social Studies," *High Points*, 37:68–73 (February), 1955.
A description of group work in a junior high school social studies class.

Leton, Donald A., "Group Processes: Some Implications in the Field of Education," *Education*, 73:135–140 (October), 1952.
Sets forth principles involved in group work and states implications that are suggestive for education. Includes discussion of group size, group readiness, group climate and discipline.

Miel, Alice, and Associates, *Cooperative Procedures in Learning*. New York: Bureau of Publications, Teachers College, Columbia University, 1952.
Filled with interesting examples from real school situations of how teachers employ small groups in their classrooms.

Noar, Gertrude, *Freedom to Live and Learn*. Philadelphia: Franklin Publishing & Supply Co., Inc., 1948.

A discussion of the organization, work, and reporting of classroom committees is included in Chapter 7.

————, *The Junior High School—Today and Tomorrow*. New York: Prentice-Hall, Inc., 1953.

Chapter 12 includes a treatment of committee work and group discussion techniques.

Seufer, Elizabeth, "Group Dynamics in Basic Business Classes," *United Business Education Association Forum*. VII, No. 8:38 (May), 1953.

A look at the group process as it occurred in a high school business class.

Simpson, Ray H., *Improving Teaching-Learning Processes*. New York: Longmans, Green & Co., Inc., 1953.

Chapter 11, "Developing Desirable Group Roles," includes a description of both student roles and teacher roles.

Spinks, Pearl, "Life Brought to Literature through Group Work," *English Journal*, 39:201–205 (April), 1950.

A description of groups at work in a high school literature class.

Strang, Ruth M., *Group Activities in College and Secondary School*. New York: Harper & Brothers Publishers, 1941.

A comprehensive treatment of group activities in all phases of school experience.

Wagner, Russell H., and Carroll C. Arnold, *Handbook of Group Discussion*. Boston: Houghton Mifflin Company, 1950.

A development of the fundamental principles of group discussion, with illustrations from adult life.

10. Guiding Learning Experiences Outside the Classroom

LEARNING is not confined to formal educational institutions such as the school. Experience is continuous for individuals, and all experiences potentially are learning experiences. We hope to control the nature and extent of learning more directly in schools through teachers, school environment, and educational methods which have been tested and found to be helpful in promoting learning.

Teachers often discover, however, that pupils do not always learn, even though teaching methods, materials, environment, and human relationships in the classroom seem to be the best. That is, they do not learn what teachers want them to learn, or they fail to learn as rapidly or as permanently as teachers hope might be the case. In contrast, teachers often are astounded by what pupils learn outside the classroom, and by the speed and permanence of that learning. We refer again to the testimony of the "Poor Scholar's Soliloquy":

In school, though, we've got to learn whatever is in the book and I just can't memorize the stuff. Last year I stayed after school every night for two weeks trying to learn the names of the Presidents. Of course I knew some of them like Washington and Jefferson and Lincoln, but there must have been thirty altogether and I never did get them straight.

I'm not too sorry though because the kids who learned the Presidents had to turn right around and learn all the Vice Presidents. I am taking the seventh grade over but our teacher this year isn't so interested in the names of the Presidents. She has us trying to learn the names of all the great American inventors.

I guess I just can't remember names in history. Anyway, this year I've been trying to learn about trucks because my uncle owns three and he says I can drive one when I'm sixteen. I already know the horsepower and

284

number of forward and backward speeds of twenty-six American trucks, some of them Diesels, and I can spot each make a long way off.[1]

This adolescent is characteristic of many youngsters of his age. Disdainful of what the school offers, or baffled by his inability to learn what is prescribed, he at the same time demonstrates competence in learning other subject matter and skills outside the school, sometimes more difficult than those the school requires.

We are not suggesting here that the school teach only those things which are seen by learners as immediate interests or values. However, when learning does not take place, it would seem that some change in method, environment, or other situational factors might be indicated. The possibilities of organized learning experiences outside the classroom, but still under the direction of the school, suggest some solutions to the problem of vitalizing education to the point where more learning takes place. There are no quick panaceas for the problems of teaching and learning; but the experimentation of many teachers with extra-mural activities urges wider use of this approach.

Such practice, however, requires an understanding on the part of teachers, pupils, administration, and parents that a redefinition of the modern curriculum includes all activities under the guidance of the school. No longer is the curriculum the sum total of all the courses of study nor can it be restricted to the four walls of a classroom. Students learn in the corridors and the cafeteria, on buses and playgrounds, in school clubs and activities. Our problem has been that we have not up to this time related and organized these learnings, or seen their implications for classroom learning. These experiences, both within and without the school, have truly been "extracurricular."

We hope that the next few years in secondary education will see greater flexibility in the daily schedules of teachers and pupils, in school buildings, in relations between the school and other community agencies, and in our conception of the school's job and the methods for doing this job. Both teachers in training and those in service will do well to prepare for the day when their classes will increasingly move out of the classroom for basic educational experiences and for experiences to supplement those in the formal classroom.

MAKING THE EXTRACURRICULUM CO-CURRICULAR

In most public high schools today, regardless of how they organize activities, pupils are urged to participate in some form of activity. In a

[1] Stephen M. Corey, "Poor Scholar's Soliloquy," *Childhood Education*, 20:219–220 (January), 1944. Reprinted by permission.

recent study of the United States Office of Education, it was indicated that two-thirds of the secondary schools in the nation schedule activity periods varying from less than 25 minutes a week to more than 275 minutes. It appears that the average school having activity periods uses from 125 to 175 minutes a week for this purpose.[2]

In many schools, however, little time within the daily class schedule has been found for these activities. The chief reason may be the unwillingness of the school to give curriculum status to pupil activities. When one sees some planless activity programs which are scheduled with inadequate supervision in after-school hours or evenings, we agree that they do not merit curricular status. Increasingly as more time within the regular school day is given to these activities, thereby giving greater assurance of the contributions of the whole staff to the program, the extent and quality of the activity program will earn for it curricular status.

In many schools, the best teaching is done in the so-called "extracurricular program." As a result, the greatest amount of learning takes place in these situations. Teachers, freed from the restrictions of mandated syllabi or from their own self-imposed concepts of what should be learned, guide informally the experiences of learners who have been given and have assumed more responsibility for their own activities. This, in short, is the best description of the conditions conducive to learning, either in or out of the classroom. Infrequently do we find them in the classroom. More frequently they characterize activity programs. The question becomes: how can the classroom be vitalized by the spirit and energy found in extra-mural activities?

The key person, as in all educational endeavors, is the teacher. His insight into the nature of and the need for pupil activity programs is absolutely necessary. Such a teacher recognizes that much of learning is dependent on such factors as (1) opportunity for exploration and discovery, (2) self-selection of activity, (3) recognition for achievement, and (4) informal, social relations which engender security. The intelligent teacher recognizes too that in the formal classroom situation most of these factors are lost in the shuffle of daily routines, of struggling to "cover ground," and of sheer numbers of pupils. A professional teacher covets therefore the opportunity to relate himself to situations where he and his students may shake off at least some of the inhibiting influences of the classroom to settle down to real work on some real interests and problems.

[2] United States Office of Education, *The Activity Period in Public High Schools* (Bulletin 1951, No. 19; Washington, D.C.: Government Printing Office, 1951), pp. 16–17.

STUDENT BODY ASSEMBLIES

For example, the student assembly program is something which has not been seen in the secondary school for its fullest potentialities. Many high school teachers and administrators regard school assemblies as useful for the observance of national holidays and other occasions, for furnishing professional, paid entertainment to pupils, and for developing student body unity and morale. We propose that frequently student convocations could be used to interpret and illustrate phases of the school instructional program not commonly experienced by all pupils.

For example, a Pan-American fiesta program produced by the modern language teacher and pupils would not only be a good learning experience for the audience but could serve to interest pupils in foreign language study. Science demonstrations of the more spectacular variety staged by teacher and pupils can serve the same purposes for boys and girls not taking science as part of their program. Countless other examples could be given from all subject fields to point up the interesting, the exciting, and the dramatic elements of learning which are present in all areas, but which frequently are displaced by the more drab aspects of the field.

To some, this contrast between classroom routines and pupil activity programs may seem overdrawn. It may be that some teachers can introduce elements of the activity program into the classroom. There are some teachers who on certain days have clubs and other kinds of activities related to the subject of the class in their own class periods. But largely, the pupil activity program is divorced from the "more respectable" subject curriculum. The latter statement in effect dramatizes the split between learners and learning in many schools. A recognition of this separation by teachers will aid in bringing the two closer together, both in and out of the classroom.

CLASS WORK AND THE ACTIVITY PROGRAM

Activity programs were first begun by teachers who saw in them opportunities to reinforce or supplement their regular class program. That is, an English teacher saw a literary club as an opportunity to encourage creative writing or to cover certain more advanced readings which were impossible in classes because of the time element or because of the heterogeneity of the class. He volunteered to sponsor it chiefly for that reason.

Cast in such a setting, it is small wonder that most students saw these kinds of activities as mere extensions of the classroom. Of more recent development, English teachers are sponsoring student activities which depart rather widely from the classroom emphases and stress such communication media as the radio, television, the movies, and the theater. These are closer to the everyday experiences of most adolescents, and to some are exciting examples of "language in action." As such, they are more suitable for an activity program than a club devoted to book reviews.

Every subject field—science, social studies, mathematics, physical education, industrial arts, fine arts, home economics, and others—all have implications for activity programs which can both supplement the classroom experience in these areas and open up completely new avenues for teachers and learners. The important learning factors for adult advisers to remember are those listed previously: (1) opportunity to explore and discover, (2) opportunity for self-selection of activity, (3) opportunity to gain recognition for achievement, (4) opportunity for informal socialization. If these are present, the chances for success are greater than in situations which are more highly structured and therefore more like classrooms.

Perhaps by now the reader may have asked himself, "Why can't such activities take place in the classroom? Why must there be an activity program?" If one sees such activities as have been suggested to be learning experiences related to a subject field, there is less reason to keep them out of the classroom. But realistically, many teachers say, "I don't have time now to cover the syllabus; my principal doesn't approve; my pupils won't pass state examinations." If these factors operate, teachers may well have to divorce such learning activities from the classroom. In this case, they become extracurricular. They are related to the curriculum, but are at best stepchildren or "poor cousins."

In other schools where greater local autonomy exists, and where administrators invite teachers to vitalize the curriculum by experimentation, the incorporation of the activity program into the curriculum is feasible and desirable. Certain administrative arrangements such as scheduling of classes, teacher assignments, and methods of procuring materials will need revision; but the net result will be greater learning and happier teachers and pupils.

For some time to come, however, the activity program as a separate entity in the school day is likely to persist. Good teachers will continue to view the activity program as co-curricular in nature and deserving as much energy and creativity as a class. It will be seen by some as supplementary to class work, by others as a new avenue for creativity and learning. In either case, the activity program is a professional responsibility of teachers and not something to be regarded as an extra burden or a "frill" of modern education.

EXTRAMURAL CONTRIBUTIONS OF TEACHING FIELDS

If learning activities which we have been describing as "extracurricular" will enjoy no more status than that for some time to come, it seems wise to consider the nature of the contributions of the various subject fields in the secondary curriculum to an activity program. We believe this is realistic from the standpoint of current practice in organizing extracurricular activities and also in recognizing teachers' responsibilities for fostering such activities.

THE LANGUAGE ARTS

This field has long enjoyed respectability, both in its classroom program and in related activities. In the past, however, language arts or English teachers have tended to sponsor somewhat narrow types of activities, leading to rather academic pursuits such as creative writing, literary appreciation, debate, declamation, and the like. The appeal of this kind of activity is limited to the more proficient student in the language arts.

Modern activity programs provide for experience with language and communication forms and skills more closely geared to everyday interests and needs. Radio, television, movies, newspapers and magazines, the theater, and group discussion are media of communication much more appropriate to twentieth century living. The development of habits, attitudes, skills, understandings, and appreciations pertinent to these cultural phenomena is more functional, and therefore more appealing to learners, than hearing book reviews, writing poetry, essays, and short stories, or engaging in formal debates. Life is not lived in this context by the majority of people. School activities should therefore be geared more realistically to the interests and pursuits of people with a view to broadening interests, refining tastes, and developing skills when appropriate. In matters of skill development, school publications offer an excellent avenue to the interests of aspiring writers and create a continuing experience for larger numbers of pupils than do literary or creative writing clubs.

This is not to say that extra-class activities in language arts should be limited to the needs and interests of pupils related to mass media of communication. There still may be room for book review groups, debating societies, and creative writing clubs. But these should come after the experiences with and through language have been provided for the rank and file of students. We say this because of our concern for making the American high school more democratic in its activity programs, and because many classroom programs in English and language arts are devoid of any sustained efforts to give experiences in connection with the modern forms of communication.

THE SOCIAL STUDIES

In this area of pupil activities we believe schools have barely scratched the surface. Most classroom activity is confined to reading and talking about man—his history, his institutions, his relations with other men, and his contemporary problems. Examination of courses of study and textbooks reveals most of the time is spent on pre-twentieth century material. As a result, activities in the extracurricular program are mostly extensions of the classroom in terms of history clubs, political science clubs, contemporary affairs study groups, and the like. The activity has been chiefly more reading and talking; thereby, it has failed to attract any but the most proficient of pupils in the social studies.

In contrast, we propose that activities stemming from this area ought to stress social action. It may be that the bulk of "material to be covered" is so staggering in the social sciences that activities in conjunction with class work seem impossible. Therefore we suggest that the extracurricular program ought to be real activity—the translation of the ideals and goals of social studies into social action.

This would mean that student groups would be fostered by social studies teachers to become active agents in school and community endeavors. Cleanup drives, housing surveys, studies of community recreational needs, campaigns to get out the vote, and programs sponsoring exchange of students with foreign lands are but a few examples of student activities growing out of social studies. Such a related program to the social studies might make this area of study more popular than recent surveys of pupil opinion have revealed it to be.

MATHEMATICS AND SCIENCE

The more exact fields of science and mathematics have in the past drawn a very select group into related activities in the extracurricular program. More often than not, they have been direct extensions of the classroom work, allowing more time for laboratory experimentation, demonstrations, or the development and application of advanced concepts in quantitative thinking. And yet most teachers of science and mathematics would insist that their fields hold general education values.

What they fail to see is that their areas do not function as general education unless learners see meaning and application for themselves in everyday life. The problem becomes one of reducing scientific and mathematical concepts and methods to the level where more people see the importance of their use in daily living.

We suggest that this can best be done by providing activities in which pupils can test for themselves these concepts and methods which seem so abstract in the classroom. Science and mathematics clubs should engage directly in home, school, and community endeavors which test and apply classroom learnings in these areas. Studies and surveys of school and community health conditions, pupil management of student accounts, surveying of home and school properties, group recommendations on school lighting, heating, ventilation, and the like, preparation of graphs and charts on school costs and other statistical information are examples of how the areas of math and science might be vitalized for more pupils. Such translation of the abstractions and symbols of mathematics and science into action programs for youth is sorely needed if these areas are not to become special education alone, primarily intended for engineers, technicians, researchers, and other professional workers.

The following description is illustrative of a community project in health, emanating from a number of classes in a high school. Frequently, this kind of project becomes too great for one class to complete, thereby requiring the cooperative planning and activity of a number of classes in a school.

Each year the students allot time to plan and carry out some worthwhile health project. The most recent one grew out of a discussion with the doctor and the nurse. They spoke of the most urgent health problems of the country. They finally agreed that the most important project to work on would be that of getting the parents of all pre-school children within the county to have their children inoculated against whooping cough and other communicable diseases.

The county was divided into zones. Each class was responsible for contacting every family within its zone.

A committee was appointed to make a form, which would include a place for each person's name, address, and age and would list most of the communicable diseases.

All students were given as many forms as needed. They were to check off any of the diseases that the child had been inoculated against. Each parent was urged to take the child to the health department on a given day.

After all families had been contacted, the forms were placed on file to be checked against the ones they would compile in the coming years.[3]

THE SPECIAL AREAS

Having paid attention to the four so-called academic areas—English, social studies, mathematics, and science—we turn now to other areas of the curriculum which have been designated as specialties, at least in the senior high school. This designation may trouble teachers of the so-called "specials" as most of them argue that their fields, or at least elements of them, are general education.

And yet by the nature of the traditional high school curriculum with its Carnegie units and its system of electives and constants, these areas are not required of all students, or if required, do not earn "full credit." As such, they are "specials," not general education.

In view of this fact, it is difficult to see why activity programs related to these special areas are often restricted to pupils regularly enrolled in classroom courses in these areas. That is, teachers of shop, agriculture, music, art, and home economics may discourage pupils from joining clubs or other activities associated with these areas if they have not had related classroom work. It would seem that the opportunity for participation in related activities should be unrestricted if teachers are really sincere about the general education value of these subject areas.

It can be said that some of the most vital activity programs in the entire school program are found in these areas. The Future Farmers of America in the vocational agriculture field is a good example. In this organization, boys have an opportunity to relate their theory and farm practice to individual and group action programs, geared to the improvement of farms, farmers, and farming generally. They subscribe to "Learning by Doing."

Other fields such as shop, home economics, music, physical education, art, and business education have been able to incorporate direct experience and activity into their programs better than the academic subjects. This may be due in part to the nature of the subject matter; but it seems likely that teachers in the special areas are able to see more clearly the importance of activity in learning, of relating verbal aspects of experience to more direct overt behavior, and of evaluating learning in terms of behavior change.

Consider the enthusiasm, interest, growth, and achievement seen

[3] Association for Supervision and Curriculum Development, National Education Association, *Developing Programs for Young Adolescents* (Washington, D.C.: The Association, 954), pp. 35–36. Reprinted by permission.

in interscholastic and intramural athletics, in concerts and marching bands, orchestras, choirs, and ensembles. To a lesser degree because of fewer numbers involved, we see the same involvement in activity programs related to art, shop, home economics, and other areas where lifelike, active participation is afforded learners. We are not arguing that the curriculum become an activity program, or that even more time and attention be given to these phases of the curriculum. Two things are suggested: (1) many things can be learned by academic teachers from the so-called "special" subjects and teachers in regard to planning, implementing, and evaluating educational experiences; (2) the academic respectability of the so-called "solids" or "constants" needs re-evaluation in terms of learning outcomes and their significance in everyday living of boys and girls.

This point of view is not revolutionary. Essentially it is conservative in the sense that we believe in the importance of the contributions of English, social studies, science, and mathematics, both for general education and for specialized pursuits. Our concern is that because of their lack of vitality and meaning for large numbers of secondary school youth, they may become the areas of school life and learning which are only endured or tolerated by many pupils so that they may participate in the activities more lifelike and significant to them. Thus we have the paradox of the "specialties" becoming general education for many pupils and the general education program developing into "specialties" for a few.

Our curriculum design, however, is such that we try to guarantee general education through constants or required subjects and special education through the electives. What is required as long as this kind of subject-area curriculum persists is a vitalizing of the required subjects by more pupil participation in active applications of these subject fields to life situations and problems, both in the regular classes and in the extracurricular program. At the same time more respectability must be granted, creditwise and supportwise, to the "special fields" and to the activities growing out of them.

This is not the ultimate resolution of the problem of greater incorporation of activity into the school program. But until the secondary school loses its inflexibility caused by Carnegie units and credits, by bells ringing every forty to sixty minutes, and by teachers and parents who give homage only to the verbal and the abstract, we will have to settle for the very occasional classroom "activities" or "projects" or "field trips," and for a well-related activity program geared to meeting the needs of adolescents with which the curriculum does not concern itself or treats in an academic fashion.

In this setting all teachers have a responsibility not only to supply creative activities for classrooms but also to foster extracurricular programs for pupils. This attitude may well be the difference between their being seen by pupils as the stereotype of the dull, pedantic person "who teaches school," and a real, live friend of pupils who guides their learning experiences into more active, lifelike situations. But even more important, vital activities in and out of the classroom may make the difference between holding students in school and having them drop out; between dull, routine lesson hearing associated with most academic classrooms and exciting, rewarding activities which culminate in behavioral changes; and between pupils who view schools and learning as a socially desirable but not particularly personally satisfying experience and young people who see in all experience, in and out of school, now and for the rest of their lives, opportunities for learning.

THE FIELD TRIP AS AN EDUCATIONAL EXPERIENCE

As long as there have been schools, there probably have been some teachers who have accompanied their classes on excursions into the near-by neighborhood in order to have a direct experience under guidance with some phase of the community. This has been particularly true of elementary schools and teachers. For some reason, people have felt that this was a more appropriate type of learning experience for children than for youth and adults. Perhaps the real reason for using this teaching method more in the elementary school than in the secondary lies in our greater concern at the secondary level for "covering ground" in books, our faith in vicarious or recalled experiences, and the difficulty of moving out of the school building under a time schedule which is more rigid and under a departmentalized organization of learning experiences.

Whatever the reasons, it has been only in recent years that secondary schools have made greater use of field trips and excursions. Improved school transportation facilities have also made possible more extended trips than into the immediate neighborhood of the school. Many communities even provide for extended tours by the senior class to a different section of the country, to some distant historical location, or to the nation's capital.

In many cases, unfortunately, these trips and excursions, whether local or extended, are not always fully exploited for their educational values. We propose to suggest at this juncture a discussion of how

PLATE 27. LEARNING ABOUT TRANSPORTATION AT FIRST HAND. A supervised field experience will reinforce classroom learnings. (Courtesy of the Civil Aeronautics Administration)

field trips may be initiated, planned, implemented, and evaluated for educational purposes.

THE POTENTIAL CONTRIBUTIONS OF FIELD TRIP EXPERIENCES

Rather than enumerating the advantages of field trips and excursions, we believe the testimony of teachers in the schools may be more persuasive. The following is from an introduction to a field trip manual of the Portland, Oregon, Public Schools:

Too often, we as teachers tend to think of education as taking place within the four walls of the classroom. We attempt to bring into the classroom, through the aid of motion pictures, radio, pictures, books and other instructional materials, many vicarious experiences which will help the child to better understand the world where he lives. This is as it should be. The greater the variety of learning experiences, the better the opportunity we have of reaching the children and making their learning experiences more meaningful and dynamic. However, because formal education has been thought of as taking place within the school we have not made extensive use of the rich resources which surround the school. Factories, banks, warehouses, docks, ships, bakeries, fire stations, rivers, and the like, are available to the teachers as instructional laboratories.

In a democracy we are striving to prepare young people to live in a complex world. It is important that in his formal educational experience the pupil understand the cultural heritage of this country. It is equally important that he learn to know and understand the living and dynamic community of which he is a part. Such learnings can be derived from books and other instructional devices, but one of the best ways to get this understanding is for the student and his teacher to visit and study the community. Field trips are not just excursions to help young people escape from the classroom. They are carefully selected experiences which the teacher and the student feel are necessary to give them a better insight into the highly complex structure of our society. By seeing how the people in the community work and play the student not only collects and tabulates the facts, but he also learns to appreciate the wide variety of jobs to be done in order to carry on the activities of the community.

As teachers, we cannot allow the school to become an island separated from the main stream of the community life. It is our job to help build bridges between the community and the school room. These should be two-way bridges which allow easy access for the children and the teachers to go out from the school to study the various facets of community life. These bridges should also make it easy for the adult members of the society to visit the school and bring into the classroom their wealth of experience and background. If we are to develop children into well informed and forward looking citizens we should make use of every opportunity to bring them into contact with every important aspect of the community activities. It is important to realize that the field trip is but the starting point of an educational experience. After the child gets back to the classroom, it is the function of the teacher to carry on what John Dewey advocates, namely, expanding the meaning of the experience. In other words, it is the function of the follow-up within the classroom to help the child realize the full meaning of the experience he has just completed. The social, political, and economic aspects of a field trip should be pointed out. All of these should be in keeping with the maturity level of the child.[4]

The Great Neck, New York, Public Schools in their field trip manual suggest the following uses for a field trip:

1. To serve as an exploratory experience to gain firsthand knowledge and information
2. To gather instructional materials and aids
3. To create and widen interest
4. To enrich classroom instruction
5. To verify previous information, class discussion, conclusions, or individual experiments[5]

THE INITIATION OF FIELD TRIPS

The second statement (Great Neck, N.Y.) suggests how field trips may originate as part of the teaching-learning process. The first possibility to be considered is the use of the field trip as a means "to

---

[4] Department of Instructional Materials, Portland Public Schools, *The Community —Our Classroom* (Portland, Ore., 1950), p. IV. Reprinted by permission.

[5] Audio-Visual Services, Great Neck Public Schools, *Educational Field Trips* (Great Neck, N.Y., 1952), p. 1. Reprinted by permission.

create and widen interest." Most teachers regard as one of their responsibilities the broadening of horizons and the creation of new interests in pupils. Assuming this responsibility frequently carries with it frustration for teachers and pupils alike, as teachers' interests frequently do not develop or expand for the learners. Mere talk about these new interests or exhortations on the importance of new concepts and experiences are not persuasive to many pupils. They must "see for themselves." With seeing may come "believing," or at least a willingness to explore further the possibilities of a new experience.

This use of field trips as a preliminary activity to a unit of work is particularly beneficial in situations where cooperative planning of the curriculum by teacher and pupils has not or cannot be done. For example, the science syllabus may ask for the teaching of conservation. This may not "click" with learners until a field trip to various points in the immediate area dramatizes the need of conservation as evidenced by soil erosion, stream pollution, destruction of parks and public lands, and the like.

Even more vital is the field trip which grows out of a problem which is identified and accepted by teachers and pupils. The trip may be used "to serve as an exploratory experience to gain firsthand knowledge and information." This purpose makes the data-gathering phase of the problem-solving approach to learning a much more vital one than having only library research. For example, in a civics class a visit to a court and interviews with a judge, bailiff, and lawyers will do more for pupils, both factually and attitudewise, than reading books, the usual procedure for research in secondary school social studies.

Another kind of purpose is "to gather instructional materials and aids." This service function of a field trip is used particularly when it is not feasible to send a whole class or when some division of labor is necessary. A committee may be sent to a community source of information, such as the public library or newspaper morgue, to secure facts without which the study in local history would be incomplete and lacking in color not supplied by usual sources.

The field trip can also "enrich classroom instruction" by making more tangible the concepts or abstractions which may have been read or discussed prior to the trip. This is an important contribution to learners who find it difficult to conceptualize or who have a meager background of experience on which to base their reading and discussion. Frequently, girls find it difficult in science to visualize machines or processes which boys have seen in the run of their everyday experience. They are handicapped until they are brought up to date by a field trip which stresses observation.

PLATE 28. A FIELD TRIP TO LOCAL INDUSTRY PROVIDES NEW INSIGHTS.
Facts, skills, appreciations, and understandings become more real
to learners in such a setting. (Courtesy of the Alameda, California,
County Schools)

Finally, there is the use of the field trip as a culminating experience.
In this case teacher and learners see the trip as a means "to verify
previous information, class discussion, conclusions, or individual
experiments." This is the reinforcement stage of learning, in which
teacher and learner review and reteach the completed unit of work.
Often this phase seems dull and repetitious to the learner in the
classroom. A trip can serve the purpose in a more vital and meaningful
way and bring a unit of work to a satisfying conclusion.

For example, the use of the field trip as a culminating experience
may be seen in a geometry class's visit to public buildings to observe
and draw architectural designs which have their origin in geometric
figures; the report of a committee interview of a local poet-historian
in his own home, as a capstone to a study of state and local writers;
and a half-day bus tour of the county by a geography class which

has been studying the effects of topography, climate, and natural resources on the economy of the county.

PLANNING THE FIELD TRIP

Preliminary planning by the teacher or a committee should begin immediately after the need for a field trip has been made evident and there is consensus on the time and place of the trip. The following may serve as a check list for contacts to be made:

I. School Authorities
 A. Permission for class to go
 B. Standard forms for parents to fill out
 C. Clearance to avoid conflicts with other school events, other transportation demands, etc.
II. Community Resource to be Visited
 A. Telephone or personal interview with responsible person, seeking permission to visit
 B. Furnish size and age of group, particular interest or purpose in visit
 C. Agree on date, time, and length of visit
III. Transportation
 A. Make arrangements with school transportation agent or public transportation company on time, place of pickup, length of trip, time of return
 B. Determine pupil fee (if any)
IV. Parents
 A. Send home with pupils brief description of purpose, time and cost of trip
 B. Request prompt return of permission slips
V. Other Contacts
 A. Eating places, if meals are required

PREPARING FOR THE FIELD TRIP

During and after these preliminary planning steps, the teacher and class should plan together for the trip. Decisions must be made on what every class member will be expected to do while on the trip. There will also be responsibilities for certain pupils as committee members charged with specific jobs. The Portland, Oregon, manual suggests the following class preparations as appropriate to cooperative group planning for a field trip:

A. Establish a definite purpose, tied in with unit.
B. List points to be observed.
C. Formulate questions to be asked.
D. Order related instructional materials (i.e., audiovisual aids, library books, pamphlets).

E. Plan committees:
    Contact committee—resource and transportation
    Finance committee—collection of fees
    Courtesy committee—brush up on manners
    Safety committee—monitors
    Recording committee—keep an account
    Materials committee—handle bulletins, related materials
    Several committees to report on various specific points to be observed.[6]

We are not suggesting that such a pattern is appropriate for all classes and purposes. It is important, however, that teacher and pupils do a very careful job on planning the trip in the interests of safety, public relations, and achievement of goals for the trip. A group trip involving from thirty to forty pupils is not a small task. It requires systematic cooperative effort on the part of everyone; for that reason it is an excellent experience for developing skills of cooperation, responsibility, and leadership.

ACTIVITIES ON THE TRIP

The trip to and from the destination can be altered so as to allow many observations to be made of points of interest, topography, and the like. Noting and listing things on the way to and from a destination can be fun and profitable. If the itinerary has been cooperatively planned, maps may be made to chart the course of the bus. This is an experience which frequently pupils could benefit from in respect to an appreciation of distances, locations, and relations, both in one's own community and in more distant areas.

Of course, the destination for the trip is the challenge of the entire venture. Here under the guidance of teacher, official guides, and others, pupils should have enough direction to know what to look for and ask about, and enough freedom to exercise initiative, self-activity, and observation within the limits imposed by the situation and group. The learners should come to a field trip destination armed with questions from themselves and the teacher, and equipped with notebooks or clipboards for recording answers. There is some value in the latter case to assigning the recording of facts, answers, and so forth to a few people so as to free others for wider observation, free questioning, picture taking, and the gathering of materials and samples.

The general conduct and effectiveness of the visit at the destination can largely be determined ahead of time by the nature and extent of the teacher's previous knowledge of what can be seen and learned, by the planning of specific activities for pupils in groups or as indi-

---

[6] Department of Instructional Materials, *op. cit.*, p. 1b. Reprinted by permission.

viduals, by provision for adequate record keeping, and by some prior attention being paid to what follow-up activities will take place after the trip.

UTILIZING THE TRIP IN THE CLASSROOM

The reconstruction of the field trip experience with emphasis on information gained, materials procured, and generalizations established is the essential culmination of a field trip. However, this can be a letdown for the pupil after the real and vital experiences of the trip itself. Enough time must be spent to clinch learnings, and yet care should be taken to close out an experience and the discussion of it before boredom sets in.

Again, the Portland and Great Neck manuals respectively furnish some suggestions for follow-up activities:

Follow-up Activities
   Thank you letters to resource telling values derived from the visit, to parents who helped, etc.
   Review instructional materials
   Pictures
   Reports
   Diagnose mistakes and difficulties
   Evaluate trip in terms of purpose
   Discuss and appraise conduct
   Record trip permanently
   Check for increased information, changed attitudes
   Teacher send report to Administration office if the resource visited was not satisfactory or cooperative, also for outstanding resource[7]
Suggested follow-up activities
   1. Reports from pupils
   2. Discussion of reports, questions by pupils and teacher, evaluating reports
   3. Writing acknowledgment letters, compositions, news releases, etc.
   4. Reading of various materials related to trip
   5. The use of a film, filmstrip, or other audiovisual material for additional information
   6. Sharing of trip experience with other classes through the use of public-address system presentation, sound recorder, school newspaper, oral reports, school displays, pamphlets, books
   7. Classroom displays and activities which could be used to illustrate or duplicate the activities observed on the trip
   8. Cooperative evaluation by pupils and teacher, and suggestions for improving future trips[8]

[7] *Ibid.*, p. 1c. Reprinted by permission.
[8] Audio-Visual Services, *op. cit.*, p. 2. Reprinted by permission.

We hope that the foregoing discussion has furnished the reader with a better understanding of the potentialities and problems of field trip organization. Three items remain for further elaboration.

Any field trip should require careful evaluation by pupils, teachers, administration, hosts or resource persons, and parents. This cooperative pooling of judgments is surely required to test the validity of claims made for this kind of direct experience. Subsequent trips can be improved, and subsequent classes should profit by the successes and failures on field trips of their predecessors. For example, the following evaluation guide would assist teacher and pupils in assessing the quality of their field trip experience.

Was the Trip a Success?
    a. Did the trip answer the pupils' questions?
    b. Did the pupils cooperate enthusiastically and well?
    c. Were the pupils enthusiastic and satisfied with trip?
    d. Were the pupils willing and eager to make assigned reports?
    e. Did the pupils abide by majority rule?
    f. Did pupils share field glasses, cameras, pictures and other materials generously?
    g. Did pupils gain a greater respect for their property and the property of others?
    h. Did pupils get a better understanding of the geography and industries of Dearborn?
    i. Did pupils gain an appreciation of Dearborn's culture such as its schools, churches, libraries, public buildings, boulevards, parks and museums?
    j. Did the trip develop in the pupils a sense of loyalty for and an appreciation of the many wonderful things in Dearborn? They should be proud of their city.[9]

In fact, we believe that such a check list might serve, with adaptations, as an evaluation guide for teachers and learners following any kind of extra-classroom activity growing out of the formal instructional program. Rephrasing the above questions in the light of preplanned goals, activities, materials, and the like would serve to focus attention on learning outcomes, both specific and general. Such attention is highly important for the continued use and success of learning experiences which take place outside the classroom under the supervision of the school.

Another outgrowth of field trips over a period of time can be the accumulation of considerable information about field resources. These should be pooled and organized into a manual on field trips, including

[9] Department of Audio-Visual Instruction, *Field Trip Handbook* (Dearborn, Mich.: The Schools, 1950), p. xviii. Reprinted by permission.

suggestions for planning, execution, and follow-up of trips, and a catalogue of outstanding places to visit, together with helpful information on these locations. For example, the following page from the Dearborn, Michigan, manual would be helpful to other teachers unfamiliar with this particular area.

PLACE: Willow Run Airport
ADDRESS: Ypsilanti, Michigan   TEL. NO. Ypsi. 3220
PERSON TO CONTACT: Mr. Weidenbach or Mr. Miller
OBJECTIVE: To see how a large airport is constructed, arranged and conducted, to provide a safe landing place for large freight and passenger planes.
THINGS TO SEE AND DO: The class will be taken through the control tower (in small groups), then through the hangars to the observation deck where they may see passenger, mail, and cargo planes landing, unloading, and taking off. If a plane is in and not due to take off for some time, you *may* be taken through a plane.
OBSERVATIONS EN ROUTE: Explain why the Expressway was built. Point out the Village of Wayne to the east of Expressway as you pass by. Point out the Kaiser-Frazer automobile plant near the airport and explain why it was built, by whom and why. Notice barrack-like buildings, built to house workers during the war.
TEACHING AIDS: Films: *An Airplane Trip* and *Behind the Scenes at the Airport*
                  Filmstrips: *Airplanes at Work* and *History of Air Transportation*
AGE OF CHILDREN PERMITTED: 8 years and up
NUMBER IN GROUP: 40 in group—not over 40
VISITING DAYS AND HOURS: Monday through Friday—8:00 A.M. to 4:30 P.M.
TIME REQUIRED FOR TOUR: 2 hours
DIRECTIONS TO GET THERE: Take M-12 Expressway until signs direct you to turn in to the air terminal.
GUIDE SERVICE: Ask for Mr. Bane. Make arrangements one week in advance.
EATING ACCOMMODATIONS: Cafeteria
ADMISSION FEE: None[10]

Finally, there remains the question of the place of the field trip in the over-all plan of an educational program. Obviously, direct experiences provide real opportunities for learning which can be used in many ways for many purposes. Realistically, it must be suggested that field trips, like any educational practice, can be overdone. If such is the case, loss in interest, of purpose and thereby of meaning, will follow. Value judgments must also be made in relation to the time, money, and effort expended. Consideration must be given to the in-

[10] *Ibid.*, p. 7. Reprinted by permission.

fringements made on other teachers' time and the possible problems in human relationships which may stem from too many field trips. On such matters involving judgments, the younger teacher does well to get the opinions of older teachers, the administration, and possibly parents in order to maintain a nice balance in providing these kinds of direct experiences.

But even though these cautions are advanced, we still argue for the use of field trips more widely than now is the case. They can be a source of genuine stimulation to students who find it difficult constantly to deal in abstractions and in vicarious experiences. To other students, it will provide challenges to leadership and going beyond the ordinary requirements of the classroom. To all students, it can be a real experience in cooperative planning and action, on a more complex level than the classroom typically affords.

SCHOOL CAMPING AS AN EDUCATIONAL EXPERIENCE

A comparatively recent development in education has been the introduction of camping under school supervision. Some school systems own their own camps and operate a year-round program, for example, in Battle Creek, Michigan; San Diego County Schools, California; and Tyler, Texas. Others operate camps on leases at certain periods of the year when weather or other situational factors permit. Still others provide limited weekend experiences or periods of a few days, utilizing state parks or private camps as facilities.

In any case, a school camping program may involve teachers in planning at the school for the camping period and/or in direct participation at the camp. For all teachers, an appreciation of the potentialities of camping is important because their pupils and their instructional time may be involved in camping. The attitudes which teachers hold toward any extra-mural school activities are the result both of their basic educational philosophy and the information and understanding they have of the activities. We propose at this point to examine some outstanding camping programs to give the reader a picture of a growing innovation in the secondary school.

GENERAL CHARACTERISTICS

Camping activities can be described as follows: social living, healthful living, work experience, recreation, and outdoor education. These activities and the educational outcomes inherent in them are justification enough for camping. But the relation of camping experiences to the school curriculum gives greater meaning and vitality to cer-

PLATE 29. THE OUTDOORS CAN BECOME A LABORATORY. Firsthand observation makes books come alive. (Courtesy of the Fayette County, Kentucky, Public Schools)

tain aspects of formal school life which frequently students do not appreciate.

The general characteristics are headed by the experiences which encourage pupils better to work in groups and to assume responsibility for their own actions. The State of Michigan Department of Public Instruction lists these social learnings as follows:

SOCIAL LIVING

1. *Planning Program*
    a. Pre-camp planning by pupils
    b. Choosing camp activities and making schedules
    c. Pre- and post-camp evaluating sessions

2. *Camper and Staff Evaluation and Planning*

    EXAMPLES: Each program group made up of pupils and teachers holds informal evaluation sessions throughout the week. They talk over the experiences of the day and make final plans for the following day.

3. *Group Living at Camp*
   There are opportunities for social experiences that occur during meal-time, recreation, and planning sessions.

   EXAMPLES: Camper hosts and hostesses are at each table during meals. Guests are invited by hosts and hostesses to eat at tables with campers and are introduced to others at the table. Program groups are entirely responsible for evening activities.

4. *Camper-Teacher Relationship*
   The teacher and campers are members of the social group, which plans and works together.

   EXAMPLE: The teacher is a member of the program group in the role both of learner and of counselor.

5. *Opportunities to Face Social Situations*
   There is an understanding of problems of race and color—difference in religion—the participation problems of "round-the-clock" living.

   EXAMPLES: All groups, regardless of color, participate in all activities. At mealtime, students plan grace acceptable to all religious groups. Menus are prepared which conform to customs and religious beliefs.

6. *Development of Individual and Group Responsibility*

   EXAMPLES: The group assumes responsibility for actions of its members. Members are responsible to the group for moral and social behavior, safety, fire precaution, plans for a party, building fires, preparing and serving food, and keeping camp clean.

7. *Rendering Service to the Social Group*
   Services to the camp, the state, and the larger community provide for effective citizenship training.

   EXAMPLE: There are many work projects, such as reforestation, stream improvement, prevention of soil erosion, and construction of camp buildings.

8. *Personal Development*
   a. Opportunities to excel in some activity
   b. Gaining a sense of security and of acceptance by the social group
   c. Acquiring skills
   d. Attaining concepts such as the organic wholeness of nature; man's dependence on a bountiful nature; man's obligation to nature and to man

9. *Democratic Participation, Planning, and Solving Group Problems*

   EXAMPLES: Campers develop their own plans for camp government;

establish standards of acceptable social behavior; formulate and implement necessary rules and regulations.[11]

To some readers, these kinds of objectives may seem rather illusory. At least, many would say that school camping cannot be justified unless there are more solid learnings which can be measured. For these reasons, greater emphasis in the literature is given to other objectives of camping education. These may be listed as follows:

HEALTHFUL LIVING

1. *Food.* Planning of menus; purchasing food; preparation and serving of meals; eating wholesome food; learning proper habits of eating.
2. *Clothing.* Learning about proper clothing for dress in the out-of-doors in all kinds of weather. Pupils plan in advance what they should wear for cold weather, for working in streams, for hiking, and the like.
3. *Shelter.* Sleeping in the out-of-doors; planning and building temporary shelters; construction of permanent cabins.
4. *Sanitation.* Food handling; care of the kitchen; safe water for drinking and bathing; washing dishes; construction of temporary pit toilets.
5. *Exercise.* Hiking; work projects; outdoor sports.
6. *Rest and Relaxation.* Adequate sleep and rest; leisure time at meals; a program of activities.
7. *Opportunities for Good Mental Health.* Fun, opportunities for leadership, recognition as a member of the social group.
8. *Development of Aesthetic Sense of Awareness.* Dignity of man, interdependence of nature.

PURPOSEFUL WORK EXPERIENCES

1. *Improvement of the Camps*
   a. Building a cabin
   b. Cleaning and redecorating buildings
   c. Building trails
   d. Construction of roads
   e. Erection of guard rails
   f. Improvement of beaches
   g. Mapping
   h. Parking areas
   i. Sanitation
2. *Reforestation*
   a. Selective cutting and study of growth of timber
   b. Cleaning and brushing
   c. Planting of seedlings
   d. Hillside beautification
   e. Scaling timber
3. *Wildlife Management*
   a. Animal population studies—census, trapping, banding, deer drives

[11] Department of Public Instruction, *Youth Love "Thy Woods and Templed Hills"* (Lansing, Mich.: The Department, 1950), pp. 4–6. Reprinted by permission.

b. Environmental improvements—building brush shelter, planting game cover, construction of bird houses

c. Study of conservation laws and the role of government agencies

4. *Fish Management*
   a. Stream improvement
   b. Building deflectors
   c. Census—shock method for determining age of fish
   d. Study of food in lakes
   e. Sounding lakes for depth
   f. Prevention of lake and stream pollution
   g. Study of conservation laws and the role of government agencies

5. *Fire-Fighting and Fire Prevention*
   a. Use of power machinery
   b. Participation in actual fire control
   c. Fire-fighting methods—fire towers, ground and air equipment, lanes, back fires

6. *Soil Conservation*
   a. Activities in controlling erosion
   b. Fertility maintenance or restoration
   c. Planting shrubs, trees, and grass cover to prevent erosion
   d. Observation of contour plowing
   e. Soil testing

7. *Gathering Useful Data*
   a. Weather records
   b. Stream-flow records
   c. Phenological records
   d. Ecological records

RECREATIONAL LIVING

1. *Social Activities in Camp*
   a. Games and play activities
   b. Singing and storytelling
   c. Dramatics
   d. Ceremonials
   e. Vespers
   f. Camp-fire programs

2. *Outdoor Activities*
   a. Hiking and excursions
   b. Cook-outs and camp-outs
   c. Swimming and boating
   d. Skating, skiing, snowshoeing
   e. Archery
   f. Photography
   g. Fly tying and bait casting
   h. Hunting and fishing
   i. Use of firearms
   j. Woodcrafts
   k. Whittling
   l. Use of camping tools
   m. Care of tools and equipment
   n. Arts and crafts

OUTDOOR EDUCATION

1. *Science.* Experiences with soil, water, weather, plants, animals, and birds.
   a. Game and fish
   b. Developing a library and simple museum
   c. Understanding of forests, soil, and water through visits to points of special interest

    d. Activities in geology through visits to stone quarry, gravel pits, etc.

    e. Weather station activities

    f. Making maple sugar

    g. Photography

    h. Study of stars

    i. Use of simple keys for identification

    j. Museum preparation, such as elementary taxidermy, foliage impression, and making casts of animal tracks

    k. Use of compass

    l. Activities involving land use and types of soil

    m. Sanitation

    n. Water testing

    o. Use of fish shocking equipment

    p. Study of poison plants and methods of protection

    q. Use of plants for food

    r. Use of fire-fighting equipment

    s. Development of nature trails

    t. Mapping and aerial photo interpretation

2. *Social Science*

    a. Land use problems and reasons for shifting population; charts and maps

    b. Study of deserted farms

    c. Indian lore and stories of lumber camps

    d. History of the area

    e. Improvement of the camp community, such as landscaping, etc.

    f. Study of local industries, such as commercial fishing, sawmills, mining, and various types of agriculture, and forestry

    g. Study of dams and electric power—watershed concept and relation to other resources

    h. Care of public property

    i. Problems of stream pollution

    j. Visiting nearby rural schools

    k. Participation in government of the camp community

    l. Recreation patterns as determined by the land and people

3. *Language Communication*

    a. Keeping daily logs and journals

    b. Trip reports

    c. Evaluation reports

    d. Storytelling with use of visual aids

    e. Written reports

    f. Reading of camp stories and legends

    g. Pre- and post-camp planning in English classes

    h. Writing letters to family and friends, to land owners, and to participating agencies

    i. Appearances before clubs and organizations to report camp experience

    j. Labeling nature trails

  k. Use of literature involving the out-of-doors
  l. Writing poetry at camp
  m. Preparation of mimeographed take-home material
  n. Preparation of radio programs

4. *Mathematics*
  a. Computing costs of food and purchasing supplies
  b. Use of compass
  c. Surveying and mapping
  d. Operation of camp store and banking
  e. Developing financial report of camp—obvious and hidden costs
  f. Drawing plans for camp buildings, bird houses and other structures
  g. Making requisitions for supplies
  h. Mathematical computations involved in logging, determining board feet, etc.
  i. Angles in determining heights of trees and buildings
  j. Studying depth and surface of lake
  k. Use of laws of leverage
  l. Determination of land values
  m. Aerial photography interpretation
  n. Meteorology
  o. Inventories of camp materials and supplies

5. *Shop*
  a. Construction of bridges, cabins, deflectors
  b. Construction of needed equipment—bird houses, feeding stations, line traps, etc.
  c. Care and use of tools
  d. Blueprints
  e. Waterfront equipment
  f. Boat repair
  g. Making a simple boat equipment
  h. Construction of same
  i. Weather instruments and housing of same
  j. Exhibits construction
  k. Hail signs
  l. Bulletin boards
  m. Outdoor museum
  n. Exhibit cases

6. *Homemaking.* Assist camp staff in:
  a. Planning menus
  b. Purchasing, preparing, and serving foods
  c. Personal sanitation
  d. Decorating
  e. Use of proper clothing
  f. Making beds
  g. Cabin sanitation

h. Social graces at meals
i. Greeting guests and introductions
7. *Music, Art, Dramatics*
   a. Camp songs and instrumental music
   b. Use of native materials
   c. Creative drawing and sketching
   d. Ceremonials, pageantry, storytelling
   e. Recreational charades
   f. Preparation of visual materials to tell stories of things seen while at camp—posters, charts, exhibits, museums, layouts, nature trail signs
   g. Preparation of take-home materials printed or mimeographed.[12]

Although the claims made for learning outcomes from camping experiences may appear extravagant, we should remember that, like any statement of objectives, these outcomes will never be fully achieved at any one time or at one place. These are potentials in camping education and by no means have all of them been achieved by any school system. The degree to which they are realized is an index of the understanding and support given by teachers to the camping program. Few will deny the desirability of these outcomes. What is required is the willingness on the part of administrators and teachers to provide more flexibility in the use of school time, and less concern over the vested interests of subject fields.

An old saw is, "The whole child goes to school." We can also say, "The whole child goes to camp." The difference lies in the setting and motivation for learning. Whether we like it or not, the formal school situation does not supply a complete or satisfying environment. The testimony of students and teachers on their camping experiences is revealed in excerpts from their evaluations:

The most impressive part of our camping trip was the good friendships which were formed among campers and teachers.
There was better opportunity at camp for each individual to show what he really could do.
We liked daily evaluations and felt that the school program would be more valuable if it could be evaluated by students.
Learned a good deal that could not be taught as effectively in a classroom.
I learned more in four days in camp that I could in four weeks reading it out of a textbook.
We felt that the whole school should have a camping experience.
If a picture or illustration is worth a thousand words, a camp-out is worth an entire textbook.

[12] *Ibid.*, pp. 6–10. Reprinted by permission.

The camp-out enabled me to get better acquainted, to get along with a group, to learn more of biology, and to have a little fun.

Careful pre-planning in the pre-camp period showed good results in camp.

The camp programs provided excellent in-service training experiences for teachers.

The camp program has implications for each field of specialization, for each subject matter area in the secondary school.

The camping program offers many possibilities for student participation, self-realization, and security.

Better camper-teacher relationships were developed that otherwise would have been impossible in the classroom.[13]

What better kinds of evidence could one ask for on the degree of pupil involvement, the sense of achievement, the variety of goals and outcomes, and the wholesome tone of the learning experiences? These are the rewards of teachers, counselors, and administrators who move learning out of the classroom occasionally to allow pupils greater access to realistic problems and to lifelike experiences in solving them.

IMPLICATIONS FOR TEACHERS OF EXTRA-CLASS LEARNING EXPERIENCES

In this chapter we have demonstrated the efficacy of guided learning experiences outside the four walls of the classroom. Examples have been given of how teachers and pupils may plan for learning situations which are difficult to realize through vicarious experience. It has been recognized that certain blocks exist for a full utilization of the total school and community environment, but we believe that careful teacher-pupil planning can eliminate many of these barriers.

This required planning is a natural concomitant for a teacher and a class engaged in problem solving. The teacher will be in a position to see some of these real blocks to direct experiences better than most students. By reason of his greater maturity and his knowledge of administrative policies and procedures, he must be constantly alert for unrealistic projects and activities proposed by students. At times he must insist on decisions based on judgments affected by these policies, by limitations of time, distance, and the like, and by other curriculum demands and objectives. And yet most teachers could incorporate more planning with students for extra-class learning experiences, and still achieve their over-all objectives. In fact, we argue that many objec-

[13] *Ibid.*, pp. 26–31. Reprinted by permission.

tives are reached more completely by vitalizing the classroom group through direct experience in the larger community.

Such planning obviously demands knowledge on the part of the teacher of the teaching and learning resources in the total school and in the community. Participation in community affairs, systematic study of the local community by an individual teacher, or preferably by a total teaching staff, and faculty-wide consideration of administrative policies which will encourage learning experiences outside the classroom—all are necessary if advances are to be made in curriculum and teaching methods.

Why does this take place so infrequently in schools? We recognize the factors of cost, time, administrative rigidity, and other blocks. However, lack of insight and understanding about the potentialities of field trips, camping, community study, and the like more frequently are a barrier. This is an indictment of both pre-service and in-service education programs.

It falls to the responsibility of teacher-preparing institutions to provide teachers-to-be with both the theoretical backgrounds for understanding extra-class learning experiences and the opportunities for trying them out in their student teaching. Observation of and participation in community agencies working with children and youth have proved effective in some teacher-education institutions. And yet the full impact of both the problems and possibilities in making the total school and community the classroom will never fully be realized until a person is on the job in the real situation.

In-service education is the key to better utilization of all-school and community resources, as is the case in most endeavors to make teaching and learning more effective. Study groups to produce manuals and resource files for better utilization of field trips, camping, and local school and community resources are becoming more common. Another recent development is Business-Industry-Education days on which teachers visit local businesses and industries, or representatives from local concerns visit classrooms. From such activities have come closer articulation between classroom and community experiences, and open doors to class groups interested in visiting and studying the community at first hand.

Such developments do not come spontaneously. They require first the insight into the potentialities for learning to be found in moving out of the classroom. Secondly, they require the energy and professional zeal to plan for the utilization of direct experience in the community. It is hoped that this chapter has furnished the reader with these understandings. There remains his responsibility to translate these understandings into action on the job.

FOR FURTHER STUDY

"The Assembly Program in the Secondary School," *Bulletin*, No. 141, National Association of Secondary School Principals, Vol. 30 (November), 1946.

A summary of the best and most successful practices in planning and developing assembly programs in 336 secondary schools throughout the country.

Carroll, John S., "Camping Education Can Vitalize the Entire School Program," *Nation's Schools*, 45:28–31 (June), 1950.

A strong endorsement of school camping as an educative experience. Consistent with principles of human development and the laws of learning.

Cronholm, L. C., and Edgar A. Lansing, "What Are the Educational Values in Planned Field Trips?" *Bulletin*, No. 210, National Association of Secondary School Principals, 39:88–92 (April), 1955.

A report of a special study and controlled project to test differences in learning outcomes between classes which had common classroom experiences, but differed in that some had related field-trip experiences and others did not.

Fedder, Ruth, *Guiding Homeroom and Club Activities*. New York: McGraw-Hill Book Co., 1949.

One of the best books available for helping teachers become proficient in their work with student activities of various kinds.

French, Will, J. Dan Hull, and B. L. Dodds, *American High School Administration*, Chaps. 13 and 14. New York: Rinehart & Co., Inc., 1951.

Excellent consideration of the place of student activities in the total school program, and their contribution to educational outcomes.

Hoffman, Betty, "School Camping Means Real-Life Learning," *National Education Association Journal*, 37: 360–361 (May), 1949.

A vivid description of a week's school camping trip involving 100 boys and girls, their parents, and teachers. Describes the phases of planning, the actual camping experience, and the follow-up activities.

Johnson, Earl S., "Field Study: An Experience in Getting Meaning," *Educational Leadership*, 10:229–233 (January), 1953.

Points out that educational field trips are not casual tours, but must be experiences in real settings where fundamental changes in perspective and meaning are produced.

Johnston, Edgar G., ed., "Vitalizing Student Activities in the Secondary School," *Bulletin*, No. 102, of the National Association of Secondary School Principals, Vol. 25 (December), 1941.

Eleven articles on various phases of student activity programs and their contribution to the pupil and the school.

Johnston, Edgar G., and Roland C. Faunce, *Student Activities in Secondary Schools*. New York: The Ronald Press, 1952.

A comprehensive treatment of student activities in the modern high school, furnishing both the theoretical justification for the "extracurriculum" and exciting examples of the programs in operation.

McKown, Harry C., *Extracurricular Activities*. Rev. ed.; New York: The Macmillan Company, 1949.

A standard textbook for courses in the field of extracurricular activities.

Rickert, M. O., "Motivation for Slow Learners," *English Journal*, 38:43–44 (January), 1949.

Describes an English class of below average high school students who organized much of their learning experience around excursions into the local community in search of better understanding of their own environment and of vocational opportunities presented for them.

Sharp, L. B., and E. DeAlton Partridge, eds., "Camping and Outdoor Education," *Bulletin*, No. 147, National Association of Secondary School Principals, Vol. 31 (May), 1947.

An excellent overview of current principles, issues, and practices in outdoor education by outstanding specialists in the field.

Smith, Julian W., "Outdoor Learning," *National Education Association Journal*, 40:262–263 (April), 1951.

An account of the development of camping education in Michigan in the 30's and 40's.

Strang, Ruth, *Group Activities in College and Secondary School*. Rev. ed.; New York: Harper & Brothers, 1946.

The first portion of the book deals with the nature and values of present-day group activities in educational institutions, followed by extensive discussion of methods of working with groups in the activity program and ways of evaluating outcomes.

Tiernan, F., "Thirty Visits to Study Community Problems," *Clearing House*, 26:149–151 (November), 1951.

The story of how a teacher of sociology and economics vitalized learning for her pupils by firsthand experience in and with the problems of their own city.

Trump, J. Lloyd, "Extraclass Activities and the Needs of Youth," in *Adapting The Secondary School Program to the Needs of Youth*, Fifty-second Yearbook of the National Society for the Study of Education; Chicago: The University of Chicago Press, 1953, Part I, pp. 160–179.

Reports the present status and trends in secondary school activity programs with some attention paid to problems or barriers in effective development of extra-class activities.

Part IV *Guiding Individual Learners*

Because a considerable proportion of the teacher's time is spent in teaching through group situations, we have devoted the major attention thus far in this book to group organization and guidance. Part II dealt with procedures for organizing the classroom so as to secure maximum learning by individuals, and Part III with the teacher's tasks in guiding group learning experiences, again so as to bring about maximum individual learning. In Part IV we turn to the closer relation of the teacher with individual pupils as he works with them on a somewhat personal basis. Chapter 11 is concerned with the means teachers can use to identify the characteristics of individual learners. Such identification is essential in modern teaching procedures which recognize the power of the individual's own drives in his learning activities. Chapter 12 presents some means whereby these individual differences, once identified, can be provided for directly. Proper provision for individual differences, we believe, is a distinguishing characteristic of the truly good teacher. Chapter 13 deals with purposes and procedures of evaluating pupil progress with emphasis on the use of evaluation to help the individual learner.

The greatest challenge modern education offers to the teacher is that of teaching adequately the various individuals who attend his classes. Teaching which really affects pupils' learning and living involves a highly individualized pupil-teacher relation. Part IV attempts to give very specific ways whereby the secondary school teacher can work successfully in these individual relations.

11. Studying the Characteristics
of Individual Learners

WE BELIEVE that the most important provisions for individual differences among pupils in the same classroom are those already treated in this book, namely, the organization of the classroom and the guidance of group activities so as to result in significant learning experiences for each boy and girl. Group learning activities which are wisely planned should provide opportunities for each member of the class to have challenging and successful experiences in terms of his needs, interests, and abilities. Such planning must be based, however, on real understanding of these individual pupils. In this chapter we turn attention to means whereby the teacher may determine the unique characteristics, including those indicated by appraisal of interests and abilities, of each boy and girl in his classroom. In Chapter 4 we have already considered the study of learners as group members and are here concerned with the teacher's direct and personal study of them as individuals. Basic to this study by teachers is the understanding of the concept we now wish to emphasize, that *teaching is guidance of individuals* in the light of their unique needs, interests, and abilities, and other characteristics.

TEACHING AS GUIDANCE OF INDIVIDUALS

Teaching in secondary schools is sometimes so divorced from guidance services and so committed to subject-matter emphases that its primary function of guiding the development of each pupil is neglected. One of the greatest lags between educational research and practice in secondary education comes at this point. On the one hand, there is a great body of facts documenting the wide differences among pupils enrolled in secondary schools, even in the same classroom. On the other, teaching practice in too many situations still ignores these facts, proceeding on the basis of expecting uniform accomplishments in assignments, recitations, and examinations.

Regardless of teaching assignments and the number and quality of special services available, the classroom teacher is the first source of guidance and direction for boys and girls in secondary schools. In general, the most effective teacher is the one who has the best relations with individual pupils—the teacher who is known to be "helpful," "interested in each pupil," and "understanding of pupils' problems" (Chapter 2). This is the teacher who believes and practices the theory that teaching is guidance of individuals.

As we see it, teaching and guidance are not discrete functions. If teaching is conceived of as direction of the traditional assign-study-recite-test type of activities, then identification of unique characteristics, interests, and abilities, and working with each individual in the light thereof may be rightly considered something separate and apart. But we do not so conceive of teaching, and instead believe that good teaching always involves understanding of individuals and working with them in the light of such understanding. Good teaching aims to help youth develop ways of thinking and behaving that will make them responsible, well-adjusted members of society. Guidance, even in the sense of specialized guidance services, aims at the same end. Hence we find it convenient to think of education as the process whereby individuals become increasingly able to solve their life problems; of teaching as the sum total of activities whereby teachers cause such education to take place; and of guidance as the way, contrasted to dictation, in which good teaching is carried on. Guidance, then, is really a description rather than just one procedure of good teaching.

At the same time, we must and do recognize that there are many specialized activities involved in teaching and education as defined. One large group of activities has to do with identifying the characteristics of individual learners and making appropriate plans for them in the light of such knowledge. Because many of these activities are frequently carried on by guidance specialists, it is convenient to call them "guidance services." We should note, however, that many of these services, including those to be described in Chapter 12, are also provided by classroom teachers.

SIGNIFICANT ITEMS TO LEARN ABOUT INDIVIDUALS

Before undertaking study of an individual pupil, the teacher needs a rather definite pattern of items to look for, fully understanding, of course, that not all items may be available or significant when a particular question regarding a certain pupil is being investigated. We

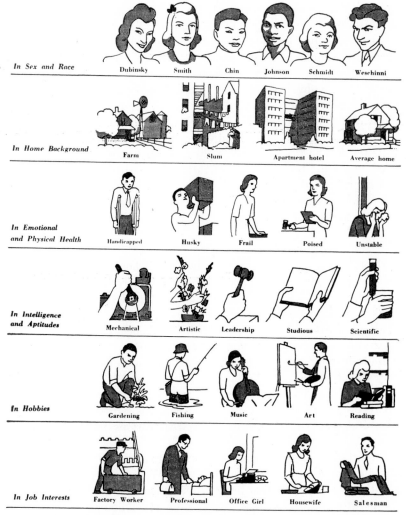

FIG. 11.   WHAT DIFFERENCES MUST THE SCHOOL CONSIDER? (Courtesy of *Planning for American Youth*, rev. ed., National Association of Secondary School Principals, 1951, p. 7)

believe, however, that effective teachers try to have as much information as possible before questions arise. Then they fill in the gaps or refresh their memories as need and opportunities develop. The items which are of frequent significance in coming to understand individual boys and girls in secondary schools are described in the following paragraphs. In general, these are the major items in which a great range of differences is customarily found within the public high school, as illustrated in the accompanying drawing (Fig. 11), and those which most frequently affect learners' motivations and learning processes in school. A summary of these items, as a guide for teachers' study and perhaps as a ready record in teachers' own files, appears in Figure 12. Some of the obvious differences (sex, race, physical maturity, and personal appearance) which are intimately related to the individual's motivations are not included in this listing. Neither are the items pertaining to the individual's relations with others that we discussed in Chapter 4. The teacher's full study and analysis of the pupil's characteristics must take into consideration these observed personal traits and interpersonal relations as well as the more intangible or less apparent factors discussed here, for all may be involved in the needs which he seeks to help the student meet.

HOME BACKGROUNDS

Experienced teachers find that the pupil's home background is important in explaining many of the other factors they need to know about him. The size of the family, the status of family life, the relations with parents, the social and economic status of the family, the kinds of learning experiences which have been had under parental supervision (or without parental supervision!), the interest of the parents in their child's schooling, and many other facts usually have very direct bearing on the interests, drives, and learning behavior of the pupil. Most, if not all of these facts, can be readily ascertained from his record, from interviews with him and his parents, and from biographical data which may be secured in various phases of the case study.

Important as these data are, they cannot rightly be regarded as adequate explanation alone of pupils' needs. We have heard many generalizations to the effect that pupils coming from certain types of homes need this or that more than pupils from other homes. It probably is true, for example, that pupils from underprivileged backgrounds exhibit, *on the average*, less ability to use language well, but it would be a very erroneous procedure to assume therefore that any pupil from an underprivileged background needs help in correct language usage. When teachers go about study of individuals seriously, they rule out predictions as to how a pupil will behave because of possibly related factors, but instead study the behavior and then try to explain it. For

INFORMATION ABOUT

_____
(Name of Pupil)

_____   _____
Class or Homeroom   (Address)

_____   _____   _____
Year   (Parent or Guardian)   (Phone)

Item and Information	Source	Date
A. HOME BACKGROUNDS		
B. PREVIOUS EDUCATIONAL EXPERIENCE		
C. INTELLIGENCE AND APTITUDES		
D. INTERESTS AND AMBITIONS		
E. PHYSICAL AND EMOTIONAL HEALTH		
F. BASIC LEARNING SKILLS		
G. OTHER INFORMATION		

FIG. 12.   FORM FOR TEACHER'S RECORD OF INDIVIDUAL PUPILS

example, the teacher determines a pupil's need for help in language usage first by hearing him speak. Later the conditions responsible for the pupil's poor language usage in his home environment are studied in order to work for his improvement.

PREVIOUS EDUCATIONAL EXPERIENCE

Of great significance also are the experiences Johnny and Mary have already had in school. The schools they have attended, the teachers they have had, the records they have made—all may offer explanations of their present expectation of and interest in school. The written record is, of course, the most readily available and perhaps the most reliable source of information about previous educational experience. But the record frequently needs supplementary explanations and interpretations to be sought by the teacher from the pupil, previous teachers, parents, and other sources. For example, the title of a subject taken and the grade on the record offer very little information, but additional items such as a course summary in the pupil's folder, an interview with the previous teacher, and Johnny's own statements as to how he reacted to and what he learned from the course may be of real value. All the items customarily included on the cumulative record—attendance, grades, test records, out-of-school activities, health, behavior—are of potential significance to teachers as they seek to learn about pupils' educational backgrounds.

INTELLIGENCE AND APTITUDES

Although intelligence-test results may easily be given too much significance in studying an individual, they are of importance in estimating a pupil's potentialities for learning. Teachers simply cannot plan wisely for each individual unless they can make reliable estimates of individual capacity to learn. In addition to the intelligence test results available in the pupil's cumulative record, the teacher is interested in the achievement record, the evidences of creative ability, the speed with which learning seems to take place, the results of any aptitude test given, and the evidences of proficiency of any sort that suggest special aptitude. Since research and experience indicate rather conclusively that the general intelligence score or quotient (I.Q.) of an individual cannot be relied upon as a prediction of all his abilities, it is particularly important that as exhaustive search as possible be made to identify all his abilities and disabilities. These aptitudes and lacks thereof become very important guides to the teacher in working out learning experiences that have challenge and promise of success for each individual.

INTERESTS AND AMBITIONS

Closely related to the previous factors are the real motivations in learning: interests, drives, ambitions, and other favorable inclinations that an individual has for certain activities. If the teacher can determine the real interests of a particular pupil and is able to devise worthwhile learning experiences which build upon these interests, individual differences are being provided for. If real interests cannot be determined or built upon, the next best thing is to find or create substitute interests that may become motivating factors in effective learning. In either case, the teacher needs a maximum amount of information from records, observation, interviews, and inventories of the interests that are important to individuals. Since the interests of the adolescent are changing at a rather rapid tempo, teachers must make this search a continuous one.

PHYSICAL AND EMOTIONAL HEALTH

The physical changes of adolescence are of such profound significance to boys and girls that teachers need to observe very carefully those taking place in their individual pupils and especially the effects in personality development. The great concern of adolescence being "Am I normal?", teachers will do well to observe their secondary school pupils' development and the appraisals they are placing on their own development. Furthermore, the changes of adolescence do affect pupils' physical needs, including those for food, rest, and exercise, and teachers should be as well informed as possible not only on the general requirements of adolescence but on any specific conditions of individual development which might affect learning activities. Adolescence is a time of great emotional development, too, and one in which emotional disturbances can easily occur if there is too much unwise interference with normal development. The typical teen-ager shows his emotions rather readily, and the teacher's problem is to find out what behavior is normal and to be expected for the typical youth and what problems exist when other types of behavior occur. Parents are frequently but not necessarily the most helpful source of information on their children's physical and emotional development, and parent-teacher conferences seem of particularly great importance during the period of secondary education. Unfortunately, they are less common than during the elementary school years.

BASIC LEARNING SKILLS

Some of the foregoing characteristics explain a further item of major importance to the teacher, that is, the ways in which his individual pupils go about their learning activities. Although information about Johnny's intelligence and aptitudes may indicate particular types of learning skills, it is still important to study these skills directly to determine the kind of help that Johnny may need in achieving his education. Unfortunately, teaching in secondary schools is sometimes carried on in almost abysmal ignorance of pupils' ways of working, because only the products of pupils' work are examined. The process, too frequently and probably because of teachers' lack of direction and overemphasis on products and the grades they receive, is one of mechanically completing written exercises without learning taking place. Copying others' work, or getting by in any other way possible is encouraged.

The teacher should examine pupils' papers and other products of learning, but the significant data come from the ways in which pupils are *seen* to read, use reference tools, do laboratory work or drawings or cooking, handle equipment in the gymnasium, laboratory, or elsewhere, study with others, or write papers. In addition to observation and analysis of pupils' ways of working, interviews with them and their parents and tests of study skills offer essential information about basic learning skills.

Some of the major types of skills needed in most or all classrooms for efficient learning activity are as follows:

Seeking information from other people
Reading for information
Viewing for information
Locating information in the library
Making notes and records for future reference
Summarizing information
Organizing data in terms of a particular problem
Manipulating equipment used in learning activities
Evaluating information

The teacher's study of individual characteristics should include observation of how pupils carry on such essential activities as the foregoing. Such observation may reveal significant needs for improvement which competent teachers can usually assist very directly and helpfully.

METHODS OF STUDYING INDIVIDUALS

As the teacher seeks to become informed about such characteristics of his pupils as just described, he learns to use various methods of studying individuals. The most readily available and usable methods for teachers include interviews, observation, pupils' work, inventories, tests, records, reports from specialists and others. Use of these methods is described in this section.

INTERVIEWS OF PUPILS AND PARENTS

The interview or teacher-pupil conference, a characteristic method used by the guidance specialist, is of potentially great value to classroom teachers in understanding their pupils but does present some difficulties. For one, the teacher cannot always conduct an interview properly—for example, in privacy—under classroom conditions. Furthermore, the teacher stands in a position of authority in the minds of many pupils and there is frequently a decided tendency to give him the answers he wants rather than those which may be more accurate. Nevertheless, teachers do use interviews frequently and effectively to learn such things as the following about pupils:

1. Facts about home backgrounds, previous educational experience, and other factors on which specific information is desired
2. Pupils' evaluations of their own progress, accomplishments, and difficulties
3. Pupils' own explanations of their behavior, ways of working, and relations with others
4. Possible interests of pupils and their own plans for appropriate learning experiences
5. What help pupils want with their outside responsibilities, classwork, and future plans

Interviews which are effective for such purposes as these are frequently held during the teacher's planning period or after school hours. Where time is not available for these purposes, teachers sometimes find it profitable to use designated class periods as conference days when committees or individuals can carry on work without teacher help and the teacher sees pupils individually in a corner of the room or an adjacent room or office. Interviews are usually arranged so that the individual pupil is not made to feel that he is being "picked on." This is accomplished by scheduling interviews on a rotation or other plan so that all pupils are interviewed.

Unfortunately, parent-teacher interviews are considerably more common in the elementary than the secondary school. For one reason, the typical elementary teacher has as potential interviewees the parents of only about 30 pupils whereas the typical secondary teacher has those of about 150 pupils. For another, parents in general follow their children through elementary grades, particularly the primary ones, more closely than later, perhaps because of the growing inde-

PLATE 30. TEACHER-PARENT-PUPIL INTERVIEWS ARE CONFERENCES
TO HELP PUPILS. Adolescents may feel better about parents coming
to see their teachers if teacher and parent do not exclude the pupil
from the conference. (Courtesy of the North Phoenix, Arizona,
High School)

pendence of children as they progress through school. Adolescents, of
course, are not happy about their parents coming for interviews if
this is not the common practice or if teacher-arranged interviews imply
that the pupils concerned are "problems."

Hence teachers who want to use parent interviews to identify pupil
characteristics, or at least to determine parental diagnoses of their
children's needs, do well to establish some pattern for interviews that
again does not "pick on" individual pupils. One practice is that of a
regular schedule of interviews by the homeroom teacher of all parents
for the homeroom concerned. These interviews may be held on days
made available at the beginning of the year or other times when children are not in attendance, or by appointments during the teacher's
planning periods or after school hours. Another pattern is that of
teacher invitations to parents, by letter or at the time of "open house"
or other general parent-teacher functions, to arrange interviews. A
frequent plan, but one that has the negative effect on pupils we men-

tioned, is that of automatically interviewing parents of children who are not achieving satisfactorily or who are having behavior problems. Granted that interviews at such times may be important, it is unfortunate for the interview to have this stigma and also for the parents whose children are not "problems" to have little or no opportunity for informing the teacher about these children.

Although there are many purposes of parent-teacher interviews other than that of informing the teacher about pupil needs, this important purpose may be served by information from parents about such matters as the following:

1. Pupils' practices of study at home
2. Parental guidance of pupils' study, radio, television, theater, youth group, and other, experiences out of school
3. Pupils' work and leisure-time activities and their relations to school
4. Parental plans, hopes, and expectations for their children

Whether the interviews are with pupils or parents or other persons, certain procedures are generally advisable. These are described in subsequent paragraphs.

The Interview Situation. Regardless of where the interview may be held, the teacher as the person arranging the interview and thereby responsible for its progress and success should provide the most comfortable, informal atmosphere possible. Whether in an office or the classroom, the interviewee will be much more at ease if the teacher is not seated behind his desk and thus more in the position of authority. If the conversation has to be held in view of other persons, perhaps in a corner of a classroom, the person being interviewed should be given some feeling of privacy by the arrangement of chairs and by the teacher's close attention to what he says despite noise, interruptions, or other distractions. The whole situation should be so arranged that the teacher seems to be saying to a parent, "I am glad you are here and I want to learn as much as possible about (the pupil) so that I can teach (him, her) better. Please make yourself comfortable and just answer a few questions that will get us started and tell me as much else as you wish. Remember this is to help (the pupil), for I want to know some things (he, she) really needs in this class."

Conducting the Interview. As just suggested, it is probably a good idea for the teacher to start the interview by asking two or three rather general questions about the pupil. In successive interviews there is little reason for the get-acquainted type of questions, but it may be a good idea to "break the ice" in some other way, such as talking briefly about some interesting incident that has occurred in the classroom, school, or community. Once rapport seems to be established, the teacher should proceed with a definite line of questions, usually preplanned, to get the particular information desired. Generally one question may lead to some that have not been anticipated, and it may frequently be desirable to digress from the planned series. However, the teacher should watch the time and check the digressions when it seems necessary to pick up some important question that has not been covered. The teacher may also wish to follow through on some leads to the pupil's needs that were not anticipated and perhaps arrange for further conversation at a later date if the interview has proved too short. Some of the problems which come up with either parents or pupils may be such that the teacher feels discussion of possible solutions is timely. However, the interviews we are considering here are primarily for the purpose of the teacher's coming to understand particular pupils, their needs, interests, and abilities, and are not primarily to give help. It may be necessary at times to restate this purpose and, especially with parents, to indicate possible future uses of the information that is being gathered. When it does seem desirable to go into planning and problem solving, any plans made, however minor and minute, should be carefully arrived at and understood by teacher and pupil or parent. If the plan involves some further conversation at another time, both teacher and interviewee should have a clear idea as to when and where that conversation may be held.

Closing the Interview. The teacher has to conduct most interviews on a fairly rigid time schedule, and for this reason may have to watch the clock more than is really desirable. The pupil or parent may need to be notified in the beginning of the teacher's time schedule, so that there will be little or no embarrassment in the teacher's closing the interview when the time arrives. A few minutes before the interview is to be closed, the teacher should check on whether the desired information is being gained and continue or redirect the questioning as indicated. He should also allow a little time to summarize what he has learned about the pupil or at least to summarize the topics that have been discussed. Perhaps he asks if there are other related items the pupil or parent wants to mention. It is particularly important to close the interview with some statement that indicates something has been accomplished. If plans have been made for the pupil, even for further interviews, these should be reviewed. Obviously, a courteous farewell and "thank you" are desirable, just as are all the other courtesies of conversation throughout the interview.

OBSERVATION

Although teachers are constantly observing their pupils, observation as a method of determining individual needs must be considerably more intensive and purposeful than is the casual glance at individuals in group situations. Chance observation, however, may note behavior that causes the teacher to undertake more systematic observation. A number of observation guides, behavior-rating scales, and similar instruments are available for teachers and guidance workers wishing to make careful studies of individual behavior.[1] Teachers may also develop their own observation guides, which may even be in the form of informal notes of items to observe for particular reasons. Among the items that may be studied through careful observation are these:

1. Facial expressions denoting interest
2. Choice of companions, playmates, teammates, persons to study and work with
3. Evidence of difficulty in hearing, vision, or speech
4. Emotional stability and nature of relations that seem to create emotional strain or disturbance
5. Proficiencies and difficulties in usual types of classroom activities
6. Choice of leisure-time activities
7. Class responsibilities volunteered for
8. Evidence of satisfaction or dissatisfaction with assignments, examinations, grades, teacher recognition, teacher disapproval

In carrying on effective observation, the teacher finds it desirable to observe the same pupil on repeated occasions in the same and different activities. For example, if observation of the pupil's use of a reference book indicates his need for special help, the teacher may wish to observe such a situation more than once to make sure there is a real difficulty, and especially to follow up special instruction with observation to make sure it helped. Repeated observations are similarly desirable in any study of pupils' ways of working. When social behavior and relations are being observed, a variety of social situations needs to be observed.

A major problem in connection with the use of observation of pupil behavior is that of time, both from the standpoint of what time is most appropriate to observe the individual and what time is available for the teacher. Obviously, observation of behavior needs to be done in such

[1] See the excellent chapter, "Observation and Rating," in Ruth Strang, *The Role of the Teacher in Personnel Work* (New York: Bureau of Publications, Teachers College, Columbia University, 1953), Chap. 8.

a way that the boy or girl being observed is not conscious of any special attention being paid him or her. Observation of ways of working can be done overtly, although even here the pupil's behavior may be affected by the knowledge that the teacher is watching and he had therefore better do as the teacher expects rather than as he usually does! Effective observation when individuals are not aware of the situation can usually be made in periods when the teacher moves from group to group. Teachers can also use periods for library work, excursions, and showing of audiovisual aids to observe individuals in these varying situations. Once teachers adopt patterns of teaching which do not involve their continuous direction of recitation or other total class activity, it is much easier to find times and opportunities for quiet observation of individuals.

PUPILS' WORK

Pupils in secondary schools do a variety of work which teachers can study: letters, stories, poems, essays, advertisements, newspaper articles, reports, minutes, summaries, outlines, notes, drawings, paintings, clay pieces, wood pieces, metal pieces, cartoons, clothing, murals, maps, charts, and others. Each of these is an index, however small, of the producer's personality. From such pieces of work, teachers may learn about the interests, skills, difficulties, and aptitudes of their pupils, and through a succession of pieces of work by the same pupil they may learn much about his general progress in learning. The pupil's work is of no use in understanding him as an individual and providing for his unique needs, interests, and abilities unless the teacher gives adequate attention to planning and review of this work. Basically, the teacher's provisions for individual differences are made as he plans with or for each pupil the individual work to be done. Such planning is necessarily based on understanding each individual and particularly on prior examination of work already done. In curriculum areas such as language arts, mathematics, industrial arts, and business education in which pupils' work can be kept for some time, teachers frequently maintain a collection of each pupil's work. In the case of written work, as in language arts, it is good practice for each pupil to maintain a folder containing his work so that both he and the teacher may periodically examine successive pieces of work to see if errors are being corrected, writing is improving, and so forth. In industrial arts or other areas in which more ambitious projects are created by the pupil, space may be assigned each pupil for temporary collections if cabinet facilities are adequate.

It should be noted that some types of pupil performance which also represent products of his learning experiences are processes rather than materials. Thus in physical education the test of pupil performance is the teacher's observation of the pupil trying a skill, engaging in a sport, or executing a dance, for example. In the science laboratory the product of work may be the completion of an experiment or the dissection of a specimen. In the shop the process of using a tool or machine correctly may be even more significant than the change seen in the object on which the tool or machine is used. Hence analysis of pupils' needs through their work or performance frequently has to involve observation of *how* they do things. As already emphasized, the process of doing even a written piece of work or other tangible product may be much more significant for the teacher's diagnosis of individual needs than the product itself.

INVENTORIES

Teachers' study of their pupils may be facilitated by use of various types of inventories which pupils may complete for teacher information. These types vary from simple completions of statements like "list all the topics you would like for us to discuss in this class" to comprehensive, published inventories of personality. An inventory is simply a pencil and paper device whereby teachers take stock of one or more items concerning their pupils through information usually supplied by the pupils themselves, although the teachers may occasionally prefer to record the data. Thus teachers may devise inventory blanks (questionnaires) on each of a great variety of items or combinations thereof, including, for example:

Data regarding amount of time given to study, radio, television, work, social affairs, and other out-of-school activities
Interest in recreation, work, social activities, study, current affairs
Types of programs listened to on radio, or viewed on television, or attended in the community
Experience in work activities at home and in the community
Knowledge about any subject or problem
Acquaintance with terms, people, places, products, and so forth
Behavior under various circumstances ("What do you do if . . . ?")
Ways of using books and other sources of information

A sample inventory of reading, radio, and motion-picture experiences is shown in Table 7.

TABLE 7

INVENTORY OF READING, RADIO, AND MOTION PICTURE EXPERIENCES

Name_____   Age_____

English Classroom_____   Grade_____

School_____   Date_____

INSTRUCTIONS

(To be read by instructor and students together, instructor reading aloud)

In order to understand how to teach the value of good reading, it is necessary to know what kinds of leisure-time reading students do. You are asked to indicate your answers to some questions so that this information may be obtained.

Your English grade will not be affected in any way by your answers.

The questions deal with your customary actions regarding your reading. You are asked to check carefully the answers which best describe what you usually do.

Key: N—never; O—often; S—sometimes.

Examples
     A. Continued stories (I read them sometimes)   .   .   .   .   N Ⓢ O
     B. Wars and crimes (I often read them) .   .   .   .   .   N S Ⓞ
     C. Amusements (I never read them or do not know them) .   .   Ⓝ S O

Think carefully about each item. Do not hurry. Circle the letter which describes your reading, radio and motion picture habits.

1. NEWSPAPERS

What parts of the papers do you read?

Comics . . . . . N S O	Current events . . . N S O
Pictures . . . . N S O	Columns . . . . N S O
Athletics . . . . N S O	Essays . . . . N S O
Crime and accidents . . N S O	Book reviews . . . N S O
Cartoons . . . . . N S O	Editorials . . . . N S O

2. MAGAZINES

What types of magazines do you read?

Romance monthlies . . N S O	Weekly news magazines . N S O
Pictorials . . . . N S O	Technical discussion . . N S O
Adventure monthlies . . N S O	Digests . . . . N S O
Humor . . . . N S O	Controversial . . . N S O
Sport . . . . . N S O	Literary . . . . N S O

3. BOOKS
What kind of books do you read?

Romance . . . . . N S O	Plays . . . . N S O
Sport . . . . . . N S O	History . . . . . N S O
Mystery . . . . . N S O	Poetry . . . . . N S O
Aviation . . . . . N S O	Biography . . . . N S O
Adventure . . . N S O	Classics . . . . . N S O

4. READING INTERESTS
In most of your reading what themes interest you?

Excitement . . . . N S O	Current news . . . . N S O
Movies . . . . . N S O	Politics . . . . . N S O
Mystery . . . . . N S O	Technical . . . . N S O
Sports . . . . . N S O	Artistic . . . . . N S O
Humor . . . . . N S O	Scientific . . . . . N S O

5. REASONS FOR READING
What reasons do you have for reading?

To pass the course . . N S O	To keep up to date . . N S O
To get good grades . . N S O	To aid conversation . . N S O
To get excitement . . N S O	To know how people act . N S O
To organize speeches . N S O	To enrich appreciation . N S O
To be amused . . . N S O	To grow intellectually . N S O

6. STYLE OF WRITERS
What kinds of style or thought do you read?

Easy words . . . . N S O	Long paragraphs . . . N S O
Exciting thought . . . N S O	Good description . . . N S O
Short paragraphs . . . N S O	Big words . . . . N S O
Factual information . . N S O	Classical references . . N S O
Concrete ideas . . . N S O	Abstract thought . . . N S O

7. KINDS OF WRITERS
What statements describe the kinds of authors whom you read?

Unheard of before . . N S O	Widely read, popular . N S O
Little known . . . . N S O	Well known . . . . N S O
Seldom discussed . . N S O	Modern but distinguished N S O
Sometimes discussed . . N S O	Read for generations . N S O
See their work often . . N S O	Praised by critics . . N S O

8. PROFIT FROM READING
What do you usually get from the time spent in reading?

"Passes the time" . . N S O	Understanding of nature . N S O
Humor . . . . . N S O	Knowledge of places . . N S O
Excitement, adventure . N S O	Knowledge of current events N S O
"I get away from myself" N S O	Knowledge of social events N S O
Vocational efficiency . . N S O	Intellectual understanding N S O

Table 7 (Continued)

9. RADIO PROGRAMS
What do you select on the dial?

"Hot" music . . . . N S O	Political commentators .	N S O
Crooners . . . . . N S O	News	N S O
Wild comedy . . . N S O	Drama	N S O
Crimes and vigilantes . N S O	Grand opera	N S O
Soft jazz . . . . . N S O	Symphony compositions .	N S O

10. MOTION PICTURES
What do you select on the screen?

Modern romance . . . N S O	Dance revues . . .	N S O
Crimes and accidents . N S O	Educational news . .	N S O
Westerns . . . . . N S O	Biographical drama . .	N S O
Aviation . . . . . N S O	Classical drama . . .	N S O
Comedies . . . . N S O	Sophisticated plays . .	N S O

Source: Pennsylvania Department of Public Instruction, *A Course of Study in English for the Secondary Schools* (Bulletin 280; Harrisburg, Pa.: The Department, 1952), pp. 240–243. Reprinted by permission.

Other such inventories may be easily prepared through the following steps:

1. Identify the item or items on which it is believed information about pupils and supplied by the latter will be significant in understanding pupil needs and interests.

2. Break each item down into subpoints about which information seems desirable.

3. Formulate questions covering each subpoint that will satisfactorily elicit the information desired.

4. Write out (type if possible) a draft of these questions, making sure that instructions are clear, that adequate space for responses is supplied, and that the type of responses called for (checks of alternate responses, "yes" or "no" ratings, or completions) will give the information desired.

5. Try out the first draft of the inventory on one or more pupils (and not the most alert) to detect ambiguous expressions, faulty instructions, and so forth.

6. Study the information from the tryout to see if it does reveal significant data about the pupil concerned, and correct the draft to eliminate insignificant items and add others that seem desirable.

7. Have the form duplicated so as to be as neat and attractive and as free from errors as possible.

In addition to teacher-prepared inventories, there are various types of inventories of personality, study practices, vocational interests, and problems and interests in general, which are commercially available. Some of these can be administered and interpreted without special training, although others are complex and better handled through a guidance specialist. Teachers should observe some of the same steps in using these published inventory blanks as in preparing their own. That is, first of all, there must be a definite reason for making an inventory, namely, that information thereby secured is considered to be significant in identifying pupil needs which the teacher can hope to help pupils satisfy. Secondly, the inventory itself—and this precaution requires its examination—must give information in a form usable by the teacher. A frequent fallacy in using these inventory blanks and also those prepared by teachers lies in the preparation of a class summary with the expectation that this information will be helpful. Although the summary may indicate areas of common need in connection with such inventories as those of study skills or current affairs interests, the more usual signicance of the inventory is with respect to the individual pupil. Thus it may be very helpful in identifying John Jones's needs to know that he spends no time at home in homework, but virtually useless to know that the average class member spends 1½ hours per day in homework. In fact, such information may be misused if it is inferred that each pupil should therefore spend 1½ hours per day in homework, for only study of John Jones as an individual would justify a judgment about his need for homework and many other types of activities.

TESTS

The field of tests and measurements is such a comprehensive one in education that teachers wishing to use tests to study their pupils—and tests are among the very best sources of information—should make use of some of the excellent publications in this field. (See "For Further Study" at the end of this chapter.) For present purposes, we should note that published, standardized tests are available to help in diagnosis of pupil difficulties, estimate of intelligence, appraisal of aptitudes, and evaluation of achievement. Many of these tests can be administered by teachers to the entire class, but some are to be administered individually either by the teacher or a person with special training. Interpretation of test results always requires care and frequently special knowledge.

In addition to the published tests, the teacher's own tests can serve some of these purposes, especially those of diagnosing difficulty and evaluating achievement. At this point it may be helpful to give some

PLATE 31. TESTS ARE IMPORTANT IN STUDYING PUPILS' APTITUDES
AND INTERESTS. Interpretation of many texts requires special care
and knowledge. (Courtesy of the Chicago, Illinois, Public Schools)

illustrative types of situations in which tests may be useful in determining pupil needs.

*To Determine Common Needs of Individuals Relative to a Particular
Subject.* In beginning work with a new class the teacher frequently
would like to know something of the status of information and skills
pertaining to the subject. At least two possible procedures may help.
First, the teacher may be able to locate some published, standardized
test relating to the subject. The first step in locating such a test may
be a conference with the school's specialist in guidance or testing. If
this person does not know of such a test or if there is no such person,
the teacher may usually locate a test through checking the *Mental
Measurements Yearbook,* the successive editions of which list with full
annotations all commercially published educational and other tests.
Other sources may be professional books in the field of tests and
measurements, books on methods of teaching in the particular curriculum field involved, and publishers' test catalogues, usually available
through the guidance specialist or principal. If at all possible, the

teacher should personally examine a sample copy of a test before deciding to use it. The second possibility is for the teacher to prepare a comprehensive test, following such procedures as suggested in Chapter 13, and give this to his class.

Regardless of the test given, the teacher wishing to use the results to determine common needs must make an analysis of the test items to discover the frequency with which each is marked incorrectly. Once it is determined which items were missed by various proportions of the class, the significance of these misses in terms of the teacher's expectations of the class has to be appraised. That is, a large number of misses is important only if the teacher feels the item is one on which common understanding is to be expected.

To Determine Individual Needs Relative to a Particular Subject. The procedures just described also result in the teacher's having information about each individual's status in the subject as revealed by the test. Whether or not this information indicates individual needs has to be decided with reference to other data about the individual, such as his abilities, learning skills, possible use of the information or other items tested. The most important use of the test in the subject comes at this point, as the teacher tries to evaluate each individual's test results in terms of other facts known about him.

Another procedure is the use of tests that are deliberately constructed so as to diagnose the difficulties which cause poor achievement. Although it may occasionally be helpful to have diagnostic results on all pupils, the sounder practice is generally to use diagnostic tests for pupils who show symptoms of difficulty. The steps in selecting published diagnostic tests are as described above, that is, getting a recommendation from a specialist or reviewing published listings and descriptions. The teacher may also prepare his own diagnostic tests for some purposes as, for example, comprehension of the textbook or use of special equipment.

To Determine Needs Relative to Basic Learning Skills. In addition to certain learning skills that may be peculiar to the subject taught, such as making correct use of a microscope in the science laboratory, there are many learning skills we described earlier in this chapter as being basic throughout and even beyond the period of secondary education. These are the skills of problem solving and especially of securing and organizing information and data in general. A number of published tests are also available pertaining to some of these skills, such as study skills and habits, and use of the library. Teachers may find it useful to construct for their classes or individual members thereof simple tests on specific skills; for example, they may develop series of questions based on reading a particular paragraph in a textbook to reveal pupils' difficulties in reading for information. Similarly, tests on the use of the textbook, common reference books, the dictionary and other tools may be constructed by the teacher so as to reveal individual difficulties in skills applied to particular materials or procedures in the classroom rather than to hypothetical situations used in the published tests. Either published or teacher-prepared tests may be used, both for screening purposes to determine what pupils have particular difficulties, and for identifying the specific difficulties individuals have, as a basis for individual help to these pupils. Frequently the same test or a similar one may be helpful in rechecking the pupil's status to determine his progress.

To Determine Other Needs the Teacher May Help the Pupil Satisfy. The teacher's general guidance function with respect to his pupils can be much more effectively discharged as he secures reliable information regarding their abilities, aptitudes, and interests. Although the teacher may be able to use tests of aptitude and ability with respect to his own area, especially in music, speech, physical education, and other subjects involving active performance, many of the more reliable tests of aptitudes and abilities are given by trained personnel. Usually some measure of general intelligence is recorded in the pupil's folder. Also, if general vocational preference or aptitude tests are given, these results would be available. In addition, the teacher can frequently have some individual testing done for pupils about whom he is especially in need of further information. The teacher should also consult any specialized help available if the tests results seem questionable or require interpretation.

RECORDS

Many types of records may be used in the study of individual pupils; in fact, the complexity of record systems in large schools sometimes prevents their effective use by teachers. In general, three types of records provide data about the pupil: those prepared by the pupil; those prepared by the teacher; and those prepared by various school personnel and maintained as school records. Brief attention is given to each type of record in the following paragraphs.

The Pupil's Own Records. Much of the record keeping we have seen done by pupils is desultory and fragmentary, perhaps because of pupils' lack of clear direction in the job. Good teaching practice, we believe, includes helping pupils to maintain some records of their learning experiences—records which are primarily for the pupils' own reference but which are available for examination by the teacher in conferences or at other times. If the record is to be a good basis for appraising pupil needs and progress, it is important that the pupil be given considerable freedom in developing a record that is suitable for his purposes. Purposes of personal record keeping include the development of skill in this important adult activity, aid in moving from one step to the next in problem solving, a guide for periodic reviewing of information compiled, and a basis for self-improvement and for teacher conferences. To aid in the development of such record systems, the following principles for organization of the record are suggested by Simpson in his helpful treatment of pupils' own records:

A. Records should be individual and original. No two learners should keep exactly the same kind of records if teaching is to be what it proposes to be, a democratic movement to develop individual differences.
B. Different parts of a record should be set up in a flexible fashion so that they can be added to as the occasion arises without recopying.
C. It is frequently advisable to make an index or a table of contents so that material can be easily found. Pagination should be flexible so that new pages may be added without recopying.
D. Ideas put into the record should be put in the learner's outline rather than copying the outline of the person who wrote the book or article from which the ideas may have come.
E. Frequently, study should be made of ways of keeping a record economically; that is, putting down the information in organized form as it is acquired rather than getting a lot of unorganized ideas and then trying to organize them after the information and background of the ideas are cold.
F. The bibliography should be set up in such a way that additional references may be added without additional recopying.[2]

Such records of pupils' learning experiences may be very useful for teacher examination in the course of a conference with the pupil or occasionally for total review. The teacher is able to detect interests, basic skills, difficulties in comprehension of instructions, and general understanding of problem-solving processes. It is highly important that the record be just that rather than a notebook which is hastily or even carefully assembled at one time simply to meet the requirement of a record. Hence the teacher needs to give very careful direction to the development of the record, as well as to its use to determine pupil difficulties and other needs.

In addition to these records of the pupil's learning experiences, several other specific types of records may be kept as appropriate to

[2] Ray H. Simpson, *Improving Teaching-Learning Processes* (New York: Longmans, Green & Co., Inc., 1953), pp. 271–272. Reprinted by permission.

the class. For example, records of how time is spent may be helpful
to any teacher seeking to work closely with individual pupils. Records
of laboratory experiments and special projects in science, industrial
arts, homemaking, agriculture, and business education are important
and have to be devised according to the nature of the enterprise. Logs
and diaries of various sorts may be utilized in any class and correspond
closely to the type of record keeping described in the previous paragraph. Records of books read, persons interviewed, films seen, and
other resources may be kept separately from the general class record.
The teacher and pupils need to plan for each class the kinds of records
that will be most helpful to the pupils and at the same time most
indicative of the needs of individual pupils. It follows that teachers
need to plan time to examine these records carefully and to follow
up with suggestions to the pupil.

The Teacher's Records. Schools generally require teachers to keep
some type of uniform record for purposes of attendance and marks
and the like. These records do not, as a rule, provide very much information about individuals other than the bare facts, and teachers usually
devise systems of notes, kept either on these records or separately,
which provide more detailed information. It is excellent practice for
teachers to have a folder on each pupil, files and space permitting, and
in this folder to place written work, anecdotal notes, test papers, notes
from home and from other teachers, information from interviews or
other sources recorded on a form like that shown in Figure 12, and
any other pertinent data. This becomes the teacher's temporary record
from which eventually some transfer may be made to the cumulative
record, and it is ordinarily destroyed after the pupil no longer is in
this teacher's class. It is a source of ready reference when problems
come up relating to the individual and during conferences with parents, the pupil, or others. Because of the difficulty of filing and storage,
teachers frequently prefer to have each pupil keep his own folder containing his work, test papers, and other items not of a confidential
nature, while they maintain for each class one folder of information
blanks about the pupils enrolled, attaching to these personal items
as needed.

The School Record. School systems increasingly use some type of
cumulative record whereby all the information considered most pertinent about pupils is entered on one record card or folder (Fig. 13).
This folder then accompanies the student from grade to grade (if kept
in the elementary teacher's possession) and school to school. In secondary schools these folders may be filed centrally, according to counseling assignments, or by homerooms. Various arrangements are also

necessary as to when and by whom information is entered on the record, and how teachers may secure records for examination. The important common principle is that any school person who has reason to do so may find in the record a considerable body of pertinent facts

This Cumulative Record Folder contains the following cards:

I	PERSONAL DATA · · · · · · · ·	· LIGHT GREEN
II	ELEMENTARY ACHIEVEMENT · · · · ·	· LIGHT GRAY
III	JUNIOR & SENIOR HIGH SCHOOL ACADEMIC RECORDS · · · · · ·	· SALMON
IV	JUNIOR & SENIOR HIGH SCHOOL SUMMARY OF GROWTH RECORDS· · · ·	· BLUE
V	HEALTH RECORDS · · · · · · · ·	· WHITE
	A. TEACHERS OBSERVATION OF PUPIL'S HEALTH	
	B. MEDICAL NURSING RECORD	
	C. CONTINUATION NOTES	
VI	TEST RECORDS · · · · · · · · ·	· YELLOW
VII	RECORD OF REFERRALS · · · · · · ·	· BUFF

FIG. 13. SAMPLE CUMULATIVE RECORD FOLDER. (Courtesy of the Arlington County, Virginia, Public Schools)

about any pupil enrolled. Good cumulative records usually include the following data:

1. Personal information—facts of birth, family history, travel and work experience
2. School history—schools attended, attendance and achievement record, courses and subjects, participation in extracurricular activities, honors and awards, disciplinary action, anecdotal notes
3. Tests—record of all standardized tests or special tests developed and given by the school to all pupils
4. Health—reports of physical and dental examinations, immunizations, illnesses, accidents

5. Educational and vocational plans—record of counseling interviews

6. Miscellaneous—photograph, special notes by teachers and counselors, and, if folder type, enclosures of autobiographies, correspondence, copies of transcripts of records

The teacher's most effective use of the cumulative record is in connection with a particular pupil rather than in reading through all records at the beginning of the year. However, it may be desirable to check all comprehensive records for items that he feels particularly pertinent to the teaching assignment, for example, the health items for the physical education class. If the records are maintained so that they reveal special interests or difficulties of pupils, all records of a class might be checked for such items. Later, as the teacher attempts to make systematic study of particular individuals, preferably all individuals, the cumulative record is a major source.

In schools that do not have such cumulative record systems, there may be various combinations of record files that reveal the same information. Although harder to maintain, the separate records (attendance, health, marks, etc.) do have the convenience at times of ready checking when only one type of record is of interest.

One frequently heard criticism of the use of cumulative records deserves comment. This is the criticism that a teacher should not know what other teachers have said or how they graded his pupils for fear it might "prejudice" him. In fact, we have heard teachers say, "I try not to listen to what other teachers say about my pupils because I don't want to be influenced." Can you imagine a competent physician not wanting to know what other physicians had found out about his patient? This criticism indicates a lack of professional attitude and a failure to recognize several significant points: (1) that good teaching requires a maximum of information about the pupil; (2) that good record keeping records facts, not judgments; and (3) that individuals do change, so that previous behavior may explain or influence but is not necessarily predictive of present behavior.

REPORTS BY SPECIALISTS

A major source of information about the characteristics of individual pupils is the report of special investigations made by the guidance specialist, social case worker, psychiatrist, or other specialist in those situations where such help is available. Ordinarily the classroom teacher refers individual pupils for investigation of their needs only after he has exhausted his own facilities and is not satisfied with what

PLATE 32. SPECIALISTS HELP IDENTIFY AND INTERPRET PUPIL CHARACTERISTICS. The counselor is explaining the significance of his scores on basic tests of abilities, interests, and personality to a high school student. (Courtesy of the Board of Education, City of New York)

he is able to learn. Frequently the referral of a pupil to the counselor, for example, is the first step in a series of conferences and arrangements that result in a different program or a special service for the pupil. The report by the specialist of his investigation of a particular pupil's problem may be a very significant lead for the classroom teacher as to further steps to be taken. Frequently this report is one of individual tests given at some earlier time and is simply consulted by the teacher in the cumulative record. More frequently, however, the teacher refers a pupil to the specialist, perhaps via the homeroom teacher or counselor as we will explain in Chapter 12, and then receives an oral or written report which may suggest steps to be taken in the classroom situation to help the pupil.

The classroom teacher's first responsibility with regard to special services is to know what services are available for his pupils, and how he may make use of them. Once this information is known, the pupils whose characteristics seem such as to indicate help by specialists can be appropriately referred by the teacher. As we have noted, the specialist may also be used in connection with the teacher's own investigations involving the choice, administration, and interpretation of tests and inventories.

OTHER TECHNIQUES

Social case workers employ a method of investigation commonly called the "case study," which is a comprehensive compilation of all the facts that can be collected to diagnose an individual's behavior and problems preparatory to developing a course of remediation. Although the teacher is rarely trained or given time to make such investigations, some of the techniques used by the case worker may be followed by the teacher in securing additional information about individual pupils. The case study would normally include all the sources of information we have described—interview, observation, examination of the pupil's work, tests, inventories, and records—and in addition, home calls and interviews with any employer, community or youth organization officer, minister, or other person who may be in a position to give pertinent information. The case study may also involve the "case conference," which is a conference of various persons most closely identified with the individual, for consideration of the information about him. In school, all of the particular pupil's current teachers, any specialists who have worked with him, and perhaps parents and other persons may come together to exchange information and planning. Although, as we have said, teachers rarely have time for such extended investigations, they may find exceedingly useful a limited number of home calls and exchange of information with other teachers of the same pupils and participation in case conferences.

In some classes, recordings are effective means of studying the individual and his needs. Especially in speech, music, and dramatics is this a helpful technique. Recordings of a discussion may also be used by the teacher and group to analyze the role of individuals in group process and thereby be helpful to the teacher in appraising the needs of individual pupils.

In addition to the types of test and inventory instruments noted, there are various rating scales and observation guides which teachers may secure in published form or prepare, for studying the behavior and performance of individuals. Essentially, either the scale or guide is a list of characteristics to be noted, with some device for recording a judgment regarding whether and to what extent each characteristic is exhibited. Thus the teacher may study an individual's needs for special help in regard to his spoken language by checking some teacher- or class-prepared scale of desirable speech characteristics.

One of the most significant techniques for the teacher's study of the individual and his needs is that of review of the pupil's own self-evaluation on whatever items are being considered. Techniques of pupil self-evaluation are considered in Chapter 13.

Many teachers make use of the autobiographies which pupils are required to write at the beginning of the year for information about their pupils. In some schools, these papers are circulated among all the teachers of the pupils concerned. In addition, to get supplementary information, it is useful to schedule appointments with all the students in a class who have written such autobiographies. With this information at hand, the teacher can find out more about the pupils' experiences and the validity of his statements than the teen-ager usually puts in formal writing.

To complete his catalogue of the various possibilities for studying individual learners, the reader might at this point review the various devices described in Chapter 4 for understanding the individual in relation to his group.

SUMMARY: HOW TO DETERMINE THE NEEDS OF INDIVIDUAL LEARNERS

The teacher who has read this chapter up to this point may well have a feeling of frustration because of the many different means which have been suggested for study of the needs of individual learners. "How am I to do all these studies and still teach my classes?" you wonder. "And how am I to know which method to use with which students?" Although these feelings may exist, we believe they are better than feelings of complacency about teaching pupils who are not really understood by the teacher and are not really learning. They are also better than frustrations which come because teachers do not know how to study individuals but realize they should, or because a single method is tried and found unsuccessful and the teacher knows no other.

This matter of understanding pupils and diagnosing their needs is a complex and challenging problem for the teacher. Pupils who are understood and who are helped with their individual problems give the teacher his greatest gratification. His major problems in understanding and helping all pupils are those of time and skill to determine and serve the needs of individuals. We believe that skill in studying individuals can be gained by interested teachers through experience in such study, provided the experience is carried on along such problem-solving lines as we have suggested. Time may be limited, but it can be found if teachers are ingenious and perhaps sacrificial. Working within the limitations that may exist, teachers can make real steps toward understanding their pupils by following these general principles:

1. Learn as much as possible about pupils, especially regarding home backgrounds, previous educational experience, intelligence and aptitudes, interests and ambitions, physical and emotional health, and basic learning skills. For this purpose, use as many of the methods of study described as are feasible: interviews of parents and pupils, observation, pupils' work, inventories, tests, records, and reports by specialists and others.

2. Wherever it is possible to help individuals make plans for their learning experiences, consult the information available about each pupil and plan with maximum reference to his needs, interests, and abilities as known.

3. For those individuals who seem to be experiencing difficulty in carrying out the plans made for and with them, endeavor to find out more about their needs, using such specialized help as available.

4. Maintain an experimental attitude toward all individuals taught, investigating as opportunity arises their apparent reactions to the successive learning experiences they are having, and seeking from these reactions, favorable or unfavorable, happy or unhappy, leads for continued planning.

FOR FURTHER STUDY

Association for Supervision and Curriculum Development, National Education Association, *Fostering Mental Health in Our Schools.* 1950 Yearbook; Washington, D.C.: The Association, 1950.
   See Part III (Chapters 12–18) for suggestions and illustrations as to ways of studying individual pupils.
Bush, Robert N., *The Teacher-Pupil Relationship.* New York: Prentice-Hall, Inc., 1954.
   Report of a ten-year study at Stanford University of teacher-pupil relationships in grades 7–14.
Cunningham, Ruth, and Associates, *Understanding Group Behavior of Boys and Girls.* New York: Bureau of Publications, Teachers College, Columbia University, 1951.
   Presents various methods for study of children in group situations.

Fenlason, Anne F., *Essentials of Interviewing*. New York: Harper & Brothers, 1952.
Detailed treatment of interview procedures.

Greene, Harry A., Albert N. Jorgensen, and J. Raymond Gerberich, *Measurement and Evaluation in the Secondary School*. New York: Longmans, Green & Co., Inc., 1954.
Chapters 1–14 deal with various problems of testing.

Hamrin, S. A., *Chats with Teachers about Counseling*. Bloomington: McKnight & McKnight, 1950.
Suggestions to teachers on interviewing and counseling teen-agers.

Hymes, James L., Jr., *Effective Home-School Relations*. New York: Prentice-Hall, Inc., 1953.
Excellent suggestions to teachers for working with parents. Although most suggestions refer to young children, many principles and some techniques are applicable to teachers of adolescents.

Langdon, Grace, and Irving W. Stout, *Teacher-Parent Interviews*. New York: Prentice-Hall, Inc., 1954.
Detailed and helpful suggestions on use and conduct of interviews of teachers and parents.

Morris, Glyn, *Practical Guidance Methods for Principals and Teachers*. New York: Harper & Brothers, 1952.
See Chapters 6 and 7 for an interesting account of how one faculty developed and used cumulative records and and case conferences for study of their pupils.

Remmers, H. H., and N. L. Gage, *Educational Measurement and Evaluation*. Rev. ed.; New York: Harper & Brothers, 1955.
Describes many types of tests and other measurements that may be used for study of individuals.

Rothney, John W. M., *The High School Student: A Book of Cases*. New York: The Dryden Press, Inc., 1953.
Through twenty-seven illustrative case studies of adolescents shows techniques and materials the teacher may use to understand individual pupils.

Simpson, Ray H., *Improving Teaching-Learning Processes*. New York: Longmans, Green & Co., Inc., 1953.
See Chapter 9 for suggestions and illustrations regarding records kept by pupils.

Strang, Ruth, *Role of the Teacher in Personnel Work*. New York: Bureau of Publications, Teachers College, Columbia University, 1953.
Part III, "Technics in Personnel Work," describes procedures, with illustrations, of studying children through observation and rating, daily schedules and other personal documents, psychological tests, projective methods, interviews, developmental records, case study, and case conferences.

Taba, Hilda, and others, *Diagnosing Human Relations Needs*. Washington, D.C.: American Council on Education, 1951.

Describes several devices found useful in the Intergroup Education Project, in diagnosing gaps in social learning of children and adolescents: diaries, parent interviews, participation schedules, sociometric procedures, open questions, and teacher logs.

Torgerson, Theodore L., *Studying Children: Diagnostic and Remedial Procedures in Teaching.* New York: The Dryden Press, Inc., 1947.

Contains useful chapters on the following techniques of child study: observation, anecdotal records, interview, home visit, tests, and case study.

12. Providing for the
Individual Learner

As we have already emphasized, the primary provision for individual learners is a methodology of teaching which involves their participation in planning. This dynamic way of working is sufficiently flexible to offer a wide range of learning opportunities appropriate to the range of needs, interests, and abilities in each class. Such a methodology is also directly concerned with the learning experiences of each pupil. We turn in this chapter from procedures of studying individual learners to provisions for them by the classroom teacher. Four major types of help for individual learners are presented: guiding the development of basic learning skills, providing special learning opportunities, using special services, and using administrative provisions.

GUIDING THE DEVELOPMENT OF BASIC LEARNING SKILLS

Basic learning skills, we pointed out in the last chapter, are really the skills of problem solving. Here we wish to describe methods whereby the teacher may help pupils acquire these skills, particularly with respect to those involved in goal-seeking activity. First, some specific ways teachers may help individual pupils sharpen the entire process of problem solving are suggested.

HELPING LEARNERS WITH PROBLEM-SOLVING SKILLS

Most teen-agers have no dearth of recognized problems. Unfortunately, the problems of greatest significance to these learners are frequently, and sometimes necessarily, beyond the scope of the classes in which they are enrolled. Also, unfortunately, youth may feel little direct and immediate concern for such pressing social problems as governmental improvement, crime and its prevention, war and peace, and even community tensions. As we suggested early in this book, however, teachers can usually find pressing problems which are related, and which may at least be used as starting points for developing interests; for these, the teachers can appropriately and profitably give direction. For example, problems of teen-agers' behavior can usually be bases for undertaking many studies in such fields as juvenile delinquency, recreation, marriage and home, and others of important personal and social concern.

Probably teachers give the most effective guidance with respect to development of skill in problem identification and selection through direction of group planning as described in Chapter 8. As groups are so engaged, teachers will note some pupils who seem to have particular difficulty in the process. For these pupils who either fail to participate in group planning or participate with seeming lack of understanding, we have found two procedures helpful. First, a conference with the pupil frequently reveals reasons for his lack of interest or understanding, and the teacher either can help the pupil relate the problem discussions to his own interests or can get clues as to ways future group discussions can be guided to secure his participation. The teacher can also identify any difficulty the pupil seems to have in problem recognition and perhaps give some suggestions on how problems are seen as such. Second, when there is too little opportunity for conferencing or when conferencing seems unsuccessful, the teacher may suggest some exercise of a written nature. For example, the pupil may be asked to review some particular experience he has had, such as a field trip, and list all the things in it that he wanted to learn more about or all the things that he did not understand and did not ask about. Such exercises still need a check by the teacher with a follow-up conference, although queries or comments on the paper may help.

Skill in the formulation of goals and plans of action for problem solution also is most effectively acquired by most individuals in group situations where various members are offering suggestions and evaluating proposals. But here, too, the teacher will note pupils who fail to participate or whose suggestions indicate complete lack of understanding of the process of problem solving. For example, there is the frequent case of the youth who sees a question and wants to answer it quickly, or have it answered superficially, rather than plan why and how it might be answered adequately. A little less familiar but more difficult is the pupil who feels that planning how to solve problems is a waste of time: "Why doesn't the teacher tell us?" Such individuals as these can usually be dealt with in the group situation and by their peers. The most difficult cases are those of pupils who have always been "told," and simply do not understand how to go about thinking through ways and means of solving problems. These are the pupils who need conferences in which the teacher asks questions to probe for their ideas about how to solve problems, however elementary, with which they are thoroughly familiar. The teacher then draws parallels with procedures being used in the class, using illustrations repeatedly. Again, written exercises may help if they cause pupils to suggest ways and means of securing answers to successively difficult problems. Frequent questioning of these pupils as to "Why did you do this?" followed by "Then how would you do this?" may also help in the extension of their problem-solving processes. The significant step for the teacher to take is to identify pupils having these difficulties and to follow through either by individual conferences or by drawing them more directly into group planning activities.

The major step of goal-seeking activity, that is, of gathering data about the problem, is usually regarded as the total learning experience. However, observation of learners frequently indicates that teachers' concentration on the learners' goal-seeking activities, without due attention to their involvement in the planning that preceded, is responsible for much aimless and fruitless searching for answers. Many pupils copy textbooks or answers to questions from the board without understanding what they are copying, and have even less understanding of the relevancy of the material to their own concerns. These are generally pupils who are not being taught with consideration of the problem-solving nature of learning. That is, these pupils are being assigned rather than involved, compelled rather than guided.

Once planning is accomplished so that individual pupils identify their goals and procedures, teachers can give most effective help to individual goal-seeking activities through many of the special learning opportunities described later in this chapter. These opportunities may be especially aimed at the skills of securing, organizing, and evaluating data to which we next turn. First, we should point out that individual pupils may also have difficulty in evaluating their problem solutions. Again, skill in this phase of problem solving usually comes through participation in group evaluation, but teachers need to be alert to the nonparticipant and to the participant who exhibits poor reasoning. The usual problem in evaluation is the tendency to accept uncritically and too hastily solutions that have been found by members of the group. Although this is to be expected of immature learners and can be met for most of them through the teacher's guidance of evaluative discussion, there may again be need for conferences and problem-solving exercises with some learners having particular difficulty. In such situations, we have found it particularly effective to emphasize questions or exercises which are of the type, "If this is so, then does it follow that . . . ?" When it obviously does not "follow," learners can be guided to reject their solutions and find better ones, and perhaps also influenced to be more critical another time.

SKILLS IN SECURING INFORMATION

In all problem-solving situations there is some type of information to be secured. In problem solving by experimentation—that is, testing of a hypothesis as to what will happen under certain circumstances—the information ("data" is the usual term) is what does happen. In problem solving by reference to experience of others, the information is the experience, recorded, witnessed, or related. It is this latter type of information with which much of pupils' learning in secondary schools is concerned and with which we are dealing here. Each of the several types of skills usually needed in securing such information is discussed in one of the following paragraphs.

Reading for Information. Reading of textbooks, supplementary books, periodicals, newspapers, pamphlets, and other printed materials is probably the most used of all skills for securing information. It is also, maybe because of its frequency and also because of its frequently poor direction, one of the most abused skills. Pupils are sometimes indiscriminately given uniform assignments of material to be read without concern for the information to be sought or their basic reading skills. Teachers who find individuals experiencing difficulty in getting information from books should not conclude that the pupils are just poor readers, but instead that these pupils need special help. The teacher's first problem in working with such pupils is diagnosis of their difficulty. The diagnosis should establish whether the pupil's difficulty is in basic reading skill, in failure to identify clearly the information sought, in lack of knowledge of how to use the book or other material, in his reading level compared to the material, or in some other particular. Usually some questioning of the pupil with the material at hand will give a simple diagnosis. If the book is simply too difficult, the teacher can suggest a simpler source. If the pupil does not know how to make use of the book, then some exercises on use of its special features may help. If there seems to be some deficiency in basic reading skill, the teacher can either refer the pupil to a reading specialist if available, or himself undertake to make a more definite analysis of the reading difficulty.

We recognize that many if not most secondary school teachers do not feel that they are qualified to teach basic reading skills. Unfortunately, these teachers will be unable to teach their pupils many other things unless the pupils can read satisfactorily. Therefore we would suggest that every prospective teacher and teacher in service take a few steps toward acquiring competence in teaching reading. Some possible steps include study of diagnostic reading tests and remedial reading materials, reading of some of the excellent publications available on reading in high schools, taking a course in a college or university on the teaching of reading, and actually working on some reading problems of individual pupils with reference to suggestions secured in these sources. In general, the following suggestions are likely to be found helpful with the pupil who has problems of basic reading skill:

1. Find a time when you can have extended sessions with this pupil—sessions in which you can develop his understanding of your desire to help and his confidence that he may exhibit his difficulties without fear of failure.

2. Use a diagnostic test, perhaps just some exercises you may develop yourself from the textbook or other source used in your class, to find out the nature of the difficulty.

3. Find something which the pupil can read with interest and understanding, regardless of its relation to the subject at hand. The librarian can help here and also with finding material that is as easy to read but more closely related to problems of the class.

4. If the reading difficulties are beyond your help, see if there is some teacher or specialist in the school who can help, if possible without penalizing the pupil by making him miss classes or by isolating him from his regular group.

5. When there seems a chance of improvement, give the pupil as much opportunity as possible to use materials he wants to read and go over the material with him as frequently as possible. Continue to find materials of increasing difficulty so long as the pupil continues to be secure in reading.

6. As far as possible, help the pupil continue in the general problem-solving activities of the class by giving him materials he can handle during periods for reading.

Many of the problems which individual pupils have in securing

information from printed sources arise from their lack of knowledge
of how to use the materials, that is, of how to use the table of contents,
index, glossaries, and other special features. Pupils can be helped in
these skills by general class sessions devoted to use of resources, but
individual pupils still need special help. Generally this special help
should develop from some conference in which the pupil's use of materials is observed and his difficulties diagnosed. The pupil can then be
given special suggestions and exercises, and repeated conferences and
observations should help him greatly.

The problem of varied reading levels is to be expected in secondary
grades, where a range of as many as eight grades in reading level is
customarily found in any unselected class. The first step in dealing with
this problem is the identification of reading levels through a good test,
and the only satisfactory provision is a range of reading materials. To
assume that all pupils in a particular class can read satisfactorily a
single book is completely unrealistic. Hence, we have included the use
of varied materials as a phase of effective teaching throughout this
book. In those increasingly few situations where teachers have only
basic textbooks for their classes, the teacher simply should not expect
uniform reading skill and must find substitutes for individual reading,
such as audiovisual aids, trips, telling, and reading in pairs or small
groups.

Using the Library for Information. Another aspect of reading for
information is the use of the school library. Before one can read for
information, regardless of how well one reads, he must be able to use
such standard library aids as the card catalogue, the *Readers' Guide to
Periodical Literature,* encyclopedias, and other reference books. Most
secondary schools provide library instruction by the librarian or
teachers. The most effective way of giving help to most pupils is to
work with them in the library with the materials concerned. In this
way the teacher or the librarian can see what the difficulties are and
help the pupil find proper ways to secure information from library
sources. Library exercises may be useful also.

Using Audiovisual Resources for Information. Despite careful group
planning for the use of audiovisual resources, some pupils will fail to
view or listen properly. The teacher's diagnosis of these difficulties
should first of all determine whether either visual or auditory deficiencies are responsible. If the pupil sees and hears satisfactorily, then
conferencing is necessary to get at the difficulties. Most frequently,
lack of interest or proper direction is responsible, and the teacher
can try to correct these situations by better planning and guidance.

If the problem seems to be one of difficulty in sustained concentration on the speaker or picture, some practice with questions or other guides to concentration may help.

Using People for Information. Pupils in secondary schools need considerable help in conducting interviews satisfactorily for getting information. Although general instruction in interviewing may be given the class, the teacher frequently finds it desirable to ask pupils who are to conduct interviews to prepare a list of questions in advance and to discuss these questions with each other. Role playing in which

PLATE 33. USING THE LIBRARY IS AN IMPORTANT PROBLEM-SOLVING SKILL. Junior high school pupils can use card catalogues and wheel card files to locate pertinent materials. (Courtesy of the Oak Ridge, Tennessee, Public Schools)

one pupil interviews another is a very useful device for teaching interview procedures and courtesies. In this way pupils can learn how to follow up questions for further information, to return the discussion to his questions when it digresses, and to record information received. The teacher can help also by the way in which he himself supplies information at the request of pupils, particularly by waiting for explicit questions and by using himself questions such as "Do you understand?" "Is this what you wanted to know?" or "Can you restate that a little more definitely?" to make sure there is good communication.

We should not overlook the use of other pupils for getting information through effective sharing of ideas and information in small groups. Frequently the best way of helping individuals who have difficulty in learning from group discussion is their inclusion in small group activities carefully guided by the teacher so as to develop better participation and involvement of each pupil. Gradual enlargement of the group may maintain continued participation of those who first seem lost in the total class situation.

Other Skills in Securing Information. The skills needed for securing information are as numerous as the sources of information, and these vary somewhat from one curriculum area to another. All areas may involve the skills we have mentioned. In addition, there are such skills as those needed for learning from experiences in the laboratories, on the playground and in the gymnasium, and from the environment in general.

Ability to secure information is acquired in the same way as other skills. Although we will analyze drill or practice in more detail later in this chapter, we may note here the three steps: (1) developing a reason for learning the skill; (2) understanding how the skill is performed; and (3) practice as necessary in the performance of the skill until it is readily and efficiently repeated when needed. Teachers who teach individual pupils well must work with each pupil to determine his status in the skills required for successful learning in the particular class, and then give as much direction as possible in correcting any difficulties pupils have. Except for the relatively unusual pupil with a special handicap, pupils whose skills are learned with full conformance to these three steps will have little difficulty in securing information. The difficulties occur most frequently when pupils do not have an understood motive for acquiring the skill or do not understand how to perform it. These difficulties are corrected in effective teaching.

SKILLS IN EVALUATING SOURCES OF INFORMATION

Guiding the immature learner to evaluate critically the information he finds recorded in printed materials, or hears or sees in audiovisual resources, or gets directly from people is a difficult, indeed perplexing, task for the teacher. As a matter of fact, the teacher has frequent difficulty in evaluating information himself. In group consideration of information, there is the advantage of having the experiences of many pupils and the teacher. But how does the teacher guide the individual pupil to weigh critically what he sees, hears, or reads?

Helping the pupil evaluate information is a rather continuous process that has to be handled in terms of each particular source of information. That is, the learner must be helped to find specific ways of checking on the information contained in a book as well as that given by a person. There are, however, certain basic criteria which apply to any source of information, and perhaps the skill pupils need most to learn is that of the critical thinking process in which these criteria are applied to whatever is read, heard, or seen. Pupils should become accustomed to answering the following questions about the information they secure and its source:

1. How does this information relate to the question being investigated? Is it what I need to know?

2. How can I be certain that this information is correct? Is there any way of checking the information?

3. How complete is the information? Is this all I need to know about the question? Where can I secure further information if needed?

Teachers use conferences to question pupils about particular information and thereby may demonstrate the kinds of questions pupils need to ask about the sources of information they consult. Pupils may become more adept in the evaluation of sources through practice directed by the teacher in examining different sources and making comparisons on some of the points listed above. Some teachers find it useful to have different pupils evaluate a particular source separately, and then compare the evaluations to discover their difficulties and misunderstandings.

SKILLS IN RECORDING AND ORGANIZING INFORMATION

As pupils go about seeking information related to problems being studied by the class, committees, or individuals, there are at least three types of purposes that may require some recording and organization of the information. First, some type of complete record or log of each major unit of work is helpful to the pupil and also to the teacher for purposes of evaluation of the unit, self-evaluation of progress, and teacher diagnosis of difficulties. Some suggestions for maintenance of this record were given in Chapter 11.

Second, there is frequent reason for notes for future reference in preparation of the log, refreshing one's memory, or further investigation. Pupils need considerable help in developing note-taking systems of their own, and teachers usually provide suggestions, practice periods, and evaluations of these systems as they are developed. Although the nature of the material may be a controlling factor, such routines as use of headings, divisions, enumerations, and underlining should be carefully explained and practiced. Pupils may profit very much from practice in note taking on reading or telling experiences with subsequent review of the notes by themselves to another person as a basis for finding inadequacies.

Third, frequently the information sought is to be reported to other persons, and some special type of note taking may be desirable for this purpose. Here again, practice is important. The practice should include (1) formulation of questions on which information is sought; (2) securing and noting this information; (3) reporting to a group on the information; (4) answering questions from the group; and (5) going back to the source for further information as needed.

PROVIDING SPECIAL LEARNING
OPPORTUNITIES FOR INDIVIDUALS

Most of the professional discussions pertaining to provision of learning opportunities for individual pupils are organized in terms of particular types of individual differences, especially those of the slow learner and the fast learner. For several reasons, we are not so organizing this discussion. First, we ourselves question whether study of individual learners as outlined in Chapter 11 will reveal such sharp and mutually exclusive categories of differences as to justify an entirely different approach for each category. Second, we believe the methodology of teaching presented in this book will provide for all but perhaps extreme types of individual differences usually not found in the general high school classroom. The use of small groups in the classroom, as described in Chapter 9, is an especially rewarding provision for individual differences. The literature is rather substantial and detailed with regard to handling the special categories of learners, and we feel readers interested in learning about techniques for special problems, such as extremely slow learners, will do well to consult some of the references given at the end of this chapter. Third, we do attempt in this chapter to give suggestions which should be helpful in dealing with varied types of individual differences, although we do not believe that any one technique is invariably the right one for a particular type of individual.

For present purposes, then, we are concerned with specific learning opportunities that may be tailored to suit individual needs, abilities, and interests as discovered by study of pupils. The effective classroom teacher can provide opportunities such as the following to give help with many different types of individual needs, interests, and abilities:

special help conferences, drill or practice, supervised or directed study, homework, individual investigations and projects, and special roles. Each of these opportunities is described in this section.

SPECIAL HELP CONFERENCES

Unfortunately, "special help" is synonymous with "staying in" in the minds of many pupils in secondary schools. Special help as punishment is entirely inconsistent with the theories of present-day teaching. As we see it, special help is substituted by the modern teacher for the tutorial system of instruction—a system that had many advantages but lacked the great asset of group stimulation and help in learning. For boys and girls presenting special learning problems—and all boys and girls at some time, usually many times, do present special problems—there is no more effective help than that which the teacher can give in a personal conference. Among the uses teachers make of the pupil-teacher conference in instruction are the following:

1. To talk with the pupil about his learning problems and outline procedures which may help him solve these problems
2. To suggest activities, projects, investigations, and other individual undertakings which may be more profitable to the learner than those which he has selected on his own or in small group planning
3. To discuss learning experiences which the pupil has missed for illness or other reasons, and plan steps whereby he may undertake these or related experiences on his own
4. To explain concepts, processes, or information which the pupil has not understood in group work
5. To answer questions the pupil has raised in class that were not appropriate for group discussion, or questions that he has asked the teacher to answer in conference
6. To give specific direction to study procedures, and observe the pupil in use of these procedures
7. To lend a sympathetic ear to the pupil's problems, and give him the security that comes from confidence in one's teacher
8. To go over specific pieces of work and test papers to help the pupil understand his difficulties, and praise him for improvement and achievement
9. To review the pupil's self-evaluation of his learning experiences, and plan next steps in the light of such evaluation
10. To outline a procedure for study of a problem of interest to the

PLATE 34. THE TEACHER HELPS INDIVIDUAL PUPILS DIRECTLY. Conferring over the pupil's work during the classroom period is frequently desirable. (Courtesy of the Board of Education, City of New York)

    pupil and beyond the interests and abilities of other class members

11. To plan learning experiences which will be related to the pupil's unique vocational interests or present work activities

12. To help the pupil plan for special roles he has in the class or school organization

As we have already indicated, time is the teacher's major problem with regard to individual conferences with pupils, whether for help to or study of individuals (and both purposes are usually accomplished in good interviews or conferences). Although before- and after-school time may have to be used, this is generally regarded as penalizing the pupil and promotes the punishment idea of special help. The best possibilities are the teacher's planning period, when its use does not deprive the pupil of participation in another needed learning experience, and the class meeting time. More extensive use of class time for teacher-pupil conferences while other learners are busy with their committee or individual studies seems generally desirable in the classrooms of secondary schools.

Assuming that mutually convenient times can be found for conferences, teachers need to take several other precautions to ensure their success. Pupils must be helped to understand that the conference is for their assistance and not for punishment, grading, or faultfinding. They need to feel that they have the teacher's sympathetic and undivided attention, difficult as it is for the teacher to give one pupil undivided attention when as many as thirty or more other pupils are in the same small classroom. Clear understanding of each other should be maintained through questions, repetitions, illustrations, and other devices which the teacher uses so that pupils attach meaning to words and phrases and concepts that is similar or identical to the teacher's own meaning. The teacher must watch for distractions and lags in the pupils' interest and attention, and change tactics as needed at such times. The usual courtesies in conference situations, such as smiles, recognition of what is said, lack of interruptions, and attention to the other's comfort, are just as important in conversations between adults and adolescents as in those between adults.

DRILL OR PRACTICE

An outgrowth or even a phase of the special help conference may well be some special practice of a needed skill by the learner. "Drill" has frequently been synonymous with memorization of terms and symbols, and in this meaning is not always applicable to the learning of skills. Skills may be memorized, but meaningless material may also be, and too frequently is, memorized as well. A skill that is really learned by an individual always has meaning, for a skill is an act or response, mental or motor, that is performed relatively identically and automatically in similar situations. Thus counting, using an index, steering an automobile, and typewriting are skills. But definitions, principles, relations, and other types of understandings that do not operate identically and automatically because of the variables they involve, are not skills, regardless of how much teachers may seek to have them memorized or drilled by pupils.

As noted earlier, there are three rather distinct stages in the acquisition of a skill: (1) the learner must purposefully undertake learning the skill; that is, a skill will no more be acquired than any other learning because it is "assigned"; (2) the learner must understand why and how the skill is performed, and guiding this understanding is the special function of the teacher; and (3) once there is this understanding, some amount of repetitive practice is desirable to fix the skill. The repetitive practice constitutes drill of a desirable nature. Unfortunately, teachers frequently fail to follow these steps in order, for pupils are sometimes required to practice skills which they neither want nor know how to perform. Drill or practice may be very effective for the individual who lacks facility in performance but wants to become more facile and does understand what it is he is trying to do. When the special help conference or other basis for teacher judgment shows that Johnny or Mary really needs drill, then the teacher can provide for it through such means as the following:

1. The teacher can himself observe or check the pupil in repeated performance of the skill at this or some other time to be arranged. Particularly can the teacher help as the pupil is just beginning drill of many types.

2. If the skill is one in which writing is useful practice, as in letter forms or business records, the teacher can arrange a time for the practice and for checking the written work.

3. If the skill involves physical manipulation, as in physical education or use of equipment, the teacher can arrange for another skilled pupil to help the learner.

4. If the skill is one of spelling, mathematical combinations, or other types in which word and symbol association is involved, the teacher can arrange for pairs of learners to check each other.

5. For most skills, the teacher can suggest ways in which the learner can provide for his own self-direction and checking.

6. The teacher may prepare drill exercises in such areas as language usage, composition, mathematics, use of books, and the like, and give these to individual learners as needed.

7. Commercially prepared workbooks may be useful with individual pupils provided the sections used are directly related to the skill in which the pupil needs practice.

The large amount of useless drill on material to be memorized or on processes which are not understood causes us to reiterate two exceedingly important principles for teachers to observe unfailingly in the guidance of practice. In the first place, the research is quite conclusive that skills are learned correctly only with reference to understanding of their use in meaningful situations. For example, the learner who does not understand the nature and purpose of interest in finance cannot possibly drill correctly on interest problems. In guiding the individual in learning skills, the teacher's first concern must be with whether he really understands the context of the skill well enough to undertake its performance. Without such understanding, no amount of drill will help the learner use the skill in situations removed from his teacher and exercises. In the second place, since the nature and amount of practice individuals need vary widely, practice must be individualized. Granted that a group of pupils may be introduced to a skill together and then given some directions for its practice, good teachers always check on each individual's performance and provide for continued practice as needed rather than assuming that all members of the group have achieved equal facility by the same practice exercises continued for the same period of time.

SUPERVISED OR DIRECTED STUDY

In many high school classes there is a somewhat mechanical division of time into a period for recitation or discussion or other total group activity (but usually, unfortunately, for recitation!) and for supervised or directed study. Frequently the division is in approximately equal periods for these two purposes. As the reader will realize by now, we believe that a more proper conception of teaching method would disfavor any such mechanical division, because the nature of the particular learning experiences under way in a good learning situation might demand an extended period for class discussion at one time, and continued extension of the period for small group or individual work at another time. However, whether the division is mechanical or flexible, good teaching method always provides for a considerable amount of time over a period of several days to be devoted to such study as use of materials, writing, conferring, and reflecting. As a matter of fact, the one situation in which even a mechanical division of time is better is that in which previously the entire period has been used for traditional recitation—some time for study promising more learning, we think!

The period for small group and individual study, whether daily or as needed, may be organized to serve several purposes. At times it may be used rather flexibly by teachers, so that they are observing particular pupils to learn more about them and are also pausing in observation to give direct help. At other times the work to be done is sufficiently well planned, so that the teacher may use the period for individual pupil-teacher conferences arranged according to some schedule. Occasionally, the work of the class may be so organized that the teacher can proceed with various items of his own daily planning, especially the examination of the pupils' work in order that questions pertaining to the work may be discussed immediately. For most of these study periods, however, we believe the teacher's time is best spent in moving from group to group and individual to individual to give such help as follows:

1. Answering questions that arise as pupils are carrying on their individual learning activities or group discussions and sharing
2. Explaining a procedure of work to an individual who is observed to be having difficulty
3. Rechecking the work of a pupil who has had difficulty, and has been given help, to see if the difficulty has been eliminated
4. Arranging pairs of learners who can help each other
5. Noting common difficulties that may necessitate an explanation to the entire group at that time, planning instruction at a later meeting of the class, or organizing a group of pupils having these difficulties to work together with the teacher for a while
6. Arranging appointments with pupils for the purposes suggested in the preceding section

Our observations in high school classrooms indicate several uses of supervised study periods which seem thoroughly undesirable. Some teachers have been observed to use most or all study periods for doing their own "homework" at their desk; this use seems completely contradictory of the term "supervised study." Other situations have been seen in which the teacher operates somewhat as a watchman in the group—watching for noise, disturbance, movement, but not for study procedures. Granted that effective study demands good working conditions, we believe that these conditions are secured by a favorable group morale rather than by the teacher's serving in a police capacity. In poor situations one frequently sees, too, an insistence on complete silence that eliminates pupils working with each other; granted, again, that good working conditions are necessary and even that some periods for reading or writing might be better without talking, really effective study frequently involves sharing an idea with another person, or asking a question, or checking one's work by another's. In these silent and uncooperative situations all assignments for study periods are uniform, and the only adaptation for individual differences is that pupils who finish their work before the end of the period are free to read, do work for other classes, or do anything else that is appropriate to the classroom.

A much better provision is a broader type of assignment or plan which provides a variety of activities suited to the needs of individual learners. Thus, instead of a study period assignment of five pages in the text on a particular topic, a more enlightened plan would be a series of suggested readings on this topic in more than one book. Each learner should be encouraged to read as much as he wishes on the topic in the classroom collection and in the text, and to prepare a list of questions about which more information is needed and which will be discussed later in class.

HOMEWORK

The general subject of homework has been widely debated in secondary education and is still a topic of much controversy among teachers and parents. Relatively little uniform homework is now assigned in elementary schools, but many secondary school teachers customarily give almost daily assignments for their pupils to complete before the next class meeting. Frequently this assignment is made before the study period so that pupils who complete the work during the latter have no work to take home. We ourselves believe that homework in the sense of uniform, regular (daily) assignments to do after school hours is generally of little value in high schools for these reasons: (1) in view of the range of needs and abilities in the typical class, there are very few occasions on which all pupils will profit from any uniform assignment, and these occasions are generally as new skills are being introduced to the total group and practice is required; (2) on such occasions as just mentioned, the practice will ordinarily be done much more profitably under the teacher's supervision than under the varying study conditions at home; (3) habits of careless work, dishonesty in copying others' work, and poor use of time are frequently strengthened rather than corrected by such homework assignments.

On the other hand, we believe that homework in the sense of particular jobs to be done after school hours in accordance with pupils' needs, interests, and abilities is indispensable in effective teaching of adolescents. For illustrations of the kind of homework teachers can use effectively to provide learning opportunities for individual pupils, note the following:

1. For pupils who are having difficulty in mastering some skill, a series of special exercises selected from the textbook, a workbook, or other source, or especially developed by the teacher, with specific directions by him as to how these exercises are to be done
2. For pupils whose school schedule is such that they are denied regular study time, arrangements for taking home materials from the classroom collection, with directions on how to use these materials
3. For pupils who have missed time in school on account of illness

or other such reasons, specific plans for study of materials used by the class during the period missed, with an arrangement for special help conferences

4. For pupils who are too easily distracted or disturbed in the classroom situation, plans for study time at home worked out with the pupils' parents

5. For pupils whose study difficulties have been carefully diagnosed and courses of remedial work planned, schedules of home activities supervised by competent persons (parents, older brothers or sisters, or tutors)

6. For pupils with special interests and abilities, plans for investigations and projects, as described in the next section of this chapter

7. For all pupils at times, suggestions of current materials, radio and television broadcasts, and community programs which should be helpful

With regard to all but the last mentioned item, the homework plan should usually be made specifically with the individual, perhaps in the course of a special help conference. Directions to an individual pupil given so that all pupils hear are frequently embarrassing to the pupil, and are seldom as well understood, received, or carried out as those given in personal conference. Any homework worth doing is worth doing right, and the teacher is clearly obliged to give directions that are clearly understood. He is also obliged to give some time to seeing or hearing about what was done. One of the reasons for careless work on the part of some pupils is undoubtedly the frustration they have experienced in trying to fulfill assignments creditably and not having any recognition from their teacher for what was done. Hence we feel homework which is worth the pupil's doing is also worth the teacher's reviewing.

SPECIAL INVESTIGATIONS AND PROJECTS

Effective guidance of group learning experiences inevitably results in many investigations and projects of an individual nature which are undertaken as individual responsibilities for committees or total classes. That is, the study of a particular problem by a committee, as described in Chapter 9, usually involves the study of related subproblems by committee members and the compilation of some composite report by the committee as a whole. Similarly, in discussions by the class as a whole, specific questions for investigations may be identified and then accepted by volunteer members of the class for study and report. In addition, many types of individual investigations and projects may be profitably undertaken by pupils at the suggestion of or with help from their teacher. It is with these special types of studies not necessarily related at all to class undertakings that we are now concerned as ways of providing for individual differences within the class.

There is rightly much interest in American education in the problem of providing adequate challenge for the gifted student. We firmly believe, as we shall note more fully later in this chapter, that the gifted are properly taught in classes grouped heterogeneously with respect to ability so that they may have the lifelike experience of working with individuals of lesser ability. The best arrangement for these students, we feel, exists in classes where imaginative and able teachers see that the gifted not only associate profitably with other pupils but that they cultivate their own mental processes and contribute to other people through carrying on extensive investigations and projects along lines of their intellectual curiosity.

A survey reported by the Office of Education in 1954 sought to determine what procedures were used effectively to meet the educational needs of rapid and slow learners in several curriculum areas. Among the pertinent findings of this survey were these: (1) special investigations and projects are prominent methods of providing for individual differences; (2) this procedure is used with both rapid and slow learners, the degree of difficulty but not necessarily the kind of project varying. Illustrating these conclusions and the findings in general regarding procedures for dealing with individual differences is the following excerpt from the summary of the section on provisions in science:

The main conclusion resulting from this study of provisions and procedures employed by science teachers considered to be extremely effective with slow learners and rapid learners is that these teachers use largely the same general provisions and procedures with both groups of pupils. However, science teachers of rapid learners use the provisions and procedures somewhat more extensively and in a few cases much more extensively.

The selected science teachers working with slow learners and the selected science teachers working with rapid learners may, based on the findings of this study, be described as teachers who help students understand scientific reasons for fire safety rules, sanitary standards, and/or first-aid practices; who include student activities which stress basic skills such as reading tables, observing experiments, and spelling common science words; who encourage students to use scientific encyclopedias and references in preparing science reports; who help students to understand how tools such as the hammer, plane, drill, and screwdriver operate; who teach students to read and evaluate science materials from newspapers; who encourage students to read stories about famous scientists; who discuss with students the qualities that help a person hold a job in industry; who encourage students to collect clippings on the uses made of science in everyday life; who guide students to note superstitions and other biases that block fair consideration of scientific evidence; who give students experiences in helping with science demonstrations; who insist that students report science experiments honestly and accurately; and who guide students to evaluate science notebook work against appropriate standards.

In addition to the above, the science teacher who is judged as especially effective in dealing with rapid learners arranges for students to become assistants for class, laboratory, and/or science-club work; stimulates students to plan and carry on projects of the experimental research type; helps students to analyze science information in statistical form; encourages students to engage in recreational reading of science fiction; helps pupils to participate in pupil-teacher planning to discover real problems for study in science; arranges for students to try competitive science examinations and aptitude tests; and announces and conducts discussions of radio, television, and movie presentations of scientific events.[1]

Special investigations and projects, like other types of homework, are usually best planned in pupil-teacher conference. However, there is not the potential element of embarrassment here that exists with regard to the assignment of a series of remedial exercises (although the gifted pupil may be sensitive to other pupils' reactions to his obviously more advanced assignments), and teachers may sometimes find it advantageous in the course of a discussion to ask an unusually able boy or girl if he or she wouldn't like to investigate some matter further. Many of these special studies, however, are related to individual interests of the pupil concerned and not to the class problem and therefore are best planned apart from the total group. Frequently the pupil himself approaches the teacher to ask how he could learn more about a given question, and this is by far the best opportunity for the teacher to suggest a line of investigation.

It should be made clear that special investigations and projects may be used profitably with pupils who are not intellectually superior. Many of the provisions for rapid and slow learners, which were included in the survey we just cited, were reported as frequently for one group as the other. Pupils who are disinterested in the class enterprise, whether bored or frustrated, may be helped by some different type of study. Pupils who are loafing may need a job in which they can find

---

[1] Arno Jewett, Dan Hull, and others, *Teaching Rapid and Slow Learners in High Schools* (United States Office of Education, Bulletin 1954, No. 5; Washington, D.C.: Government Printing Office, 1954), p. 58. This survey includes provisions in English, social studies, mathematics, science, home economics, and industrial arts.

PLATE 35. PUPILS CAN BE HELPED THROUGH SPECIAL JOBS. The choice of pupils to take leadership in the class is an opportunity to provide for individual differences. (Courtesy of the Board of Education, City of New York)

more reason to work. Those who are reticent in group discussion may speak out more easily in terms of some unique study they have been guided to make. Pupils who think and learn more slowly in general may display surprising ability when helped to work on a project for which they do have aptitude. In short, good teaching method includes provision of learning experiences especially tailored to the individual pupil who seems to need more individuality in his experiences than comes through even the best planning of total class and small group work.

SPECIAL ROLES

We described fully in Chapter 7 the use of various special roles in the class organization to promote good working relations. Here we merely wish to call attention to the fact that these same roles can also serve the purpose of providing for the individual differences in the classroom. That is, the withdrawn child may be helped by being given a role such as that of secretary which brings him slowly into group activities; the overly aggressive child by one such as reporter which gives him satisfactions that overcome the frustrations he has experienced; the slow learner by one which capitalizes on his special aptitude; the fast learner by one which makes him share his abilities with the less able.

The teacher's dilemma is whether to let boys and girls decide the assignment of such special functions to pupils, that is, to have the individuals volunteer or be chosen by their classmates, or to assign pupils to these jobs. The former procedure creates better feelings of responsibility by the group and by the individuals who choose or are elected to special jobs; the latter procedure, assignment by the teacher, more likely results in the matching of roles with the needs of learners. Our experience indicates that this is really not the "either-or" proposition it might seem. Elections can be guided by teachers through setting of qualifications so as to result in better choices than might be made otherwise. Volunteers can also be invited or choices among them made on the basis of agreed-upon qualifications. Teachers may also suggest to individual pupils that perhaps they should volunteer for particular group responsibilities. There may be jobs for which the class by vote asks the teacher to designate pupils. There may also be instances in which it seems so important for the welfare of the group that a pupil with proven competence for the job at hand be chosen, for example, in the choice of a leader of a group taking a field trip, as to make it preferable for the teacher to name the pupil rather than to risk either abiding by an unfortunate choice or having to veto one.

USING SPECIAL SERVICES TO HELP
INDIVIDUAL LEARNERS

As long as the secondary school was a relatively small, selective school with a generally homogeneous, college-bound population and a somewhat uniform college-preparatory program of studies for all who attended, there was little recognition of need for the corps of specialists one finds today in the large metropolitan high schools of the United States. During the twentieth century as the proportion of youth attending high school has grown from approximately 30 to 80 per cent, with a consequent expansion in size of the pupil enrollment in individual schools and in the program of studies and other curriculum provisions of the school, wider functions than classroom teaching have been developed and various new staff positions added. In a metropolitan high school enrolling some 2,700 students which one of us has frequently visited, the staff includes the following positions, for example, to provide special services to students:

Dean of Boys	"Guidance" teachers (several,
Dean of Girls	part-time)
Counselor	Nurse
Coordinator of student activities	Registrar

Positions for providing special services in other secondary schools include, in addition to the above, social case workers, physicians, psychologists, psychiatrists, teachers of remedial classes, teachers of special (gifted) classes, teachers of handicapped children, coordinators of placement, directors of testing and research, and others.

Smaller schools, of course, cannot provide so many special services for individual students. However, there has been increasing recognition of the obligation of the high school to provide various services; and even in the absence of special personnel, many small schools depend on itinerant or volunteer services and also expect classroom teachers to spend more time in counseling and referral of students to private services than was formerly true. Increasingly, therefore, persons in training for positions in secondary schools need to familiarize themselves with the kind of services secondary schools do provide to individual students and how teachers may themselves give some of the less technical services and coordinate all services given members of any classroom group for which they may have this responsibility.

THE CLASSROOM TEACHER AS COORDINATOR OF SPECIAL SERVICES

The simplest relation of the classroom teacher to persons providing special services is that found in the elementary school organized on the self-contained classroom basis. In this, the usual, plan one elementary teacher has a group of pupils throughout the day for an entire year. This teacher knows his or her pupils well and is alert to the needs of individual pupils for consultation with the nurse, the psychologist, the social case worker, or other special service person. Hence this teacher can easily serve as a coordinator of special services as shown in Figure 14. In the departmentalized program of the high school the situation is much more complex, for no pupil has a single teacher all day all year; usually each pupil has five or six teachers each day, with frequent change of program and teachers at midyear. Not one of these teachers can as easily be the coordinator of special services for any of the five classes he usually teaches daily as can the elementary teacher.

One of several alternatives for relating the services to classroom teachers may be followed in high schools having various special

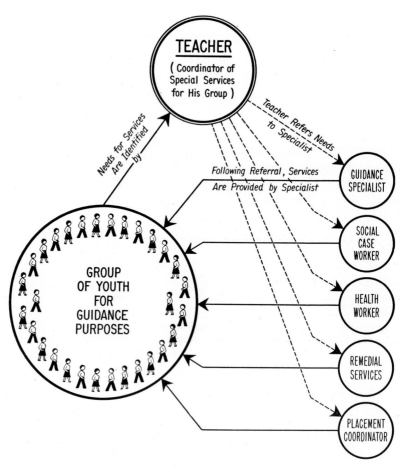

Fig. 14. The Classroom Teacher as Coordinator of Special
Services

services available to their enrollees. First, there may be no effort to provide for any coordination of services by classroom teachers, and the role of the teacher is simply to refer pupils to specialists whenever needed. Although this simplifies referrals, it also means that no one is assuming responsibility for making sure that all boys and girls are getting the benefit of available services or that individual boys and girls are benefiting from referrals made. Of course, if each teacher is carefully studying individual pupils and their records and calling on specialized help as needed, the plan might work, as it does in the small school where all the teachers know and frequently discuss individual pupils.

Second, all students may be assigned to homerooms and each homeroom teacher designated as the person responsible for records, referrals, and other phases of coordinating the special services for the particular group of students involved. Under this plan the homeroom teacher functions as shown in Figure 14. Although this plan fixes responsibility, it does not necessarily assure a relation between the homeroom teacher and members of the homeroom group that is close enough for the teacher to be able to know the pupils and their needs well. Frequently the homeroom period is very brief and the teacher does not have the group in any teaching situation. Sometimes the homeroom teacher will also have his homeroom group as one of his classes and this arrangement provides for a closer relation that may help.

Third, each pupil may be assigned to a counselor, and the counselor made responsible for the records, advisement, and referrals of his counselees. If the number of counselees is small enough, this arrangement may be better than the homeroom plan, but frequently the number is not small and the counselor has no relation with his counselees other than a very few brief interviews annually.

Fourth, some type of core curriculum plan (Chapter 14) is becoming common, especially in junior high schools. This plan provides for each learning group involved to have two or more class periods with the same teacher and for this teacher to serve as the coordinator of special services for the group. The core teacher usually has much the same relation to the secondary school core group as the elementary teacher to the elementary self-contained classroom group.

Fifth, a promising type of organization in large junior high schools is the "little school" plan as illustrated in Table 8, in which one group of four or five teachers has the same sections of a grade. That is, the "little school" consists of 125 to 175 boys and girls who have the same teachers. These teachers work together in planning for their classes, and compare problems and ideas regarding individual learners. Here coordination is done for the "little school" by the faculty group as well as by each teacher for his particular homeroom section. This plan provides for the informality and intimacy of the really small school as described earlier. The schedule illustrated makes possible a core-

TABLE 8. SCHEDULE OF PUPILS AND TEACHERS IN A "LITTLE SCHOOL" ORGANIZATION

SCHEDULE OF PUPILS

Homeroom No.	Period 1	Period 2	Period 3	Period 4	Period 5	Period 6
7–1 Mrs. Smith	English-Soc. Stud. Mrs. Smith		Science Mr. Jones	Art Miss Wills	Phys. Ed.	Math. Mr. Ellis
7–2 Miss Cox	Math. Mr. Ellis	English-Soc. Stud. Miss Cox		Science Mr. Jones	Phys. Ed.	Art Miss Wills
7–3 Miss Wills	Art Miss Wills	Math Mr. Ellis	English-Soc. Stud. Mrs. Smith		Phys. Ed.	Science Mr. Jones
7–4 Mr. Jones	Science Mr. Jones	Art Miss Wills	Math. Mr. Ellis	English Miss Cox	Phys. Ed.	Soc. Stud. Miss Cox
7–5 Mr. Ellis	Soc. Stud. Miss Cox	Science Mr. Jones	Art Miss Wills	Math. Mr. Ellis	Phys. Ed.	English Mrs. Smith

SCHEDULE OF TEACHERS

Teacher	Period 1	Period 2	Period 3	Period 4	Period 5	Period 6
Mrs. Smith (H.R. 7–1)	English-Soc. Stud. 7–1		English-Soc. Stud. 7–3		Planning	English 7–5
Mr. Jones (H.R. 7–4)	Science 7–4	Science 7–5	Science 7–1	Science 7–2	Planning	Science 7–3
Miss Wills* (H.R. 7–3)	Art 7–3	Art 7–4	Art 7–5	Art 7–1	Planning	Art 7–2
Mr. Ellis (H.R. 7–5)	Math. 7–2	Math. 7–3	Math. 7–4	Math. 7–5	Planning	Math. 7–1
Miss Cox (H.R. 7–2)	Soc. Stud. 7–5	English-Soc. Stud. 7–2		English 7–4	Planning	Soc. Stud. 7–4

* Since these five homeroom groups, that is, the "little school," have Art for twelve weeks, followed by Music for another twelve weeks, and then by General Shop the last twelve weeks, the teacher having this schedule (Miss Wills) will change each twelve weeks.

curriculum plan for four of the five sections, and by rearrangement all sections can have a core-type schedule.

Under any of these alternatives, the classroom teacher should assume considerable responsibility for studying the needs of boys and girls and for obtaining and using the services of specialists in relation to these needs. As coordinator of special services, he needs to know what services are available and which students need what services, to arrange for such needed services, and to follow up on each referral to help boys and girls secure maximum help. If there is no coordinating responsibility fixed by homeroom, core, "little school," or counseling groups, the teacher secures available help as needed by individuals in all his classes. If responsibility is fixed by homerooms, most or all teachers will be assigned homerooms and have the coordinating function described for their homeroom groups, and will refer individuals in other classes to their respective homeroom teachers. If counselors are responsible for coordinating special services, the classroom teacher refers students to the appropriate counselors. Under the core plan, the core teacher serves as coordinator of special services and other teachers refer individual pupils to the core teacher. Attention is now turned to the types of special services that are needed and may be available and to the responsibility of the classroom teacher relative to each type. This information should clarify the teacher's function as coordinator.

GUIDANCE SERVICES

We are considering as guidance services for present purposes the services to individual students usually rendered by guidance specialists, whose titles may be any of these or others: dean, counselor, guidance teacher, director or coordinator of guidance, director of testing, student advisor. The services relating to individual pupils provided by these persons[2] usually include some of the following:

1. Administration and interpretation of tests of a variety of sorts, and advisement of teachers and pupils concerning the implications of test results
2. Counseling of individuals with respect to their educational, vocational, and personal interests, problems, and plans
3. Referral of pupils with special psychological, physical, emotional,

---

[2] See for an excellent, more extended treatment of this topic, Chapter VI, "Guidance Specialists as Resource Persons," in Association for Supervision and Curriculum Development, National Education Association, *Guidance in the Curriculum* (1955 Yearbook; Washington, D.C.: The Association, 1955).

and other problems to specialists who can give assistance with these problems

4. Studies of individual pupils' behavior, accomplishments, and difficulties in out-of-school situations, including those in employment

5. Maintaining records of pupils and systems of communication with teachers and others so that needed information about individual pupils is available to all concerned

6. Advising teachers on adjustments to be made in the classroom situation for individual pupils, and parents on adjustments indicated for the home

Classroom teachers who have the advantage of services of these types can find them of great usefulness in providing for the individual needs, interests, and abilities of their pupils. Communication between the teacher and the specialist is essential and is usually handled through such arrangements as the following:

1. Guidance specialists make available to the teacher responsible for a particular homeroom, core, or other group, the pertinent individual records for this group with such interpretations as necessary of the information and its use.

2. When group tests are given, either as a routine part of the testing program or upon request of the teacher, the guidance specialist provides some interpretation of the data and may confer with the teacher about the implications of test results for teaching or further individual testing of particular pupils.

3. Teachers who wish further information about certain pupils consult with the guidance specialist regarding the need, and arrangements are made for such testing, counseling, or other studies as are possible.

4. In larger schools the teacher makes such a written referral as shown in Figure 15, and the guidance specialist reports back to the teacher. If need for a conference is indicated, one is arranged on the initiative of either teacher or guidance person.

5. In the case of a pupil presenting particularly acute guidance problems, a conference may be arranged by either the responsible teacher or the guidance specialist of all school personnel and perhaps parents and others who have pertinent information or need for information.

6. A periodic conference may be scheduled between the guidance specialist and each homeroom or other teacher having responsibility for one group of pupils to discuss any individual problems either wishes.

FORM ORS-46 (REVISED)
1-54

OAK RIDGE PUBLIC SCHOOLS

REQUEST FOR GUIDANCE SERVICE

Pupil_____ Birthdate_____ Date_____

School_____ Teacher_____ Grade_____

Parent_____ Address_____ Phone_____

State the problem for which the child is referred.

Do you think the parents are aware of the problem?

State a convenient time for a conference with Guidance personnel.

Please do not write below this line: the space is for use in the Guidance Office.

Date received_____ Assigned to_____

Disposition:

Fig. 15. Form for Referral of a Pupil to a Guidance Specialist. (Courtesy of the Oak Ridge, Tennessee, Public Schools)

7. Cumulative records may be stored either in the custody of the
teacher or the guidance specialist or even in the main office, with
some plan whereby the other persons needing access to these records
may readily see them.

8. Arrangements for pupils to see guidance specialists, at the request

of the specialist, the pupil, or the teacher, are usually either made by the responsible teacher or with information to the latter.

In summary, the classroom teacher is the original guidance advisor for the pupils assigned as his responsibility either for specific guidance purposes, as in the homeroom plan, or for all pupils taught, in the absence of such a plan. When there is a homeroom or similar plan for coordinating special purposes, each teacher is still responsible for studying all his pupils and for securing further information through referrals or otherwise from the homeroom teacher.

To illustrate these relations, in a high school having a homeroom plan for coordination of special services, Miss Jones, an English teacher, wishes information about the apparently poor reading ability of John Smith, a tenth-grader. She secures his cumulative record from Mr. Williams, John's homeroom teacher, and notes that his reading test scores had consistently been average or better through the ninth grade. She does find a notation to the effect that John had appeared preoccupied and disinterested in his English class in the ninth grade. Questioning of John gives little information about his reading ability and interest, although he does state that his new job after school prevents him from doing any outside reading or other study. Hence Miss Jones suggests to Mr. Williams that he find out more about John's outside work, his study habits, and any other items that would explain his poor work in English. Mr. Williams does talk with John and finds that this pupil says he is having financial problems, is having to work a great deal, and expects to leave school just as soon as he is sixteen. Mr. Williams wants to discourage this, but feels that he does not have enough information about John's home situation, future interests, and abilities to counsel the boy. He therefore arranges an interview of John with the boys' counselor, Mr. Dykes. In due time, Mr. Dykes reports back that he has conferred with John and his parents and also John's employer, and has been able to work out a reduced program of work until June for John with the prospect of full-time employment during the summer. He hopes this will keep John in school and suggests that Mr. Williams should keep in touch with John's school work and let Mr. Dykes know if further problems develop. He also notes that John's work on a newspaper route has developed his interest in the newspaper business, where he will work in the summer, and suggests that this fact be reported to John's teachers. Mr. Williams talks with Miss Jones about the facts of the case thus revealed, and Miss Jones works out for John some special reading and projects dealing with newspaper publishing.

In the example just given, three persons were really carrying on guidance services for an individual pupil. First, the English teacher was trying to teach John as an individual, discovering his needs and interests and planning instruction accordingly. Secondly, the home-room teacher was serving as a coordinator of information about John and therefore as a liaison between the classroom teacher and the guidance specialist. Thirdly, the guidance specialist, the boys' counselor for the school, was securing information about the boy that was not readily available to teachers and working out arrangements outside the school, with information to those concerned, that seemed promising for the pupil's continued and better education. This seems to us a proper way of relating the services of guidance specialists to the classroom teacher.

If in our example there had been no homeroom teacher, the English teacher would have gone directly to the counselor, and the problem might have been worked out just as we described. But if we can imagine that the mathematics, science, history, and physical education teachers also come to Mr. Dykes, who perhaps counsels several hundred students, to get information about John Smith, it is obvious that Mr. Dykes would soon be unable to take care of all the requests made of him. Hence the homeroom teacher would serve a helpful clearinghouse function in reporting to these other teachers and thereby eliminating the necessity of the counselor's having four additional teacher interviews or even written reports to handle with regard to the same case.

SOCIAL CASE WORKERS

Larger school systems and indeed many large schools employ persons variously designated by such terms as "visiting teacher," "attendance worker," "student welfare officer," or "social case worker." Such persons usually make more thoroughgoing investigation of problems of absenteeism, behavior, and the like than are possible for the guidance specialist having the in-school functions we have just described. Ordinarily, referral of cases to these case workers is made by the guidance specialist. For example, if in our previous example the counselor's study of John Smith's record had revealed the need for a comprehensive investigation of home and employment conditions, and a case worker had been available for this purpose, the counselor would likely have referred the investigation. Or, if the original indication of John's difficulties had been that of persistent attendance problems, the homeroom teacher might have referred the case directly to the case worker for an investigation.

In smaller high schools the work of the counselor and social case worker may be centered in one person. In very small ones having no special service personnel, the classroom teacher frequently conducts his own investigation. In fact, this is probably the ideal situation, assuming adequate qualifications of the teacher and a close acquaintance of teacher with pupils and their families. Special services, we should note, have developed largely as a result of the increasing size and complexity of the high school organization. However, they also bring specialization on the part of special service personnel to a degree rarely possible for the classroom teacher. The resultant problem is that of coordinating the special services with the work of the classroom teacher, so that the individual pupil has at all times one person by whom his complete record is known and made available for consultation and supplementary investigation when there is need. For this reason, the best arrangement seems to be the combination of home-room or core teachers as coordinators with well-organized and well-staffed special services, including social case workers.

CLINICAL SERVICES

Two general and frequently related types of clinical services are available for dealing with individual problems in the large schools. The more usual type is the health clinic, frequently a facility in the school serviced by a school or public health nurse and perhaps by one or more part-time physicians. Local arrangements vary so much as to how these services operate as to make generalization impossible. The other type of clinical service has to do with mental, emotional or behavior, and related problems and includes the services of psychologists, psychiatrists, and other specialists. Considerable screening is usually essential in referral of problems for clinical examination and treatment, if treatment is provided. Generally, therefore, these services (not including routine and emergency health services) are available only through a specific routine which involves referral by the school's chief guidance specialist or principal. The specialist or principal, of course, has to be in turn informed of the original problem by the teacher or teachers who first identify the need for clinical examination. Teachers in schools having clinical services available need specific information on the nature of these services and the channeling of referrals, and with this information can make excellent use of the services in caring for particular individuals.

EMPLOYMENT SERVICES

Many boys and girls in secondary schools have problems of employment on which schools give help. Some are employed part-time and need special programs to permit or help their work; teachers may make fine contributions to problems of individual differences by assisting in such cases as that of the John Smith we described. Others need part-time employment, and the teacher who determines this fact may help through the school's placement service, the counselor, or the teacher's own effort. Still others need help in finding a job after graduation, and the school's placement service, whatever its nature, can be of direct assistance.

In metropolitan areas youth who leave school to work are frequently enabled to continue their high school program in evening school, and teachers and guidance workers can help through planning with such students for their continuation programs. Various types of apprenticeship training programs, Diversified Cooperative Training, and other work experience programs offer teachers opportunity to work with boys and girls to secure work experience and educational training at the same time. Correspondence courses are available to students in school and to employed youth in many states, especially in those having large rural populations, to provide subjects required for graduation and other purposes, and teachers may again give help in advising youth about enrolling for such courses.

SERVICES FOR THE HANDICAPPED

Although special facilities and instructional programs for the physically and mentally handicapped are much more widely provided at the elementary than the secondary level, increasing provision is being made at the latter. In the absence of such facilities and programs within the school, teachers and guidance specialists can advise parents and youth on facilities which may be available elsewhere. In many instances, teachers must simply make the best adaptation possible within the regular classroom, referring pupils with marked handicaps to whatever facilities may become available for them as rapidly as possible.

Since the markedly handicapped boy or girl is usually not to be found in the secondary school, the following suggestions pertain to the teacher's role with respect to handicaps that may exist in his classes and for which special help is available:

1. Refer students who seem to have visual, hearing, or speech defects for examinations, and be guided by the findings as to next steps.

2. Investigate the health records of students who have obvious physical handicaps to determine whether further referral is indicated and what special care is needed in the classroom.

3. Consult with the guidance specialist about pupils who seem to have very low mental abilities to determine the facts and whether some other placement in school might be desirable and, if not, what special provisions need to be made for such pupils in the classroom.

4. Most important, be as widely acquainted as possible with the special facilities of the school and community for dealing with handicapped children, and work with guidance specialists, if available, in referring cases to appropriate facilities.

5. In the case of boys and girls temporarily out of school but able to study, refer to teachers of homebound children if available and, if not, communicate with the pupils or parents to provide as much guidance as desirable and possible in helping such pupils to continue their work satisfactorily.

REMEDIAL SERVICES

In many larger secondary schools various so-called "remedial" classes or other types of opportunities are provided, especially in reading, speech, composition, and mathematics. Frequently these classes are not remedial in the true sense at all, but are simply sections of a subject in which pupils with low test scores or other records are placed. Sometimes they are organized through placing pupils in them who have failed a related course; this is especially true of summer school classes. Remedial services, as we see it, should be based on careful diagnosis of disabilities, and provided in those cases where there are definitely "remedial" procedures as in speech correction. In the best situations these classes are not "classes" in the usual sense, that is, in lieu of some other credit-carrying class, but are provided for whatever period needed and on a somewhat tutorial basis. That is, the speech, reading, or language specialist is available to help pupils referred to the special service for whatever time is necessary and desirable. In these situations the specialist keeps the responsible teacher or teachers informed of the pupil's progress, suggests ways of helping the pupil in the regular classrooms, and works out a schedule of special help so that the pupil misses a minimum of regular class activities.

These remedial services are sometimes and appropriately described as reading, speech, language, or mathematics "laboratories." They are staffed by teachers especially competent in the skills concerned, and pupils who need help may even arrange on their own volition to get this. We ourselves feel that with the great range of differences in the population of the large high school, such service centers should and will see considerable expansion in the years ahead. They represent a very fine development of provisions for the individual needs of learners.

SERVICES FOR THE GIFTED

In recent years a considerable number of educators and laymen have expressed concern in publications and public statements about the neglect of the gifted student in high school. These statements, plus the generally increasing recognition of the need to provide for individual differences in our schools, have led to considerable experimentation in various types of programs and services for gifted children. The 1954 Office of Education report of a survey of provisions for rapid and slow learners included the following administrative provisions, listed in order of occurrence in the schools included, for rapid learners only:

College-preparatory curriculum
Pupils permitted to carry above-normal class load for graduation credit
Elective classes in advanced or specialized subjects (journalism, electronics, calculus, etc.)
Remedial sections for able pupils whose performance is below capacity
Teachers assigned on basis of training and experience with rapid learners
Pupils sectioned in classes which do 2 years' work in 1; or 3 years' work in 2, etc.[3]

Also, the following provisions were reported as being made for both rapid and slow learners:

Teachers furnished guidance information pertinent to pupils
Teachers assigned on basis of traits and interest suitable for work
Regular classes furnished advanced study materials and additional learning aids. (See Plate 36.)
Space, furniture and equipment for flexible grouping in classes and activities
Ability (homogeneous) classes. (Pupils grouped according to I.Q., reading ability, previous grades, social maturity, etc.)
Individualized instruction outside of regular class hours
Job placement services
Supervised work experience
Summer-school sessions provided
Credit given for demonstrated achievement regardless of time spent in class
Transfer to special school encouraged
Flexible graduation requirements as to credits.[4]

[3] Jewett, Hull, and others, *op. cit.*, p. 8.
[4] *Ibid.*

PLATE 36. CONCRETE LEARNING AIDS HELP ALL LEARNERS. Classroom situations like this give each learner opportunity to ask or
answer questions according to his understanding of a common
problem. (Courtesy of the Lakewood, Ohio, Public Schools)

Major types of administrative provisions for individual differences
are described in greater detail in the following section.

ADMINISTRATIVE PROVISIONS FOR
INDIVIDUAL DIFFERENCES

The variety and complexity of provisions made within the administrative structure of high schools for serving the individual differences
of pupils are beyond the scope of this book. Teachers certainly need
to be aware of these provisions, however, in order to use them where
available and possible and to work as faculty members for desirable
provisions. In the following paragraphs we are therefore identifying
certain major common types of administrative provisions and
indicating a point of view regarding them.

GROUPING OF PUPILS

Probably the most frequent administrative provision for individual differences is some type of homogeneous grouping, usually by general ability or by proficiency in the subject. Thus, when there are several sections of the same subject, pupils may be classified as fast, average, and slow with respect to the subject, and assigned to sections accordingly. In the junior high school where sections are maintained intact in the required subjects, the sections may be organized on the basis of so-called "general ability."

The primary argument for this type of grouping is that it facilitates mastery of the subject, since the teacher can presumably adjust the work more easily to one level. Teachers who advocate homogeneous grouping generally believe that *the* purpose of instruction is mastery of subject matter, and that this purpose is more important than learning to work with peers of greater or lesser ability. In view of the research showing the difficulty of achieving homogeneous grouping and the paucity of conclusive evidence of its effects on achievement, we question whether this argument holds up. Furthermore, the purpose of class organization is not identical mastery of the subject but rather the maximum understanding of related problems of which pupils are capable. Grouping pupils heterogeneously gives slower pupils the advantage of help and stimulation of others, and faster pupils the opportunity to help others and also to move at their own rate. We ourselves believe that administrative policies of grouping on bases other than ability, probably on a random basis in organizing sections of the same class, will in the long run be better provision for individual differences than ability grouping. We do recognize that the elective system itself results in a type of homogeneous grouping, sometimes by ability as well as interest, which wisely used may be very useful in providing for individual differences.

THE ELECTIVE SYSTEM OF CLASSES AND ACTIVITIES

In most high schools pupils have some choice as to their areas of concentration ("majors," or "curricula," are frequently used terms) and also choices of subjects to be taken within these areas. For example, a typical student planning to attend a liberal arts college would have about two-thirds of his courses specified and the other third elective. Sometimes the recommendations of school personnel are such that pupils may feel they really have little to elect. Nevertheless, the average high school student has some choice of classes and a wider choice of so-called "extracurricular" activities. In making these choices, he has freedom to follow his own interests, needs, and abilities, and in larger high schools the advantage also of guidance specialists to advise him regarding the suitability of various classes and activities for his future plans. Guidance is quite desirable in these larger schools when one considers the statistic one of us acquired at a high school of about 2,700 enrollees, that it would take approximately twenty-six years to complete at the usual rate all the courses offered there and that one could belong to at least two different clubs each of these years, there being over sixty clubs in the school.

PROGRAM ADJUSTMENTS

A frequent and highly desirable method of providing for individual differences in the secondary school is that of adjusting the program of an individual to suit his particular needs. Thus a pupil needing to work may be given an abbreviated schedule, or a pupil especially interested in a vocational area and needing to go to work at an early date may be given a double program of studies in the area concerned, or a pupil having difficulty with a particular teacher may be given a chance with another if there is reason to think the teacher relation is responsible for the difficulty. School administrators vary in their attitudes toward making such adjustments, of course, just as teachers vary in their attitudes toward making adjustments in teaching situations. In general, there is probably no more important type of provision for individual differences than a policy of administration which assumes that a chief function of program planning for pupils is that of suiting the program to the individual. Where this policy prevails, pupils are transferred from class to class, schedule to schedule, or even school to school, as there is reason to believe such a transfer would help, and matters of promotion and graduation are also administered with concern for the individual pupil.

FACILITIES FOR CURRICULUM PLANNING AND IMPROVEMENT

Wise planning of teachers for individual differences involves their careful, cooperative planning of the school curriculum as a whole and of the instructional program for each group of learners, and their wide participation in various types of improvement programs. Part V of this book describes in some detail these planning and improvement processes. Our present point is that an essential provision for individual differences of pupils is that of adequate facilities for school personnel to engage in these processes. The facilities needed include such items as planning periods, times for departmental and faculty meetings, clerical help in preparing materials, leadership and consultative help in curriculum study, in-service education, and cooperative research. Good administrative leadership sees that faculty organization and the school budget are so set as to facilitate planning and improvement.

ADEQUATE RESOURCES

Of all these significant provisions for individual differences, the fundamental and indispensable one seems to be that of resources. Resources include resourceful teachers, specialists, and materials personnel. The term also covers the tools which personnel must have available for dealing with individual differences: adequate libraries, audiovisual equipment and materials, tests and other materials for diagnosis and appraisal of individual differences, well-equipped laboratories and gymnasiums, records and files, and many other physical items which are essential in the successful provision of a good education for all learners.

The reader may conclude from the foregoing statements that all one needs in order to care for individual differences is a generous school budget. Unfortunately, schools with generous budgets do not necessarily spend their funds to provide well for all individual differences. In addition to a budget adequate to supply all the resources mentioned above, including competent personnel, there must be administrative policies and personnel which direct proper expenditure of the budget. Given an adequate budget, enlightened administrative policies, and an able administrator interested in providing for individual differences, the teacher can be assured that only his own limitations will restrict the development of an instructional program which will meet individual needs, interests, and abilities to a maximum extent. And teachers who are employed in these situations usually have few limitations! We hope that all our readers will have or find just such situations. To those who do not, remember that as a teacher you can do much to create a more favorable budget and administrative policies by the pupil and parent attitudes you help develop as well as by your direct participation in school policy making. In short, maybe it is up to the teachers to provide for individual differences even to the point of helping to create favorable administrative provisions.

FOR FURTHER STUDY

Association for Supervision and Curriculum Development, National Education Association, *Guidance in the Curriculum*. 1955 Yearbook; Washington, D.C.: The Association, 1955.

See especially Chapter 6, "Guidance Specialists as Resource Persons," and Chapter 11, "Guiding through Teaching."

Berthold, Charles A., *Administrative Concern for Individual Differences.* New York: Bureau of Publications, Teachers College, Columbia University, 1951.
A survey of administrative provisions for individual differences.

Blair, Glenn Myers, *Diagnostic and Remedial Teaching in Secondary Schools.* New York: The Macmillan Company, 1947.
Detailed descriptions of procedures for diagnosing difficulties in the three R's and related areas and for remedial work in these areas.

Butler, Frank A., *The Improvement of Teaching in Secondary Schools.* 3rd ed.; Chicago: The University of Chicago Press, 1954.
See Chapters 13 and 14 for a review of provisions for individual differences, including diagnostic and remedial procedures.

Cook, Walter W., "Individual Differences and Curriculum Practice," *Journal of Educational Psychology,* 39:141–148 (March), 1948.
A penetrating analysis of the need for changed curriculum practices to provide for individual differences.

Dodds, B. L., "That All May Learn," *Bulletin,* No. 185, National Association of Secondary School Principals, 23:1–235 (November), 1939.
A comprehensive summary of theory, research, and practice dealing with the educationally neglected (nonacademic) high school pupil.

Educational Policies Commission, *The Education of the Gifted.* Washington, D.C.: National Education Association, 1950.
The philosophy and practice of education of gifted children.

Gray, William S., ed., *Improving Reading in All Curriculum Areas.* Chicago: The University of Chicago Press, Supplementary Educational Monograph No. 76, November, 1952.
The proceedings of the 1952 Conference on Reading at the University of Chicago include many suggestions for improving reading skills in high school subjects.

Jewett, Arno, J. Dan Hull, and others, *Rapid and Slow Learners in High Schools.* U.S. Office of Education Bulletin, 1954, No. 5; Washington, D.C.: Government Printing Office, 1954.
A survey of provisions made for rapid and slow learners in grades 7–12 in schools enrolling more than 300 pupils.

Kelly, Janet A., *Guidance and Curriculum.* Englewood Cliffs, N.J.: Prentice-Hall, Inc., 1955.
Devoted to the thesis that guidance and curriculum can be united in a "guidance-curriculum centered program." Part III, "Bridging the Gap," offers helpful suggestions for cooperation of teachers and special guidance personnel.

Koos, Leonard V., *Junior High School Trends.* New York: Harper & Brothers, 1955.
See Chapters 6, 7, and 8 for descriptions of some provisions in junior high schools for individual differences.

Mort, Paul R., and William S. Vincent, *Modern Educational Practice*. New York: McGraw-Hill Book Co. Inc., 1950.

This catalogue of brief descriptions of educational practice includes many items relating to provisions for individual differences of pupils.

National Society for the Study of Education, *Education of Exceptional Children*. Forty-ninth Yearbook of the Society; Chicago: The University of Chicago Press, 1950, Part II.

Principles and practices of education of various types of exceptional children.

Simpson, Elizabeth A., *Helping High School Students Read Better*. Chicago: Science Research Associates, Inc., 1954.

Techniques for improving reading skills.

Strang, Ruth, Constance M. McCullough, and Arthur E. Traxler, *Problems in the Improvement of Reading*. New York: McGraw-Hill Book Co. Inc., 1946.

Principles and practices of improving reading at all levels. Chapters 8, 9, and 10 deal, respectively, with improvement of reading in English, mathematics and science, and social studies.

Thorndike, Robert L., "How Children Learn the Principles and Techniques of Problem-Solving," in *Learning and Instruction*. Forty-ninth Yearbook of the National Society for the Study of Education; Chicago: The University of Chicago Press, 1950, Part I, Chap. 8.

See especially pages 210–215 for suggestions on helping learners to develop the techniques of problem solving.

13. Evaluating Pupil Progress

EVALUATION is an essential and continuous phase of helping individual learners. Most of the procedures we described in Chapter 11 for studying the characteristics of individual learners are evaluative procedures. The means of providing for individual differences presented in Chapter 12 involve frequent re-evaluation to determine whether progress is being made. Although the same procedure may be used for original diagnosis as for later checking of progress, our present concern is with the latter step. We seek in this chapter to explain the ways in which evaluation of the pupil's progress may help him make greater progress. Following consideration of the nature and purposes of evaluation, specific techniques of teacher, pupil, and group evaluation are treated.

WHAT IS EVALUATION?

Evaluation occurs every time a judgment is made. We are constantly evaluating our feelings, the weather, the people we meet, our success in whatever we are undertaking. Evaluation is the process of making a judgment as to the value of something. In terms of this chapter, evaluation is the process of making a judgment as to the progress of pupils. One's judgment depends, of course, on the values one holds. Thus the teacher who feels the important value is that of ability to recall subject matter may evaluate very favorably the progress of the pupil who scores high on recall tests. The same pupil may feel the important value is that of scoring high on the teacher's tests and he, too, evaluates very favorably his progress. Another pupil may regard test scores as a fairly unimportant value and evaluate his progress quite differently, even though he, too, makes high scores.

Although pupils, parents, and teachers are constantly evaluating pupil progress, traditional methods of recording and reporting marks have placed the burden of responsibility for evaluation on the teacher's shoulders. These burdens are sometimes so heavy that teachers tend to place an emphasis on marks that detracts from the real process of making judgments about the progress of pupils—judgments that can be far more significant in terms of helping pupils than the recording of A's, B's, C's, and so forth, on their report cards. In this chapter we are concerned with the entire process of evaluating pupil progress, including techniques of recording and reporting. In this process pupils, parents, and teachers have responsibilities, we believe, because all can and do make valid judgments about pupil progress that may help learners make better progress. Some of these relations and the whole concept of evaluating pupil progress may be better explained by examining some of the issues that are involved.

ARE MEASUREMENT AND EVALUATION THE SAME?

The terms "measurement" and "evaluation" are sometimes, but erroneously, used synonymously. To evaluate the progress of the pupil is to make a judgment as to the value (adequacy, quality, and so forth) of his progress. To measure progress is to express it in terms of some standard of measurement, as months or years or norms. The teacher makes an evaluation of a pupil's progress when he concludes that the pupil has become proficient in the use of tools in the industrial arts shop. This evaluation may be based in part on counting the number of tools and operations with which there is proficiency, a matter of measurement. Similarly, the English teacher might measure the pupil's English usage by a test on common usage. The measurement itself is useless as an evaluation but may be very helpful in evaluation. The raw score made on the test means little but when compared with other scores or a norm (the score that has been established as an average or median), it indicates the position of a particular pupil with respect to others. For purposes of evaluation, the pupil's score on a second test given after an interval of instruction provides a much better basis for determining progress. The difference between scores is a measurement, and the judgment as to whether the difference is enough is an evaluation.

In evaluation the element of expected progress is present, whereas in measurement only actual progress is determined. Thus, in evaluating Johnny's reading progress, the teacher determines his reading level. Following a period of instruction a retest measures his progress. The teacher evaluates by comparing this measure with the expected progress. To sum up, measurements are data which may be useful in evaluation.

WHAT CAN BE EVALUATED?

Teachers frequently assert that pupil progress with respect to only certain kinds of educational goals can be evaluated. Thus it is said that attitudes, feelings, behavior, even understandings, cannot be evaluated, but skills and knowledges can. What these people are really saying is that progress with respect to some goals cannot be measured in the usual objective, quantitative terms. Actually, recent developments in the field of tests and measurements have provided measures of objective and quantitative types for attitudes and the like, but even without such measures these goals can be evaluated. For example, observation of pupils' behavior provides perhaps the most reliable data as to their progress in the items of behavior observed.

We believe that progress in any particular in which progress is sought can be evaluated. That is, any goal toward which individuals work becomes a standard of value whereby an evaluation can be made. If a goal in the homemaking class is to develop good taste in the choice of clothing, for example, "good taste" becomes a value to be applied in the evaluation of pupil progress. If the class develops some standards of good taste, both the girls and their teacher may evaluate their choices of clothing by these standards. Periodic appraisal (evaluation at a particular time) of the clothing chosen by an individual girl provides data for determining her progress in use of good taste. Without such group standards, the appraisal of good taste may be more difficult and certainly less objective, but there can still be evaluation of the individual's progress in use of good taste by whatever standards of taste the evaluator uses. If the goal toward which progress is sought can be identified, however subjectively and individually, then judgment can be reached as to the progress made.

In other words, we believe that pupils and teachers can evaluate progress only if they can define the values they seek. If the value sought is known, then one's status regarding that value can be determined or appraised, and comparison of status from time to time becomes the basis of evaluating progress.

WRITTEN TESTS AND EVALUATION

Evaluation and testing are also frequently confused. The confusion disappears if we keep in mind that we can evaluate progress toward any goal we can define but that we can test progress toward certain goals adequately only by written means. Thus a pupil and his teacher might agree that an important goal for him is greater courtesy in his interpersonal relations. This goal might be defined in some detail as to types of courtesies in which improvement is desirable. Written tests might be used to determine the pupil's ability to recall when such expressions as "Thank you" and "Pardon me" should be used, but these tests would be a very inferior method of determining the pupil's progress toward the real goal of *being* more courteous.

The distinctions already drawn between evaluation and measurement apply in the present case since tests are forms of measurements. However, written tests have so typically been the only form of measurement used in secondary education that particular emphasis needs to be given here to their relation to evaluation. That relation is one of a single means to some end: tests give one type of evidence as to progress which may be considered in evaluating. In some instances, test results may be the only reliable type of evidence, and in others tests may be completely inadequate or even lacking. For example, written tests on the meaning of scientific concepts may be the best evidence to be secured on progress in understanding these concepts, but written tests on how to hit a baseball would be poor substitutes for performance in the batter's box.

MARKING SYSTEMS AND EVALUATION

As we have already indicated, evaluation in education has been greatly influenced by marking systems, so much that in many teaching-learning situations it appears that the values being sought are marks alone. In these very situations, however, one hears pupils and teachers expressing judgments about the value or lack of value of what is being done, so that we can be sure certain evaluations are being made independently of the struggle for passing marks.

Remembering that an evaluation is a judgment of the value of something, marks are simply means of recording and reporting somebody's, usually the teacher's, judgment or evaluation. Although the bases on which marks are determined may be inadequate and poor and may even have nothing to do with pupil progress, the marks nevertheless represent an evaluation in terms of whatever value the marker determined. Unfortunately, marking systems generally record and report evaluations of pupils' present achievement rather than of their recent progress, and achievement is frequently on the basis of comparison of pupils with each other.

Thus there is a twofold relation between marking systems and evaluation. In the first place, the necessity of assigning marks to pupils is a major, sometimes the only, reason for procedures of evaluation.

This purpose may determine the whole nature of the evaluative process, as it has generally done in encouraging schemes of examinations, required readings and papers and projects, and similar devices which are motivated by the teacher's need to assign marks to pupils. In the second place, marks are usually the chief, if not the only, record made of evaluation. Thus the main source of information about pupil progress resides in the records and transcripts of their academic grades. We feel that these relations provide a very inadequate basis for evaluation which exists to help learners, and hope in this chapter to help teachers understand more important purposes and uses of evaluation than those related to academic marks.

WHEN DOES EVALUATION TAKE PLACE?

To many, perhaps most, students the one time that evaluation takes place is the examination period. But in modern teaching-learning theory, evaluation is seen as a continuous process that is taking place simultaneously with learning experiences. Formal evaluations are held when examinations are given, marked, and results considered, and also when pupil-teacher conferences are held, group planning is done, or check lists are completed to appraise experiences. But informal evaluation is occurring as pupils and teachers ask themselves how they are doing, as they wonder about better ways of working, and as they reflect on their desires and satisfactions. The difficult job of the teacher in evaluating pupil progress is to find means of getting at the honest and significant evaluative evidence that does not easily emerge in the formal evaluation situations.

WHO EVALUATES?

The reader is undoubtedly aware by now that we believe all concerned with the teaching-learning process are evaluating pupil progress: the teacher, pupils, and parents. In practice, only the teacher's evaluation may be considered in recording and reporting marks and even in planning for and helping the individual learner, but the learner has his own evaluation and his parents may have theirs, too, if they are following his school progress. Evaluation which really helps pupils should involve use of all possible sources of evaluative evidence and be a cooperative process, we believe. Therefore in this chapter we include information about techniques to be used in the pupil's self-evaluation, the teacher's evaluation, and cooperative evaluation of pupil progress.

PURPOSES OF EVALUATING PUPIL PROGRESS

The authors' emphasis on the broader functions of evaluation as compared with those of marking systems makes it necessary for us to define more exactly than we have thus far just what these functions are. The whole process of evaluation is essential to school improvement, we believe, but here we are concerned with evaluation only in regard to the progress of individual pupils. In this connection we see four major purposes of evaluation.

HELPING LEARNERS ACHIEVE SELF-UNDERSTANDING AND IMPROVEMENT

The unique function of evaluation as contrasted with some of the more limited processes of tests and measurements is that of helping the learner achieve greater understanding of himself and thereby make fundamental improvements. In his analysis of the problem of the role of the school in promoting self-understanding, Jersild emphasizes the great importance of measures to meet this need:

There is a need of staggering magnitude for doing something in our education program to help children and youth acquire realistic attitudes of self-acceptance. A large proportion of the young people now entering adulthood are burdened with anxiety, hostility, defensive attitudes toward themselves and others, feelings of guilt, inferiority, or other forms of self-disparagement and self-distrust. They struggle not only with the real dangers and thwartings in our troubled world but with unresolved childhood problems. They are beset with conflicts arising from unrealistic concepts and unhealthy attitudes which they carry from childhood into adult life.[1]

We are fully aware that no procedures of evaluating pupil progress will within themselves assure the solution of these problems described by Jersild. On the other hand, we see as the primary purpose of evaluation the provision of opportunities for youth to learn more about themselves, and particularly more about their strengths and difficulties and consequent needs for further progress. Learning is so utterly dependent on the learner's own motivations that evaluation devices which cause self-examination and self-motivation of subsequent actions deserve high priority in educational method. The other purposes of evaluation of pupil progress which we shall mention are wholly subordinate to this one of self-understanding and self-motivation and can be justified, we believe, only as they relate to the primary purpose. Thus it is important to inform parents of their children's progress in order for

[1] Arthur T. Jersild, *In Search of Self* (New York: Bureau of Publications, Teachers College, Columbia University, 1952), p. 5.

children to have parental help in reaching greater self-understanding. We do believe that parents can help in this way and therefore that informative reports to parents are desirable.

GUIDING TEACHERS IN WORKING WITH INDIVIDUAL LEARNERS

We explained fully in Chapter 11 the importance of evaluative data in teachers' understanding of their pupils. Direct help to individual learners can come only as the teacher understands the needs of these pupils. Needs are revealed not only by measures of the individual's present status but even better by evidence of his progress over a period of time in meeting these needs. The help the teacher can give, knowing the individual's needs and progress, depends on the individual's understanding of these matters himself, but the teacher can promote such understanding once the facts of evaluation are at hand. Furthermore, the evaluation of a pupil's progress helps the teacher evaluate his own work with the pupil and plan needed redirections.

GUIDING PARENTS IN WORKING WITH THEIR CHILDREN

As we explained above, parents can give their children help in understanding themselves and planning for self-improvement. Wise parents use reports of their children's progress as a basis for discussion and planning with the children rather than as threats and coercions. This kind of parental help does necessitate a type of evaluation and evaluation report, which clearly defines the progress pupils are making and indicate lines of needed improvement rather than the traditional marks which, standing alone, give no accurate statement either of progress or needed improvement. That is, A's appearing on a report card under English usually merely tell the parent that his child stands high in this subject, but not whether he stands as high as he should or whether there are any aspects of English in which the pupil should make improvement.

PROVIDING RECORDS FOR FUTURE REFERENCE

Each of the foregoing purposes of evaluation necessitates records of evaluation that can be referred to by the pupil, teacher, and parent. In addition, the pupil's further development is aided by the activities of other teachers, guidance counselors, college advisors, and employers. Although the evaluation record is frequently used as a selective device, even this step, wisely taken, may be of use to the pupil at a later time in eliminating him from occupations or training programs for which his record does not indicate proficiency. It is essential that teachers and counselors have access to as accurate records of past performance as possible to do well their jobs with pupils.

STEPS IN EVALUATING PUPIL PROGRESS

The essential steps in evaluation are (1) to define the goal being sought; (2) to collect evidence on the realization of the goal; (3) to make a judgment as to whether the achievement is satisfactory; and (4) in the light of the value determined, to plan next steps. These steps take on more specific meanings when the concern is evaluation of progress. They are restated and explained in this section accordingly.

DEFINING THE PROGRESS DESIRED

Although the teacher and pupils may have set up as a learning goal such an inclusive purpose as "respecting the rights of others," the evaluation of an individual's progress toward this goal has to be more specific if he is to be helped. Under most desirable conditions, each pupil would set up for himself some concrete behavior to be achieved in relation to the rights of others. Thus one pupil might aim to give others more opportunity to participate in discussion by being less of a monopolist himself, another might try to restrain himself in the cafeteria line, and still another might determine to be more friendly with classmates he has ignored in the past. Since emphasis is on "progress" rather than just "doing something," there is need for some indication of present behavior which can be compared later with behavior at that time. The first pupil might note that he is usually one of the most talkative members of the class and would even profit by some record of his participation in discussion. The second might need a record of the frequency or at least the occurrence of reproof from the cafeteria monitor for his boisterousness or pushing in line, and the third a check of the pupils in the class whom he has usually ignored. In addition to these measures of present status with respect to the behavior involved, there is also needed some prediction of progress. In the instances used, these predictions might be general, such as monopolizing discussion less, behaving correctly in the cafeteria, and being friendly with all classmates. In other instances, such as skills in throwing a basketball or spelling science terms correctly, there might be much more quantitative descriptions of desired progress. The significant step is that of defining for each pupil, if possible by that pupil himself perhaps in cooperation with the teacher, the kind of behavior desired. Some estimate is needed also of the difference between the new or modified behavior and the old. This definition and estimate provides a basis for later evaluation of progress.

Once the desired behavior or goal is defined and there is a reckoning of the difference sought, it becomes a relatively easy matter for the individual and perhaps his teacher or other helper to collect evidence as to progress. The collection of evidence is the step at which evaluation techniques, as usually conceived, come into play: tests, diaries, progress charts, observation records, and other techniques described later in this chapter. The means for collecting evidence depend, of course, upon the kind of behavior involved. If the behavior is a way of working, techniques of self-analysis and observation are most applicable. If it is a skill, tests of performance, written or otherwise as is appropriate, must be used. If it is reflective thinking, problem situations, hypothetical or real, may be needed. If it is an attitude, situations and written tests may determine change. The important step here is to define the kinds of situations in which the desired behavior will be revealed and to plan for checking on the presence or absence of the behavior in such situations. Thus, if progress in correct use of personal pronouns is sought, conversational situations and written materials can be assumed to be places wherein such use can be noted. The pupil can plan to keep a record of his errors as noted by himself and others and periodically check on their extent.

MAKING JUDGMENTS REGARDING PROGRESS

Probably some of the most effective judgment making, evaluation, is done wholly informally as the pupil, with or without his teacher, sees that he has behaved or not behaved in a specific instance in the way desired. For purposes of continued improvement, however, some more systematic type of judgment making is usually necessary. The traditional type is the monthly, six-weeks', semester, or annual examination. Although examinations do have contributions to make in the total scheme of evaluation, they are not adequate for all purposes. The nature of the progress desired necessarily determines the kind and time of systematic evaluation. If the goal is a long-term one, such as learning how to use library materials to secure information, there can be identified specific skills which can be set as short-term goals with plans made to evaluate progress within some reasonable, convenient period. Thus learning how to use the *Readers' Guide* might be a goal assumed by all members of the class and a definite time agreed upon for checking on progress. In the light of this check, individual members of the class might redefine their goals and set for themselves further periods for use of the *Guide* and evaluation thereof, while others might go on to other library tools.

Whatever the basis and time for systematic judgment making, the process is uniformly that of looking at the evidence of progress in relation to the original prediction as to the type of behavior desired and deciding whether the progress is satisfactory. Thus the pupil who characteristically uses the term "ain't" might aim to eliminate this usage from his vocabulary and agree with his teacher upon a scheme for keeping a record of the usage for a six-weeks' period. If at the end of that time, there is still evidence that he uses the word, he admits that his original aim has not been met completely in the six weeks and that he needs further checks. Similarly, the pupil who is dissatisfied because he is not sure what occupational choice he should make may plan with his counselor for a series of investigations over the first semester of his senior year in the expectation that he will hit on the right choice within this period. At the end of the semester when he returns for reporting to the counselor on his investigations, he reviews these and finds that he still is uncertain of his choice but that he has virtually eliminated three earlier possibilities. The judgment in such a case might be that good progress has been made because some possibilities have been eliminated.

PLANNING FOR FURTHER PROGRESS

Returning to the example of the pupil who wanted to quit using "ain't," his evaluation showing that he had reduced but not eliminated this usage would likely lead to a conclusion that he should continue his efforts. The pupil who was investigating vocational choices would also likely choose to continue his investigations of possible occupations. Similarly, most desired behavior requires periodic appraisal and judgment and planning for next steps. In group situations, one of the chief contributions of the teacher is to help boys and girls size up their progress and plan for next steps. In terms of the teacher's help to individual pupils, planning for further progress is really a highly individualized matter most effectively done through personal conference.

TECHNIQUES OF PUPIL SELF-EVALUATION

Regardless of the procedure used for collecting evaluative evidence, all effective evaluation becomes self-evaluation. That is, pupil progress is ultimately motivated by the pupil's own planning, and this planning has to be based on some type of evaluative evidence. This evidence may come directly through the pupil's own processes, or he may accept—and acceptance is itself an act of self-evaluation—the evidence from his teacher, the learning group, or others. In this section we are concerned with the methods the pupil may use for getting evaluative evidence about his own progress.

SELF-EVALUATION THROUGH COUNSELING

Indirect methods of teacher counseling can be of very great value to youth in thinking through their own problems, goals, and accomplishments. Teachers who make effective use of this aid to self-evaluation become adroit in conferencing with pupils to push the latter's thinking on such successive questions as, "What improvements are you trying to make in (the class)?" "Why are you trying to make these improvements? How are you going about it? Do you think you are making progress? Why?" Given good rapport between teacher and pupil, this kind of conferencing is probably as productive for the pupil as any amount of written evaluative exercises. But responses to such questions under pressure of marks and in the tension of a situation that promises to affect the pupil's status in the class are not likely to effect self-evaluation that is either honest or dynamic. Teachers who wish to help pupils in self-evaluation through counseling techniques may find it desirable to try this on an exploratory basis with pupils whose responses can be relied upon before undertaking systematic use of the technique.

SELF-EVALUATION THROUGH CHARTS AND CHECK LISTS

A variety of materials are used to help pupils in self-evaluation through checking themselves on some form provided by the teacher. For example, Table 9 illustrates a form used by pupils to check their progress in a unit of work in social studies. In this illustration, the form is first checked by the pupil with a grade assigned himself on the various items, and then a conference is held with the teacher to discuss the evaluation. Similar check lists, with or without the marking system, might be prepared for use by pupils in connection with units of work in any curriculum area.

Self-marking progress charts are also maintained by pupils in many classes. Progress graphs can be worked out in connection with any type of learning activities in which there are quantitative estimates of work accomplished or errors made as in shop jobs or spelling drill. The chief utility of these devices lies in their ready answer to the question, "How am I doing in (the class)?"

TABLE 9
INDIVIDUAL PUPIL EVALUATION

Name_____   Unit Topic_____

Period_____Date_____   _____

DIRECTIONS: Below is listed a chart of *your* individual progress while studying the above named unit topic. *You* are to evaluate *your own* progress, quite frankly and objectively, and then list a numerical grade in the column indicated for each week. In determining grades, take into consideration *your* own interest, ability, suggested ideas, cooperation, and attitudes. Upon completion of this form, your teacher will have an individual conference with you, and from time to time we will discuss your progress in the below-mentioned items as well as your total use of skills in reading, writing, spelling, listening, and understanding others.

EXPLANATION OF NUMERICAL MARKS: AVERAGE:

4—Superior effort and progress   A—4.0
3—Good effort and progress   B—3.0
2—Average effort and progress   C—2.0
1—Below average effort and progress   D—1.0
0—Unsatisfactory effort and progress

EVALUATION

Item	Weekly grade 1	2	3	Final grade	Comment
1. Offering suggestions and ideas for organizing and planning unit					
2. Understood and planned individual and committee work					
3. Found and used resource material					
4. Reading accurately with understanding					
5. Originality in thought and work					
6. Speaking effectively (not memorization)					
7. Used notes in preparation of talk					
8. Listened attentively to other talks					
9. Written work neat, used accurate bibliography					
10. Allowed ample time to prepare material					
11. Took notes during talks given by others					
12. Cooperation with others					

TEACHER'S COMMENTS: _____

                                      Student's signature

                                      _____

                                      Teacher's signature

The teacher may wish to keep on hand a supply of evaluation forms whereby each pupil can check his participation in discussion and planning activities. Such a form may be a simple list of questions like the following:

How Did I Do Today?

Yes No

Did I get said what I wanted to?
Did I talk more than I should have?
Did I talk less than I should have?
Were the ideas I presented worth presenting?
Did I help the class make progress?
Did I pay attention to others?
Did I help make this class worth while?

We have found that occasional use of such simple check lists may help class members considerably in their participation practices.

USE OF TESTS FOR SELF-EVALUATION

Tests made by the teacher and by pupils, as well as standardized tests, may be of substantial help in self-evaluation. For example, test exercises prepared by the teacher to help pupils check up on their reading comprehension, or their skill in using a book, or their ability to find materials in reference books or other library resources, may be very useful guides to pupils in determining areas of needed improvement. Similarly, standardized tests on any of these and other work skills may be self-administered and scored, and then study given to errors and their correction.

When test results can be disassociated from marks and pupils see the utility of tests as evidence of their need for improvement, self-correction of the teacher's tests can be a valuable experience. Teachers frequently arrange for pairs of pupils to check each other's papers and then go over the errors as a way of securing a measure of objectivity and of promoting sharing of information. Even where examinations are commonly used as a basis for giving marks, practice tests may be useful means of stimulating pupils' self-evaluation and subsequent learning.

Self-correction of papers of all kinds offers the same opportunity for the student to find his own difficulties. Of course, there has to be some guidance from the teacher or group as to how the paper is to be corrected. Once this is understood and the grade motive removed, pupils can advance their own self-understanding by reviewing critically their own work. As a matter of fact, this skill of reviewing one's own work is a very important one frequently neglected in the secondary school classroom.

Another type of test that helps in self-evaluation is the one which is primarily a list of questions that induce some self-analysis. Thus an examination covering a unit of work in local government in the civics or government class might consist of such questions as these:

What are the chief ideas about government in ——— that you have acquired as a result of this unit?

Explain how these ideas have helped or will help you.

What other questions do you have about government in ———?

How can you find out the answers to these questions?

Are you satisfied with your work in this unit? Why or why not?

USE OF RECORDS FOR SELF-EVALUATION

Any types of records kept by pupils may be helpful in their self-evaluation activities: diaries and logs, time schedules, plans and accomplishments, written statements of progress for parents, periodic summaries and evaluations. Each of these types is briefly described in a following paragraph.

Diaries and Logs. Many teachers encourage their pupils to maintain a notebook that is to be a diary or daily log of their activities in connection with the class concerned. Under each day the pupil writes a brief summary of what he did before, during, and after the class that related to the work under way in the class. Pupils may be asked to spend a few minutes at the end of each period filling in this information, and periodically, perhaps once a week, time is provided for a check of the diaries for the pupils to reach any conclusions as to the value of what they have done for the class. Pupils may be organized in pairs to check each other's diaries, and occasionally the teacher may check the diary of a pupil who seems to need help. Primarily, however, the record is the pupil's own as a basis for his self-determination of the nature and value of his activities.

Time Schedules. In classes involving a considerable amount of individual activity, either in or out of the class period, it may be helpful to pupils to keep a record of the use of time for the class. Thus, in classes in homemaking, agriculture, and industrial arts which emphasize projects in these fields, it may be important for pupils to keep records of the time devoted to various phases of projects under way. Comparison of time schedules with other pupils and checking with teachers may indicate good and poor uses of time. Similarly, pupils in music, art, typing, creative writing, and similar classes that involve considerable outside practice or original work may find it desirable to keep time schedules from day to day to discover times that are best for their work as well as those that are poor. Accurate records of total time usage throughout the day for a week or so may also help pupils find cases of imbalance in their time expenditure.

Plans and Accomplishments. In connection with units of work, teachers frequently give pupils guidance in maintaining records of plans and accomplishments according to some similar form. Thus pupils may be asked to organize notes or even to prepare summaries on a mimeographed sheet with headings on the following points:

Class Purposes	What I Achieved
My Own Plans	What I Should Do Next

The teacher may have this record turned in periodically as the unit progresses, for study and suggestions which he wishes to make. It is an especially good basis for pupil-teacher conferences in connection with the unit or work. Some suggestions one teacher made for using this type of material follow:

Weekly evaluation sheets have been used with core classes at different times and with different groups ranging from the ninth through the twelfth grade. Originally they were planned by the teacher to help pupils evaluate their successes and failures on a short time basis. As time went on a number of other values showed up through the use of the sheets.

They may be reviewed by pupils at card-marking time if it is a class in which pupils evaluate themselves. It is thus possible for a boy or girl to look back over the past weeks and recall incidents which otherwise might be forgotten. These items may then become part of his card-marking evaluation.[2]

Of course, the threat of marks may make for falsification or "dressing up" of records of this type, just as it does in other instances, and our only suggestion to meet this problem is a clear understanding between pupils and the teacher as to the bases on which marks are to be given. If the basis is one of progress and it is understood that progress will be marked in accordance with the teacher's and pupil's agreement as to the latter's plans, then it is to be expected that the pupil must show specific evidence of accomplishment. This is an entirely different basis from expectation of uniform achievement on tests or even of notebooks containing uniform answers to questions, outlines of readings, and notes on discussions.

Statements to Parents. A device that serves several purposes, includ-

[2] Evaluation Committee, Metropolitan Detroit Bureau of Cooperative School Studies, "Pupil Self-evaluation" (Detroit: The Bureau, no date), p. 2. Mimeographed.

ing that of pupil self-evaluation, is the written statement of the pupil to his parents telling them what he has been accomplishing in a particular class. An illustrative letter from a junior high school pupil reporting on his activities in connection with a unit of work, "The Resources of the United States," follows:

Dear Mother and Father:

We have been studying about "The resources of the United States" in the seventh grade. When we started to work, the teacher had us tell what resources we knew about. She put these on the blackboard, and we decided which ones to study more about. So far we have studied about climate, food crops, cotton, and oil. We will study some others later.

I was interested most in cotton, because I had never seen any growing. We saw a film about cotton which showed us how it grows, is picked, cleaned, baled, and made into cloth. We also read about how cotton is raised in the South, and about some of the inventions and products. Miss Cox brought us some samples of cotton cloth and other products. We are going to visit the cotton mill next week.

When we started this study, the teacher had us write down what we wanted to learn. I put down just two questions because I really didn't know much about resources. I put down: What are the resources of the United States? How is cotton grown? I know a lot more about these questions now, but I have a lot more questions to study up on now.

Miss Cox and I talked about some of my written work and decided I should do more writing for practice. So I have been writing reports on my reading and she goes over them. She says I am doing better, and I haven't misspelled a word this week. I didn't talk much in our planning sessions at first, but I have been working on a committee and now have more to say. I like this kind of work very much. I believe I am learning more this year than last.

I will write you more about our study when we finish it.

Your son,

Similarly, pupils may write statements to their parents about units completed, particular activities, a day's work, a month's work, a committee project, some special exercises, or other pieces of work that to summarize in this way will help. Teachers using this type of self-evaluative report usually suggest items to be covered in the statements, such as what the class is working on, what particular activities the pupil has been doing, and how he feels he has gotten along. Frequently, parents are invited to discuss the report with their children and make suggestions as to how the latter may make further improvement. Sometimes a form letter from the teacher covering the report and inviting some reaction, with space provided for this purpose, is helpful.

SELF-DRILL FOR SELF-EVALUATION

We should not neglect the self-evaluative possibilities of the typical drill procedures. Pupils frequently have reason to drill themselves on formulas, meanings, spellings, mathematical combinations, and other learnings which need to become somewhat automatic. As they do this, if the drill is carried on intelligently, there is an element of self-evaluation. Thus the boy or girl who is memorizing spellings may go over a list of words and note the number of words about which he isn't sure, look these up, go over the list again and continue noting errors or uncertainties until there are no errors or questions. Such drill repeated from time to time gives the pupil a basis for determining progress and need for further study.

REFLECTIVE THINKING AS SELF-EVALUATION

All of these approaches to self-evaluation have in them one or more steps at which reflection by the pupil is the critical point in sizing up his progress. It is this whole process of reflection which a problem-solving emphasis in methodology should stimulate. It is also at this step of critical evaluation that most pupils have difficulty. Particularly if the pupil has been accustomed, as many or most have, to someone else doing his evaluations for him, it is difficult for him to think through the evidence and reach a conclusion as to the worth of his activities. Without this step, no check list, report, or set of notes is of real value in self-evaluation. Hence teachers need to give a great deal of attention to the thought processes indicated by pupils' analysis of their own work. Counseling as described in the beginning of this section is probably the most certain way in which the teacher can help the individual pupil look critically at his own work. It may be helpful first for the teacher to go over with the entire group the steps in the evaluative process and probably to take one or two pupils' own self-evaluations as examples of how the pupil analyzes the data he has in order to come to a judgment of the worth of his work.

TECHNIQUES OF EVALUATION BY THE TEACHER

The techniques described in Chapter 11 for studying individual pupils are also techniques for studying their progress. Since we dealt rather fully with the use of interviews, observations, inventories, tests, and records in that chapter, we are here simply noting how successive uses of these devices may serve the purpose of evaluating pupil progress.

If teachers conduct interviews or conferences with pupils in the manner we described, successive interviews with the same pupil may be very helpful to the teacher in reaching a judgment about the pupil's progress. For example, if the initial interview with a pupil shows that he has some difficulties in the basic arithmetical processes needed for algebra, the algebra teacher might recommend a series of exercises in an arithmetic book and give some suggestions on how the pupil can acquire skill through these exercises. At the next interview, if the teacher has reviewed his analysis and recommendations for the pupil concerned, it will be a logical step to go over the pupil's work and check quickly on his present ability in these skills. As an example of a situation in which there can be a somewhat less objective evaluation, we may note the frequent one in which there is an evident lack of interest in the class. If this lack of interest is noted in the first interview and the teacher makes some suggestions about things the pupil might do that will be more interesting, successive interviews would get evidence regarding the outcomes of these activities and the pupil's apparent interest thereafter. The important principle in use of interviews for evaluating pupil progress is that of continuity in lines of investigation. Unless successive interviews are related to one another through planning and reviewing each one, the teacher has little basis on which to judge progress. Therefore the wise teacher makes some type of notes during or after each interview and in the subsequent interview brings conversation around to points noted for follow-up.

OBSERVATIONS

Teachers often use observations of pupils to reach judgments about their progress. Thus the physical education teacher watches pupils' development in physical skills, the typing teacher their typing skills, the history teacher their understanding of historical and other social relations, and all teachers watch pupil development in communication skills and in general interpersonal relations. Unfortunately, the large number of pupils taught under the departmentalized schedule and the tendency toward total class activity sometimes make it difficult if not impossible for the teacher to become sufficiently sensitive to the unique development of each pupil to be able to detect differences in successive observations. As a result, frequently it is only the pupil having difficulty of one sort or another who is called most easily to the teacher's attention and is therefore observed most carefully. To solve this problem, teachers whose classes are in areas in which observation can be most profitable, especially in laboratories and other situations in which there is considerable physical activity, may work out schemes of work that assure some successive, deliberate observation of each pupil. Where such observation is possible, the teacher notes pupils' needs, makes suggestions, and in later observation checks on whether the writing, sewing, cooking, jumping, or typing, and so forth is being performed more correctly.

The check list presented in Table 10 was prepared by a group of graduate students (mostly teachers in service) for their use in observ-

TABLE 10

EVIDENCES OF EFFECTIVE LEARNING
(A Guide for Teacher Observation and Evaluation of
Learning Processes)

	IS THIS EVIDENCE PRESENT IN THE CLASS?	
	Yes	*No*
I. EVIDENCES OF SUSTAINED SATISFACTION OF LEARNERS		
A. Various facial expressions, for example, frown, smile, raised eyebrows	....	....
B. Good participation (oral and otherwise) .	....	....
C. Personal expression of pupils to teacher .	....	....
D. Cooperation in doing services for the group	....	....
E. Promptness in attendance and work . .	....	....
F. Consistent use of good work habits . .	....	....
II. EVIDENCES OF PROBLEM DEFINING AND SOLVING		
A. Realistic questions from pupils . . .	....	....
B. Systematic collection of facts pertaining to a definite question or topic	....	....
C. Reflection on thought questions before answering	....	....
D. Reluctance to accept ready-made solutions	....	....
E. Systematic organization of materials to arrive at definite conclusions	....	....
F. Personal identification of own needs . .	....	....
G. Tendency to think ahead to the end result	....	....
H. Participation in school and community projects	....	....
I. Self-confidence in overcoming a particular problem	....	....
J. Apparent reliance on facts in solving problems	....	....

	IS THIS EVIDENCE PRESENT IN THE CLASS?	
	Yes	*No*

III. EVIDENCES OF ASSOCIATION OF PAST AND PRESENT
EXPERIENCES OF LEARNERS

A. Derivation of meanings of unfamiliar words used in context . . . .

B. Recognition of cues relating to behavior based on past experiences . . . .

C. Self-identification with personalities who are socially acceptable . . . .

D. Use of creative media to show clarification of thinking . . . .

E. Illustration of material read or discussed by own experiences . . . .

F. Modification of behavior in the classroom because of past experiences . . . .

IV. EVIDENCES OF THE CONTROL OF THE PROBLEM
SITUATION

A. Easy adjustment to a new situation . . ..

B. Proficient utilization of available resources ....

C. Increased independence in doing work successfully . . . .

D. Increased ease in communicating understandingly regarding the problem . . . .

E. Improved ability to give and receive constructive criticism . . . .

F. Continued use of good work habits . . ..

V. EVIDENCES OF PERFORMANCE

A. Correct performance in substitute situations ....

B. Overt, correct performance of skills . . ..

C. Application in real situations of behavior learned at school . . . .

ing and evaluating learning processes in the classroom. Although intended for teacher use in appraising the status of the class as a whole, it might be equally useful in observation of individual pupils by the teacher, in pupils' evaluation of the class, and in pupils' self-evaluation. The emphasis here is on real evidences of learning rather than on tests or products only. Repeated use of such a check list for observation of individual pupils would be particularly helpful in evaluating pupil progress.

PLATE 37. PUPILS' WORK INDICATES THEIR PROGRESS. Probably the most frequently used source for checking pupil progress is such completed pieces of work as these. (Courtesy of the Fayette County, Kentucky, Public Schools)

PUPILS' WORK

Probably the most frequently used source for checking pupil progress is the pupil's work. As pointed out in Chapter 11, the product of his learning processes is not always a reliable source of information about the pupil's needs, although it obviously is to be included among the important sources. Certainly, products in the shop and other laboratory situations, creative pieces of writing and other work, and similar results of pupil activity give significant evidence of the pupil's progress when compared from time to time. As we suggested earlier, it is good practice to keep samples of pupils' work for this purpose of comparison. Thus the English teacher's folder of papers written by each pupil, perhaps maintained by the pupils, is an excellent source for study by teacher and pupil to detect whether errors are being eliminated, ideas being expressed better, handwriting being improved, and the like.

Typical marking practices which involve evaluation only of present status in comparison with some standard of achievement make what we consider an unfortunate and inadequate use of pupils' work. That is, the teacher sometimes devotes considerable time and energy to finding errors in pupils' work and assigning marks thereon, but gives no attention to the meaning of these errors in terms of progress made since previous pieces of work were submitted nor to directions in which the pupil should make improvement. We believe that just a little more time and energy devoted to keeping samples of successive pieces of work, or making notes about them when their storage is impractical, and comparing these from time to time would be ever so much more rewarding in terms of the motivation to pupils' learning than A's, B's, C's, D's, or F's only. Also, when we consider the time spent in trying to compute these marks and their usual lack of reliability, however carefully computed, it seems probable that the same amount of time might be much more effectively spent in making the studies of progress and giving pupils specific suggestions on how improvement can be made. Furthermore, if marks must be given, a mark on progress can probably be computed as reliably as one on status; thus, the A given a paper would be interpreted to mean "excellent progress since your last paper."

INVENTORIES

As we noted in Chapter 11, an inventory is simply a pencil and paper device whereby teacher or pupils take stock of one or more items concerning the latter. Since progress evaluation involves taking stock at different times to see what progress has occurred, the inventory is particularly appropriate in evaluating pupil progress. Thus the teacher who takes inventory of his pupils' reading habits through such an inventory as illustrated in Chapter 11 (pp. 334–336) might administer this form a second time and compare the responses of individual pupils on the two inventories to see what changes occurred during the interval. Similarly, inventories might be repeated in connection with any of the uses listed as follows in Chapter 11:

Data regarding amount of time given to study, radio, television, work, social affairs, and other out-of-school activities
Interest in recreation, work, social activities, study, current events
Types of programs listened to on radio, viewed on television or at community activities
Experience in work activities at home and in the community
Knowledge relative to any subject or problem
Acquaintance with terms, people, places, products, and so forth
Behavior under various circumstances ("What do you do if" . . . ?)
Ways of using books and other sources of information.

TESTS

Testing and evaluating, we noted earlier, are not synonymous. In fact, we regard tests as a special form of inventory and their uses in evaluating pupil progress as the same as those just described for inventories. A test is a device for taking stock of pupils' abilities, difficulties, achievement, aptitudes, or other characteristics. As instruction is planned to improve pupils' stock of such characteristics, successive tests should give a sound basis for determining progress. The distinctive feature of tests for purposes of evaluating pupil progress is their ready adaptation to quantitative measures. That is, scores made by a pupil on successive, identical or similar tests readily permit comparison of scores to determine the individual's gain. Several specific uses of tests for evaluating pupil progress are described below.

Standardized Achievement Tests. Standardized achievement tests are available in practically all secondary school subjects[3] and have great usefulness for diagnosing group and individual needs as well as for evaluating individual progress. If the test is valid for the instruction concerned, that is, if its items relate to the material studied by the class, then comparison of test scores made by the same individual on successive uses of the test can be very helpful in determining progress. The standardized test has two particular advantages for this purpose. First, many tests are published in different forms of the same difficulty so that scores made on different forms are comparable, and yet one cannot assume that a correct response on the second test is due to the item having been remembered from the first form and memorized for the test. Second, the makers of standardized tests provide means of comparing scores with norms, age or grade or percentile rankings, so as to make the comparison of successive scores more meaningful.

Tests of Basic Learning Skills. The tests of basic learning skills which we described in Chapter 11 have particular utility in evaluating pupil progress. Since learning in many curriculum fields is dependent on such skills as securing information from books and other published sources, evaluating information in these sources, and using evidence in reaching conclusions—all skills which can be tested through pencil-and-paper exercises in most subjects—repeated tests of proficiency

---

[3] See Harry A. Greene, Albert N. Jorgensen, and J. Raymond Gerberich, *Measurement and Evaluation in the Secondary School* (New York: Longmans, Green & Co., Inc., 1954), for chapters which include materials on standardized tests, on each of the major secondary school curriculum areas as follows: language arts, Chapters 15 and 16; foreign languages, 17; social studies, 18; mathematics, 19; sciences, 20; fine arts, 21; industrial and practical arts, 22; business education, 23; and health and physical education, 24.

give evidence not only of progress which has been made but clues as to further progress to be expected in the subject through use of these skills. These tests may be procured in published form or prepared by the teacher. Probably some of the most effective testing for work skills is done through the teacher's preparation of exercises on the use of books and other sources of information that are being regularly used in the class. Thus a test may be prepared that requires correct use of the table of contents, index, glossary, and other special features of the textbook. This test may be so constructed that the items are keyed under each of the special features, and a record kept of pupils having difficulty in use of the index, for example. After some practice of these skills, another test of a similar nature may be administered and analyzed to determine if particular pupils continue to have the same difficulties. This type of test may be used to advantage in any class in which there is use made of printed materials.

Teacher-prepared Achievement Tests. A variety of teacher-prepared achievement tests may be used for several purposes in evaluating pupil progress. Pretests on a unit of work (Chapter 14) which is followed by use of the same test or a similar one give some measure of pupil progress in acquiring the information and understandings tested. Tests for this purpose may be either *essay* or *objective*. Thus, in introducing a unit on "The industrialization of the United States" in American history, the teacher might use an essay test including such questions as, "Why do we have labor unions in the United States?" "What effect has the expansion of industry had on population movement? School enrollment?" An objective test item covering one of these questions and to which only one answer would be correct might be of the multiple-response type as follows:

( ) The expansion of industry in the United States brought about a movement of the population from
   a. Rural to urban areas
   b. Urban to rural areas
   c. Suburban to downtown areas
   d. Inland to coastal areas

The objective test items are more easily scored and analyzed but usually do not reveal so well the pupils' real understanding or lack thereof regarding a topic.

Tests on successive units may be used to determine the position of individual pupils in relation to each other, and this information may reveal unusual progress or lack thereof. In objective testing, some measure of central tendency, usually the *median* or the middle score—

for example, the sixteenth score in a ranked distribution of thirty-one scores—is used for this purpose. In essay testing, the papers may be arranged in various groups according to quality, and a relative position assigned each, or marks may be given the papers. In either case the relative position may be compared from test to test.

Tests based on specific learning experiences such as field trips, films, discussions, and readings may be used to identify pupils who failed to get expected understandings from these experiences. Subsequent tests on similar experiences may then be used as a check to see whether progress is made by these pupils in successful learning. Problem-type tests ("What would you do if . . . ?") can be used repetitively to determine individual pupils' progress in problem-solving skills.

The usefulness of good teacher-prepared tests is so extensive that we believe it important for every teacher to have abilities in test construction. Among the procedures you may follow for developing these abilities are the following:

1. Examine critically the tests used in your own college courses. Do they test what they are supposed to? Do they discriminate between those who are doing well and doing poorly in the course? Can they be scored fairly easily?

2. Practice making tests in your student teaching and get the reactions of your critic teacher and college supervisor. Try to make all kinds of test items: essay, problem, objective including multiple-response, true-false, completion, matching.

3. Read some of the books on tests and measurements such as those cited in "For Further Study" at the end of this chapter, and especially study the publications on testing in your particular subject field that you will undoubtedly learn about in a special methods course.

4. Try making out a test on parts of this book, perhaps this chapter, and have your instructor criticize your test items. To illustrate how to do this, as well as several types of test items, we are listing below some sample items based on the introductory statements in this chapter under the heading "What Is Evaluation?":

Essay. What is the difference between testing and evaluation?
True-False. (The student is directed to check either the F (False) or T (True) column.)
    The use of A's, B's, C's, and so forth, is essential in good systems of evaluation.
Completion. (The student fills in all blanks.)
    Evaluation is the process of making a judgment as to the _____ of something.
Multiple-Response. (The student circles the letter of the correct response.)

An essential step in evaluation of pupil progress is
a. Placing marks in the cumulative record
b. Identifying the pupil's status with regard to the value concerned
c. Using objective tests at the beginning and end
d. Developing an objective standard of measurement

The reader is referred to some of the standard works in tests and measurements cited at the end of this chapter for further information regarding construction of the foregoing and other types of test items.

RECORDS

We described in some detail in Chapter 11 the teacher's use of three types of records for study of the needs of individual pupils: the pupil's own records, the teacher's records, and the school's records. Each of these types of records may also be very useful in the teacher's efforts to evaluate pupil progress. Just as the pupil evaluates his own progress through keeping the kind of records noted earlier in this chapter, the teacher may occasionally check these records to note both the progress made in record keeping and the progress revealed in other respects. The teacher's folder on each pupil, the collections of the pupils' work, or the record sheet showing periodic judgments regarding class participation, speaking and reporting skills, and similar items may be consulted frequently to determine how individual pupils are progressing. The cumulative record does not show progress under way in a particular class, of course, but is used to learn pupil needs in which progress can be determined by the teacher as he works with the pupil concerned.

TECHNIQUES OF EVALUATION BY GROUPS

The major uses of group evaluation are in connection with group planning as described in Chapter 8 rather than in the evaluation of individual pupils' progress. However, group evaluations may be used in at least two ways to help in evaluation of pupil progress: (1) for direct evaluation of the individual, and (2) for stimulation of the individual's own self-evaluation. These uses are described in this section.

GROUP EVALUATION OF INDIVIDUAL PROGRESS

In connection with small group or committee work, some teachers place responsibility on the small group for evaluating the contributions, achievement, or progress of each of its members. For example, as a part of its final written report, the committee may list the jobs each

PLATE 38. GROUP SUMMARIES AND REVIEWS OF INFORMATION ARE
BASES OF INDIVIDUAL SELF-EVALUATION. Such summaries may cause
individual pupils to evaluate their own understanding. (Courtesy
of the National Education Association)

member performed. Also, the work of individual committee members
may be rated on some basis such as "outstanding," "good," "poor," and
"unsatisfactory" by other members, although this is a harsh and usually
unsatisfactory procedure if these evaluations are related closely to
teachers' marks. Another technique is that of committee ratings of
individual progress through marks defined as "accomplished more than
we expected," "accomplished about what we expected," and "accomplished less than we expected." Small groups may also vote on members who have made the most contributions or progress; sometimes
this vote is done by an entire class at the conclusion of a unit of work.
In general, we have found the most satisfactory procedure to be that
of committee reports which include definite statements as to the contributions of each member, with the responsibility being that of the
teacher to weigh the pupils' contributions and to compare them with
previous ones to determine progress. We also think it good practice
for committee members to rate each other's oral reports to the class,
perhaps handing each other notes of comments.

STIMULATION OF PUPIL SELF-EVALUATION

In general, all types of group evaluation have possibilities for stimulating individual self-evaluation. Thus a discussion by the class on how well its members have worked together on a particular project is likely to cause some individual pupils to reflect on their own successes or failures in working with others. Reports by the class observer (Chapter 5) or total class discussion of why a particular session was good or poor may cause individuals to evaluate their own participation in the session. Review of what has been learned about a particular topic may stimulate individual pupils to ask themselves if they have really learned what is being said. Checking by teacher and pupils of such a list of evidences of effective learning as shown in Table 10 causes many of those checking to apply some, maybe all, points to themselves to see if they were showing these evidences. It is largely because of the incentive to self-evaluation given by group evaluation that we feel it highly desirable for some time to be given to discussion or other forms of group evaluation in every class frequently, perhaps every day. As pupils become concerned about how well the class is doing and how it can be better, we are satisfied that they will become personally involved and look at their individual roles in the total group.

INTERPRETING PUPIL PROGRESS

As we see their relation to evaluating pupil progress, marking systems constitute a somewhat classic example of "the tail wagging the dog." That is, a marking system is simply a device for recording and interpreting pupil progress, but the system has become so important in the motivation of school work that pupils and parents and perhaps even teachers lose sight of the really subordinate relation of marks to the progress they symbolize. We hope this chapter may make some contribution to readers' understanding of the true relation.

Despite this confusion in relations, it is very important to have a way of recording and reporting pupil progress. Whether the marks are in percentages, letters, or some other symbols seems less important than the significance given them. Unfortunately, the usual interpretation is one of relative achievement. That is, it is usually assumed that an A represents a very high achievement, higher than the majority of a class would likely attain. This interpretation ignores the progress idea, since a pupil who achieves considerably less than is to be expected of him may still have the highest test scores of anyone in the class, while another pupil who scores much lower may be outstripping the teacher's expectations. Since the public in general regards marks as symbols of relative achievement, we expect that teachers will need to continue to give marks of this type. However, we believe there are methods that may be successfully used to report pupil progress as well. Several of these are briefly described in this section.

MARKS DEFINED IN TERMS OF PROGRESS

In some secondary schools the letter marks are used as usual, except that on the report forms they are defined in terms of progress. Thus on these report forms such explanations of marks as the following appear:

A—Outstanding progress
B—Better than expected progress
C—Average progress; could do better
D—Less progress than expected
F—Little or no progress

Although such a marking system has possibilities if teachers and parents and pupils could perceive the usual marks of achievement as having new meanings, in general the marks are assigned and understood as though the explanations were in the more usual terms of achievement. Because of the general association of letter marks with relative achievement rather than individual progress, we suspect that some better and different type of symbols should be used when it is really progress that is being interpreted.

USE OF TWO MARKS

Many reporting systems use two types of marks: one for achievement and one for progress or effort. For example, the junior high report cards (a different one used for each subject) illustrated in Figure 16 are devised so that an X is placed in the column for the appropriate quarter to show any aspect of a subject (such as "related skills" in English) in which improvement is needed, and so that for each subject two marks are given. One of these is for "achievement" and is of the usual letter type. The other is for "effort" and is numerical as follows:

1. Superior
2. Satisfactory
3. Unsatisfactory

These numerical marks are also used for checking the identical "Personal and Social Growth" items on the back of each card (the cards for all subjects taken by the pupil are sent home in a pocket of the

Subject: English Teacher:						
Success in English depends upon growth in the following areas:	Quarters					
	1	2	3	4	Final Exam	Final Grade
1. Reading						
2. Writing						
3. Speaking						
4. Listening						
5. Related skills						
ACHIEVEMENT						
EFFORT						
Name Homeroom						

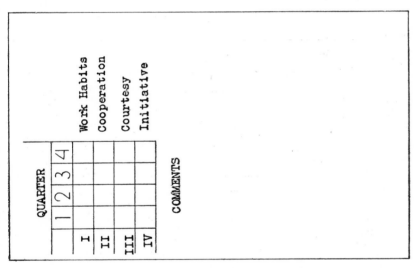

Fig. 16. SAMPLE REPORT CARD USING DIFFERENT MARKS FOR ACHIEVEMENT AND EFFORT. (Courtesy of the Fayetteville-Manlius Central School, Fayetteville, New York)

report folder) and on the folder (by both the homeroom teacher and pupil).

Other systems use similar arrangements, including the symbols O (outstanding), S (satisfactory), and U (unsatisfactory) for progress. These two-mark systems have the advantage of meeting the expectation of marks for achievement and at the same time providing some indication of pupil progress as distinct from achievement. Unfortunately, the values of such systems are sometimes lost on pupils and parents who pay attention only to the achievement mark.

CHECK LISTS OF PROGRESS

Usually in addition to marks of achievement, many reporting systems include some type of check list marked by the teacher to show progress in specific learning goals. Such a check list is illustrated in Table 11. It may be prepared by each subject department, even by individual teachers, or for optional use by various departments and teachers (as in the illustration), or for uniform use of the same check list by all teachers. Its usefulness is in showing to parents and pupils the teacher's evaluation of progress and needs in specific terms, and thus in helping the learner make further progress.

TABLE 11

SAMPLE CHECK LIST OF PUPIL PROGRESS

Name_____   Course_____
Grade and Year_____   Teacher_____
Days Absent_____   No. of Times Tardy_____

Teachers have checked only the items considered relevant at the time of reporting for which they had adequate data	*A check mark in this column indicates satisfactory growth and achievement*	*A check mark in this column indicates exceptional growth and achievement*	*A check mark in this column indicates need for greater growth and achievement*
LANGUAGE ARTS			
Reading skills . .	....	....	....
Reading interests .	....	....	....
Participation in discussions .	....	....	....
Written expression .	....	....	....
Spelling	....	....	....
STUDY AND WORK HABITS			
Efficient use of materials . . .	....	....	....
Efficient use of time .	....	....	....
Standards of achievement . . .	....	....	....
Conscientiousness .	....	....	....
Industry	....	....	....
Promptness . . .	....	....	....
Neatness	....	....	....

Teachers have checked only the items considered relevant at the time of reporting for which they had adequate data	*A check mark in this column indicates satisfactory growth and achievement*	*A check mark in this column indicates exceptional growth and achievement*	*A check mark in this column indicates need for greater growth and achievement*
UNDERSTANDING AND MASTERY OF THE SUBJECT MATTER . .	....	....	....
PERSONAL-SOCIAL DEVELOPMENT			
School citizenship .	....	....	....
Social sensitivity . .	....	....	....
Courtesy	....	....	....
Tolerance . . .	....	....	....
Leadership . . .	....	....	....
Self-direction . .	....	....	....
Creativeness . . .	....	....	....
Reliability . . .	....	....	....
Cooperation . . .	....	....	....

Source: Herbert L. Coon (chairman) and others, "Reporting to Parents in the Ohio State University School" (Columbus: Ohio State University School, 1953), p. 32. Mimeographed.

LETTERS TO PARENTS

In some schools teachers are encouraged to write occasional letters to parents reporting on their children's progress. In others, letter-type reports are issued periodically, perhaps twice a year. Because of the time-consuming nature of letter reports, they are infrequently used in secondary schools, although most report cards provide space for teachers' comments and many individual teachers do use these spaces or write letters to parents as the occasion demands.

PARENT-TEACHER CONFERENCES

Conferences are becoming common methods of reporting pupil progress to parents of elementary school children, and some use is being made of them in secondary schools, most frequently in connection with pupils who are having considerable difficulty. In an increasing number of schools conferences between the homeroom teacher, and sometimes all teachers, and parents of entering children are expected. The advantages of the conference for learning about the individual pupil cited in Chapter 11 apply in evaluating pupil progress. The following report of a parent-teacher conference on pupil progress is illustrative of the kinds of matters that may be discussed in these conferences and also of the written summary for later reference:

OHIO STATE UNIVERSITY—UNIVERSITY SCHOOL

CONFERENCE WITH PARENTS

Date_____ April 6, 1953 _____.   Child's Name___ William Reach ___

Present: Mrs. Reach, Mr. Schmidt

Reason for Conference: To discuss Bill's academic progress

Points Discussed:
1. Bill has shown some improvement in his work, especially in spelling and the general neatness of his English compositions.
2. He is somewhat delinquent in all his classes as far as meeting deadlines is concerned. He lacks enthusiasm and interest.
3. Bill has better than average ability but does not make the best use of this ability.
4. Bill wants to enter engineering college upon graduation from high school.

Agreements or Recommendations:
1. The counselor will hold a conference with Bill to discuss his progress.
2. He will need to be impressed with the necessity of budgeting time and meeting deadlines.
3. He will need to recognize the importance of changing his work habits if he hopes to succeed in college.
4. Perhaps Bill should be persuaded to give increased consideration to his second vocational choice—business—since engineering may be beyond his ability.
5. Bill may have to drop some of his out-of-class activities.
6. Though Bill should develop self-direction and self-discipline, he will, occasionally, need to be pushed toward and frequently reminded of the goals he is seeking.

Frank Schmidt [4]
Signature

SUMMARY: USING EVALUATION TO
HELP LEARNERS

In this chapter we have treated evaluation as a way to help, rather than to force, the individual's learning activities. Evaluation of pupil progress has been described as a process of making judgments about

---

[4] The University School, *op. cit.*, p. 34. Names used in this quotation had been changed by the editors of the report.

the progress of pupils. This process, to be of value, must result in the individual's own determination of the value of his activities and therefore of his further needs in learning situations. Thus, the teacher's primary responsibility is that of aiding pupils to develop effective means of self-evaluation. Although evaluation by the teacher and others is also necessary, we have treated all types of external evaluation as means to the ultimate end of pupils' self-understanding and self-motivation. We have recognized, of course, that teacher evaluation of pupil progress is essential to the teacher's successful, direct help to individual pupils.

FOR FURTHER STUDY

Buros, Oscar Krisen, ed., *Mental Measurements Yearbook.* Highland Park, N.J.: Gryphon Press, various dates.
Comprehensive catalogue of published tests of all types.
Burton, William H., *The Guidance of Learning Activities.* 2nd ed.; New York: Appleton-Century-Crofts, Inc., 1952.
See for many helpful suggestions Chapter 19, "The Measurement and Evaluation of Learning Outcomes"; Chapter 20, "The Diagnosis of Learning Difficulties"; and Chapter 21, "Marking and Reporting Progress."
Coon, Herbert L. (chairman) and others, "Reporting Student Progress, Grades Seven through Twelve." Columbus: The Ohio State University School, 1953. Mimeographed.
Compilation of various types of reports to parents used in the Ohio State University School.
Greene, Harry A., Albert N. Jorgensen, and J. Raymond Gerberich, *Measurement and Evaluation in the Secondary School.* New York: Longmans, Green & Co., Inc., 1954.
Chapters 15–25 deal with measurement and evaluation in the various subject fields usually included in the secondary school curriculum.
Harris, Fred E., *Three Persistent Educational Problems: Grading, Promoting, and Reporting to Parents.* Bulletin of the Bureau of School Service, College of Education, University of Kentucky, Vol. 26, No. 1 (September), 1953.
Considers issues, practices, and new developments regarding these problems.
Jennings, Helen Hall, *Sociometry in Group Relations.* Washington, D.C.: American Council on Education, 1948.
Presents adaptations of sociometric devices for diagnosing interpersonal relations in school groups as used in the Intergroup Education Project.
Jersild, Arthur T., *In Search of Self.* New York: Bureau of Publications, Teachers College, Columbia University, 1952.
See Chapters 19–21 on self-evaluation.

Jordan, Arthur M., *Measurement in Education*. New York: McGraw-Hill Book Co., Inc., 1953.

Chapters 5–13 deal with measurement in the various subject fields at both elementary and secondary levels, as appropriate. A chapter (19) on statistical methods is included.

Kurtz, John J., and Esther J. Swenson, "Student, Parent, and Teacher Attitudes toward Student Achievement," *School Review*, 59:273–279 (May), 1951.

Shows interrelation between attitudes toward school, achievement, and education, and actual achievement.

Remmers, H. H., and N. L. Gage, *Educational Measurement and Evaluation*. Rev. ed.; New York: Harper & Brothers, 1955.

This standard text in educational measurement deals with measures of achievement, abilities, adjustment, attitudes, environment and background, and physical characteristics.

Simpson, Ray H., *Improving Teaching-Learning Processes*. New York: Longmans, Green & Co., Inc., 1953.

See Chapter 7, "Basic Considerations Related to Developing Evaluative Abilities," and Chapter 8, "Developing Self-evaluation."

Sims, Verner M., "Evaluating Progress toward the Satisfaction of Needs," in *Adapting the Secondary School Program to the Needs of Youth*. Fifty-second Yearbook of the National Society for the Study of Education; Chicago: The University of Chicago Press, 1953, Part I, Chap. 14.

This careful analysis of the evaluation job of the classroom teacher cites and interprets various significant studies related to the problem.

Smith, Eugene R., and Ralph W. Tyler, *Appraising and Recording Student Progress*. New York: Harper & Brothers, 1942.

One of the reports of the Eight-Year Study of the Progressive Education Association, and a significant departure in the literature on evaluation at that time. Part I deals with the development and use of evaluation instruments, and Part II with records for guidance and transfer of students.

Thorndike, Robert L., and Elizabeth P. Hagen, *Measurement and Evaluation in Psychology and Education*. New York: John Wiley & Sons, Inc., 1955.

Includes chapters on intelligence and achievement tests, testing programs, teacher-made tests, and marks and reporting.

Wrinkle, William L., *Improving Marking and Reporting Practices in Elementary and Secondary Schools*. New York: Rinehart & Company, Inc., 1947.

Describes and illustrates various systems of marking and reporting.

Part V The Teacher's Role in Planning and Improving Instruction

The ways of working with secondary school pupils we have described thus far do not just happen in the classroom situation. For most if not all teachers, and certainly for all beginning teachers, dynamic classroom procedures are based on careful planning by the teacher. Experienced teachers change from ineffective to effective procedures only as they deliberately plan to change. Good planning is an essential aspect of a dynamic methodology.

In this final part of our book we turn to systematic analysis and description of the processes of planning and improving teaching. Improvement involves evaluating one's ways of working, and searching for and trying out different ways. Since these improvement processes necessitate planning at each stage, planning and improvement are almost inextricably related phases of teaching. Chapter 14 deals with the teacher's planning of his total instructional program, Chapter 15 with the detailed steps in the planning he takes from day to day, and Chapter 16 with means of improving instruction.

The pressures high school teachers experience as they work with different learning groups in each class period sometimes result in lack of attention to proper planning. Successful pupil-teacher planning must be based on careful teacher preparation. Inadequate plans create insecurity and further pressures. Hence we believe that no part of teaching method is more critical to the teacher's happiness and effectiveness than that of his own planning and improvement efforts, both long term and day to day. Time, care, and skill here may make the difference between success and failure in teaching.

14. Planning the Organization
of Instruction

WE HAVE NOTED the need for teacher planning in connection with many problems of teaching method already considered in this book. Effective guidance of learning activities in general requires a considerable amount of advance planning on the teacher's part. In this chapter consideration is given to the teacher's tasks in planning the instructional program as a whole for each class he teaches. We are concerned here with the major problems of planning: setting purposes, delimiting the general framework of instruction of a class for a year (or semester), and planning large divisions of instruction (units of work). Before dealing with these problems specifically, we need to relate the teacher's planning process to the total curriculum plan and to analyze the process itself.

PLANNING IN RELATION TO THE
CURRICULUM ORGANIZATION

The nature of the teacher's planning depends somewhat on the philosophy and practice of curriculum organization in the school as a whole. In secondary schools one finds just two distinct patterns of organization in practice. Typically and almost universally, classes are organized around *subjects,* each taught for one period (usually in a six-period school day) per day. In many schools, especially junior high schools, various modifications of the subject organization have been introduced for a part of the school day. These various modifications we are grouping under the heading "The Core Organization."

THE SUBJECT ORGANIZATION

The predominant pattern of the curriculum of secondary schools is that of subject organization. Characteristically, the secondary school's curriculum consists of various subjects, further divided into courses, and "extracurricular" activities. Although these activities frequently follow a rather flexible pattern according to pupils' interests, the subjects are typically considered as "the curriculum" and the activities as "extracurricular." And even if subjects and activities are on a co-curricular basis, the teacher's instructional duties, with which we are here concerned, are usually assigned in terms of subjects. Teachers "teach" classes and "sponsor" activities!

In these classes organized around subjects, one finds quite varying degrees of flexibility in organization. Thus one teacher plans for his class in biology on the assumption that there are certain fixed divisions of this subject, such as life processes, that must serve as the bases of instructional organization, whereas another plans with his pupils to organize instruction around almost any problem having to do with living things. However, there is always some reference even in the latter teacher's planning to the question, "What can be included in biology?" That is, the notions as to accepted content of the subject concerned influence the teacher's planning. This is of considerable importance, for without such notions there is greater freedom but less direction of planning.

THE CORE ORGANIZATION

Although the term "core curriculum" is used to describe many quite different patterns of curriculum organization, we see most of these as clearly distinct from the subject pattern. In general, core curriculum may be considered as one plan for organizing and scheduling instruction in a major portion of the program of general education, that is, the program to provide for the common needs of all pupils in the school. Usually, the core is scheduled for a longer period than the individual subject class, and is organized around some of the common personal and social problems of members of the core classes.

One finds almost as wide a range of practice in organizing instruction in core classes as in the usual subject fields. The core frequently is scheduled in lieu of certain subjects, especially social studies and language arts, and in such cases may be little more than a double period in which the subjects are taught separately as usual. In some instances at the other extreme the core has no assumed content and merely provides an opportunity for teacher and pupils to pursue whatever problems they feel appropriate and desirable. Probably in most instances there are some assumptions as to the content of the core organization, but fewer assumptions than with regard to any subject. Therefore in planning core, units of work may usually be organized which cut across subject lines and include materials related to problems of living instead of divisions of a subject. That is, the teacher in a core curriculum organization usually, but not necessarily, has greater freedom in planning the instructional pattern than does the teacher in a subject organization.

OTHER TYPES OF CURRICULUM ORGANIZATION

The organization of the curriculum in broad fields is becoming increasingly common in secondary schools. Thus social studies rather than the separate subjects of history, geography, and civics is the pattern widely used in junior high schools and to a lesser extent in senior high schools. Similarly, general science fuses materials from several science subjects, and language arts from communication fields. However, the broad field is still a subject type of organization and there is assumed some broad framework of content to be considered in planning instruction. In general, there is greater flexibility in the choice of subject matter in the broad fields than in the traditional subject organization.

Some secondary schools have experimented with organizing the curriculum in relation to social functions of living and other analyses of life activities. In general, these experiments have not changed the basic curriculum framework, but have simply guided the teacher in a core or subject organization in selecting subject matter and experiences that relate to these social functions, such as consumption of goods and services, protecting life and health, or getting a living. Thus, where such plans exist, the teacher's planning is given some direction other than the logic of subjects as to criteria for selecting subject matter.

Similarly, the interests, needs, and problems of learners may be a basis for organizing instruction. In secondary schools this plan of organization is most usually used, as already noted, in relation to the activity program, that is, the "extracurricular" activities as separate from the program of studies. Also, these bases operate in setting up new courses for particular groups of adolescents having common needs and interests, such as personal typing, auto mechanics, and cosmetology. And, of course, good planning in the core and subject organization is based on consideration of the interests, needs, and problems of pupils concerned. In general, however, the framework of the curriculum of secondary schools is organized around subjects, social problems, life activities, or other centers determined by adults rather than around the immediate, felt interests and needs of pupils.

THE PLANNING PROCESS

In order to clarify the various steps in planning, we are drawing an analogy between the teaching-learning process and an automobile trip. This analogy is not too farfetched, because a comprehensive, good organization of learning experiences is a trip through partially unknown territory to some predetermined destination (the learning goal).

SETTING DESTINATIONS

Many kinds of automobile trips are made—those for business, for pleasure, for combined pleasure and business purposes, for emergencies, and so forth. Similarly, there are varying purposes of learning experiences in the classrooms of secondary schools. In some the goals are partially set by state law as, for example, the common requirement of a year's instruction in American history. Learning destinations are also influenced by local requirements of the board of education. For example, a unit of work on local government may be specified as a part of the civics or American history course, or a unit on narcotics in the general science course. In neither case, however, are the specific goals, learning experiences, and general nature, pleasurable or otherwise, of the unit specified.

School faculties and departmental groups usually exert more influence on the setting of specific learning destinations than state and local regulations. Agreement as to achievement standards in skill subjects, units of work to be included in particular courses, number and kind of projects in homemaking, agriculture, and other prevocational courses may set definite destinations for learning groups. In most cases, it is probably true that learning goals can be largely determined by the teacher, usually in cooperation with learners. Just as the family planning a vacation trip may have to choose a destination within various limitations, such as time and funds, the learning group must usually set purposes within some general framework of limitations.

Since learning groups in secondary schools are usually organized by subjects, the relation of possible goals to the nature of the subject included sets one limit. Thus the development of muscular coordination may be an appropriate purpose for the class in physical education but not for that in Latin. Other limitations are set by any general

PLATE 39. SCHOOL PLANNING GROUPS DETERMINE THE INSTRUCTIONAL FRAMEWORK. Such planning sessions as this by a group of mathematics teachers are essential in a good school program. (Courtesy of the Waco, Texas, Public Schools)

framework of goals that may have been stated by the faculty or its curriculum planning committees; by any official course of study or teacher's guide; by the range of experiences possible in terms of materials, trips, and people; and, perhaps most important, by the teacher's imagination and ingenuity. The factors which control the family's choice are influenced by such basic matters as the vacations taken by their friends, their experiences on previous vacations, their ideas of pleasure and rest, and their general socioeconomic status. There are also such basic factors in setting learning purposes as community and general social ideals, professional standards and expectations, previous experiences of the teacher and learners, public opinion, and the activities of pressure groups.

Knowing fixed destinations, even the traveling man with his directed itinerary may consider other destinations. Certainly the teacher will give major study to all the possible learning goals for his class, whether he is setting them for a year, a month, or a single period. In so doing, he needs to consider all the factors which enter into the setting of alternatives: the possibilities of the curriculum area involved, the social and professional expectations already mentioned, the interests of pupils and himself, and the practical factors of time and resources. Choices must be made: important destinations which pupils cannot reach must be eliminated, as must be goals which are considered as outside the functions of the school. Desirable objectives toward which the teacher feels incompetent to give guidance, or for which resources are lacking, must be deferred. Thus setting destinations for the learning group, as for the travelers, is a matter of lining up all the possible goals and then eliminating those which are impractical.

CHOOSING ROUTES

Once the traveler has chosen his destination, or accepted one assigned by his employer, the route of travel must be selected. Similarly, when one or more purposes of learning experiences has been chosen, the nature of these experiences needs to be planned. This process of planning may be best illustrated at this point by comparison of the family's choice of a vacation route and the learning group's choice of a unit of work.

First, we should note that a *unit of work* is a major division of instruction, built around some single idea, theme, problem, or purpose and including such subject matter and activities as are related and important to learners in developing the idea, theme, problem, or purpose. As we noted earlier in this chapter, any systematic organization of instruction must be organized around some type of center; these centers are the ideas, themes, problems, or purposes that give unity. In the core organization these centers may be pupil needs and interests, social functions of living, or aspects of the subjects included. Units of work in social studies may be organized around social problems, movements, or historical periods; in English, around problems of communication, types of literature, historical periods, social problems; in science, around environmental problems, scientific forces, generalizations; in mathematics, around mathematical processes, problems of living; in homemaking, around problems of home living, processes of cooking and sewing, aspects of housekeeping; and so forth. That is, within each curriculum area there are alternative bases of organizing instruction, and the teacher must decide which basis or combination of bases to use; but always there is some organization even if it is as inadequate as chapters in the textbook or daily lessons.

In planning possible units of work, the teacher uses somewhat the same procedure as the family that goes about choosing its vacation route wisely. The family, through the father or some other designated member, gets together all the information available about possible routes. Thus, if a family living in Chicago wishes to spend a week in Florida and can be away a total of two weeks, they will secure various road maps and planned routes from gasoline companies, automobile associations, and other agencies that provide these services. Friends who have taken the trip will be asked how they traveled and the advantages and disadvantages of different routes. Then the family will sit down together and talk over the various possibilities, and decide whether to take a scenic drive down the Gulf Coast route, a shorter route through the mid-South and central Florida, or to pick up some mountain scenery through east Tennessee and on down the east coast of Florida.

Similarly, the American history teacher desiring to develop a unit of work on the meaning of American democracy may wish to accumulate alternative road maps for the unit. The nearest parallel to the vacationers' road map would be a *resource unit* on democracy, for a resource unit is a compilation of suggested learning experiences and resources from which teachers may make choices for particular units of work. The teacher might consult several such resource units: those prepared by local committees of teachers, those available from other school systems, and perhaps some available in published form. Perhaps no such helps are available, and he will have to compile possible learning routes by examining suggestions in the textbook, teachers' guide, *unit plans* (outlines of units of work for particular learning groups) of previous years, unit plans of other teachers, collections of pamphlets on democracy, articles in professional journals describing other teachers' experiences with such a unit, and similar sources. He may find that the many possible routes include a study of the development and interpretation of the United States Constitution, a systematic study of the definitions of democracy available in our American literature, a chronological review of great movements in American history aimed to improve democratic processes, some comparisons of democratic practices in the school and in the community, and so forth. At this point it is probably time for him to do as the head of the vacationing family, and talk over with his pupils the various possible routes. It is important to note, however, that he has the alternatives clearly in mind and a great deal of information about each before he invites pupils to share in the decision. Again, we emphasize that effective pupil-teacher planning must be based on careful teacher planning. In cooperative planning processes, the pupils may be invited to secure information about possible routes, too, but they are guided in getting the information. The family head would not ask his children to decide what route to take to Florida without giving them information about possible routes, nor would he direct them to find out what routes are possible unless they had sufficient background in United States geography, map reading, and related areas and skills to know where to go to get the information. At the same time, he would have them consult neighbors and friends who had taken the same route, read travel folders, and secure other information by means they knew how to employ.

To summarize, the process of choosing routes toward a given learning destination involves two steps: (1) the determination by the teacher, usually in advance of discussion with the learning group, of possible routes through study of resource units and/or other materials indicated; and (2) the selection by pupils and teacher of a particular route or unit of work. We should note that cooperative selection of a unit of work involves the teacher's own planning of how to guide the discussion-planning process as well as of possible routes.

CHANGES EN ROUTE

Once the family has selected its route to Florida, one road map or series of maps will guide the way; and once the teacher and learners have selected their route, one *unit plan,* which we shall illustrate more fully later, will serve as the teacher's road map. The unit plan may be a marked-up resource unit or unit plan of another year or teacher or better, be the teacher's own outline prepared in the light of his examination of alternative plans and of his cooperative planning with learners.

Whatever the road map of the family or the unit plan of the teacher, changes should and usually do occur on the way. The family finds that they want to make a side trip which was not anticipated, or that there is a detour, or that their time is going faster or slower than expected. And the teacher finds that some learning experience in the unit plan seems less interesting as the time comes for its beginning, or that some unexpected learning difficulties demand a side trip to learn to use reference books, or that some experiences in studying the Constitution suggest to learners the desirability of having interviews with lawyers which take time not anticipated in the plan. Wise travelers and wise teachers allow plenty of flexibility in their plans to take care of unexpected developments.

For instance, the teacher of our example may have chosen with the class in American history to undertake a unit of work on the meaning of democracy built around the first ten Amendments to the United

States Constitution. After studying the background of these Amendments, the class might take them up one by one to understand their meaning for American citizens. The teacher might find that this study became simply a matter of memorizing the Amendments themselves and that the pupils really did not understand or want to understand their real significance. Accordingly, he decides to abandon the Amendment-by-Amendment approach and instead guides the pupils to reading and discussing some of the great cases tried before the Supreme Court relating to these Amendments. Particular interest is revealed in the Fifth Amendment because of current investigations by congressional committees. The unit of work shifts to a study of the Fifth Amendment and its use by persons testifying in regard to alleged subversive activities. Interest again shifts, this time to subversive activities, and the teacher plans another revision of the unit of work to get at the relation of subversive activities to democracy and the comparison of basic principles of democratic and undemocratic societies. This planning is still concerned with the original unit problem, but the route shifts. Before the study is completed, the teacher brings the pupils back to the ten Amendments, because the analysis of democratic government versus undemocratic government reveals that these ten Amendments are rights our citizens enjoy because of our democratic government. Thus the original destination is not changed any more than the family's, but the route may be modified considerably. Actually, the destination might be changed in both cases if circumstances arise which make it desirable: the family might decide that its vacation could be better spent on the Gulf Coast of Mississippi than in Florida, and the teacher might decide to shift the unit to the meaning of communism. In either case, however, the underlying purpose (vacation, appreciation of democracy) is served, though another trip may be necessary to get at the original vacation or unit plan.

Throughout the trip the family is evaluating their route: whether they are seeing what they had hoped for, whether it is taking too long or too little, whether every member is getting something for the ride. The father and mother are likely to spend some time each evening with the road maps, and throughout the unit of work the teacher and learners are evaluating whether their study is interesting and profitable. The teacher, like the parents, must spend time each day sizing up the situation. "Are we approaching the basic purposes? Is our timing good? Is every learner being sufficiently involved? What changes must be made in the unit plan?" Thus, teacher planning is continuous. Starting with an over-all purpose, the destination, the teacher begins a plan, completes it with learners, guides their learning experiences, and daily reviews and modifies the plan in the light of new needs and problems which are observed. And when the destination is finally reached by the family, a backward look may be taken to decide whether this was the best route and whether it should be followed again; similarly, the teacher looks backward to decide where important steps were missed and whether the experience as a whole was sufficiently satisfactory to indicate that some related unit might be tried with another learning group another time. This type of evaluation, although really just commonplace looking backward, is an essential phase of good teacher planning.

MAKING RECORDS FOR FUTURE PLANNING

The family that goes at its vacation planning systematically will keep some kind of record of its trip—perhaps an expense account, a marked-up road map, some souvenir folders, even a diary or log. The teacher who sees planning as an essential phase of his job will also keep records that will make future related units of work easier and more successful. Thus he may mark up his original unit plan, if written, to show changes from time to time. He may keep records of materials used, tests given, interviews and trips, and pupils' achievement, and he may collect samples of pupils' work, newspaper and magazine clippings, and unusual pamphlets and other materials. All these materials become his *unit record*, the log of the unit of work.

Particularly important in the family log would be the opinions of family members about the trip. These might not be written out, because the family would store these opinions in their memory to consider next year when they again begin vacation planning. But for the teacher, the learners of this year will not be on hand, and these evaluative items need to be written into the record. Hence the unit record usually contains some notes by the teacher regarding learners' reactions and progress and perhaps evaluative papers or check lists, or a summary thereof, prepared by them. This is important evidence to consider when the teacher again takes up planning for the unit of work on democracy or even planning of alternative units, for perhaps the evidence will indicate that this was not a good unit of work, at least as developed.

WHO PLANS?

The foregoing analysis of planning, with the analogy of travel and teaching, shows that all members of the learning group, as of the family, have opportunity to participate in planning. It also shows that leadership is necessary, that of the parents in family planning and that of the teacher in instructional planning. Someone must guide the inexperienced and immature members of the family and of the learning group to information about alternatives as a basis for cooperative decision. There may be situations in which the destinations are so fixed and the routes so clearly marked and without good alternatives that the father has to explain to the family there are no choices. There are probably some situations in teaching where pupil choices cannot be made; for example, our social expectations leave no choice as to the study of the meaning of democracy, even of the United States Constitution, and teachers must explain this to pupils. Thus the teacher may involve pupils in many phases of planning, but his is the responsibility for leadership. Specifically, we believe that the responsibilities of the teacher in planning instruction include provision for the following steps, which require the cooperation of others to make the teacher's task more successful:

1. Setting major purposes
2. Planning the over-all organization of instruction
3. Planning units of work
4. Planning from day to day, class to class
5. Securing resources for the learning group
6. Developing records to help future planning

These steps have already been defined and illustrated by analogy in this section. In the remainder of this chapter and in Chapter 15 each step is considered more systematically through explanation of techniques and materials to be used by teachers in secondary schools.

SETTING MAJOR PURPOSES OF INSTRUCTION

The task of establishing educational purposes is one of the essential steps in curriculum planning—a step so complex and important as to justify treatment beyond the scope of this book.[1] The logical order of curriculum planning is illustrated in the accompanying table. As it indicates, major curriculum goals are properly set by the cooperative planning of all groups involved in school operation. Actually, the first five steps in curriculum planning are logically taken by groups

---

[1] See for an extended treatment of this step a publication in which one of us collaborated, J. Galen Saylor and William M. Alexander, *Curriculum Planning* (New York: Rinehart & Company, Inc., 1954), Chapter 7.

of professional and lay persons before the classroom teacher individually sets up plans for instruction of specific learning groups. In practice, teachers find that goals and over-all plans are not always so established, for in many instances the only prior plans of which one can find record are those adopted from textbooks and perhaps departmental syllabi or examinations. Regardless of the extent of prior curriculum planning, the teacher must answer for each learning group, "Where must we go? Where else might we go? What is the total list of destinations to strive to reach?" In the following paragraphs, suggestions are offered as to how the classroom teacher may go about answering these questions and developing his own statement of purposes for each class he is to teach.

TABLE 12

THE LOGICAL ORDER OF STEPS IN CURRICULUM PLANNING

WHO	DOES	WHAT? (*for example*)
I. DETERMINES CURRICULUM GOALS		
A planning group representing citizens, boards of education, professional personnel, parents, and pupils	decides on major goals to be sought by the schools:	Understanding of the responsibilities of American citizenship.
II. OUTLINES CURRICULUM DESIGN		
The system planning group	develops the broad framework of the curriculum:	To use subject type of design and to include certain required subjects in social studies.
III. DEFINES THE SCOPE OF THE CURRICULUM		
The system planning group	indicates major areas and problems of living around which instructional units may ultimately be organized in relation to I and II:	The problem of participation in voting and other civic processes.
IV. DEFINES THE SEQUENCE OF THE CURRICULUM		
The system planning group	suggests levels at which emphasis may appropriately be given to each area or problem, or to aspects thereof:	For senior high school, voting in local, state, and national elections.
V. PLANS RESOURCE UNITS		
School planning groups	by levels or departments plan resource units for major areas or problems and aspects thereof:	A resource unit on "Voting."

Source: Saylor and Alexander, *Curriculum Planning*, p. 400.

WHO	DOES	WHAT? (*for example*)
VI. MAKES UNIT PLANS		
Individual teachers	make unit plans for each learning group:	A unit plan for an 11A American history class on "Voting in U.S. Presidential Elections."
VII. DEVELOPS LEARNING EXPERIENCES		
The learning group	plans and carries on learning experiences related to the unit plan, usually through units of work:	An experience in using voting machines in connection with the above-named unit or plan.

CONSULT WRITTEN STATEMENTS OF PURPOSES

In most schools some statement of purposes for instruction as a whole, if not for particular departments or courses, is usually available. These statements may be in the form of educational purposes for the system as a whole or for the individual school or for subject departments. The beginning teacher may hope for some printed statement of the system's or school's philosophy or purposes to be given him when he reports for work.

The purposes of instruction in particular subject fields, even individual courses, are also frequently to be found in written form, usually in *courses of study* or other *curriculum guides*. A course of study is usually an outline of instruction in a particular field, and more general curriculum guides simply suggest various principles and plans of organizing instruction. These publications may be issued by state departments of education, the city or county school system, or the individual school or department. Even where detailed statements of purposes are not available in comprehensive form, the departmental group or individual teachers may have prepared brief statements of purposes for particular courses. The teacher beginning instruction in any new course should ask for all such statements as are available.

HELP FORMULATE STATEMENTS OF PURPOSES

Whether or not such statements as described above are available, the individual teacher helps himself and his school by working with other teachers in determining purposes. If statements are already prepared, he can review these at the beginning of the year with other teachers to determine which seem applicable for the boys and girls to be taught this particular year and in the classes he is assigned to teach. If statements are not available, planning with other teachers is a profitable way of developing them.

In larger schools where several teachers are teaching in the same department, departmental planning is common. Here the beginning teacher may receive considerable direction by learning how other teachers have set up instructional purposes, and by sharing with them in determining purposes for particular groups. In the smaller school where each teacher handles all instruction in a given instructional area or perhaps in more than one area, the teacher may share in setting school purposes and in planning with others for points of emphasis to be made in various areas.

Such planning among teachers in no way takes the place of the cooperative teacher-pupil planning emphasized in this book. The final selection of purposes and related learning experiences is properly done in learning group situations, but our present interest is in the preparation which teachers must make for these situations. Also, we must emphasize the fact that some purposes are fixed and must be predetermined and planned for by the teacher.

PREPARE A WORKING STATEMENT OF PURPOSES FOR
EACH LEARNING GROUP

After consulting any and all written statements of purposes and working with other teachers in preparing new or revised statements, the individual teacher still needs to set up a working guide for English 7A, Biology 10B, Mathematics I, or whatever his teaching assignments may be. Furthermore, even if he has five classes all in English 10A or some other single course, a statement of purposes is rightly prepared for each of the five classes. Although the major purposes may be much the same, it is unlikely that each learning group will have sufficient identity of previous experience, of competence in skills, and of other characteristics to justify uniform instructional purposes. Hence the working guide of instructional purposes should not be completed until the teacher and pupils have set these so far as possible in accordance with the suggestions regarding cooperative planning given in Chapter 8. This working statement may be first developed as a blackboard summary with the class and finally prepared in written form. The teacher should guide the development of such a statement of purposes in accordance with the following general principles.

The Statement Should Be Comprehensive. The total list of purposes should include all the skills, understandings, and behaviors which the teacher hopes learners will achieve in the total period of their relations, that is, the school year or semester. The list should reflect the teacher's analysis of purposes which are fixed by requirements or general expectations and also by his study of other desirable purposes.

In general, the teacher is better off to be ambitious in this preliminary planning, for it seems better to eliminate purposes found unattainable than to completely neglect purposes which are desirable. This merely means that purposes which seem desirable and probably attainable should be listed, not those considered impossible.

Purposes Should Be Stated in Terms of Pupil Performance. Educational objectives are frequently stated in terms of what the teacher does rather than what the pupil does, and sometimes the purposes are therefore thought to be achieved after the teacher has performed. Since our only real criterion of successful teaching is pupil performance, it is more direct, logical, and helpful to state the purposes originally as pupil "to-do's." Thus we believe that the statement "to behave courteously" is a more significant one than "to stress courtesy." Similarly, the teacher has a better guide to planning and evaluation in the purpose "to distinguish between statements of fact and opinion" than in "to give practice in critical reading," or "to understand the effect of inflation on wages and prices" as compared with "to show the inflationary spiral."

Practice in stating instructional purposes in terms of pupil performance will help in the process of refining and eliminating objectives. Frequently the conversion of a statement from teacher to pupil terms will itself reveal the impossibility or difficulty of attaining the purpose. For example, the English teacher who thinks of the wide differences of background and ability in his English I class may find considerably more ambitious, if not impossible, the purpose "to use correctly all parts of speech" than "to show how to diagram sentences." Perhaps he will decide to change the statement to some more modest one, such as "to improve in the correct use of language."

The Purposes Included Should Be Realistic. A great many statements of educational purposes seem very idealistic and unattainable when viewed in relation to the learners, teachers, and resources involved. Perhaps because of this frequent characteristic, many teachers are apathetic about reading or preparing statements of purposes. Too, there is usually an impression that purposes are merely statements on paper which should look right but which need have no relation to what goes on in the classrooms. Such statements are of little worth in educational planning. Teachers sincerely interested in having good instructional plans will do far better to stick to words and phrases that have meaning in terms of what is possible and attainable. For example, the purpose "to understand the present in the light of the past" is frequently stated in history and seems wonderful, but analysis of many classroom practices in teaching history suggests that the "light" of the past frequently never turns to the present. A more realistic purpose might be "to understand some current social problems by analysis of their chronological background and development" or, perhaps even more realistically, "to understand the nature of our industrial society and its problems by studying the industrialization of the United States."

Purposes that are realistic are based on thorough understanding of the learners as well as of the subject matter that might be included. Thus, "to appreciate the literary qualities of the American novel" may be a rather farfetched purpose for a group of boys and girls whose reading has been largely confined to school textbooks and comic books. A more realistic purpose for the English teacher to have for such a group may be "to enjoy reading a good American novel." Similarly, "to appreciate the significance of the family in American life" may be a large order for learners whose family living has been broken and unhappy, and it may be that the social studies or homemaking or core teacher will do better to work with the class toward the purpose "to understand some factors which make for happy family living." Just the use of modifiers may make statements of purposes more realistic; for example, "to appreciate *some* contributions of science to mankind" seems considerably more attainable than "to appreciate *the* contributions of science to mankind" in the ninth-grade general science class.

The List of Purposes Should Be Flexible. For many reasons, the statement should be so prepared and used as to have a high degree of flexibility. In the first place, it is an initial statement prepared at the beginning of the year, and many circumstances may develop in the school or community to make it desirable to eliminate or add purposes. In the second place, as there is more involvement of pupils in planning, the teacher's initial expectations of their purposes and performance may have to be modified. In the third place, as teachers work together in curriculum planning, there may be need to experiment with the attainment of different purposes from those originally anticipated. Any one or combination of such reasons may make it desirable to reconsider and modify the statement of purposes.

As already indicated, the initial statement is primarily a working guide to give direction to teacher-pupil planning activities and to the development of unit plans. Without such a statement, instruction is likely to be planless, either drifting from one thing to another without reason or sticking to some mechanical outline, such as that of the textbook, without the teacher or learners having any conception of what their learning destinations are. The other extreme is a statement of purposes in terms of minimum essentials, which inhibits the teacher if he really regards the purposes as absolutes to be achieved by all learners. Thus the purpose "to be able to type sixty words per minute without error," if regarded as a minimum essential for all learners in the typewriting class, might make the teaching of typewriting become primarily a matter of coaching and drilling the slow typists. Such a purpose as "to improve in speed and accuracy to the best of one's ability" is a much more flexible statement that provides for the individual differences of learners and for some creative work by the teacher in dealing with both slow and rapid typists. In summary, flexibility is secured through (1) statements which are themselves flexible, that is, not stated in absolute terms, and (2) flexible use of statements, that is, making modifications as needed.

PLANNING THE FRAMEWORK OF INSTRUCTION

Once the teacher's study of his teaching assignment has resulted in a statement of purposes for each class, the next step is an over-all organization or framework of instruction. Here, as in setting purposes, his job may be facilitated and guided by any written curriculum guides of the school or system. With or without such guides, there are the jobs of determining major divisions of the year's work and of planning for each such major division. These two steps are considered in this and the following section. First, however, attention is given to the possible relation of the school's or system's curriculum plan to the teacher's planning.

USING CURRICULUM GUIDES

For convenient reference, written curriculum guides may be classified as follows:

1. Statements of philosophy, purposes, objectives, and so forth
2. General guides to the framework of the curriculum as a whole
3. Guides (courses of study) to learning experiences for specific areas and levels
4. Resource units and related materials
5. Descriptions of practices in the schools
6. Guides to curriculum planning

We have already indicated the use of statements of philosophy in developing the teacher's own definition of purposes. We are interested now chiefly in the teacher's use of the other types of guides listed above, and will also note the use of resource guides, descriptions of practices, and other guides to planning later in this chapter.

Faculties or committees which have developed guides to the framework of the curriculum as a whole usually will have settled the major issue of curriculum organization. Any general guide should indicate whether the organization is subject, broad field, core, or some other type, and thereby provide bases for organizing and selecting learning experiences. In such situations the teacher's first job in organizing instruction is to understand the point of view and procedures suggested in the guide and their applicability to organizing instruction for his own classes.

Courses of study are in effect plans for organizing instruction in specific subjects or broad fields, usually by grade levels. They vary in breadth from a general course of study in science, grades 7 to 12, for example, to a specific course of study in biology, grade 10. Where very specific courses of study are available and are adopted *in toto* by the teacher, his preliminary planning of instructional organization is over. However, just beginning with his first class meeting may be the dissatisfaction of both teacher and pupils with a plan of procedure that was developed without reference to the backgrounds, interests, and competencies of the teacher and pupils. The wise teacher uses such a course of study as a guide to his own planning. Thus he may select some of the recommended units of work, or combine some of those recommended into new ones, or take one merely as a point of departure, or he may decide to plan his own organization through such an analysis as suggested in the next section and then check this against the course of study.

A growing number of school systems give the teacher specific aid in curriculum planning through providing resource units, descriptions of classroom practices, and other guides to some of the tasks involved. Thus teachers are given bulletins offering suggestions such as are contained in this chapter, but with reference to a particular school or school system. How to organize instruction, how to plan units of work, how to evaluate pupil progress, and how to select resources for learning are problems common to all teachers, and about which curriculum-planning groups may well give suggestions in specific bulletins. Such bulletins give local illustrations pertinent to these problems, and list persons, places, and materials available locally for the teacher's help. Beginning teachers will do well to secure copies of all such aids available in the school of their initial employment and to use these aids thoroughly and wisely. Such materials are particularly important, as we shall see later, in planning units of work and in anticipating an organization of units. They are almost indispensable in a core curriculum organization.

PLATE 40. VARIED MATERIALS SHOULD BE CONSULTED IN PLANNING INSTRUCTION. Here a planning group is engaged in examining textbooks. (Courtesy of the Fayette County, Kentucky, Public Schools)

ORGANIZING THE INSTRUCTIONAL FRAMEWORK FOR
A PARTICULAR GROUP

Whether or not there is help for the teacher in the form of written curriculum guides, an instructional organization for each learning group must be developed. With good guides available, his job is primarily one of selection and adaptation of materials as just described. Without them, he must create a tentative organization. We propose here some principles to be observed either in adapting or creating a framework.

There are two fundamentally different bases for organizing instruction. One is the logical pattern of subject matter, the other the psychological pattern of the learner's own purposes. Although, as we pointed out early in this chapter, the core organization facilitates the use of learners' purposes, they may also be consulted in a subject organization. Regardless of the instructional pattern, each learner develops his own organization of purposes and learning experiences, selecting from those which may have been organized for the total group. Even the pattern which the teacher sees as an organization around learners' purposes is not likely to correspond to the unique purposes of each learner. However, an organization that gives major importance to learners' problems and purposes facilitates adaptation by individual pupils, and hence good planning usually gives much consideration to learners' own purposes.

The chief utility of patterns of curriculum organization other than the subject one lies in their lack of an inherent logical organization and hence their ready adaptation to an instructional organization based on learners' own problems. Thus the teacher planning an organization of instruction within a core curriculum or for a new problems-type course is not faced with the dilemma of whether to follow the logic of the subject or the interests of learners. At the same time, he has very little basis on which to plan an organization and will need to make plans of a highly tentative type for initial instruction only.

Each subject area has its own logical organization. Thus the logical organization of history is around chronology; of literature around literary types; of chemistry around chemical elements; of biology around types and processes of life; of agriculture around products; and so forth. But learners in the history class may not be interested in chronological periods as such, but in current or unusual events and problems; in literature classes, the interest may be certain themes, or characters, or authors; chemistry, chemical phenomena of everyday life; agriculture, labor-saving machinery and farm income. Hence effective planning of instructional organization in a subject area needs to work out a set of organizing centers that represents the best reconciliation possible of the logic of the subject and the interests of learners. This planning may be accomplished by use of such a form as suggested and illustrated in the accompanying form. Even in situations where a curriculum guide suggests a specific instructional organization it may be worth while to check this organization by use of such a form.

As shown in Figure 17, the teacher using this device for planning the instructional framework writes in the first column one major organizing center (each center is written up separately) suggested by analysis of youth needs and of the logic of the subject. This information he may have from his own knowledge or from the curriculum guide. In the second column he lists the related interests of boys and girls of the class concerned. Here the experienced teacher will be at an advantage, for he has had opportunity to observe these interests from year to year. The inexperienced teacher may have to accept the evidence from other teachers or from published sources regarding interests to be expected; or, perhaps better, he may hold up his planning until he has had opportunity to get acquainted with the learning group and take some preliminary inventory of their interests by check list

Subject (s) _____

Grade _____

School _____

MAJOR PURPOSES OF INSTRUCTION (USE REVERSE IF NECESSARY)

1.
2.
3.
4.
5.
6.
7.
8.
9.
10.

–A– An Area of Instruction Considered Important by the Teachers (Complete B, C, D, E, F for each area)	–B– Related Interests of Pupils Which Research and Our Judgment Indicate as Significant	–C– Units of Work Suggested by Pupils and Teachers as Related to the Area and to These Interests	–D– Purposes of Instruction to Be Emphasized in Each Unit (Use numbers as above)	–E– Skills to Be Emphasized in Each Unit (Use numbers from separate list)	–F– Sections (or Teachers) and Dates Unit Was or Will Be Taught

FIG. 17. FORM FOR USE IN PLANNING THE ORGANIZATION OF INSTRUCTION

or discussion. In the third column, the teacher records what seem to be units of work which represent an approach through pupil interests to the broad area. In the fourth column, the units are checked for their relevance to instructional purposes; in the fifth, basic skills to be emphasized are listed; and in the sixth, a record is kept of the use of each unit. This form with minor modifications may be used for recording plans for several classes of the same or different teachers. Prepared as a large wall chart, it may be a helpful basis for planning and/or recording units of work by a departmental or other group of teachers.

Several problems arise in making this kind of analysis. First, what does the teacher do about areas for which no interests are identified? If there is no known interest in a particular area, the question becomes one of whether understanding of that area is essential to understanding others; if so, it should be related to the others, and if not, perhaps it should be eliminated.

Second, in what sequence should the areas and units be arranged? The answer to this question depends a great deal on the nature of the subject; for example, mathematics, foreign language, and some science subjects do have an internal sequence which cannot very well be violated. In other fields, especially English and social studies (and in the core organization), sequence is much less inherent and teachers can afford to plan from one unit of work to another in the light of pupil interests and current developments. Wherever possible, it is probably a good working principle to select in advance one or two areas for the first few weeks and regard any subsequent sequence, if planned at all, as very tentative and subject to pupil-teacher planning processes.

Third, there is the related question of how much time to give to each major division of the year's work. This question in particular is one which we believe must be left unanswered or answered only very tentatively in advance. Particularly during the first year of teaching, the teacher needs to feel his way and determine on the basis of pupil interests and achievement how intensively and thoroughly to go into any unit of work. It may be well to set up an approximate length of time, say four to six weeks, for the first large unit, and then decide on the basis of experience with this plan how much time to allow for other ones. Even after the first year, teachers find that the same or related units take varying amounts of time with different learning groups, because of differences in the pupils and their previous experiences, interests, and other factors. So time allotments are best made on a very flexible basis, and even those recommended by the curriculum guide should be considered highly tentative.

PLANNING UNITS OF WORK

Earlier in this chapter in our analogy of the automobile trip, we noted the meaning of "unit of work" and related terms. Because of the frequent confusion of terminology in instructional organization, these terms are defined here rather specifically. A *resource unit* is a compilation of suggested learning experiences and resources related to some broad area. From this compilation, teachers may choose ideas, materials, and procedures to be used in their unit plans. A sample resource unit is reproduced in Appendix III. A *unit plan* is a teacher's outline of the unit of work he hopes to develop with a learning group. The *unit of work* is the actual organization of learning experiences related to the unit topic, problem, or other source of unity, as developed in the learning situation; that is, the unit of work is what actually happens. The *unit record* is the record of the unit of work, that is, a sort of diary, log, or summary. In the analogy we compared the resource unit with the compilation of road maps and planned routes for a trip, and the unit record with the marked-up road map or the diary kept by the traveler.

Thus the unit of work is one of the major divisions of the instructional organization or framework discussed in the preceding section; the resource unit is a source for getting ideas and materials; the unit plan is the teacher's own outline for the unit of work; and the unit record is some account of what happened. In the following paragraphs consideration is given to the nature of a good unit of work, the use of resource units, and the preparation of unit plans.

THE NATURE OF A GOOD UNIT OF WORK

The teacher's planning of the organization of instruction for a particular learning group should result in a list of organizing centers or areas: unit problems, themes, topics, generalizations, projects or other sources of unity. The nature of each unit of work, however, is yet to be determined and should be carefully planned in terms of learners concerned. Whether the unit of work is a division of instruction in the core curriculum, specific subjects, or other curriculum patterns, there are certain principles we have found important in developing the detailed unit plan. These principles may be summarized as follows:

1. *The Unit of Work Should Be Organized around a Significant Problem or Other Source of Unity.* There are really two basic principles involved in this statement: first, that the unit of work should be organized around *a* source of unity, and second, that the source should

be *significant*. Units of work sometimes lack unity; that is, the activities and resources involved do not contribute to learners' understanding of the central idea. For example, the teacher sometimes divides instructional organization by time periods (semesters, months, reporting periods, and the like) and calls the resulting blocks "units" when there may be no real unity in the material taken up lesson by lesson. Again, the ideas involved are sometimes so broad that learners never clearly sense the relatedness of specific learning experiences to the unit idea; for example, a unit on "consumer chemistry" in the chemistry course would not likely succeed in tying together all the consumer applications to be made in the course.

"Significance" has a dual connotation: a unit of work should be both philosophically and psychologically appropriate. That is, it should be important or significant in terms of what boys and girls ought to learn and also in what they can and want to learn. A unit of work on "electronics" might be philosophically appropriate for ninth-graders but psychologically inappropriate; one on "science magic" might be psychologically but not philosophically appropriate; and one on "personal cleanliness and sanitation" might conform to both criteria of significance.

2. *The Unit of Work Should Aid in the Progressive and Balanced Development of Learners.* As suggested earlier, it may be very difficult to plan the right sequence of units of work in the beginning of the year. Frequently one unit of work produces interests that cannot be anticipated in advance—interests that may lead into some unit of work that the teacher had not expected to follow. For example, the civics teacher might plan a sequence of units dealing with national government that follow the traditional organization of the executive, legislative, and judicial branches, and later find that the pupils became more interested in the political aspects of the executive branch and wanted to go into the study of political parties next, although this unit had been planned for some months later. Although the logical organization would be sacrificed in so doing, the teacher would likely prefer to follow the progression indicated by the pupils' interest. That is, "progressive" development of learners has to be defined in terms of specific learners; it is their progress with which teachers are concerned, not the progress of the subject matter. Progressive development is secured by the kind of planning along the instructional route that is sensitive to pupil interests, intelligent about avoiding undesirable repetitions, and alert to the needs of boys and girls for related information and skills.

In this same civics class, the learners' development would not be very well balanced in terms of instructional purposes if the entire year were spent on national government. "Balance" is secured by setting purposes which are themselves balanced, and, further, by selection and planning of units of work which in the aggregate give attention to each purpose commensurate to its importance.

It should also be noted that progressive and balanced development is approached within the unit of work as well as in the choice of units. Units of work which provide for a great deal of work at the same level and type do not make for progressive and balanced learning. Pupils studying a unit on breakfast foods in the homemaking class would not progress very far by repeating the preparation of the same breakfast foods day after day nor would their knowledge of foods and their preparation become very well balanced. Similarly, pupils studying radio broadcasting in the speech class would need to have more of a variety of experiences than those of announcing and making speeches.

3. *The Unit of Work Should Provide for the Individual Differences of Learners.* In the final analysis, the extent to which the unit of work provides for continuity and balance in learning must be determined by evaluation of its results for different learners. That is, the experience which appropriately comes next for one learner is not necessarily the same as that for another; and what one needs for balanced development may not be what another needs. Hence good unit planning anticipates a variety of experiences that may be had by different learners in terms of their needs and interests. Thus the English teacher planning a unit on work on "Becoming a good conversationalist" recognizes that his pupils are at varying stages of development in their conversational abilities. Some pupils need a great deal of experience in just the social amenities of conversation; others need help in finding a greater variety of conversational topics; and others lack the basic skills of good English usage. The unit plan must then assume varying situations, different subgroups for specific purposes, different written conversations for study, and other alternatives to meet the needs of all members of the group.

Planning for individual differences is a much broader matter than choosing reading materials of different levels of difficulty, important as this task is. As we noted in Chapter 12, there must also be planning for distribution of responsibilities in accordance with individual abilities and needs, for drill in using whatever types of skill are involved, for the organization of committees and subgroups which will accord best with pupil needs and interests, and for use of varied resources such as visual aids, field trips, and interviews in terms of the readiness of different pupils for these resources.

4. The Unit of Work Should Be Developed on an Experimental Basis. Even though it has been carefully planned with reference to full resource units, a good unit of work develops in the classroom situation and through the day-by-day, period-by-period evaluation of the teacher and learners. Alternatives must be chosen in terms of what seems best at the time; needs that were not anticipated have to be met; interests which were not aroused as hoped for must be fanned anew or abandoned. Unless the unit of work is carried on in an attitude of experimentation—that is, with constant evaluation and modification of plans as needed—it may become as fixed and ineffective as a series of uniform assignments in a single textbook. Just as the traveler reconsiders his route and travel plans along the way, and makes the modifications which his experience indicates as desirable, the teacher reconsiders and revises his unit plan as need is indicated by observation and evaluation of pupil progress and interest.

THE USE OF RESOURCE UNITS AND MATERIALS

Many secondary school teachers have the advantage of well-planned resource units prepared by their own teacher groups, which may be consulted for valuable leads in developing unit plans. In general, the authors believe that the most effective use of resource units is made by those who participate in their preparation, and therefore recommend as an important phase of curriculum planning, teacher cooperation in the preparation of these materials. In many school systems, provision is made for departmental and cross-departmental groups to prepare resource units in connection with their curriculum planning activities. These resource units are then made available to all interested teachers, and provide a most helpful source of ideas and materials for the development of unit plans. The teacher ·beginning his planning for a particular instructional responsibility should inquire for copies of all such resource units as may be appropriate.

Although time consuming, the preparation of resource units is probably as valuable planning activity as can be engaged in by classroom teachers. The process of preparation includes the following steps:

1. Agreement on the form of the resource unit—such items as the following are usually included:

    a. Statement of the unit problem
    b. Groups (grades, curriculum areas) for whom the unit plans related to this resource unit might be prepared
    c. Desired learnings hoped for in this unit (sometimes developed fully to include subject matter of the unit)
    d. Possible learning experiences related to the problem

e. Specific teaching-learning aids that may be used

f. Techniques for evaluating units of work and pupil progress in these units, related to the resource unit

2. Determination of major areas around which resource units need to be developed

3. Collection of materials already available related to these areas, such as written unit plans, bibliographies of printed and audiovisual materials, tests, and list of places for field trips

4. Designation of responsibility for different divisions of the resource unit, and preparation of the various sections

5. Critical sharing by the entire group of the materials which individuals have prepared

6. Careful editing of the entire resource unit by one person

The authors recognize that many readers of this book may not have resource units available in their schools and may not be able to organize teacher groups for the preparation of these materials. To these readers in particular, we offer a number of suggestions as to procedures which may give help somewhat equivalent to that available in resource units prepared by teacher groups in the local situation:

1. *Consult Published Resource Units.* Series of resource units have been published by the National Council for the Social Studies and the National Association of Secondary School Principals (*Problems in American Life Series*), the North Central Association of Colleges and Secondary Schools (*Unit Studies in American Problems*), the Consumer Education Study, National Association of Secondary-School Principals (*Consumer Education Series*), and other professional organizations. Many resource units are also published by school systems and made available for sale or exchange.

2. *Find Leads to Units of Work in Your State and Local Curriculum Guides.* Many school systems and state departments of education which do not publish resource units as such do publish curriculum guides for various curriculum areas. In these curriculum guides, teachers may find many outlines or accounts of possible units as well as lists of materials and other resources that will be helpful in the development of their own unit plans.

3. *Read Accounts of Units of Work in Professional Journals and Publications.* Several of the professional journals of interest to secondary school teachers, which are listed in Appendix II, frequently include descriptions of classroom experimentation prepared by the teachers carrying on the experimentation. Yearbooks and monographs prepared by the professional organizations also frequently include

descriptions of classroom work, as do professional books like this one. In preparing specific units, teachers may also check through library tools (*Education Index* and card catalogues) for references on the particular unit problem with which they are concerned.

4. *Develop Resource Files of Your Own.* Every teacher really needs a set of vertical files, even if the school system provides teacher-prepared resource units and the school library has a comprehensive vertical file. Teachers who have their own files of resource materials usually find them more meaningful and usable because they were collected personally.

The preparation and maintenance of a vertical file of resource materials is not very difficult and only takes a little extra time for the teacher who reads and studies and experiments anyway. The following simple suggestions may help you get one started:

1. Get a set of file folders and, if possible, one or more file drawers.

2. Put headings on these folders to correspond approximately to major divisions of your instructional organization, that is, major units of work you have taught, or expect to teach, or hope eventually to teach.

3. As you read and study in preparation for teaching and also for purely personal reasons, clip or note or collect such items as the following when related to the headings you have developed:

    a. news clippings
    b. cartoons
    c. stories and jokes
    d. magazine articles
    e. pictures
    f. lists of materials
    g. maps and charts
    h. tables of statistics and other data
    i. reviews of books, films, and plays
    j. advertisements
    k. pamphlets

4. Similarly, clip or note or collect such materials, even though you have no related headings in your file, if you think you might later want to use the material. You can and should eventually prepare additional folders.

5. Wherever possible, note the source on the material so that you can get additional copies if needed. Also, to expedite filing, note on the material the heading you had in mind.

6. File the materials periodically in your folders, indicating by a note in the other folder(s) concerned, cross references to materials you might want to use in more than one connection.

7. Also include in these files materials from your teaching wherever related to the headings: bibliographies, unit plans and records, tests, evaluation summaries, samples of pupils' work, and the like.

8. Periodically (unless your files are unlimited) screen through your materials to reduce their bulk and also to reacquaint yourself with possible sources and leads.

PREPARATION OF UNIT PLANS

Once instructional purposes have been set, the major divisions of the instructional organization tentatively planned, and resource materials secured relative to each possible unit of work, the preparation of the unit plan is not very complex. The job primarily is one of matching goals hoped for with possible learning experiences and resources, perhaps chosen from the relevant resource units and materials.

The unit plan, regardless of the curriculum area and level involved, should provide for at least the following items:

1. Definition of the unit problem and the learnings desired in connection with the unit
2. Means of introducing the unit and carrying on pupil-teacher planning in its development
3. Lists of learning experiences related to the unit problem, including lists of appropriate materials and other resources
4. A brief outline of some one or more culminating activities for summarizing the unit learnings
5. A plan of evaluation of pupil achievement and of the unit itself

Published curriculum guides which contain sample unit plans are available in many local school systems and are excellent aids in teacher planning.

FOR FURTHER STUDY

Alberty, Harold, *Reorganizing the High School Curriculum.* Rev. ed.; New York: The Macmillan Company, 1953.
This significant text on the high school curriculum is particularly helpful with regard to the core curriculum.

Association for Supervision and Curriculum Development, National Education Association, *Developing Programs for Young Adolescents.* Washington, D.C.: The Association, 1954.
Briefly surveys current practices in junior high school education and proposes problems and procedures for improvement.

Board of Education of the City of New York, *Suggestions to Teachers of*

Experimental Core Classes. Curriculum Bulletin, 1950–1951 Series, No. 2; New York: The Board, 1951.

This guide for developing the core program in grades 9 and 10 in the New York City Schools contains many suggestions for planning the organization of instruction.

Burnett, Will, and Bernice Burnett, "Core Program in Action," *Education,* Vol. 73, No. 5 (January), 1953.

A special issue describing core programs in considerable detail. Includes reports of recorded core-class sessions.

Consumer Education Study, National Association of Secondary School Principals, *Consumer Education Series.* Washington, D.C.: The Study, various dates.

Series of resource units in consumer education.

Draper, Edgar M., and Gordon Gardner, "How to Construct a Resource Unit," *Clearing House,* 26:267–270 (January), 1952.

A brief, usable description of the characteristics and divisions of a resource unit.

Faunce, Roland, and Nelson Bossing, *Developing the Core Curriculum.* New York: Prentice-Hall, Inc., 1951.

Chapters 6–10 deal particularly with procedures of teaching in the core curriculum.

Harap, Henry, *Social Living in the Curriculum.* Nashville: Division of Surveys and Field Services, George Peabody College for Teachers, 1952. Part II describes practices in unit development at each grade level and gives particular attention to classroom procedure.

Klohr, Paul R., "The Resource Unit in Curriculum Reorganization," *Bulletin,* No. 171, National Association of Secondary School Principals, 34:74–77 (May), 1950.

A brief report of the author's doctoral study on the nature, organization, and uses of resource units.

Leonard, J. Paul, *Developing the Secondary School Curriculum.* Rev. ed.; New York: Rinehart & Company, Inc., 1953.

This basic text on the high school curriculum includes three helpful chapters (15–17) on unit work and includes many excerpts of units for illustrative purposes.

Miel, Alice, and Associates, *Cooperative Procedures in Learning.* New York: Bureau of Publications, Teachers College, Columbia University, 1952.

Presents many illustrations of cooperative planning and suggests techniques for dealing with various problems in using cooperative procedures.

National Council for the Social Studies and National Association of Secondary School Principals, National Education Association, *Problems in American Life Series.* Washington, D.C.: The Association, various dates.

A series of resource units in social studies.

Noar, Gertrude, *Freedom to Live and Learn.* Philadelphia: Franklin Publishing & Supply Co., Inc., 1948.

Illustrates an experimental approach to curriculum planning in a junior high school.

Romine, Stephen A., *Building the High School Curriculum*. New York: The Ronald Press Company, 1954.

See Part III for suggested procedures of planning the curriculum framework and also units of work.

Saylor, J. Galen, and William M. Alexander, *Curriculum Planning for Better Teaching and Learning*. New York: Rinehart & Company, Inc., 1954.

Especially related to this chapter are Parts III ("How Shall the Curriculum Framework Be Organized?") and IV ("How Shall We Plan the Curriculum for Better Teaching?").

Wright, Grace S., *Core Curriculum Development: Problems and Practices*. U.S. Office of Education Bulletin 1952, No. 5; Washington, D.C.: Government Printing Office, 1952.

Illustrates practices in various types of core-curriculum organization.

15. Planning from Day to Day

IN CHAPTER 14 we were concerned with the relatively long-term planning processes that teachers need to employ at the beginning of the year and also at or near the beginning of each major instructional division or unit of work. Regardless of how carefully and adequately this long-term planning may have been done, there is always the need for the teacher's own planning from day to day and from one class period to the next. This daily planning is especially important in maintaining continuity and interest in learning.

MAINTAINING CONTINUITY AND INTEREST

Even if the teacher follows all the suggestions relating to continuity and interest we have presented in previous chapters, these important values may be lost between consecutive meetings of the same class—unless, that is, adequate care is taken by the teacher to relate these meetings to each other and to the changing interests of adolescents. Hence most of the tasks and techniques described in this chapter deal with the teacher's planning or preparation in the interim between class sessions: outlining the class meeting, arranging facilities and securing resources, study of pupils' records and work, preparation of materials for pupils, study of subject-matter materials, and making records for future references.

PLANNING EACH CLASS MEETING

In addition to the advance planning of the major divisions of instruction, the units of work, and the cooperative planning in the classroom with boys and girls, teachers need to make specific plans for each class meeting. The value of formal plans of a fixed, uniform type is

460

quite limited, particularly when these are prepared a week or even a month in advance as required in some schools; but the teacher's daily plans, following whatever form he finds most useful, are essential. For example, a sample plan for a week's lessons prepared in connection with a unit in senior high American history on "The Threats to Our American Heritage" follow:

For the First Day

INTRODUCTORY ACTIVITIES

1. List on the blackboard questions concerning democracy and communism already suggested by pupils:
   a. How does the daily life of an American family compare with that of a Russian family?
   b. What about the Communist party in the United States today?
   c. What do we mean by propaganda? Does the United States use it?
   d. Is there communism in our government?
   e. How can the Communists hide behind the Fifth Amendment?
   f. Who is a "fellow-traveler"?
2. Ask if pupils feel they know enough about communism and our Constitution, and add other questions.
3. Appoint a class committee to prepare a bulletin board comparing the rights and benefits of peoples in a democratic society with those in a communistic one.
4. Discuss current ideas held by students regarding communism.
5. Distribute the list of possible sources of information about communism and the United States Constitution.

PLAN FOR TUESDAY

1. Select a topic in connection with the Constitution or communism.
2. Prepare to do research work in the library.

For the Second Day

PROBLEMS

1. Arrange class reports for all pupils.
2. Begin research work in the library.

PROCEDURE

1. Put on the blackboard the various reports to be given and agree on the individuals (or groups) who will give these reports. (Have the class secretary take these notes down for later reference.)
2. Go over the ideas of the bulletin board committee, and let them begin work.
3. Use the remainder of the period in the library for individual work.

PLAN FOR WEDNESDAY

1. Plan to do additional library work.
2. Continue work by the bulletin board committee.

For the Third Day

PROBLEM

1. Complete library work.

PROCEDURE

1. Take class to library for work on reports.
2. Arrange for bulletin board committee to work in classroom.

PLAN FOR THURSDAY

1. Begin class reports on the Constitution.
2. Read in text (or other source) the Preamble, Article I, and Article II of the United States Constitution.

For the Fourth Day

PROBLEMS

1. Discussion of why our Constitution was adopted and its relation to democratic government.
2. Explanation of the Constitution's provisions for the legislative and executive branches.

PROCEDURE

1. Begin class reports on
   a. The history of our Constitution
   b. The Preamble as a democratic expression
   c. Democracy and the legislative branch
   d. Democracy and the executive branch

QUESTIONS FOR DISCUSSION

1. Why were the Articles of Confederation considered inadequate for the newly formed thirteen states?
2. What are the democratic guarantees in our Constitution?
3. What are enumerated or delegated powers? Implied powers?
4. Why is the Constitution a *democratic* document?
5. How can a President be removed?

PLAN FOR FRIDAY

1. Read Articles III through VII and the Amendments.
2. Begin reports on communism.

For the Fifth Day

PROBLEM

1. Begin to examine just exactly what communism is and what its threats are to us as individuals and to the United States.

PROCEDURE

1. Begin discussion of questions on the Constitution.
2. Begin oral reports on
    a. What is communism?
    b. Comparison between the views of Jefferson and Washington and those of Lenin and Marx
    c. The Communist party in the United States
    d. The causes of communism
3. Begin discussion of these questions:
    a. Is there free enterprise in Russia?
    b. Compare the idea of private ownership in America with that of state ownership in Russia.
    c. What are the aims of communism?
    d. How do standards of living in Russia compare with those in the United States? Why?
    e. Could communism become our form of government under the Constitution?
    f. Does the Fifth Amendment protect us? Should it be repealed?
    g. How important is the Communist party in America today?

PLAN FOR MONDAY

1. Continue reports on communism.
2. Continue discussion of above questions.[1]

In large metropolitan schools where substitute teachers unacquainted with the class or its teacher may be used in the teacher's absence, some such simple, uniform record of plans may be desirable as is shown in Figure 18. However, even this type of uniform lesson plan is unnecessary if effective use is made of the blackboard or the class recorder's notes. Some schools simply ask each teacher to leave each day either on the blackboard, in notes on his desk, or on lesson plan forms (supplied teachers on request to the principal) some record (of plans and/or names of class members or other teachers who can tell the plans) that might give a substitute teacher a basis for instruction. With the advantage of this flexibility, teachers may devise their own system of record keeping.

As we have already stated, it is usually desirable to end the class

---

[1] These plans were provided the authors by William H. Thomas, social studies teacher, Miami Edison Senior High School, Miami, Florida, in January, 1955.

meeting with a brief summary of what has been done at that meeting and what should follow. If the teacher jots this down, or has it jotted down by the class recorder, the basic outline for the next meeting is

Date: Teacher:

Class: Period:

	Notes
Unit of Work:	
Problem/Purpose for Today:	
Procedures:	
Planning Ahead:	
Special Announcements, etc.:	
Pupils/Committees to See:	

Fig. 18.   Form for Daily Plans

set and further planning is mostly a matter of filling in the outline. Although the nature of the outline varies with the curriculum area, the unit of work under way, and the general procedure followed in the classroom, it should always answer certain questions which follow.

WHAT SHOULD THE CLASS HOPE TO ACCOMPLISH
IN THIS MEETING? WHY?

In general, each class meeting should be devoted to a phase, part, subordinate question or problem, or other division of the unit of work. Thus the meeting may be for such different yet related purposes as planning a unit of work; organizing committees to undertake study of questions involved in the unit of work; working as committees; using library materials related to some particular question or questions; hear-

ing a visiting speaker; seeing a film; discussing a particular topic or problem; reporting on individual readings or interviews; hearing committee reports; planning, taking, or summarizing a field trip; practicing some skill; writing papers under direction; discussing errors made in some papers; carrying on laboratory experiments; learning to use a new tool or learning aid; or some combination of such purposes. In each of these examples, it is to be noted, there is something to be accomplished and this "something" usually relates to something else that follows or preceded. Sometimes it may be quite desirable to spend a meeting on a topic or skill completely unrelated to the unit of work, but this is the exception rather than the custom. Such exceptions may be caused by the unexpected presence of a noted resource person, an unexpected and significant local or school development, or some similar event. Regardless, the daily outline should show the central thing to be accomplished, and why. In the foregoing illustrative daily plans the thing to be accomplished was indicated as "problem." It is important for the written plan or outline of the daily class meeting to indicate what accomplishment is hoped for, both to remind the teacher to have this idea reiterated at the beginning of the meeting and to help him focus his planning and conduct of the class on the question.

WHAT PROCEDURES SHOULD BE FOLLOWED?

Probably the longest and most detailed section of the outline most teachers make for each meeting is the section on procedures. For this section, the teacher wisely lists the maximum number of things to do which seem at all possible for the meeting, recognizing that time may not permit each of these to be done. Inexperienced teachers, or most teachers beginning some new procedure, may find it desirable to indicate in some detail how each step is to be taken, by whom, with what directions, and so forth. If the procedure is a class discussion, it may be desirable to list specific questions that may stimulate the discussion. If there is to be directed study for the entire group or some subgroup, the teacher may need to list specific directions to be given for the study. If there is to be use of a visual aid, introductory and follow-up questions may need to be listed. If there is to be committee work, suggestions and resources for the committees are needed.

As teachers become more accustomed to a variety of procedures, only such a brief listing of these as shown in the sample plans may be necessary. Probably the test of what detail is necessary is the teacher's feeling of security as the class undertakes each procedure. If he feels more at ease with a detailed outline of what to do, then such an outline should be available as long as this feeling persists. In time, he will likely find it unnecessary. On the other hand, if he is annoyed at having to refer to his outline during the class meeting, he may find it better to think through, even write out, his procedures carefully in advance but to have only the briefest of listings actually before him in the classroom. Some teachers find it desirable to prepare a detailed outline, go over it carefully in advance of the class meeting, and have it safely available in a closed folder, but to conduct the class meeting from memory so far as possible with only occasional reference to the notes when memory fails as to planned next steps.

WHAT NEXT STEPS SHOULD BE ANTICIPATED?

The plan for a particular class meeting always anticipates what may follow if each meeting is a part of a larger division of work. Although the plans may go awry or pupil-teacher planning may result in quite different alternatives than those really expected by the teacher, it is still wise to have some expectations. In the majority of cases the plans actually developed at the end of the meeting will be similar to those anticipated, and in all cases they will be better plans as a result of the teacher's having thought through directions to be taken. It is important, of course, that the teacher's expectations, however definitely formulated and written down in the outline, be considered tentative and subject to revision in the light of what happens during the class meeting.

WHAT END-OF-MEETING SUMMARY OR EVALUATION
MAY BE DESIRABLE?

Some type of summary of the discussion, plans, understandings, or agreements reached is desirable at the end of virtually all meetings. The outline should assure this by listing one or more possible types of summaries. For example, if the meeting is planned as a discussion, a summary by the recorder, teacher, or entire class may be indicated. If the meeting is devoted to committee work, a one-minute summary by each committee of what it has done may serve to end the meeting constructively and to point to next steps. Similarly, some type of summation can be planned for almost any type of class activity.

In addition, as described earlier, some type of end-of-meeting evaluation—discussion, check list, teacher's observations—is frequently desirable. The teacher's outline may desirably list questions to be asked to elicit group evaluation, or questions to which pupils are to respond in writing, or the titles of any duplicated check lists to be used.

WHAT MISCELLANEOUS ITEMS MUST BE TAKEN CARE OF?

Class meetings can rarely be exclusively devoted to work on the plans made at the previous meeting. Usually some things happen in the interim, or were overlooked in the previous meeting, or simply occur to the teacher in the process of planning, that need to be cared for. Perhaps some pupil needs to be reminded or given special help in performance of a job he has failed to do, or group members are to be told of a new resource that would help them, or some new equipment in the laboratory needs to be demonstrated. Rather than depend on memory alone for these items, many teachers find it desirable to jot them down on the outline. If the teacher refers to the outline just before the beginning or close of the meeting as a regular routine, he can make sure that these matters are cared for.

ARRANGING PHYSICAL FACILITIES

The arrangement of tables and chairs, exhibits, displays, special collections, bulletin boards, and other equipment is a definite, time-consuming, and important part of the teacher's daily preparation for each class. Each of these jobs does not have to be performed every day, and some of them can be shared with learners, but the teacher's constant thoughtfulness and alertness about them are prerequisite to successful learning experiences.

One of the most perplexing problems in high school teaching is that of arrangement of a single classroom to meet the needs of each of the five or more learning groups usually assigned teachers in the completely departmentalized program. If all classes are in the same subject, and this is rarely the situation, the teacher may fall into the fallacy that he can follow the same plan day in and day out. Such an assumption is completely contrary to all we know about good teaching, for each group of learners presents the range of interests, capacities, and difficulties of its individual members, and since each of these individuals is unique, the ranges do not coincide. Whether the classes are in the same or varying subjects, the teacher needs to find ways of working within the classroom that permit ready adaptation of facilities to the needs of each different class. Some of the following suggestions may be found helpful:

1. Find an arrangement of chairs (assuming movable ones) that permits rearrangement, each period if necessary, with the least confusion and loss of time. Most teachers find that a circular arrangement of chairs, or tables with chairs around them, is the most easily adapt-

PLATE 41. ALL NEEDED AVAILABLE PHYSICAL FACILITIES SHOULD BE USED. Corners in the classroom or in vacant rooms of the building may be used for small group work. (Courtesy of the Fayette County, Kentucky, Public Schools)

able one. Small circles can be readily formed for group work, or the larger circle can be made into an open oval for seeing the blackboard or other visual aid.

2. Blackboard space permitting, reserve a small section for each different class and use this for recording plans or other data to be left on the board for the next meeting. If this is done, it is important that there still be considerable space left free for use during the class meeting.

3. Bulletin board and display space also permitting, reserve a section for the use of each class. If space does not permit such an arrangement, leave some space free for daily use for whatever purposes develop and some other space that rotates for display use from class to class, perhaps on a weekly basis.

4. If there is a classroom library, maintain some central collection that may be used by all classes, and special collections, changed as new units are undertaken, for each class.

Many other suggestions on the problem of physical facilities are given in Chapter 3. Perhaps our most important suggestion is that the teacher experiment with whatever facilities he has to find their maximum utility for his various classes. In such experimentation he will be looking most of all for arrangements that have flexibility, so that no class will be restricted completely to arrangements that suit the needs only of some other class. Flexibility involves such arrangements as suggested above and also a willingness on the part of pupils, the teacher, the custodians, and the administration to make frequent rearrangements, perhaps with each period of the day, even if this requires strong muscles, extra cleaning, and occasional scratching of the floor and furniture.

SECURING RESOURCES FOR LEARNING

The proper selection and use of resources for learning is a task in which teachers need rather specific preparation and experience. In this section we shall deal with basic principles to be considered in selecting resources, types of resources from which selections may be made, and procedures to be followed in identifying possible resources. It is suggested that in addition to study of such principles, teachers in preparation and in service should observe and experiment with the use of resources, and familiarize themselves with some of the basic sources of help (see "For Further Study" at the end of this chapter) on technical problems associated with audiovisual and other resources.

THE NATURE OF RESOURCES FOR LEARNING

Traditional practices of teaching have glorified the textbook as the one resource for learning. Without seeking to minimize the very real importance of textbooks in learning, the authors wish to emphasize that any source from which a learner secures help in solving his learning problem is a resource for him. Since learners vary widely in their experiential backgrounds and abilities, they do not make uniformly good use of the same resource. What one can learn from a book, another may have to learn from being told. What one learns from one book, another may have to learn from a different book. That is, resources for learning need to be as varied as are the abilities of boys and girls to learn. Hence the teacher needs a very broad concept of the role of resources in learning: that whatever sources, human or material, are helpful to his pupils, are resources to be considered in the planning of instruction.

TYPES OF RESOURCES

As just stated, the possible number of resources is almost infinite. In another publication, one of us has catalogued and described in some detail various types of resources for learning.[2] The classification only is reproduced here as a guide for teachers as to the great range of possible resources from which selections must be made in planning instruction:

Human Resources
　　The teacher as a resource person
　　Learners as resources for each other
　　　　Pairs of learners
　　　　Learners whose unique experiences help others
　　　　Learners whose special competencies help others
　　　　Learners in special roles in group situations
　　　　Learners as liaison with outside resources
　　School personnel as resources
　　Community people as resources
Environmental Resources
　　General classrooms
　　Special-purpose rooms: shops, laboratories, band room, library, audio-visual, rooms for handicapped learners, medical facilities, kitchen, homemaking apartment, museum, and so forth
　　All-school facilities: auditorium, theater, cafeteria or lunchroom, gymnasium, corridors
　　School grounds
　　Resources in the community: institutions, businesses, industries, farms, terminals, museums, libraries, governmental offices, radio and television stations, newspaper plants, telephone and telegraph offices, post offices, theaters
　　Resources beyond the local community
Printed Resources
　　Textbooks
　　Study and testing materials
　　Classroom library materials
　　School library materials
　　Newspapers and magazines
　　Free and inexpensive printed materials
　　Printed resources in home and community
Audiovisual Materials
　　Pictures, slides, and film strips
　　Exhibit pieces
　　Maps, globes, and charts
　　Motion pictures
　　Recordings and transcriptions
　　Radio and television

[2] See Chapter 14, "Selection and Use of Resources for Learning," in J. Galen Saylor and William M. Alexander, *Curriculum Planning* (New York: Rinehart & Company, Inc., 1954).

CRITERIA FOR SELECTING RESOURCES

Although the teacher might like to have a different resource for each learner, such practical limitations as availability, budget, space, and teacher ability make necessary some choices of resources to be used. Furthermore, when alternative resources are possible, choices need to be made as to which to use in particular learning situations with particular learners. Hence some basic principles or criteria for selecting resources are essential. We propose the following as being of major importance.

Relevancy. The teacher must first determine the relevancy or appropriateness of a given resource to the problem at hand. Textbooks published before the event of present interest occurred are not relevant, nor are speakers who can speak fluently and interestingly but not on the matter at hand. Relevant resources are those which pertain to and shed light on the problem of the unit of work or a division thereof. The teacher's selection of resources must involve sufficient study of these to determine their relevancy. In other words, the teacher's own preparation (planning) must include careful examination of materials which he may recommend for pupil use. The effective teacher does not send pupils to the library to see what books are available on a particular topic, but sends them to see certain books he recommends and also to check specific tools for other similar books.

Utility. Resources may have relevancy without utility; for example, literature in a foreign language may be relevant to a unit in literature, but it is not useful until translated into English. Frequently people who have had experiences which would be most relevant to problems being studied by boys and girls are unable to communicate this information effectively to the latter. Reading materials in particular lack utility because of the variations in individual reading levels. Thus a textbook written at the level of the ninth grade lacks utility for those ninth-grade pupils whose reading level may be as low as the fifth grade. Teachers can appraise the utility of a given resource only by knowledge of the material and with reference to the needs and abilities of the learners by whom it might be used.

Availability. The very practical factor of availability eliminates many resources that might qualify by all other factors. However, this criterion is sometimes applied in a more absolute fashion than necessary; for example, a book which is needed might not be in the classroom or even the school library, but by a little effort could be secured from the public or some other library in the community. Similarly, neither the teacher nor the learners may have had experiences in travel that would illuminate some social studies topic, but a little checking of other school personnel or persons in the community might yield just the right person. So application of the criterion of availability means considerable study on the teacher's part of all the potential resources that may be available. For this purpose, he will find very helpful whatever files or publications the school or school system may have regarding places to go, people to use, materials to see, and so forth.

Accuracy. Other things being equal, the teacher will select the resource that gives most accurate information on the problem at hand. Sometimes biased materials may be purposefully used to teach boys and girls to detect bias, but teachers must exercise care in selecting materials, especially free and inexpensive pamphlets and visual aids, to be certain that the biases involved are known. Although textbooks are frequently selected by persons other than the teacher, he must also endeavor to be acquainted with possible inaccuracies in their content and if possible to be able to refer youngsters to other sources on problems about which the textbooks may be either inaccurate or not up to date.

Economy. The cost of resources is frequently a determining factor in their selection. Using the school bus or private transportation at either the school's or the pupils' expense is uneconomical when a single person could come to the school and explain equally well what pupils might learn from the field trip; but frequently pupils would not learn as well from the explanation, so the factors of utility and economy have to be reconciled. Although the use of uniform textbooks is sometimes defended on the grounds of economy, it is poor economy to buy a book per pupil which only half the pupils can use intelligently. It may be better to buy sets of more than one book at or near the same cost and get maximum pupil use. Teachers who apply the criterion of economy to the selection of resources may need the help of administrators in setting up and expending budgets, and they may also need considerable practice in appraising utility in relation to costs.

IDENTIFYING POSSIBLE RESOURCES

Before actually applying the foregoing criteria and selecting resources for learners, possible resources must first be identified. These steps may be combined through reference to records and written evaluations of resources. Hence many schools keep files of some type of evaluation records of different resources. In the absence of such a school file, the teacher's own set of evaluations may be useful. Inventories of unusual resources, particularly people, are also very helpful. Many schools maintain a file on pupil resources within the school

PLATE 42. TEACHERS STUDY RESOURCES AT FIRST HAND. These
teachers are studying near-by natural resources with guidance of
consultants from the state game and fish commission. (Courtesy
of the Oak Ridge, Tennessee, Public Schools)

somewhat like the one on human resources which we explained in
Chapter 5 (Fig. 7).

Such a guide for selecting an individual boy or girl to share his or
her unique experience or competence with a class can be of great help
to the individuals selected as well as to the classes concerned. Similar
card files, giving more data regarding addresses and phone numbers,
can be very useful in identifying community resource persons. Reference to such files of community and pupil resource persons is a ready
way of identifying human resources. Suggestions for locating some of
the other, somewhat less readily accessible, resources are given in the
following paragraphs.

Identifying Resources in the Community. The problem of identifying community resources is of consequence only in the larger communities where teachers cannot easily have firsthand acquaintance with

all the resources. Even in the smaller communities, however, there may be the problem of the teacher's lack of awareness of the usefulness of commonplace scenic sights, businesses, farm areas, and the like. In the larger communities, at least three types of help may be available to the teacher desiring to become acquainted with possible resources.

First, a growing number of school systems are providing direct help to teachers through tours and other firsthand contact with community resources. Preplanning days may be used by groups of teachers, especially new teachers, to visit museums, libraries, industries, and other community resources. Other possibilities include use of occasional faculty meeting time for a firsthand study of some particular resource, arrangement of Saturday or other off-hours' trips for interested teachers, summer workshops on community resources, and arrangements of special times for beginning teachers to visit some resources. The assumption in all such arrangements is that once teachers have themselves visited or otherwise used a local resource, they will be in a better position to make wise use of this with their classes—much the same idea as the teachers' preview of a film that might later be used with their pupils.

Second, to supplement or in lieu of firsthand experience, many school systems prepare guides to community resources. These range from simple lists of places to which classes may be taken to more elaborate mimeographed or printed guides that give complete information about a large variety of community resources. A sample page of the latter type of guide is shown in Chapter 10. Frequently the information about community resources may be included in curriculum guides and in relation to particular curriculum areas or resource units. Another very usable type of guide is a card file maintained by the individual school or the subject department or even the individual teacher. The card system has the advantage of flexibility, so that new resources can easily be inserted and resources found undesirable can be eliminated.

Third, many teachers have to rely on the advice of persons who are more familiar with community resources. Principals, supervisors of instruction, curriculum coordinators, and department heads may give a great deal of concrete help to teachers through having readily available information about possible resources. In the larger high schools some one person may be charged with responsibility for maintaining this information, especially if there is a card file or other inventory available.

Our chief suggestion to the teacher is that he find out what help there is available to him in identifying and selecting community resources. The same advice applies to the various other resources. That is, in most schools there is some person or persons, file or files, or other source of help, and the teacher needs to know first of all who or what this source is.

Library Resources. The obvious way of identifying library resources is to visit, study, and use the school library. Many secondary schools provide some type of orientation to the library for new teachers, and this practice is of great help to the beginner. Unfortunately, the orientation sometimes is too concerned with rules and regulations of the library and its use, and the teachers do not get acquainted with the collection itself until months later as they have necessity. As early as possible, teachers need such items of information as the following about the library if they are to make effective selection and use of its resources:

1. General range of library holdings
2. Library holdings in the particular teaching field
3. Available tools (catalogues, indexes, and so forth) for locating library materials
4. Systems of withdrawal of materials by the teacher and by classes
5. Arrangements for classroom collections
6. Arrangements for borrowing materials from other libraries
7. Services provided by the librarian in regard to reading lists, reserves, locating materials, teaching library usage, and so forth
8. Opportunities for teachers to browse, to order materials, to see new materials as received

Testing Materials. As indicated in Chapter 11, wise use of published testing materials for diagnosing and working with pupil difficulties and abilities requires careful selection of these resources. In many secondary schools some guidance person serves as the coordinator of these materials and can readily help the teacher locate appropriate materials. Where these services are not available, the teacher can frequently get help from the principal, a supervisor, or some state or local school testing service. If the teacher has to rely purely on his own knowledge of testing resources, some of the frequently published bibliographies of tests should be secured and consulted, and samples requested of tests that seem appropriate.

Free and Inexpensive Materials. A great variety and tremendous amount of material is published in America and abroad and made available to schools free or at very low cost. These materials include those published by governmental, professional, commercial, and special interest agencies, and range from scholarly, scientific productions to sheer advertising. Most of the materials fail to meet the criteria presented earlier in this chapter with regard to use by particular high school classes, but even so, there remains an abundance of materials that do have possibilities. As we noted earlier, even the very biased productions may be useful in presenting and analyzing differing opinions on particular problems.

Some school systems have found the problem of selecting and using free and inexpensive materials sufficiently important to develop policies concerning them. These and other systems frequently provide bibliographic service for teachers. In other situations teachers are perfectly free to use any materials they desire, but are given no direction or help in identifying and selecting materials. In such situations teachers will find very helpful some of the various services available as guides to free and inexpensive materials. In addition to the frequent listings of pertinent materials to be found in the professional journals of various curriculum areas (for example, *Social Education, English Journal, Mathematics Teacher*), occasional compilations of materials are published by the Association for Supervision and Curriculum Development (see the pamphlet, *Using Free Materials in the Classroom*); the National Association of Secondary-School Principals (see *Catalog of Free and Inexpensive Aids for High Schools* and also periodic reviews of materials in the Association's *Bulletin*); the Division of Surveys and Field Studies, George Peabody College for Teachers (see the publication, *Free and Inexpensive Learning Materials*); and other agencies. Also, the following comprehensive services are available:

Standard Catalog for High School Libraries, with semiannual supplements, published by The H.W. Wilson Company, New York, lists pamphlets under Dewey decimal classification.

Booklist, published monthly by American Library Association, Chicago, includes lists of free and inexpensive materials and government publications.

School Life, published monthly, October through June, by the United States Office of Education, Washington, D.C., includes a section on government publications of special educational interest.

Educators' Index to Free Materials, published annually by Educators Progress Service, Randolph, Wisconsin, gives an annotated list of free charts, films, maps, exhibits, and so forth.

Selected United States Government Publications, issued biweekly by the Superintendent of Documents, Government Printing Office, Washington 25, D.C., lists with prices publications of various governmental branches.

Audiovisual Resources. Larger school systems that have audiovisual aids collections usually publish some type of guide to these resources which serve as the teacher's source for identifying possible aids.

In other situations where aids are procured through state or other agencies, the guides published by these agencies are similarly available. In many larger high schools one person may be designated as coordinator of audiovisual aids, and his help can be sought in locating possible materials. In lieu of these services or to supplement them when teachers wish to check for more extensive listings, the following index publications may be consulted:

Educational Film Guide (New York: The H.W. Wilson Company). Cumulated annual catalogue with supplement service.

Educators' Guide to Free Films and Slidefilms (Randolph, Wis.: Educators Progress Service). Lists films and slidefilms; revised annually.

Filmstrip Guide (New York: The H.W. Wilson Company). Cumulated annual catalogue of filmstrips, with monthly supplement service.

Various listings of recordings, paintings, and other aids are also published periodically by the United States Office of Education and the Department of Audio-Visual Instruction, National Education Association. Guides to local radio and television programs are available in the daily press, and advance listing of the major networks may be secured without charge upon request.

. . . . .

In concluding this section on the selection of resources, it should be reiterated that resource units prepared in advance by groups of teachers as described in Chapter 14 provide great help to teachers in their day-by-day planning. That is, the original screening of resources is done by the group who prepare the resource unit and the teacher is spared the great expenditure of time essential to tracking down all the possibilities from which to make a selection. To illustrate this use of resource units, we are reproducing excerpts herewith of the section on bibliography which appears in a resource unit, "Who Are Americans? An English Unit for Grade Nine," in the Denver *Guide for Teaching the Language Arts* (1953):

The bibliography for this unit is by no means complete. No attempt has been made to include all the materials which could be used in connection with this unit.

Presented here, however, is a sampling of easy and more difficult reading material which should interest ninth graders. The grade placements indicated are taken largely from the *Children's Catalog* and from several intercultural bibliographies. In a few cases the grade placement has been estimated. Because these grade placement indications are not always precise, teachers themselves will wish to look over the books and choose those which are most suitable for their classes. School librarians should be consulted concerning additional materials.

Suggestions for audio-visual materials and teacher reference have also been included in this section.

Fiction [*45 items listed as the following*]

Allee, Marjorie Hill. The Great Tradition. Boston: Houghton, 1937 (8–9)
Tells the story of Merritt Lane's college life at the University of Chicago. Brings in the relationships among a small group of girls who share an apartment. Includes a problem of prejudice against a Negro student.

Biography [*25 items listed as the following*]

Antin, Mary. Promised Land. Boston: Houghton, 1912 (9)
An autobiography of a Jewish girl who emigrates from Poland to the United States at the age of twelve. Describes her first impressions of America.

Short Stories, Poems, Plays, Essays, and Articles [*9 items listed as the following*]

Association for Childhood Education. Told under the Stars and Stripes. New York: Macmillan, 1945 (5–8)
Contains short stories about people of various national and racial origins in America. Some stories are below ninth grade level in interest.

Other Nonfiction [*13 items listed as the following*]

Ansley, Delight. The Good Ways. New York: Crowell, 1950 (9–)
Describes the philosophy of founders of the world's great religions and emphasizes the likenesses. Supplements Fitch's One God. More difficult but well worth reading.

Pamphlets and Magazines [*6 items listed as the following*]

Alpenfels, Ethel J. Sense and Nonsense about Race. New York: Friendship Press, 1946, 25¢
Presents scientific information about races in a clever, informal style. It is the type of material that the teacher would wish to discuss with the pupils as they read it.

References for Teachers [*5 items listed as the following*]

Americans All: Studies in Intercultural Education. Sponsored by Department of Supervisors and Directors of Instruction of the N.E.A., National Council of Teachers of English, and Society for Curriculum Study. Washington, D.C.: Department of Supervisors and Directors of Instruction of the N.E.A., 1942 (Available in the Professional Library of the Denver Public Schools.)

Audio-Visual Materials

Suggestions for audio-visual aids given in this section are by no means comprehensive. Since the Department of Special Services is constantly purchasing new materials for use in the schools, teachers should consult the audio-visual aids listings in their own buildings before ordering materials for the unit.

Films and filmstrips listed below are available through the Department of Special Services of the Denver Public Schools and can be used to bring out and emphasize the aims of this unit:

1. Films [*15 items listed as the following*]
   Americans All, sound, 16 minutes
   A March of Time film. Focuses attention on racial and religious tensions and what a community can do about them.

2. Filmstrips [*Several items explained*]

3. Records
   The following records, which should be ordered separately by title and number, are available through the Department of Special Services of the Denver Public Schools: [13 items listed][3]

If the teacher has the advantage of lists of resources like the foregoing, the problem of identifying possible learning resources is solved and his day-to-day planning regarding resources consists primarily of selecting appropriate resources from a list in the unit and arranging for the use of these. In the absence of such resource units, the teacher's work in identifying and selecting resources amounts to the preparation of materials which may subsequently serve him as resource units, provided he maintains adequate records of what he finds and uses.

STUDY OF PUPILS' RECORDS AND WORK

Time in daily preparation must also be devoted to study of pupil records and work. Questions that arise about particular pupils and their problems require checking of these pupils' cumulative records, and perhaps inquiry of other teachers and guidance personnel. As we noted in Chapter 11, sometimes conferences with the pupil and/or his parents may be desirable.

Although the modern secondary school teacher does not require pupils to do a great deal of busy work, he does challenge pupils to do various sorts of work, depending on the curriculum area involved: essays, outlines, summaries, reviews, drawings, maps, charts, and many kinds of products in the shops and laboratories. We believe it sound reasoning to expect the teacher to take time to examine any piece of work which pupils are expected to prepare. Improvement is much more likely to come when learners are given specific criticisms and

[3] Denver Public Schools, *A Guide for Teaching the Language Arts* (Denver, Colo.: The Schools, 1953), pp. 123–128. Reprinted by permission. (Bracketed notes supplied to abstract material omitted except for sample items.)

suggestions on their products. Without such criticisms and suggestions, learners may simply be permitted to continue to make the same errors, and indeed this is one of the major objections to uniform assignments of homework, neither prepared under supervision nor checked by the teacher. It is better to expect less work and make good use of it for improvement purposes than to expect a great deal of work which is simply filed away, destroyed, or returned unmarked.

Notes for the cumulative record and the reports of pupil progress must also be prepared for the purposes we defined in Chapter 13. If pupils' work is evaluated and recorded as it is submitted, the report of progress is a matter of inspecting the records and arriving at marks that represent the teacher's best appraisal of progress during the reporting period. If there is no such record, the teacher must rely on time-consuming final examinations and/or purely subjective estimates of the pupils' progress.

A frequent mistake in teaching is the use of pupils' work for marking purposes only. When papers and other products are returned to the pupil with marks only supplied by the teacher, the pupils naturally arrive at the conclusion that the only purpose of turning in work is to get a mark. Accordingly, there are overlooked such basic purposes as discovering one's errors and how to overcome them, learning what improvement has been made since the last piece of work, and getting suggestions for the next steps in carrying on the type of work involved. As already indicated, teachers who use pupils' work effectively make sure that each piece of work examined is returned with constructive suggestions on good and poor points, means of improvement, and next steps.

PREPARATION OF MATERIALS FOR PUPILS

Good planning and teaching involves the preparation of various materials from time to time. Time and facilities permitting, such materials as unit outlines, lists of readings, suggested learning activities, and other items relating to each unit of work are very helpful to pupils. Instructions for using equipment, preparing papers and other work, directions for committee and field activities can be duplicated for economy of time in explanation. Evaluation check lists and tests are frequently needed. Reliance on commercially prepared materials such as workbooks is common, particularly when there are lack of time and facilities for typing and duplicating and also the pressure of many large classes; but the use of materials prepared by the teacher for his own classes is usually much more effective.

In preparing these materials, teachers may save time and make better materials if they will take such safeguards as these:

1. Prepare a rough draft of the outline, instructions, and so forth first, and actually try out this draft with a few pupils.

2. Correct the rough draft for errors caught in the tryout, such as terms pupils do not understand, ambiguous expressions, and instructions that are not clear.

3. Edit the material carefully to make it appear properly spaced, uniform in style, and as attractive as possible before being duplicated. Oversight in these steps sometimes results in carelessly prepared material that sets poor examples for learners as well as fails to secure the results expected by the teacher.

STUDY OF THE SUBJECT-MATTER MATERIAL

Although good teachers do not necessarily "know all the answers," they are and should be expected to have considerably wider understanding of most problems dealt with by learners than the latter. Regardless of how thorough their preparation for teaching may be, teachers on the job have very frequent need to review the information being sought by their pupils, to check for additional information that may be needed, to look up particular questions that were asked and could not be answered at the time, and to keep current their information on developments in their curriculum areas.

The means for study of pertinent subject matter necessarily vary with the subject involved. Thus the social studies teacher needs to read current materials widely, while the business education teacher may need to concentrate on keeping abreast of local business developments and facilities. Regardless of the field, a few sources for study are common and need to be consistently used by teachers:

1. Texts and supplementary materials used by pupils
2. Popular magazines which include articles relating to the teaching field
3. Professional journals in the field of interest (Appendix II)
4. Book reviews (those books which are pertinent and available) appearing in these periodicals and the book review sections of daily newspapers
5. A good daily newspaper
6. Radio and television programs, public meetings, and programs of local organizations, which are pertinent to the field of interest

MAKING RECORDS FOR FUTURE REFERENCE

Teachers necessarily devote some time each day to record keeping. Some record-keeping jobs such as those pertaining to pupil attendance and supplies are prescribed by the school and vary too widely in their nature for explanation here. Certain other jobs are voluntary with the teacher and usually do not have to follow a prescribed form. Three such jobs are commented on in this section.

First, the organization of instruction by units of work is more effectively done if some type of unit record is maintained. As we suggested in Chapter 14, this record may be as simple as an annotation of the unit plan. If there is no written unit plan, the record may be primarily a collection of materials developed in the course of the unit. Even with a unit plan, the teacher will help future planning by maintaining in a single unit folder copies of such materials as reading lists, tests, directions, recorders' reports, evaluation check lists, sample pupil papers, and notes or summaries regarding final summations and evaluations.

Second, the day-by-day outlining of each class meeting is helped by some post-meeting check of the outline for that meeting. We have found it useful to spend a few minutes following each meeting in checking over the outline, noting by checks ($\sqrt{}$) or cross-outs (X) items that were and were not cared for and writing in matters that were not included in the outline but happened. If the teacher is able to prepare the outline for the meeting at the same time, such notes may be unnecessary although they do help for reference days or weeks later. Frequently teachers find it desirable to check the outline immediately after the meeting (while classes are changing). Then outlines for the following day may be prepared in the planning period or after school by reference to this checked-off outline.

Third, records need to be maintained with regard to individual pupils. The picture of the teacher with grade book in hand, marking each pupil's answer to the questions of the recitation, is one too many of us recall from high school days and one that we fervently hope will be recalled by increasingly few people. At the same time, teachers do need records pertaining to the individual learner: anecdotes, test results, notes on participation, notes on conferences, samples of work, and the like. These records, whether maintained in the school's cumulative record or the teacher's own temporary file, as is better, have to be prepared as classroom events make them desirable.

In addition to these three major types of the teacher's own record keeping, there are various other recording and writing tasks in planning which we have mentioned. In summary, they are as follows:

1. Checking the blackboard notes or recorder's notes on plans
2. Duplicating records or summaries
3. Preparing tabulations of evaluative check lists or summaries of end-of-meeting suggestions
4. Preparing request forms for resources
5. Completing evaluation forms, or annotating inventory records, on resources

THE TEACHER'S DILEMMA: WHEN TO PLAN

The authors realize that the teachers' study of the chapter up to this point may result in a feeling of frustration as to how they can ever do all the jobs of planning we have described and emphasized as essential to good teaching. The authors have experienced this dilemma, too, and know very well how hard it is to work with youngsters the full school day and then spend the time required for planning the next day's work. Faced with this dilemma, we have had to choose between two alternatives: first, find the time and do effective teaching; or, second, slide through the easiest way, using last year's plans, teaching sections of the same course in exactly the same way (one preparation for two or more classes), and ignoring many things that should be done. We believe that the conscientious teacher must reject the latter alternative and somehow find the time to do effective planning. For this teacher, several possibilities of time are available.

PRE-SCHOOL AND POST-SCHOOL PLANNING DAYS

An increasing number of school systems are providing time within the school year (contract period) for teachers to plan on both group and individual bases. The time provided varies from two or three days at the beginning of the year to as much as one month or more divided between the beginning and end of the year. Occasionally planning days are scattered through the school year, one each six weeks, for example. These planning days occur when no pupils come to school and the school faculties work together in total and small groups and as individual teachers, on some planned schedule. Such days offer a wonderful opportunity for teachers to prepare resource units and other major jobs of curriculum planning, and also give the individual teacher a chance to work out unit plans, select resources, and so forth. Unfortunately, not all teachers have these opportunities, and their time before and after the pupils' term is their own; it may still be better to use it than to meet one's first classes without preparation.

DAILY PLANNING PERIODS

Most secondary schools provide teachers with a daily planning period, usually on the basis of five periods for classes and one for planning. Although this forty to sixty minute period is inadequate for all the jobs of daily planning we have described, it is exceedingly helpful if not dissipated. Teachers find that the most effective use of the daily period is for checking pupils' records and work, arranging facilities, and seeing individual pupils and teachers, and perhaps making daily plans. The tasks of unit preparation and the teacher's study cannot be as readily broken off on the time schedule as the foregoing duties.

AFTER-SCHOOL TIME

We believe wholeheartedly that teachers deserve leisure time in as great amount as other professional workers. On the other hand, we also believe that to merit our professional status, we must be as well prepared for our jobs as other professional people. Our school day is generally somewhat shorter than the working day of other people, although out-of-school activities and various types of meetings do make heavy inroads on the period after three o'clock (or whenever pupils are dismissed). In general, an average of two hours' after-school time each school day for preparation does not seem an unreasonable expectation of the secondary school teacher. When this time is spent is, of course, the teachers' problem. However, many school administrators do encourage them to do their planning at school, so that when they do go home, even if it is at the five o'clock hour of many other workers, their time is free for personal purposes until the next morning. Most teachers find that work late at night, and at other times when relaxation is desirable, is rarely done as well as that accomplished within a reasonably full working day.

PROPER USE OF CLASS PERIODS

Although we unhesitatingly reject any use of class periods which leaves the pupils unsupervised and unaided, we do emphasize the fact that some planning is done best with learning groups. Pupil-teacher planning, as we have described it, is an essential phase of good teaching and relieves the teacher of making all the decisions and knowing all the answers. Furthermore, proper arrangement of the class schedule provides frequent time for the teacher to work with small groups and individuals while other groups and individuals are doing their work. Good classroom management should make it rarely necessary for the teacher to have to meet with committees and individuals, other than those with personal problems, outside the class period. Hence proper use of the class periods will itself free afterschool time for the teacher's own planning.

FOR FURTHER STUDY

Alcorn, Marvin D., Richard A. Houseman, and Jim R. Schonert, *Better Teaching in Secondary Schools.* New York: Henry Holt & Co., Inc., 1954.
A brief chapter (4), "Daily Planning," includes four illustrative lesson plans.

Association for Supervision and Curriculum Development, National Education Association, *Toward Better Teaching.* 1949 Yearbook; Washington, D.C.: The Association, 1949.
Contains many fine illustrations of planning.

————, *Creating a Good Environment for Learning.* 1954 Yearbook; Washington, D.C.: The Association, 1954.
Excellent illustrations of planning resources and facilities for classroom instruction.

Bossing, Nelson L., *Teaching in Secondary Schools.* 3rd ed.; Boston: Houghton Mifflin Company, 1952.
Part IV, "Teaching Techniques of the Class Period," includes material on daily planning, assignments, use of questions, review and practice, illustrations, radio and television.

Cronbach, Lee J., ed., *Text Materials in Education.* Urbana: University of Illinois Press, 1954.
Study of writing, functions, and use of textbooks.

Dale, Edgar, *Audio-visual Methods in Teaching.* Rev. ed.; New York: The Dryden Press, Inc., 1954.
A standard, comprehensive text on the use of audiovisual materials in teaching.

Division of Surveys and Field Services, George Peabody College for Teachers, *Free and Inexpensive Learning Materials.* Nashville: The Division, various dates.
An annotated, classified list of materials; reissued every few years.

East, Marjorie, *Display for Learning.* New York: The Dryden Press, Inc., 1952.
Specific instructions on the preparation and use of visual materials in the classroom.

Grambs, Jean D., and William J. Iverson, *Modern Methods in Secondary Education.* New York: The Dryden Press, Inc., 1952.
See pages 83–103 for these authors' treatment of teacher planning.

Kinder, James S., *Audio-visual Materials and Techniques.* New York: American Book Co., 1953.
Complete description, with many illustrations and specific instructions, of the use of many audiovisual resources.

Kinney, Lucien, and Katharine Dresden, *Better Learning through Current Materials.* 2nd ed.; Stanford University, Calif.: Stanford University Press, 1952.
Presents and evaluates in detail procedures and materials proven valuable in classes participating in an extended study of the use of current materials.

Miel, Alice, and Associates, *Cooperative Procedures in Learning.* New York: Bureau of Publications, Teachers College, Columbia University, 1952.
See especially Chapter 2, "Planning Use of Time," and Chapter 3, "Planning for Improvement and Care of Physical Surroundings."

Rivlin, Harry N., *Teaching Adolescents in Secondary Schools.* New York: Appleton-Century-Crofts, Inc., 1948.
See Chapter 15 on suggestions for planning the opening days of the school year.

Saylor, J. Galen, and William M. Alexander, *Curriculum Planning for Better Teaching and Learning.* New York: Rinehart & Company, Inc., 1954.
See Chapter 13, "Planning and Developing Learning Experiences with Learners," and Chapter 14, "Selection and Use of Resources for Learning."

Umstattd, James G., *Secondary School Teaching.* Boston: Ginn & Co., 1953.
Part 1 contains materials dealing with various problems of planning instruction.

16. The Teacher's Role in the
Improvement of Instruction

WE FEEL that high school teachers, indeed teachers in general, have an obligation to themselves and to the profession to pursue the continuing improvement of their work. Throughout this book we have emphasized an experimental approach to teaching—an approach that recognizes the role of change in society and education and the need for continuous adaptation of educational method to changing conditions. In this final chapter we deal more directly with several important means of such adaptation or improvement: self-evaluation, help from others, curriculum planning, in-service education, and experimentation. First, we wish to review the necessity of continuing improvement of teaching.

THE QUEST FOR IMPROVEMENT IN TEACHING

One's attitude toward improvement of teaching is related very closely to one's basic philosophy of education. If education is conceived to be primarily a matter of transmitting prescribed information in the most palatable doses possible to children and youth, then improvement is seen to be necessary only in terms of arriving at proper formulas for dispensing information at times and in amounts appropriate to the children and youth taught. In general, teachers who operate on the basis of this philosophy soon arrive at such formulas and tend to feel that further improvement is essentially a matter of keeping the information up to date. Periodically they may revise the formulas as information is added or deleted, and occasionally they may change the sugar-coating.

On the other hand, education may be interpreted more fully as the more dynamic process of guiding the experiences of boys and girls so that they will become more resourceful and adept in achieving important purposes they have or accept, including the acquisition of needed knowledge. Then improvement in teaching is viewed as a persistent purpose, which even the best teacher never accomplishes so completely that further improvement is not to be sought. This philosophy recognizes the many variables in the teaching-learning situation which cannot be arrayed in such mechanical relations as to make possible an absolute formula for best teaching that will apply in any classroom at any time. Examination of some of these variables will help us perceive the need of a continuous quest for better teaching.

CHANGING HUMAN ELEMENTS IN THE TEACHING-LEARNING SITUATION

The information-dosing concept of teaching tends to overlook the highly important human elements of the teaching-learning situation. Even those situations in which there is need for emphasis on telling and assigning types of teaching activities have to be guided by the teacher with full consideration of the human elements. Individual learners do not respond in the same way to what is told or assigned, nor can it be expected that different classes, composed as they are of different individuals, will generally develop the same group feeling about what they are told or assigned. Comparisons by a teacher of various classes as "good" or "poor" are frequently expressions of his feeling of satisfaction or dissatisfaction over the individual and group reactions to the same teacher activities. When the teacher who feels that a particular class is "poor" perceives that this estimate may be indicative of the need for a different procedure and undertakes to make a change, he frequently finds that the class becomes "good."

Obviously, teachers do develop procedures that seem to work well with all classes. Generally, however, these are procedures which enlist pupil participation and build on class interests rather than teacher activities that require no active interaction with learners. For example, procedures for conducting a discussion can be used successfully with different groups of the same general maturity, because they are aimed at getting the group members to define their own topics and make their own contributions. But when the teacher follows such a procedure with one group and then attempts to lead another into defining the same topics and making the same contributions, he has changed procedures and cannot expect equivalent results.

Despite their many common general characteristics, adolescents do differ from one another. No two of them learn in exactly the same way, and certainly no two groups of thirty or more different adolescents can be expected to have had the same previous experiences and present feelings toward one another and their teacher that would make for identical results in the teaching-learning situation.

It is not to be concluded from this emphasis on variations between the human elements in different teaching-learning situations that improved ways of working cannot be found from one situation to the next. Improvement in the human relationships of the classroom consists of the increasing ability of the teacher to have effective relations with the widely varying individuals he teaches from period to period, year to year. Mostly it is a matter of growing adaptability to the complexities of changing personalities. Such improvement may come with experience in the classroom, but not necessarily so. Teachers who do not seek to become more adaptable, but instead attempt to classify boys and girls as "fast" and "slow" or "good" and "poor," and use procedures for each classification without attempting to understand individual pupils are not seeking improvement. Increasing adaptability in human relationships comes with growth in abilities to study individuals, to analyze the dynamics of groups, to identify oneself with others. These abilities can be cultivated through further education of the teacher and sharpened by experience. In view of the ever growing body of research and practice in the field of human relationships, plus the ever changing individuals and groups we teach, we question whether any of us should anticipate becoming so expert in these abilities that further improvement would not be possible. Our own experience indicates that the most important approach to improvement is the development of a fundamental interest in informed study of the human elements of the teaching-learning situation. This type of study is carried on with every group the effective teacher teaches, always with the expectation of doing a better job than would be done otherwise.

CHANGES IN ENVIRONMENTAL FACTORS

Changes in the environmental factors which affect the teaching-learning situation also challenge the teacher to adapt his ways of working to new or changing environments. Improvements in school buildings and classrooms are being widely made in connection with the great expansion of school facilities necessitated by increasing enrollments, and these changes facilitate quite different ways of teaching from those usually followed in the traditional classroom with its fixed seating and lack of ready arrangements for small group activities. Even more significant are the changing conditions of social life in the

PLATE 43. MODERN SCHOOL FACILITIES BOTH NECESSITATE AND
FACILITATE DIFFERENT TEACHING METHODS. Such a modern school
library offers splendid possibility for individual and group study.
(Courtesy of the Oak Ridge, Tennessee, Public Schools)

community and the world with their inevitable effects on the experiences, past, present, and future, of children and youth.

One of the major criticisms frequently made of education, and especially secondary education, is the lag between educational practices and social conditions. Although this same criticism is made of social institutions in general, we who teach are nevertheless challenged to examine the facts and make such modifications of our practices as we can and should in the light of the evidence. Common observation usually provides evidence enough of the lag. Just compare the facilities of home and community for learning from television, radio, motion pictures, advertising, pictorial magazines, and other media with those of the average school. Or compare the information on social and scientific developments available in current magazines and newspapers with that being presented in many classrooms by textbooks which cannot be up to date and teachers who can be but are not! Or evaluate the abilities of school graduates to carry on the activities essential in the adult life of the community—for example, making a living, purchasing and using goods and services, taking part in civic affairs, managing a home and rearing children. The secondary school alone cannot be expected to educate youth for optimum performance of all these activities by graduation time, but it is reasonable to expect the school to provide a program aiming at development of basic skills and understandings related to each such life activity. Particularly should be expected the development of problem-solving abilities which will equip youth for the rapidly changing conditions and problems of modern life.

In view of the changing environment in which teaching takes place, perhaps it is this last aim which schools make paramount. And here the evidence of lag is all too convincing. Too much of our high school teaching has been in terms of facts and absolutes at the time, which are soon disproven by new social and scientific developments. For example, we recall from our own high school days in the 1920's "learning" that the League of Nations would outlaw international war, Russia was too backward a nation to become a world power, aviation was too dangerous for commercial development, prices were controlled only by the operation of supply and demand, and many other generalizations which have been completely disproved by subsequent developments. We hope that today's high school teachers as well as all of the other educational influences—press, radio, television, movies, and others—are seeking different types of learning. The United Nations for example is another effort, one we hope will succeed, to outlaw international war. Nations rise and fall in their world influence. Jet plane propulsion is another event in the sequence of development of the great aviation industry. Prices and other economic phenomena may be controlled by political and social action, whether we like it or not, as well as by economic principles. There are other open-ended generalizations to leave youth with a speculative and interested attitude toward the future and their responsibility for making future developments of even greater significance in human welfare than those of the past. Since we who teach cannot know all the conditions under which our pupils will live after they leave our classrooms, our most significant teaching is to help them understand the phenomena of present environmental conditions and acquire skills and attitudes which will help them adapt to, even participate in creating, new environmental conditions. This kind of teaching is challenging and hard, but also highly satisfying and rewarding.

How can the teacher possibly teach with full use of present environ-

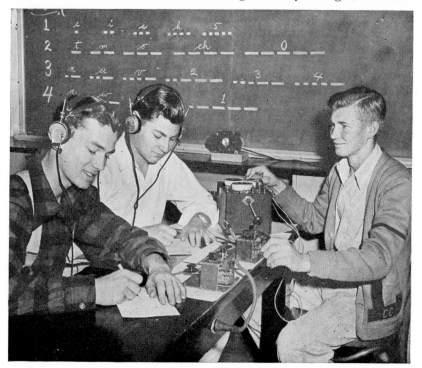

PLATE 44. MODERN COMMUNICATION SYSTEMS PROVIDE AND DEMAND NEW MATERIALS AND TECHNIQUES. Members of a high school class in radio are practicing receiving code. (Courtesy of the Long Beach, California, Public Schools)

mental factors and with some eye to the future environments in which his pupils will live? He can do this only by applying himself through intellectual inquiry to understanding as far as possible the social developments related to his fields of particular interest and the professional developments with respect to informed use of the school and community environment. Reading and keeping up with the news, and participation with his colleagues in organized in-service education and curriculum planning programs, are his best ways of continuing improvement, that is, of continuing, intelligent adaptation of his ways of working to a changing social and physical environment.

NEW TEACHING MATERIALS AND TECHNIQUES

Change also occurs with respect to teaching materials and techniques, and it is in these areas that in-service education, curriculum planning, and experimentation are most frequently concerned. The great body of professional literature and the varied possibilities of in-service education projects developed by school systems and teacher-education institutions leave most secondary teachers little excuse for not keeping up with developments in their teaching fields.

There are two basic approaches to the use of new teaching materials and techniques to improve teaching, both of them commendable and both involving classroom experimentation. One is the search for new materials and techniques developed and used by others, and the other the creation of new materials and techniques by the teacher. This latter approach is frequently termed "classroom research" and is a technique of great significance to teachers. Actually, either approach may be research, since the investigation of the usability of someone else's materials in one's own classroom involves the seeking of evidence to establish conclusions, and this we consider research. The one differ-ence of some importance between the two approaches is the way in which a teacher proceeds to make improvement. If the search is for others' materials or techniques, the investigation is first of all a survey of what is available. If it is new materials the teacher desires, such common sources as catalogues, indexes, curriculum guides, advertise-ments, and exhibits are surveyed. If it is new techniques one wishes, they are located through visiting other teachers, discussions, reading professional journals and research studies.

There is a very wide gap between educational practice and research which might be narrowed greatly by more consistent and widespread efforts of teachers to put into classroom practice the discoveries of better materials and techniques. For example, exact knowledge of the great range of individual differences among children and youth in school has been accumulating for a generation. Paralleling the devel-opment of this knowledge has been a large amount of research on ways of dealing effectively with individual differences in the class-room. We know rather certainly that better teaching practice involves use of varied materials and other resources for learning, organization of learning groups on various bases, working with small groups and individuals as well as the total class, and many other practices which we have described fully in this book. Nevertheless, one may still visit many high school classrooms in which there is observed use of a single textbook and few if any other materials, conduct of the class as a total group for all purposes, and complete reliance on the recita-tion as the method of teaching. Teachers who desire to improve their ways of working with learners need to keep abreast of professional research, general literature, and best practices in order that their classes may have the advantage of the best materials and techniques available to them and found effective in their own classrooms.

Whatever the original approach may be, there is sooner or later introduction of some changed practice in the classroom. Although we conceive of experimentation as being more than simple tryout, that is, as including the collection of evidence, we do recognize the frequent feeling of teachers that they want to "try something different." This feeling is usually the basis of improvement, and what the teacher does about it reflects a critical decision. If the feeling is pushed aside and nothing different happens, the situation is not improved and the teacher frequently becomes unhappier and less effective. If the teacher simply turns to something new because of a chance suggestion or as the only alternative known, without any real thinking through of the underlying problems in the situation, the odds are that there will be little improvement. But if the teacher does analyze more carefully the situation, identify the problem involved, weigh alternative solutions, and then try out something that appears a possible step towards improvement, facts can be collected and conclusions reached which sooner or later improve the situation. This is experimentation of the sort we need on the part of all who teach if continuing improvement of education is to take place.

TEACHER IMPROVEMENT

Improvement of the teacher himself is both a means and an end in the improvement of instruction. That is, we teachers become better persons and teachers through improving our ways of working with learners, the environment, and teaching materials; and these ways of working also improve as a result of our general personal and professional betterment. As the teacher is finding ways and means of securing greater satisfactions in his work, he inevitably is becoming a better-adjusted individual, more adept in his personal relations, more intelligent about his job, more open-minded about educational problems and practices. Sometimes his efforts may be bent directly toward achieving these personal improvements. Thus, in Chapter 2, we suggested some steps the prospective teacher or teacher in service might take to improve in specific personality traits. Whatever steps may be ultimately taken by the teacher toward improvement in his work, we believe it fundamental that he accept fully certain basic principles regarding improvement and apply these throughout his career. The principles we believe most significant are these:

1. Because of the variables in teaching, especially the human vari-

ables, there is not and cannot be some absolute standard of performance which once achieved cannot be improved.

2. Since the interpersonal relations of teacher and pupils are most
critical in determining the quality of the educational process, the
teacher should seek for optimum relations with each successive individual and group taught.

3. The most reliable evidence regarding the nature of interpersonal
relations has to do with the feelings people have for each other, and
the teacher should therefore develop means of appraising the feelings
pupils have for him and those he has towards pupils and of changing
his behavior in directions indicated as desirable as far as he finds it
possible to change.

4. The inevitability of change in education should be understood
and accepted, and teachers therefore should regard their practices at
any given time as simply the ones then used and keep an open and
inquiring outlook for new and better practices.

5. Since improvement is always relative to some appraisal of present
performance in terms of some concept of desirable performance, it is
necessary both to formulate, with frequent review, concepts of desirable performance and to appraise at frequent intervals one's progress
toward such performance.

6. Improvement is a process of learning and one in which the
learner, the teacher, must determine and seek his own goals; that is,
improvement of teaching occurs as teachers improve themselves, and
it cannot be forced by other persons any more than can other teaching
processes.

This last principle, as well as some others, indicates the need for
teacher self-evaluation as a basis for all improvement. In the next section attention is given to self-evaluation as a specific approach to
improvement; but readers should keep in mind that formal use of self-
evaluation instruments, helpful as these may be, is not the only way
teachers size themselves up and enter into improvement efforts. Before
any of the other approaches—securing help from others, engaging in
organized curriculum study, participating in in-service education activities, carrying on classroom experimentation—can result in improvement, the teacher must consciously, however casually or deliberately,
recognize a need for improvement. This recognition involves evaluation of himself. In making improvement, as we have already emphasized, there must also be experimentation. Hence we should conclude
that some type of self-evaluation and of experimentation are always
present in improvement efforts.

IMPROVEMENT THROUGH SELF-EVALUATION

In addition to the informal self-evaluation all of us constantly use as we wonder how well we are doing, there are at least three more definite patterns frequently used in connection with the improvement of teaching. These patterns are described briefly in the following paragraphs.

USE OF EVALUATION INSTRUMENTS PREPARED BY OTHERS

Teacher-rating scales, self-evaluation check lists, and other instruments for evaluating teaching and teachers have been prepared in great variety and number. Although the use of rating scales by administrators for the purpose of deciding whether to retain, place on tenure, or advance teachers has declined, there are still available a number of rating forms, which may be used by a person other than the teacher concerned, and scores determined for teacher performance. Such scales are sometimes used by both the teacher and another person and the two confer on their respective ratings. As an example of such a relatively simple form—one that has been widely used in connection with evaluations of secondary schools, especially for accrediting purposes—Figure 19 reproduces the check list on "Professional Qualifications" from the *Evaluative Criteria* of the Cooperative Study of Secondary-School Standards. In schools which engage in evaluations using these *Evaluative Criteria,* individual teachers may check themselves on this page and then the visiting committee member(s) may check the same page.

Probably the most extensive use of rating scales at present is that of the teacher's own voluntary application, since there has been rather widespread criticism of external rating of teachers through use of these scales. In some schools copies of published rating scales are made available to teachers for such use as they may desire. In others, rating scales or other types of evaluation check lists are prepared by individual administrators or committees, and copies given teachers with the suggestion that they use them to evaluate their own performance.

In general, there is limited value in the use, even for self-evaluation, of rating scales and check lists which have been developed without participation by those who evaluate themselves. Teachers who attempt to use such forms frequently are uncertain as to their meaning. Also, frequently a teacher may not agree in philosophy with the makers of the form, and his application of the form to his own practices merely convinces him that it does not apply or that those who devel-

PROFESSIONAL QUALIFICATIONS

The following checklist and evaluation items are applicable only to members of the instructional staff. All of these items should be checked and evaluated by the individual teacher and reviewed by the administrative head of the school.

CHECKLIST

This teacher as a professional worker

( ) 1. Shows evidence of understanding the contribution of his area of teaching to the educational needs of pupils.

( ) 2. Shows a willingness to cooperate with other teachers in meeting the educational needs of pupils.

( ) 3. Shows evidence of planning carefully for instructional activities.

( ) 4. Willingly changes plans and procedures in instructional activities when conditions suggest such changes (e.g., different philosophy of classification of pupils, community needs or activities, out-of-school activities of pupils).

( ) 5. Provides flexibility in adapting instructional activities to new or changing conditions which develop within the classroom.

( ) 6. Provides opportunities for pupils to participate in *planning* instructional activities.

( ) 7. Provides opportunities for pupils to participate in *conducting* instructional activities.

( ) 8. Provides opportunities for pupils to participate in *evaluating* the results of instructional activities.

( ) 9. Gives evidence of increasing interest and skill in studying growth and development of individual pupils.

( ) 10. Adapts instruction to the needs of individual pupils.

( ) 11. Makes effective use of supplementary aids (e.g., audio-visual aids).

( ) 12. Makes effective use of community resources (e.g., industries, museums, parks, school grounds, local history, members of community).

( ) 13. Provides opportunities for pupils to participate in both individual and group activities.

( ) 14. Conducts procedures in assignments, examinations, and evaluations of pupil achievement in such a manner as to encourage individual integrity on the part of pupils.

( ) 15. Keeps accurate records of pupil achievement.

( ) 16. Participates in the in-service training program of the staff.

( ) 17. Assists in establishing cooperative relationships with parents and other members of the community.

( ) 18.

( ) 19.

EVALUATIONS

( ) *a. How effectively are plans and preparations made for instructional activities?*

( ) *b. To what extent are instructional activities conducted democratically?*

( ) *c. How skillfully are instructional activities carried out?*

( ) *d. How satisfactory are relationships with school associates?*

( ) *e. How satisfactory are relationships with members of the community?*

( ) *f. How satisfactory is the attitude toward teaching as a profession?*

COMMENTS

FIG. 19. FORM FOR EVALUATING PROFESSIONAL QUALIFICATIONS. (Courtesy of the Cooperative Study of Secondary School Standards, *Evaluative Criteria,* 1950 ed., p. 282)

oped it did not understand good teaching—and examination of some forms would indicate he might be right! The greatest weakness in the use of such a form lies in the fact that it gives the teacher no guidance in understanding the philosophy and practices of good teaching on which the form is based. As stated by a national committee on teacher rating in the following analysis of the use of rating forms prepared by others, this weakness may be overcome by in-service education:

These self-evaluation forms do not describe or characterize desirable practice; hence they do little to help the teacher gain a better understanding of what constitutes good teaching. While the teacher is asked to rate or evaluate himself on a number of characteristics, he is not given guidance as to what constitutes best practice. His own concept of good teaching would be the basis for self-evaluation. Of course, such plans are usually one aspect of a more complete program of in-service education, so that the teacher gains a better understanding of good teaching from his participation in other phases of the program. If this is true, then the evaluation form would simply be a method of directing the teacher's attention to desirable elements in teaching which have already been considered and described in other ways. Unless the self-evaluation forms examined by the committee are used in conjunction with a well-rounded in-service growth program, they would be of little value in stimulating teachers to do a better job with boys and girls.[1]

Teachers who are given and asked to use evaluation forms prepared by others should seek as much information as possible about the philosophy on which these forms are based. Perhaps questions to this end may lead to decisions to study the whole problem further and even to develop self-evaluation guides which will be more meaningful to those concerned.

Despite the weaknesses mentioned and even if there is no in-service education or development of local guides, there may still be some values in the use of forms prepared by others. These forms may suggest ways in which the individual teacher may develop his own self-evaluation check list, or they may indicate criteria which have not occurred to the teacher and which he wishes to investigate, or they may be sufficiently intelligible and appropriate to the teacher's own philosophy as to suggest points on which improvement is needed. At worst, they can call to teachers' attention the need for self-evaluation and stimulate their own evaluative processes, even though the forms

[1] Association for Supervision and Curriculum Development, National Education Association, *Better Than Rating* (Washington, D.C.: The Association, 1950), p. 51.

may offer no direct help and in fact be thoroughly objectionable. Hence, in the absence of any other plan for self-evaluation, teachers might do well to secure some forms prepared by others and look them over as one basis of considering the whole idea of self-improvement.

GROUP DISCUSSION AS A BASIS FOR SELF-EVALUATION

A procedure that does not have the weaknesses of evaluation forms prepared by others is that of development of self-evaluation guides through processes of group discussion by the teachers who are to use them. Thus an entire faculty, a departmental group, a group of beginning or probationary teachers, or any other group of teachers may work through the development of a statement which represents their composite thinking about the characteristics of good teaching, or good teachers. This statement then is available to each for his own self-evaluation. The leader of a group working on such a statement may find it profitable to use such an initial discussion guide as that shown in Table 13.

Several advantages may accrue from this process of self-evaluation. First of all, the discussion itself may serve to iron out disagreements in practice and point of view, to help teachers' thinking about the need for improvement, and to suggest ideas and techniques that will help in improvement. Second, the final statement has meaning to the participants, and their subsequent (or immediate) application of the criteria to their own teaching should therefore reveal strengths and weaknesses much more clearly than some form which uses terms and ideas they do not understand or accept. Third, self-evaluation is usually occurring as the statement is developed, and steps toward improvement may not have to wait on the teacher's finding time to work through the entire evaluation form. Because of these advantages, faculty groups concerned with improvement of teaching may advisedly undertake periodic study of criteria for self-evaluation of teaching. It is important that any such study be regarded as a beginning point in improvement, and that statements prepared at any one time be reviewed from time to time thereafter; such review makes it possible to note criteria that are found poor or not applicable, to incorporate new ideas, and to allow teachers who have joined the faculty since the statement was developed a chance to understand and criticize it. Such reviews, frequently amounting to new studies, have all the potential advantages of the initial study if those who prepared the original statement are willing to have it criticized and rewritten.

Table 13

Essentials of Good Teaching

A discussion guide

This discussion guide was developed to describe a *process* of good teaching. It is expected that this outline will be used as a starting point in faculty, departmental, grade level, or committee groups wishing to develop their own ideas of the essentials of good teaching.

	COMMENTS
ESSENTIALS	(*Is each item an essential of good teaching?*)

I. FORMULATING COOPERATIVELY WORTH-WHILE GOALS AND PLANS

1. Making flexible, suitable plans for and with each individual, each small group, and the total group . . . .
2. Selecting a variety of resources that will serve the curriculum goals . . . .
3. Providing adequate opportunity for pupil-teacher planning . . . .
4. Getting pupil understanding of reasons for and nature of cooperative planning . . . .
5. Encouraging each individual to assume his share of responsibility for planning . . . .
6. Selecting cooperatively, where possible, long-term and intermediate goals . . . .
7. Choosing goals appropriate to accepted school purposes . . . .
8. Agreeing on rules and limits for the group . ...

II. CREATING A GOOD LEARNING ENVIRONMENT

1. Developing pupil responsibility for keeping a functional, attractive classroom . . . .
2. Encouraging informal, friendly working conditions conducive to learning . . . .
3. Having adequate materials available for each learning experience . . . .
4. Arranging materials to secure full use . . ..
5. Using all space to maximum advantage . . ..
6. Arranging furniture in so far as possible to meet the needs of small groups and of the total group . . . .
7. Handling ventilation and lighting for comfort of pupils . . . .

| | COMMENTS |
| ESSENTIALS | (*Is each item an essential of good teaching?*) |

8. Minimizing disruptive effects of distractions from the outside . . . .

III. STIMULATING CREATIVE ACTIVITY ON THE PART OF THE INDIVIDUAL LEARNER
1. Encouraging each individual to develop his own ideas . . . .
2. Stimulating the use of a variety of media and techniques for self-expression . . . .
3. Demonstrating and encouraging an experimental attitude . . . .
4. Promoting recognition of creative effort . . ..

IV. EVALUATING PROGRESS CONTINUOUSLY
1. Making evaluation a part of, rather than separate from, the learning process . . . .
2. Developing and using devices and techniques for self-evaluation by teacher and pupils and for group evaluation . . . .
3. Using test results and other evaluative measures to help teacher and pupils learn more about their abilities, their needs, and their progress . . . .
4. Guiding the group in summarizing, recording, and analyzing progress toward its chosen goals and in restating goals accordingly . . . .

V. GUIDING LEARNERS INDIVIDUALLY AND IN GROUPS IN THEIR LEARNING EXPERIENCE
1. Making each experience meaningful through such means as using problem-solving devices, finding information and using it, choosing from a wide variety of materials—maps, charts, slides, periodicals, films, community resources, field trips . . . .
2. Organizing activities around a significant theme, objective, or problem . . . .
3. Carrying on challenging and creative activities for each learner . . . .
4. Providing activities for the development of self-direction and personal responsibility . . ..
5. Making oneself available to pupils and parents for conferences and help . . . .

ESSENTIALS	COMMENTS (*Is each item an essential of good teaching?*)
6. Utilizing group study and research periods as time for planning and individual conferences	....
7. Organizing different types of work areas within the classroom	....
8. Encouraging an awareness of need for, and acceptance of, group standards	....

Source: Prepared in 1954 by the following graduate students at the University of Miami: Del Barrett, Eloise Bates, Herbert Blinn, W. H. Charlton, Blanche Cox, Helen Gwaltney, Philip Paul Hurst, Irving Nissman, Irving Tannenbaum.

DEVELOPING ONE'S OWN SELF-EVALUATION GUIDE

The self-evaluation guide which has most meaning to the individual teacher is the one he prepares himself. That is, the criteria he most willingly and successfully applies to his own teaching are those which represent his personal philosophy of teaching. As we see it, the major usefulness to the teacher of statements of criteria or self-evaluation forms prepared by others lies in the help they may give him in formulating his own beliefs. When an individual asks himself evaluative questions in the privacy of his own reflections, he depends on questions he considers important.

In view of this influence of one's point of view, we believe that teachers should try to verbalize their own beliefs about what is good teaching, and that they should check their beliefs against those of other people and, especially, about what research and best practice indicate to be good teaching. For example, we have tried to present in this book a consistent point of view regarding good teaching practices—practices we consider sound in terms of accepted educational theory and research. Although we do not expect our readers to agree with all the ideas we have presented, we would hope that many of them will evaluate their own beliefs about good teaching in terms of the ideas here. Where there is conflict in these ideas, we further hope the reader will examine the bases of our own beliefs, and if these seem irrefutable, modify his own ideas so as to make them consistent with those we have presented. From such a process should come some rather definite group of concepts the reader could then apply to his own teaching. Whether this is done through a written list of questions, or a list plus a scale to indicate the degree of performance, or simply by reflection is a matter for the individual to settle. The important idea is for teachers to recognize the necessity of evaluating their own teaching performance in the light of accepted concepts of what constitutes good teaching. Unless the teacher does accept the necessity for looking critically at himself and working on the problems revealed thereby, we know that he will not make real improvement. Once a teacher accepts self-evaluation as an important part of his work, we are confident that he will find satisfactory bases and techniques for making the evaluation, and equally confident that he will try to make needed improvements in his teaching performance.

IMPROVEMENT THROUGH HELP FROM OTHERS

The teacher's greatest source of help in improving his work is in the contributions of other people. Some of these contributions come to the teacher vicariously through publications and other means, some come through group improvement efforts such as organized curriculum planning and in-service education, and still others come through direct, individual-to-individual contacts. In this section we are dealing with the helpful contacts which any teacher can have practically for the asking.

HELP FROM OTHER TEACHERS

Beginning teachers especially rely on the help of other teachers. The obvious need of the beginner for frequent information and advice leads many principals to set up plans whereby each new teacher is given one experienced teacher to serve as a "big brother" or "big sister." Such plans, and even the more informal questioning of the experienced teacher next door, are quite helpful in the orientation of the beginner, but do not necessarily assist in the teacher's improvement. Effective use of one's colleagues to solve one's own teaching problems involves the kind of atmosphere and arrangements in which requests for advice do not imply a weakness on the part of the questioner and in which the questioner feels perfectly free to follow or not to follow the advice. Some characteristics of this kind of situation which teachers may help to create in their schools are given here:

1. Teachers frequently invite other teachers to their classes to see some piece of work in progress, either to give recognition to the pupils, or to help the guest teachers evaluate what is being accomplished, or to diagnose some situation that seems to need change.

2. Beginning teachers (particularly in larger schools where several beginners are employed) are given special conference periods to

which they may invite experienced teachers of their own choice to discuss questions asked by the beginners.

3. Occasional meetings of an informal nature are arranged of all the teachers having a particular planning period, to promote acquaintance and to discuss work under way in each classroom as a basis for later conversations between teachers doing related work or having related problems.

4. Pupils and their parents are discouraged from making adverse criticisms to their teachers of other teachers, and are encouraged to express these criticisms to the teachers concerned.

5. Teachers refrain from making adverse criticisms of other teachers except to the teachers concerned, and are encouraged by each other to pass along constructive suggestions.

6. Administrators and supervisors refrain from seeking information about teachers from third parties, and treat as confidential those matters which are told them in confidence.

7. Administrators and supervisors seek to bring together teachers who can help each other by referring one teacher to another or by creating informal situations where topics of mutual interest can be discussed.

8. Teachers who seek advice from other teachers state their questions honestly and fully, usually prefaced by some such question as "Have you ever had a problem like this?"

9. Teachers who give advice to others describe their experience in equally honest terms such as, "Yes, I did have that problem and I found something that helped me but it might not help you."

10. In all discussions of teaching problems, teachers avoid guilt accusations, "I told you so's," and other attitudes that tend to discourage sharing of problems, confidences, and experiences.

11. In all teacher relationships each individual shows respect for the personality of the other, avoiding "better than thou" attitudes and expressions.

12. Experienced teachers avoid attitudes of condescension and statements which indicate that inexperienced teachers are always (or ever) ignorant, ineffective, or untrained.

We realize that there may be few school situations in which all of the foregoing characteristics are uniformly present. We believe, however, that such seemingly utopian situations can be created by wise leadership, and especially by the efforts of teachers to practice good human relationships and professional ethics. As more and more beginning teachers practice these principles they will influence experienced teachers who may not have seen such principles at work before. As teachers not accustomed to working in these ways see others doing so, and as they realize these are more accepted and approved ways than those of selfishness, intolerance, condescension, skepticism, and ill will, a utopia in teacher relations may be approached.

HELP FROM SUPERVISORS

In the twentieth century our whole concept of supervision has changed from one of inspection and rating to one of help and improvement. Most persons now employed as school supervisors, including principals who give time to supervision, and persons entitled department heads, consultants, coordinators, and directors, think of their job primarily as that of giving help to teachers in improving instruction. Unfortunately, the concept of inspection or "snoopervision" still holds on in the minds of some teachers and supervisors, and sometimes supervisors who intend to help find that teachers expect to be rated or ordered rather than helped. Occasionally it may also be true that teachers who expect to be helped find themselves rated instead. We believe that every teacher is entitled to know by whom he is rated, if at all, and by whom he may be helped. If rating and helping are done by the same supervisor, then the teacher is also entitled to know what, if any effect, his asking for help has on his ratings—in fact, on just what bases he is rated.

The great majority of high school teachers usually have at least one supervisory person to whom they can go for help without fear of being rated low because they express a problem. In smaller schools the principal is usually the only source of supervisory help, but he is frequently a source of very great help. In addition, even in smaller schools there may be some supervisor for the county or district who is available for help on various sorts of problems. In the larger high schools, in addition to the principal and one or more system-wide supervisors, department heads are frequently given time for conferencing with teachers on their instructional problems.

Our chief suggestion to the beginning teacher is that he find out as exactly as possible just what supervisory help is available to him—both the persons and the kind of help they can give Frequently school systems provide orientation programs for new teachers in which all persons who have supervisory responsibilities are fully identified. If this is not the case, the beginning teacher should inquire of his administrative head—department head or principal—as to the availability of supervisory services. Once the services are identified, then the more rapidly they are called upon for help, the more effective their use by the beginning teacher. Our experience indicates that beginners are frequently loath to call on supervisors, due perhaps to the hold-over concept of "snoopervision" we mentioned and also perhaps to some unfortunate experience with the college supervisor of student teaching. When this reluctance exists, it behooves the supervisors to promote their services, possibly to the extent of systematic classroom visits and conferences with beginning teachers to dispel fears and prejudice.

Experienced as well as inexperienced teachers can make profitable use of supervisory services in improving instruction. Unfortunately, in some situations the current supervisors may have different concepts of supervision than their predecessors, but some of the same teachers who worked when inspection was the concept are still teaching and the concept has not changed in their minds. Again, the supervisor must promote his services with these teachers. Teachers should expect clear-cut statements of purpose by supervisors who visit their classrooms, and who arrange for conferences and other opportunities for securing help. Once the purposes are understood, and rapport is established between teacher and supervisor, we believe that understandings can be reached which make possible effective help to the teacher.

Teachers secure help much more readily from supervisors when clear explanations are given of the duties and ways of working of the latter. We would suggest to our readers that they ask for such explanations in their schools if there is not clear understanding. Once supervisory services have been explained, it still is to be observed whether the individuals involved behave as explained. In the event that promised help is not forthcoming or if supervisors' actions are inconsistent with announced policies, teachers will do well to examine their own relations with the supervisors. Perhaps they have failed to ask for help, or maybe they have been "standoffish," or maybe there is just needed closer acquaintance. It must be remembered that the teacher has to be as sincere and active in seeking help as the supervisor in giving it, for this seeking of help is learning, too, and the teacher learns only as he really wants and tries to learn. That is, the supervisor can offer help, but he cannot make the teacher use the help he offers even if it is the best available help the teacher could possibly secure. We realize fully that there are ineffective supervisors, just as there are ineffective teachers, but we believe that the foregoing suggestions will result in the identification and eventual improvement of such supervisors, or in their elimination if they cannot be improved. Our emphasis here, and we believe it a very important one, is on the teacher's responsibility for understanding and using supervisory help. To this end we offer further the following specific suggestions:

1. Ask your supervisor to give you the help he can reasonably be expected to give, such as the names of people to see, materials to examine, techniques to try, rather than to solve problems with which he is necessarily unacquainted, such as the behavior of individual learners he does not know.

2. Expect your supervisor to suggest ways in which you can solve your own problem, rather than solutions which are ready-made.

3. State your reason for seeking improvement and help clearly, indicating your dissatisfactions and difficulties in enough detail so that the supervisor is able to understand the problem.

4. Invite the supervisor to visit your classroom and help you analyze a problem whenever the problem is one that can be seen by classroom observation.

5. Be sure you understand clearly the supervisor's suggestions, and arrange for subsequent conferences if further explanations seem or become necessary.

6. Express freely your disagreements or misgivings regarding suggestions made by the supervisor, and seek alternative suggestions from him when those made first seem unacceptable.

HELP FROM OTHER SCHOOL PERSONNEL

In addition to the help teachers receive from each other and from supervisory personnel, a variety of other resource persons is usually available on the school staff. The *librarian* is ordinarily an invaluable asset to the teacher seeking improvement through better use of materials. The *person in charge of audiovisual aids* can be equally valuable. The *guidance personnel* serve many helpful functions with respect to the study and handling of problems of boys and girls. *Building maintenance personnel* can be of real assistance in better room arrangement. The *school secretary* may provide important aid in preparing materials, arranging for field trips, contacting resource persons, and undertaking many other tasks in the improvement of instruction.

In general, there are as many special sources of help as there are school personnel assigned special functions. The teacher's first responsibility in using these persons as aids in improving instruction is to know their identity and functions. Hence an important part of the orientation program for teachers is that of clear identification of the special services available to help pupils and teachers. Once identified, the services should be used as frequently as desirable and as early as possible in order that the teacher may become experienced in their correct use. Most of the suggestions made in the preceding sections apply to the use of these special personnel. To summarize these suggestions, the steps for wise use of other people as helpers in improving instruction are these: (1) know what helps are available; (2) request the help clearly and directly with respect to appropriate problems; (3) use the suggestions (materials, people, services, techniques) experimentally, that is, to see whether they work, rather than automatically; and (4) continue to seek and use other persons as helpers in the same way as new needs develop.

We should not leave this discussion of the utility of people in improving instruction without pointing out the importance of pupils as helpers. Our point of view is that effective teaching uses boys and girls continuously to seek improvement, for we have emphasized throughout this book the importance of cooperative planning and evaluation of learning experiences. When learners are involved in making plans, they, too, are responsible for the success of these plans. The greatest help pupils can give is their active participation in the classroom program, and teachers can secure this participation by the many means we have described. From time to time there may be dissatisfactions on the part of the teacher which he may advisedly express to pupils, and evaluation and planning sessions at such times may be significant steps in improvement projects. Thus in classes operating on these cooperative bases, the members are continually helping themselves and each other to have better experiences rather than having to jump in during emergencies to help out the teacher.

IMPROVEMENT THROUGH CURRICULUM PLANNING

We have discussed the teacher's role in curriculum planning in Chapter 14. Here we merely wish to emphasize the point that participation in curriculum planning is an approach to improvement and to note in summary fashion the various opportunities for the teacher to participate.

If curriculum planning is conceived of as a process only of outlining the content of subjects and writing syllabi or courses of study, the help teachers receive from participation in such a process is very limited. We conceive of the process as the much broader one of planning the entire instructional program, that is, the curriculum of the school. All teachers participate in this process at least to the extent that they plan the experiences of their own classes, for plans of particular classes are parts of the total curriculum plan. We believe, however, that teachers will become better teachers by participating in curriculum planning on a broader basis, too. As they sit with curriculum councils (Fig. 20) and hear evaluations of the school program, or with faculty planning groups and participate in discussions of school-wide aims and programs, or with departmental groups and plan specific resource units, they are broadening their experience and acquiring greater personal resources for improving their instruction.

A detailed organization of the individual school for curriculum planning is depicted in Figure 20 and explained in another publication[2] in which one of the present authors collaborated. Teacher participation in such group planning is the most effective way we know for teachers to increase their understanding of the school program and thereby become more effective leaders in the program. Specifically, organized curriculum planning may result in such increased understandings to assist teacher improvement as the following:

1. Parent and pupil reactions to the school program as expressed in lay and student councils
2. Effective ways (or ineffective ways) of working demonstrated in the various types of curriculum planning groups
3. Purposes to be served by the school as determined through councils and accepted by the faculty planning group
4. The total program of the school and the relation or lack thereof of its various parts
5. The work of the different departments and individuals in the school as reflected in the faculty planning group
6. School policies as determined in the faculty planning group
7. Services available to the teacher from committees and individuals in the school, as organized by curriculum planning groups
8. Curriculum plans for the department concerned, including resource units with their wealth of suggestions
9. Plans for curriculum evaluation developed in curriculum planning groups
10. Plans for experimentation developed in the various planning groups

Teachers whose school systems have well-developed plans for curriculum study and improvement are likely to find continuing improvement of instruction relatively easy. It is also likely that in these systems a larger proportion of teachers will be actively participating in improvement efforts, and more actual improvement will be occurring

[2] See J. Galen Saylor and William M. Alexander, *Curriculum Planning* (New York: Rinehart & Company, Inc., 1954), pp. 546–555.

STEP 1 – PLANNING CURRICULUM PURPOSES AND POLICIES

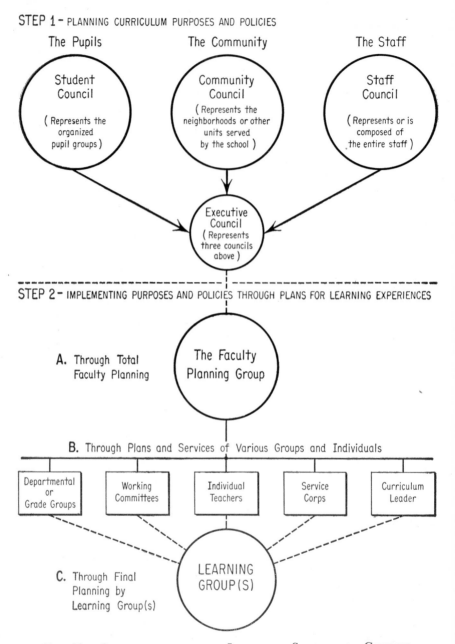

FIG. 20. ORGANIZATION OF THE INDIVIDUAL SCHOOL FOR CURRICULUM PLANNING

than in those systems in which curriculum planning is casual or non-existent above the classroom level.

IMPROVEMENT THROUGH IN-SERVICE EDUCATION

Although all the improvement efforts we have described thus far in this chapter may be considered as education of teachers in service, we would like in this section to describe certain specific ways of teacher improvement on the job, which are more usually classified as in-service education. Such in-service education activities which are widely available to high school teachers include professional reading, university courses, professional meetings, conferences and study groups, and workshops.

PROFESSIONAL READING

Professional reading, like reading for learning of any sort, is best done in connection with specific purposes. Teachers seeking to get ideas or descriptions or research or materials bearing on particular problems need to know the usual sources for identifying pertinent writings and to have access to these sources and the writings. Their professional training should have resulted in such skills as use of the *Education Index* to locate periodical literature, of the *Review of Educational Research* and the *Encyclopedia of Educational Research* to locate research studies, and of the card catalogue and other sources to find books. They should also be accustomed to using bibliographies appearing in recent books or other publications to identify related additional materials. If they have these skills and there are library facilities available, location of pertinent materials is relatively simple. If they do not have the skills but do have library facilities, the librarians will help. If they lack library facilities, the problem may be more difficult. Most communities in which there are no school or other libraries housing professional materials for teachers have some sort of extension library service, which the teacher may learn about and use. If no library service is available, the teacher can subscribe to as many periodicals as possible, buy some pertinent books, and perhaps use summer periods for university study or free days for trips to near-by libraries.

Regardless of the library facilities available, the teacher will do well to make thorough use of at least three periodicals secured through professional memberships: (1) the state education journal, (2) the *Journal* of the National Education Association, and (3) the journal(s) of the respective subject field (Appendix II). In addition to the general professional articles and news notes, these journals usually offer such help as announcement of new publications, lists of pamphlets and visual aids, and specific articles which may relate to the teacher's problems or suggest problems which should be attacked.

There is a very considerable body of educational literature, ever growing and improving, which should not be neglected by teachers in their efforts to improve teaching. Sometimes the very bulk of the literature may discourage teachers from its use, and this is why we urge the thorough use of at least three periodicals, in part as guides to the selection of other pertinent material. Most of the problems which concern teachers have also concerned other teachers, and usually there is an article or book, maybe many, which contain some solutions others have found. Hence professional materials should be regarded and consulted as resources of high priority in efforts to improve teaching. Larger school systems in recognition of this fact usually maintain some type of professional library. Individual schools frequently maintain a professional section in the school library or a separate professional collection or shelf. If no such arrangements exist, teachers can make their own collection by sharing their personal copies of professional magazines and books. The prospective teacher may confidently expect therefore some opportunity for professional reading once on the job, and devote some time in his training program to acquainting himself with the sources of helpful materials and the use of library tools that will be particularly helpful in his teaching field and in teaching in general. In this connection we hope that readers of this book make frequent use of the bibliographies ("For Further Study") at the end of our chapters, both in connection with courses using this book as a text and as a source of suggestions for further reading on problems encountered on the job.

PROFESSIONAL MEETINGS, CONFERENCES, AND STUDY PROGRAMS

Most teacher organizations provide worth-while in-service education opportunities through their programs for members. In addition to the annual meetings of national and state organizations with their array of speakers, exhibits, and discussion sessions, there are the various local organizations with more frequent meetings attended by considerably higher proportions of their membership than is true of the national and some of the state organizations. In recent years there has been a decided trend toward program planning in professional associations which emphasizes small group meetings around specific problems, clinics, demonstrations, and other types of meetings designed to give specific aid to teachers in their quest for improving teaching.

PLATE 45. EXHIBITS OF TEACHING MATERIALS ARE HELPFUL. Such collections of teacher-prepared, pupil-prepared, and commercial materials deserve careful study by teachers. (Courtesy of the, Philadelphia, Pennsylvania, Public Schools)

State and local classroom teachers' associations have also rendered fine help to their members through organizing conferences in which teachers can frequently get many ideas as to techniques and materials to be tried out in their own classroom situations.

School systems, sometimes in cooperation with teachers' associations, are also developing many types of professional meetings to provide specific help on instructional problems. One-day institutes on general or specific teaching problems, clinics on problems of pupils, demonstrations with learners, exhibits of teacher-prepared or pupil-prepared materials, joint parent-teacher meetings, pre-school and post-school conferences of several days, orientation meetings, social gatherings, and recreational events are examples of the kinds of programs teachers may find organized and supported by school systems. Also, many schools and teacher organizations arrange various kinds of continuing study programs. Some of these programs organized by schools are designed to give help on system-wide or school-wide problems such as reporting to parents, using local resources, and guidance of pupils. Others may be organized around problems suggested by teachers, with the school administration assuming responsibility for employing consultative leadership to help participants in the study programs. Similarly, local professional associations may organize voluntary study groups whose members are interested in working together for a number of sessions on common problems. Sometimes study programs are undertaken in cooperation with the parent-teacher association or other group. However organized, any of these meetings, conferences, and study groups may be helpful to teachers in improving their work provided the following conditions prevail:

1. The teachers who participate in the meetings have opportunity to suggest problems and programs and to participate as frequently and actively as possible in advance planning.

2. Participation is on a voluntary basis, particularly when meetings are held on an after-hours schedule.

3. Meetings are held in places and at times that are convenient to the participants.

4. There are varied types of programs, including plenty of opportunity for getting acquainted and for discussion.

5. Recommendations for action are welcomed by the school administration, and there is frequent demonstration of the use of recommendations presented.

6. The resources—people and materials—available for these sessions are adequate.

7. The leaders create a permissive atmosphere, and participants use the opportunity to share their problems, feelings, contributions, and experimentation.

It should be noted that these criteria in general apply as well to a school faculty meeting as to some less usual kind of professional meeting. Faculty meetings can be organized and conducted in such a way as to be of very significant help to faculty members. In these meetings as well as the others we have described, the cooperation of teachers in preparing agenda or programs, participation in discussion, and in doing all the jobs incidental to well-planned and organized meetings is essential. In short, teachers can do much to make their meetings helpful and successful, just as learners in the classroom can make their learning experiences worth while. In both types of learning situations the designated leader does have to invite participation sincerely and enthusiastically, and the group members have to respond equally sincerely and enthusiastically if there is genuine learning.

A wide variety of courses for teachers is available in the teacher-education institutions of the United States. Many teachers can take advantage of these courses in their own or near-by communities at local institutions or by extension arrangements, throughout the school year. In many communities special courses are offered to give individual teachers and even entire faculties help on specific problems. Other teachers can take university work only in the summer since they must travel to more distant centers. Unfortunately, degree and certification requirements frequently prescribe the courses that must be taken, and these courses do not necessarily deal with the teaching problems which concern the enrollees. In many cases, however, teachers have considerable freedom in their choice of courses. Also, some college and university instructors organize their courses by some of the same cooperative planning procedures we have recommended for use by high school teachers, so that enrollees in courses taught by these instructors may get help regardless of any apparent unrelatedness of course titles to teachers' problems.

Our experiences in teaching teachers, both in courses specially organized for in-service education and in courses required for graduate degrees in education, indicate that teachers can do much to make their courses helpful. Although the university instructor must make possible the participation of teachers in planning these courses, he can be helped to see the need for such cooperation. Once he has made participation possible, the enrollees must assume some responsibility for the success of the course. Specifically, teachers enrolled in college and university courses may help to make these courses suit their needs through such actions as the following:

1. Solicit opportunities to participate in planning some of the agenda and activities of the course by asking at appropriate times whether particular problems could be considered or particular activities could be undertaken.

2. If opportunities to participate in planning are given, take full advantage of them by suggesting sincerely and clearly the questions on which help is desired.

3. Be as anxious to contribute as to receive experiences and ideas.

4. Bring to class meetings specific materials, cases, statements, and so forth, which help the individual who brings them to stick to the facts of a problem and to explain these facts clearly to other individuals.

5. Use requirements of term papers, projects, and the like, if there

are such requirements, as opportunities to work on specific problems or classroom experiments.

6. Use the resources provided or recommended by the instructor as fully as possible, and when these resources seem inadequate ask him to suggest others.

7. When evaluations are made of the course, give honest and careful criticisms and suggestions.

8. Whenever possible, select a course on the basis of advice from the instructor or others in position to give such advice as to its proba-ble relevance to your interests and problems.

9. If other persons from your school are also taking courses and you have common problems, enroll in the same course for the advantage of working together in the course and in the school.

10. Seek personal conferences with the instructor to get his help on problems and also to give the help in evaluating and planning the course he frequently seeks in individual conferences.

WORKSHOPS

The workshop, first introduced by the Progressive Education Asso-ciation at Ohio State University in 1936, has become a very popular and common arrangement for various types of educational study and planning. Workshops are now conducted under the auspices of pro-fessional organizations, teacher-education institutions, and school sys-tems, and frequently under the joint auspices of two or more such agencies. The most common type of workshop and probably the type most valuable for and pertinent to in-service education for improving instruction is that organized and supported by a school system for its personnel. Frequently held in cooperation with a local or near-by teacher-education institution, and thereby offering university credit, such workshops are usually held in public school facilities, operate on a regular school day schedule (for example, 8:30 A.M. to 3 P.M.), and may extend from one to six weeks. Characteristic features of the workshop programs of this type include the following:

1. Workshop participants usually identify in advance some of the instructional problems to be considered in the workshop, and resources —consultants, materials, and others—are selected in terms of these problems.

2. A variety of activities is planned to provide both a breadth of learning experiences and full opportunity for intensive work on the problems selected.

3. The workshop organization provides for considerable activities in small groups organized around unifying factors, such as mutual

problems, common interests, jobs to be done, or teaching fields, or some combination of these factors, so as to facilitate discussion, planning, and problem-solving activities.

4. Emphasis is placed on the problems, policies, and resources of the school system through such means as presentation and study, and sometimes preparation and revision, of school bulletins and curriculum guides; use of local personnel as discussion leaders and resource people; field trips to community resources; preview of locally available audiovisual aids; and joint meetings with parents and pupils.

5. The organization and schedule of the workshop is maintained on as flexible basis as possible so that provision may be made for meetings and other activities which were not anticipated and are found to be desired by participants.

6. Usually a planning, steering, or scheduling committee of participants works with the director throughout the workshop to plan and evaluate daily, and to develop plans for total workshop evaluation and recommendations for future workshops and for the school system.

7. Workshop participants are encouraged to criticize policies and procedures of the school system, and to make recommendations through their group reports or group representatives for improvements.

Some of these characteristics are revealed in Table 14, showing the schedule of a workshop held in 1954 for about 450 elementary and secondary teachers of the Dade County Schools, Miami, Florida.

In this particular workshop, the working groups were organized on an alphabetical basis so that teachers of various departments might work together on common instructional problems. Opportunities were also provided for meetings by departments during the first week of the workshop, which was also the post-school conference for all school personnel, when all secondary school teachers in Dade County spent one period per day in departmental meetings planned in advance by departmental committees.

In general, we believe this type of workshop program to be as promising for improvement of teaching as any in-service education opportunity available in American school systems. Its advantages probably lie in the relatively relaxed opportunity for extended and intensive study and discussion, the homogeneity of the people and problems, and the active participation in planning of those concerned. Teachers who are new to school systems are particularly fortunate if they can participate in such a workshop just before beginning the school year and thus secure an acquaintance and orientation which would come much more slowly with the routine of their jobs.

TABLE 14

DAILY SCHEDULE FOR THE 1954 DADE COUNTY CONTINUING WORKSHOP
CORAL GABLES HIGH SCHOOL

June 21–July 2, 1954

ACTIVITY	SECTION A *Elementary* (*Groups 1–5*)	SECTION B *Elementary* (*Groups 6–10*)	SECTION C *Secondary* (*Groups 16, 17*)
ASSEMBLY (Singing, devotionals, highlight talks—auditorium)	8:30–9:00	8:30–9:00	8:30–9:00
FIRST GROUP MEETING (In own classroom) *	9:00–10:30	10:30–11:45	9:00–10:30
LABORATORY (Various centers for demonstration work)	10:30–11:30	12:45–1:45	1:00–2:00
LUNCH (Cafeteria)	11:30–12:30	11:45–12:45	12:00–1:00
WORK PERIOD (Library, etc.)	12:30–2:00	9:00–10:30	10:30–12:00
FINAL GROUP MEETING In own classroom) *	2:00–3:00	1:45–3:00	2:00–3:00
COMMITTEE MEETINGS AND CONFERENCES WITH CONSULTANTS	3:00–3:30	3:00–3:30	3:00–3:30

* Each workshop group (about thirty persons) has its own classroom for group meetings and for committee work when desired during the work period. The group's consultant uses this classroom for conferences during the consultant's unassigned time. Each group is as organized in advance and remains constant in personnel.

OTHER TYPES OF IN-SERVICE EDUCATION

As we noted earlier, any activity that contributes to teachers' solution of problems in their jobs can be considered as in-service education. In addition to all the activities we have already described in this chapter, there are in-service educational potentialities in other activities such as the following:

Travel in the United States and abroad
Work in occupations other than teaching
Visitation of other schools and classrooms
Writing professional articles

Making professional speeches

Participating in community activities

Participating in general cultural and recreational activities

Practicing in varied situations such basic skills needed in teaching as speaking, interviewing, writing, recording, finding information, carrying on research

IMPROVEMENT THROUGH EXPERIMENTATION

As we noted earlier in this chapter, experimentation is a significant step toward improvement in teaching. The real test of the teacher's self-evaluation, use of help from others, curriculum planning, or in-service education is whether change for the better in his teaching practices occurs. In this section we will explain and illustrate a plan of experimentation that includes procedures which help the teacher decide whether change is for the better.

THE NATURE OF EXPERIMENTATION IN TEACHING METHOD

Good teaching method, as we see it, is always experimental. That is, teachers who are guided by the modern point of view of teaching we have tried to present in this book are always seeking ways of working with their pupils which are maximally effective. Because one of these teachers finds that a particular way of working seems effective with a particular group at a particular time, he does not assume that the same way will be most effective with all groups at all times. He never concludes that his ways of working are the best possible, but simply that these ways of working represent the best pattern of teaching that he has as yet developed. Experience, he recognizes, will reveal deficiencies in these patterns and add new ways of working which will be better if proper care is taken. The quest for improvement is continuous, not necessarily because his teaching is "bad," but because increasing experience, properly directed and evaluated, means increasing learning for the teacher and therefore increasing effectiveness in his teaching method.

Teachers who accept and practice this experimental method are constantly engaging in experimentation. They recognize the necessity of testing their theories of teaching through formulating hypotheses stemming from these theories and collecting evidence which will support or negate the theories. The teacher who is not experimental teaches day after day, class after class, without deliberately seeking to evaluate or improve these teaching experiences. His experiencing is perhaps interesting—he may even feel it successful—but there is never the challenge and reward that comes with controlling experiences so as to make successive ones different and better. He never questions his practices and their underlying theories. The one teacher simply accepts pupil disinterest as inevitable or unfortunate and allows disinterest to continue from one day and one class to the next without trying to do anything for the better; he does not look critically at his assumptions regarding interest. Believing interest is significant, the other teacher looks for a reason for disinterest and tries out successive hunches to increase interest until he finds effective modifications of his procedures. The first teacher perhaps expends less energies in his teaching, although he may waste much time and effort scolding pupils for what he feels is their failure, but he is denied the great satisfactions that come with seeing improvement result from experimentation.

This process of experimentation is the scientific method of inquiry applied to teaching method. Experimentation is both a characteristic of the method itself and a particular process of studying and improving this method. Experimental teaching method continuously seeks improvement through the process of experimentation. This process has certain distinct steps that we will define and illustrate in a subsequent section. First, however, we should note that there are several different concepts of experimentation. One is the concept of simple *problem solving*. For example, Miss Smith observed that her general science class was very restless at its Monday meeting and suspected this was due to the fact that the pupils had not done any reading of the text in preparation for the recitation. Hence she decided to try out a plan of having a brief period right then for reading the text. After some twenty minutes the discussion continued, there was less restlessness, and Miss Smith concluded that she had solved the problem for the time being. There is a constant procession of similar problem situations in teaching, and teachers are constantly having to think through these problems and try out solutions. Although the term "experimenting" is frequently used in connection with things that are tried out, there is little of the attempt to seek evidence and evaluate the tryout solutions which characterizes the more scientific process of experimentation.

Another concept is that of *controlled experimentation*, which has been a characteristic method of research in the field of methodology. To illustrate, we may assume that Miss Smith decided to investigate scientifically the use of a study period within the general science class meeting time so as to reach some generalization regarding this problem. Perhaps Miss Smith wished to do a study for a graduate degree at some teacher-education institution which required controlled experiments for graduate theses. She would then seek to set up two classes equivalent to each other on a maximum number of factors and teach one (the control group) by a recitation procedure only, and the other (the experimental group) by a combined study-recitation procedure. Data would be gathered regarding the comparative achievement of the two groups over a semester or year and statistical procedures used to determine whether the difference in achievement was sufficiently significant to support a generalization as to the superiority of one method over the other. Although this method has been widely used in educational research, the contradictory findings as to the value of various methods lead one to suspect that the variables supposedly eliminated are not, and that they are perhaps more important than the specific method.[3] Furthermore, the reservations usually attached to the generalizations of these studies frequently make the conclusions of little worth, and the statistical processes are sometimes too complicated for use in ordinary classroom experimentation.

A third concept of classroom experimentation and one more nearly synonymous with that we are presenting is the idea of *action research*. Action research, or research to guide action, is characterized by one of its major proponents, Stephen M. Corey, as follows:

> Those who engage in action research do so primarily because they wish to improve their own practices. Action research is conducted in the heat of combat, so to speak. It is conducted by teachers or supervisors or administrators in order that they may know, on the basis of relatively objective evidence, whether or not they are accomplishing the things they hope to accomplish.[4]

To use Miss Smith's general science class for another illustration, this time for one of classroom action research or experimentation, we may suppose that she had been concerned for some time about the apparent disinterest of many members of the class in the recitations she conducted. She decided to try out a hunch that interest would increase if she would give the pupils more opportunity to participate in planning the class meetings. Accordingly, she used a questionnaire to find out what the general reaction of class members was to the present procedure and shared a tabulation of the reactions with the class. She then asked for suggestions from the class as to new procedures which would be more to their liking. Among the suggestions

[3] See William M. Alexander and Samuel Ersoff, "Schools for Adolescents: Instructional Procedures," Chapter VI, in *Review of Educational Research*, 24 : 54 (February), 1954.

[4] Stephen M. Corey, *Action Research to Improve School Practices* (New York: Bureau of Publications, Teachers College, Columbia University, 1953), pp. 142–143.

generally agreed upon were the use of audiovisual aids, field trips, and demonstrations. During the next six weeks Miss Smith scheduled several films, took the class on two field trips, and demonstrated several concepts presented in the textbook. At the end of that time she repeated the questionnaire and compared the results with the earlier tabulation. The marked increase in favorable reactions, plus her general observation of greater interest in the class, convinced her that the original hunch was right; that is, that interest was greater after pupils were given more opportunity to participate in planning. Note that Miss Smith did not conclude that audiovisual aids, field trips, and demonstrations constituted the way to teach general science. In fact, she now plans to continue experimentation with different types of learning experiences, and takes up further inquiry of the class as to those which they find valuable and would like to use more frequently. Thus she is off to investigation of another hunch or series of hunches, this time about effective learning experiences for this particular class.

THE STEPS IN CLASSROOM EXPERIMENTATION

Four steps are involved in classroom experimentation: defining the problem; formulating a tryout solution or hypothesis; gathering data about the hypothesis; and reaching conclusions from the data. Although the logical order of these steps is as listed, it should be noted that the hunch or hypothesis sometimes develops before the problem is analyzed, that the tryout solution is sometimes initiated before it has been carefully formulated, and that conclusions are sometimes reached simultaneously with—and sometimes, erroneously, before!—the collection of data. In the interest of more reliable conclusions, teachers should conduct their experimentation with attention to each of these steps. They are defined more carefully in the following paragraphs.

Defining the Problem. In the case of Miss Smith and the general science class, there was a clearly recognized problem, namely, the lack of interest of many class members. Before Miss Smith could properly proceed with experimentation, it was essential that she recognize this problem and see it as a question for investigation. Her problem was not properly why students are disinterested in general, or what is wrong with classes in general, but what situation would have increased interest on the part of the members of this particular class. Similarly, teachers need to define problems for experimentation rather exactly. It is not enough to be dissatisfied with a situation; for experimentation to flourish, the teacher must inquire into the basis of the dissatisfaction and ask ultimately what actions he may undertake to get a more favorable situation. Experimentation is undertaken not to find causes of unfavorable situations, but rather to find remedies on the basis of some supposition as to cause.

Formulating a Hypothesis. Once the specific question for investigation is clearly identified—for example, what conditions would produce increased interest in Miss Smith's general science class—a tentative answer must be decided upon. This tentative answer is the solution, hunch, or hypothesis to be tried out. Inexperienced investigators usually encounter considerable difficulty in formulating hypotheses, as the tendency is to state hunches that cannot be tested under existing circumstances. For example, Miss Smith's hypothesis might have been that increased interest in the general science class would result from having a laboratory period. But since the school's schedule did not permit a laboratory period, this could not be tried out, and therefore such an answer to the problem would have been an idle conjecture, however shrewd, of no value to Miss Smith and the present class. The element of practicability must be given considerable weight in the teacher's classroom experimentation. More fundamental research which does not seek answers to present problems for purposes of immediate improvement deals with hypotheses that require special conditions for investigation. Classroom action research has to deal with hypotheses that can be investigated in the present classroom situation.

Gathering Data Regarding the Hypothesis. The critical step of gathering evidence distinguishes the type of experimentation we are describing from mere problem solving and also from the more fundamental research, including controlled experimentation, which seeks to reach generalizations true of larger populations than that with which the research is conducted. Perhaps the real distinction lies in the degree of confidence one can have in the conclusion: the more adequate and reliable the evidence, the greater confidence in general one can have in the conclusions. In classroom experimentation there are very real limitations on the types and extent of evidence teachers can gather. We noted, however, in Miss Smith's case that her evidence, simple as it was, regarding the comparative reactions of class members before and after the experimentation and also her own observations of pupil interest, seemed perfectly satisfactory as a basis for conclusions. She could have confidence in these so long as she did not seek to make generalizations justified by neither the original hypothesis nor the data.

Sometimes we fail to recognize the availability of a great many sources of evidence as to the success of our efforts to improve teaching. Among the sources which may provide data for the teacher who is experimenting are the following:

Opinions of the teacher, other teachers and special school personnel, pupils, and parents

Observation of individuals and groups by the teacher and others

Achievement records based on tests of various sorts

Performance tests administered periodically with reference to skills of various sorts

Rating scales used by the teacher and others to estimate pupil behavior

Evaluations of teaching made by pupils and observers

Records of pupils' use of the library and other resources for learning

Comparisons of pupils' work at various times

Recordings of group evaluations of experimental practices

Interviews with pupils to determine their reasons for individual reactions to experimental practices

Inventories of pupils' activities

The teacher who is carrying on experimental practices has to rely rather heavily on before-and-after types of evidence, since comparison of one group with another is generally inconsistent with the purpose of classroom experimentation. Hence, whenever experimentation is undertaken, it is a wise precaution to collect some systematic evidence regarding conditions which are related to the behavior it is hoped to change. Afterward in the process or at the end of experimentation similar evidence can be collected and comparisons made. Most of the types of evidence listed above can be collected and compared in this way.

Reaching Conclusions from the Data. The one question to be answered in all experimentation is, "Do the data support the hypothesis?" Although subordinate conclusions may be developed, the fundamental interest in the experiment is to find out whether the situation is different when the experimental factor is introduced. Thus Miss Smith concluded that interest in her general science class was greater when pupils had participated in planning. She did not rightly conclude that pupil participation caused great interest, although she may have thought so, because her hypothesis was not concerned with the complex factor of causation. Actually, completely extraneous factors may have been in part the cause of the greater interest. Very likely, the mere fact of being involved in experimentation stimulated greater interest on the part of pupils, for we know from research and experience that people like to be involved in experimentation. This fact, however, merely underlines the desirability of experimentation in general. We noted, too, that Miss Smith did not and could not conclude that the learning experiences used in the experiment were necessarily better learning experiences, for this was not the subject of her investigation. Her one concern was to secure greater interest on the part of the class, and the evidence showed this result was attained.

The essence of classroom action research lies in just such attempts as Miss Smith's to find better situations than those with which there is dissatisfaction. This is also the distinguishing characteristic of experimental teaching. Experimental teachers—teachers whom we consider to be good teachers becoming better—have only to join the quest for improvement and take carefully the steps we have just outlined as they find points in which improvement seems feasible and desirable. We may now list certain conditions in which this kind of teaching thrives that teachers can help create.

THE CONDITIONS OF EFFECTIVE EXPERIMENTATION

The prerequisite of all successful experimentation is a philosophy on the part of the teacher that experimentation is a necessary, accepted, and desirable phase of teaching method. Without this philosophy, experimentation is superficial, uncertain, or nonexistent. Teachers who have the philosophy will put it to work under almost any teaching conditions, but we believe they will experiment more effectively if such conditions as the following prevail:

1. Teachers cooperate with each other in experimentation by undertaking joint experiments, relieving each other of routine duties at times, helping in the extra duties experimentation sometimes involves, and by providing counsel and assistance as requested.

2. There is a healthy respect for experimentation on the part of administrators, the faculty as a whole, pupils, and parents.

3. Faculty and other decisions are customarily made on the basis of facts and there is in general reliance on evidence in reaching conclusions.

4. Freedom of discussion prevails in faculty meetings, and teachers are encouraged to express their dissatisfactions and to work together in finding more satisfying conditions.

5. Routines are waived when possible and necessary in order to facilitate experimentation in the classroom.

6. The administration encourages experimentation and cooperates as far as possible in providing facilities and in giving recognition to those who experiment.

7. Supervisory or other consultative assistance is available to help teachers organize and carry on experimentation.

EXPERIMENTATION AND DYNAMIC TEACHING

As we see it, experimentation is an integral part of dynamic teaching. Indeed it is the force which prevents teaching from becoming static. Even the problem-solving approach to teaching and learning we have presented in this book would become static if hypotheses stemming from the theory of problem solving were not constantly tested. For example, central in this theory of methodology is the belief that no single pattern of teaching techniques will work effectively in all situations. We would urge our readers who have or develop confidence in the efficacy of certain techniques to seek evidence regarding these techniques. If our hypothesis is correct, they will find reason to experiment further with other techniques, and again and again we believe they will discover evidence of the inadequacy of any single pattern of procedure.

Also central in the dynamic methodology is the belief that experience in problem-solving processes will help learners become increasingly able to think through critically their own problems. Teachers should constantly be testing this theory through evaluating pupils' growth in reflective abilities as they work together in attacking learning problems by the scientific method of inquiry.

Similarly, the authors hope readers will test in their own classrooms the theories of effective teaching we have presented. However, we recognize the fact that the teacher's most significant experimentation is that which tests the hypotheses stemming from his own beliefs about teaching. If this experimentation follows the procedures described, and if the teacher modifies his practices and theories as the evidence indicates, we feel certain that his teaching will take on increasingly dynamic qualities.

EXPERIMENTATION IS REWARDING

Lest the teacher decide that experimentation is much work for nothing, we close our discussion with a strong reminder that experimentation is rewarding. Sometimes the rewards are intangible, but we believe that some of our greatest rewards as teachers are the intangibles of feelings of personal satisfaction with a job well done, of the gratitude and praise of our pupils, and of the respect of our colleagues. In addition, there are sometimes more material rewards, such as salary increases for outstanding performance, promotion to supervisory and administrative positions, opportunities to write and speak professionally, fellowships and scholarships for advanced study, and other honors and opportunities which are given to those teachers who have demonstrated special merit and professional zeal. We believe, however, that the teacher must decide whether or not to experiment so far as possible without concern for the rewards, one way or the other. The fundamental decision for the teacher is whether to do the best job possible with each group of pupils taught or whether to be content to coast along doing whatever comes with least exertion. If he sincerely wants to do an ever better job, there is no choice but to experiment, and it is equally certain that experimentation will bring the great inner satisfaction of knowing that he is moving forward rather than standing still or going backward. For such teachers, there are many and varied opportunities for recognition in the profession.

SUMMARY: THE TEACHER'S ROLE IN IMPROVING INSTRUCTION

In this final chapter of our book on teaching method, we have presented a challenge to readers to undertake improvement as an essential phase of good teaching method. We sincerely believe that teachers do have an obligation to work for better teaching throughout their professional careers. Furthermore, we are well aware of the many evidences that all teaching is not of the caliber deserved by the children and youth of America. The one and only way that better teaching can be done is for teachers themselves to work for continuing improvement. This is our responsibility and our opportunity.

This point of view has been expressed here in specific ways by which teachers in secondary schools can work toward improved teaching. We have suggested ways of self-evaluation, of getting help from others, of participating in curriculum planning, of specific in-service education, and of classroom experimentation. In closing this chapter and our book, we wish to express the conviction that each teacher has to work out for himself the best ways of seeking self-improvement but that he has no choice, ethically, other than to continue the quest for improvement throughout his career. We hope that what we have written will point the way to the rich rewards of teaching that becomes ever more effective and ever more satisfying for teachers and learners alike.

FOR FURTHER STUDY

Association for Supervision and Curriculum Development, National Education Association, *Better Than Rating*. Washington, D.C.: The Association, 1950.

Analyzes teacher rating practices and proposes as better alternatives various procedures for teacher improvement.

————, *Developing Programs for Young Adolescents*. Washington, D.C.: The Association, 1954.

Part III suggests steps needed in providing better programs, including instruction, for young adolescents.

Beecher, Dwight E., *The Evaluation of Teaching*. Syracuse, New York: Syracuse University Press, 1949.

Describes various procedures for the evaluation of teaching.

Benne, Kenneth D., and Bozidar Muntyan, *Human Relations in Curriculum Change*. New York: The Dryden Press, Inc., 1951.

A book of selected readings on the analysis and management of human relations in curriculum change.

Cantor, Nathaniel, *The Teaching-Learning Process*. New York: The Dryden Press, Inc., 1953.

See pages 269–283 for "Some Characteristics of a Professional Teacher."

Chase, Stuart, *Roads to Agreement*. New York: Harper & Brothers, 1951.

Deals with methods of effective human relations that may be suggestive of means for teacher improvement.

Corey, Stephen M., *Action Research to Improve School Practices*. New York: Bureau of Publications, Teachers College, Columbia University, 1953.

A useful guide for planning and conducting cooperative research in the field of classroom instruction.

Gruber, Frederick C., and Thomas Bayard Beatty, *Secondary School Activities*. New York: McGraw-Hill Book Co., Inc., 1954.

Suggestions for carrying on each type of student activity in secondary schools.

"High Schools for Tomorrow," *Teachers College Record*, 56:355–420 (April), 1955.

This special issue on secondary education contains several articles on emerging and needed changes in secondary schools.

Kelley, Earl C., *The Workshop Way of Learning*. New York: Harper & Brothers, 1951.

Primarily a report of a workshop for teachers held at Wayne University, this book describes workshop procedures as a way of teaching.

Macomber, Freeman Glenn, *Teaching in the Modern Secondary School*. New York: McGraw-Hill Book Co., Inc., 1952.

See Chapter 10, "Evaluating Teaching and Learning," especially pages 248–254 for a "Self-Evaluation Inventory for the Good Teacher."

National Commission on Teacher Education and Professional Standards, National Education Association, *The Teacher and Professional Organizations*. Washington, D.C.: The Association, 1952.

History, objectives, work, and accomplishments of professional organizations, and the obligations and benefits of teacher participation.

Saylor, J. Galen, and William M. Alexander, *Curriculum Planning for Better Teaching and Learning.* New York: Rinehart & Company, Inc., 1954.
Chapter 16 gives suggestions and illustrations regarding teacher participation in organized curriculum-planning activities.

Sharp, George, *Curriculum Development as Re-education of the Teacher.* New York: Bureau of Publications, Teachers College, Columbia University, 1951.
Analysis of changes in teachers essential to curriculum improvement.

Wann, Kenneth D., "Teachers as Researchers," *Educational Leadership,* 9:489–495 (May), 1952.
Reports teachers' evaluations of their participation in cooperative curriculum research.

Appendix 1

A LIST OF SELECTED FILMS, FILMSTRIPS, AND
RECORDINGS ON PUPILS, TEACHERS, AND
TEACHING METHODS IN THE SECONDARY SCHOOLS

1. FILMS

Age of Turmoil (20 min.)

This film is concerned with early adolescence—approximately the
period from thirteen to fifteen years. It focuses on the behavior that
reflects the emotional turmoil of this age group—giggling, destructive
criticism of school, unrealistic ideas of their own future, hours spent in
seemingly useless activity, and so forth. Most of the scenes are set in
the home and show the mother and father making appropriate and
occasionally inappropriate responses. Different personality types have
been selected to illustrate this budding stage, such as the leader or the
quiet type. (McGraw-Hill)

Broader Concept of Method: Part I—Developing Pupil Interest (13 min.)

This film presents a frank picture of the teacher-dominated, lesson-
hearing type of recitation, and shows typical effects of this method on
student attitudes, responses, and learning. It then shows alternative techniques to achieve broader educational objectives. Draws comparison
between formal recitation and informal, group discussion type of class
sessions. In the latter, students are permitted to share in the planning of
their work, and are thereby stimulated toward worth-while and meaningful learning experiences. This atmosphere of freedom of discussion
leads to a suggestion for a class project that is readily accepted by the
students. (McGraw-Hill)

*Broader Concept of Method: Part II—Teacher and Pupils Planning and
Working Together* (19 min.)

Development of the project begun in Part I is continued here. Students
are shown learning to work together, to organize themselves into functional groups, to make and carry out plans for investigation, to present

530

their findings and recommendations in a final report, and to put into practice some of their recommendations. This group participation results in evidence of reflective thinking and self-expression, plus a growing ability to evaluate properly the things learned as a result of this class experience. The film shows how the teacher can provide tactful guidance in the solution of difficulties encountered by the various groups. Techniques shown are readily applicable to other class situations in which students share in the planning and implementing of their work. (McGraw-Hill)

Importance of Goals (19 min.)

The case of thirteen-year-old Tommy illustrates the principle that all education is essentially a process of attaining basic, meaningful goals. (McGraw-Hill)

Maintaining Classroom Discipline (14 min.)

By contrasting methods of handling the same class, this film explores techniques for securing proper class conduct and attitudes. First is shown a class where teacher and students seem to be pulling in opposite directions and where school work is neither instructive nor pleasant. Analysis indicates that the teacher has failed to stimulate the students' interest, and they have sought a natural relief from boredom in misbehavior. Small incidents, mishandled, soon develop into serious problems. The film then returns to the starting point and shows how the same situations could be handled more adroitly by the same teacher with the same class, under the same conditions. By contrast, the film establishes basic principles of method which help toward productive and mutually satisfactory class control. (McGraw-Hill)

Meaning of Adolescence (16 min.)

In our society, the years of adolescence are often years of insecurity and difficult adjustments. This film is episodic in treatment and revolves about two adolescents, a boy and a girl, and their family. The five major adjustments to adult life are outlined—physical maturity, social living, getting along with the opposite sex, settlement of religious doubts, and the establishment of a sound moral code. (McGraw-Hill)

Meeting the Needs of Adolescents (19 min.)

What can parents do to prepare their child for the future? This film deals with a family that includes a seventeen-year-old girl and a fourteen-year-old boy. It shows how their basic physical needs are met, how their mental development is stimulated and directed, how they are guided in their spiritual growth, and how parents can develop the social consciousness which will make their children good companions in later life. The film points out what parents can do to help constructively and indicates some of the needless worries that parents have about their teen-agers. (McGraw-Hill)

Motivating the Class (19 min.)

A young student teacher of mathematics learns that adequate motivation is basic to all good teaching, and is obtained by translating the values of the subject matter into terms the pupils .can understand (McGraw-Hill)

Near Home (25 min.)

This is a film about good teaching. To illustrate several principles that are basic to good teaching, a class and teacher study the community in which they live. In the study of the community, the pupils and the teacher can be observed in a learning process that takes advantage of an inherent interest in things near by. (International Film Bureau)

Physical Aspects of Puberty (19 min.)

This film describes the physical changes of puberty. By means of animation, it shows the functioning of the endocrine glands, the gonadotropic hormone, male and female reproductive systems, secondary sex characteristics, and other physical changes. Normal variations in the adolescent pattern of physical development can have social repercussions, and behavior problems that seem emotional are often based on this variation in rate of physical growth. (McGraw-Hill)

Practicing Democracy in the Classroom (21 min.)

This film makes the point that the teaching of good citizenship in schools can be done more effectively through democratic methods than through laissez faire and authoritatian methods. It demonstrates what is meant by "democratic teaching techniques" by portraying students in an up-to-date classroom being taught by the democratic method. (Ency. Brit.)

Problem of Pupil Adjustment: Part 1—The Dropout (20 min.)

This is a case study of a boy who should be graduating with his high school class; but instead, he quit school after freshman year and since then he has drifted from one mediocre job to another. He is only one of the "dropouts," one of the nearly 50 per cent of all high school freshmen who quit school before they are graduated. Steve left school as soon as the law allowed. A life-adjustment program, with class subjects related to the interests of boys and girls, might be the answer for Steve and those other "dropouts" in our schools today. (McGraw-Hill)

Problem of Pupil Adjustment: Part 2—The Stay-In (19 min.)

This is the study of an actual school that holds an enviable record for reducing its "dropouts" to less than 5 per cent of its total student population. It shows clearly what can be done to meet this problem when individual pupil needs are met in a school program that stresses learning in terms of adjustment to actual everyday living. When such enrichment is added to a school curriculum, pupils begin to see the relation between their in-school and out-of-school lives—a relation that is meaningful and challenging and absorbing. The "dropout" problem ceases to exist, for the ground on which it flourishes has been removed. (McGraw-Hill)

Social-Sex Attitudes in Adolescence (22 min.)

This film is concerned with the growing understanding of the meaning of sex in the teen-ager. It shows how teen-agers meet, and are helped to meet their main problems in becoming aware of and adjusted to the opposite sex. A boy and girl are taken through their entire adolescent experience, which culminates in their marriage at the end of the film. We see how, as children, they were given sex education in the home, how they became increasingly aware of the opposite sex, how they began dating different kinds of boys and girls until they had a fairly clear idea of the kind of person they wanted to marry, how they handled such problems as petting, and how they finally met, discovered and shared their common interests, fell in love and married. (McGraw-Hill)

Using the Classroom Film (22 min.)

This film demonstrates accepted methods of teaching with classroom films. It follows the teacher as he selects and previews the film, as he prepares the film lesson, and as he guides classroom discussion before and after screening the EBFilm *Wheat Farmer*. It presents a variety of worth-while learning activities growing out of the film experience. A stimulating portrayal of basic techniques and possibilities of teaching with films. (Ency. Brit.)

We Plan Together (20 min.)

This film was produced by Horace Mann-Lincoln Institute of School Experimentation. It was prepared to help teachers in preparation and teachers in service, as well as interested laymen and students, gain a better understanding of the process of cooperative planning in education. It shows an eleventh-grade group planning cooperatively for learning in their core class over a period of several months. (Teachers College, Columbia University)

Discussion in Democracy (10 min.)

This presents the basic principles of leading a group discussion and illustrates their use by a group of high school students. It opens by showing two boys and two girls discussing what they can do to decrease the number of fires in their community and getting into an argument because they are not following an organized plan of discussion. Then it shows the group leader discussing fire prevention with the chairman of the city council, accepting his suggestions for organizing their study of the situation, and assigning each student a specific problem. As each student reports his findings to the group, appropriate scenes illustrate his report. Alice visits the fire department to learn about staff needs and the fire-fighting methods employed; Howard examines the cost of various types

of new fire engines and explains their improvements over older models;
and Betty investigates the cost of fires to the community. Then the film
pictures the group discussing the problem in terms of the data reported
and formulating recommendations to the city council. When one student
raises the question, "What can the school do?" the film shows the group
discussing in an orderly manner a plan for a fire-prevention campaign in
the school. Comments that this discussion was successful because the
group followed an organized plan, gathered pertinent information, and
used it in arriving at a conclusion. (Coronet, 1948)

Learning to Understand Children—A Diagnostic Approach (21 min.)

This film presents the case study of an emotionally and socially
maladjusted girl of fifteen. It includes diagnostic techniques, such as
observation of her behavior, study of her previous records, personal
interviews, home visitation, and recommendations for remedial measures.
(McGraw-Hill)

Learning to Understand Children—A Remedial Program (23 min.)

This film is a continuation of the case study of the maladjusted girl in
which the teacher develops a plan for remedial action by making use
of the girl's talent in art. (McGraw-Hill)

Practicing Democracy in the Classroom (22 min.)

This was filmed in Kalamazoo, Michigan. It shows how a teacher,
along with fellow-members of his faculty, some parents, and students,
worked out a satisfactory approach to the problem of teaching a course
in American history by using methods that give students a chance to
develop the knowledge, skills, and attitudes of a desirable citizen of a
democracy. (Ency. Brit.)

The Problem Method: Part I—Defining the Problem and Gathering Information (18 min.)

This film shows how pupils in a social studies class become aware of
the existence of pressure groups and their influence on legislation. With
the help of the teacher, the pupils are led to define the problems. The
procedures are shown which were employed in gathering and sharing
information. (McGraw-Hill)

The Problem Method: Part II—Using Information to Solve the Problem (16 min.)

This film is a continuation of Part I. It shows how the information that
is gathered by the class is used to solve the problem. Various hypotheses
are suggested as possible solutions to the problem. With the help of the
teacher, the class is led to see the need for a set of criteria against which
each hypothesis can be tested. The criteria are developed by pupils, and
the process of thinking that was involved in testing each hypothesis and
in arriving at a solution is shown. The experience gained in the solution of
the main problem leads the class to a consideration of a local problem.

The film suggests the importance of the problem method in preparing students for democratic living. (McGraw-Hill)

2. FILMSTRIPS

Adolescent Development Series (McGraw-Hill, 1953, silent, black and white). Five filmstrips to accompany motion pictures with the same titles: *Meaning of Adolescence,* 34 frames; *Physical Aspects of Puberty,* 34 frames; *Age of Turmoil,* 36 frames; *Social-Sex Attitudes in Adolescence,* 35 frames; *Meeting the Needs of Adolescents,* 34 frames.

Cooperative School Plant Planning (Ind. U and Ed. Film Lib. Assn., 1952, 100 frames, silent with captions, color). Presents a functional approach to dynamic group action as applied to the community planning of school buildings. Outlines the roles of the board of education, the superintendent of schools, the educational consultant, the architect, the engineer, other experts, children, teachers, and citizens of the community as they take part in a cooperative school plant-planning procedure. Many details of administration are covered, as well as ways in which cooperating groups and individuals can benefit.

Core Curriculum Class in Action (Wayne U, 1949, 50 frames, silent with captions, black and white). Follows a typical ninth-grade core class from its first class meeting through various teacher-pupil planned activities and the final evaluation of the work done. Answers such questions as "How does a class organized on a core plan operate?" "What are its objectives and how are they set?" "How is pupil-teacher planning accomplished?"

Personal Problems of Adolescent Youth (Ohio State U, 1953, 43 frames, silent, black and white). Designed for adult groups and teachers in service who desire a deeper understanding of adolescent difficulties.

The Teacher and Public Relations (NEA, 1952, 50 frames, silent with captions, black and white). How to build an appreciation of the professional skills and achievements of teachers, why we teach what we teach, how we teach, homework assignments, reports to parents, public relations values of co-curricular activities, making parents partners, and working with community groups.

Teacher Education (Secondary) (McGraw-Hill, 1948, silent, black and white). Five filmstrips to accompany motion pictures with the same titles: *Learning to Understand Children: I, A Diagnostic Approach,* 37 frames; *Learning to Understand Children: II, A Remedial Program,* 34 frames; *Maintaining Classroom Discipline,* 43 frames; *Broader Concept of Method, Part I; Developing Pupil Interest,* 33 frames; *Broader Concept of Method; Part II, Teacher and Pupils Planning and Working Together,* 37 frames.

Your Educational Philosophy—Does It Matter? (Wayne U, 1952, 40 frames, silent, black and white). This filmstrip, through a presentation of two different philosophies in action, shows the need for every teacher to have a sound philosophy as a frame of reference for work with children.

3. RECORDINGS

Case Problems in Guidance (Wayne U, 78 rpm). Three 10″ records entitled *Disorder—Then What?, Developing Group Responsibility, Tom Is Truant.* One side of each record presents, in dramatic form, a school situation with guidance implications. The remaining side gives the manner in which the teacher concerned handled the situation. Discussion questions are presented at the close of each side.

The descriptions of the preceding films, filmstrips, and recordings are based on material from the following sources:

1. *Conference Bibliography,* Tenth Annual National Conference of the National Commission on Teacher Education and Professional Standards, 1955.
2. *Educational Film Library,* 1954–1956, School of Education, Syracuse University, Syracuse, N. Y.

Appendix II

A CLASSIFIED LIST OF SELECTED EDUCATIONAL PUBLICATIONS AND THEIR SOURCES IN THE UNITED STATES

(The number after each publication title indicates the number of issues per year.)

1. GENERAL IN SCOPE AND CIRCULATION

NEA Journal—9, $5
Journal of the National Education Association
Joy Elmer Morgan, Editor
1201 Sixteenth Street Northwest
Washington 6, D.C.
Progressive Education—7, $4.25
Archibald W. Anderson, Editor
105 Gregory Hall
University of Illinois
Urbana, Illinois
School Life—9, $1.25
John H. Lloyd, Managing Editor
Federal Security Agency
Office of Education
Washington 25, D.C.

2. ADMINISTRATION

Bulletin of the National Association of Secondary-School Principals—8, $5
National Association of Secondary-School Principals of the National Education Association
Paul E. Elicker, Editor
1201 Sixteenth Street Northwest
Washington 6, D.C.

3. ART

Art Education—5, $2
Journal of the National Art Education Association
Italo L. deFrancesco, Editor
State Teachers College
Kutztown, Pennsylvania

4. BUSINESS EDUCATION

Business Education (UBEA) Forum—8, $4 to nonmembers
United Business Education Association, a department of the National
Education Association
Hollis P. Guy, Executive Secretary
1201 Sixteenth Street Northwest
Washington 6, D.C.

5. CURRICULUM

Educational Leadership—8, $3.50
Official Organ, Association for Supervision and Curriculum Develop-
ment, National Education Association
George Denemark, Editor
1201 Sixteenth Street Northwest
Washington 6, D.C.

6. ENGLISH

English Journal, The—9, $4
W. Wilbur Hatfield, Editor
211 West Sixty-eighth Street
Chicago 21, Illinois

7. EXCEPTIONAL CHILDREN

Exceptional Children—8, $3
Journal of the International Council for Exceptional Children
Francis E. Lord, Editor
Michigan State Normal College
Ypsilanti, Michigan

8. HEALTH, PHYSICAL EDUCATION, AND SAFETY

*Journal of the American Association for Health, Physical Education and
Recreation*—10, $5
Ella H. Wright, Editor
1201 Sixteenth Street Northwest
Washington 6, D.C.

9. INDUSTRIAL ARTS

Industrial Arts Teacher—5, $2.50
American Industrial Arts Association
D. Arthur Bricker, Executive Secretary
123 East Ninth Street
Cincinnati 2, Ohio

10. LANGUAGE TEACHING

Modern Language Journal—8, $2.50
American Federation of Modern Language Teachers Associations
Julio delToro, Managing Editor
University of Michigan
Ann Arbor, Michigan

11. MUSIC

Music Educators Journal—6, $2
C. V. Buttelman, Managing Editor
64 East Jackson Boulevard
Chicago 4, Illinois
Washington Office:
NEA Building
1201 Sixteenth Street Northwest
Washington 6, D.C.

12. PARENT EDUCATION

National Parent-Teacher; The P.T.A. Magazine—10, $1.25
Eva Grant, Editor
Editorial and Subscription Offices
600 South Michigan Boulevard
Chicago 5, Illinois

13. PSYCHOLOGY AND MENTAL HYGIENE

Journal of Educational Psychology—8, $7
Warwick and York, Publishers
10 East Center Street
Baltimore 2, Maryland
Mental Hygiene—4, $6
National Association for Mental Health
George S. Stevenson, M.D., Director
1790 Broadway
New York 19, New York

14. SCIENCE AND MATHEMATICS

Mathematics Teacher—8, $3
M. H. Ahrendt, Business Manager

National Council of Teachers of Mathematics
1201 Sixteenth Street Northwest
Washington 6, D.C.
Science Teacher, The—6, $3
National Science Teachers Association
Robert H. Carleton, Editor
1201 Sixteenth Street Northwest
Washington 6, D.C.

15. SECONDARY EDUCATION

California Journal of Secondary Education—8, $3
Robert N. Bush, Editor
California Association of Secondary School Administrators
Haviland Hall
Berkeley 4, California
Clearing House, The—A Journal for Modern Junior and Senior High
School Faculties—9, $4 (formerly *Junior-Senior High School Clearing
House*)
Forrest E. Long, Editor
207 Fourth Avenue
New York 3, New York
Publisher: Inor Publishing Company
(same address)
High School Journal—8, $2
Samuel M. Holton, Editor
School of Education
University of North Carolina
Chapel Hill, North Carolina
School Review—9, $4.50
Publisher: University of Chicago Press
5750 Ellis Avenue
Chicago 37, Illinois

16. SOCIAL STUDIES

Social Education—8, $4
Journal of the National Council for the Social Studies
Lewis Paul Todd, Editor
1201 Sixteenth Street Northwest
Washington 6, D.C.

17. SPEECH EDUCATION

Quarterly Journal of Speech, The—4, $3.50
H. F. Harding, Editor
Speech Association of America
Ohio State University
Columbus 10, Ohio

18. VISUAL EDUCATION

Educational Screen—10, $3
Official Organ of the Department of Audio-Visual Instruction of the
National Education Association
Paul C. Reed, Editor
64 East Lake Street
Chicago 1, Illinois

19. VOCATIONAL EDUCATION, GUIDANCE, AND HOMEMAKING

American Vocational Journal—10
Official Publication of the American Vocational Association (subscrip-
tion included in $3 individual and $2 affiliated membership fees.
Library or school subscription, $2)
M. D. Mobley, Editor-in-Chief
1010 Vermont Avenue Northwest
Washington 5, D.C.
Journal of Home Economics—10, $5
Mary Hawkins, Editor
Official Journal of the American Home Economics Association
1600 Twentieth Street Northwest
Washington 9, D.C.
Personnel and Guidance Journal, The—8, $6 (Formerly *Occupations*)
American Personnel and Guidance Association
William D. Wilkins, Editor
1534 O Street Northwest
Washington 5, D.C.

In addition, numerous local, state, and regional teachers' associations
publish materials of value to both pre-service and in-service educators.
State departments of education usually have publications of interest. The
above are too numerous for listing here.

(The information on educational associations and publications given above
is based on material from America's Education Press, Twenty-fourth Yearbook of the Educational Press Association of America, 1953.)

Appendix III

MONEY AND YOU

A Resource Unit in General Education*

I. THE UNIT PROBLEM

One of the guiding principles of education is to teach boys and girls to do better those desirable things that they are likely to do anyway. Most young people face the problem of money management. More than ever before, the adjustment of boys and girls to our economic and business life demands a constructive attitude toward business, a clear understanding of its functions, and the ability and skill to use its goods and services effectively.

The proper management of the family income is imperative in attaining goals or satisfactions in life. Young people need to realize that the spending of their income should be carefully planned by democratic processes within the family group in order to obtain the greatest value possible for each individual. Information concerning ways of budgeting and keeping of accounts will help them to accept their responsibility with greater efficiency.

II. WHERE? WHEN? WHY?

This unit was organized to be taught in ninth- or tenth-grade General Business classes. Since it contains "probability learnings" for all youth, this unit could well be adapted for use in homemaking or social studies classes, or for twelfth-grade classes in effective living. "The tools of learning—reading, writing, spelling, and arithmetic—are also the tools of business." Thus subject matter in language arts and mathematics is included. Relation of this unit to others to be used and the desires and needs of the students involved will best determine when and where this unit can be taught most effectively.

* Adapted from a unit prepared by Don Ali and Carroll Waggoner, students at the University of Miami School of Education, June, 1955.

Many of the activities listed may be adapted to fifth- and sixth-grade classes in arithmetic.

III. DESIRED LEARNINGS ACQUIRED OR HOPED FOR

A. Desired concepts
1. That freedom from economic want can be achieved by careful planning
2. That financial security is obtained through planning in advance for the use of the family income
3. That wise money management means getting the greatest possible satisfaction from the money we have
4. Etc.

B. Specific learnings
1. To think clearly of the relation between the amount of money earned and the amount of money available for spending
2. Ability to make a budget of income and expenditures
3. Ability to keep the records necessary to determine whether thrift habits are being formed
4. Etc.

C. Desired growth in language arts
1. To motivate interest in reading
2. To improve penmanship in letters and numbers
3. To facilitate improvement in oral and written reports
4. To increase vocabulary especially related to budgeting and using a checking account, and to improve ability to spell

D. Desired growth in arithmetic
To improve accuracy and speed in the four fundamentals: addition, subtraction, division, and multiplication

E. Desired social outcomes
1. An appreciation of the importance of business in our democratic society
2. Understanding that in business one must be able to get along with people
3. Understanding that budgeting and thrift are essential in satisfactory home and family life as well as in business
4. etc.

IV. LEARNING EXPERIENCES

Activities for budgeting
1. As a committee project, interview a businessman to find out how a business manages its money.
2. On a separate sheet of paper, make two columns, one headed "Wants," the other "Needs." List your own wants and needs. In a month, check back to see if they are the same.

3. Talk to some grown-ups that you know quite well, possibly your parents or neighbors. Ask them what they think is the smallest possible amount of money that they would need per week (or per month, or per year) in order to live happily. Jot down this figure, and make a note to yourself indicating whether or not you would be satisfied to live as they do.

4. On the slip of paper which you will receive, write down the smallest amount of money you think you would need per week in order to live happily—not as a child living with your parents, but as a young working person. We're all curious about what others think; so we'll let a committee summarize these figures. Then we shall compare our figures with national average incomes.

5. You have been asking how large an allowance a high school student should have, and we haven't been able to decide on any definite amount. Let's make a list of the different things for which students spend their allowance. We shall use this list to try to figure out how much spending money the average student needs.

6. It would help our class to answer this question on allowances if each of you would keep track of your personal expenses for a week. The list of expenditures which you compiled will make a good chart for this purpose. Start filling in the spaces today. At the end of the week we shall collect your charts and make some conclusions.

MY PERSONAL EXPENSES

Date	Mon.	Tues.	Wed.	Thurs.	Fri.	Sat.	Sun.	TOTALS
Transportation								
Lunches								
Candy, treats, etc.								
Amusements, hobbies, sports								
Church, charities								
Clothing, cleaning								
School supplies								
Savings, unusual								
TOTALS								

7. If possible, secure a sample budget of some public institution, such as a city, county, township, church, or hospital. If possible, get the proper official to explain how the budget is constructed and how it operates.

8. Ask two former students, one a career girl and the other a young housewife, to visit the class and tell about their experiences in using budgets and methods of recording household accounts.

9. List ten things for which high school boys and girls spend money that you would consider luxuries. Name five items that you consider necessities.

10. Have four or more students in the class prepare and present a skit using a family conference on money management as the theme.

11. Read portions of *Mamma's Bank Account*, by Kathryn Forbes, Harcourt, Brace, 1943, or—if possible—have it given as a dramatic reading.

12. Arrange a large board display showing, on one half, dollar bills going into a home; on the other half, pictures of articles and services for which a family spends income. The home, in the center, could be represented by a picture of a house with a picture of a family superimposed upon it.

13. Income—means to an end
    Pupils read from the following references in order to gain a better understanding of income:

    Justin and Rust, *Today's Home Living*, pp. 304–310
    Graves, Skinner, and Swenson, *The Family and Its Relationships*, pp. 184–188
    Shultz, Hazel, *The Young Consumer*, pp. 67–103

    Class discusses the questions:

    What is money?
    What are the sources of money income?
    What is real income?
    What factors, other than money, can contribute to the family income?
    What personal services can the individual render in the home which make an addition to the family income?

14. A committee investigates data on the range of incomes in the United States and the percentage of families in each income bracket. The committee reports its findings for class discussion.

    From personal knowledge, are these figures what one would expect?
    What income groups are largest?

15. Individuals investigate the average income that may be expected in the vocation they plan to enter and then decide whether or not the real compensation for work always has money value.

16. Each pupil lists the services that are given by the community without direct charge and which contribute to the social income of a family. The class as a whole or a committee may compile a complete list from the individual lists.

Which of these community services does your family use?

Does the Federal government contribute to personal and family income?

17. The film, *Your Thrift Habits,* may be shown to give suggestions for answering the following questions about budgeting of personal incomes.

What is a budget?

What examples of plans can be found in other phases of living?

What can a budget do to help one gain more satisfaction from expenditure of personal income?

What items would appear in a personal budget?

Why should budget records be simple?

Why should a budget be revised from time to time?

18. For specific help in starting a budget, the class reads references in Smith, Bahr and Wilhelm, *Your Personal Economics,* pp. 68–80. The class then discusses these questions:

What are the five steps to follow in making a budget?

Why should budget records be simple?

Why should a budget be revised from time to time?

19. The film, *Why Budget?,* or the filmstrip, *Budgeting for Better Living,* will give an opportunity to contrast personal and family budgets. Class discusses the differences.

Why is making a family budget more complicated than making a personal budget?

Who should make the family budget?

What are some of the things which influence the family plan?

Which items are in a family budget that are not in a budget for a single person?

What kind of training in early childhood would prepare one for participating in a family conference to plan a budget?

20. An outside speaker from the Household Finance Corporation or some other agency interested in family spending plans might talk to the class about planning for the use of income.

21. Making a budget

A family has decided to try budgeting. The members have discussed their income and expenses and have agreed upon what things are important to them. What form can they use to set up their budget and their system of accounts?

The class may explore the literature available for suggestions as to forms that might be used. Each student decides which form she or he likes best.

Enough of these pamphlets, or similar ones should be obtained in advance so that each student may have one:

Money Management—Your Budget
The Family Money Manager
Budget Control of Family Finance
Personal Money Management

After examining the pamphlets the class may discuss:

What are the four steps that would give a basis for a budget?
What do we want our money to buy?
What are flexible expenses: How can they be handled in the plan?
How may past unpaid bills be considered?
What item in the budget is going to make possible the fulfillment of wishes?
What can be done if expenses exceed the income?

When the items that are to be included in the budget have been decided upon, the next question to be settled is the amount of income that may be allotted fairly to each item. To determine this, the class could be divided into committees to get factual information from home, neighbors, and friends on amounts spent for different items. The committees report to the class.

What does it cost to own an automobile?
What taxes are paid on the homes that are owned?
What is the scale of rent?
How much will it cost for the college education of the children?
What figures are available on the cost of feeding the family?
What are the operating costs, such as light, heat, and water?

Since some people consider standard budget proportions as reliable guides for the percentages to be assigned to various items, one student or a committee may study these as given in different texts and report to the class.

Are the figures right for all families?
How are they influenced in the amount of income? by the tastes or standards of living of the families?
What is the relation between the size of the house or the size of the family and the operating costs?

By means of class discussion, a representative family is set up. The class members are divided into groups, and each group works out a budget for that family. These are reported to the entire class for comparison, revision, and evaluation.

22. Spelling and vocabulary building:

barter	checks
counterfeit	depositors
medium of exchange	joint account
minting	signature card
uniformity	disbursements
budget	amount
commission	check stub
expenditures	drawer
flexible	payee
reserve	verify
cash balance	blank endorsement
cashbook	clearinghouse
procedure	full endorsement
source	endorser
treasurer	restrictive endorsement
certified check	bank statement
endorse	outstanding checks
interest	reconciliation
security	service charge
receipt	stopping payment

For a light-hearted approach to the difficult vocabulary of General Business courses, encourage your students to construct "chuckleful" true-false test questions on some of the terms. You might call them *Daffynitions.* The idea has real merits:

1. It stimulates interest in vocabulary (and that is something!)
2. Each statement leads naturally into a *correct* redefinition.
3. It provides a point of committee activity that is profitable.
4. It interests everyone in the school in General Business.
5. It humanizes you and the course.

Examples:

1. A *receipt* is a description of how to bake a cake.
2. A *clearinghouse* is a pretty house with a large clearing in front of it.
3. A *medium of exchange* is a bookie.
4. One who can find treasure on a submerged coral reef is a *treasurer.*
5. *Minting* is the process of preparing the mint for a Kentucky Colonel's mint-julep.

23. On page 4 of *Moderns Make Money Behave* is an account of the financial problems of the Logan family. Using the plan for managing money on pages 11–15, set up a budget for the

Logans which will get them out of debt and provide them with the things they need.

24. Check your daily newspapers for current stories about family situations which reflect either good or poor financial management. Use these stories as material for class discussion.

V. TEACHING-LEARNING AIDS

A. Printed aids

BOOKS, BUDGETING

1. Baxter, Laura, Margaret Justin, and Lucile D. Rust, *Our Home and Family*. Philadelphia, Lippincott, 1940, Chap. 2.
2. Bonde, Ruth L., *Management in Daily Living*. New York: The Macmillan Company, 1944.
3. Brindze, Ruth, *How to Spend Money*. New York: Vanguard, 1935.
4. ————, *Johnny Get Your Money's Worth*. New York: Vanguard Press, 1938.
5. Bryson, Lyman, *Facing the Future's Risks*. New York: Harper & Brothers, 1953.
6. Dana, Margaret, *Behind the Label*. Boston: Little Brown & Co., 1938.

   Dodd, J. H. South, *Applied Economics*. Western Co., 1945.
8. Donaldson, E. F., *Personal Finance*. New York: The Ronald Press Company, 1948.
9. Donham, Agnes S., *Spending the Family Income*. Boston: Little, Brown and Co., 1933.

   Suggests standards for savings, shelter, food, clothing, operating expenses, and ways of distributing income. Will be especially useful for groups working in areas of family money management.

10. Finke, Mary B., and Helen Knox, *Moneywise—The Intelligent Woman's Guide to Everyday Finance*. New York: Putnam, 1950. $3.50

    Basic information on banks, insurance budgets, and the like. While written primarily for women, this book will be interesting reading for high school students, as well as other adults. Part I deals with everyday affairs, for example, savings, credit, checking accounts. Part II suggests items to be considered in planning for the future, such as insurance and estate planning.

11. Floyd, Oliver Reed, and L. B. Kinney, *Using Dollars and Sense*. New York: Newson & Co., 1942.

12. Groves, Ernest Rutherford, Skinner and Swenson, *The Family and Its Relationships.* Chicago: J. B. Lippincott Co., 1948.
13. Hamblen, Stewart Belknap, and Godfrey Frank Zimmerman, *Wise Spending.* New York: Harper Brothers, 1941.
14. Harris, Florence L., and Treava E. Kauffman, *Young Folks at Home.* Boston: D. C. Heath, 1948.

> A course in home economics for junior high school girls. Places special emphasis on "Spending the Family's Money" in Unit V (pages 174–245). Includes suggested activities and bibliography.

15. Janzen, Cornelius Cicero, and O. W. Stephenson, *Everyday Economics.* New York: Silver Burdett Co., 1941.
16. Jordan, David F., and Edgar F. Willett, *Managing Personal Finances.* New York: Prentice-Hall, 1945. 418 p. Rev. ed.

> A detailed discussion of many of the problems of money management. Discusses such topics as business cycles, buying on credit, installment credit, etc. Easy reading for high school students and adults. Should be available as a reference for any group working on problems of personal finance.

17. Justin, Margaret M., and L. M. O. Rust, *Today's Home Living,* Philadelphia: J. B. Lippincott and Co., 1947.
18. Lasser, J. K., and S. F. Porter, *How to Live within Your Income.* New York: Simon and Schuster, 1948.

> Written in an encouraging, almost coaxing, vein, this book includes chapters on wise buying, choosing between renting and building a home, how to secure loans, how to minimize the income tax, and various other problems of money management.

19. Moore, W. L., and Howard E. Wheland, *Record Keeping for Everyone.* Cincinnati: South-Western Publishing Co., 1951.

> This book attempts to give the pupil the basic understanding of business transactions and simple acceptable ways of recording them.

20. Nickell, Paulena, and J. M. Dorsey, *Management in Family Living.* New York: John Wiley and Son, Inc., 1948.
21. Owens, David F., *Controlling Your Personal Finances.* New York: Prentice-Hall, Inc., 1937.
22. Shields, Harold Gustav, and W. H. Wilson, *Business-Economic Problems.* Cincinnati: South-Western Publishing Co., 1935. Pp. 61–86 for budgeting.

B. Visual aids

Budgeting For Better Living. 108 frames, 25 min., script; 35 mm. Household Finance Corporation, 191 Michigan Avenue, Chicago, Illinois. Free rental.

> Outline of budgeting procedure. Suitable for money management, consumer education, or family living groups. The financial ups and downs of a typical family are portrayed.

C. Other aids
1. Alumni
2. Businessman
3. Families
4. Faculty
5. Field Trips

VI. EVALUATION

SAMPLE TESTS

A. *Thrift*

Part I. Matching

Read the explanations in the right-hand column. Select the word in the left-hand column that means the same as the explanation, and put the number of this word in front of the explanation.

1. Thrift
2. Memorandum
3. Principal
4. Budget
5. Occupation
6. Interest
7. Balance
8. Expense
9. Receipt
10. Benevolence
11. Allowance

( )   1. A definite plan for the distribution of time or money so that one may gain benefit from it.

( )   2. The money paid out.

( )   3. An amount of money that is paid for the use of money.

( )   4. Avoidance of waste of any kind.

( )   5. An act of kindness.

( )   6. The business, trade, or employment of a person.

( )   7. An informal record of things that should be remembered.

( )   8. A sum of money that interest is paid on.

( )   9. The difference between the total of the receipts column and the total of the payments column.

( )   10. Money taken in.

Part II. True and false

If you believe that any of the following statements are true, place a *T* on the line following the statement; if you think it is false, place an *F* on the line following the statement. DO NOT GUESS. Two points will be taken off for each incorrect answer, and one point shall be taken off for blanks.

1. A budget guarantees a person that he will save a definite sum each week. _____
2. The United States is richer in all things than it was 50 to 100 years ago. _____
3. Thrift is a good habit to apply throughout life. _____
4. The longer savings are invested, the more rapidly they increase. _____
5. It is necessary that one save funds for unusual expenses. _____
6. The income from interest may be more than the principal if invested for a number of years. _____
7. It is possible to have an increase in prosperity and wealth in the United States without saving. _____
8. Savings that are invested increase because of interest. _____
9. A person should include such items as medical and dental services under the heading, "Household." _____
10. The amounts spent are entered in the Receipts column of your personal income and expense record. _____
11. Each class of expenses must be recorded separately in your personal income and expense record so that the total of that class may be compared with the allowance of that expense. _____
12. When the columns are added in the personal income and expense record, they are entered first in pencil.
13. The total difference between the Receipts column and the Payments column in the personal income and expense record is the total amount spent. _____
14. An estimate of expenses is based on incomplete information. _____
15. Life insurance premiums are charged to household expenses. _____

Part III. Completion

Fill the blank in each statement with the word or words which best complete the statement. Only one-half credit will be given for words that are spelled incorrectly.

1. The interest on $1,000 for 1 year at 5 per cent is _____.

2. The five steps in successful budgeting are _____,

_____,

_____,

_____,

_____.

3. Family budget making should be a project undertaken by _____.

4. Money management is learned by making use of _____.

5. In a problem of interest, $100 is the _____, 4 per cent is the _____, and one year is the _____.

6. We save for the purpose of attaining our _____ in life.

7. A thrifty person saves _____ and _____.

8. A person must know his _____ so he can estimate his expenditures in a thrifty manner.

9. The difference between the total of the Receipts column and the total of the _____ column is the cash on hand.

10. A guide for family budgets is _____ budgets.

Part IV. Multiple choice

Read each statement carefully, and select the word or words which best answer the statements. Write the letter of this answer on the line provided in front of the number of the statement.

1. The greatest differences in family expenses are likely to be found from month to month in (a) benevolences, (b) food, (c) family welfare, (d) rent. _____

2. A budget of money is needed to (a) make it possible for one to spend more, (b) increase income, (c) decrease waste, (d) guide one to save and spend wisely. _____

3. To show the amount of money on hand at the beginning of a new week, the balance is written in the (a) Payments column, (b) Receipts column, (c) Explanation column, (d) none of these. _____

4. It is advantageous for a person to start saving at an early age because (a) savings will increase yearly if invested wisely, (b) it is easier to save while young, (c) his income is no doubt larger now than in the future, (d) if he doesn't save now, he never will. _____

5. The total of all the savings and expense columns should equal the total of the (a) Receipts column, (b) Payments column, (c) Explanation column, (d) none of these. _____

6. A budget of time is needed because it (a) makes

Part IV. Multiple choice (continued)

duties easier, (b) aids thrift by planning, (c) aids in
using time to best advantage, (d) none of these.   _____

7. A family needs a budget more than an individual
   because (a) the family can save a larger amount,
   (b) the family income is smaller than the individual's
   income, (c) there are many standard budgets made
   to fit a family income, (d) the different members of a
   family have so many wants that it is difficult for them
   to save.   _____

8. An allowance is (a) a sum of money paid out, (b) a
   fixed share or amount, (c) an act of kindness, (d) an
   informal record.   _____

B. A student opinionnaire on personal and family finances

Here are some statements about which there are many differences
of opinion. Please place a check mark in the blank which best
expresses your degree of agreement or disagreement with the
statement. Your answers will in no way affect your grade or
standing in class.

SA, Strongly Agree; A, Agree; U, Undecided; D, Disagree;
SD, Strongly Disagree

	SA	A	U	D	SD
1. Money is one of the most important things in life.					
2. Some people just do not have enough money to budget.					
3. A person can take a prepared budget and use it as his own.					
4. Parents should decide the amount of their children's allowance.					
5. Adolescents should be paid for some of the regular work they do at home.					
9. One should always save regardless of the amount.					
10. Buying on credit encourages one to buy things one can't afford.					
11. Parents should let their young people find out what it means to earn by encouraging them to earn some of their own money.					
12. A child is a big money investment to his parents, and therefore he has an obligation to them.					

	SA	A	U	D	SD
13. Deciding how to spend the family income should be a family project.					
14. Father should have more authority as to how the family income should be spent because he earns the money.					
15. Mother should control the purse strings, giving father his weekly allowance.					
16. Parents should let young people select their own clothes.					
17. How each person chooses to spend his allowance should be an individual decision.					
18. The only time most people talk about money is when someone is unhappy.					
19. A person should pay back money that he borrows from his parents.					
20. Each family should make its own individual budget to fit its needs.					
21. Money matters should be discussed before marriage in the light of day rather than in the moonlight.					
22. Women are not supposed to know anything about business affairs.					
23. Newlyweds should be able to start housekeeping on the same economic level as their parents.					
24. Working children should pay room and board if they live at home after graduation.					
25. A wife adds to the family income when she performs her homemaking duties.					
26. When people get old and helpless their children should take the responsibility for caring for them.					

C. Other Evaluation Techniques—interviews, self-rating scales, etc.

Index

557